www.wadsworth.com

www.wadsworth.com is the World Wide Web site for Wadsworth and is your direct source to dozens of online resources.

At *www.wadsworth.com* you can find out about supplements, demonstration software, and student resources. You can also send email to many of our authors and preview new publications and exciting new technologies.

www.wadsworth.com
Changing the way the world learns®

SIXTH EDITION

SOCIAL WORK WITH GROUPS
A Comprehensive Workbook

Charles Zastrow
University of Wisconsin–Whitewater

THOMSON

BROOKS/COLE

AUSTRALIA • CANADA • MEXICO • SINGAPORE • SPAIN • UNITED KINGDOM • UNITED STATES

THOMSON
★
BROOKS/COLE
™

Social Work with Groups: A Comprehensive Workbook
Charles Zastrow

Executive Editor: *Lisa Gebo*
Assistant Editor: *Alma Dea Michelena*
Editorial Assistant: *Sheila Walsh*
Technology Project Manager: *Barry Connolly*
Marketing Manager: *Caroline Concilla*
Advertising Project Manager: *Tami Strang*
Project Manager, Editorial Production:
    Rita Jaramillo
Art Director: *Vernon Boes*
Print Buyer: *Doreen Suruki*

Permissions Editor: *Stephanie Lee*
Production Service: *Buuji, Inc.*
Text Designer: *John Edeen*
Copy Editor: *Kristina Rose McComas*
Cover Designer: *Katherine Minerva*
Cover Image: © *Peter Guttman/Corbis*
Cover Printer: *Phoenix Color Corporation*
Compositor: *Buuji, Inc.*
Printer: *Edwards Brothers–Ann Arbor*

For more information about our products, contact us at:
Thomson Learning Academic Resource Center
1-800-423-0563

For permission to use material from this text or product, submit a request online at
http://www.thomsonrights.com.

Any additional questions about permissions can be submitted by email to thomsonrights@thomson.com.

Thomson Higher Education
10 Davis Drive
Belmont, CA 94002-3098
USA

Asia (including India)
Thomson Learning
5 Shenton Way
#01-01 UIC Building
Singapore 068808

Australia/New Zealand
Thomson Learning Australia
102 Dodds Street
Southbank, Victoria 3006
Australia

Canada
Thomson Nelson
1120 Birchmount Road
Toronto, Ontario M1K 5G4
Canada

UK/Europe/Middle East/Africa
Thomson Learning
High Holborn House
50/51 Bedford Row
London WC1R 4LR
United Kingdom

Library of Congress Control Number: 2004113117

ISBN 0-534-53481-3

To Kathy

My wife and soulmate

Contents

■ **CHAPTER THREE**

Group Dynamics: Leadership   59

Preface

What inspired this book? In the spring of 1983, I was teaching my first group-work course to an undergraduate social work class. Before the start of the semester, I wrote a number of lectures about group dynamics and how groups are used in social work practice with socialization groups, task groups, decision-making and problem-solving groups, self-help groups, and therapy groups. At the start of the semester, I dutifully began giving these lectures. Soon, however, I began sensing that the lectures were not being well received. During the third week, a student stayed after class and said, "I'm afraid this may hurt my grade, but most of the students in this class feel that you can't teach a group-work class with only lectures. The only way students will learn how to run groups is by having the experience (in class or out of class) of leading groups." I thought about it for a few days and decided the student was exactly right. With the students' consent, I redesigned the whole course, with the basic thrust being to have the students take turns in leading the class on group-work topics that we mutually agreed upon. Because at that time there was no social work group text to facilitate this process, I attempted to write one. The first edition of this text was published in 1985.

The basic assumption of this text is that the best way for students to learn how to run groups is by leading groups in class. The classroom thus becomes a laboratory for students to practice and develop their group leadership skills. This text is designed to facilitate this laboratory approach to undergraduate and graduate group-work courses. (The prior edition of this text was entitled *Social Work with Groups: Using the Class as a Group Leadership Laboratory*.)

This edition provides additional opportunities for students to gain proficiency in social group work skills through the inclusion of numerous "skill-building" exercises that have been added in various sections of each chapter. The new title of this text, *Social Work with Groups: A Comprehensive Workbook*, reflects this emphasis on using skill-building exercises to facilitate students developing group leadership skills.

■ PLAN OF THE BOOK

Each chapter is designed according to the following format:

1. The goal or goals of the chapter are stated.
2. Theoretical material is presented on how the goals can be achieved. If the goal is to learn how to handle disruptive members of a group, for example, the chapter describes appropriate strategies.
3. Several "skill-building" exercises are then interspersed throughout each chapter, and also at the end of each chapter. These exercises give students practice in acquiring the skills described in the chapter.

At the end of the book is a Group Treatment Theories Resource Manual (GTTRM). To highlight the uniqueness of the GTTRM, material is presented in modules, rather than chapters. This GTTRM presents three prominent theories of counseling that are widely using by social workers in working with treatment groups: rational therapy, behavior therapy, and reality therapy. It is not necessary for the instructor to cover all three of these theories of group intervention. Rather, it is suggested that he or she (perhaps with the consultation of other faculty in the program) decide which of the three intervention theories described in the GTTRM are most important for students to learn to best serve clients in the school's geographic area.

■ USING THE BOOK

After the instructor covers the introductory material contained in the first chapter, it is suggested that students (either individually or in small groups) take turns preparing and conducting future class sessions by summarizing the theoretical material in the chapters and leading the class in related exercises. (Students may also be given the opportunity to select a topic not covered in the text.) A booklet that can be packaged with this text contains theoretical material and class exercises on five topics that may be used as a resource for class presentations by students. This booklet is entitled *Strategies for Working with Specific Social Work Groups*.

The "skill-building" exercises in this text may be used in a variety of ways. The assigned leader (who may be the instructor, a student, or a small group of students) for a chapter may use the exercises in the following ways: (1) The assigned leader may request that the other students complete certain exercises as a homework assignment prior to the next class period; the exercises are then reviewed when the class next meets. (2) The assigned leader may have the other students complete one or more exercises during the class. (3) The instructor may assign certain exercises as written homework to be submitted for evaluation. The pages of this workbook are perforated for easy removal. (4) The instructor may have each student complete several exercises and then place them in a portfolio, which the instructor may periodically review for evaluation purposes.

Students should make their presentations stimulating, interesting, and educational by speaking extemporaneously rather than reading and by adapting chapter topics using personal observations or research. Students should also prepare and distribute handouts that summarize the key points of their presentations and should move around the classroom to maintain and increase the interest of the class. The use of technological resources, such as Microsoft® PowerPoint®, is also suggested.

For further study, students and instructors can visit the Brooks/Cole Social Work website (http://socialwork.wadsworth.com), an invaluable source of information that reinforces and augments the concepts presented in this text. The Social Work website contains online quizzing, text-specific content (including related Web links), a link to the NASW Code of Ethics in the Student Resources section of the site, and downloadable Microsoft® PowerPoint® slides.

■ ACKNOWLEDGMENTS

Sincere thanks are extended to the following contributing authors: Lisa A. Curtis, Grafton H. Hull, Jr., Karen Kirst-Ashman, LaVonne Cornell-Swanson, Virginia Dotson, Michael O. Koch, Thomas P. Troast, Carey Tradewell, Daniel Paul Vega, and Michael Wallace. Vicki Vogel is recognized for helping to prepare the manuscript and for preparing the ancillary materials. Karen Thomson is also acknowledged for her assistance in preparing the ancillary materials.

About the Author

CHARLES ZASTROW, MSW and PhD, is Professor in the Social Work Department, University of Wisconsin–Whitewater. He has worked as a practitioner in a variety of public and private social welfare agencies and has chaired 14 social work accreditation site visit teams for the Council on Social Work Education (CSWE). He recently was, for six years, a member of the Commission on Accreditation of CSWE. He is currently the chair of the Commission on Educational Policy of CSWE. He is a member of: The Association for the Advancement of Social Work with Groups, the National Association of Social Workers, the Council on Social Work Education, and NASW Register of Clinical Social Workers. He is licensed as a Clinical Social Worker in Wisconsin. In addition to *Social Work with Groups*, he has written several other books, including the following textbooks: *Introduction to Social Work and Social Welfare* (8th ed.), *The Practice of Social Work* (7th ed.), and *Understanding Human Behavior and the Social Environment* (6th ed.) (with Dr. Karen Kirst-Ashman).

■ CONTRIBUTING AUTHORS

Lisa A. Curtis, MA
Professional Journalist
Milwaukee, Wisconsin

Virginia Dotson, PhD
Psychotherapist and licensed
psychologist
Milwaukee, Wisconsin

Karen K. Kirst-Ashman, MSW, PhD
Professor
Department of Social Work
University of Wisconsin–Whitewater

Michael O. Koch, PhD
Psychotherapist and licensed
psychologist
Milwaukee, Wisconsin

**LaVonne J. Cornell-Swanson, MSW,
ACSW, LICSW, PhD**
Assistant Professor
Department of Social Work
University of Wisconsin–Eau Claire

Carey Tradewell Monreal
President/CEO
The Milwaukee Women's Center
Milwaukee, Wisconsin

Thomas P. Troast, PhD
Psychotherapist
Milwaukee, Wisconsin

Daniel Paul Vega, MSW, LCSW
Clinical social worker
Tacoma, Washington

Michael Wallace
Instructor
Department of Social Work
University of Wisconsin–Whitewater

CHAPTER ONE

Groups: Types and Stages of Development

GOALS

Each group develops a unique character or personality because of the principles of group dynamics. This chapter presents a brief history of social group work and introduces the primary types of groups in social work. Models of the stages in the development of a group over time are summarized. Differences between reference and membership groups are described, and several ice-breaker exercises are presented. Guidelines on how to conduct classroom exercises are summarized.

Every social service agency uses groups, and every practicing social worker is involved in a variety of groups. Social work with groups is practiced in adoption agencies, correctional settings, halfway houses, substance abuse treatment centers, physical rehabilitation centers, family service agencies, private psychotherapy clinics, mental hospitals, nursing homes, community centers, public schools, and many other social service settings. To effectively serve clients in human service systems today, social workers in generalist practice positions must be trained in group methods. Often, social workers serve as leaders and participants in myriad groups requiring skills ranging from simple to complex. The beginning social worker is likely to be surprised at the diverse groups in existence and excited by the challenge of practicing social work in many different settings.

HISTORICAL DEVELOPMENT OF GROUP WORK

The roots of group social work began in the settlement houses, the YMCAs and YWCAs, Boy Scouts and Girl Scouts, and Jewish centers of the 1800s.[1] These agencies focused on providing group programs for people considered "normal." Recipients of early group services came for recreation, informal education, friendship, and social action. Euster notes that these recipients "learned to cooperate and get along with others socially; they enriched themselves through new knowledge, skills, and interests, and the overall state of society was bettered through responsible involvement in community problems."[2]

Settlement Houses

The first settlement house, Toynbee Hall, was established in London in 1884; many others were soon formed in large U.S. cities.[3]

Many of the early settlement house workers were daughters of ministers. Usually from middle and upper class families, they would live in a poor neighborhood so they could experience the harsh realities of poverty. Using the missionary approach of teaching residents how to live moral lives and improve their circumstances, early settlement workers sought to improve housing, health, and living conditions; find jobs for workers; teach English, hygiene, and occupational skills; and improve living conditions through neighborhood cooperative efforts. The techniques settlement houses used to effect change are now called social group work, social action, and community organization.

Settlement houses emphasized "environmental reform," but they also "continued to struggle to teach the poor the prevailing middle-class values of work, thrift, and abstinence as the keys to success."[4] In addition to dealing with local problems through local action, settlement houses played important roles in drafting legislation and organizing to influence social policy and legislation.

The most noted leader in the settlement-house movement was Jane Addams of Hull House in Chicago. She was born in 1860 in Cedarville, Illinois, the daughter of parents who owned a successful flour mill and wood mill.[5] After graduating from Rockford Seminary in Rockford, Illinois, she attended medical school briefly but was forced to leave due to illness. She then traveled for a few years in Europe, perplexed as to what her life work should be. At the age of 25, she joined the Presbyterian church, which helped her find a focus for her life: religion, humanitarianism, and serving the poor. (She later joined the Congregational church, now known as the United Church of Christ.) Addams heard about the establishment of Toynbee Hall in England and returned to Europe to study the approach. The staff of college students and graduates, mainly from Oxford, lived in the slums of London to learn conditions firsthand and to improve life there with their own personal resources, including financial ones.

Jane Addams returned to the United States and rented a two-story house, later named Hull House, in an impoverished neighborhood in Chicago. With a few friends, Addams initiated a variety of group and individual activities for the community. Group activities included a literature reading group for young women, a kindergarten, and groups that focused on social relationships, sports, music, painting, art, and discussion of current affairs. Hull House also provided services to individuals who needed immediate help such as food, shelter, and information on and referral for other services. A Hull House Social Science Club studied social problems in a scientific manner and then became involved in social action efforts to improve living conditions. This group worked successfully for passage of Illinois legislation to prevent the employment of children in sweatshops. Addams also became interested in the various ethnic groups in the neighborhood. She was fairly successful in bringing the various nationalities together at Hull House where they could interact and exchange cultural values.

The success of Hull House served as a model for the establishment of settlement houses in other areas of Chicago and many other large cities in the United States. Settlement-house leaders believed that by changing neighborhoods, they could improve communities, and by altering communities, they could develop a better society. For her extraordinary contributions, Jane Addams received the Nobel Prize for Peace in 1931.

Young Men's Christian Association (YMCA)

The founder of the Young Men's Christian Association, George Williams,[6] was born and reared on a small farm in England. He stopped attending school at the age of 13 to work on his father's farm, but at 14, he became an apprentice to a draper (a manufacturer and dealer of cloth and woolen materials) and learned the trade. He grew up in a religious environment and joined the Congregational Church at the age of 16. At 20, he moved to London and worked for another drapery firm. Like Williams, the business owner, George Hitchcock, was deeply religious and allowed his new employee to organize prayer meetings at work.

The size of the prayer circle gradually grew, and the meetings featured Bible reading as well as prayers. The success of this group inspired Williams and his associates to organize similar groups at other drapers' establishments. The prayer circle Williams formed with 12 fellow employees marked the beginning of YMCAs. In 1844, the resulting prayer circles at 14 businesses formed an association called the Young Men's Christian Association. Each group conducted weekly religious services that included prayer, Bible readings, and discussions of spiritual topics.

The YMCA soon began to expand its activities. Prominent speakers from various fields of public and scholarly life addressed its members. An office was selected, and Protestant clergy in France, Holland, and other countries were persuaded to form YMCAs. Gradually, the programs were expanded to meet the unique needs of the communities in which the YMCAs were located.

In 1851, Thomas V. Sullivan, a retired mariner, picked up a religious weekly in Boston and read about the YMCA movement in London.[7] Sullivan gathered a few friends and established the first YMCA in the United States. Similar to the London association, the U.S. movement spread quickly to other communities. In only seven years, YMCAs were serving communities throughout the United States.

The U.S. YMCA had many firsts. It was the first organization to aid troops during wartime in the field and in prison camps. It pioneered community sports and athletics, invented volleyball and basketball, and taught water safety and swimming. It devised an international program of social service similar to that of the Peace Corps. It originated group recreational camping, developed night schools and adult education, initiated widespread nondenominational Christian work for college students, and reached out to assist foreign students. From an origin that involved a narrowly focused religious objective, YMCAs have expanded their objectives in a variety of directions. The success of YMCAs helped spur the first Young Women's Christian Association, formed in Boston in 1866.[8]

TYPES OF GROUPS

There are a variety of groups that occur in social work—social conversation, recreation-skill building, educational, task, problem-solving and decision-making, focus, self-help, socialization, treatment, and sensitivity and encounter training. According to Johnson and Johnson, a group may be defined as two or more individuals in face-to-face interaction, each aware of positive interdependence as they strive to achieve mutual goals, each aware of his or her membership in the group, and each aware of the others who belong to the group.[9]

Social Conversation

Social conversation is often employed to determine what kind of relationship might develop with people we do not know very well. Since talk is often loose and tends to drift aimlessly, there is usually no formal agenda for social conversations. If the topic of conversation is dull, the subject can simply be changed. Although individuals may have a goal (perhaps only to establish an acquaintanceship) such goals need not become the agenda for the entire group. In social work, social conversation with other professionals is frequent, but groups involving clients generally have objectives other than conversation, such as resolving personal problems.

Recreation/Skill Building

Recreational groups may be categorized as *informal recreational groups* or *skill-building recreational groups*.

A recreational group service agency (such as the YMCA, YWCA, or neighborhood center) may offer little more than physical space and the use of some equipment to provide activities for enjoyment and exercise. Often activities such as playground games and informal athletics are spontaneous, and the groups are practically leaderless. Some agencies claim that recreation and interaction with others help to build character and prevent delinquency among youths by providing an alternative to street life.

In contrast to informal recreational groups, a skill-building recreational group has an increased focus on tasks and is guided by an adviser, coach, or instructor. The objective is to improve a set of skills in an enjoyable way. Examples of activities include arts and crafts, and sports such as golf, basketball, and swimming, which may develop into competitive team sports with leagues. These groups are frequently led by professionals with recreational training rather than social work training, and the agencies involved include the YMCA, YWCA, Boy Scouts, Girl Scouts, neighborhood centers, and school recreational departments.

Education

While the topics covered vary widely, all educational groups teach specialized skills and knowledge, such as classes on child-rearing, stress management, parenting, English as a foreign language, and assertiveness training. Orientations offered by social service organizations to train volunteers fall into this category as well. Educational groups usually have a classroom atmosphere, involving considerable group interaction and discussion; a professional person with expertise in the area, often a social worker, assumes the role of teacher.

Task

Task groups are formed to achieve a specific set of tasks or objectives. The following examples are types of task groups that social workers are apt to interact with or become involved in. A *board of directors* is an administrative group charged with responsibility for setting the policy governing agency programs. A *task force* is a group established for a special purpose and is usually disbanded after the task is completed. A *committee* of an agency or organization is a group that is formed to deal with specific tasks or matters. An *ad hoc committee,* like a task force, is set up for one purpose and usually ceases functioning after completion of its task.

Problem Solving and Decision Making

Both providers and consumers of social services may become involved in groups concerned with problem solving and decision making. (There is considerable overlap between task groups and these groups; in fact, problem-solving and decision-making groups can be considered a subcategory of task groups.)

Social service providers use group meetings for objectives such as developing a treatment plan for a client or a group of clients, or deciding how best to allocate scarce resources. Potential consumers of services may form a group to meet a current community need. Data on the need may be gathered, and the group may be used as a vehicle either to develop a program or to influence existing agencies to provide services. Social workers may function as stimulators and organizers of these group efforts.

In problem-solving and decision-making groups, each participant normally has some interest or stake in the process and stands to gain or lose personally by the outcome. Usually, there is a formal leader, and other leaders sometimes emerge during the process.

Focus

Focus groups are closely related to task groups and problem-solving and decision-making groups. They may be formed for a variety of purposes, including (1) to identify needs or issues, (2) to generate proposals that resolve an identified issue, and (3) to test reactions to alternative approaches to an issue. A focus group is a

> A group convened to discuss a specific issue or single topic, often with the aid of questionnaires and a moderator who actively keeps the conversation oriented to that topic. Such groups are often established to acquire information and generate ideas that would not be as accessible through individual interviews.[10]

A Self-Help Group: Parents Anonymous[a]

Parents Anonymous (PA), a national self-help organization for parents who have abused or neglected their children, was established in 1970 by Jolly K. in California. For four years before forming the group, Jolly had struggled with an uncontrollable urge to severely punish her daughter. One afternoon she attempted to strangle the child. Desperate, she sought help from a local child-guidance clinic and was placed in therapy. When asked by her therapist what she could do about her problem, Jolly developed an idea. As she explained, "If alcoholics could stop drinking by getting together, and gamblers could stop gambling, maybe the same principle would work for [child] abusers, too." With her therapist's encouragement she formed "Mothers Anonymous" in 1970 and organized a few chapters in California. Nearly every major city in the United States and Canada now has a chapter, and the name has been changed to Parents Anonymous because fathers who abuse their children are also eligible to join.

PA is a crisis intervention program that offers two main forms of help: a weekly group meeting and personal and telephone contact. Members share experiences and feelings during weekly meetings and learn to better control their emotions. During periods of crisis, personal and telephone contact is especially important, particularly when a member feels a nearly uncontrollable desire to take anger or frustration out on a child. Parents may be referred to PA by a social agency (including protective services), or be self-referred as parents who recognize that they need help.

Cassie Starkweather and S. Michael Turner describe why abusive parents would rather participate in a self-help group than receive professional counseling.

It has been our experience that most [abusive] parents judge themselves more harshly than other, more objective people tend to judge them. The fear of losing their children frequently diminishes with reassurance from other members that they are not the monsters they think they are.

Generally speaking, PA members are so afraid they are going to be judged by others as harshly as they judge themselves that they are afraid to go out and seek help. Frequently our members express fears of dealing with a professional person, seeing differences in education, sex, or social status as basic differences that would prevent easy communication or mutual understanding.

Members express feelings of gratification at finding that other parents are "in the same boat." They contrast this with their feelings about professionals who, they often assume, have not taken out the time from their training and current job responsibilities to raise families of their own.[b]

PA emphasizes honesty and directness, since parents who are prone to abuse their children have learned to hide this problem because society finds it difficult to acknowledge. In contrast to society's tendency to deny the problem, the goal of PA is to help parents admit that they are abusive. The term abuse is used liberally at meetings, and this insistence on frankness has a healthy effect on members. Abusive parents are relieved because they have finally found a group of people able to accept them as they are. Furthermore, only when they are able to admit they are abusive can they begin to find ways to heal themselves.

During meetings parents are expected to actually admit to beating their child or engaging in other forms of abuse, and the members challenge each other to find ways to curb these activities. Members share constructive approaches to anger and other abuse-precipitating emotions and help each other develop specific plans for dealing with situations that have resulted in abusive episodes. Members learn to recognize danger signs and to take action to avoid abuse.

Leadership is provided by a group member selected by other members. The leader, called a chairperson, is normally assisted by a professional sponsor who serves as resource and back-up person to the chair and the group. The social worker who assumes the role of sponsor must be prepared to perform a variety of functions, including teacher-trainer, broker of community services needed by parents, advocate, consultant, and counselor.

---

[a]Adapted from *Introduction to Social Work and Social Welfare,* 8th ed., by Zastrow. © 2004. Reprinted with permission of Brooks/Cole, a division of Thomson Learning, Inc.
[b]Cassie L. Starkweather and S. Michael Turner, "Parents Anonymous: Reflections on the Development of a Self-Help Group," in *Child Abuse: Intervention and Treatment,* eds. Nancy C. Ebeling and Deborah A. Hill (Acton, MA: Publishing Sciences Group, 1975), p. 151.

Two examples of a focus group are a nominal group (described in Chapter 4) and a brainstorming session (described in Chapter 6).

A *representative group* is another version of a focus group. Its strength is that its members have been selected specifically to represent different perspectives and points of view in a community. At best, the representative group is a focus group that reflects the cleavages in the community and seeks to bring diverse views to the table; at worst, it is a front group for people who seek to make the community *think* it has been involved.

Self-Help and Mutual-Aid

Self-help groups are increasingly popular and often successful in helping individuals overcome social or personal problems. Katz and Bender provide a comprehensive definition:

> Self-help groups are voluntary, small group structures . . . usually formed by peers who have come together for mutual assistance in satisfying a common need, overcoming a common handicap or life-disrupting problem, and bringing about desired social and/or personal change. The initiators and members of such groups perceive that their needs are not, or cannot be, met by or through existing social institutions. . . . They often provide material assistance as well as emotional support, they are frequently "cause"-oriented, and promulgate an ideology or [set of] values through which members may attain an enhanced sense of personal identity.[11]

Alcoholics Anonymous, developed by two recovering alcoholics, was the first self-help group to demonstrate substantial success. In *Self-Help Organizations and Professional Practice,* Powell describes a number of self-help groups that are now active.[12]

Closely related to self-help groups are mutual-aid groups, and the terms are sometimes interchangeable. Mutual-aid groups are informal or formal associations of people who share certain problems and meet regularly in small groups with professional leaders to provide emotional support, information, assistance in problem solving, and other help for each other.

Many self-help groups use individual confession and testimony techniques. Each member explains his or her problem and recounts related experiences and plans for handling the problem. When a member encounters a crisis (for example, an abusive parent having an urge to abuse a child), he or she is encouraged to call another group member, who helps the person cope. Having experienced the misery and consequences of the problem, group members are highly dedicated to helping themselves and their fellow sufferers. The participants also benefit from the "helper therapy" principle; that is, the helper gains psychological rewards.[13] Helping others makes a person feel worthwhile, enabling the person to put his or her own problems into perspective.

Most self-help groups are "direct service" in that they help members with individual problems. Other self-help groups work on community-wide issues and tend to be more social-action oriented. Some direct service self-help groups attempt to change legislation and policy in public and private institutions. Others (parents of children with a cognitive disability, for example) also raise funds and operate community programs. However, many people with personal problems use self-help groups in the same way others use social agencies. An additional advantage of self-help groups is that they generally operate with a minimal budget. (For further discussion, see Chapter 8.)

Socialization

The primary objective of most socialization groups is to develop attitudes and behaviors in group members that are more socially acceptable.[14] Developing social skills, increasing self-confidence, and planning for the future are other focuses. Leadership roles in socialization groups are frequently filled by social workers who work with groups for predelinquent youths to curb delinquency; youths of diverse racial backgrounds to reduce racial tensions; and pregnant, unmarried young females to help them make plans for the future. Elderly residents in nursing homes are often remotivated by socialization groups and become involved in various activities. Teenagers at correctional schools are helped to make plans for returning to their home community. Leadership of all the groups mentioned in this section requires considerable skills and knowledge to help the group to foster individual growth and change.

Treatment

Treatment groups are generally composed of members with severe emotional, behavioral, and personal problems. Leaders of such groups must have superb counseling and group leadership skills, including the ability to accurately perceive the core of each member's response to what is being communicated. Group leaders must also have the personal capacities to develop and maintain a constructive atmosphere within a group. As in one-on-one counseling, the goal of treatment groups is to have members explore their problems in depth and then develop strategies for resolving them. Three treatment approaches (reality therapy, behavior therapy, and rational therapy) are described in the Group Treatment Theories Resource Manual (located at the end of the text). These three treatment approaches can be used to change dysfunctional behaviors and unwanted emotions of group members.

In summary, to be a competent group therapist the professional should have superb interviewing and counseling skills, a working knowledge of the principles of group dynamics (described in Chapters 1, 2, 3, 4, 5, and 6 of this text), and a working knowledge of contemporary therapy approaches, three of which are described in the Group Treatment Theories Resource Manual, located at the end of this text.

Group treatment has several advantages over one-on-one therapy. The "helper" therapy principle generally is operative. Members at times interchange roles and become the helper for someone else, receiving psychological rewards and putting their own problems into perspective in the process. Group treatment also allows members with interaction problems to test new approaches. In addition, research has shown it is generally easier to change the attitudes of an individual in a group than one-on-one.[15] Group treatment permits a social worker to treat more than one person at a time and represents a substantial savings of professional time. (Treatment groups are discussed more fully in Chapter 12.)

Sensitivity and Encounter Training

Encounter groups, sensitivity training groups, and T (training)-groups all refer to a group experience in which people relate to each other in a close interpersonal manner and self-disclosure is required. The goal is to improve interpersonal awareness. Barker defines a sensitivity group as

> a training and consciousness-raising group rather than one that meets to resolve psychosocial or mental disorders. Such groups typically consist of 10 to 20 members and a leader, called a trainer or facilitator. The members participate in discussions and experiential activities to demonstrate how groups function, to show how each member tends to affect others, and to help them become more aware of their own and other people's feelings and behaviors.[16]

An encounter group may meet for a few hours or over a few days. Once increased interpersonal awareness is achieved, it is anticipated that attitudes and behaviors will change. For these changes to occur a three-phase process generally takes place: *unfreezing, change,* and *refreezing.*[17]

Unfreezing occurs in encounter groups through a deliberate process of interacting in nontraditional ways. Our attitudes and behavior patterns have been developed through years of social experiences. Such patterns, following years of experimentation and refinement, have now become nearly automatic. The interpersonal style we develop through years of trial and error generally has considerable utility in our everyday interactions. Deep down, however, we may recognize a need for improvement but are reluctant to make the effort, partly because our present style is somewhat functional and partly because we are afraid to reveal things about ourselves. Unfreezing occurs when we decide certain patterns of our present behavior need to be changed, and we are psychologically ready to explore ways to make changes.

A Socialization Group: A Group at a Runaway Center

New Horizons, located in an older home in a large midwestern city, is a private, temporary shelter where youths on the run can stay for two weeks. The facility is licensed to house up to eight youths; however, state law requires that parents be contacted and parental permission received before New Horizons can provide shelter overnight. Services include temporary shelter, individual and family counseling, and a 24-hour hotline for youths in crisis. Since the average stay at New Horizons is nine days, the population is continually changing. During their stay, youths (and often their parents) receive intensive counseling, which focuses on reducing conflicts between the youths and their parents, and on helping them make future living plans. The two-week limit conveys the importance to residents and their families of resolving the conflicts that keep them apart.

Every evening at seven, a group meeting allows residents to express their satisfactions and dissatisfactions with the facilities and program at New Horizons. All the residents and the two or three staff members on duty are expected to attend. The meetings are convened and led by the staff, most of whom are social workers. Sometimes, the group becomes primarily a "gripe" session, but the staff makes conscientious efforts to improve or change situations involving legitimate gripes. For example, a youth may indicate that the past few days have been "boring," and staff and residents then jointly plan activities for the next few days.

Interaction problems that arise between residents, and between staff and residents, are also handled during a group session. A resident may be preventing others from sleeping; some residents may refuse to share in domestic tasks; there may be squabbles about which TV program to watch; some residents may be overly aggressive. Since most of the youths face a variety of crises associated with being on the run, many are anxious and under stress. In such an emotional climate, interaction problems are certain to arise. Staff members are sometimes intensely questioned about their actions, decisions, and policies. For example, one of the policies at New Horizons is that each resident must agree not to use alcohol or narcotic drugs while at the shelter. The penalty is expulsion. Occasionally, a few youths use some drugs, are caught, and expelled. Removing a youth from this facility has an immense impact on the other residents, and at the following meetings staff members are expected to clarify and explain such decisions.

The staff also presents material on topics requested by residents during meetings. Subjects often covered include sex; drugs; homosexuality; physical and sexual abuse (a fair number of residents are abused by family members); avoiding rape; handling anger, depression, and other unwanted emotions; legal rights of youths on the run; being more assertive; explaining running away to relatives and friends; and human services available to youths in the community. During such presentations, considerable discussion with residents is encouraged and generally occurs.

The final objective of the group is to convey information about planned daily activities and changes in the overall program at New Horizons.

Tubbs and Baird describe the unfreezing process in sensitivity groups:

Unfreezing occurs when our expectations are violated. We become less sure of ourselves when traditional ways of doing things are not followed. In the encounter group, the leader usually does not act like a leader. He or she frequently starts with a brief statement encouraging the group members to participate, to be open and honest, and to expect things to be different. Group members may begin by taking off their shoes, sitting in a circle on the floor, and holding hands with their eyes closed. The leader then encourages them to feel intensely the sensations they are experiencing, the size and texture of the hands they are holding, and so forth.

Other structured exercises or experiences may be planned to help the group focus on the "here-and-now" experience. Pairs may go for "trust walks" in which each person alternately is led around with eyes closed. Sitting face to face and conducting a hand dialogue, or a silent facial mirroring often helps to break the initial barriers to change. Other techniques may involve the "pass around" in which a person in the center of a tight circle relaxes and is physically passed around the circle. Those who have trouble feeling a part of the group are encouraged to break into or out of the circle of people whose hands are tightly held. With these experiences, most participants begin to feel more open to conversation about what they have experienced. This sharing of experiences or self-disclosure about the here and now provides more data for the group to discuss.[18]

The second phase of the process involves making changes in attitudes and behavior, which are usually facilitated by spontaneous feedback as to how a person "comes across" to others. In everyday interaction, spontaneous feedback seldom occurs, so ineffective interaction patterns are repeated. In sensitivity groups, feedback is strongly encouraged, as the following interaction illustrates:

Carl: All right (*in a sharp tone*), let's get this trust walk over with and stop dilly-dallying around. I'll lead the first person around—who wants to be blindfolded first?

Judy: I feel uncomfortable about your statement. I feel you are saying this group is a waste of your time. Also, this appears to be your third attempt this evening to "boss" us around.

Jim: I also feel like you are trying to tell us peons what to do. Even the tone of your voice is autocratic and suggests some disgust with this group.

Carl: I'm sorry. I didn't mean it to sound like that. I wonder if I do that outside the group too?

Such feedback provides us with new insights on how we affect others. Once problem interactions are identified, that member is encouraged to try out new response patterns in the relative safety of the group.

The third and final phase involves "refreezing," a term that is not an accurate description since it implies rigidity within a new set of response patterns. On the contrary, by experimenting with new sets of behaviors, a group member becomes a growing, continually changing person who becomes increasingly effective in interacting with others. In terminating a sensitivity group, the leader may alert the participants to be "on guard" as old behavior patterns tend to creep back in.

Sensitivity groups usually generate an outpouring of emotions, as do treatment groups. Sensitivity groups provide an interesting contrast to treatment groups. In treatment groups, each member explores personal and emotional problems in depth and then develops strategies to resolve them. Sensitivity groups generally do not directly attempt to identify and change specific emotional or personal problems, such as drinking, feelings of depression, or sexual dysfunctions. The philosophy behind sensitivity groups is that by simply increasing personal and interpersonal awareness, people will be better able to avoid, cope with, and handle specific personal problems that arise.

Despite their popularity, sensitivity groups remain controversial. In some cases, inadequately trained and incompetent individuals have become self-proclaimed leaders and enticed people to join through sensational advertising. If handled poorly, the short duration of some groups may intensify personal problems; for example, a person's defense mechanisms may be stripped away without first developing adaptive coping patterns. Many authorities on sensitivity training disclaim the use of encounter groups as a form of psychotherapy and discourage those with serious personal problems from joining such a group. Carl Rogers, in reviewing his own extensive experience as leader/participant, echoes these concerns:

> Frequently the behavior changes that occur, if any, are not lasting. In addition, the individual may become deeply involved in revealing himself and then be left with problems which are not worked through. Less common, but still noteworthy, there are also very occasional accounts of an individual having a psychotic episode during or immediately following an intensive group experience. We must keep in mind that not all people are suited for groups.[19]

In some cases the popularity of sensitivity groups has led some individuals to enter harmful groups with incompetent leaders where normal ethical standards have been abused. Shostrom has identified some means by which those interested in encounter groups can prevent exploitation: (1) Never participate in a group of fewer than a half-dozen members. The necessary and valuable candor generated by an effective group

Contrasting Goals of Treatment Groups versus Sensitivity Groups

TREATMENT GROUPS

Step 1: Examine problems in depth.

Step 2: Develop and select, from various resolution approaches, a strategy to resolve the problem.

SENSITIVITY GROUPS

Step 1: Help each person become more aware of herself and how she affects others in interpersonal interactions.

Step 2: Help a person develop more effective interaction patterns.

cannot be dissipated, shared, or examined by too small a group, and scapegoating or purely vicious ganging up can develop. (2) Never join an encounter group on impulse—as a fling, binge, or surrender to the unplanned. (3) Never stay with a group that has a behavioral ax to grind. (4) Never participate in a group that lacks formal connection with a professional who has proper credentials.[20]

After reviewing the research on the outcome of sensitivity groups, Lieberman, Yalom, and Miles provide an appropriate perspective for those interested in the intensive group experience:

> Encounter groups present a clear and evident danger if they are used for radical surgery to produce a new man [person]. The danger is even greater when the leader and the participants share this misconception. If we no longer expect groups to produce magical, lasting change and if we stop seeing them as panaceas, we can regard them as useful, socially sanctioned opportunities for human beings to explore and to express themselves. Then we can begin to work on ways to improve them so that they may make a meaningful contribution toward solving human problems.[21]

INITIAL DEVELOPMENT OF GROUPS

The process of establishing and conducting groups varies significantly, depending on the type of group and the specific purposes to be achieved. However, for a group to reach its maximum potential, there are still some unifying or common elements to be addressed prior to establishing the group. These factors described in this section include determining a group's objectives, size, open-ended or closed-ended status, and duration. In addition, since specific pitfalls or dilemmas characterize certain types of groups, plans must be made to prevent or handle problems should they arise.

Determining Objectives

Careful consideration must be given to the objectives for a group being formed in order to select effective members. For example, problem-solving groups often require the expertise of professionals in other disciplines—professionals whose skills and knowledge directly contribute to the accomplishment of group goals; some of these professionals may have backgrounds, training, and perceptions that differ from those of the social worker. While this approach produces a group with a wealth of expertise, it creates additional demands on the leader. When the members have diverse backgrounds and interests, other difficulties include problems encountered in setting goals, prioritizing goals, and determining tasks to be performed. Educational groups, on the other hand, are usually composed of members who share a common interest in a particular area, such as child-rearing skills. Individuals with similar needs join an educational group primarily to gain rather than dispense information. This tends to make leadership easier. Because potential members of treatment groups (unlike those of problem-solving or educational groups) often have diverse problems, and may in addition have interactional difficulties, a much more thorough screening of members is required. Therefore, it is essential that the objectives or purposes of each group be established at the beginning because they have a significant impact on the process of membership selection and other aspects of functioning.

Size

The size of a group affects members' satisfactions, interactions, and the amount of output per member. Although smaller groups are generally rated more favorably, larger groups are often more successful in resolving complex problems.[22] While members in larger groups experience more stress and greater communication difficulties, they usually bring a greater number of problem-solving skills and resources to the group as a whole. Since each person has fewer opportunities to interact in a large group, some members feel inhibited and reluctant to talk. As the size of the group increases, discussion generally hinges on the input of the most frequent contributor, who assumes a dominant role. As a result, the gap in participation widens between the most frequent contributor and the other members of the group.

In his research on group size, Slater found that groups of five people were considered most satisfactory by members themselves and

> most effective in dealing with an intellectual task involving the collection and exchange of information about a situation; the coordination, analysis, and evaluation of this information; and a group decision regarding the appropriate administrative action to be taken.[23]

In a group of five members, a number of different relationships can be formed with a moderate level of intimacy. Several individuals can also act as "buffers" who deal with strained situations or power plays. If a vote is needed to resolve a dispute, obviously a two-two split can be avoided. In groups smaller than five, Slater observed, the members were inhibited from expressing their ideas through fear of alienating one another and thereby destroying the group. In groups of more than five, members also felt inhibited and participated less often.

Groups with an even number of members tend to have higher rates of disagreement and antagonism than those with an odd number, apparently because of the possible division of the group into two equal subdivisions.[24] For each task to be accomplished, there is probably an optimal group size. The more complex the task, the larger the optimal size, so that the knowledge, abilities, and skills of many members are available to accomplish the task. A group should be large enough to allow members to speak freely without being inhibited and small enough to permit a moderate level of intimacy and involvement.

Open-Ended versus Closed-Ended Groups

Whether the group will be open-ended, with new members added as old members leave, or whether the membership will remain constant until termination (closed-ended) should be determined at the outset. *Open-ended groups* provide a measure of synergism through the addition of new members. As new individuals join, they provide a different viewpoint, even though they usually are gradually socialized into group norms and practices by the older members. The impact of such changes is not all beneficial, however. The constant change in membership may inhibit openness and detract from the sense of trust needed before certain subjects are broached. In addition, open groups are likely to "have members at different levels of commitment to the process and members [who are not] at the same stages of development."[25]

A *closed-ended group* can often function more effectively because it has a relatively constant population and often operates within a specified time frame.[26] Although the premature loss of members can seriously damage such a group's effectiveness, a leader must deal with member termination in both open and closed groups and plan for this eventuality.

Duration

The duration of a group has two related components: the number of sessions and the length of each session. Many groups meet for one to two hours once or twice a week for a specified number of weeks. Meeting for one to two hours tends to optimize productive activity and behavior. Meeting lengths shorter than one hour usually do not allow sufficient time to thoroughly discuss the issues that are raised. In meetings that last longer than three hours, members tend to become drowsy, frustrated, and unable to concentrate. Although a meeting length of one to two hours appears to be a guideline for optimal functioning in many groups, at times pressing issues may necessitate a longer meeting to process and conclude group business. Obviously, if a crisis occurs five minutes before the end of the meeting, the group leader should not conclude the session. By the same token, some discussions can become so intense that they could last indefinitely and accomplish little. A pragmatic approach to terminating each meeting or series of meetings within a set time frame will enhance the group's respect for the leader and foster the group's development.

Setting meetings in which there are three or four (or more) days between meetings usually allows the members some time to work on tasks that are designed to accomplish their personal goals and the goals of the group. For example, in educational groups, members can study and complete homework assignments between meetings. In treatment groups, members can carry out homework assignments designed to reduce or resolve personal problems.

■ STAGES OF GROUPS

The steps involved in planning and implementing educational, treatment, and socialization groups are similar to the procedures followed by social workers who deal with individual clients:

GROUPS	INDIVIDUALS
intake	intake
selection of members	assessment and planning
assessment and planning	intervention
group development and	evaluation and termination
intervention	
evaluation and termination	

Inexperienced group leaders usually expect a smooth transition from one stage to another and are disappointed if this does not occur. Therefore, many new practitioners tend to force the group out of one stage into another instead of allowing the natural growth process to evolve. Experience will demonstrate the futility of these efforts as, barring unforeseen circumstances, each group will move at its own pace and eventually arrive at the same destination. Groups that skip stages or whose development is otherwise thwarted will often return to a previous stage to complete unfinished business. While groups do sometimes become mired in one stage, these occurrences are less common than generally thought. The procedures for establishing socialization, educational, and treatment groups are briefly summarized in the following material and expanded upon throughout the text.

Intake

During intake, the presenting concerns and needs of prospective members are identified. Judgments that some or all of these people could benefit from a group approach are made. An agreement is often formulated between the members of the group and the group leader about tentative group goals (see Chapter 4). This stage may also be referred to as the contract stage, as the leader and the members make a commitment to pursue the situation to the next step.

Selection of Members

Individuals most likely to benefit from a group should be selected as members. Selecting a group requires attention to both descriptive and behavioral factors.[27] A decision needs to be made whether to seek homogeneity or diversity in these factors. There are few guidelines as to when diversity and when homogeneity of these factors will be most effective and efficient. Age, sex, and level of education are *descriptive factors* that may create homogeneity or foster diversity within the group. In groups of children and adolescents, the age span among members must be kept relatively small because levels of maturity and interests can vary greatly. Similarly, same-sex groupings may facilitate achieving group goals for pre-adolescents, but for middle-adolescent groups there may be specific advantages to having representation from both sexes.

The *behavioral attributes* expected of a group member will also have a major effect on the attainment of group objectives. For example, placing several hyperactive or aggressive youngsters in a group may be a prelude to failure. Members may be selected for their value as models for appropriate behavior or because they possess other personal characteristics expected to enhance the group. As a general rule, the best judgment regarding a member's potential contribution to the group is obtained by looking at past behavioral attributes.[28]

Assessment and Planning

A more in-depth assessment and statement of goals and plans for action occurs during this phase. In reality, this step is completed only when the group ends because the dynamic nature of most groups requires an ongoing adjustment of goals and intervention plans. Goals should be time-limited with a reasonable chance for attainment, and the leader should ensure that all goals are clearly stated to aid in later evaluations. Clarification of goals also eliminates hidden agendas.

Group Development and Intervention

Numerous models of group development have evolved. Three of these models are described in the next section of this chapter, entitled "Models of Group Development over Time."

Evaluation and Termination

To think of evaluation as a specific point in the life of a group is perhaps not realistic since evaluation must be an ongoing process. The decision to terminate a group may be based on the accomplishment of group or individual goals, the expiration of a predetermined period of time, the failure of the group to achieve desired ends, the relocation of the leader of the group, or a shortage of funds to keep the group going.

The termination of a group often produces the same reactions that characterize the termination of other significant relationships, including the feeling of being rejected. The group leader must be aware of these potential feelings and help group members terminate with a minimum of difficulty. Additional material on how to terminate a group is presented in Chapter 13.

◼ MODELS OF GROUP DEVELOPMENT OVER TIME

Groups change over time. Numerous framework models have been developed to describe these changes. The models of group development described here are (1) the Garland, Jones, and Kolodny Model, (2) the Tuckman Model, (3) the Northen and Kurland Model, and (4) the Bales Model.

Garland, Jones, and Kolodny Model

Garland, Jones, and Kolodny developed a model that identifies five stages of development in social work groups.[29] By describing and understanding the various kinds of developmental problems in groups, leaders can more effectively anticipate and respond to the reactions of group members. The conceptualization of Garland et al. appears particularly applicable to socialization, therapeutic, and encounter groups; to a lesser extent, the model is applicable to self-help, task, problem-solving and decision-making, educational, and recreation/skill groups.

Emotional closeness among members is the central focus of the model and is reflected in *struggles* that occur at five stages of group growth: preaffiliation, power and control, intimacy, differentiation, and separation.

Preaffiliation

In the first stage, *preaffiliation,* members are ambivalent about joining the group, and interaction is guarded. Members test out, often through approach and avoidance behavior, whether they really want to belong. Because new situations are often frightening, members attempt to protect themselves from being hurt or taken advantage of, maintaining a certain amount of distance and attempting to get what they can from the group without taking many risks. Even though individuals are aware that group involvement will make demands that may be frustrating or even painful, they are attracted because of rewards and satisfying experiences in other groups. These former positive ramifications are transferred to the "new" group. During this first stage, the leader tries to make the group appear as attractive as possible "by allowing and supporting distance, gently inviting trust, facilitating exploration of the physical and psychological milieu, and by providing activities if necessary and initiating group structure."[30] This stage ends gradually as members begin to feel safe and comfortable within the group and to view its rewards as worth a tentative emotional commitment.

Power and Control

In the second stage, *power and control,* the character of the group begins to emerge. Patterns of communication, alliances, and subgroups begin to develop. Individuals assume certain roles and responsibilities, establish norms and methods for handling group tasks, and begin to ask questions. Although these processes are necessary to conduct meetings, they also lead to a power struggle in which each member attempts to gain greater control over the gratifications and rewards to be received from the group. A major source of gratification for any group is the leader, who influences the direction of the group and gives or withholds emotional and material rewards. At this point, members realize that the group is becoming important to them. This second stage is transitional, with certain basic issues requiring resolution: Does the group or the leader have primary control? What are the limits of the power of the group and of the leader, and to what extent will the leader use his power?

This uncertainty results in anxiety and considerable testing by group members to gauge limits and establish norms for the power and authority of both the group and the leader. Rebellion is not uncommon, and the dropout rate in groups is often highest at this stage. During this struggle the leader should (1) help the members understand the nature of the power struggle, (2) give emotional support to help members weather the discomfort of uncertainty, and (3) help to establish norms to resolve the uncertainty. Group members must trust the leader to maintain a safe balance of shared power and control. When that trust is achieved, group members make a major commitment to become involved.

Intimacy

In the third stage, *intimacy,* the likes and dislikes of intimate relationships are expressed. The group becomes more like a family, with sibling rivalry exhibited and with the leader sometimes referred to as a parent. Feelings are more openly expressed and discussed, and the group is viewed as a place where growth and change take place. Individuals feel free to examine and make efforts to change personal attitudes, concerns, and problems, and there is a feeling of "oneness" or cohesiveness. Members struggle to explore and make changes in their personal lives, and to examine "what this group is all about."

Differentiation

During the fourth stage, *differentiation*, members are freer to experiment with new and alternative behavior patterns because they recognize individual rights and needs, and they communicate more effectively. Leadership is more evenly shared, roles are more functional, and the organization itself is more efficient. Power problems are now minimal, and decisions are made and carried out on a less emotional and more objective basis. Garland and Frey note:

> This kind of individualized therapeutic cohesion has been achieved because the group experience has all along valued and nurtured individual integrity. . . .
>
> The worker assists in this stage by helping the group to run itself and by encouraging it to act as a unit with other groups or in the wider community. During this time the [social] worker exploits opportunities for evaluation by the group of its activities, feelings and behavior.[31]

The differentiation stage is analogous to a healthy functioning family in which the children have reached adulthood and are now becoming successful in pursuing their own lives. Relationships are more often between equals, and members are mutually supportive and able to relate to each other in more rational and objective ways.

Separation

The final stage is *separation*. Group purposes have been achieved, and members have learned new behavioral patterns to enable them to move on to other social experiences. Termination is not always easily accomplished, as members may be reluctant to move on and may display regressive behavior to prolong the existence of the group. Members may express anger or may psychologically deny that termination is approaching. Garland and Frey describe the leader's (or social worker's) role this way:

> To facilitate separation the [social] worker must be willing to let go. Concentration upon group and individual mobility, evaluation of the experience, help with the expression of the ambivalence about termination and recognition of the progress which has been made are his major tasks. Acceptance of termination is facilitated by active guidance of members as individuals to other ongoing sources of support and assistance.[32]

Exercise 1.1: The Garland, Jones, and Kolodny Model

GOAL: This exercise is designed to help you analyze groups in terms of the Garland, Jones, and Kolodny Model.

Write a description of a group that you have participated in that has at least some of the group development stages identified by the Garland, Jones, and Kolodny Model. Identify the stages of your group that are consistent with the model. Also describe any developmental stages of your group that are inconsistent with this model.

Tuckman Model

Tuckman reviewed over 50 studies, primarily of limited-duration therapy and sensitivity groups, and concluded that these groups go through the following five predictable developmental stages: forming, storming, norming, performing, and adjourning.[33] Each stage will be briefly described.

Forming

Members become oriented toward each other, work on being accepted, and learn more about the group. This stage is marked by a period of uncertainty in which members try to determine their places in the group and learn the group's rules and procedures.

Storming

Conflicts begin to arise as members resist the influence of the group and rebel against accomplishing their tasks. Members confront their various differences, and the management of conflict often becomes the focus of attention.

Norming

The group establishes cohesiveness and commitment. In the process, the members discover new ways to work together. Norms are also set for appropriate behavior.

Performing

The group works as a unit to achieve group goals. Members develop proficiency in achieving goals and become more flexible in their patterns of working together.

Adjourning

The group disbands. The feelings that members experience are similar to those in the "Separation Stage" of the Garland, Jones, and Kolodny Model described in the previous section.

Exercise 1.2: The Tuckman Model

GOAL: This exercise is designed to help you analyze groups in terms of the Tuckman Model.

Write a description of a group that you have participated in that has at least some of the group development stages identified by the Tuckman Model. Identify the stages of your group that are consistent with the model. Also describe any developmental stages of your group that are inconsistent with this model.

Northen and Kurland Model*

Northen and Kurland focus on stages of group development and point out that each stage has its own developmental issues that must be attended to and at least partially resolved before the group can move into the next stage.[34] Northern and Kurland propose a four-stage model with emphasis on socio-emotional themes.

Inclusion–Orientation

The main socio-emotional theme of this stage, as the title implies, is whether or not group members will feel included. This stage is typically marked by anxiety and uncertainty as group members become acquainted with the group leader and each other. "The major task for the members is to become oriented to the group and to decide to be included in the group's membership."[35]

Uncertainty–Exploration

The major theme of this stage has to do with group members' uncertainty regarding issues of power and control. The socio-emotional issue pertains to conflict, especially in relationship to the group leader. Group members at this stage explore and test their relationship with the leader and each other in order to establish roles and develop trust and acceptance.

Mutuality–Goal Achievement

At this stage, the group is characterized by mutual aid and problem solving. Socio-emotional patterns among group members show greater self-disclosure, empathy, and mutual acceptance. Conflict and differences are dealt with as a means to achieve both individual and group goals.

---

*The description of this model was written by Michael Wallace, MSW, instructor at the University of Wisconsin–Whitewater.

Separation–Termination

The final stage focuses on the socio-emotional issues of separation and termination. Members at this stage may be reluctant to leave the leader and the group. The task here is to help prepare members for termination, deal with any unfinished business, and, most importantly, help group members transfer what they have learned in group to life outside the group.

Exercise 1.3: The Northen and Kurland Model

GOAL: This exercise is designed to help you analyze groups in terms of the Northen and Kurland Model.

Write a description of a group that you have participated in that has at least some of the group development stages identified by the Northen and Kurland Model. Identify the stages of your group that are consistent with the model. Also describe any developmental stages of your group that are inconsistent with this model.

Sequential Stage Models of Group Development

The three models of group development that were just described are sequential stage models. (These models are the Garland, Jones, and Kolodny Model; the Tuckman Model; and the Northen and Kurland Model.) Despite the variable nature of the stages of group development described in these three models, these models contain similar stages. As can be seen in Table 1.1, the various phases of group development can be divided into three phases: beginning, middle, and end.

In sequential models, the beginning stages of groups are concerned with planning, organizing, convening, and orientation. The beginnings of groups tend to be characterized by an emergence of group feeling. However, group feeling does not emerge without a struggle. Power issues and conflicts between members often emerge. The leader can help resolve power issues and conflicts by encouraging members to discuss and seek to resolve the power issues and conflicts that arise. (Strategies to resolve conflicts and power issues are described in Chapter 6.)

Although some work is accomplished in all stages of a group's development, most occurs in the middle stage. At the beginning of the middle stage, the conflicts over roles, norms, and power issues found in the later part of the beginning stage give way to the

■ **TABLE 1.1 Sequential Stage Models of Group Development**

Development Stage	Garland, Jones, and Kolodny	Tuckman	Northen and Kurland
Beginning	Preaffiliation Power and control	Forming	Inclusion–Orientation Uncertainty–Exploration
Middle	Intimacy Differentiation	Storming Norming Performing	Mutuality–Goal Achievement
End	Separation	Adjourning	Separation–Termination

members learning effective patterns of working together. Greater group cohesion appears. When this occurs, members concern themselves with the work necessary to accomplish the specific tasks (and achieve the goals) that have been agreed upon.

The end stage of a group is characterized by the completion and evaluation of the group's efforts, and by members terminating their contact with one another in this specific group. In this stage, tasks groups tend to make decisions, finish their business, produce the results of their efforts, and celebrate the accomplishments. On the other hand, treatment group members (because they have focused on emotional and behavioral issues) often experience the termination of the group as an emotional loss. They are pleased that they have made progress in resolving their issues but have a reluctance to lose the support they have received from the group. Termination is more fully described in Chapter 6: Task Groups and in Chapter 12: Treatment Groups.

For the interested reader, a relational model of group development stages in women's groups is described in Chapter 7.

Bales Model

The stages described in the models of group development that were just discussed are sequential-stage models, since they specify sequential stages of group development. In contrast, Robert F. Bales developed a recurring-phase model.[36] Bales asserted that groups continue to seek an equilibrium between task-oriented work and emotional expressions, in order to build better relationships among group members. (Task roles and social/emotional roles performed by members of a group are specified at some length in Chapter 3.) Bales asserts that groups tend to oscillate between these two concerns. Sometimes a group focuses on identifying and performing the tasks that will lead to achievement of its goals. At other times, the group focuses on building the morale and improving the social/emotional atmosphere of the group.

The sequential-stage perspective and the recurring-phase perspective are not necessarily contradictory. Both are useful for understanding group development. The sequential-stage perspective assumes that groups move through various stages while dealing with a series of basic themes that surface when they are relevant to the group's work. The recurring-phase perspective assumes that the issues underlying these basic themes are never completely resolved and tend to recur later.

■ GROUP COHESION

Group cohesion is the sum of all the variables influencing members to stay in a group. It occurs when the positive attractions of a group outweigh negative implications a member might encounter. The word *cohesion* is derived from Latin and can be translated literally as the "act of sticking together." A group's level of cohesion is constantly changing as events alter each member's feelings and attitudes about the group.

The extent of a member's attraction to and involvement in a group can be measured by his or her perceptions of the payoffs and costs. They are infinite because they vary from individual to individual, but the following lists offer a brief indication of possibilities:

PAYOFFS	COSTS
companionship	being with people one dislikes
attaining personal goals	expending time and effort
prestige	criticism
enjoyment	distasteful tasks
emotional support	boring meetings

The higher the level of attraction (payoffs), the greater the attractive qualities of cohesion.

An individual's willingness to risk and to become involved in a group depends to a large extent on the degree to which his needs for belonging are met. Often, members join groups to help meet the need to belong. Membership in a group or a person's willingness to share himself or herself often hinges on the degree of acceptance experienced in the group. The climate in a group is a crucial factor in determining the actual sense of belonging that members achieve. Clearly, the need for belonging can be a powerful factor in joining and remaining a member of groups.

Obviously, group members are most attracted to group meetings when friendly, pleasant interactions take place. Besides feeling relaxed, members are more apt to share their ideas and relate to others within the group. Initially, ice-breaker exercises can help members become more comfortable, and goals can be set that incorporate the personal goals of members (see Chapter 4). The more members feel involved in making decisions, the more they will feel that their views are respected.

Highly cohesive groups have low rates of absenteeism and low turnover in membership. In addition, members are generally motivated to complete assigned tasks, and they are apt to conform to group norms. They are more willing to listen, accept suggestions, and defend the group against external criticism. Because a group provides a source of security, it often rewards members by becoming a support system that reduces anxiety, heightens self-esteem, adds meaning to living, and often helps members resolve personal problems. Therefore, membership in a cohesive group enhances a member's psychological health by transmitting feelings of being valued, accepted, and liked.

Members should be rewarded for jobs well done rather than coerced or manipulated, to help create a cooperative atmosphere, not a competitive one. Again, pleasing interactions, rather than a constant war of words or negative banter, increase a group's cohesion. If a difficult situation arises, a problem-solving approach should be used. A win-lose approach usually decreases cohesion (see Chapter 6).

Trust among group members is another necessary condition for effective communication, cooperation, and cohesion. When distrust exists, individuals will not disclose sensitive personal information or commit their resources to accomplishing group goals. Even though some groups have "built-in" prestige, being a member of certain groups can potentially damage a member's reputation (for example, a member of a board of directors of a nursing home beset by a well-publicized scandal involving extensive patient abuse).

A group's cohesion will generally decrease when there is a long-term disagreement on how to define or resolve a major problem. Unreasonable or excessive demands on members, such as forcing a shy person to give a speech, will also sharply reduce the group's attractiveness. Dominating members and those who engage in repulsive behavior are certainly not large drawing cards. Scapegoats who are blamed for difficult situations may react aggressively or drop out. Finally, cohesion can be decreased if outside activities of the members are curtailed because of the group. For example, a student group that meets two or three nights a week may interfere with study time, exercising, and socializing.

Exercise 1.4: Variables That Impact Group Cohesion

GOAL: This exercise is designed to help you understand the variables that contribute to group cohesion.

1. Describe a highly cohesive group (perhaps a sports team, a group at school, or a church group) that you participated in. Identify the variables that contributed to group cohesion.

2. Describe a group that you participated in which had very little cohesion. Identify the variables that led this group to have very little cohesion.

■ MEMBERSHIP AND REFERENCE GROUPS

A *membership group* is a group in which a person belongs or does not belong. However, some people are marginal members of a group. For example, everyone enrolled at a college campus is a member of the student body, but some students are only marginal members because they are not involved in any campus activities. Carol works nearly full-time in the evening and does not live on campus, but she does attend classes. She identifies primarily with the people she works with, and other students influence her very little. Carol, then, has limited psychological membership in the student body and only minor identification with the campus. Full psychological membership in a group occurs only when a person is positively attracted to the group and accepted as a member. The more fully a person is a member of a group, the greater will be that person's commitment to accomplishing group goals.

Individuals who aspire to membership in a group will act as the members act. Students who want to be admitted to a fraternity or sorority, for example, will act like members to increase their chances of being admitted. Aspiring members are psychologically identifying with the group, even though they are not members.

Voluntary membership is freely chosen while *involuntary membership* is required. Social workers often work with involuntary groups in prison settings, mental hospitals, residential treatment facilities, and schools, where members are often uninterested, hostile, or disruptive.

Practically all of us are members of a variety of groups. Jim, for example, is a family member, a Roman Catholic, a PTA member, a forward on a basketball team, a member of the National Association of Social Workers, and a member of the local board of Planned Parenthood. Occasionally there are conflicts because the groups may schedule meetings at the same time and have different norms and values. Planned Parenthood's views on birth control and abortion, for example, differ from those espoused by the Catholic Church. To resolve this dilemma, Jim can compartmentalize his values by accepting Planned Parenthood's views on abortion and birth control and most of the Catholic doctrine except the church's views on abortion and birth control. The resolution of conflicts resulting from multiple membership is often attained through much anxiety and great personal cost.

Reference groups are groups whose influence we accept and identify with. In the example given earlier, Carol is a member of a student body and a work group. Since she primarily identifies with her work group, it serves as a reference group for her, but the student body does not. Reference groups have two distinct functions: (1) normative, for members who seek to conform to their positions and standards for behavior; and (2) decision-making, for members who use group standards, or norms, as the basis for making and evaluating decisions.

Some members of a group are referents who influence and are influenced by other members. In a large group, only a small subgroup of members are referents. These referents "make sense" to other members (who identify with them) as they are viewed as experts or authorities, or have most of the power. Occasionally, people select a reference group in terms of an issue. For example, Jim uses Planned Parenthood as a reference group to express his feelings on birth control and abortion, while he uses the Catholic Church as a reference group for his views on suicide, euthanasia, life after death, and morality.

Exercise 1.5: Understanding Membership and Reference Groups

GOAL: This exercise is designed to help you understand the concepts of reference groups and membership groups.

1. **Identify a group that you are a member of, which is not a reference group for you. Why is it not a reference group for you?**

2. **Identify a group that you are a member of, which is also a reference group for you. Describe why you identify with this reference group.**

■ BREAKING THE ICE

In most newly formed groups, the leader has the initial responsibility of seeking to create an atmosphere in which members feel comfortable. Members of a new group are apt to have a number of concerns: "Will I be respected and accepted?" "Will this group be worth my time and effort?" "Will I feel embarrassed or inferior?" "Will I be able to form new friendships?" "Are the other members the kind of people I will like?" "What will my roles and responsibilities be—and will I like them?" "Will I have a leadership role?" "Will others expect more of me than I am capable of giving?" "Will my personal goals or expectations be realized?" "If I find I do not like or enjoy this group, is there a nice way to get out?"

To help members become comfortable, the leader might use an ice-breaker exercise. (Several such exercises are described at the end of this chapter.) Such exercises are designed to help members become acquainted with one another, introduce themselves, reduce anxieties, and facilitate communication. Each group has a unique personality. In most social work groups, the leader attempts to create an atmosphere in which the members trust one another and want to share their thoughts and ideas. Ice breakers are an important step in establishing such an atmosphere.

As a student, you have probably observed that each class has a unique personality. Norms are established in their first few sessions, for example, as to whether students will share and discuss their opinions and beliefs. If a norm of "silence" is established, the instructor generally ends up doing practically all the talking. Such a class becomes a "chore" for the instructor and also for the students. Many of the ingredients that go into determining whether a class will establish a norm of "talking" or of "silence" are unknown. Certainly, a norm of talking is facilitated by ice breakers.

Ice-breaking exercises can also accomplish specific objectives, such as obtaining information on the members' expectations for the group. One such ice breaker is described at the end of this chapter. Before we consider ice breaker exercises, the pitfalls, ethics, and guidelines on conducting classroom exercises will be summarized.

■ EXPERIENTIAL LEARNING

It is important that social work students receive experiential training in classes to prepare them for the realities of social work practice. Social workers encounter many sensitive situations in the course of their work: divorce, suicide, child abuse and neglect, incest, and death. In a classroom, a qualified instructor observes the level of psychological stress in participants, provides feedback on how to better handle sensitive situations, and intervenes if necessary. After students graduate and begin working with clients, such guidance is seldom available. Therefore, it is vital that they develop their skills through practical classroom applications before they venture into real group counseling situations.

Classroom exercises offer a variety of payoffs. They can illustrate key theoretical concepts, clarify values, or help students develop skills such as assessment and intervention. They are generally fun and often teach students more effectively than other mechanisms. Exercises also help students get acquainted, build group cohesion, and increase group morale.

Ethics and Guidelines for Conducting Exercises

1. The leader has the tasks of explaining the objectives, describing the steps, beginning the exercise, keeping the members on task and on time, modeling appropriate values and skills, leading the members in discussing and evaluating the exercise after it is conducted, and being alert to the emotional reactions of the members to the exercise.

2. Generally, the more enthusiasm the instructor displays for class exercises, the more enthusiasm the students will display.

3. Students learn in different ways. Some will be more responsive and learn more from exercises than others.

4. The learning needs of the students should determine the kinds of exercises used. Leaders may want to modify the exercises in this text to meet special learning needs. In designing or modifying an exercise, leaders should consider the following questions: Is this the best exercise to accomplish the learning objectives? Should the exercise be modified to better fit the characteristics of the group? How can processing of the exercise be best accomplished? Is there sufficient class time to conduct the exercise? Is the group too large or too small for the exercise? Are the required materials available? What problems may arise? Is there sufficient time to process problems?

5. To allot enough time, the leaders should estimate how much time each step in the exercise will take.

6. When an exercise is introduced, group members should be informed of the objectives, given an overview of what will occur, and encouraged to ask questions. Members have a right to expect clear information before beginning the exercise. To build trust, the leader should not give false information or incorrect answers to questions. If an accurate answer (to a question raised before the exercise is conducted) will reveal information the exercise is designed to convey, the leader may say, "It is best to delay answering this question as the exercise is designed to reveal the answer."

7. The instructor should always be present when an exercise is being conducted.

8. The leader should have specific educational objectives for each exercise and be able to articulate these objectives. Students have the right to know what the objectives are. (If stating the objectives at the beginning will "give away" a point hidden in the exercise, the objectives should be carefully explained at the end.)

9. The leader should carefully plan each exercise and be qualified to conduct it. The exercises in this text are explained in considerable detail. The leader should prepare for each exercise by reading and visualizing the steps, and by thinking about how this specific class might respond.

10. A few exercises may arouse strong emotions because they may touch an area in which a student is struggling. The instructor should thus observe students closely, be prepared to talk privately with such students after class, and be aware of appropriate counseling resources for students whose psychological stress is severe.

11. The instructor should seek to establish a supportive, caring, and respectful atmosphere among the students.

12. The class should understand the importance of keeping sensitive personal information confidential.

13. Once the objectives and format of an exercise are explained, student participation should be voluntary. Students who do not wish to participate should be excused with the understanding that every student is expected to participate in most of the exercises.

14. No exercise should be so secretive or sensitive that other faculty could not be invited to observe.

15. It is generally better to use one or two exercises to demonstrate a point than to use several.

16. If a number of exercises are conducted during a term, the instructor should seek to have each student take an active role in at least some of them. Special efforts should be made to involve those students who are quiet and nonassertive.

17. The instructor should critique student skills or behavior in a positive way. The student should not be made to feel inferior, incompetent, or inadequate. When a shortcoming is pointed out, the student should also be praised for what she or he did well. The feedback should focus on behavior rather than on the person, on

observations rather than on judgments. A problem-solving approach in which shortcomings are identified and alternatives for improvement provided works well. The feedback should focus on sharing ideas and information rather than on giving advice. The instructor should never embarrass a student in front of classmates, and sensitive subjects should be covered in a private meeting with that student.

18. The instructor should provide encouragement by being positive and by praising, at one time or another, each student for such actions as making positive contributions, putting forth effort, displaying progress, showing unique skills, or being perceptive and respectful of others.

19. After completion, each exercise should be discussed and evaluated in an open, relaxed atmosphere. Students must feel free to raise questions, express thoughts and concerns, and discuss the merits and shortcomings of the exercise. Such an evaluation brings about closure, which is important, and helps the leader improve the exercise for future use.

20. Even the most carefully designed exercises sometimes fail. An important instruction may have been left out. The students may be distracted by other concerns and fail to give the exercise their undivided attention. The exercise may be poorly designed. When an exercise flops, it is generally best to acknowledge that things did not go as planned. Attempting to cover up an obvious flop will only cause students to question the honesty and effectiveness of the leader. Humor can "take the edge off," and the leader may be able to achieve the learning objectives by using another closely related exercise. At times, an exercise may be a complete loss. How the instructor reacts will be a factor in determining the student's confidence in the instructor. In addition, an appropriate reaction will help students learn how to respond to failures in groups they lead. Since humans are fallible by nature, some exercises will not achieve the desired objectives, and instructors should learn from such mistakes.

Pitfalls to Avoid in Conducting Class Exercises

1. Class exercises are not designed to solve emotional problems. Certainly the leader should not seek to meet his or her emotional needs through such exercises.
2. Class exercises should not be used simply to fill class time. They should have legitimate teaching objectives and value.
3. An exercise should not be used if there is insufficient time to discuss or process the activity.
4. Exercises should not replace other forms of instruction, such as lectures.
5. Although some students enroll in social work and psychology courses to solve their own personal problems, experiential exercises should *not* encourage students to disclose material they will later regret having divulged. If extremely personal information is revealed, the class atmosphere must be supportive. Subsequent discussion should be more generalized and objective.

◼ GROUP EXERCISES

GOAL: The following exercises are designed to help break the ice in new groups and are just a sample of the many ice-breaker experiences available. The group leader should select exercises appropriate to specific groups and modify them as needed.

Exercise A: Getting Acquainted

The leader asks the members to sit in a circle and explains that the goal is to get acquainted. The group is asked to make a list of what they would like to know about each other, such as name, year in school, major, and reason for taking course. An interesting item the leader may decide to add is "most embarrassing moment" or "tell us something about you that would surprise us." The list should be written on a blackboard or flip chart. One by one the members, including the leader, respond to the listed items. The leader should then ask if there is additional information the members want to know about him or her, including training and professional experience, and should answer all questions except those considered too personal.

Exercise B: Introducing a Partner

Follow the same format as in Exercise A. The only variant is that after the items are listed, the members pair off and gather the information from their partners. If there is an uneven number of members, form one subgroup of three. Allow five minutes for information gathering. Partners then introduce each other to the group.

Exercise C: Personal Expectations for the Group

The leader asks the members to introduce themselves. Possible items that might be covered are the following:

Name
Year in school
Major
Paid experience in social work
Volunteer experience in social work
Most embarrassing experience (for humor)
Reason for taking course
Personal expectations for the class or group
Something about you that would surprise us

This ice breaker is useful as a first step in seeking to identify the personal goals of members. The leader's goals and objectives for the group should then be given. A discussion may well ensue, and it should focus on setting group goals. The leader should be flexible, seeking to set goals that meet legitimate expectations of the members. If one or more expectations are beyond the objectives of the group, the leader should tactfully indicate this and explain why.

Exercise D: Searching for Descriptors

The leader passes out a list of descriptors designed for a specific group. (A *descriptor* is a word or phrase that identifies an item.) Some possibilities are listed below. Each group member then finds three others who say "yes" to specific descriptors. (The number "three" may be increased or decreased.) Each member should then give a completed list to the leader. The exercise may be ended by asking the members what items of interest they learned about others.

SAMPLE DESCRIPTORS

Likes professional football	Owns a car
Is a Leo	Has water-skied
Plays golf	Has traveled in Mexico
Likes classical music	Has meditated
Has had a paid or volunteer	Likes to jog
job in social work	Enjoys riding horses
Is dating somewhat steadily	Has flown airplanes
or is married	Attends church regularly
Has received a speeding ticket	

CHAPTER TWO

Social Group Work and Social Work Practice

GOALS

This chapter presents a conceptualization of social work practice. We will see that social work with groups is an integral component of social work practice. The chapter also summarizes the conceptualization of social work practice that is presented in the Educational Policy Statement of the Council on Social Work Education for baccalaureate degree programs and master's degree programs in social work.

What do social workers do? How is social work different from psychology, psychiatry, guidance and counseling, and other helping professions? What is the relationship between social work and social welfare? What knowledge, skills, and values do social workers need to be effective? This chapter will seek to address these questions. There have been a number of other efforts to address these same issues.[1] This chapter is largely an effort to integrate these prior conceptualizations. The purpose of this chapter is to describe social work as a profession and thereby assist social workers and other interested persons in understanding and articulating what social work is and what is unique about the social work profession.

■ DEFINITION OF SOCIAL WORK

Social work has been defined by the National Association of Social Workers (NASW) as follows:

> Social work is the professional activity of helping individuals, groups, or communities to enhance or restore their capacity for social functioning and to create societal conditions favorable to their goals.
>
> Social work practice consists of the professional application of social work values, principles, and techniques to one or more of the following ends: helping people obtain tangible services; providing counseling and psychotherapy for individuals, families, and groups; helping communities or groups provide or improve social and health services; and participating in relevant legislative processes.
>
> The practice of social work requires knowledge of human development and behavior; of social, economic, and cultural institutions; and of the interaction of all these factors.[2]

Much of the material in this chapter is adapted from *The Practice of Social Work,* 7th ed., by Zastrow. © 2003. Reprinted with permission of Brooks/Cole, a divison of Thomson Learning, Inc.

The term *social worker* is generally applied to graduates (with bachelor's or master's degrees) of educational programs in social work who are employed in the field of social welfare. A social worker is a *change agent,* a helper who is specifically employed for the purpose of creating planned change.[3] As a change agent, a social worker is expected to be skilled at working with individuals, groups, families, and organizations, and in bringing about community changes.

■ RELATIONSHIP BETWEEN SOCIAL WORK AND SOCIAL WELFARE

The goal of social welfare is to fulfill the social, financial, health, and recreational requirements of all individuals in a society. Social welfare seeks to enhance the social functioning of all age groups, both rich and poor. When other institutions in our society (such as the market economy and the family) fail at times to meet the basic needs of individuals or groups of people, then social services are needed and demanded.

Barker defines social welfare as

a nation's system of programs, benefits, and services that help people meet those social, economic, educational, and health needs that are fundamental to the maintenance of society.[4]

Examples of social welfare programs and services are foster care, adoption, day care, Head Start, probation and parole, public assistance programs (such as Food Stamps), public health nursing, sex therapy, suicide counseling, recreational services (Boy Scouts and YWCA programs), services to populations-at-risk (such as the elderly), school social services, medical and legal services to the poor, family planning services, Meals on Wheels, nursing home services, shelters for battered spouses, services to persons with acquired immune deficiency syndrome (AIDS), protective services for victims of child abuse and neglect, assertiveness training, encounter groups and sensitivity training, public housing projects, family counseling, Alcoholics Anonymous, runaway services, services to people with developmental disabilities, and rehabilitation services.

Almost all social workers are employed in the field of social welfare. There are, however, many other professional and occupational groups working in the field of social welfare, as illustrated in Figure 2.1.

■ WHAT IS THE PROFESSION OF SOCIAL WORK?

The National Association of Social Workers defines the social work profession as follows:

The social work profession exists to provide humane and effective social services to individuals, families, groups, communities, and society so that social functioning may be enhanced and the quality of life improved. . . .

The profession of social work by both traditional and practical definition, is the profession that provides the formal knowledge base, theoretical concepts, specific functional skills, and essential social values which are used to implement society's mandate to provide safe, effective, and constructive social services.[5]

Social work is thus distinct from other professions (such as psychology and psychiatry) as it is the profession that has the responsibility and mandate to provide social services.

A social worker needs training and expertise in a wide range of areas to be able to effectively handle problems faced by individuals, groups, families, organizations, and the larger community. While most professions are becoming more specialized (for example, most medical doctors now specialize in one or two areas), social work continues to emphasize a generic (broad-based) approach. The practice of social work is analogous to the old general practice of medicine. A general practitioner in medicine (or family practice) has training to handle a wide range of common medical problems faced by people, while a social worker has training to handle a wide range of common social and personal problems faced by people.

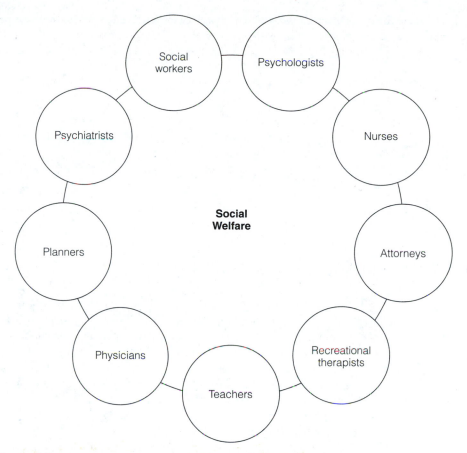

Figure 2.1
Examples of professional groups within the field of social welfare

Professional people staffing social welfare services include attorneys providing legal services to the poor; urban planners in social planning agencies; physicians in public health agencies; teachers in residential treatment facilities for the emotionally disturbed; psychologists, nurses, and recreational therapists in mental hospitals; and psychiatrists in mental health clinics.

Exercise 2.1: Your Areas of Interest in Social Work

GOAL: This exercise is designed to help you identify the social work areas that you desire to work in.

1. **Rank the following five client systems in the order that you prefer to work with them (with 1 indicating your first choice).**

   _____ **Individuals**
   _____ **Families**
   _____ **Groups**
   _____ **Organizations**
   _____ **The larger community**

2. **Describe the reasons for your ranking order.**

3. **Describe the areas of social work (such as services to battered spouses) that you prefer to work in. Also specify your reasons for your selected areas.**

■ GENERALIST SOCIAL WORK PRACTICE

There used to be an erroneous belief that a social worker was either a caseworker, a group worker, or a community organizer. Practicing social workers know that such a belief is faulty because every social worker is involved as a change agent in working with individuals, groups, families, organizations, and the larger community. The amount of time spent at each level varies from worker to worker, but every worker will, at times, be assigned and expected to work at these five levels and therefore needs training in all of them. A generalist social worker has the skills, and utilizes those skills, to work with the following five client systems: individuals, groups, families, organizations, and communities.

A generalist social worker is trained to use the problem-solving process to assess and intervene with the problems confronting individuals, families, groups, organizations, and communities. Anderson has identified three characteristics of a generalist social worker: (1) The generalist is often the first professional to see clients as they enter the social welfare system; (2) the worker must therefore be competent to assess clients' needs and to identify their stress points and problems; and (3) the worker must draw on a variety of skills and methods in serving clients.[6]

Brieland, Costin, and Atherton define and describe generalist practice as follows:

The generalist social worker, the equivalent of the general practitioner in medicine, is characterized by a wide repertoire of skills to deal with basic conditions, backed up by specialists to whom referrals are made. This role is a fitting one for the entry-level social worker.

The generalist model involves identifying and analyzing the interventive behaviors appropriate to social work. The worker must perform a wide range of tasks related to the provision and management of direct service, the development of social policy, and the facilitation of social change. The generalist should be well grounded in systems theory that emphasizes interaction and independence. The major system that will be used is the local network of services. . . .

The public welfare worker in a small county may be a classic example of the generalist. He or she knows the resources of the county, is acquainted with the key people, and may have considerable influence to accomplish service goals, including obtaining jobs, different housing, or emergency food and clothing. The activities of the urban generalist are more complex, and more effort must be expended to use the array of resources.[7]

Hull defines generalist practice as follows:

The basic principle of generalist practice is that baccalaureate social workers are able to utilize the problem solving process to intervene with various size systems including individuals, families, groups, organizations, and communities. The generalist operates within a systems and person-in-the-environment framework (sometimes referred to as an ecological model). The generalist expects that many problems will require intervention with more than one system (e.g., individual work with a delinquent adolescent plus work with the family or school) and that single explanations of problem situations are frequently unhelpful. The generalist may play several roles simultaneously or sequentially depending upon the needs of the client, (e.g., facilitator, advocate, educator, broker, enabler, case manager, and/or mediator). They may serve as leaders/facilitators of task groups, socialization groups, information groups, and self-help groups. They are capable of conducting needs assessments and evaluating their own practice and the programs with which they are associated. They make referrals when client problems so dictate and know when to utilize supervision from more experienced staff. Generalists operate within the ethical guidelines prescribed by the NASW Code of Ethics and must be able to work with clients, coworkers, and colleagues from different ethnic, cultural, and professional orientations. The knowledge and skills of the generalist are transferable from one setting to another and from one problem to another.[8]

The crux of generalist practice involves a view of the situation in terms of the person-in-environment conceptualization (described in an upcoming section in this chapter) and the capacity and willingness to intervene at several different levels, if necessary, while assuming any number of roles. The case example in the box "Generalist Practice Involves Options Planning" illustrates the approach of responding at several different levels in a variety of roles.

This text should facilitate readers' learning a generalist practice approach in social work by describing a variety of assessment and intervention strategies. Through learning these strategies, readers can then select those approaches that hold the most promise in facilitating positive changes in clients (who may be individuals, groups, families, organizations, or communities).

■ THE CHANGE PROCESS

A social worker uses a *change process* in working with clients. (Clients include individuals, groups, families, organizations, and communities.) The Council on Social Work Education in EPAS (Educational Policy and Accreditation Standards) identifies 10 skills that are needed for social work practice:

1. Engaging clients in an appropriate working relationship.
2. Identifying issues, problems, needs, resources, and assets.
3. Collecting and assessing information.
4. Planning for service delivery.
5. Using communication skills, supervision, and consultation.
6. Identifying, analyzing, and implementing empirically based interventions designed to achieve client goals.
7. Applying empirical knowledge and technological advances.
8. Evaluating program outcomes and practice effectiveness.
9. Developing, analyzing, advocating, and providing leadership for policies and services.
10. Promoting social and economic justice.[9]

The first eight skills, interestingly, provide an excellent framework for conceptualizing the change process in social work.

Phase 1: Engaging Clients in an Appropriate Working Relationship

Let's examine the change process in the case example entitled "Generalist Practice Involves Options Planning." Recall that four teenagers were expelled for drinking beer at school during school hours. The first step in the change process is to identify all potential clients. The second step is to engage them in an appropriate relationship.

Generalist Practice Involves Options Planning

Jack Dawson is a social worker at a high school in a Midwestern state. Four teenagers have been expelled (consistent with school board policy) for drinking alcoholic beverages at the school during school hours. Mr. Dawson assesses the situation and identifies the following potential courses of action. He can serve as an advocate for the youths by urging the school board and the administration to reinstate the youths. Mr. Dawson is aware that the expulsions are upsetting not only to the youths and their parents but also to the police department and the business community (because expelled youths tend to spend the day on city streets). He can involve the four teenagers in one-to-one counseling about their expulsion and their drinking patterns. He can involve these youths (along with others having drinking problems) in group counseling at the school. He can function as a broker to have the youths receive individual or group counseling from a counseling center outside the school system. He can ascertain the willingness of the parents to become involved in family therapy and serve as a broker to link the interested families with a counseling center that offers family therapy. He can raise the issue (to parents, to the business community, to the police department, to the school administration, and to the school board) of whether expulsion from school for drinking alcoholic beverages is a desirable policy. (Perhaps a better school system policy, in cases like this, is to place the youths on "in-school suspension," where they are required to stay in a study room for a few days.) Expulsion is a drastic measure that may adversely affect the futures of these youths. Mr. Dawson can serve as an organizer and a catalyst to encourage interested parents and school staff to use the incident as a rationale for incorporating educational material on alcohol and other drugs into the curriculum. (The selected courses of action will depend on a variety of factors, including a cost-benefit analysis of each course.)

In this case example, there are a number of "potential clients." Clients are the people who sanction or ask for the worker's services, those who are the expected beneficiaries of the service, and those who have a working agreement or contract with the worker. Using this definition, the four teenagers who were expelled from school (and their parents) are potential clients as they are the expected beneficiaries of the services. The high school is a client as it has a contractual agreement with the worker, Mr. Dawson. (The high school is also a client here because it asks Mr. Dawson for assistance with this situation.) The other students in the school (and their parents) are also potential clients as they are expected beneficiaries of his services.

In order to be effective, it is essential that a worker seek to form appropriate, professional relationships with all potential clients. A working relationship is facilitated when the worker reflects empathy, warmth, and sincerity.

Phase 2: Identifying Issues, Problems, Needs, Resources, and Assets

The first step in phase 2 is to identify issues, problems, and needs. Only then can the available resources and assets be determined.

The school social worker, Jack Dawson, identifies a variety of issues (questions/concerns/problems), including the following: Do the youths have a drinking problem? Were the youths, disenchanted with the school system, displaying their discontent by breaking school rules? What short-term and long-term adverse effects may the expulsions have on the youths? Will the expulsions have an adverse effect by marking these youths as "trouble makers" and thereby leading them into further delinquent behavior? How will the parents of these youths react to the drinking and to the expulsions? What effects will the expulsions have on other students at the school? (A possible positive effect: The expulsions may be a deterrent to other students who consider violating school rules. A possible negative consequence: The expulsions may encourage other students to violate school rules in order to be expelled and relieved of the obligation to attend school.) Will the expulsions create problems for merchants in the community if the expelled youths spend their days on the street? Is the school policy of expelling youths for drinking on school grounds constructive or destructive? Does the school system have a responsibility to add a drug-education component to the curriculum? Do certain aspects of the school system encourage youths to rebel? If so, should these aspects be changed?

Based on the initial identification of issues, problems, and needs, the social worker must then determine what resources and assets are available to confront the situation. This comprehensive list will serve as a guide during the next phase (collecting and assessing information).

Mr. Dawson is aware that the high school has a number of resources and assets to confront these issues. A number of professionals (teachers, psychologists, other social workers, nurses, and guidance counselors) are available to provide services, including assistance in developing and implementing new programs to address the identified problems, needs, and issues. If need be, the school has funds to hire one or more consultants who are experts in alcohol and drug issues. The school also has an established bureaucracy (including a school board) that has procedures and policies for establishing new programs. State and federal grant money may be available for initiating drug prevention programs.

Phase 3: Collecting and Assessing Information

In this phase, an in-depth collection and analysis of data are undertaken to provide the social worker with answers to the issues and problems raised in Phase 1. On some of the issues, useful information can be obtained directly from the clients (including the youths in this example). Thus, the question of whether the youths have a drinking problem can be answered by meeting with them individually, forming a trusting relationship, and then inquiring how often they drink, how much they consume when drinking, and what problems they have encountered while drinking. For the remaining issues raised in Phase 1, information must be collected from other sources. For example, the issue of short- and long-term adverse effects of the expulsion on the youths may be answered by researching the literature on this topic.

Assessment is the process of analyzing the data to make sense of it.

Phase 4: Planning for Service Delivery

After information is collected and assessed, Mr. Dawson and other decision makers in the school system need to decide whether the school system should provide services in this situation. (Often such a decision involves an assessment as to whether the prospective clients meet the eligibility requirements of the agency.) The decision to provide services in this case is easy to make, as the school system has an obligation to provide services to all enrolled students. The next decision—which services to provide—is dealt with in phases 5–7.

Phase 5: Using Communication Skills, Supervision, and Consultation

Effectiveness as a social worker is highly dependent on the worker's communication skills—both oral and writing skills. (Many agency directors assert that writing skills are as important as interviewing and counseling skills—as workers need to document assessment and treatment plans, as well as write court reports and the other reports required by the agency.) Also important are the worker's capacities to give presentations; be a witness in court; and communicate effectively with clients, staff, and professionals at other agencies.

Every agency administrator wants social workers who are "team players" and who respond to supervision in a positive manner—that is, who do not become defensive when critical comments and suggestions are given. (In this case example, Mr. Dawson has frequent meetings with his supervision, Dr. Maria Garcia, Director of Pupil Services at the high school, about what courses of action he should take.)

Workers also need to know when consultation may be beneficial and then be willing to utilize such consultation. Thus, after contacting the state's Department of Public Instruction, Mr. Dawson finds that a department consultant, Dr. Raul Alvarez, has considerable expertise in nationwide alcohol and drug prevention and treatment programs. Dr. Alvarez is available to the school at no direct charge. The two arrange to meet and discuss pertinent issues in Mr. Dawson's community and which programs Dr. Alvarez feels may fit well with this situation.

Phase 6: Identifying, Analyzing, and Implementing Empirically Based Interventions Designed to Achieve Client Goals

The case example summarizes a variety of interventions that are valid and consistent with the common purposes, values, and ethics of the social work profession. There are several potential interventions for this case. Mr. Dawson can seek to involve the four youths in one-to-one counseling about their drinking patterns and their expulsions. He can offer group counseling at the school for the four youths and for other students that have drinking problems. Or, he can seek to have the four youths receive individual or group counseling from a counseling center outside the school system. Mr. Dawson could also seek to have the youths and their parents receive family therapy from a counseling center outside the school system. Yet another intervention strategy is to raise the issue (with parents, the business community, the police department, the school administration, and the school board) as to whether expulsion from school for drinking alcoholic beverages is a desirable policy—perhaps "in-school suspension" would be a better policy. An additional intervention strategy is to incorporate educational material on alcohol and other drugs into the curriculum.

Mr. Dawson discusses these strategies with Dr. Alvarez and obtains his thoughts (based on the results of interventions in other communities) as to which will be most cost effective. (Cost-benefit analysis compares resources used to potential benefits.) Only rarely are social workers able to pursue *all* worthy interventions because of time and resource limitations.

Mr. Dawson selects the preventive approach as one intervention—that is, he will work to expand the health curriculum to include material on alcohol and other drugs. Numerous questions related to this intervention now arise for Mr. Dawson. What specific material should be covered in a drug-education program? Which drugs should be included? (Mr. Dawson knows that describing certain drugs, such as LSD, may cause some parents to ask whether educational material about seldom-used drugs might encourage some youths to experiment.) *Where* should the drug-education component be added to the curriculum—in large assemblies with all students required to attend? In health classes? In social science classes? Will the school administration, teachers, school board, students, and parents support a proposal to add this component to the curriculum? What strategy will be most effective in gaining the support of these various groups?

As a first step in this phase, Mr. Dawson meets with his immediate supervisor, Dr. Garcia, to discuss these issues and to generate a list of alternative strategies. Three strategies are discussed:

1. An anonymous survey could be conducted in the high school to discover the extent of alcohol and other drug use among students. Such survey results could document the need for drug education.
2. A committee of professional staff in the Pupil Services Department could develop a drug-education program.
3. The Pupil Services Department could ask the school administration and the school board to appoint a committee representing the school board, the administration, the teachers, the students, the parents, and the Pupil Services Department. This committee would explore the need for, and feasibility of, a drug-education program.

Mr. Dawson and Dr. Garcia decide that the best way to obtain broad support for the drug-education program is to pursue the third option. Dr. Garcia meets with the high school principal, Mary Powell, who after some contemplation agrees to explore the need for such a program. Ms. Powell asks the school board to support the formation of a committee. The school board agrees, a committee is formed, and it begins holding meetings. Mr. Dawson is appointed by Dr. Garcia to be the Pupil Services' representative to this committee.

Mr. Dawson also decides to pursue the following additional interventions: (1) seek to involve the four youths in one-to-one counseling about their drinking patterns and their expulsions—however, only one youth comes to see him on a regular basis; the other three have a pattern of making excuses for not coming, and (2) seek to change the policy of expelling students from school for drinking alcoholic beverages on school grounds to an in-school suspension policy. For conciseness, this text will focus on the preventive approach—that is, adding educational material on alcohol and other drugs to the curriculum.

Phase 7: Applying Empirical Knowledge and Technology

One of the first questions raised by committee members during initial deliberations is, "If a drug-education program is developed, what specific drugs should it include?" Some committee members, as expected, are concerned that providing information about drugs not currently in use among young people in the community may encourage the use of such drugs. As a result, the Pupil Services Department is asked to conduct a student survey to identify the mind-altering drugs currently in use and to discover the extent of such use.

A second related issue arising in the committee is the broader question of whether a drug-education program has preventive value or whether such a program might promote illegal drug use. Mr. Dawson responds by suggesting that Dr. Alvarez meet with the committee to discuss this issue. Dr. Alvarez then shares information on the preventive value of a variety of drug-education programs across the nation.

After 14 months of planning and deliberation, the committee presents its proposal for drug education to the school board. Their program is designed to be part of the health curriculum in the district's middle school and high schools.

The drug-education program contains the latest research-based knowledge on drugs commonly used by young people in the community and includes the following: mind-altering effects, characteristics of physical and psychological dependency, and withdrawal and long-term health effects. The curriculum also contains research-based information on the most effective treatment approaches, ways a family can cope with a drug-abusing member, how to confront a friend or relative who is abusing, the dangers of driving under the influence of drugs, associations between drug use and sexually transmitted diseases (including AIDS), suggestions for people concerned about their own drug use, and practical ways to say "no" to drugs.

Helpful technologies in this program include computer databases that contain effective drug-education programs in other school systems, software for processing surveys of student drug use and attitudes in the district, and current films and videotapes that offer age-appropriate drug-education material.

Phase 8: Evaluating Program Outcomes and Practice Effectiveness

To evaluate this preventive approach, the Pupil Services Department decides to conduct an annual survey of a random sample of students to assess the extent of drug use/abuse and to elicit students' thoughts about the merits and shortcomings of the drug-education program. The Pupil Services Department also decides to survey parents to elicit their thoughts on the merits and shortcomings of the program, and to obtain their suggestions for improvement. Such surveys provide a way to monitor and evaluate the program's outcomes.

The final phase of any intervention is termination. The committee that developed the drug-education program has its final meeting after the school board approves the proposal. Most members experience mixed emotions at this meeting. They are delighted that their task is successfully completed, but they feel some sadness because this group, which has become an important and meaningful part of their lives, is now ending. (With any committee, if a close working relationship has formed among members, termination is often a painful process. As issues were addressed, some dependency may have developed, and as a result members may experience a sense of loss when termination occurs.) (Chapter 13 describes termination and evaluation in greater detail.)

■ A VARIETY OF ROLES

In working with individuals, groups, families, organizations, and communities, a social worker is expected to be knowledgeable and skillful in filling a variety of roles. The particular role selected should (ideally) be determined by what will be most effective, given the circumstances. The following material identifies some, but certainly not all, of the roles assumed by social workers.

Enabler

In this role, a worker *helps* individuals or groups to articulate their needs, clarify and identify their problems, explore resolution strategies, select and apply a strategy, and develop their capacities to deal with problems more effectively. This role model is perhaps the most frequently used approach in counseling individuals, groups, and families, and is used in community practice—primarily when the objective is to help people organize to help themselves.

(It should be noted that this definition of the term *enabler* is very different from the definition used in reference to chemical dependency. There the term refers to a family member or friend who facilitates the substance abuser in persisting in the use and abuse of drugs.)

Broker

A broker links individuals and groups who need help (and do not know where to find it) with community services. For example, a wife who is physically abused by her husband might be referred to a shelter for battered women. Nowadays even moderate-sized communities have 200–300 social service agencies and organizations. Even human services professionals are often only partially aware of the total service network in their community.

Advocate

The role of advocate has been borrowed from the law profession. It is an active, directive role in which the social worker represents a client or a citizens' group. When a client or a citizens' group needs help and existing institutions are uninterested (or openly negative and hostile), the advocate's role may be appropriate. The advocate provides leadership in collecting information, arguing the validity of the client's need and request, and challenging the institution's decision not to provide services. The purpose is not to ridicule or censure a particular institution but to modify or change one or more of its service policies. In this role, the advocate is a partisan who is exclusively serving the interests of a client or a citizens' group.

Empowerer

A key goal of social work practice is *empowerment,* the process of helping individuals, families, groups, organizations, and communities increase their personal, interpersonal, socioeconomic, and political strength and influence. Social workers who engage in empowerment-focused practice seek to develop the capacity of clients to understand their environment, make choices, take responsibility for those choices, and influence their life situations through organization and advocacy. Empowerment-focused social workers also seek a more equitable distribution of resources and power among different groups in society. This focus on equity and social justice has been a hallmark of the social work profession, as practiced by Jane Addams and other early settlement workers.

Activist

An activist seeks basic institutional change; often the objective involves a shift in power and resources to a disadvantaged group. An activist is concerned about social injustice, inequity, and deprivation. Tactics involve conflict, confrontation, and negotiation. Social action is concerned with changing the social environment in order to better meet the recognized needs of individuals. The methods used are assertive and action-oriented (for example, organizing welfare recipients to work toward improvements in services and increases in money payments). Activities of social action include fact-finding, analysis of community needs, research, dissemination and interpretation of information, organizing activities with people, and other efforts to mobilize public understanding and support on behalf of some existing or proposed social program. Social action activity can be geared toward a problem that is local, statewide, or national in scope.

Mediator

The mediator role involves intervention in disputes between parties to help them find compromises, reconcile differences, or reach mutually satisfactory agreements. Social workers have used their value orientations and unique skills in many forms of mediation (for example, divorcing spouses, neighbors in conflict, landlords and tenants, labor and management, and contenders for child custody). A mediator remains neutral, not siding with either party in the dispute. Mediators make sure they understand the positions of both parties. They may help to clarify positions, identify miscommunication about differences, and help both parties present their cases clearly.

Negotiator

A negotiator brings together people in conflict and seeks to bargain and compromise to find mutually acceptable agreements. Somewhat like mediation, negotiation involves finding a middle ground that all sides can live with. However, unlike a mediator (who maintains a neutral position), a negotiator is usually allied with one side or the other.

Educator

The educator gives information to clients and teaches them adaptive skills. To be an effective educator, the worker must first be knowledgeable. Additionally, the worker must be a good communicator so information is conveyed clearly and readily understood by the receiver. An educator can teach parenting skills to young parents, instruct teenagers in job-hunting strategies, and teach anger-control techniques to individuals with aggressive tendencies.

Initiator

An initiator calls attention to a problem or to a potential problem. It is important to recognize that sometimes a potential problem requires attention. For example, if a proposal is made to renovate a low-income neighborhood by building middle-income housing units, the initiator will be concerned that low-income residents could become homeless if the proposal is approved (because these current residents may not be able to afford middle-income units). Because calling attention to problems usually does not resolve them, the initiator role must often be followed by other kinds of work.

Coordinator

Coordination involves bringing components together in an organized manner. For example, a multiproblem family may need help from several agencies to meet its complicated financial, emotional, legal, health, social, educational, recreational, and interactional needs. Frequently, someone at an agency must assume the role of case manager to coordinate services from different agencies and avoid both duplication of services and conflict among the services.

Researcher

At times every worker is a researcher. Research in social work practice can involve reading literature on topics of interest, evaluating the outcomes of one's practice, assessing the merits and shortcomings of programs, and studying community needs.

Group Facilitator

A group facilitator serves as a leader for a group discussion in a therapy group, an educational group, a self-help group, a sensitivity group, a family therapy group, or a group with some other focus.

Public Speaker

Social workers occasionally talk to a variety of groups (e.g., high school classes; public service organizations such as Kiwanis; police officers; staff at other agencies) to inform them of available services or to argue the need for new services. In recent years, a variety of new services have been identified (for example, family preservation programs and services for people with AIDS). Social workers who have public speaking skills are better able to explain services to groups of potential clients and funding sources, and are apt to be rewarded (including financially) by their employers for these skills.

Exercise 2.2: Your Interest in Various Social Work Roles

GOAL: This exercise is designed to help you identify the social work roles in which you would like to become involved.

1. Check one of the following for each of the indicated roles.

	I desire to become involved in this role	Uncertain	I do not want to become involved in this role
Enabler			
Broker			
Advocate			
Empowerer			
Activist			
Mediator			
Negotiator			
Educator			
Initiator			
Coordinator			
Researcher			
Group Facilitator			
Public Speaker			

2. **Describe your reasons for selecting the particular roles in which you desire to become involved.**

3. **Describe your reasons for selecting the particular roles in which you do *not* want to become involved.**

■ A SYSTEMS PERSPECTIVE

Social workers are trained to take a systems perspective on their work with individuals, groups, families, organizations, and communities. A systems perspective emphasizes looking beyond the presenting problems of clients in order to assess the complexities and interrelationships of their problems. A systems perspective is based on systems theory. Key concepts of general systems theory are *wholeness, relationship,* and *homeostasis*.

The concept of *wholeness* means that the objects or elements within a system produce an entity greater than the additive sums of the separate parts. Systems theory is antireductionistic, asserting that no system can be adequately understood or totally explained once it has been broken down into its component parts. (For example, the central nervous system is able to carry out thought processes that would not be revealed if only the parts were observed.)

The concept of *relationship* asserts that the pattern and structure of the elements in a system are as important as the elements themselves. For example, Masters and Johnson have found that sexual dysfunctions primarily occur due to the nature of the relationship between husband and wife, rather than to the psychological makeup of the partners in a marriage system.[10]

Systems theory opposes simple cause-and-effect explanations. For example, whether a child will be abused in a family is determined by a variety of variables and the patterns of these variables, such as parents' capacity to control their anger, relationships between child and parents, relationships between parents, degree of psychological stress, characteristics of the child, and opportunities for socially acceptable ways for parents to ventilate anger.

The concept of *homeostasis* suggests that living systems seek a balance to maintain and preserve the system. Jackson, for example, has noted that families tend to establish a behavioral balance or stability and to resist any change from that predetermined level of stability.[11] Emergence of the state of imbalance (generated either within or outside the marriage) ultimately acts to restore the homeostatic balance of the family. If one child in a family is abused, that abuse often serves a function as indicated by the fact that if that child is removed, a second child is often abused. Or, if one family member improves through seeking counseling, that improvement will generally upset the balance within the family, and other family members will have to make changes (such changes may be adaptive or maladaptive) to adjust to the new behavior of the improved family member.

Ecological theory is a subcategory of systems theory and has become prominent in social work practice, as discussed in the next section.

■ MEDICAL MODEL VERSUS ECOLOGICAL MODEL

From the 1920s to the 1960s most social workers used a medical model approach to assessing and changing human behavior. This approach, initiated primarily by Sigmund Freud, views clients as *patients*. The task of the provider of services is first to diagnose the causes of a patient's problems and then to provide treatment. The patient's problems are viewed as being inside the patient.

Medical Model

In regard to emotional and behavioral problems of people, the medical model conceptualizes these problems as *mental illnesses*. People with emotional or behavioral problems are then given medical labels such as schizophrenia, paranoia, psychosis, and insanity. Adherents of the medical approach believe the disturbed person's mind is affected by some generally unknown internal condition that is thought to result from a variety of possible causative factors: genetic endowment, metabolic disorders, infectious diseases, internal conflicts, unconscious uses of defense mechanisms, and traumatic early experiences that cause emotional fixations and prevent future psychological growth.

The medical model has a lengthy classification of mental disorders defined by the American Psychiatric Association. The major categories of mental disorders are listed in Table 2.1.

The medical model approach arose in reaction to the historical notion that the emotionally disturbed were possessed by demons, were mad, and were to be blamed for their disturbances. These people were "treated" by being beaten, locked up, or killed. The medical model led to viewing the disturbed as in need of help, stimulated research into the nature of emotional problems, and promoted the development of therapeutic approaches.

The major evidence for the validity of the medical model approach comes from studies that suggest that some mental disorders, such as schizophrenia, may be influenced by genetics (heredity). The bulk of the evidence for the significance of heredity comes from studies of twins. For example, in some studies identical twins have been found to have a concordance rate (that is, if one has it, both have it) for schizophrenia of about 50 percent.[12]

Keep in mind that the rate of schizophrenia in the general population is about 1 percent.[13] When one identical twin is schizophrenic, the other is 50 times more likely than the average to be schizophrenic. This suggests a causal influence of genes but not genetic determination, as concordance for identical twins is only 50 percent, not 100 percent.

■ TABLE 2.1 Major Mental Disorders According to the American Psychiatric Association

DISORDERS USUALLY FIRST DIAGNOSED IN INFANCY, CHILDHOOD, OR ADOLESCENCE include, but are not limited to, mental retardation, learning disorders, communication disorders (such as stuttering), autism, attention-deficit/hyperactivity disorder, and separation anxiety disorder.

DELIRIUM, DEMENTIA, AND AMNESTIC AND OTHER COGNITIVE DISORDERS include delirium due to alcohol and other drug intoxication, dementia due to Alzheimer's disease or Parkinson's disease, dementia due to head trauma, and amnestic disorder.

SUBSTANCE-RELATED DISORDERS include mental disorders related to abuse of alcohol, caffeine, amphetamines, cocaine, hallucinogens, nicotine, and other mind-altering substances.

SCHIZOPHRENIA AND OTHER PSYCHOTIC DISORDERS include delusional disorders and all forms of schizophrenia (such as paranoid, disorganized, and catatonic).

MOOD DISORDERS—emotional disorders such as depression and bipolar disorders.

ANXIETY DISORDERS includes phobias, post-traumatic stress disorder, and anxiety disorders.

SOMATOFORM DISORDERS—psychological problems that manifest themselves as symptoms of physical disease (for example, hypochondria).

DISSOCIATIVE DISORDERS—problems in which part of the personality is dissociated from the rest (for example, dissociative identity disorder, formerly called multiple personality disorder).

SEXUAL AND GENDER IDENTITY DISORDERS include sexual dysfunctions (such as hypoactive sexual desire, premature ejaculation, male erectile disorder, male and female orgasmic disorders, and vaginismus), exhibitionism, fetishism, pedophilia (child molestation), sexual masochism, sexual sadism, voyeurism, and gender identity disorders (such as cross-gender identification).

EATING DISORDERS include anorexia nervosa and bulimia nervosa.

SLEEP DISORDERS—insomnia and other problems with sleep (such as nightmares and sleepwalking).

IMPULSE-CONTROL DISORDERS—the inability to control certain undesirable impulses (for example, kleptomania, pyromania, and pathological gambling).

ADJUSTMENT DISORDERS—difficulty in adjusting to the stress created by such common events as unemployment or divorce.

PERSONALITY DISORDERS—an enduring pattern of inner experience and behavior that deviates markedly from the expectations of the individual's culture, is pervasive and inflexible, has an onset in adolescence or early adulthood, is stable over time, and leads to distress or impairment. Examples include paranoid personality disorder, antisocial personality disorder, and obsessive-compulsive personality disorder.

OTHER CONDITIONS covers a variety of disorders, including parent-child relational problems; partner relational problems; sibling relational problems; child victims of physical abuse, sexual abuse, and neglect; adult victims of physical abuse and sexual abuse; malingering; bereavement; academic problems; occupational problems; identity problems; and religious or spiritual problems.

Source: Diagnostic and Statistical Manual of Mental Disorders–IV, Text: Revision, by the American Psychiatric Association, 2000, Washington, DC: American Psychiatric Association.

Exercise 2.3: Understanding the Major Mental Disorders

GOAL: This exercise is designed to assist you in understanding the major mental disorders. Briefly describe people you know who have the mental disorders identified in Table 2.1. For confidentiality reasons, do not use the real name of the person. (The following is an example of a desired brief description. Fred, age 67, was diagnosed with Alzheimer's disease five years ago. He is now in an assisted-living facility. His wife visits him nearly every day.)

Ecological Model

In the 1960s, social work began questioning the usefulness of the medical model. Environmental factors were shown to be at least as important in causing a client's problems as internal factors. Research also was demonstrating that psychoanalysis was probably ineffective in treating clients' problems.[14]

Then social work shifted at least some of its emphasis to a *reform approach* that seeks to change systems to benefit clients. The enactment of the anti-poverty programs, such as Head Start, is an example of a successful reform approach.

In the past several years, social work has focused on using an *ecological approach*. This approach integrates both treatment and reform by conceptualizing and emphasizing the dysfunctional transactions between people and their physical and social environments. Human beings are known to develop and adapt through transactions with all elements of their environments. An ecological model gives attention to both internal and external factors. It does not view people as passive reactors to their environments but rather as active participants in dynamic and reciprocal interactions.

It tries to improve the coping patterns of people in their environments to obtain a better match between an individual's needs and the characteristics of his or her environment. One emphasis of an ecological model is on the person-in-environment, which is conceptualized in Figure 2.2.

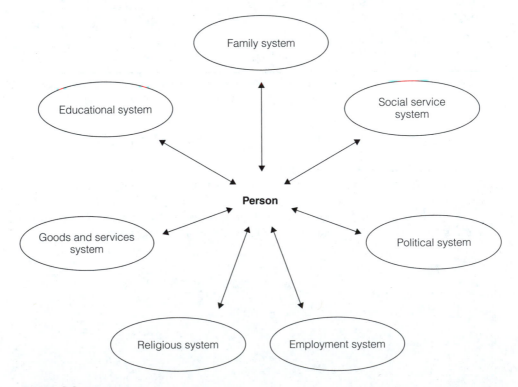

Figure 2.2
Person-in-environment conceptualization

People in society continually interact with many systems, some of which are shown in this figure.

Figure 2.2 suggests that people interact with many systems. With this conceptualization, social work can focus on three separate areas. First, it can focus on the person and seek to develop problem-solving, coping, and developmental capacities. Second, it can focus on the relationship between a person and the systems he or she interacts with and link the person with needed resources, services, and opportunities. Third, it can focus on the systems and seek to reform them to meet the needs of the individual more effectively.

The ecological model views individuals, families, and small groups as having transitional problems and needs as they move from one life stage to another. Individuals face many transitional changes as they grow older, such as learning to walk, entering first grade, adjusting to puberty, graduating from school, finding a job, getting married, having children, children leaving home, and retiring.

Families have a life cycle of events that also require adjustment for engagement, marriage, birth of children, parenting, children going to school, children leaving home, and loss of a parent (perhaps through death or divorce).

Small groups also have transitional phases of development. Members of small groups spend time getting acquainted, gradually learn to trust each other, begin to self-disclose more, learn to work together on tasks, develop approaches to handle interpersonal conflict, and face adjustments to the group's eventual termination or the departure of some members.

A central concern of an ecological model is to articulate the transitional problems and needs of individuals, families, and small groups. Once these problems and needs are identified, intervention approaches are then selected and applied to help individuals, families, and small groups resolve the transitional problems and meet their needs.

An ecological model can also focus on the maladaptive interpersonal problems and needs in families and groups. It can seek to articulate the maladaptive communication processes and dysfunctional relationship patterns of families and small groups. These difficulties cover an array of areas, including interpersonal conflicts, power struggles, double binds, distortions in communicating, scapegoating, and discrimination. The consequences of such difficulties are usually maladaptive for some members. An ecological model seeks to identify such interpersonal obstacles and then apply appropriate intervention strategies. For example, parents may set the price for honesty too high for their children. In such families, children gradually learn to hide certain behaviors and thoughts, and even learn to lie. If the parents discover such dishonesty, an uproar usually occurs. An appropriate intervention in such a family is to open up communication patterns and help the parents understand that if they really want honesty from their children, they need to learn to be more accepting of their children's thoughts and actions.

Two centuries ago, people interacted primarily within the family system. Families were nearly self-sufficient. In those days, the *person-in-family* was a way of conceptualizing the main system for individuals to interact. Our society has become much more complex. Today, a person's life and quality of life are interwoven and interdependent upon many systems, as shown in Figure 2.2.

Exercise 2.4: Understanding the Medical Model and the Ecological Model

GOAL: This exercise is designed to help you understand the Medical Model and the Ecological Model.

In understanding why people become involved in dysfunctional behavior (such as being anorexic, committing a crime, or becoming a batterer), which model (the Medical Model or the Ecological Model) do you believe is more useful? State the reasons for your choice.

■ GOALS OF SOCIAL WORK PRACTICE

The National Association of Social Workers has conceptualized social work practice as having four major goals.[15]

Goal 1: Enhance the Clients' Problem-Solving, Coping, and Developmental Capacities

Using the person-in-environment concept, the focus of social work practice at this level is on the "person." With this focus, a social worker serves primarily as an *enabler*. In the role of an enabler, the worker may take on activities of a counselor, teacher, caregiver (i.e., providing supportive services to those who cannot fully solve their problems and meet their own needs), and behavior changer (i.e., changing specific parts of a client's behavior).

Goal 2: Link Clients with Systems That Provide Resources, Services, and Opportunities

Using the person-in-environment concept, the focus of social work practice at this level is on the relationships between persons and the systems with which they interact. With this focus, a social worker serves primarily as a *broker.*

Goal 3: Promote the Effective and Humane Operation of Systems That Provide Resources and Services

Using the person-in-environment concept, the focus of social work practice at this level is on the systems people interact with. One role a worker may fill at this level is that of an *advocate*. Additional roles at this level are the following:

Program developer seeks to promote or design programs or technologies to meet social needs.

Supervisor seeks to increase the effectiveness and efficiency of the delivery of services through supervising other staff.

Coordinator seeks to improve a delivery system through increasing communications and coordination among human service resources.

Consultant seeks to provide guidance to agencies and organizations through suggesting ways to increase the effectiveness and efficiency of services.

Goal 4: Develop and Improve Social Policy

The focus of Goal 4 is on the statutes and broader social policies that underlie available resources. Major roles of social workers at this level are *planner* and *policy developer*. In these roles, workers develop and seek adoption of new statutes or policies and propose elimination of ineffective or inappropriate statutes and policies. In these planning and policy development processes, social workers may take on an advocate role and, in some instances, an activist role.

The Council on Social Work Education (CSWE) is the national accrediting body for social work education in the United States. It defines the purpose of social work as follows:

> The social work profession receives its sanction from public and private auspices and is the primary profession in the development, provision, and evaluation of social services. Professional social workers are leaders in a variety of organizational settings and service delivery systems within a global context.
>
> The profession of social work is based on the values of service, social and economic justice, dignity and worth of the person, importance of human relationships, and integri-

ty and competence in practice. With these values as defining principles, the purposes of social work are:

- To enhance human well-being and alleviate poverty, oppression, and other forms of social injustice.
- To enhance the social functioning and interactions of individuals, families, groups, organizations, and communities by involving them in accomplishing goals, developing resources, and preventing and alleviating distress.
- To formulate and implement social policies, services, and programs that meet basic human needs and support the development of human capacities.
- To pursue policies, services, and resources through advocacy and social or political actions that promote social and economic justice.
- To develop and use research, knowledge, and skills that advance social work practice.
- To develop and apply practice in the context of diverse cultures.[16]

This definition of the purpose of social work is consistent with the four goals of social work mentioned previously. However, it adds four additional goals of social work, as follows.

Goal 5: Enhance Human Well-Being and Alleviate Poverty, Oppression, and Other Forms of Social Injustice

The social work profession is committed to enhancing the well-being of all human berings. It is particularly committed to alleviating poverty, oppression, and other forms of social injustice. About 15 percent of the U.S. population has an income below the poverty line. Social work has always advocated for developing programs to alleviate poverty, and many practitioners focus on providing services to the poor.

Poverty is global, as every society has members who are poor. In some societies, as many as 95 percent of the population lives in poverty. Social workers are committed to alleviating poverty, not only in the United States but also worldwide. Alleviating poverty is obviously complex and difficult. Social work professionals work with a variety of systems to make progress in alleviating poverty, including educational systems, health care systems, political systems, business and employment systems, religious systems, and human services systems.

Oppression is the unjust or cruel exercise of authority or power. In our society, a number of groups have been oppressed—including African Americans, Latinos, Chinese Americans, Native Americans, women, people with disabilities, gays and lesbians, various religious groups, and people living in poverty. (The listing of these groups is only illustrative and certainly not exhaustive.) Social injustice occurs when some members of a society have less protection, fewer basic rights and opportunities, or fewer social benefits than other members of that society. Social work is a profession that is committed not only to alleviating poverty but also to combating oppression and other forms of social injustice.

Goal 6: Pursue Policies, Services, and Resources through Advocacy and Social or Political Actions That Promote Social and Economic Justice

Social justice is an ideal condition in which all members of a society have the same basic rights, protection, opportunities, obligations, and social benefits. Economic justice is also an ideal condition in which all members of a society have the same opportunities to attain material goods, income, and wealth. Social workers have an obligation to help groups at risk increase their personal, interpersonal, socioeconomic, and political strength and influence through improving their circumstances. Empowerment-focused social workers seek a more equitable distribution of resources and power among the various groups in society. Diverse groups that may be at risk include those distinguished by age, class, color, disability, ethnicity, family structure, gender, marital status, national origin, race, religion, sex, and sexual orientation.

Goal 7: Develop and Use Research, Knowledge, and Skills That Advance Social Work Practice

Social workers are expected to contribute to the knowledge and skill base of social work practice. Included in this expectation is the responsibility of social workers to objectively assess their own practice and to assess the programs and services they provide.

Goal 8: Develop and Apply Practice in the Context of Diverse Cultures

Our society is changing rapidly. By the middle of the 21st century, nearly half of the U.S. population will be people of color. Because of demographic changes and other social trends, human service practitioners and organizations will increasingly deal with people who are more diverse, politically more active, better informed, and more aware of their rights. These trends will demand significant changes in the nature, structure, and quality of human service organizations, and also changes in the sensitivity, knowledge, and skills of social service providers. There is thus a need for ongoing efforts to develop new approaches to preparing culturally competent social workers. In order to become culturally competent, a social worker needs to (1) become aware of culture and its pervasive influence; (2) learn about her or his own culture; (3) recognize her or his own ethnocentricity; (4) learn about other cultures; (5) acquire cultural knowledge about the client she or he is working with; and (6) adapt social work skills and intervention approaches to the needs and styles of the cultures of these clients.

Exercise 2.5: Your Interest in Achieving the Goals of Social Work

GOAL: This exercise is designed to help you identify your interest in the activities associated with the eight goals of social work.

1. **Check the boxes that identify your interest level in each of the eight goals of social work.**

	Highly interested	Somewhat interested	Uncertain	Somewhat disinterested	Not interested
Goal 1					
Goal 2					
Goal 3					
Goal 4					
Goal 5					
Goal 6					
Goal 7					
Goal 8					

2. **For goals in which you are "Highly interested," state the reasons for your decisions.**

3. For goals in which you are "Somewhat disinterested" or "Not interested," state the reasons for your decisions.

■ A PROBLEM-SOLVING APPROACH

In working with individuals, families, groups, organizations, and communities, social workers use a problem-solving approach. Steps in the problem-solving process can be stated in a variety of ways. Below is a simple statement of this process:

1. Identify as precisely as possible the problem or problems.
2. Generate possible alternative solutions.
3. Evaluate the alternative solutions.
4. Select a solution or solutions, and set goals.
5. Implement the solution(s).
6. Follow up to evaluate how the solution(s) worked.

(Note that another conceptualization of the problem-solving approach is the change-process view of social work practice, which was described earlier in this chapter.)

Exercise 2.6: Applying the Problem-Solving Approach

GOAL: This exercise is designed to assist you in applying the problem-solving approach.

Describe a dilemma that you faced (or are currently facing) in which you used the six stages of the problem-solving approach. In your description, describe what you did for each of the six stages.

■ MICRO, MEZZO, AND MACRO PRACTICE

Social workers practice at three levels: (1) *micro*—working on a one-to-one basis with an individual, (2) *mezzo*—working with families and other small groups, and (3) *macro*—working with organizations and communities or seeking changes in statutes and social policies.

The specific activities performed by workers include, but are not limited to, the following:

Social Casework

Aimed at helping individuals on a one-to-one basis to meet personal and social problems, casework may be geared to helping the client adjust to his or her environment, or to changing certain social and economic pressures that adversely affect an individual. Social casework services are provided by nearly every social welfare agency that provides direct services to people. Social casework encompasses a wide variety of activities, such as counseling runaway youths; helping unemployed people secure training or employment; counseling someone who is suicidal; placing a homeless child in an adoptive or foster home; providing protective services to abused children and their families; finding nursing homes for stroke victims who no longer need to be confined to a hospital; counseling individuals with sexual dysfunctions; helping alcoholics acknowledge they have a drinking problem; counseling those with a terminal illness; being a probation and parole officer; providing services to single parents; and working in medical and mental hospitals as a member of a rehabilitation team.

Case Management

Recently a number of social service agencies have labeled their social workers *case managers*. The tasks performed by case managers are similar to those of caseworkers. The job descriptions of case managers vary from service area to service area. For example, case managers in a juvenile probation setting are highly involved in supervising clients, providing some counseling, monitoring clients to make certain they are following the rules of probation, linking clients and their families with needed services, preparing court reports, and testifying in court. On the other hand, case managers at a rehabilitation center for people with a cognitive disability are apt to be involved in providing job training to clients, counseling clients, arranging transportation, disciplining clients for unacceptable behavior, acting as an advocate for clients, and acting as liaison with the people who supervise clients during their nonwork hours (at a group home, foster home, residential treatment facility, or their parents' home). Hepworth and Larsen describe the role of a case manager as follows:

> Case managers link clients to needed resources that exist in complex service delivery networks and orchestrate the delivery of services in a timely fashion. Case managers function as brokers, facilitators, linkers, mediators, and advocates. A case manager must have extensive knowledge of community resources, rights of clients, and policies and procedures of various agencies, and must be skillful in mediation and advocacy.[17]

Barker defines case management as follows:

> A procedure to plan, seek, and monitor services for a variety of agencies and staff on behalf of a client. Usually one agency takes primary responsibility for the client and assigns a case manager, who coordinates services, advocates for the client, and sometimes controls resources and purchases services for the client. The procedure makes it possible for many social workers in an agency, or in different agencies, to coordinate their efforts to serve a given client through professional teamwork, thus expanding the range of needed services offered. Case management may involve monitoring the progress of a client whose needs require the services of many different professionals, agencies, health care facilities, and human service programs.[18]

Group Work

The intellectual, emotional, and social development of individuals may be furthered through group activities. In contrast to casework or group therapy, it is not primarily therapeutic, except in a broad sense. Different groups have different objectives, such as socialization, information exchange, curbing delinquency, recreation, changing socially unacceptable values, and helping achieve better relations between cultural and racial groups. For example, a group worker at a neighborhood center may, through group activities, seek to curb delinquency patterns and change socially unacceptable values; or a worker at an adoption agency may meet with a group of applicants to explain adoption procedures and help applicants prepare to become adoptive parents. Activities and focuses of groups vary: arts and crafts; dancing; games; dramatics; music; photography; sports; nature study; woodwork; first aid; home management; information exchange; and discussion of such topics as politics, sex, marriage, religion, and career selection.

Group Treatment

Group treatment is aimed at facilitating the social, behavioral, and emotional adjustment of individuals through the group process. Participants in group treatment usually have emotional, interactional, or behavioral difficulties. Group treatment has several advantages over one-to-one counseling, such as the operation of the *helper therapy* principle, which maintains it is therapeutic for the helper (who can be any member of a group) to feel he or she has been helpful to others.[19] In contrast to one-to-one counseling, group pressure is often more effective in changing maladaptive behavior of individuals, and group treatment is a time saver as it enables the therapist to treat several people at the same time. A few examples in which group treatment might be used are for individuals who are severely depressed, have drinking problems, are victims of a rape, are psychologically addicted to drugs, have a relative who is terminally ill, are single and pregnant, are recently divorced, or have an eating disorder.

Family Treatment

A type of group treatment aimed at helping families with interactional, behavioral, and emotional problems, family treatment can be used with parent-child interaction problems, marital conflicts, and conflicts with grandparents. A wide variety of problems are dealt with in family treatment or family counseling, such as disagreements between parents and youths on choice of friends and dates, drinking and other drug use, domestic tasks, curfew hours, communication problems, sexual values and behavior, study habits, and grades received.

Community Organization

The aim of community organization is to stimulate and assist the local community to evaluate, plan, and coordinate efforts to provide for the community's health, welfare, and recreation needs. It perhaps is not possible to define precisely the activities of a community organizer, but such activities are apt to include encouraging and fostering citizen participation, coordinating efforts between agencies or between groups, public relations and public education, research, planning, and resource management. A community organizer acts as a catalyst in stimulating and encouraging community action. Agency settings where such specialists are apt to be employed include community welfare councils, social planning agencies, health planning councils, and community action agencies. The *term community organization* is now being replaced in some settings by such labels as *planning, social planning, program development, policy development,* and *macro practice.*

　　Barker defines community organization as

An intervention process used by social workers and other professionals to help individuals, groups, and collectives of people with common interests or from the same geographic areas to deal with social problems and to enhance social well-being through planned collective action. Methods include identifying problem areas, analyzing causes, formulating plans, developing strategies, mobilizing necessary resources, identifying and recruiting community leaders, and encouraging interrelationships between them to facilitate their efforts.[20]

Policy Analysis

Policy analysis involves the systematic evaluation of a policy and the process by which it was formulated. Those who conduct such an analysis consider whether the process and the result are clear, equitable, legal, rational, compatible with social values, superior to the alternatives, cost-effective, and explicit. Frequently such an analysis identifies certain shortcomings in the policy, and those conducting the policy analysis then usually recommend modifications designed to alleviate these shortcomings.

Administration

Administration is the activity that involves directing the overall program of a social service agency. Administrative functions include setting agency and program objectives, analyzing social conditions in the community, making decisions relating to what services will be provided, employing and supervising staff members, setting up an organizational structure, administering financial affairs, and securing funds for the agency's operations. Administration also involves setting organizational goals, coordinating activities toward the achievement of selected goals, and making and monitoring necessary changes in processes and structure to improve effectiveness and efficiency. In social work, the term *administration* is often used synonymously with *management*. In a small agency, administrative functions may be carried out by one person, while in a larger agency several people may be involved in administrative affairs.

Other areas of professional activity in social work include research, consulting, supervision, planning, program development, and teaching (primarily at the college level). The ability to study and evaluate one's own practice and to evaluate programs is an important skill for a social worker. Skills essential for social work practice are described further in the next section. Generalist social workers are expected to have an extensive knowledge base, to possess numerous skills, and to adhere to a well-defined set of professional social work values.

Exercise 2.7: Identifying Your Interest in Various Social Work Activities

1. For each of the following activities, check the box that indicates your level of interest in engaging in it.

	Highly interested	Somewhat interested	Uncertain	Somewhat disinterested	Not interested
1. Social Casework					
2. Case Management					
3. Group Work					
4. Group Treatment					
5. Family Treatment					
6. Community Organization					
7. Policy Analysis					
8. Administration					

2. For the activities that you checked "Highly interested," state the reasons for your selections.

3. For the activities that you checked "Somewhat disinterested" or "Not interested," state the reasons for your selections.

▪ KNOWLEDGE, SKILLS, AND VALUES NEEDED FOR SOCIAL WORK PRACTICE

Knowledge

In EPAS (Education Policy and Accreditation Standards), the Council on Social Work Education has categorized the following fundamental knowledge that accredited baccalaureate and master's degree programs must provide to social work students:

A. Values and Ethics

Social work education programs integrate content about values and principles of ethical decision making as presented in the National Association of Social Workers Code of Ethics. The educational experience provides students with the opportunity to be aware of personal values; develop, demonstrate, and promote the values of the profession; and analyze ethical dilemmas and the ways in which these affect practice, services, and clients.

B. Diversity

Social work programs integrate content that promotes understanding, affirmation, and respect for people from diverse backgrounds. The content emphasizes the interlocking and complex nature of culture and personal identity. It ensures that social services meet the needs of groups served and are culturally relevant. Programs educate students to recognize diversity within and between groups that may influence assessment, planning, intervention, and research. Students learn how to define, design, and implement strategies for effective practice with persons from diverse backgrounds.

C. **Populations-at-Risk and Social and Economic Justice**

Social work education programs integrate content on populations-at-risk, examining the factors that contribute to and constitute being at risk. Programs educate students to identify how group membership influences access to resources and present content on the dynamics of such risk factors and responsive and productive strategies to redress them.

Programs integrate social and economic justice content grounded in an understanding of distributive justice, human and civil rights, and the global interconnections of oppression. Programs provide content related to implementing strategies to combat discrimination, oppression, and economic deprivation and to promote social and economic justice. Programs prepare students to advocate for nondiscriminatory social and economic systems.

D. **Human Behavior and the Social Environment**

Social work education programs provide content on the reciprocal relationships between human behavior and social environments. Content includes empirically based theories and knowledge that focus on the interactions between and among individuals, groups, societies, and economic systems. It includes theories and knowledge of biological, sociological, cultural, psychological, and spiritual development across the life span; the range of social systems in which people live (individual, family, group, organizational, and community); and the ways in which social systems promote or deter people in maintaining or achieving health and well-being.

E. **Social Welfare Policy and Services**

Programs provide content about the history of social work, the history and current structures of social welfare services, and the role of policy in service delivery, social work practice, and attainment of individual and social well-being. Course content provides students with knowledge and skills to understand major policies that form the foundation of social welfare; analyze organizational, local, state, national, and international issues in social welfare policy and social service delivery; analyze and apply the results of policy research relevant to social service delivery; understand and demonstrate policy practice skills in regard to economic, political, and organizational systems, and use them to influence, formulate, and advocate for policy consistent with social work values; and identify financial, organizational, administrative, and planning processes required to deliver social services.

F. **Social Work Practice**

Social work practice content is anchored in the purposes of the social work profession and focuses on strengths, capacities, and resources of client systems in relation to their broader environments. Students learn practice content that encompasses knowledge and skills to work with individuals, families, groups, organizations, and communities. This current includes engaging clients in an appropriate working relationship; identifying issues, problems, needs, resources, and assets; collecting and assessing information; and planning for service delivery. It includes using communication skills, supervision, and consultation. Practice content also includes identifying, analyzing, and implementing empirically based interventions designed to achieve client goals; applying empirical knowledge and technological advances; evaluating program outcomes and practice effectiveness; developing, analyzing, advocating, and providing leadership for policies and services; and promoting social and economic justice.

G. **Research**

Qualitative and quantitative research content provides understanding of a scientific, analytic, and ethical approach to building knowledge for practice. The content prepares students to develop, use, and effectively communicate empirically based knowledge, including evidence-based interventions. Research knowledge is used by students to provide high-quality services; to initiate change; to improve practice, policy, and social service delivery; and to evaluate their own practice.

H. Field Education

Field education is an integral component of social work education anchored in the mission, goals, and educational level of the program. It occurs in settings that reinforce students' identification with the purposes, values, and ethics of the profession, fosters the integration of empirical and practice-based knowledge, and promotes the development of professional competence. Field education is systematically designed, supervised, coordinated, and evaluated on the basis of criteria by which students demonstrate the achievement of program objectives.[21]

As indicated, baccalaureate and master's degree programs are mandated to provide this foundation curriculum content. In addition, master's programs provide "advanced curriculum content," which the Council on Social Work Education in EPAS describes as follows:

The master's curriculum prepares graduates for advanced social work practice in an area of concentration. Using a conceptual framework to identify advanced knowledge and skills, programs build an advanced curriculum from the foundation content. In the advanced curriculum, the foundation content areas . . . are addressed in greater depth, breadth, and specificity and support the program's conception of advanced practice.[22]

Master's programs offer "concentrations" from which students can choose their specialization. A concentration component should build knowledge, values, and skills for advanced practice in an identifiable area. Areas frequently offered by master's programs include fields of practice, problem areas, populations-at-risk, and intervention methods or roles.

Core Practice Skills

There have been a number of efforts to articulate the essential skills for entry-level social work practice positions. A few of these conceptualizations will be presented to indicate contemporary thinking about core practice skills. It should be noted that there are a number of similarities between these conceptualizations, but there is *not* yet full agreement on these core skills.

Baer has identified the following 10 competencies as essential for successfully performing the responsibilities of entry-level social work positions:

1. Identify and assess situations in which the relationship between people and social institutions needs to be initiated, enhanced, restored, protected, or terminated.
2. Develop and implement a plan for improving the well-being of people, based on problem assessment and the exploration of obtainable goals and available options.
3. Enhance the problem-solving, coping, and developmental capacities of people.
4. Link people with systems that provide them with resources, services, and opportunities.
5. Intervene effectively on behalf of populations most vulnerable and discriminated against.
6. Promote the effective and humane operation of the systems that provide people with services, resources, and opportunities.
7. Actively participate with others in creating new, modified, or improved service, resource, or opportunity systems that are more equitable, just, and responsive to consumers of services; work with others to eliminate unjust systems.
8. Evaluate the extent to which the objectives of the intervention plan were achieved.

9. Continually evaluate one's professional growth and development through assessment of practice behaviors and skills.

10. Contribute to the improvement of service delivery by adding to the knowledge base of the profession as appropriate and supporting and upholding the standards and ethics of the profession.[23]

NASW has identified the following abilities, closely related to conceptualizing essential skills, as being needed for social work practice:

Speak and write clearly.
Teach others.
Respond supportively in emotion-laden or crisis situations.
Serve as a role model in a professional relationship.
Interpret complex psychosocial phenomena.
Organize a workload to meet designated responsibilities.
Identify and obtain resources needed to assist others.
Assess one's performance and feelings.
Participate in and lead group activities.
Function under stress.
Deal with conflict situations or contentious personalities.
Relate social and psychological theory to practice situations.
Identify the information necessary to solve a problem.
Conduct research studies of agency services or one's practice.[24]

In EPAS, the Council on Social Work Education mandates that accredited baccalaureate and master's programs in social work programs must provide content on the following 10 skills, which we discussed in detail earlier in the chapter:

1. Engaging clients in an appropriate working relationship.
2. Identifying issues, problems, needs, resources, and assets.
3. Collecting and assessing information.
4. Planning for service delivery.
5. Using communication skills, supervision, and consultation.
6. Identifying, analyzing, and implementing empirically based interventions designed to achieve client goals.
7. Applying empirical knowledge and technological advances.
8. Evaluating program outcomes and practice effectiveness.
9. Developing, analyzing, advocating, and providing leadership for policies and services.
10. Promoting social and economic justice.

The acquisition of social work skills depends partly on innate ability and partly on learning experiences. Social work education programs facilitate the learning of these skills by presenting theoretical material to students (such as material on how to interview), by monitoring and critiquing students who are practicing applying these skills (for example, videotaping students in simulated counseling situations), and by extensively supervising students in practicum courses.

Values

Should the primary objective of imprisonment be rehabilitation or punishment? Should a father who commits incest be prosecuted if publicity in the community is likely to lead to family breakup, or should an effort be made through counseling to stop the incest and keep the family intact? Should a wife who is occasionally abused by her husband be encouraged to remain with him? Should an abortion be suggested as one alternative for resolving the problems of someone who is single and pregnant? Should youths who are considered uncontrollable by their parents be placed in correctional schools? If a client of a social worker threatens serious harm to some third person, what should the worker do? If a client indicates he is HIV-positive and continues to persist in behavior that places his partner in danger of contracting the disease but refuses to warn the partner of the peril, what should the social worker do? All of these questions involve making decisions that are largely based on values. Much of social work practice is dependent upon making such decisions.

NASW has identified the following broad-based values as necessary in social work practice:

- Commitment to the primary importance of the individual in society.
- Respect for the confidentiality of relationships with clients.
- Commitment to social change to meet socially recognized needs.
- Willingness to keep personal feelings and needs separate from professional relationships.
- Willingness to transmit knowledge and skills to others.
- Respect and appreciation for individual and group differences.
- Commitment to developing clients' ability to help themselves.
- Willingness to persist in efforts on behalf of clients despite frustration.
- Commitment to social justice and the economic, physical, and mental well-being of all in society.
- Commitment to a high standard of personal and professional conduct.[25]

The Code of Ethics of the National Association of Social Workers identifies a number of values that social workers are obligated to adhere to. (A copy of this Code appears at www.naswdc.org.)

Because values play a key role in social work practice, it is essential that social work educational programs (1) help students clarify their values, (2) foster the development of values in students that are consistent with professional social work practice, and (3) help students analyze how values impact professional practice.

Goals of Social Work Education

The Council on Social Work Education in EPAS identifies the purposes and goals of social work education as follows:

The purpose of social work education are to prepare competent and effective professionals, to develop social work knowledge, and to provide leadership in the development of service delivery systems. Social work education is grounded in the profession's history, purposes, and philosophy and is based on a body of knowledge, values, and skills. Social work education enables students to integrate the knowledge, values, and skills of the social work profession for competent practice.

Among its programs, which vary in design, structure, and objectives, social work education achieves these purposes through such means as:

- Providing curricula and teaching practices at the forefront of the new and changing knowledge base of social work and related disciplines.
- Providing curricula that build on a liberal arts perspective to promote breadth of knowledge, critical thinking, and communication skills.
- Developing knowledge.
- Developing and applying instructional and practice-relevant technology.
- Maintaining reciprocal relationships with social work practitioners, groups, organizations, and communities.
- Promoting continual professional development of students, faculty, and practitioners.
- Promoting interprofessional and interdisciplinary collaboration.
- Preparing social workers to engage in prevention activities that promote well-being.
- Preparing social workers to practice with individuals, families, groups, organizations, and communities.
- Preparing social workers to evaluate the processes and effectiveness of practice.
- Preparing social workers to practice without discrimination, with respect, and with knowledge and skills related to clients' age, class, color, culture, disability, ethnicity, family structure, gender, marital status, national origin, race, religion, sex, and sexual orientation.

- Preparing social workers to alleviate poverty, oppression, and other forms of social injustice.
- Preparing social workers to recognize the global context of social work practice.
- Preparing social workers to formulate and influence social policies and social work services in diverse political contexts.[26]

Objectives of Social Work Education

The Council on Social Work Education in EPAS has specified the foundation program objectives for both baccalaureate and master's degree programs. These objectives, which follow, highlight much of the knowledge, values, and skills needed for social work practice. (The symbols "B6" and "M6" apply, respectively, to baccalaureate programs and master's degree programs.) Graduates of baccalaureate and master's degree programs in the United States are expected to demonstrate the ability to:

1. Applying critical thinking skills within the context of professional social work practice.
2. Understanding the value base of the profession and its ethical standards and principles, and practice accordingly.
3. Practice without discrimination and with respect, knowledge, and skills related to clients' age, class, color, culture, disability, ethnicity, family structure, gender, marital status, national origin, race, religion, sex, and sexual orientation.
4. Understand the forms and mechanisms of oppression and discrimination and apply strategies of advocacy and social change that advance social and economic justice.
5. Understand and interpret the history of the social work profession and its contemporary structures and issues.
B6. Apply the knowledge and skills of generalist social work practice with systems of all sizes.
M6. Apply the knowledge and skills of a generalist social work perspective to practice with systems of all sizes.
7. Use theoretical frameworks supported by empirical evidence to understand individual development and behavior across the life span and the interactions among individuals, and between individuals and families, groups, organizations, and communities.
8. Analyze, formulate, and influence social policies.
9. Evaluate research studies, apply research findings to practice, and evaluate their own practice interventions.
10. Use communication skills, differentially across client populations, colleagues, and communities.
11. Use supervision and consultation appropriate to social work practice.
12. Function within the structure of organizations and service delivery systems, and seek necessary organizational change.[27]

In stating these objectives, the Council on Social Work Education notes: "A program may develop additional objectives to cover the required content in relation to its particular mission, goals, and educational level."[28]

Graduates of master's degree programs are also required by the Council on Social Work Education to meet the objectives of the concentration that they specialize in, as specified in the following statement:

> Graduates of a master's social work program are advanced practitioners who apply the knowledge and skills of advanced social work practice in an area of concentration. They analyze, intervene, and evaluate in ways that at highly differentiated, discriminating, and self-critical. Graduates synthesize and apply a broad range of knowledge and practice with a high degree of autonomy and skill. They refine and advance the quality of their practice and that of the larger social work profession.[29]

A Greater Focus on Outcomes

The Council on Social Work Education is a specialized accreditation entity. A number of specialized accreditation entities exist, such as the American Bar Association, which accredits law programs throughout the United States. The fairly large number of higher-education accreditation entities in the United States are accountable to the Council for Higher Education Accreditation (CHEA). CHEA is thus the association that accredits higher-education accreditation entities in the United States. (Membership on CHEA is primarily composed of representatives from chancellors and presidents of U.S. colleges and universities.)

In recent years, CHEA has mandated that the higher-education accreditation entitles that it accredits must have a greater focus on outcomes. As a result, the Council on Social Work Education now requires that accredited baccalaureate and master's programs in social work must demonstrate that students in social work programs are in fact attaining the stated objectives of those programs. Thus, faculty now strongly focus on students attaining these objectives, and they also measure the extent to which students attain these objectives.

■ SOCIAL GROUP WORK AS A COMPONENT OF SOCIAL WORK PRACTICE

Social work practice involves providing humane and effective social services to individuals, families, groups, organizations, and communities. Social work with groups has considerable overlap in providing social services to individuals, families, organizations, and communities. The skills, knowledge, and values needed for effective social work practice with groups are very similar to the skills, knowledge, and values needed for effective social work practice with individuals, families, organizations, and communities.

The material in this text on verbal communication, nonverbal communication, problem solving, interviewing, counseling, and contracting, is applicable to social work practice with both individuals and groups. A family, as described in Chapter 9, is a subtype of a group. The close relationships between a group and an organization are described in Chapter 10. Finally, the close relationships between a group and a community are also described in Chapter 10. Acquiring the skills, values, and knowledge needed for effective practice with groups will simultaneously increase a social worker's ability to work effectively with individuals, families, organizations, and communities.

■ GROUP EXERCISES

Exercise A: Options Planning

GOAL: This exercise is designed to help students gain an awareness of how generalist social workers generate options for combatting social problems.

The leader briefly describes generalist social work practice and indicates that options planning is one important aspect. The leader should state the purpose of this exercise, ask students to form subgroups of about five students, then read the first vignette to the subgroup. Give them about ten minutes to arrive at their options. Then ask the subgroups to share their options with the class. Seek to stimulate class discussion of various options. Proceed with the remaining vignettes in the same manner.

VIGNETTE #1

Blackhawk High School has recently had significant increases in the number of female students who have become pregnant. Many of these students become single mothers who face a number of obstacles in providing quality child care while trying to continue their education. The community is becoming increasingly concerned about the rising pregnancy rate and the difficulties these young mothers are encountering. The principal of the school requests that the school social worker, Ms. Gomez, do something to "fix" these problems. What are realistic options that she might initiate and pursue?

VIGNETTE #2

Milton College wants to better educate its students, faculty, and other staff about HIV and AIDS. Education is currently recognized as the best way to curb the spread of HIV and AIDS and combat HIV and AIDS discrimination. The president of the college requests that the social work department take the lead in developing educational approaches for use on campus. What realistic educational formats (such as peer education, workshops, and in-service training seminars) can be introduced to educate students, faculty, and other staff in these areas?

VIGNETTE #3

Mr. Komarek is a social worker for a public welfare department in a small rural community that has no shelter for homeless individuals or families. Community leaders have asked the county public welfare department to do something about the increasing number of homeless in the community. The director of the agency, responding to community pressure, assigns Mr. Komarek to head up a task force (i.e., a committee) to combat the homeless problem. What realistic options could be pursued by Mr. Komarek and this task force?

VIGNETTE #4

The mayor of a large city has appointed a task force to develop recommendations for improving living conditions in the inner city. The inner city has high rates of unemployment, crime, drug and alcohol abuse, births outside of marriage, substandard housing, high school dropouts, homeless individuals and families, gang activity, and homicides. A great many people are receiving public assistance. Ms. Taylor, a social worker and social planner employed by United Way, is appointed to this task force. What realistic recommendations for improving living conditions should be advanced by this task force?

Exercise B: Social Work with Groups and Generalist Practice

GOAL: This exercise is designed to help students acquire a working knowledge of key terms used in social work.

Step 1. The leader states the purpose of this exercise. Indicate that social workers must be able to describe to others what the profession of social work is and how it is distinct from other professions. Students form subgroups of about five students each. The leader asks each subgroup to discuss answers to the first of the following four questions. Give the subgroups about ten minutes to arrive at an answer. Then ask them to share their answers with the class. After this process is completed, the leader may summarize the answer to this question given in this chapter, and may compare it with the answers arrived at by the subgroups. The answers from the class may be better than the answers in the text.

Step 2. Proceed with the remaining three questions in a similar manner.

QUESTIONS

1. Define social work and social welfare, and describe the relationship between the two.
2. Define the profession of social work and describe how it is distinct from such other helping professions as psychology and psychiatry.
3. Define the terms "social worker" and "generalist social worker."
4. Describe how social work practice with groups is distinct from, but similar to, social work practice with other client systems—that is, individuals, families, organizations, and communities.

CHAPTER THREE

Group Dynamics: Leadership

GOALS

Is the statement "He's a born leader" valid, or is leadership a learned characteristic rather than an inherited trait? This chapter describes four major approaches to leadership, including the trait approach, and defines effective group leadership functions, roles, and techniques. This chapter asserts that the use of power is a necessary component of group functioning. Five bases of power are described, and the different consequences of using these bases and the effects of unequal power in groups are also discussed. Material is presented here on how to start and lead a group.

Leadership occurs whenever one person in a group influences other members to help the group reach its goals. Because all group members influence each other at various times, each individual exerts leadership. However, a difference exists between being a designated leader—a president or chairperson—and engaging in leadership behavior. A *designated leader* has certain responsibilities, such as calling meetings and leading discussions, while *leadership* refers to influential behavior in general.

■ APPROACHES TO LEADERSHIP

Four major approaches to leadership theory—trait, position, leadership style, and distributed functions—are summarized in the following sections.

The Trait Approach

Aristotle observed: "From the hour of their birth some are marked for subjugation, and others for command." This trait approach to leadership, which has existed for centuries, assumes that leaders have inherent personal characteristics, or traits, that distinguish them from followers. This approach asserts that leaders are born, not made, and emerge naturally instead of being trained. It has also been called the "great man" or "great woman" theory of leadership. According to Krech, Crutchfield, and Ballachey, who reviewed research studies on leadership traits, a leader needs to be perceived as (1) a member of the group he or she is attempting to lead, (2) embodying to a special degree the norms and values central to the group, (3) the most qualified group member to accomplish the task at hand, and (4) fitting members' expectations about how he or she should behave and what functions he or she should serve.[1]

Some research on personality traits indicates that leaders tend to be better adjusted and more dominant, extroverted, "masculine," and interpersonally sensitive than their followers. Other traits, such as intelligence, enthusiasm, dominance, self-confidence, and egalitarianism, have also been found to characterize leaders.[2] Although potential leaders tend to have more positive attributes than other group members, they cannot be so successful that members perceive them as "different." For example, Davis and Hare found that "B" students were the campus leaders, while the more intelligent "A" students were considered "grinds" who occasionally were treated as outcasts for being "curve wreckers."[3] Also, the member who talks most has been found to win most decisions and so becomes the leader, unless he talks too much and antagonizes other group members.[4]

Two postulated leadership traits that have received considerable attention are charisma and Machiavellianism. We will take a brief look at each of these traits.

Charisma

Charisma has been defined as "an extraordinary power, as of working miracles."[5] Johnson and Johnson give the following definition of a charismatic leader:

> The charismatic leader must have a sense of mission, a belief in the social-change movement he or she leads, and confidence in oneself as the chosen instrument to lead the movement to its destination. The leader must appear extremely self-confident in order to inspire others with the faith that the movement he or she leads will, without fail, prevail and ultimately reduce their distress.[6]

Some charismatic leaders appear to inspire their followers to love and be fully committed to them. Other charismatic leaders offer their followers the hope and promise of deliverance from distress.

Charisma has not been precisely defined, and its components have not been fully identified. The qualities and characteristics that each charismatic leader has will differ somewhat from those of other charismatic leaders. The following leaders all have been referred to as charismatic, yet they differed substantially in personality characteristics: John F. Kennedy, Martin Luther King Jr., Julius Caesar, General George Patton, Confucius, Gandhi, and Winston Churchill.

One flaw with the charisma approach to leadership is that people who are viewed as having charisma tend to express this quality in a variety of ways. A second flaw is that many people do well as leaders without being viewed as having charisma. For example, many group therapists are effective in leading groups even though they are not viewed as charismatic.

Exercise 3.1:   The Charismatic Leader

GOAL: This exercise is designed to assist you in identifying charismatic people and understanding the various characteristics that lead a person to be charismatic.

1. **Write the names of three people you identify as being charismatic. These may be presidents, political leaders, religious leaders, teachers, acquaintances, and so on. For each person you identify, list the characteristics that cause this person (in your view) to be charismatic.**

2. **For the three people you wrote about, identify the charismatic characteristics that all three individuals appear to have in common.**

3. **Do any of these people have unique charismatic characteristics (that is, characteristics that are not held by the other two)? If "yes," identify the person and describe his or her unique characteristics.**

Machiavellianism

Niccolò Machiavelli (1469–1527) was an Italian statesman who advocated cunning, deceit, and duplicity as political methods rulers should use for increasing their power and control. Machiavelli was not the originator of such an approach; earlier theorists conceptualized leadership in terms of manipulation for self-enhancement. However, the term *Machiavellianism* has become associated with the notion that politics is amoral and that any means should be used to achieve political power. Machiavellian leadership is based on the concepts that people (1) are basically fallible, gullible, untrustworthy, and weak; (2) are impersonal objects; and (3) should be manipulated so that the leader can achieve his goals.

Christie and Geis conclude that Machiavellian leaders have four characteristics:

1. They have little emotional involvement in interpersonal relationships—it is easier to manipulate others if "followers" are viewed as impersonal objects.
2. They are not concerned about conventional morality; they take a utilitarian view (what they can get out of it) rather than a moral view of their interactions with others.
3. They have a fairly accurate perception of the needs of their followers, which facilitates their capacity to manipulate them.
4. They have a low degree of ideological commitment; they focus on manipulating others for personal benefit, rather than on achieving long-term ideological goals.[7]

While a few leaders may have Machiavellian characteristics, most do not. Today very few groups would function effectively or efficiently with Machiavellian leaders.

In recent years the trait theory of leadership has declined in popularity, partly because research results have raised questions about its validity. For example, different leadership positions often require different leadership traits. The characteristics of a good leader in the military differ markedly from those of a good group therapy leader. Moreover, traits found in leaders have also been found in followers. Though qualities such as high intelligence and a well-adjusted personality may have some correlation with leadership, many highly intelligent people never get top leadership positions, and some highly intelligent leaders (Adolf Hitler, for example) have been emotionally unstable. The best rule for leader selection involves choosing individuals with the necessary skills, qualities, and motivation to help a group accomplish its goals.

Exercise 3.2: Machiavellian Leaders

GOAL: This exercise is designed to assist you in understanding the characteristics of Machiavellian leaders.

Some authorities view Joseph Stalin, Adolf Hitler, and Saddam Hussein as Machiavellian leaders. Identify three people you view as Machiavellian leaders. (These people may include one or more of the leaders just mentioned.) For each person you list, write the characteristics he or she had (or has) that are Machiavellian in nature.

The Position Approach

In most large organizations, there are several levels of leadership, such as president, vice-president, manager, supervisor, and foreman. The position approach defines leadership in terms of the authority of a particular position. It focuses on studying the behavior, training and personal background of leaders in high-level positions.

Studies using the position approach, however, have revealed little consistency in how people assume leadership positions. Obviously, individuals may become leaders with little related training (in family businesses, for example), while others spend years developing their skills. Also, individuals in different leadership positions have been found to display a variety of appropriate behaviors. For example, a drill sergeant in basic military training is not expected to be empathetic, but a sensitivity group leader is. It is difficult to compile a list of leadership traits by using this approach. Not surprisingly, the position approach has shown that what constitutes leadership behavior depends upon the particular requirements of the position.

Another problem with the position approach is that it is difficult to define which behavior of a designated leader is leadership behavior and which is not. Certainly not all of the behavior of a designated authority figure is leadership behavior. For instance, an inexperienced individual in a position of authority can mask incompetence with an authoritarian attitude. Also, the leadership behavior among group members who are not designated leaders is difficult for the position approach to explain, because this approach focuses its attention on designated leaders.

The Leadership-Style Approach

Because researchers on the trait and the position approaches were turning out contradictory results, Lewin, Lippitt, and White focused on examining leadership styles. Their research uncovered three—authoritarian, democratic, and laissez-faire.[8]

Authoritarian Leaders

These types of leaders, who have more absolute power than democratic leaders, set goals and policies, dictate the activities of the members, and develop major plans. The leader alone is the purveyor of rewards and punishments and knows the succession of future steps in the group's activities. Authoritarian leadership is generally efficient and decisive. One of the hazards, however, is that group members may respond out of necessity and not because of commitment to group goals. The authoritarian leader who anticipates approval from subordinates may be surprised to find that backbiting and bickering are common in the group. Unsuccessful authoritarian leadership is apt to generate factionalism, behind-the-scenes jockeying for position among members, and a decline in morale.

Democratic Leaders

In contrast, democratic leaders seek the maximum involvement and participation of every member in all decisions affecting the group and attempt to spread responsibility rather than concentrate it. Democratic leadership can lead to slow decision making and confusion, but it is frequently more effective because of the strong cooperation that emerges from group participation. Interpersonal hostilities between members, dissatisfactions with the leader, and concern for personal advancement all become issues that are discussed and acted upon. With democratic leadership, the private complaining that is kept behind the scenes in the authoritarian approach usually becomes public. When this occurs, such conflicts can be more openly and readily confronted and dealt with. Once this public conflict has been resolved in a democratic group, however, a strong personal commitment usually develops, which motivates members to implement group decisions rather than to subvert them. The potential for sabotage in an authoritarian group is high and therein lies the major advantage of the democratic style. The democratic leader knows that mistakes are inevitable and the group will suffer from them, but he or she must learn to stand back and allow the democratic process to continue without interference.

Depending on the situation, authoritarian or democratic leadership may be more effective, assuming members' expectations about appropriate behavior for each situation are met.[9] When group members anticipate a democratic style, as they do in educational settings or discussion groups, the democratic style is utilized well. When members anticipate forceful leadership from their superiors, as in industry or the military, individuals accept a more authoritarian form of leadership.

Laissez-Faire Leaders

These leaders participate very little, and group members are generally left to function (or flounder) with little input. Group members seldom function well under a laissez-faire style, which may be effective *only* when the members are committed to a course of action, have the resources to implement it, and need minimal leadership to reach their goals. For example, laissez-faire leadership may work well in a college department in which the faculty members are competent, conscientious, and responsible, and have the resources to meet their objectives.

Exercise 3.3: Authoritarian, Democratic, and Laissez-Faire Leaders

GOAL: This exercise is designed to help you understand these three types of leadership styles.

1. **Identify someone who used an authoritarian style in leading a group. State what the leader did that led you to conclude his or her style was authoritarian. Also state what the reactions of the other group members were to this authoritarian style.**

2. Identify someone who used a democratic style in leading a group. State what the leader did that led you to conclude his or her style was democratic. Also state what the reactions of the other group members were to this democratic style.

3. Identify someone who used a laissez-faire style in leading a group. State what the leader did that led you to conclude his or her style was laissez-faire. Also state what the reactions of the other group member were to this laissez-faire style.

The Distributed-Functions Approach

Because different leadership styles are required in different situations (even within the same group), research in recent years has focused more on how leadership functions are distributed. The distributed-functions approach disagrees with the "great man," or trait, theory of leadership and asserts that every member of a group will be a leader at times by taking actions that serve group functions. Leadership is defined as the performance of acts that help the group maintain itself and reach its goals. Leadership functions include setting goals, selecting and implementing tasks, and providing resources to accomplish group goals while maintaining the group's cohesion and satisfying the needs of individual members. The functional approach involves determining what tasks, or functions, are essential to achieve group goals and how different group members should participate.

With this approach, the demands of leadership are viewed as being specific to a particular group in a particular situation. For example, cracking a joke may be a useful leadership tactic in certain situations if it relieves tension. But when other members are revealing intense personal information in therapy, humor may be counterproductive and therefore inappropriate leadership behavior.

Many individuals who fear taking a leadership role are uncertain about leadership functions and feel they lack the proper qualities of a leader. Amazingly, even the most fearful and anxious students have already taken on many leadership roles and nearly everyone has assumed leadership responsibilities by adolescence. Functional leadership involves a learned set of skills that anyone with certain minimal capabilities can acquire. Responsible membership is the same thing as responsible leadership because both maintain the group's cohesion and accomplish its goals. Since people can be taught leadership skills and behaviors, the implication of this theory is that nearly everyone can be taught to be an effective leader.

Exercise 3.4: Applying the Distributed-Functions Approach

GOAL: This exercise is designed to show you that you already have taken on leadership functions in a group.

The distributed-functions approach asserts that every member of a group will be a leader at times by taking actions that serve group functions. Identify a group that you are currently in or that you were a member of in the past. Describe the actions you took that were useful to the group. (When you made positive contributions to this group, you were taking on leadership responsibilities.)

■ LEADERSHIP ROLES

Task and Maintenance Roles

Through considerable research on problem-solving groups, Bales has identified two specific leadership functions: the task specialist and the social/emotional, or group maintenance, specialist.[10] All groups, whether organized for therapeutic reasons, problem solving, or other purposes, rely on members performing task roles and group maintenance roles satisfactorily. *Task roles are those needed to accomplish specific goals set by the group.* They have been summarized by Johnson and Johnson as follows:

Information and Opinion Giver: Offers facts, opinions, ideas, suggestions, and relevant information to help group discussion.

Information and Opinion Seeker: Asks for facts, information, opinions, ideas, and feelings from other members to help group discussion.

Starter: Proposes goals and tasks to initiate action within the group.

Direction Giver: Develops plans on how to proceed and focuses attention on the task to be done.

Summarizer: Pulls together related ideas or suggestions and restates and summarizes major points discussed.

Coordinator: Shows relationships among various ideas by pulling them together and harmonizes activities of various subgroups and members.

Diagnoser: Figures out sources of difficulties the group has in working effectively and the blocks to progress in accomplishing the group's goals.

Energizer: Stimulates a higher quality of work from the group.

Reality Tester: Examines the practicality and workability of ideas, evaluates alternative solutions, and applies them to real situations to see how they will work.

Evaluator: Compares group decisions and accomplishments with group standards and goals.

The Johnsons have also identified *group maintenance roles,* which strengthen social/emotional bonds within the group:

Encourager of Participation: Warmly encourages everyone to participate, giving recognition for contributions, demonstrating acceptance and openness to ideas of others; is friendly and responsive to group members.

Harmonizer and Compromiser: Persuades members to analyze constructively their differences in opinions, searches for common elements in conflicts, and tries to reconcile disagreements.

Tension Reliever: Eases tensions and increases the enjoyment of group members by joking, suggesting breaks, and proposing fun approaches to group work.

Communication Helper: Shows good communication skills and makes sure that each group member understands what other members are saying.

Evaluator of Emotional Climate: Asks members how they feel about the way in which the group is working and about each other, and shares own feelings about both.

Process Observer: Watches the process by which the group is working and uses the observations to help examine group effectiveness.

Standard Setter: Expresses group standards and goals to make members aware of the direction of the work and the progress being made toward the goal, and to get open acceptance of group norms and procedures.

Active Listener: Listens and serves as an interested audience for other members, is receptive to others' ideas, and goes along with the group when not in disagreement.

Trust Builder: Accepts and supports openness of other group members, reinforcing risk taking and encouraging individuality.

Interpersonal Problem Solver: Promotes open discussion of conflicts between group members in order to resolve conflicts and increase group togetherness.[11]

Each of the foregoing task and maintenance functions may be required periodically within a group, and effective group members (and leaders) are sensitive to these needs.

A task leader emerges in many groups because he or she has the best ideas and does the most to guide discussions. Since this person concentrates on a task, and generally plays an aggressive role in moving the group toward the goal, hostility is apt to arise and the task leader may be disliked. Concurrently, a second leader may emerge: a social/emotional specialist who concentrates on group harmony and resolves tensions and conflicts within the group. In groups with an official leader, the leader is expected to be both the task specialist and the social/emotional specialist. In groups without an official leader, these two functions are generally assumed by two different emergent leaders. When social/emotional group maintenance needs are met, a group will continually improve its task effectiveness. However, when maintenance needs are ignored, a group's task effectiveness deteriorates.

Hersey and Blanchard have developed a situational theory of leadership that points out when leaders should focus on task behaviors, on maintenance behaviors, or on both.[12] In essence, the theory asserts that when members have low maturity in terms of accomplishing a specific task, the leader should engage in high-task behaviors and low-maintenance behaviors. Hersey and Blanchard refer to this situation as *telling*—the leader's behavior is most effective when the leader defines the roles of members and *tells* them how, when, and where to do needed tasks. The task maturity of members increases as their experience and understanding of the task increases. For moderately mature members, the leader should engage in high-task behaviors and high-maintenance behaviors. This combination of behaviors is referred to as *selling*. The leader should not only provide clear directions about role and task responsibilities, but also use maintenance behaviors to get the members to "buy into" the decisions that have to be made.

Hersey and Blanchard also assert that when the group members' commitment to the task increases, so does their maturity. When members are committed to accomplishing the task and have the ability and knowledge to complete the task, the leader should engage in low-task behaviors and high-maintenance behaviors. This is referred to as *participating*. Finally, for groups in which members are both willing and able to take responsibility for directing their own task behavior, the leader should engage in low-task and low-maintenance behaviors; this is referred to as *delegating*. Delegating allows members considerable autonomy in completing the task.

Exercise 3.5: Your Task and Maintenance Contributions to a Group

GOAL: This exercise is designed to assist you in understanding your task and maintenance contributions to a group.

1. Identify a group you are currently participating in or have participated in at same time. Briefly describe this group, including its goals.

2. Review the list of task roles and then describe your task contributions to this group.

3. Review the list of maintenance roles and then describe your maintenance contributions to this group.

Other Roles

The designated group leader has a special obligation to assume, or to assist others in assuming, timely and appropriate task and maintenance roles. Each leader is also responsible for a variety of functions, which range from setting initial policies to planning for termination. To meet the needs and particular developmental stage of a group, a leader may be required to assume any of the previously described roles as well these:

Executive: Coordinates the activities of a group.
Policy Maker: Establishes group goals and policies.
Planner: Decides the means by which the group shall achieve its goals.
Expert: Offers ready source of information and skills.
External Group Representative: Serves as official spokesperson.
Controller of Internal Relations: Controls the group structure and in-group relations.
Purveyor of Rewards and Punishments: Promotes, demotes, and assigns pleasant or unpleasant tasks.
Arbitrator and Mediator: Acts as both judge and conciliator, and has the power to reduce or increase factionalism within the group.
Exemplar: Serves as a model of behavior for other members.
Ideologist: Serves as the source of group beliefs and values.
Scapegoat: Serves as the target for members' frustrations and disappointments.

■ POWER AND INFLUENCE IN GROUPS

Although the use of power in human interactions is often viewed negatively, it is, in fact, a normal part of relationships because people are frequently influencing and being influenced by one another. The terms *power* and *influence* will be used interchangeably in this chapter. Both terms refer to the capacity of an individual to motivate others to carry out certain actions or to behave in a particular way. Earlier in this chapter, leadership was defined as one member of a group influencing other members to achieve group goals and promote group maintenance. In an effective group, each member at times takes a leadership role by performing task and maintenance functions. Task functions move the group forward; maintenance functions improve the social/emotional atmosphere of the group.

In making decisions, group members present their views and opinions in an effort to influence group members. For example, some members attempt to incorporate their personal goals into the group's goals or to promote the strategies for action they want implemented. Members influence each other to commit their time and resources to the group. Controversies are usually settled through mutual influence, as members seek acceptable compromises or solutions. The use of power is indeed a necessary component of effective group functioning, and it is natural and generally desirable for every member to influence other members in the pursuit of both personal and group goals.

Every group member has a need to control what happens in a group because people join groups to attain personal goals they cannot achieve individually. If members do not exert power, their chances of achieving their personal goals are minute, and they are apt to become apathetic and disengage themselves from the group.

When group members are cooperating, power is asserted in the same direction, and members encourage each other to put forth greater effort, as they would on a sports team. However, when members are competitive or have incompatible goals, their assertions of power conflict. Republican and Democratic congressional representatives, for example, are constantly competing with each other, and their efforts to influence frequently clash.

Group members in conflict sometimes resort to manipulation; that is, they influence others for their own purpose or profit. Often, this manipulation is dishonest or unfair, for it involves the use of power for one's own benefit at the expense of other members. When people say they do not want to have power over others, they usually mean they do not want to manipulate others. If group members feel coerced by threats or discover they are manipulated in other ways, they usually react with anger, distrust, resentment, and retaliation. Manipulation, then, is a destructive kind of power because it decreases cooperation and can cause serious maintenance problems. "Influencing with integrity" is in contrast to manipulation. In a group, influencing with integrity involves seeking to influence the group in a direction that is in the group's best interests.

An effective group member is skillful in influencing others in a positive way. The amount of power a member has depends on how valuable his or her resources are. If a member has vital resources that are also available to others, that member will have less power. Interestingly, it is *not* a person's *actual* resources that determine power; instead, it is the *perception* of the other group members as to the value of a member's resources. It is possible to have vital resources but little power if these resources are ignored or unknown. It is also possible to have great power but few vital resources if members exaggerate the importance of such resources.

■ POWER BASES IN GROUPS

French and Raven have developed a framework for understanding the extent to which one group member influences another by identifying five bases of power: reward, coercive, legitimate, referent, and expert.[13] This framework allows group members to analyze the source of their power and offers suggestions on when, and when not, to use their power to influence others.

Reward Power

Rewards include such things as promotions, pay increases, days off, and praise. Reward power is based on B's (one member's) perception that A (another member or the entire group) has the capacity to dispense rewards or remove negative consequences in response to B's behavior. This power will be greater if the group members value the reward and believe they cannot get it from anyone else. Group members will usually work hard for someone who has high reward power and communicate effectively with her. Reward power can backfire, however, if group members feel they are being conned or bribed. If reward power is used by A in a conflict situation with B, B is apt to feel he is being bribed and controlled, and may eventually refuse to cooperate.

Coercive Power

The ability to fire a worker who falls below a given level of production is a common example of coercive power, which is based on B's perceptions that A can dispense punishments or remove positive consequences. Coercive power stems from the expectation on the part of B that he will be punished by A if he fails to conform to the required standards set by A. The distinction between reward and coercive power is important. French and Raven note that reward power will tend to increase the attraction of B toward A, while coercive power will decrease this attraction. If coercive power is used by A to attempt to settle a conflict, it often increases B's hostility, resentment, and anger. Threats often lead to aggression and counterthreats; for example, military threats often increase conflict between rival countries. Coercive power may exacerbate conflict by leading both A and B to distrust each other and to retaliate against each other. Therefore, whenever possible, coercive power should not be used to settle conflicts.

Legitimate Power

Legitimate power is directly related to an internalized value or norm and is probably the most complex of the five power bases. Legitimate power is based on the perception by B that A has a legitimate right to prescribe what constitutes proper behavior for him and that B has an obligation to accept this influence. Cultural values constitute one common basis for legitimate power and include intelligence, age, caste, and physical characteristics as factors determining power. For example, in some cultures the aged are highly respected and are granted the right to prescribe behavior for others. The legitimate power inherent in a formal organization is generally determined by a relationship between positions rather than between people. A supervisor in a factory, for instance, has the inherent right to assign work. A third basis for legitimate power is a legitimizing agent; for example, an election. The election process legitimizes a person's right to a position that already had a legitimate range of power associated with it.

The limits of legitimate power are generally specified at the time that power is assigned (e.g., in a job description). The attempted use of power outside of this range will decrease the legitimate power of the authority figure and decrease her attractiveness and influence.

Referent Power

Referent power occurs when one individual, A, influences another, B, as a result of identification. Identification in this context means either a feeling of oneness with A or a desire for an identity such as A's. The stronger the identification of B with A, the greater the attraction to A and the greater the referent power of A. Verbalization of referent power is "I am like A, and therefore I will believe or behave as A does," or "I want to be like A, and I will be more like A if I believe or behave as A does." In ambiguous situations (that is, situations where there are no objective right or wrong beliefs or opinions), B will seek to evaluate his thoughts, beliefs, and values in terms of what A thinks, believes, and values. In ambiguous situations B is apt to adopt the thoughts, beliefs, and values of the individual or group with which B identifies. French and Raven note that B is often not consciously aware of the referent power that A exerts.

Expert Power

Accepting a physician's advice in medical matters is a common example of expert influence, which is based on the perception that a person has knowledge or expertise that is the source of power. Another example would be accepting a counselor's suggestions. Experts can influence B (the responder) only if B thinks that A (the expert) has the right answer and B trusts A. The range of expert power is more limited than that of referent power because the expert is seen as having superior knowledge or ability only in specific areas. French and Raven note that the attempted exertion of expert power outside the perceived range will reduce that power because confidence in the expert seems to be undermined.

French and Raven theorize that for all five types, the stronger the basis of power, the greater the power. Referent power is thought to have the broadest range. Any attempt to use power outside the prescribed range is hypothesized to reduce the power.

Exercise 3.6: The Power Bases in This Class

GOAL: This exercise is designed to assist you in understanding and applying the power bases that were developed by French and Raven.

This class can be reviewed as being a group. For each of the listed power bases, answer the following: Who in this class has this power base? Have these people engaged in actions that demonstrated this power base? If "yes," write down these actions.

Reward Power:

Coercive Power:

Legitimate Power:

Referent Power:

Expert Power:

■ EFFECTS OF UNEQUAL POWER

The effectiveness of a group is improved when power is based upon expertise and competence, and is relatively equal among members. Members are more committed to implementing decisions when they feel they have had a fair say in making a decision. If a group is dominated by a few powerful members, the low-power members are likely to feel less committed to carrying out the decisions they perceive as being made by the powerful members. When power is relatively balanced, however, the members are generally more cooperative with each other.

Unequal power often leads to distrust between the high- and low-power members. The low-power members fear they will be manipulated and are reluctant to share their thoughts completely with the high-power members because they believe that if they express views in opposition to the views of the high-power members, they are apt to receive fewer rewards and may be coerced. High-power members avoid revealing weaknesses because they fear the low-power members may come to think they are undeserving of their power and seek to grasp it. The problem-solving capacity of groups is generally increased when members have fairly equal power or when the group has flexible and gradually changing power patterns that tend to equalize influence among group members.

Power based on authority or popularity can dramatically reduce the problem-solving capacities of groups when the tasks require expertise and competence. High-power people generally believe that low-power people really do like them because they see themselves as benevolent. They generally believe that low-power people communicate honestly with them and do not hide valuable information from them. When low-power members express dissatisfaction, however, high-power people frequently are not benevolent. Instead, they perceive that the low-power people are "making waves" and "not appreciating what is being done for them." In such situations high-power people may withhold rewards and use threats and coercion. These reactions usually intensify the conflict and polarize the two sides.

When threatened, high-power people may maintain power by instituting rules or norms that legitimize their power and make it illegal to change the status quo.[14] After the South lost the Civil War, for example, the white power structure in the South sought to maintain its power by keeping schools, restaurants, and public restrooms segregated. Processes were established that prevented many black people from voting, and few were hired for high-status positions. Numerous state and local laws were enacted to legitimize this segregation.

High-power people may also maintain their position by creating severe penalties for attempting to change the status quo. Blacks in the South were lynched for such offenses as seeking to be served in white restaurants. In addition, high-power members may seek to deter low-power members from rebelling by dispensing a variety of rewards to those low-power members who support the status quo.

Halle has observed that the greater a person's power becomes, the less sufficient it seems because the requests and claims upon it increase faster than the capacity to fulfill them.[15] For example, although the United States has become very powerful in the past 50 years, requests for domestic and military help from other countries have increased more rapidly than the country's ability to fulfill them. The power of the United States thus seems insufficient.

How do low-power people relate to high-power people? There are a variety of strategies. One is to emphasize and exaggerate the degree to which high-power people like them, overestimating their goodwill.[16] Low-power people using this strategy direct much of their attention and communication to high-power people, seeking to remain on good terms with them.

A second strategy for low-power people is to become apathetic and submissive. Authoritarian leadership often breeds this reaction. A third strategy is to become angry and rebel; rebellion sometimes leads to destructive violence.

Low-power people can use a variety of strategies to change the distribution of power.[17] One is to endear themselves by frequently complimenting high-power people and agreeing with them. The hope is that high-power people will come to depend on them and reward them with more power. A second strategy is to develop personal resources and organizations so that they are less vulnerable to exploitation and less dependent upon high-power people. This strategy builds a separate power structure. A third strategy is to build coalitions with other parties. Right-to-life groups, for example, have formed a coalition with leaders in the Roman Catholic Church in an attempt to make abortions illegal. A fourth strategy is to use existing legal procedures to bring pressures for change. The Civil Rights movement has used the court system extensively to force the power structure to make changes. A fifth strategy involves low-power members organizing and using confrontation techniques to force the power structure to change.

Perhaps the best known authority on using power confrontation techniques was Saul Alinsky.[18] Alinsky and his associates organized many citizens' groups to confront established power structures. For example, in the 1960s Alinsky was working with a citizens' group known as the Woodlawn Organization in the inner city of Chicago. City authorities had made commitments to this organization to improve several conditions in the neighborhood. When it became clear the commitments would not be honored, however, the Woodlawn Organization sought ways to pressure the city into meeting its commitments. The proposed solution was to embarrass city officials by tying up all the lavatories at O'Hare, one of the world's busiest airports. Alinsky describes this effort as follows:

> An intelligence study was launched to learn how many sit-down toilets for both men and women, as well as stand-up urinals, there were in the entire O'Hare airport complex and how many men and women would be necessary for the nation's first "shit-in."
>
> The consequences of this kind of action would be catastrophic in many ways. People would be desperate for a place to relieve themselves. One can see children yelling at their parents, "Mommy, I've got to go," and desperate mothers surrendering, "All right—well, do it. Do it right here." O'Hare would soon become a shambles. The whole scene would become unbelievable and the laughter and ridicule would be nationwide. It would probably get a front page story in the London *Times*. It would be a source of great mortification and embarrassment to the city administration. It might even create the kind of emergency in which planes would have to be held up while passengers got back aboard to use the plane's toilet facilities.
>
> The threat of this tactic was leaked (. . . there may be a Freudian slip here . . . so what?) back to the administration, and within 48 hours the Woodlawn Organization found itself in conference with the authorities who said they were certainly going to live up to their commitments and they could never understand where anyone got the idea that a promise made by Chicago's City Hall would not be observed.[19]

Community change efforts through group projects are often enjoyable!

Exercise 3.7: Groups of Equal Power and Unequal Power

GOAL: This exercise is designed to help you understand the effects of equal power and unequal power among members in a group.

1. **Describe a group that you participated in where group members had approximately the same amount of power.**

2. **Describe a group that you participated in where a few group members had most of the power and the rest of the members had very little power.**

3. **Which group were you most attracted to? What were the reasons for this attraction?**

4. **Review the section on the effects of unequal power. Describe how these research results are consistent or inconsistent with your experiences of being in a group of equal power and then in a group of unequal power.**

■ GUIDELINES FOR FORMING AND LEADING A GROUP

The theory of leadership emphasized in this chapter is the distributed-functions approach, which asserts that every group member takes on leadership responsibilities at various times, and every effective action by a member is simultaneously an effective leadership action. Being a designated leader is not that different from taking on leadership roles. This section will summarize a number of suggestions for how to form and lead a group effectively.

Homework

The key to successful group leadership is extensive preparation. Even experienced leaders carefully prepare for each group and for each group session.

In planning for a new group, the following questions must be answered: What is the purpose or general goals of the group? How can these goals be achieved? What are the characteristics of the members? Do some members have unique individual goals or needs? What resources are needed to accomplish group goals? What is the agenda for the first meeting? What is the best way for members to suggest and decide on the specific goals of the group? Should an ice-breaker exercise be used? Which one? Should refreshments be provided? How should the chairs be arranged? What type of group atmosphere will best help the group accomplish its tasks? What is the best available meeting place? Why has the leader been selected? What do the members expect from the leader?

To plan the first meeting, a leader should view the group as a new member would view it. Here are a few questions a new member might have: What will be the goals of this group? Why am I joining? Will my personal goals be met? Will I feel comfortable? Will I be accepted? Will the other members be radically different in terms of backgrounds and interests? If I do not like this group, can I leave gracefully? Will other members respect what I have to say, or will they laugh and make fun of me? By considering such concerns, the leader can plan the first meeting to help other members feel comfortable and to clarify the goals and activities of the group.

Before the first meeting, it is *absolutely essential* that a leader identify the group's needs and expectations as precisely as possible. A group whose leader and members disagree on goals cannot succeed.

There are a variety of ways to identify what the members want. The leader may have an opportunity to ask them before the first meeting. If that is not possible, the leader can at least talk to the organizer of the meeting about the group's expectations. The first meeting is always a good time to clarify the group's goals. The leader also needs the answers to the following questions:

1. How many members are expected?
2. What are their characteristics: age, socioeconomic status, racial and ethnic background, gender, educational/professional background?
3. How knowledgeable are the members about the topics the group will be dealing with?
4. What are the likely personal goals of the various members?
5. How motivated are the members to accomplish the purposes for which the group is being formed? Voluntary membership usually indicates greater motivation. Individuals who have been ordered by a court to participate in an alcohol rehabilitation program, for example, have little motivation and may even be hostile.
6. What values are the members likely to have? While being careful to avoid stereotyping, a leader must understand, for example, that teenagers on juvenile probation will differ significantly from retired priests.

In planning a meeting, it is helpful for a leader to visualize how the meeting will go. For example, a leader may want to visualize the following first meeting:

The members will arrive at various times. I will be there early to greet them, introduce myself, assist them in feeling comfortable, and engage in small talk. Possible topics that are apt to be of interest to these new members are _____, _____, and _____.

I will begin the meeting by introducing myself and the overall purpose of the group. I will use the following ice-breaker exercises for members to introduce themselves and get acquainted. I will ask the group to give me a list of four or five items they would like to know about the other members. Then the members will introduce themselves and respond to the items. I will also respond to the items and encourage the members to ask questions about me and the group.

After the ice-breaker exercise, I will briefly state the overall purpose of the group and ask for questions. Possible questions are _____. My answers will be _____.

We will proceed to the agenda, which has been mailed to the members. During the discussion of each agenda point, the following questions may arise: _____. My answers are _____.

The kind of group atmosphere I will seek to create is democratic and egalitarian. Such an atmosphere is best suited for encouraging members to become committed to the group goals and to contribute their time and resources. I will create this atmosphere by arranging the chairs in a circle, by drawing out through questions those who are silent, by using humor, and by making sure I do not dominate the conversation.

I will end the meeting by summarizing what has been covered and the decisions that have been made. We will set a time for the next meeting. I will finally ask if anyone has any additional comments or questions. Throughout the meeting I will seek to establish a positive atmosphere, partly by complimenting the members on the contributions they make.

If a group has met more than once, the leader needs to review the following kinds of questions. Have the overall goals been decided upon and clarified? If not, what needs to be done in this clarification process? Is the group making adequate progress in accomplishing its goals? If not, what are the obstacles that must be overcome? Is the group taking the most effective course of action to reach its goals? What is the agenda for the next meeting? What activities should be planned? Will successful completion of these activities move the group toward accomplishing its overall goals? If not, which other activities will? Is each member sufficiently motivated to help the group accomplish its goals? If not, why? What might be done to stimulate their interest?

Planning a Session

In planning a session, the leader must keep the group's overall goals—as well as those for that session—in mind. (For material on how to set group goals, see Chapter 4.) To be effective, the leader must know exactly what should be accomplished in each session and make sure that all the items on the agenda contribute to the goals. Here is a checklist that may help leaders plan successful group sessions. An effective leader will do the following:

1. Select relevant content. The material should not only be relevant to the specific goals for the session but also to the backgrounds and interests of the participants. Time-management advice for college students, for example, probably will be different from that for business executives. Time-saving tips for students will likely focus on improving study habits; business executives will be more interested in how to manage time in an office setting. An excellent way to evaluate possible material is to define precisely how it will be valuable to members of the group. The leader should ask: "If a group member wants to know why he or she should know this, can I give a valid reason?" If that question cannot be answered precisely, the material should be discarded and replaced with more relevant material.

2. Use examples. Examples help to illustrate key concepts and stimulate the participants. People tend to remember examples more readily than statistics or concepts. Vivid case histories that illustrate the drastic effects of spouse abuse, for instance, will be remembered much longer than statistics on the extent of spouse abuse.

3. Present materials in a logical order. It is generally desirable to begin by summarizing the agenda items for the session. Ideally, one topic should blend into the next. Group exercises should be used in conjunction with related theoretical material.

4. Plan the time. Once the content of a session is selected and organized, the time each segment requires should be estimated. Accurate estimates will help determine whether planned material and activities are appropriate for the allotted time. A good leader also knows what material can be deleted if time is running short and what can be added if the session progresses more rapidly than planned. Substitute activities must also be available to replace speakers who fail to appear or films that fail to arrive.

5. Be flexible. A variety of unexpected events may make it desirable to change the agenda during a session. Interpersonal conflict between members may take considerable time, or it may become clear that subjects related to the group's overall purpose are more valuable for the group to focus on than the prepared agenda.

6. Change the pace. People pay attention longer if there is an occasional change of pace. Long lectures or discussions can become boring. Group exercises, films, guest speakers, breaks, debates, and other activities will help vary the tempo of a meeting or session. In group therapy, one way to change the pace is to move from one member's problems to those of another. Lectures can be more stimulating if the instructor:

- speaks extemporaneously instead of reading material
- walks around the room occasionally, rather than standing or sitting in one place
- draws out participants by asking questions

(An excellent way to learn how to give more stimulating presentations is to observe the nonverbal and verbal communication patterns of dynamic speakers.) It is critical to use appropriate transitions so that the topics blend into one another smoothly.

Relaxing before You Start a Meeting

Before beginning a meeting, the leader is likely to be nervous about how the session may go. Some anxiety, in fact, is helpful because it increases alertness and that will make the leader more attentive, producing a better meeting. Too much anxiety, however, reduces effectiveness. Relaxation techniques that can alleviate excessive anxiety are described in Chapter 11. They are highly recommended and include walking, jogging, listening to music, meditating, and being alone to clear the mind. Effective group leaders generally learn they can reduce their level of anxiety through using one or more relaxation techniques. Practice in leading groups also builds confidence and reduces anxiety.

Cues upon Entering the Meeting Room

It is essential that a leader be on time, but arriving early is better because it allows the leader to see that materials, seating arrangements, refreshments, and any other needs are in place as planned. The leader will also have an opportunity to observe the members before the group begins. He or she can gain information about the interests of the participants from their age, gender, clothes and personal appearance, conversation, and interaction with one another. An effective leader observes such cues and uses them to create an initial bond with the participants. For example, this author was asked to give a workshop on suicide prevention to a high school class. Upon arriving, I was informed by the teacher that one of the students in the class had recently committed suicide. Instead of beginning with my planned presentation, I asked each student to write down, anonymously, one or two concerns or questions that they had about suicide. We then had a lively discussion based on their questions and concerns. Such a discussion was probably more valuable than the formal presentation (which I never gave) because it focused on their specific questions and concerns.

Seating Arrangements

Seating is important for several reasons. It can affect who talks to whom, influence leadership roles, and, as a result, affect group cohesion and morale. In most groups members should have eye contact with one another. The group leader must be able to make eye contact with everyone to obtain nonverbal feedback on what the members are thinking and feeling.

A circle is ideal for generating discussion, encouraging a sense of equal status for each member, and promoting group openness and cohesion. The traditional classroom arrangement, on the other hand, has the effect of placing the leader in a position of authority. It also tends to inhibit communication because members can easily make eye contact only with other members seated nearby.

Tables have advantages and disadvantages. They provide a place to write and to put work materials, and some members feel more comfortable at a table because they can lean on it. But tables restrict movement and may serve as barriers between people.

The leader should thus carefully consider the use of tables. In business meetings or other "working" sessions, for example, tables are necessary. In therapy groups, however, tables are seldom used. When work surfaces and written communication are required, small tables in a circle can be an effective arrangement.

The shape of the tables can also influence the way group members interact. If the table is rectangular, the leader traditionally sits at one end, becomes the head of the table and the "authority," tends to do more talking, and has a greater influence on the discussion than other group members. A round or square table, however, establishes a more egalitarian atmosphere. The "head of the table" effect can also be reduced by placing two rectangular tables together to make a square.

In new groups, or even established ones, members are likely to sit next to friends. If it is important for everyone in the group to interact, the leader may want to ask people to sit next to individuals they do not know. People are most apt to talk to others sitting at right angles to them and then to those next to them. Those sitting directly across receive less communication, and those sitting anywhere else are even less likely to be addressed.

Introductions

The leader's credentials should be summarized at the first meeting to give the group a sense of confidence that the leader can fulfill the expectations of the members. If the leader is being introduced, a concise summary of the leader's credentials *for the expected role* is desirable. If the leader is introducing herself, the important credentials should be summarized in an informative but modest way. The summary should be made in a way that helps create the desired atmosphere—whether it be formal or informal, fun or serious, or whatever. An excellent way to handle the introductions in many groups is to use an ice-breaker exercise as described in Chapter 1.

It is highly desirable for the leader to learn the names of all group members as quickly as possible. This requires extra attention, and name tags can help everyone be more comfortable sooner. Members appreciate being called by name because it affirms their importance.

If the group is small, the members can introduce themselves individually, perhaps using an ice breaker. In addition to the usual personal information, it is helpful for members to state their expectations for the group as they introduce themselves. This helps uncover hidden agendas that are incompatible with the goals of the group. If a stated expectation is beyond the scope of the group, the leader should tactfully point this out to avoid later frustration or dissatisfaction.

Clarifying Roles

The leader of a group should be clear as to his or her roles and responsibilities. If they are unclear, the leader may want to discuss them with the group. One way of doing this is for the group to select goals and then make decisions about the tasks and responsibilities that *each* member will have in working toward the goals of the group. In most situations it is clearly a mistake for the leader to do the bulk of the work. Generally, the group will be most productive if all members make substantial contributions. The more members contribute to a group, the more likely they are to feel a part of the group. Such positive feelings will benefit everyone.

Even if the leader is certain of the appropriate roles, others may be confused or may have different expectations. If there is any doubt, the leader should explain the roles clearly. If group members indicate different expectations, the group should then make decisions about who will do what.

In explaining his or her role the leader should be modest about personal skills and resources, attempting to come across as a knowledgeable person rather than an authority figure who has all the answers. The leader must also be prepared to explain the reasoning behind exercises and other actions or activities. The leader's role will vary from group to group and from situation to situation.

Agenda

Most meetings are more effective if the leader provides an agenda several days beforehand. Ideally, all members of the group should have an opportunity to suggest items for the agenda. The agenda should be briefly reviewed at the start of the meeting to give each member a chance to suggest additions, deletions, or other changes. In some meetings it may be appropriate for the group to discuss, and perhaps vote on, the suggested changes in the agenda.

Additional Guidelines for Leading a Group

This section briefly summarizes additional suggestions for effectively leading a group. Future chapters will expand on the following guidelines:

1. Understand that leadership is a shared responsibility. Every member will take on leadership roles at times. Designated leaders should not seek to dominate a group or believe they are responsible for directing the group in all of its task and maintenance functions. In fact, productivity and group cohesion are substantially increased when everyone contributes.
2. Use decision-making procedures best suited for the issues facing a particular group. (See Chapter 6 for a discussion of a variety of decision-making procedures and their consequences.)
3. Use a problem-solving approach to handle the issues and problems facing the group. (See Chapter 6 for a summary of how to use the problem-solving approach.)
4. Create a cooperative atmosphere rather than a competitive one. (See Chapter 4.)
5. View controversy and conflict as natural and desirable for resolving issues and arriving at good decisions. In resolving conflicts, seek to use a no-lose, problem-solving approach rather than a win-lose approach. (See Chapter 6.)
6. Generally, seek to confront members who are hostile or disruptive (Chapter 4).
7. Use appropriate self-disclosure (Chapter 5).
8. Seek to create an atmosphere of open and honest communication. (See Chapter 5 for ways to improve verbal communication and be an active listener, and for ways to improve nonverbal communication.)
9. Provide stimulating, relevant content and exercises that illustrate the concepts and help members try out suggested new behaviors. In an assertiveness group, for example, theoretical material on how to be more assertive should be followed by practice in being more assertive. (The chapters in this text use this format.)
10. Give attention to how to end a session. A few minutes before the session is scheduled to conclude, or when the group has exhausted the subject, a brief summary emphasizing the major points to be remembered leaves the group with a sense of achievement and signals the end of the session. Additional ways to end a session are described in Chapter 13.

Leaders are not born. They are made—through training, practice, and experience. By learning how to lead groups effectively individuals become more aware of themselves, grow as people, become more self-confident, feel good about themselves, develop highly marketable skills, learn to improve interpersonal relationships, and help themselves and others accomplish important tasks. Everyone reading this text has the potential to become an effective group leader. This chapter has sought to demystify leadership by describing what an effective leader does and is. It is now up to you to further develop your capacities in being a leader. You can do it!

■ STANDARDS FOR SOCIAL WORK PRACTICE WITH GROUPS

As the name suggests, the Association for the Advancement of Social Work with Groups, Inc. (AASWG) is an international professional organization that seeks to promote and advance social work practice with groups. Its offices are incorporated in New York. This organization has formulated the following standards for social work practice with groups. These standards begin with this preamble:[20]

> These standards reflect the distinguishing features of group work as well as the unique perspective that social workers bring to their practice with groups. Central to social work practice with groups is the concept of mutual aid. The group worker recognizes that the group, with its multiple helping relationships, is the primary source of change. The group worker's role is one primarily of helping members work together to achieve the goals that they have established for themselves.
>
> By design, these standards are general, rather than specific. They are applicable to the types of groups that social workers encounter in the full range of settings in which they practice. Further, the standards allow the individual practitioner to apply a variety of relevant group work models, within the more general mutual aid framework.
>
> Section I identifies essential knowledge and values that underlie social work practice with groups. In Sections II through V, worker tasks in the pre-group, beginning, middle, and ending phases of the group are identified, as is specific knowledge that may be needed by the worker in each phase.

I.   CORE KNOWLEDGE AND VALUES

A. Familial, social, political, cultural context of member identity, interactional style, and concern
   members are viewed as citizens
   members are capable of change and capable of helping one another
B. Attention to the whole person
   systems perspective used in assessment and intervention
   person and environment
   bio-psycho-social perspective
   member-in-group
   group-in-community
C. Competency-based assessment
   emphasis on member strengths as well as deficits
D. Mutual aid function
   group consists of multiple helping relationships
   worker's primary role is one of helping members to help one another
E. Groups characterized by democratic process
   members are helped to own the group
   equal worth of members and worker
   worker is not all powerful "expert"
   worker to group and worker to members
   relationships characterized by egalitarianism and reciprocity
F. Emphasis on empowerment
   group goals emphasize individual member growth and social change
   group worker promotes individual and group autonomy
G. Worker's assessment and interventions characterized by flexibility and eclecticism

H. Small group behavior
  group as an entity separate and distinct from individual members
  phases of group development foster change throughout the life of the group
  recognition of how group process shapes and influences individual member behavior
I. Groups formed for different purposes and goals
  group type (e.g., education, problem-solving, social action) influences what worker does
  and how group accomplishes its goals
J. Monitoring and evaluation of success of group in accomplishing its objectives through
  observation and measurement of outcomes and/or processes

II. GROUP WORK IN THE PRE-GROUP PHASE

Tasks:
A. Identify common needs of potential group members
B. Plan and conduct outreach, recruitment of members
C. Secure organizational support and sanction for group, if needed
D. Address organizational resistance to groups, if needed
E. Screen and prepare members for group, when appropriate
F. Secure permission for members' participation, when needed
G. Develop compositional balance, if appropriate
H. Select appropriate group type, structure, and size
I. Establish meeting place, time, and so on that promote member comfort and cohesion
J. Develop and articulate verbally and/or in writing a clear statement of group purpose that
  reflects member needs and, where appropriate, agency mission
K. Develop and articulate clear statement of worker role that reflects the group's purpose
L. Use preparatory empathy to tune into members' feelings and reactions to group's
  beginning

Knowledge Needed:
A. Organization's mission and function and how this influences nature of group work
  service
B. Social and institutional barriers which may impact on the development of group work
  service
C. Issues associated with group composition
D. Human life cycle and its relationship to potential members' needs
E. Cultural factors and their influence on potential members' lives and their ability to
  engage in group and relate to others
F. Types of groups and their relationship to member needs
G. Specific types of individual and social problems that lead to a need for group

III. GROUP WORK IN THE BEGINNING PHASE

Tasks:
A. Provide clear statement of group (and, if necessary, agency) purpose and worker role
B. Elicit member feedback regarding perception of needs, interests, and problems
C. Encourage members to share concerns and strengths with one another
D. Facilitate connections between members and members and worker
E. Encourage awareness and expression of commonalities among members
F. Monitor group for manifestations of authority theme and, when needed, respond
  directly
G. Assess impact of cultural differences between members and between members and
  worker and address directly when needed
H. Assist group in establishing rules and norms that promote change and growth
I. Use of self to develop cohesion among members and comfort with worker
J. Assist members in establishing individual and group goals
K. Clarify link between individual and group goals
L. Help members to establish a beginning contract which provides clarity and direction to
  their work together
M. Promote individual autonomy and empowerment of members
N. Create and maintain environment of sociocultural safety

Knowledge Needed:

A. Group dynamics in beginning stage of group
B. Causes/manifestations of resistance to change among members and in external environment

IV. GROUP WORK IN THE MIDDLE PHASE

Tasks:

A. Point out commonalities among members
B. Reinforce connection between individual needs/problems and group goals
C. Encourage and model supportive, honest feedback between members and between members and worker
D. Use here and now/process illumination to further group's work
E. Help members use role playing, behavioral rehearsal, and other verbal and non-verbal activities to accomplish individual and group goals
F. Monitor norms that govern group's work
G. Assess group's progress toward its goals
H. Re-contract with members, if needed, to assist them in achieving individual and group goals
I. Identify obstacles to work within and outside group's boundaries and deal with directly
J. Clarify and interpret communication patterns between members, between members and the worker, and between the group and others external to the group
K. Identify and highlight member conflict, when needed, and facilitate resolution
L. Summarize sessions

Knowledge Needed:

A. Group dynamics in the middle phase
B. Role theory and its application to members' relationships with one another and with worker
C. Communication theory and its application to verbal and non-verbal interactions within group and between group and others external to group
D. Member interactions as manifestations of sociocultural forces of race, class, gender, sexual orientation, etc.
E. Member interactions as manifestations of psychodynamic factors
F. Purposeful use of verbal and non-verbal activities

V. GROUP WORK IN THE ENDING PHASE

Tasks:

A. Identify and point out direct and indirect signs of members' reactions to ending
B. Share worker's ending feelings with members
C. Assist members in sharing their feelings about endings with one another
D. Help members identify gains they have made and changes that have resulted from their participation in the group
E. Assist members in applying new knowledge and skills to their daily lives
F. Encourage member feedback to worker
G. Help members honestly reflect on and evaluate their work together
H. Develop plans for continuation of service or referral of members, as needed
I. Assess individual member and group progress
J. Evaluate impact of group experience on individual members and external environment

Knowledge Needed:

A. Group dynamics in the ending phase
B. Formal and informal resources which maintain and enhance members' growth
C. Influence of past losses and separations in lives of members and worker on group's ending

■ GROUP EXERCISES

Exercise A: Desensitizing Fears of Leading a Group

GOAL: To identify the specific fears about being a designated leader for a group and to provide information to reduce those fears.

Step 1. The group leader should state the purpose of this exercise. Each student should then be handed a sheet of paper and instructed to complete, anonymously, the sentence "My specific fears about being a designated leader of a group are . . . ." The leader should emphasize that the completed statements will be collected and discussed.

Step 2. The responses should be collected in a way that ensures anonymity and then read aloud. After a concern is read, the students should suggest ways of reducing the concern. If a concern involves handling hostile members, for example, the class, with help from the instructor, may suggest strategies for coping with them. If a member fears that he or she does not have the traits needed to lead a group, it may be pointed out that research has found that no specific traits distinguish leaders from followers and that the distributed-functions theory of leadership asserts that practically anyone can be trained to be a leader.

Step 3. After Step 2 is completed, the group leader or the instructor may want to summarize key points on how to lead a group and explain that future sessions will explore these points in greater depth.

Exercise B: Task Functions and Group Maintenance Functions

GOAL: To show that at times nearly everyone takes a leadership role in groups that involves performing task and group maintenance functions.

Step 1. The group leader should indicate that this exercise will elicit the class's thoughts on what criteria should be used for admitting students into the social work program at this campus. The leader should then explain that the Council on Social Work Education (the national organization that accredits social work programs) requires every program to have criteria for admitting students. There is considerable variation in criteria among the programs in this country. Common criteria include a minimum grade-point average and a vaguely defined "aptitude for social work."

Step 2. The class then forms subgroups of five or six students and each selects an observer. The observers then form a group in another room or hallway. The subgroups should not begin discussing their primary task until the observers return.

Step 3. The observers are told that their task is to record *significant* task and group maintenance functions performed by each member of their subgroup. The leader may need to explain that task functions are statements designed to help the subgroup accomplish its task and that group maintenance functions are statements made to strengthen the social/emotional aspects of group life. Observers should be given a handout that summarizes the task roles and group maintenance roles developed by Johnson and Johnson, which appear in this chapter. The observers will be asked after the exercise is over to summarize to their subgroup how each member contributed through certain task and group maintenance functions.

Step 4. The leader and observers return to the subgroups. The subgroups are informed that their task is to develop criteria for admitting students to the social work program at this campus. The subgroup is free to suggest various criteria but should probably begin by discussing: (1) whether a grade-point average should be used for admission and what it should be, and (2) how "aptitude for social work" should be defined and measured.

Step 5. The subgroups should work for 20 to 30 minutes, and each should then state and explain its proposed criteria. Time should then be called and each subgroup should be asked to indicate to the class what criteria was arrived at.

Step 6. The group leader should indicate that one of the purposes of this exercise is to demonstrate that most members in a group assume leadership roles by carrying out task and group maintenance functions. The leader should then define task and group maintenance functions.

Step 7. Each observer summarizes to his or her subgroup, but *not* to the whole class, the significant task and group maintenance functions performed by each member.

Step 8. End the exercise by asking members if they have any thoughts or comments.

Exercise C: Power Bases

GOAL: To practice analyzing influence attempts in terms of power bases.

Step 1. The group leader explains the purpose of the exercise, describes the five bases of power developed by French and Raven, and briefly discusses the effects of using each base.

Step 2. The class divides into subgroups of three members each and answers the following questions:

1. What bases of power does the instructor of this course have?
2. What bases of power does a student in this class have?
3. What is the primary power base the instructor has?
4. What is the primary power base a student has?

Step 3. The subgroups share their answers to these questions by having one member from each subgroup write the answers on the blackboard. The class then discusses the reasons for the similarities and differences between the answers arrived at by the subgroups.

Step 4. In all likelihood the instructor will be seen as having much more power than the students. The group leader should summarize the effects of unequal power on communication and on relationships within a group (as described in this chapter). Students then discuss how they feel when an instructor attempts to present herself on a level equal or superior to students. Further, what are the positive and negative aspects of each relationship?

Exercise D: Types of Influence

GOAL: To increase awareness of feelings toward the following three types of influence: personal challenge, coercive power, and manipulation.

Step 1. The instructor explains the purpose of the exercise and asks students to visualize each of the following situations. The instructor should pause after each situation and allow students time to write their responses.

Narrative 1. Visualize an academic situation in which you worked hard on something because it presented a personal challenge and because you expected to grow as a person through meeting this challenge. Briefly describe this situation on a sheet of paper and summarize your feelings about the challenge motivating you to work hard.

Narrative 2. Visualize a work situation in which someone sought to use coercive power to make you do something. Briefly describe this situation on a sheet of paper and summarize your feelings about it.

Narrative 3. Visualize a situation in which someone sought to manipulate or con you into doing something. Briefly describe this situation on a sheet of paper and summarize your feelings when you discovered this.

Step 2. The students then form subgroups of three members each to share what they wrote and discuss how they felt about each situation. If any student does not wish to share these personal thoughts, that is acceptable.

Step 3. The students think of situations in which using coercive power and manipulation would be desirable and then discuss the situations.

CHAPTER FOUR

Group Dynamics: Goals and Norms

GOALS

Just as a baseball team has a short-term goal of winning a game and a long-term goal of clinching a pennant, individuals and groups must identify short-term and long-term goals to function effectively. This chapter provides guidelines on setting goals, defines hidden agendas, describes the differences between competitive and cooperative groups, and presents an overview of the nominal group approach. All groups have norms, and this chapter describes their importance, examines how they are formed, and discusses group pressures to conform. Various types of hostile or disruptive group members are identified, and methods are suggested for handling their uncooperative behavior.

A goal is an end toward which an individual or group of people is working. It is an ideal or a desired achievement that people value. A personal goal is a goal held by a member of a group. A group goal is a goal held by enough members of a group that the group can be said to be working toward achieving it.

All groups have goals, and every individual who joins a group has personal goals. Groups generally have both short-range and long-range goals. The short-range goals should be stepping-stones to the long-range goals. Group goals are important for several reasons. The effectiveness and efficiency of the group and its procedures can be measured by the extent to which goals are achieved. Goals guide groups and their members by giving the group's programs and efforts direction. Conflicts between group members are often resolved according to which position is most helpful in achieving group goals. Group goals are also a strong motivating force that stimulates members to work together. Once members make a commitment to achieve a certain goal, they will feel an obligation to put forth their abilities, efforts, and resources to achieve it.

A member's commitment to a group goal will depend on (1) how attracted this member is to the group, (2) how attractive the goal appears, (3) how likely it appears the group can accomplish the goal, (4) the ability to measure progress toward achieving the goal and the ability to measure when the goal is attained, (5) the rewards the group and the member will receive when the goal is attained, (6) the challenge presented by the goal, as a moderate risk of failure is usually more challenging than a high or low risk of failure,[1] and (7) the types of interactions the member will have with other group members in working toward the goal (some ways of interacting are more enjoyable and rewarding than others).

Setting group goals is the first step in measuring the effectiveness of a group. Once goals are set, the tasks necessary to accomplish the goals must be determined. Next, responsibilities for carrying out the tasks must be agreed upon or assigned, and deadlines for completing those tasks set. As the process proceeds, the extent to which deadlines have been met and tasks achieved must be evaluated. The final measurement is whether the group has achieved its goals. An effective group is one that has considerable success in achieving its goals. (The processes of setting group goals, determining the tasks for accomplishing the goals, assigning tasks to each member, and setting deadlines for accomplishing the tasks are, in reality, also the components of forming contracts with group members about expectations. Contracts and group goals should be reviewed periodically as the group progresses and revised if necessary.)

Group members will be more motivated to achieve group goals if they are involved in setting those goals. Through involvement, members will be (1) more likely to have their personal goals become a component of the group goals, (2) more aware of the importance of choosing these goals, and (3) more committed to providing their resources to achieve the goals.

■ PERSONAL GOALS

The personal goals of members may be *very* diverse. In a stress management group, for example, some members may join because they want to learn how to relax, others because they are lonely and want companionship, and still others because their spouses urged them. Some may join because they have heard good things about the group leader and want to "check it out." A few may join because they do not believe stress is destructive and want to convince others of this belief.

While some members are acutely aware of their personal goals, others may not be. For example, freshman social work majors sometimes attend a meeting of the Student Social Work Club at the urging of a faculty member without having given much thought to their personal goals and objectives.

The more similarity there is between the personal goals of members and the goals of the group, the more attracted to the group the members are likely to be, and the more willing to provide their resources and energies to the group. If the personal goals of the group are homogeneous (alike), members are more apt to agree on group goals, to work together toward achieving those goals, and to be happier with the group. Heterogeneous personal goals do not necessarily spell failure for a group, but they do require special attention.

Exercise 4.1: Identifying Your Personal Goals

GOAL: We need to identify our personal goals in every group we participate in so that we then can select the kinds of group activities that will allow us to achieve our personal goals and thereby result in the group being personally useful to us. This exercise is designed to assist you in setting personal goals.

Specify the personal goals that you have in this class. Your personal goals should include a summary of the knowledge, skills, and values you want to acquire and perhaps also the grade you hope to attain.

Hidden Agendas

When members have heterogeneous personal goals, hidden agendas are more likely to develop. (If members have homogeneous personal goals, these goals are apt to become group goals, and hidden agendas are less likely to arise.) A *hidden agenda* is a personal goal held by a member but unknown to other group members, which interferes with the group's efforts. At times, hidden agendas can be very destructive. For example, I have participated in groups where an individual observed the comments and actions of others to obtain evidence to bring legal harassment charges. Usually, however, hidden agendas are less destructive than this and may consist of little more than a lonely person's wish to monopolize the group's "air time" with insignificant small talk. Because this type of behavior can slow progress severely, group goals should incorporate, to some extent, the personal goals of its members. Leaders can also minimize the effects of hidden agendas by making the group's goals clear at the outset.

Certain signals suggest hidden agendas. A member may fail to contribute or may say and do things that impede group activities. When hidden agendas appear to exist, the consequences of confronting a member about disruptive behavior must be evaluated. If the consequences appear beneficial, then the member should be confronted, either openly or privately. Whatever method of confrontation appears to be most beneficial should be used. Sometimes, however, hidden agendas are best left undisturbed. For example, a group member who has recently experienced the death of a spouse may use a nontherapy group to ventilate pain. In this situation, it may or may not be constructive to confront the person.

When confronting a member about a hidden agenda, avoid blaming or criticizing. The confrontation should lead to a trusting, open discussion of the issue. If the hidden agenda is rational and legitimate, extensive efforts should be made to help the member. Alternatives for resolving the concern could be explored and one or more implemented to resolve the problem. (Later in this chapter additional suggestions are given on how to confront someone.) Perhaps the goals of the group can even be revised to incorporate the more personal issue, or perhaps the member can be helped to achieve the personal goal outside the group. A group member grieving over the death of a spouse, for example, may be referred to a counselor or to a survivors' group where the grief can be expressed and worked out more effectively.

Exercise 4.2: Hidden Agendas and Their Effects

GOAL: This exercise is designed to help you understand hidden agendas, their effects, and how you can more effectively respond to someone who has a hidden agenda in a group.

1. **Describe a group that you participated in where one of the other members had a hidden agenda that was eventually revealed. What was the hidden agenda? How did this hidden agenda adversely impact the group?**

2. **How effective were the other group members in handling this hidden agenda?**

3. **As you reflect on how the other group members handled this hidden agenda, is there a course of action that could have been taken that would have dealt with this hidden agenda more effectively? If "yes," describe this course of action.**

4. Describe a hidden agenda that you had when participating in a group. How did your hidden agenda impact the group?

ESTABLISHING GROUP GOALS

Although group goals can be developed in a variety of ways, the procedures in the following sections are recommended because they involve group members in the decision-making process. After the leader shares his or her views on the goals of the group, members are asked to explain their own reasons for joining—that is, their personal goals. Working together, the leader and group members discuss the merits of the goals presented and discuss additional goals, refining and rewording them until a final list is developed. Decision-making procedures as outlined in Chapter 6 may be used to resolve conflicts and attain agreement. The final list should be typed and distributed to each member for reference.

Alternatively, the group leader may interview each member before the first meeting about personal and group goals, and then develop a composite list to present at the first meeting of the group. This list is then discussed and amended until a majority of members are satisfied. A less effective way to determine group goals is for the leader to attempt to "sell" the group a set of goals he believes is preferable. If group goals are prescribed in this manner or by the constitution of the group, they should still be fully discussed by members, who may refine and reword them.

Effective groups usually follow a variation of the following format. Long-range goals are set first, and efforts are made to state these goals in operational and measurable terms. Short-range goals are then established and prioritized as to their importance in achieving the long-range goals. Tasks are also identified to achieve short-range goals and then ranked according to their importance. For high-priority tasks, specific responsibilities are assigned to group members, and deadlines are set for completion. Future evaluations then identify the progress being made in achieving the tasks and goals.

Operational and Measurable Goals

An *operational goal* is one that can be directly translated into courses of action to achieve the goal. A goal such as "Each member of this class will be able to describe the difference between personal and group goals" is operational. Students could put this goal into action by studying the first part of this chapter and then taking a test that asks them to define both terms. The test scores measure whether the class reached the goal.

A *nonoperational goal* is one that cannot be achieved through specific actions. "Everyone in this class will learn how to cure all emotional and behavioral problems," for example, is nonoperational because treatment approaches have not been developed to treat successfully all people who have emotional and behavioral problems. A goal that is nonoperational is *much* harder to achieve. For instance, it may be centuries before we know whether it is possible to treat all emotional and behavioral problems successfully.

In practice, groups should strive to develop operational goals so that a course of action can be developed and the goal more readily achieved. "Helping students to better manage stress in their lives through instructing them in meditation," for example, is much more operational than "Seeking ways to help students better manage stress."

Group goals should also be measurable. For example, the goal "Having everyone in this class become a great group leader" is very difficult to measure *without* criteria to use in judging what constitutes a great leader. In contrast, the following goal is more measurable: "By the end of this semester, every student in this class will have demonstrated that she or he can lead a group at a level that the instructor deems *satisfactory*." One way to make this goal operational is by having the students take turns being a group leader. For each session the instructor then rates the student who leads the group as doing a "satisfactory" or "less than satisfactory" job. Students who receive a "less than satisfactory" rating can be given additional opportunities to lead the class and have their performance rated again. Progress toward this goal is simply measured by counting the number of students who receive an overall "satisfactory" rating.

Operational, measurable goals are valuable for a variety of reasons. They help guide the members and the group in planning and working on tasks. A group that is unclear as to what its goals are will be even more confused as to what specific tasks are needed to reach those goals. Operational and measurable goals also measure the effectiveness of the leader because the leader's actions can be judged in terms of movement toward group goals. Clear goals, in fact, often make leadership easier because the group knows what it is trying to achieve and is less likely to question a leader's actions that move the group toward its goals.

In addition, operational and measurable goals make it easier to communicate the purpose of the group to other groups and to nonmembers. Such goals also help evaluate progress. Each course of action can be assessed to determine its payoffs in attaining goals. The group can easily determine whether a course of action should be continued or abandoned. Clear goals and documented progress toward those goals are especially valuable when accountability is required by funding sources or others. A final advantage is that conflicts between members can often be resolved by determining which position appears to best help the group reach its goals. When conflicts arise in groups that do not have measurable and operational goals, there is no logical way to determine whose view has higher payoffs. As a result, the conflict is not apt to be resolved and may force the group to spend more time maintaining harmony than completing its work.

Forming clear goals that are operational and measurable is a lengthy, time-consuming process. The goal-setting stage is often when a group flounders the most. It occurs early in the life of a group, when members are also testing their interest and commitment and when interpersonal relationships are being formed. Arriving at goals the members can support often takes much longer than anticipated. The value of setting clear goals, however, far outweighs the time and effort saved by accepting goals that are vague and that may later be seriously challenged. Johnson and Johnson note, "The more time a group spends establishing agreement on clear goals, the less time it needs in achieving them—and the more likely it will be that the members will work effectively for the common outcome."[2]

Research has found that groups have a better chance to be effective when the following are met:

1. The goals are clear, operationally defined, and measurable.
2. The members see the goals as being relevant, attainable, meaningful, and acceptable.
3. Both personal and group goals can be attained by the same activities and tasks.
4. The goals are viewed as challenging and have a moderate risk of failure.
5. The resources needed to accomplish the tasks are available.
6. There is high coordination among group members.
7. The group members maintain a cooperative rather than a competitive atmosphere.[3]

Exercise 4.3: Group Goals and Personal Goals in This Class

GOAL: This exercise is designed to assist you in understanding the dynamics between group goals and personal goals.

1. Specify the group goals that the instructor wants for this class. (Usually, the "Course Objectives" section of the syllabus will specify the group goals desired by the instructor.) In his or her lectures, the instructor may have identified additional desired group goals.

2. Have all the students in the class "accepted" the desired group goals of the class? If "no," describe why you believe some students have not accepted the instructor's group goals.

3. Did the instructor ask the students for additional group goals that they desired for the class. If "yes," did the students suggest additional group goals? If "yes" to this question, what were the additional group goals that were suggested—and were they adopted for this class?

4. Do you believe some members of the class have personal goals or hidden agendas that are inconsistent with the group goals? (These personal goals or hidden agendas may include "not wanting to study very much" or "wanting help in resolving a personal dilemma.") If "yes," specify these inconsistent personal goals or hidden agendas.

5. Earlier in Exercise 4.1 you identified your personal goals for this class. Are your personal goals consistent with the group goals? If some are inconsistent, please specify these inconsistent personal goals.

Competition versus Cooperation

Groups tend to have either a cooperative or a competitive atmosphere. A cooperative group is marked by open and honest communication, trust, pooling of resources, and cohesion. Research into problem-solving groups has found a number of positive consequences of a cooperative group atmosphere. Cooperation among members increases creativity, coordination of effort, division of labor, emotional involvement in group accomplishment, helping and sharing, interpersonal skills, cooperative attitudes and values, positive self-attitudes, congeniality among group members, positive attitudes toward the group and tasks, divergent thinking, acceptance of individual and cultural differences, and problem-solving skills.[4]

A cooperative group atmosphere results when the personal goals of group members are perceived to be compatible, identical, or complementary. An example of a highly cooperative group is a football team where the main goal of each member is to win, and the main goal of the team is to win. In a cooperative group, each member seeks to coordinate his or her efforts with those of other group members to achieve the goals of the group. In establishing a cooperative atmosphere, rewards to members must be based on the quantity and quality of group performance, rather than on individual performance.

In contrast, a competitive atmosphere is usually destructive. Competition exists when the members perceive their personal goals to be incompatible, different, conflicting, or mutually exclusive. In a highly competitive group, a member can achieve a goal only if the other group members fail to obtain their goals.[5] A group interview of several applicants for a job vacancy such as an audition for a play, for example, is intentionally competitive. Each member seeks to accomplish personal goals while seeking to block other group members from accomplishing theirs. The negative consequences of competition in problem-solving groups are numerous. Competition decreases creativity, coordination of effort, division of labor, helping and sharing, and cohesion. Competition promotes ineffective communication, suspicion and mistrust, high anxiety about goal accomplishment, competitive values and attitudes, negative self-attitudes, animosity between group members, and negative attitudes toward the group and its tasks. Competition also encourages the rejection of differences of opinion, divergent thinking, and cultural and individual differences. A competitive atmosphere leads to low effectiveness in solving complex problems.[6]

Are there any situations in which competition is beneficial? There are a few. For example, in team sports coaches have discovered it is beneficial to have highly talented athletes compete for starting positions. Such competition generally encourages athletes to work harder. But even in team sports, successful coaches know that a key to winning is instilling a sense of team effort (that is, cooperative atmosphere), so that each player focuses not on individual recognition but on helping the team win by playing the role he or she has been assigned.

Kelly and Stahelski examined the question of what happens when a competitive person joins a group that has a cooperative atmosphere.[7] Since cooperative groups are much more effective in solving problems than competitive groups, the question is significant. Three consequences were found to occur. The competitive behavior of the new member leads the other members to behave competitively. The competitive person views the former cooperative members as having always been competitive. The former cooperative members are generally aware that their competitive behavior is largely a consequence of the new member's competitiveness. Thus, it appears that one competitive person can change a cooperative group into a competitive group.

The positive characteristics of a cooperative group are readily destroyed by a competitive person. All of the following decrease when a competitive person joins a formerly cooperative group: trust, congeniality among members, openness of communication, and problem-solving orientation.[8] Why does a competitive person have such a strong, destructive effect? Apparently, the cooperative members realize the competitive person will, if given a chance, take advantage of their cooperativeness and use it to his or her personal advantage. In many situations their only recourse to prevent exploitation is to become competitive. Thus, even though cooperation is by far the most effective atmosphere in problem-solving groups, it takes only one competitive person to change the atmosphere to a destructive, competitive one. If a cooperative group is to survive, the members must work together to reduce feelings of competitiveness among the members.

Exercise 4.4: The Effects of a Competitive Group Member

GOAL: This exercise is designed to help you understand the effects of a competitive group member and to then reflect upon what a group might constructively do to minimize the adverse effects of a competitive member.

1. **Describe the behavior of a competitive person in a group in which you participated. Did the competitive behavior adversely impact the group? If "yes," please specify the adverse effects.**

2. **When a competitive person adversely impacts a group, what constructive course of action might the other group members take in order to minimize the adverse effects?**

■ THE NOMINAL GROUP APPROACH

The nominal group approach, developed by Delbecq and Van de Ven, can be used as an aid in formulating group goals.[9] This approach is a problem-identification technique for designing or modifying programs and involves meeting with potential users to assess their needs. A nominal group is "a group in which individuals work in the presence of others but do not verbally interact."[10] By simply allowing group members to list their needs on paper *without group discussion,* each member's personal views can be ascertained. Too often in the past, new programs have been developed by "experts" who lacked a clear picture of the needs of their consumers, with the result being the creation of programs which ineffectively serve consumers. So, the prime objective of the nominal group approach is to identify the needs of the consumer group (that is, the potential users of a new service) in order to develop a program that effectively serves them.[11]

A nominal group meeting can be conducted within a half-hour or an hour; it has often been used by university faculty to identify topics students wish to have covered in classes. For example, the nominal group approach was used by the social work department at the author's university in connection with an elective workshop in grief management.[12] Enrollment was limited to 30 students. At the first class meeting, the students were asked, using a nominal group approach, "What specific topics do you want covered in this course?" The specific steps in conducting a nominal group are described in Exercise C at the end of this chapter. (The responses given in the grief management class appear in Table 4.1.)

When a nominal group is used with a subgroup of a consumer group, care should be taken to obtain a representative cross section of the consumer group. Before using the nominal group approach, the subgroup should be informed of the purpose of the study. However, the researchers should generally *not* provide any information on what they think should be the results of using the nominal group approach so as not to bias the participants.

■ TABLE 4.1 Highest Ranking Topics for Grief Management Course

Topics	Number of Votes
1. Suicide	13
2. Getting over the loss and loneliness that result from the death of someone else	9
3. The terminally ill and how to relate to them	9
4. Funeral director—guest speaker	9
5. AIDS	8
6. Getting over the loss of a close relationship	8
7. Coping skills for myself and others	8
8. Hospice movement—guest speaker	8
9. How to come to terms with your own death	7
10. Should one be permitted to take one's own life?	7
11. How to change fears and negative attitudes about death	6
12. Communication with survivors (that is, people who have had someone close to them die)	6
13. Sudden Infant Death Syndrome	6
14. Life after death	5
15. How to help others (parents) deal with the death of someone close (children)	4

Research on the merits of the nominal group approach suggests that it is superior to brainstorming and to other types of group interaction for generating information relevant to a problem situation. It elicits more suggestions and covers more areas of interest.[13] (Brainstorming has the shortcoming that the items first suggested tend to set the direction for future items that are generated.) The nominal group is designed to receive input from all group members rather than just the more vocal or aggressive ones, as often happens in conventional group discussions. Evaluation of items is avoided, which substantially reduces the pressure against expressing minority opinions or unconventional ideas. Conflicting, incompatible ideas are tolerated. Furthermore, the approach appears to save time, as it can be conducted faster than interacting group processes.[14] The nominal group approach has a gamelike quality, as the group generates creative tension, which appears to stimulate individuals to do their best in suggesting items.

■ GROUP NORMS

Group norms are rules that specify proper group behavior. To be a norm, a rule must be accepted by a majority of the group. If a person recognizes a norm and believes the benefits of conforming outweigh the consequences of deviating, the norm can influence that person's behavior. At first, members may conform because of pressures from the group. As time passes, though, members generally internalize norms and conform automatically. Norms provide one of the most important mechanisms of social control over members of groups and over society as a whole.

Every group has norms. If you frequently socialize with a certain group of students, for example, your group will gradually set norms as to what is acceptable and unacceptable behavior at gatherings. Your classes will have certain norms as well, covering smoking, chewing bubble gum, arriving late, absences, meeting deadlines, raising a hand before speaking, and cheating on exams.

Some norms are set formally—bylaws and constitutions of organizations, for instance, specify responsibilities for the officers. Other norms are set informally. During a department meeting the department chair may frown at a faculty member who is reading her mail. If that faculty member responds to the nonverbal communication and puts aside her mail, other faculty members may observe the nonverbal interaction and decide never to read their mail during meetings. Through this process a norm against reading mail has informally been established.

Norms have an "ought to" or "must" quality, and they vary in importance. There are strong pressures to obey and, in some cases, severe penalties for violating *important* norms—confidentiality in therapy groups, for example. If a member violates confidentiality by revealing personal information about another member to others outside the group, he may be penalized by expulsion from the group. Failure to obey less important norms, such as not belching at meetings, generates only mild disapproval and little or no penalty.

Members are often only subconsciously aware of many of the norms that are guiding their behavior. If one were to ask a group member to define her group's norms, she would probably be able to list only a few because many norms are taken for granted. Norms relating to dress, promptness, or foul language are often given little thought by group members.

When a person enters a new group, he generally feels strange and uncomfortable because he is unaware of the norms. So he searches for clues to norms, asking himself such questions as these: What is appropriate to disclose, and what is not? Who is in the "in" group, and who is left out? Is smoking permissible? Can I tell a joke? Do members raise their hands before speaking? What role does each member play? Is the group competitive or cooperative? Are there hidden agendas? Are there coalitions? Which members are more powerful?

■ HOW NORMS ARE LEARNED AND DEVELOPED

Some group norms are fairly universal, so new members who have worked in groups before will be aware of many norms that are likely to be operating. For example, an individual who joins a therapy group will expect other members to be honest, open, and self-disclosing. Many groups have norms such as reciprocity (if someone does something kind or helpful for you, you should do something kind or helpful in return), fair play (don't lie or cheat to get what you want), social responsibility (you should help those who need it), and shared air time (everyone should have a chance to talk and no one should monopolize the conversation).

New members learn norms by talking privately with a group member they trust. They may ask questions like this: Who has the power? Is it acceptable to say or do such and such? Are there coalitions in the group? Do some members have hidden agendas? Are there personal matters that some members are sensitive about? Someone who is overweight, for example, may express discomfort with comments on dieting, and other members may individually decide not to mention dieting when the overweight person is present.

Although norms are learned in a variety of ways, the most common way is through positive and negative reinforcement. Through a process of trial and error, members identify which of their behaviors are accepted and rewarded by the group and which are judged inappropriate or destructive. Another way members identify norms is through "modeling," which involves learning through observing another member's behavior.

Some norms are in the bylaws, constitution, minutes, and/or other documents of a group or organization. For example, there may be guidelines for placing an item on the agenda, the duties and responsibilities of the officers, and the decision-making procedures for resolving crucial issues. Furthermore, norms can take the form of role expectations that can be official or unofficial. Officially, the chair of a group is expected to call and run meetings; the secretary keeps minutes. Unofficially, a wealthy member is expected to make donations when the group needs funds. Likewise, a member who is skilled at reducing tension is expected to ease the tension level when it gets too high.

Some norms develop less formally through nonverbal communications. For example, the leader of a therapy group may shake her head in disapproval of one member mimicking another. The other members note the gesture and then individually (without discussion) decide not to mimic anyone in the group in the future.

Some norms become known only after they are violated. Napier and Gershenfeld give an example:

A minister may preach about justice and racial equality and may urge his congregation to live according to these principles, all of which they accept from him. However, when he marches in a picket line, the congregation may rebuke him for transcending his position. He may be sanctioned with a statement to the effect that ministers may preach about justice and equality, but action on social issues is for others. In this situation, neither the minister nor the congregation knew the norm existed until an action took place that was contrary to the norm; the congregation then made known the violation by the threat of sanctions.[15]

New norms may develop from suggestions on group policy or procedures made by group members. For example, a member may suggest, "In order for an item to be placed on the agenda, the members must be informed of it at least 48 hours prior to the meeting to give them an opportunity to think about it." If the group approves of the suggestion, it becomes a policy and a norm.

Exercise 4.5: Group Norms in This Class

GOAL: This exercise is designed to assist you in identifying group norms and understanding the processes that led to their development.

1. **Specify the group norms that exist for proper behavior in this class.**

2. **Identify the processes that occurred that led to these group norms. (For example, the department may have standards for acceptable behavior in a class. The NASW Code of Ethics has statements on confidentiality, honesty, and opposition to making racist and sexist remarks. The Educational Policy and Accreditation Standards of the Council on Social Work Education has statements on diversity, populations at risk, and promoting social and economic justice. The instructor may have made statements about proper behavior in this class. Some students may have made statements about what they view as offensive remarks and behaviors.)**

■ CONFORMITY

Conformity means yielding to group pressure. To conform, a group member must experience conflict between the influences exerted by the group (group norms) and his or her personal values. A member experiencing this type of conflict has two options—announce an independent position or conform by agreeing with the group's position in either an expedient or a true manner. The *expedient conformer* can outwardly agree but inwardly disagree, while a *true conformer* agrees both outwardly and inwardly.

There have been a number of classic studies of conforming behavior. Sherif examined what has been called the "autokinetic effect" of conformity.[16] In his experiment subjects in a darkened room were asked to judge how far a dot of light moved. Although the light *appeared* to move, it actually did not (the autokinetic effect). Each subject saw the dot of light and made a series of individual judgments as to how far it moved. The subjects were then brought together in groups of three to judge how far the light moved. Their judgments tended to converge into a group standard. Later, when they again viewed the light by themselves, they tended to retain the group standard as their answer. The essential finding was that when a situation is ambiguous and there is no objective way of determining the "right" answer, members rely on the group to help define reality. In real life this finding means that membership in a group determines much of what individuals will see, learn, think about, and do.

Asch also examined conforming behavior and investigated what happens when an individual's judgment conflicts with that of other group members.[17] The experiments involved two sets of cards, as shown in Figure 4.1.

Subjects from psychology classes who volunteered for the experiment were arranged in groups of seven to nine. They were seated at a table and asked to state in turn which line was closest in size to the standard. In the control groups, practically all subjects chose Line 2. The responses in the experimental groups, however, were of greater interest. In the experimental groups all of the group members except for *one subject* were accomplices of the experimenter. The *subject* was always seated so that he would give his opinion last. All of the accomplices chose the same wrong line. When it came to the subject's turn, he was faced with relying on his own judgment or conforming to the group's judgment, even though he probably perceived it as wrong. In a variety of similar studies, Asch found that more than one-third of the subjects conformed to the group judgment. Such a high level of conformity is amazing considering there was no overt group pressure to conform, the situation was not ambiguous, and the subjects did not know each other.

According to Schachter, everyone has a need to evaluate the "rightness" of feelings, opinions, values, and attitudes as well as the extent of abilities. He conducted studies to demonstrate that in the absence of objective, nonsocial means of evaluation, a person

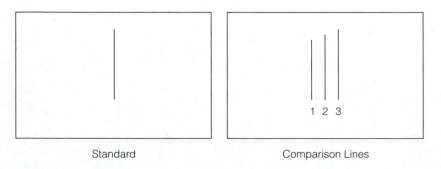

Standard   Comparison Lines

Figure 4.1
Cards in Asch comformity studies

will rely on other people as comparative points of reference. He called this the theory of social comparison. A study by Schachter and Singer provides support for this theory.[18] Subjects were aroused by an injection of adrenaline and then exposed to the actions of a peer. In some cases, the peer (actually the experimenter's confederate) behaved in a highly euphoric manner, while for other subjects he acted as if he were angry. The experimenters predicted that those subjects who did not have an appropriate explanation for the physiological sensations aroused by the drug (because they had been uninformed or misinformed about the drug and its effects) would imitate the inappropriate behavior of the confederate and interpret their feelings in a manner consistent with the confederate's behavior. The predictions were confirmed. Furthermore, the control subjects, who were either informed of the effects of adrenaline or did not receive the injection, displayed few imitative responses of the confederate. To a large extent, then, the peer defined social reality for the experimental subjects (that is, those subjects injected with adrenaline who did not receive an explanation of the physiological sensations aroused by the drug).

A number of conclusions have been drawn from conformity research and are summarized as follows:[19]

1. Group pressure influences behavior, even when the bogus group consensus is obviously wrong. In one study, for example, 50 military officers were asked to indicate which of two figures shown side by side, a star and a circle, was larger in area. The circle was clearly about one-third larger, but under group pressure 46 percent of the officers agreed with the bogus group consensus that the star was larger.

2. Many people can be pressured into yielding on attitudes and opinions even on personally significant matters. For example, the same 50 military officers were asked, first privately and then later under group consensus conditions, to consider the statement: "I doubt whether I would make a good leader." In private none of the officers expressed agreement, but under unanimous group pressure, 37 percent expressed agreement.

3. Although yielding occurs more often on difficult, subjective items than on easy, objective ones, there are extremely large individual differences. A few people yield on almost all items, a few on none. Most yield on some and not on others.

4. When people are retested privately on the same items some time later, a major part of the yielding effect disappears because the person tends to rely on personal judgment. Yet, a small part of the yielding effect remains, indicating group pressure can change attitudes.

5. As a group increases in size, the pressure to yield increases and more yielding occurs. When a person is opposed by only one other person, there is very little yielding. Yielding is markedly reduced when a person has the *support* of one other person (a partner) in the group.

Apparently a dissident opinion has a tremendous effect in strengthening the independence of like-minded people.

In a dramatic study involving conformity Milgram demonstrated that subjects in an experimental situation would administer electric shocks of dangerous strength to another person when instructed to do so by the experimenter.[20] (The other person, unknown to the subject, did not actually receive the electrical shocks.) Even when they were instructed to give increasingly strong shocks and the victim protested in anguish, most subjects followed the experimenter's orders. This series of studies on obedience demonstrated that people will yield to "authoritative" commands even when the behavior is incompatible with their own normal moral standards of conduct. Milgram suggested that his studies help us understand why the German people complied with the unethical commands of Hitler. Group pressures, especially when viewed as authoritative, have a tremendous effect on a person's actions, attitudes, and beliefs.

Exercise 4.6: Your Yielding to Group Pressure

GOAL: This exercise is designed to help you understand that all of us have yielded (at one time or another) to group pressure. The exercise also helps you understand your feelings about yielding.

1. **Describe a group that you participated in, in which you yielded to group pressure. Specify the issue or action that you yielded to. (If you have difficulty in identifying a time when you yielded, feel free to identify an issue in which you yielded to pressure from your parents.)**

2. **Specify your thoughts and feelings during the time when you yielded. Also specify your thoughts and feelings after you yielded.**

3. **If you had to do it over, would you still yield? Why or why not?**

Idiosyncrasy Credits

Every member of a group gains credits (and increased status) by exhibiting competence and conforming to the expectations applicable at a given time. Eventually, these credits allow a person to break the norms and rules of the group without being chastised. To some extent, after credits have been accumulated, nonconformity to general procedures or expectations serves as a confirming feature of one's status and further enhances one's position. Yet there is a limit to the number of idiosyncrasy credits awarded. Nonconformity beyond this limit will result in a dramatic decrease in status and perhaps even in rejection by the other group members.[21] For example, a star basketball player at a college may eventually be kicked off the team if he or she continues to be arrested for criminal activity.

Exercise 4.7: Understanding Idiosyncrasy Credits

GOAL: This exercise is designed to show you the effects of idiosyncrasy credits.

1. Describe someone's behavior that violated the norms of a group to which you belong or belonged. (Perhaps it was during a time when you went out for a night on the town with a group of friends.)

2. Was this norm violating behavior tolerated by the other group members, or did the group reject this person? If the behavior was tolerated or excused by the other group members, was it because this person had idiosyncrasy credits? If "yes," what were the bases of these credits (such as "he or she does many positive things for the group")?

■ DO'S AND DON'TS OF NORMS

Norms should be established that will improve the group's capacity to function effectively, such as starting meetings on time or cooperating rather than competing. Because norms exist only to allow the group to function effectively, nonfunctional norms should be identified and then either discarded or replaced with more appropriate standards. In some settings, it is desirable to write down crucial norms. In group homes for delinquent youths, for example, all the rules about smoking, drinking, curfew hours, attending school, and domestic duties should be posted so that the residents are fully aware of them. The consequences of violating these norms should also be clearly written out.

Important norms should be enforced immediately after a violation and as consistently as possible. If norms are not enforced, they will lose their effectiveness, and a new norm (that it is OK to break such a rule) may begin to emerge. In most social service settings, social workers *must* follow through on consequences when clients violate important norms. Social workers lose their credibility with clients when consequences do not follow violations. Most centers serving runaways, for example, clearly spell out that residents cannot use alcohol or drugs while at the center. Residents who do are asked to leave. In one center, workers failed to expel a resident caught using alcohol, and the next day most of the residents were drinking beer.

Group leaders should personally attempt to model the norms they believe are important. At a group home, for example, residents will not keep their rooms clean if the group leader's office is a mess.

■ PROBLEMS OF CONFORMITY

Hostile or disruptive members who fail to conform to group norms may be present in any group, even in those where membership is voluntary. However, they are more likely to be found in involuntary groups. Involuntary members often (at least at initial group meetings) wish they were a thousand other places than at the meeting. They may be angry and believe the time spent in the group will be completely wasted.

An involuntary client is one who is compelled to be a recipient of a social worker's (or another professional person's) services. For example, an individual may be required to be a recipient by a court order, by incarceration, or by family or employer pressure.

The following are a variety of settings in which social workers encounter involuntary clients: correctional institutions, protective services, mental-health facilities, certain public schools, group homes, residential treatment facilities, nursing homes, and hospitals. In each of these settings, social workers may be expected to lead groups of unwilling clients.

Types of Disruptive Behavior

Unwilling group members can display counterproductive behavior. To more vividly describe some of these disruptive behaviors, we will look at the behaviors as if they were characters or personalities.

The Bear

This person openly expresses anger, rage, frustration, resentment, and hostility. The bear may be unhappy as a member of the group or with what is happening in the group. Discontent can be expressed in a variety of ways: verbally, by attacking other members of the group; nonverbally, by facial expressions; or physically, by aggressively pushing and shoving another member.

The bear who directly expresses unhappiness in an active fashion can also express unhappiness in passive-aggressive ways through indirect aggression. Bach and Wyden have called indirect aggression "crazy-making."[22] Indirect aggressors maintain a front of kindness but find subtle, indirect ways of expressing their anger, rage, or frustrations. Bach and Wyden label direct aggression "clean fighting" because feelings are expressed openly and can be identified and resolved. "Dirty fighters" use indirect tricks and never clearly express their feelings, which often causes a great deal of pain and can destroy effective communication in a group. Most disruptive behaviors involve an element of indirect aggression.

If you have a relationship with a "dirty fighter," he or she will identify what will "press your buttons" (that is, "get your goat"). When the "dirty fighter" is angry or frustrated with you, he or she will casually and subtly "press these buttons" to get you going.

The Eager Beaver

This person volunteers to do crucial tasks but has little intention of completing them and is simply seducing other members into believing he or she is a willing contributor. The eager beaver may partially perform some of the tasks to show good faith but then employ a variety of excuses to explain why the tasks cannot be completed on time.

The Clown

This disrupter is rarely serious. He or she is always joking and clowning around, even when the other members want to be serious. A clown inhibits other members from expressing their thoughts and feelings because they fear they may be ridiculed.

The Conformity Power of Groups

The power of groups over individuals is great, as shown by the following examples.

On February 4, 1974, Patty Hearst, a college student and daughter of a wealthy publishing magnate, was kidnapped by the Symbionese Liberation Army, an ultraradical group. She was forcibly dragged from her home in Berkeley, California, taken to a house by her abductors, and placed in a closet. For several days, she remained in this closet with no lights. She was blindfolded, her hands were bound, and she was given food but was unable to dispose of her body wastes. Besides making constant threats against her life, her captors told her that her family had abandoned her by not complying with the kidnap demands. She was informed that her parents said it was all right with them if she was put to death. At times, Patty was also sexually assaulted by her captors. After a number of weeks passed, she was released from the closet. A few days later she was taken to a bank where (according to Ms. Hearst) her captors forced her to participate in a bank robbery. She was given a gun to use during the robbery, and one of her captors (armed with a gun) kept an eye on her. After this robbery, she was taken back to her place of captivity and informed that she was now guilty of bank robbery and murder, and that the FBI would shoot her on sight. For the next several months, Ms. Hearst conformed because of this pressure and joined her captors in committing additional crimes and in trying to avoid apprehension by the police. After her apprehension 19 months later, she claimed that she had committed bank robbery and other crimes because she was brainwashed by her captors. She was given a light prison sentence for her role in the robberies.

In the 1960s Jim Jones, a minister, started a religious commune called the People's Temple Movement in San Francisco, California. Gradually, the members were asked to give all their personal property to the People's Temple. In return, the Temple provided food, shelter, social services, and social and spiritual programs. Jones had considerable charisma and was successful in seducing the members to center their whole lives around the Temple and its activities. To gain further control over his followers, Jim Jones took them to an isolated area in the jungles of Guyana, South America. Rumors that the members were being sexually and physically abused and were being treated as slaves filtered back to California. In response to these complaints, Congressman Leo Ryan and a small staff went to Guyana to investigate the People's Temple Movement. Jim Jones ordered Ryan killed so that he could not report on the abuses he saw. Ryan was shot to death. Jim Jones then concluded that the United States would take strong retaliatory action and urged his followers to take their own lives en masse so they could be reunited in paradise. More than 900 men, women, and children committed mass suicide by drinking a fruit punch containing cyanide.

The power of conformity is also exhibited in religious cults such as Hari Krishna, the Moonies, and Scientology, whose members are able to convince typical white, middle-class college youths to join and forgo their education, career goals, families, and material possessions.

Source: Adapted from "Patty's Own Story," *Wisconsin State Journal,* Sept. 24, 1975, pp. 1–2.

The Psychoanalyzer

Continual analysis of what other members are doing and saying is the psychoanalyzer's forte. He or she often uses psychological terms and delights in analyzing what others really mean and what is wrong with them. The psychoanalyzer often slows down a group by getting members to engage in mind-reading rather than task completion. Other members are inhibited from expressing their thoughts and feelings; they fear they may be analyzed as having psychological problems.

The Withholder

A withholder has important information or resources that would help the group accomplish its task but intentionally withholds assistance. He or she is more interested in watching the group struggle and spin its wheels.

The Beltliner

Everyone has a psychological "beltline" under which are subjects that he or she is extremely sensitive about. Beltline items may include physical characteristics, intelligence, past behavior, past unhappy events, or personality characteristics. An overweight person, for example, may be highly sensitive about comments related to obesity.

Members who make subtle negative comments about the sensitive areas of other members threaten group cohesion and morale. A beltliner is a dirty fighter.

The Guiltmaker

A group member may attempt to control others by making them feel guilty. The guiltmaker traps the group into helping him or her with personal needs and goals, rather than working toward group goals. The guiltmaker uses such common expressions as "You never do anything for me" and "All I've done for you and this is the thanks I get" to trigger the guilt response.

The Catastrophe Crier

By exaggerating the seriousness of a problem, a catastrophe crier would have group members believe that consequences will be not minor but disastrous. Since the catastrophe crier focuses only on examining the severity of the problem and not on developing and implementing problem-solving approaches, he or she intensifies a problem rather than solving it.

The Subject Changer

This person does not want a group to deal with crucial issues or with controversy and conflict. When difficult situations arise, he or she tries to change the subject. If successful, a subject-changer prevents the group from dealing with crucial topics. There are a variety of reasons for seeking to change a subject; for example, the changer may detest heated debates or may fear the debate will reveal something he or she wishes to keep hidden.

The Whiner

A whiner continually complains about one thing or another without taking action to resolve the problem. Because the whiner seeks attention and sympathy from other members, he or she slows down a group in accomplishing its tasks.

The Benedict Arnold

If a group is competing with another group, a betrayer, or "Benedict Arnold," supplies confidential information to the other group. This person may encourage people outside the group to ridicule or disregard it, or slyly have the group's funding cut back. Inside the group this member may attempt to prevent the group from accomplishing its goals. People appointed to head departments at state and federal levels, for example, are expected by the public to be voices for the growth and progress of that department. But some appointees have betrayed this trust by a hidden agreement with the appointers to be a "hatchet man" and cut the services and funding requests of their departments.

The Trivial Tyrannizer

Instead of honestly sharing concerns, frustrations, and discontent, this member annoys a group with constant interruptions and digressions. He or she may arrive late for meetings and leave early, fail to show up for crucial meetings requiring everyone's attendance, or bring up concerns that the group has already acted on. Besides raising trivial questions about the wording of the minutes, for instance, this person may yawn or read something when other members are speaking.

The Shirker

A group member may be disruptive simply by failing to do anything for the group. When assigned certain tasks, the shirker will evade these responsibilities by using a variety of excuses.

The Power Grabber

A power grabber may attempt to become the group leader or the power source behind the group leader by convincing other members that he or she has more expertise than anyone else in the group or by buying the support of others with money, favors, or promises. A power grabber may create conflicts that make the leader look bad and sabotage the efforts of the leader, even though he or she may not assume leadership power.

The Paranoiac

Because he or she is excessively or irrationally suspicious and distrustful of others in the group, the paranoiac always feels picked on. Much of this person's time is spent defending himself or herself and finding fault with other group members. Paranoiac individuals often feel that other members must be discredited before they can amass enough evidence to discredit the paranoiacs.

It should be noted that some disrupters are intentionally aware of the effects of their behavior. Most of the previous examples are of this type. On the other hand, some disrupters are acting out of unconscious personal needs and therefore may not be aware their behavior is having a disruptive effect. The following suggestions on handling disruptive behavior apply whether the disrupter is aware or unaware of the effects of his or her behavior.

Handling Disruptive Behavior

Hostile and disruptive behavior can be handled in three basic ways: (1) members can be allowed to continue to be disruptive and the effects can be ignored or minimized; (2) the leader can confront members about their disruptive behavior; and (3) other group members can confront the disruptive behavior. The approach chosen should be based on what method will be most helpful to the group.

Minimizing Disruptiveness

If a disruptive group member is allowed to express discontent to the group, he or she may become less disruptive as time goes on through a ventilating process. When a member is disruptive, it is often helpful for the leader to ask the person tactfully to express his or her concerns. The group may then decide to deal with the concerns, especially those that are legitimate. With some concerns resolved, the disruptive group member may become more satisfied with the group and begin to feel the group has something to offer.

Let us assume, for example, that a man is angry and embarrassed about being sent to "Group Dynamics," a group consisting of people found guilty of driving while intoxicated. This man may be angry that he got a ticket while others who drink and drive have not been caught and "sentenced" to the group by a judge. At the initial meetings, he may aggressively ask a litany of questions: "What is the purpose of the group?" "What evidence is there that the group will do any good?" "What does one have to do in the group to pass?" "What qualifications does the group leader have for leading this group?" "Has the group leader ever been intoxicated while driving?" "If not, how can the leader understand what the members are thinking and feeling?" "If so, how can the leader be hypocritical by attempting to 'play therapist' when he or she has similar problems?" "Will members be forced to reveal personal things?" "What is the purpose of each of the group exercises?" "Does the leader believe the people in this group are drunks?"

The leader can handle these concerns by allowing this man to air his views and by providing honest answers. Furthermore, the group leader may acknowledge that she would also be angry if placed in that member's position. This approach seeks to allow members to ventilate their concerns, to answer their questions, and to convey understanding of their unhappiness. The goal is to create an atmosphere in which the group will be receptive to the content and exercises that will make the group effective.

Leader Confrontation

The group leader can confront the member about his disruptive behavior with other group members present or at a private meeting. The choice of private or group confrontation should be based on which will be most beneficial. If other members are present, they may be able to elaborate on the ways in which the member's behavior is disrupting the group and emphasize the seriousness of the problem. A disadvantage of group confrontation is that a hostile member may feel he or she is being "ganged-up on."

During a confrontation, the group leader should seek to fully and assertively express concerns in a nonblaming way by using I-messages (see Chapter 5 for I-messages and Appendix 1: Module 2 for assertiveness).[23] Some confronters make the mistake of primarily using the two types of you-messages: solution and put-down messages. Solution messages order, direct, command, warn, threaten, preach, moralize, or advise. Put-down messages blame, judge, criticize, ridicule, or name call.

I-messages consist of a nonblaming description of the effects of the disruptive member's behavior on the group or on the leader. The group leader simply tells the member which behavior is disruptive and then leaves it up to that member to take responsibility for changing it. I-messages generally lead to honesty and openness in a relationship, while you-messages usually reduce communication and polarize relationships.

Sometimes simply confronting a member with her disruptive behavior will lead to a change because she may not be aware of the behavior's negative effects. Once informed, she may alter the behavior or reveal reasons for being disruptive. For example, the disruptive member may be resentful because she has not been assigned more responsibilities in the group. Assigning that person more tasks may lead not only to a cessation of the disruptive behavior but also to her becoming a contented, productive member. When concerns underlying the disruptive behavior are resolved, it often ceases. In such a confrontation, the leader must tactfully ask questions to identify the reasons for the disruptive behavior.

However, confrontation may not always stop the behavior, for the disrupter may either continue along the same line or switch to another method of disruption. A "clown," for example, may become a "subject changer" or a "betrayer." If the disruptive behavior continues after a confrontation, the group leader can ignore the disruptive behavior as much as possible and minimize its effects, or confront the member again. In choosing the second alternative, the group leader must clearly inform the member that adverse consequences will result, explain those consequences, and follow through on implementing them if disruptive behavior continues.

For example, a group leader may inform a disruptive member in a court-imposed Group Dynamics class that he has four choices: (1) to participate in meetings and get as much out of them as possible; (2) not to participate but to attend in order to meet the court's requirement; (3) to attend and continue disrupting the class, with the court then being informed of his disruptive behavior; or (4) not to come to class, in which case the lack of attendance will be documented, the court notified, and that person's driver's license possibly suspended.

Some students tend to monopolize a class by rambling on about topics only remotely connected to what is being discussed. Usually, simply informing them privately about the rambling and the need to share "air time" solves the problem. However, a few students continue rambling even after the first confrontation. They are then informed privately that they must raise their hands before talking and will be called on only once or twice each session, depending on the class. Furthermore, indicate that if they try to talk before raising their hands, the class members will be asked if they believe some people are using up too much class time. If the answer is "yes," the class will then be asked to set rules for sharing class time. The second confrontation has always resulted in less rambling.

Group Confrontation

The third approach is to have another group member, rather than the leader, confront the disruptive member; the same guidelines apply here that were described earlier for such a confrontation. There are certain situations in which the confrontation is best handled by someone other than the leader. For example, several years ago a social work department at a large eastern university recruited someone from another university to chair the department. A faculty member in that department had wanted the position and felt cheated. When the new chair came, this faculty member refused to do any departmental tasks and was at times verbally disruptive during faculty meetings. Two other faculty members in this department met with the disgruntled party to explain the reasons he was not selected, to allow him to express his resentment, and to politely request that he seek to be more cooperative because it was in everyone's best interests. This confrontation was quite successful and changed the disgruntled faculty member's attitude.

If confrontation is necessary, a decision has to be made by the group leader and by other concerned members about who should do it. Generally, the decision should be based on who appears to have the best chances of influencing the disruptive member.

Reducing the Likelihood of Disruptive Behavior

Group members are less apt to be disruptive when their personal goals are identified and incorporated into the group goals. By involving all group members in setting goals and making decisions, the group's communication, cohesion, and problem-solving effectiveness are likely to increase. An autocratic leadership style discourages commitment while a democratic style promotes it. Moreover, autocratic leadership is less satisfying to members and may lead to disruptive behavior. Group goals that are clear, operational, and measurable also tend to increase members' satisfaction and commitment to the group, and reduce frustrations, as discussed earlier in this chapter.

A cooperative atmosphere leads to higher morale, open and honest communication, more effective problem solving, and increased group cohesion and satisfaction. As discussed earlier in this chapter, a competitive atmosphere is more apt to lead to disruptive behavior.

If some members are disruptive in similar ways, the group can discuss the effects of the disruptions in a nonblaming way and set "house rules" for handling disconcerting behavior. For example, three or four people who are smoking may be irritating the nonsmokers. House rules may be established as to when and where smoking may take place. Or some members may be habitually late. This problem can be discussed, and the group can agree on some rules regarding meeting times and tardiness.

Disruptive behavior usually decreases if the group leader is well organized, covers relevant and interesting material, and effectively helps the members reach decisions and accomplish goals. A group leader should also pay attention to meeting the social/emotional needs of members and actively strive to have all members participate in making decisions. He or she cannot play favorites and must follow through on what is initiated. If the group leader has serious problems in one or more of these areas, discontent and disruptive behavior will probably increase.

The more assertively and competently the leader presents himself or herself, the more trust and confidence the group members will display. If the leader is aggressive, the members will usually feel angry or intimidated and respond either aggressively or passive-aggressively. If the leader is nonassertive, the members will tend to have a low level of confidence in the leader and may begin asking whether a new leader should be selected.

If a group is not functioning well, the leader should confront the group with his or her concerns and ask the group to help identify the reasons so that changes can be made. Depending on the circumstances, these can be identified at a group meeting or through written reports that ensure anonymity. Using this confrontational approach, the leader commits himself or herself to working with the group to make changes. For example, I taught a practice course in which hardly anyone was asking questions or making comments. During the fifth week of the class, I confronted the class in the following manner: "I think we've got a problem. This is the fifth week of this practice class, and no one is saying anything. To make this class go, we need to start talking. One of the first skills that social workers need is the ability to talk. I'm not convinced that people in this class can talk. So far, it's been mainly me that's been talking. Now, I'm going to shut up and let you talk. I want you to tell me why you're not talking. I'm a big boy. I can take whatever you have to say." After a few minutes of silence, some students began talking, and we ended up having a lively discussion. Basically, the students said I was primarily lecturing, which led them to be passive, and they requested exercises to try out the theories and principles I was presenting. In future classes, I adjusted my teaching approach to include exercises. After this confrontation, the students became more verbal in future sessions (though still not as verbal as I desired).

When members are forced to attend a group they do not want to attend, as in the case of involuntary clients, the group leader may begin by saying something like, "I know most of you really don't want to be here, and I wouldn't either if I were forced to come. I wonder if we might begin by talking about your anger and unhappiness about being here?" Then the group leader should attempt to convey the purposes of the group, what is going to happen, and how the members can satisfy the minimal requirements for "passing." The group leader can mention that members can (1) choose to actively participate and get as much out of the group as possible, (2) remain silent and listen to what others have to say, (3) vent their anger and unhappiness in disruptive ways (which will probably anger and alienate others in the group) or, (4) refuse to come, which will have certain consequences. The group leader can then indicate that he or she cannot control their behavior, so the choice among these alternatives is up to each member. Such an approach almost always leads the involuntary clients to choose either the first or second alternative, perhaps because such an approach leads these clients to conclude that the leader is understanding of their anger—and they then focus on making the best choices in this predicament.

Sometime during the life of the group, one or more members may struggle with the leader for control. There are a variety of ways to handle a power struggle. (1) The person (or persons) may be given limited leadership responsibilities. This "second-in-command" approach may satisfy the member, who may become very helpful. He or she may accomplish important group tasks or, in therapy groups, prove to be a useful "co-counselor." (2) The group leader and the member desiring to be the leader can meet privately and work out a shared leadership arrangement to present to the group or identify the changes that the member would like to see made. (3) The leader may display in a tactful manner (through words and actions) that he is the person best qualified to lead the group. (Following this strategy a political campaign-like atmosphere sometimes occurs, with the leader and the aspiring leader acting as competing candidates, both seeking to impress other group members with their leadership qualifications.) (4) The group leader can resign, ask the members whom they wish to have as their leader, and indicate that he or she would again take the position if the group so desired. (5) Another strategy is to ask for a vote of confidence. If a majority vote of support is not received, the group leader promises to step down. By rallying her resources and supporters in a display of strength, a group leader can usually show the aspiring leader that a take-over attempt is futile. (6) Finally, the group leader can threaten the aspiring leader with certain adverse consequences. Sometimes these threats boomerang and motivate the aspiring leader to work harder or are used to convince other group members that the present group leader lacks moral integrity.

Exercise 4.8: Handling Disruptive Behavior of a Group Member

GOAL: This exercise is designed to help you better handle the disruptive behavior of a group member.

1. **Describe the disruptive behavior of someone who was also a member of a group in which you were involved.**

2. How did the disruptive behavior impact the group?

3. What actions (if any) did the other group members take to attempt to minimize the effects of the disruptive behavior? Were these actions effective?

4. If the actions were not effective, review the material in this text on handling disruptive behavior. What actions might have been taken by you (or by other group members) to more effectively handle the disruptive behavior?

■ GROUP EXERCISES

Exercise A: Setting Personal and Group Goals

GOAL: To identify personal goals for this class and to set group goals.

Step 1. The group leader begins by explaining the purpose of the exercise. Then, the group leader should explain what operational and measurable goals are and summarize their importance.

Step 2. Each member makes a list of personal and group goals for the class on a sheet of paper. The instructor should also prepare a list of group goals for the class.

Step 3. A listing should be made on the blackboard of the personal and group goals suggested by each student (inform students that they have a right to privacy and do not need to identify their personal goals). The instructor's list of group goals should also be put on the blackboard.

Step 4. The class should then discuss the personal and group goals listed on the blackboard and decide what the goals for the class will be. (The group leader should have previously read the material in Chapter 6 on procedures for decision making.) In arriving at class goals, it should be made clear that since the instructor is responsible for the course, he or she may exclude or add any group goal.

Step 5. After group goals are established, the following questions should be discussed with the group:
1. Are all of these goals operational and measurable? If not, how can they be improved?
2. What difficulties were encountered in setting group goals?
3. Did it take longer than expected?
4. Did anyone become frustrated at some point? Why?
5. How satisfied is the group with the goals that were set?
6. How does the group feel about the instructor having a greater say as to what the group's goals should be?
7. Are these goals realistically attainable?
8. Are these group goals compatible with personal goals?
9. Are individuals committed to work toward attaining these group goals?

Exercise B: A Sphinx Foundation Grant

GOAL: To observe what happens when some members are cooperative while others are competitive.

Step 1. The group leader explains that the exercise involves setting goals. Students are to assume that the Sphinx Foundation has awarded $100,000 to the students and faculty in this social work program to improve the program and/or social services in the community surrounding the campus. The task of the class is to arrive at recommendations as to how these funds should be used. The class is divided into three equal subgroups.

Step 2. Each subgroup meets for 15 minutes to develop proposals. A representative then presents the proposals to representatives of the other two subgroups.

Step 3. The three representatives meet in the center of the room for 15 minutes to present the proposals to each other and work toward a decision for the class. The three subgroups observe the negotiations. A subgroup cannot meet with the other subgroups, but members in a subgroup may talk among themselves. The subgroups may not talk with their representatives, but they may send written messages.

Step 4. The representatives should next confer with their subgroups for five minutes.

Step 5. The representatives then meet in the center of the room for five minutes to attempt to reach an agreement. Next, they meet with their subgroups for five minutes. And, finally, they meet again in the center of the room to seek to reach a final agreement.

Step 6. Discuss the following questions:
1. Was an agreement reached? Why or why not?
2. Did the representatives and the subgroups attempt to be cooperative or competitive? Why? What were the results of being primarily either cooperative or competitive?
3. Were the proposals primarily designed to benefit students, the department, or social services in the community? Why was this particular focus the major emphasis?
4. What are the representatives' feelings about this exercise? Did the representatives feel pressure from their subgroup? If so, what type of pressure?
5. How were decisions made within each subgroup, and how did the representatives make decisions?

Exercise C: The Nominal Group Approach

GOAL: Demonstrate how to conduct a nominal group.

Step 1. The leader begins by describing what a nominal group is and how it can be used. The leader then explains that the goal of the exercise is to identify shortcomings in the college's social work program by obtaining the views of the participants as to their wants and needs. In a classroom setting it is not necessary to obtain a representative cross section of the group because the students compose the total population of potential users.

Step 2. The participants are randomly divided into small groups of five to eight students. Each group should be seated around a separate table. (When tables are not available, classroom desks can be arranged in groups of five to eight with only limited inconvenience.)

Step 3. The leader distributes a sheet of paper containing a question participants must answer in writing. (An alternative to distributing a sheet of paper is to write the question on the blackboard.) One question that might be used is the following:

> Without mentioning names, what do you see as the shortcomings of our social work program?
>
> Please—No talking

Step 4. For 15 to 20 minutes, the participants privately list their responses to the question. No talking is permitted during this time.

Step 5. One member of each group is designated as recorder. The recorder asks each group member to state a shortcoming and lists each response on flip-chart sheets with a magic marker in full view of other members. This process continues until each member has given all of his or her responses. Listing is done separately for each group. Each response is recorded exactly as each member states it, and there is no discussion.

Step 6. The flip-chart sheets are then posted on the wall with masking tape near the group involved. A brief, informal discussion follows and focuses on clarifying what the ideas mean. There are two different approaches to reviewing the items: (1) all items are made known to the whole class, or (2) each group briefly reviews only the items recorded for its group. Both approaches appear to work. For smaller groups, the first is usually used. When the total number of listed items becomes very large, the second approach is generally more effective.

Step 7. Once the participants are familiar with the items on the flip-chart sheets, each is asked to list on index cards the five items he or she feels are most important.

Step 8. These items are handed in anonymously and then tabulated on the flip-chart sheets, or each student can simply check five items on the flip-chart sheets with a magic marker. These results are then briefly discussed with the students. (The instructor may well find it desirable to share the results with the other faculty in the department, and a faculty meeting may be arranged to discuss and take action on the highly rated items.)

Exercise D: The Autokinetic Effect

GOAL: To show that in ambiguous situations individuals will rely on the group to help define reality.

NOTE: This exercise is a variation of the study on the autokinetic effect discussed earlier in the chapter.

Step 1. For this exercise the group will need a room that can be completely darkened. The group leader explains that this study will determine each student's capacity to judge how far a dot of light moves in a darkened room. The class sits at the back of the room with pencil and paper ready to record their answers. With all lights off, the leader places a small flashlight at the front of the room and secures it so it will not move. The flashlight is then turned on for 30 seconds, then off, and students are asked to record how far they think the light moved. (The room remains dark.) The process is conducted two more times. During this part of the exercise, the students are asked not to talk with each other and to save their answers for later discussion. The lights are then turned on.

Step 2. The students form subgroups of three members toward the back of the room, and the room goes dark. The light is turned on three separate times for approximately 30 seconds. However, after each time the light is turned off, the students discuss and arrive at a group consensus as to how far the light moved. Each student records his or her group's consensus.

Step 3. With the lights back on, the students are informed that they will again be tested individually and that they are not to talk with anyone during this part of the exercise. The process is repeated. Each time the flashlight is turned off, the students are to record (in the dark) how far the light moved.

Step 4. Nine or ten volunteers write their answers to the nine trials on the blackboard—the first three done individually, the second three through group consensus, and the final three again individually.

Step 5. The class discusses whether these results are consistent with previous studies on the autokinetic effect, where the final three judgments tend to converge to a group standard. (In making this comparison, note whether the final three judgments are closer to the middle three group judgments than were the first three judgments.)

Step 6. The leader may or may not summarize at this point the results of the Asch studies and other studies done on conformity.

Exercise E: Identifying and Changing Group Norms

GOAL: To give practice in identifying norms that exist in a group and to assess whether some of these norms should be changed.

Step 1. The group leader explains what group norms are and states the purpose of this exercise. The class then forms subgroups of three or four students. Each subgroup makes a list of norms that exist in the class.

Step 2. From this list, the subgroups identify a few of the norms that they would like to see altered and propose changes.

Step 3. A representative from each subgroup writes its list of norms on the blackboard, circling the norms the subgroup wants changed.

Step 4. A class discussion follows. Are the subgroups generally in agreement or disagreement as to the norms that exist in the class? For the norms that are circled, a representative from each subgroup should state why the subgroup would like to see these norms changed and present the subgroup's suggestions for replacing these norms. The class should then discuss whether the changes are desirable. (Since the instructor has primary responsibility for how the class is conducted, the instructor has the right to veto any suggested change.)

Exercise F: An Ornery Instructor

GOAL: To help develop an awareness of norms that exist in the group and to look at what happens in a group when the leader acts under a new set of norms.

Step 1. This exercise is perhaps best done by the instructor. The instructor begins the class in a fashion very different from what he or she generally does. For example, the instructor may dress much more, or much less, formally. If chairs are generally in a circle, they should be put in rows. If the instructor generally engages in small talk before starting the class, this should be avoided. If the instructor comes across as a warm person, he or she should attempt to come across as a cold person. The instructor may take roll, for instance, and announce that from this point forward a student's grade will be dropped one full grade for each missed class period. The instructor may openly criticize students who arrive late or who otherwise disrupt the class in minor ways. The instructor may indicate he or she is unhappy with the way the class is going, and therefore new rules will be implemented: roll call will be taken each day; there will be a quiz every week; each student's attitude and participation in the class will now count as 30 percent of the final grade; any student who fails to take an exam at the scheduled time or who does not get a paper in on time will receive no higher than a D in the course; and the students will be graded down severely if they do not participate in class.

Step 2. After 10 or 15 minutes of this uncharacteristic behavior, the instructor should explain the real purpose of the exercise, which involved the intentional violation of existing norms. The instructor then asks what the class was thinking and feeling when he or she applied a new set of norms in the class. The instructor may conclude by stating that norms are very important in guiding the direction of a group and that significant changes in norms often lead to confusion and resistance.

Exercise G: How Group Decisions Affect Values

GOAL: To show how group decisions affect individual values.

Step 1. The group leader explains that the purpose of this exercise is to help students assess their values. The leader then distributes the following questionnaire, explains that the results will be anonymous, and instructs students not to talk while filling it out. The class then forms subgroups of five or six members. The questions are as follows:

1. Do you believe gay and lesbian teachers should be allowed to teach young children?
    a. Definitely
    b. Probably
    c. Undecided
    d. Probably not
    e. Definitely not
2. Do you believe individuals who have such a profound cognitive disability that they will never function beyond a six-month mental age level should be kept alive at taxpayers' expense?
    a. Definitely
    b. Probably
    c. Undecided
    d. Probably not
    e. Definitely not
3. Do you believe people have a right to take their own lives?
    a. Definitely
    b. Probably
    c. Undecided
    d. Probably not
    e. Definitely not
4. Should teenage females be allowed to have an abortion on demand without the consent of a parent?
    a. Definitely
    b. Probably
    c. Undecided
    d. Probably not
    e. Definitely not
5. Would you allow your child to attend classes at a school that a child with AIDS is also attending?
    a. Definitely
    b. Probably
    c. Undecided
    d. Probably not
    e. Definitely not

Step 2. The questionnaires are collected and kept separate for each subgroup. The subgroups are then asked to discuss each topic and arrive at a single answer for each question. Each subgroup should be given an additional questionnaire on which to record its answers.

Step 3. After the subgroups have completed Step 2, each member should again fill out the questionnaire anonymously. Again, the questionnaires for each subgroup should be kept separate.

Step 4. Prior to conducting this exercise, the group leader should arrange to have the instructor tabulate the results. The results should be recorded according to the following format:

Subgroup A

		Number of students selecting this alternative		
		Prediscussion Replies	Group Decision Replies	Postdiscussion Replies
Question 1	a.			
	b.			
	c.			
	d.			
	e.			
Question 2	a.			
	b.			
	c.			
	d.			
	e.			
Question 3	a.			
	b.			
	c.			
	d.			
	e.			
Question 4	a.			
	b.			
	c.			
	d.			
	e.			
Question 5	a.			
	b.			
	c.			
	d.			
	e.			

Step 5. During a break, the responses for all the subgroups are put on the blackboard or entered on a transparency according to the format listed in Step 4. The following questions should then be discussed: Do the prediscussion replies differ from the postdiscussion replies? If "yes," what are the reasons some members changed their views? Do group discussions and group decisions appear to influence value judgments by students? When students answered the individual questionnaire after the group decision did they feel a conflict between the group view and their personal values? If "yes," how did they feel about this conflict, and how did they attempt to resolve it?

Exercise H: Confrontation and I-Messages

GOAL: To practice confrontation and using I-messages.

Step 1. The group leader begins by explaining the goals of the exercise. Then, I-messages should be described. I-messages are a nonblaming description of the effects of another's behavior on you. In using I-messages, the sender does not necessarily have to use the term "I"; the key is to describe the effects of another's behavior on you in a nonblaming way, without being critical or suggesting solutions. (See Chapter 5 for a more detailed description of I-messages.)

Step 2. The following situations involving confrontation use role playing, and the "confronter" is urged to use I-messages. Two different students should be asked to volunteer for each role play and are given the following instructions.

Role play 1. You're a group leader, and a member of your group has been 10 to 15 minutes late for every meeting. His habitual tardiness has been disruptive, and you fear that other members may follow this person's example and also arrive late. Your task is to confront this member about being late.

Role play 2. You're a group leader, and there has been interpersonal conflict in the group that is not being dealt with because each time efforts are made to deal with the conflict, Jim (or Jill) either makes a joke of it or changes the subject. Your task is to confront Jim (or Jill) about this.

Role play 3. You're a nonsmoker, along with most other group members. Jean (or John) usually sits next to you and frequently smokes a cigarette, which you find increasingly irritating. Your task is to confront Jean (or John) about this.

Role play 4. You're a group member, and the group has been going nowhere because goals have not been established. The leader appears confused and uncertain about group procedures. The group is composed of students who are supposed to advise the social work faculty on curriculum and departmental policies. You are aware that this is the first group the leader has led. Your task is to confront the leader and explain that you and other members feel confused and frustrated because it appears that the group has been floundering.

Step 3. After each role play, discuss how well each confronter (1) assertively expressed his or her concerns and (2) used I-messages to express the concerns.

Exercise I: Confronting and Being Confronted by Others

GOAL: To practice tactfully confronting a partner about his or her group performance and to receive feedback on group performance.

NOTE: The instructor should lead this exercise, because it may generate strong emotions in the participants.

Step 1. The group leader explains the purposes of the exercise. Before beginning, the group leader indicates that some members need to work on controlling their disruptive behavior. The group leader should also explain that other issues may be brought up in the confrontation. The group leader briefly summarizes the following ways in which members are disruptive to suggest areas that the confronting student may want to mention tactfully to his or her partner.

The Bear	The Eager Beaver
The Psychoanalyzer	The Beltliner
The Guiltmaker	The Withholder
The Clown	The Catastrophe Crier
The Subject Changer	The Whiner
The Benedict Arnold	The Trivial Tyrannizer
The Shirker	The Power Grabber
The Paranoiac	

Step 2. Next, each member pairs up with another. The instructor explains that the task of each student is to confront his or her partner tactfully about behavior related to group performance that he or she might work on. First, one student is the confronter and the other the listener; then roles are reversed. The group leader should emphasize the importance of (1) first complimenting the partner on demonstrated strengths to balance out the negative feelings that may result from the confrontation, (2) using I-messages, and (3) being tactful and making the confrontation as positive as possible.

Step 3. After the confrontations, the instructor asks the students how they felt about the experience and encourages discussion of the positive and negative aspects of the exercise.

CHAPTER FIVE

Verbal and Nonverbal Communication

GOALS

To be effective, group members and social workers must be able to communicate their thoughts and feelings accurately. This chapter presents a model of communication, describes factors that interfere with the communication process, and offers guidelines on how to communicate more effectively. Sigmund Freud noted, "He that has eyes to see and ears to hear may convince himself that no mortal can keep a secret. If his lips are silent, he chatters with his fingertips; betrayal oozes out of him at every pore."[1] This chapter also summarizes material on nonverbal communication and demonstrates how nonverbal communication can be used to better understand other people.

All cooperative group interaction, whether verbal or nonverbal, depends upon effective communication. Through communication members argue, trade insults, debate issues, arrive at group goals, assume tasks and responsibilities, laugh, and work out differences. Effective communication occurs between two or more people when the receiver interprets the sender's message in the way the sender intended. The meaning of a communication is the response it elicits in the receiver, regardless of the intent of the sender.

■ A MODEL OF COMMUNICATION

Although most people think they understand what communication is all about, they are not fully aware of the process that goes on whenever people share ideas. This section will briefly summarize the process. We will begin by assuming that you, a sender, want to express a thought or a feeling.

The first thing you do is translate your thoughts and feelings into symbols (usually spoken words, but also nonverbal signals) that others can understand. This process is called *encoding*. Finding the precise symbols to express what you think or feel can be difficult. The next step is to *send the message*. There are a number of ways of sending a message: by letter, e-mail, telephone, note, spoken word, touch, posture, gestures, and facial expressions. When your message reaches a receiver, the receiver *decodes* the message by interpreting it in terms of thoughts or feelings that mean something to the receiver. The completed process is shown in Figure 5.1.

This process is one-way communication, in which a sender directs a message to a receiver. Most communication is a two-way process, however, as the initial sender

Figure 5.1
A model of communication

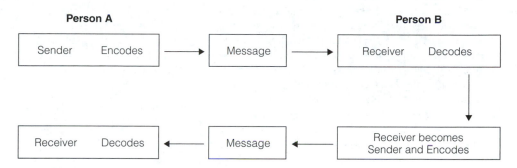

Figure 5.2
A model of two-way communication

directs a message to a receiver and the receiver responds. Two-way communication is diagrammed in Figure 5.2.

With effective communication, what the receiver decodes is what the sender sends. However, frequently something goes wrong. A friendly joke is taken as an insult. A subtle request is missed. A constructive suggestion is taken as a put-down.

Our model identifies the areas in which misinterpretations may occur. First, the sender may have difficulty putting into symbolic form the thoughts and feelings he or she wishes to express. Second, the message may not be sent effectively. There may be too much noise for the sender to be fully heard, or the sender may not speak loudly enough. Although nonverbal cues tend to be ambiguous, words also have a variety of meanings and may connote something different from what the sender intends. Third, during the decoding process the receiver may misunderstand the sender's message as a result of several factors, including physiological factors; individual attitudes, values, beliefs, defense mechanisms, and stereotypes; and perceptual factors, such as not listening. Later in this chapter we will take a closer look at how each of these factors influences communication.

One-Way Communication

Some groups and many corporations use one-way communication. The boss or group leader gives instructions and orders, or makes announcements to the other group members, who are not allowed to respond with their thoughts, feelings, and ideas. In one-way communication, the listener's role is only to receive the sender's messages and to carry out instructions and orders. The advantages of one-way communication are that messages and instructions are given quickly, and the boss does not have to deal with the questions and concerns of the listeners. In authority hierarchies, messages are often passed down through several levels.

Some studies have examined what happens when information is passed through several people using one-way communication.[2] As the message is passed along, it tends to become more simplified and distorted because of the three psychological processes of leveling, sharpening, and assimilation. First, receivers reduce or *level* the amount of information because they recall less information than they receive. In successive mes-

Erroneous Interpretations of Words

Language is symbolic, and meanings often rest more in people than in words themselves. Moreover, each word in any language can be interpreted in a variety of ways, which often leads to misunderstandings. A tragic example concerns Japan during the summer of 1945. In late July, Japanese governmental leaders knew they had been beaten and wanted to end the war. When the Potsdam Declaration issued by the Allied Forces called upon Japan to surrender, Premier Suzuki informed the Japanese press on July 28 that his response was *mokusatsu*. He apparently intended this word to mean "to withhold comment," which was supposed to be a signal to the Allied Forces that Japan was preparing to surrender. Unfortunately, the word *mokusatsu* can also be translated into "to ignore." The Japanese press hastily translated Premier Suzuki's statement into English and chose the wrong meaning, and Radio Tokyo broadcast to the world that the Suzuki cabinet had decided to ignore the Potsdam ultimatum. Suzuki's cabinet was furious about his choice of words and the message that was broadcast. The United States government responded on August 6 by dropping an atomic bomb on Hiroshima, and a few days later on Nagasaki. Hundreds of thousands of people were needlessly killed.

Source: William J. Coughlin, "The Great Mokusatsu Mistake," in *Looking Out/Looking In*, by Ronald B. Adler and Neil Towne, 3d ed. (New York: Holt, Rinehart, and Winston, 1981), pp. 303–305.

sages, fewer details are mentioned and fewer words are used. Second, a few high points become dominant and readily remembered or *sharpened*, while much of the remainder is forgotten. Third, the receivers interpret or *assimilate* much of the message in terms of their own unique personalities and reference frames. This process involves changing the unfamiliar to some known context, leaving out material that seems irrelevant, and substituting material that gives meaning in terms of the receiver's frame of reference.

Directive or Coercive Communication

A variation of one-way communication involves feedback, which McGregor has labeled *directive* or *coercive* communication.[3] With this approach, a chairperson delivers a message, and group members have an opportunity to seek clarification. The feedback is limited to determining how well the members understand the message. When the chair determines that the members understand the message, communication ceases. This type of communication is based on the premise that the chair's view on an issue is in the best interest of the group or organization. Directive or coercive communication has an advantage over simple one-way communication because there is a process in place to determine whether members understand the message.

Problems with One-Way Communication

Some serious drawbacks exist to one-way and directive communication. The members may have valuable information that could improve the group's productivity, but because it is not communicated to the chair, it is never considered. In addition, details of the original message are lost, and the original message is distorted as it is passed from one level to another. These distortions will reduce the coordination between hierarchy levels and sometimes result in ineffective implementation of the chair's directives. In addition, the morale of the group and the commitment of members to carry out the directives are substantially reduced when the members have no input into the decision-making process. A major defect of U.S. corporations in the past has been that communication was usually a one-way process. Japanese corporations tended to produce higher quality products at lower cost, partially as a result of the positive two-way communication between workers and management. In Japanese companies, workers identify their concerns and offer suggestions for improving productivity in periodic meetings with management. (Many U.S. corporations have now moved toward implementing two-way communication between workers and management.)

Two-Way Communication

Some groups use two-way communication, which allows all members to participate fully. There are numerous benefits to be gained through this type of interaction. Since minority opinions are encouraged and often expressed, two-way communication improves cohesion, group morale, trust, and openness. Conflicts and controversies are resolved through higher quality solutions as the resources and ideas of all the members are pooled. Although two-way communication is almost always more productive and effective than one-way communication, it is much more time consuming.

Problems with Two-Way Communication

The authority hierarchy also affects two-way communication because high-status people tend to talk more, and most messages are directed to high-status members. Often members with little power take few risks and avoid frank remarks because they fear the consequences. High-authority members are often reluctant to reveal their limitations and vulnerabilities for fear of appearing weak and undeserving of their status. This tendency of high-authority members also reduces honest and open communication.

When there are sharp differences in status and authority among members, a cooperative atmosphere should be established to encourage the full participation of all members. Also, if the group is to be effective, group norms must indicate that the ideas and opinions of all group members are valuable and essential.

Exercise 5.1: The Emotional Effects of One-Way Communication

GOAL: This exercise is designed to assist you in understanding the emotional impact of one-way communication.

1. **Describe a situation where someone (perhaps an employer, a parent, or a teacher) used one-way communication with you.**

2. **How did you feel when you were not allowed to voice your opinion, were not allowed to share your thoughts, and were not allowed to ask a question?**

3. **Were you motivated to do what the person who used one-way communication wanted you to do?**

■ PERCEPTION

Let us go back to the model of communication presented at the beginning of the chapter. Among the areas in which communication can go awry is the receiver's perception of the sender's message. The message perceived by the receiver depends not only on the encoding processes of the sender but also on the receiver's decoding, or interpretation. For example, the receiver may *add* to the sender's message. If a student of the opposite sex tells you, "You really look nice today," you may perceive that the sender is really saying, "I'd like to be romantically involved with you." A receiver also may *not fully comprehend* everything the sender is saying, just as an undergraduate may not fully grasp all the details of a sophisticated, abstract lecture given by a senior faculty member. Finally, a receiver may *distort* portions of the message because, for example, it cannot be heard clearly.

What a receiver perceives, then, *becomes the message.* This message may be fully accurate, partially accurate, or completely inaccurate. An ink blot test demonstrates that there are huge variations in what individuals perceive in an ill-defined or nebulous communication. The perception of any sender's message is based on the receiver's experiences, the receiver's needs, and the sender's actual message. Because a receiver's response is always a combination of what is seen, heard, *and* happening within the receiver at that moment, it is unlikely that two people will ever perceive the same thing in exactly the same way.[4] This response process can be easily demonstrated by counting the number of triangles in Figure 5.3.

The number of triangles that you count will depend on the number of ways you look at the diagram and define a triangle. People count as few as one triangle and as many as twenty. Obviously, then, more complex messages are even more difficult to interpret accurately.

The Perceptual Process

Since receivers are exposed to much more input than they can possibly handle, perceptions are organized to attach meaning to individual experiences. The first step of this process is to *select* data considered important enough to interpret.

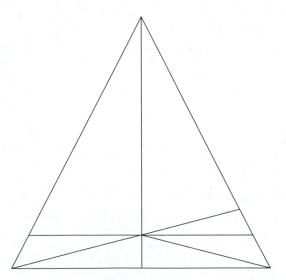

Figure 5.3
How many triangles can you count in this diagram?

Several factors cause receivers to select certain messages and ignore others. For example, stimuli that are *intense* (loud, large, or bright) stand out; someone who laughs loudly at a party will attract more attention than people who are quiet. *Repetitious* stimuli also attract attention and are widely used by advertisers. For example, Smokey the Bear—who reminds people to be careful to avoid starting forest fires—has become a symbol through repetitive advertising. Since a *change in stimuli* attracts attention, the constant noise level of cars going by will be tuned out, but any unusual sound will get our attention. *Motives* often determine the information selected from an environment. If an individual is hungry while traveling, he is much more apt to notice billboards advertising food and restaurants. If a person has a hobby or becomes an expert in some area, relevant information is also more likely to be observed. A group member sensitive about a certain subject is much more likely to pay attention to a comment even remotely related to his sensitive area.

The second step of the perceptual process is to *organize* data in some meaningful way. To make sense of human behavior, for example, people will interpret a specific behavior in terms of their favorite theories. If we believe in psychoanalytic theory, we will attempt to understand or interpret behavior according to a psychoanalytic model. If we believe in the principles of cognitive behavior theory, our interpretation of the same behavior will be very different. A psychoanalyst would say that a single woman who becomes pregnant has an unconscious desire (such as wanting to hurt her father or mother) that leads her to become pregnant. In contrast, a cognitive behavioral specialist would say that she decided to have intercourse because she believed that the anticipated rewards outweighed the potential consequences.

Group members constantly select what is important to remember and respond to, and organize messages in order to interpret and react to them. In the organizational process, past experiences, knowledge of human behavior, beliefs, values, attitudes, stereotypes, and defense mechanisms lead individuals to hear and see what they want. Information that supports a person's views is remembered, while information that forces individuals to question their firm beliefs and attitudes is often ignored or forgotten.

Physiological Influences

Each individual perceives the world in a unique way because of a number of physiological factors. Although only one world exists "out there," each person perceives a somewhat different world because of our own perceptual hardware.

Taste
There are fairly wide variations in the ways people experience taste. Although there are four basic types of taste—sweet, sour, salty, and bitter—individual taste buds permit considerable variation. Experiments have shown that litmus paper treated with PTC (phenylthiocarbamide) will taste salty, bitter, sweet, or sour, or have no taste at all, depending on who tastes it.[5] Arguments and discussions concerning the palatability of food often center on which food tastes better, but the simple fact is that the same food tastes different to different people.

Smell
There are also wide variations in the sense of smell. Odors pleasing to one person are repulsive to others. Such variations in perception thus affect communication.

Temperature
Sensitivity to temperature also varies greatly. Some people may be perspiring at 70°F, while others may be shivering. When a person has a fever, his or her perception of the "ideal" temperature changes, for example, and disagreements over appropriate temperatures in offices and houses are frequent.

Hearing

Noisy environments (factories, rock clubs, airports) have contributed to hearing loss, and people with significant uncorrected hearing losses are apt to miss parts of communications in a group. Often, they are forced to "fill in" by guessing the sounds they cannot hear, reading lips, and observing nonverbal communication.

Vision

People who are color-blind, farsighted, nearsighted, or otherwise visually impaired perceive objects differently from people who have good vision. Sherri Adler briefly describes how her poor vision affected communication with her husband, Ron:

> Since I've known Ron we've had some experiences that have caused communication problems because of our differences in vision: He has perfect eyesight, and even when I'm wearing contacts he can see better than I can.
>
> A few summers ago we drove to Colorado. I would get angry (and frightened) when he continuously passed cars on narrow two-lane roads, and he would get mad at me for following slow-moving cars for thirty minutes without passing. When I explained that I just couldn't see as far up the road as he could, we realized that we didn't see things the same way and that our safety would be threatened if I was to drive the way he wanted me to.[6]

Other Physiological Factors

Other physiological factors also influence our perception. If we are relaxed and well rested, we are apt to perceive a joke played on us by a friend as being humorous, and we are likely to laugh heartily. However, if we are in ill health, under high stress, fatigued, tired, hungry, thirsty, or nearly asleep, that same joke may not seem funny. All of these physiological factors have a substantial effect on our perceptions and the way we relate to people. For some women, the menstrual cycle plays a role in shaping moods and perceptions, and thus it may affect communication. There is some evidence that men may also have a four- to six-week physiological cycle of high periods and low periods.[7] Both males and females have a daily cycle in which a number of changes occur in sexual drive, body temperature, alertness, tolerance to stress, and mood, largely due to hormonal cycles.[8] Because of these daily changes, the prime time for productive work varies with individuals.

Sociopsychological Influences

Sociopsychological factors, including defense mechanisms, beliefs, attitudes, values, and stereotypes, influence what we perceive.

Defense Mechanisms

A defense mechanism is a psychological attempt to avoid or escape from painful conditions such as anxiety, frustration, hurt, and guilt. An individual's defense mechanisms are usually activated when he or she faces information that conflicts with his or her self-image. Defense mechanisms preserve self-concept and self-esteem, and soften the blows of failure, deprivation, or guilt. Common defense mechanisms will be briefly summarized in the following sections.

> *Rationalization:* One of the most common defense mechanisms is rationalization, the development of a logical but false explanation that protects a person's self-concept. Group members who use this mechanism actually believe the excuses they have dreamed up. For example, a student who fails an exam may blame it on poor teaching or having to work outside of classes rather than acknowledging the real reasons, such as not studying.
>
> *Projection:* By using this defense mechanism, group members can unconsciously attribute their unacceptable ideas and impulses to others. An example would

be a person who wanted to make himself look good by making others look bad. Psychologically, this person does not want to admit to himself that he has such selfish motives. So, he projects the selfishness onto others by believing they are trying to make him look bad, which then justifies his own negative behavior.

Denial: An individual can escape psychic pain by rejecting or denying reality. When people are confronted with a serious loss, they are likely to initially deny it. For example, a person can deny that a loved one has died. Many alcoholics deny they have a drinking problem.

Reaction Formation: Group members can avoid facing an unpleasant truth by acting opposite to the way they feel. Individuals who are angry and cannot admit it to others or themselves often act as if there is nothing wrong. By using the reaction-formation defense mechanism, sad and lonely individuals can act as if they are the life of the party, laughing and telling jokes. Also, people at funerals who are grieving deeply may behave as if everything is fine. The defense mechanism of denial is generally involved in reaction formation, as the individual seeks to deny painful facts, events, or feelings.

Compensation: This mechanism involves offsetting a real or fancied defect or inferiority by creating a real or fancied achievement or superiority. A recently divorced father may attempt to soften his children's pain by buying them expensive toys. Also, just as unhappily married college students can avoid dealing with their marriage by putting all their energies into their studies, people who have "failed" in their careers and personal life can compensate for their failure by getting "high" on alcohol and drugs.

Identification: When you were seven or eight you had heroes or heroines that you idealized and imitated. Some adults hide their real feelings in certain situations and instead of being themselves imitate someone they admire. The problem with this mechanism is that people "hooked" on identification cannot respond to a situation genuinely. They deny their real feelings and instead act as their hero would.

Fantasy: This mechanism involves using fantasy to dull the pain of reality. It is not uncommon, for example, for an unhappy adopted child to fantasize that her natural parents are exalted, loving people who will one day rescue her. Everyone daydreams, but most people soon return to reality. Some fantasies, however, endure and have destructive effects. For example, a former client of mine thought he could bring his deceased mother back to life by bringing female corpses to his home. After digging up several graves, he was arrested.

Regression: Some adults regress to an infantile or childlike state when ill or in trouble, with the subconscious goal of receiving more care and attention. When certain group members are confronted about their failings, they shed tears in an attempt to be excused for not fulfilling crucial commitments.

Isolation: The separation of an object (idea, experience, or memory) from the emotions associated with it results in the person showing no emotion to the object. This mechanism makes it possible for an individual to avoid the pain of anxiety, shame, or guilt. For example, a person uses this mechanism when discussing a violent act he or she has committed and shows no emotion.

Displacement: This mechanism occurs when hostile or aggressive feelings are vented against safer objects or people rather than against those who caused the feelings. A husband who has had a frustrating day at work, for example, may verbally or physically abuse his wife, children, or family pets.

Undoing: When a person feels guilty about some act or wish, she can undo her guilt by acting in a manner that reflects the reverse of this act or wish. The classic example is an unfaithful spouse who lavishes attention on his or her mate.

Exercise 5.2: Using Defense Mechanisms

GOAL: This exercise is designed to assist you in better understanding defense mechanisms.

1. **Reread the list of defense mechanisms discussed in this section. List the ones that you remember someone else using. Indicate for each who the user was (first name only) and describe how this person used the defense mechanism.**

2. **List the defense mechanisms that you remember using yourself. Describe how you used each of these mechanisms.**

Although everyone uses defense mechanisms to cope with unpleasant situations, defense mechanisms can become destructive when perception of reality becomes seriously distorted. The following example illustrates how defense mechanisms can severely distort a message. (Names have been changed in this example.)

Dr. Nystrom was recruited from a different university to chair the social work department at a medium-sized midwestern university. Three weeks after the start of the first semester, four students came to Dr. Nystrom's office to complain about the teaching of Dr. Weller, a new faculty member. Dr. Nystrom asked the students to present their concerns to Dr. Weller, but the students wanted to remain anonymous. Dr. Nystrom then asked the students to specify their concerns. Next, he informed Dr. Weller of the concerns. Weller appeared stunned and said little.

The next day Dr. Weller barged into Dr. Nystrom's office. "I know my teaching is good," she declared. "I spent most of last night trying to figure out what's happening. It is clear to me there is nothing wrong with my teaching. I've concluded that you are turning students against me."

(This is rationalization and projection.) Dr. Nystrom was unable to convince Dr. Weller that he was not turning students against her, and their relationship deteriorated. Ever since then, Dr. Weller has been convinced that Dr. Nystrom is seeking to have her contract terminated. Dr. Weller has continued to receive low student evaluations but has rationalized them with excuses, such as ill health and claiming that faculty in the department are turning students against her. This paranoia has had a destructive effect on departmental morale.

Communication That Fosters Defensiveness

Gibb has found that we are more likely to respond defensively to certain types of communication and that defensiveness is *reciprocal*.[9] If a sender begins to respond defensively, the receiver will react by putting up defenses, which will then increase the sender's defensiveness. Gibb has identified six types of messages that increase a receiver's defensiveness: evaluative, controlling, manipulative, indifference, superiority, and certainty.

Any message perceived as *evaluative* or *judgmental* increases the receiver's defensiveness. When an individual is being evaluated or rated, he or she is more on guard. In contrast, nonblaming communication reduces defensiveness.

Communication meant to *control* behavior or thoughts also increases defensiveness. For example, when a salesperson aggressively attempts to sell a product, many customers react defensively. Gibb indicates that defensiveness is decreased when the sender projects a willingness to share in the solution of a problem, for example, "Let's find a solution that works for both of us."

Defensiveness also increases when people discover that someone is trying to *manipulate* them. Since people would rather be asked to do something directly than be tricked into doing it, manipulative communication leads to distrust and defensiveness. An honest request may not always produce an immediate positive response, but it will lead to more open and honest communication and support in crucial situations.

Indifference to another person's feelings and thoughts increases defensiveness by conveying a lack of concern and implying that the person involved is not important. Defense mechanisms then allow the receiver to maintain a sense of value to offset the indifference. Gibb has found that empathy reduces defensiveness and is much more beneficial to relationships than indifference.

When someone relates to us in a *superior* way, we often become angry, tune that person out, or use defense mechanisms to maintain our self-respect. Some individuals go to great lengths to cut the superior person "down to size." Relating on an *equal basis* is much more conducive to openness, sharing, and reducing defensiveness. Instructors who relate to students as equals, for example, are using better educational and communication methods than instructors who attempt to impress students with their superior position and knowledge.

The final type of communication that, as Gibb notes, increases defensiveness is *certainty*. This type involves messages from people who steadfastly assert that their way of doing things is the *only* way or who act as if they have all the answers. Gibb notes that people who work hard at demonstrating certainty usually feel insecure and inferior; their certainty is a reaction formation. In this case, defensiveness can be reduced when openness to new information and ideas is communicated.

Defensiveness is probably the greatest barrier to effective communication, and should be avoided. Messages should be sent in ways that do not make either senders or receivers defensive.

Exercise 5.3: Defensive Communication

GOAL: This exercise is designed to assist you in understanding the types of communication that fosters defensiveness.

For each of the following types of communication, describe a time when someone used this type of communication with you, and also describe your emotional reactions in each situation.

a. Evaluative or judgmental communication:

b. Communication to control you:

c. Communication to manipulate you:

d. Indifferent communication:

e. Superior communication, which suggested you were inferior:

f. Certainty communication:

Beliefs, Values, and Attitudes

Individuals use their beliefs, values, and attitudes to select, interpret, and organize information. If a member in a group is liked, her comments receive more attention and support. Dislike sparks disagreement or strenuous opposition. Sometimes a group member will dislike another so intensely that he automatically votes against every motion that person makes, even those to his direct benefit.

The importance of beliefs and values in communication can be illustrated with a few examples. If parents are conservative and strongly opposed to interracial marriages, they will probably be opposed to interracial dating. A Roman Catholic who strongly opposes abortions will feel close to a speaker who supports that belief and be repelled by someone who favors choice. Deeply religious individuals often become threatened when someone professes that some other religion than theirs is the one, true religion. Finally, people with different sexual values will usually avoid discussing sexuality with each other.

Beliefs have a major impact on perception and sometimes lead to inaccurate interpretations of a message. For example, some people incorrectly believe that others are generally attempting to control them or put them down. Under this system of belief, they are apt to misinterpret general statements, jump to conclusions, and become defensive. Open and honest communication is unlikely to occur. This type of misinterpretation of messages has also been called the tendency to *personalize* messages.

Stereotypes

Stereotypes are fixed mental images of a group that are applied to all its members. Stereotypes may be partially accurate or completely erroneous. You can discover some of the stereotypes you hold by considering the mental images you get in response to the following phrases: "a macho male," "a Republican," "a welfare mother," "a policeman," "a homosexual," "a handicapped person," "an ex-con." For most of these phrases, you probably were able to get a mental picture of such people, and you probably have beliefs about their lifestyles, values, interests, and attitudes. During your first interaction with someone who fits into one of these categories, you are apt to respond in terms of your preconceived expectations. For example, if you distrust and fear police officers, you will probably be guarded in what you say and do if you meet an officer, and you will be apt to end the interaction as rapidly as possible.

■ SELF-DISCLOSURE

One of the main reasons we are not fully understood when we communicate is that we do not fully express what we are thinking and feeling. We often ponder how much we should share about our thoughts and feelings. What are the costs and benefits of self-disclosure?

Self-disclosure has been defined as "the process of deliberately revealing information about ourselves that is significant and that would not normally be known by others."[10] Some people are *over*disclosers in that they either talk too much about themselves or they talk revealingly about themselves at inappropriate times. If a student social work club is discussing a proposal for a new course on aging, for example, it would be inappropriate for a student to indicate that she has periodically thought about suicide. *Under*disclosers do not want others to know them intimately and speak very little about themselves even when the situation calls for it. An underdiscloser may encourage friends to share their personal concerns but then refuse to talk personally about herself. Appropriate self-disclosure can be defined as the right amount of self-revelation at the right time.

The risks of self-disclosure have been described by Jourard: "When you permit yourself to be known, you expose yourself not only to a lover's balm, but also to a hater's bombs. When he knows you, he knows just where to plant them for maximum effect."[11] The risks of self-disclosure include subsequent criticism, laughter, disapproval, or rejection, as well as a danger that the information may be used against the individual involved. If a student discloses to a class that he has a drinking problem, there is always the danger that someone in the class may inform a potential employer.

People fail to disclose appropriately for many reasons. Some may fear closeness, rejection, and criticism, or they may be ashamed of their thoughts, feelings, or past actions. In certain instances, disclosure will put pressure on a group member to change; for example, a person may be reluctant to acknowledge that he has a drinking problem because he knows that if he acknowledges the problem there will be pressure put on him to give up drinking (which he does not want to do). Jourard asserts that self-disclosure is necessary for psychological health and growth because people cannot be themselves unless they know themselves.[12] Through self-disclosure a person can know himself better; nonetheless, many cannot or will not face troubled parts of themselves and so resist self-disclosure.

If thoughts and feelings are not shared, an individual is not accurately communicating what she is really thinking and feeling and will not be fully understood. Honest and open relationships that are meaningful are based on self-disclosure with people accepting individuals as they are. A close, meaningful relationship is probably possible with mutual self-disclosure.

The question of whether to disclose can be answered by following a simple guideline. Individuals should self-disclose when the potential benefits outweigh the potential risks; making realistic judgments about the potential benefits and risks is the hard part. A leader of a therapy group usually should self-disclose if the information will be therapeutic for group members. For example, if members have drinking problems, a leader who shares her personal experiences with drinking could provide useful information and increase rapport with those members who are struggling with their drinking problems. On the other hand, a leader who is still emotionally involved with a problem usually *should not* self-disclose, or group members may view her as a client rather than a therapist. If a leader of a group of battered women tearfully relates a sexual assault, members may feel that she cannot be objective in dealing with their situations.

It is also important to remember that there are degrees of self-disclosure; you do not have to tell everything. It is possible to share some opinions, feelings, thoughts, or experiences while reserving riskier information. By observing the reactions of the receivers, senders can better determine whether it is in their best interests to reveal more.

What is disclosed should be relevant to the present relationship with the receivers. For example, a romantic relationship could disintegrate if past sexual relationships were disclosed. Most people know their partners have had previous sexual experiences, but few want to hear the intimate details.

Exercise 5.4: Feeling Good after Self-Disclosure

GOAL: This exercise is designed to assist you in understanding that self-disclosure, at times, is beneficial.

1. **Describe something personal that you self-disclosed, and afterwards were glad that you did. Further describe why you were glad you self-disclosed.**

2. Not all self-disclosure is beneficial. Describe your thoughts as to when you should and should not self-disclose.

The Johari Window

Luft and Ingram developed a graphic model of self-disclosure in groups known as the *Johari* (taken from the authors' first names, Joe and Harry) *Window*.[13] Diagram A in Figure 5.4 represents everything there is to know about you—your needs, dislikes, past experiences, goals, desires, secrets, beliefs, values, and attitudes. However, you do not know everything about yourself. You are aware of some things and unaware of other things, as diagrammed in Figure 5.4(B). In addition, the frame can be divided to show

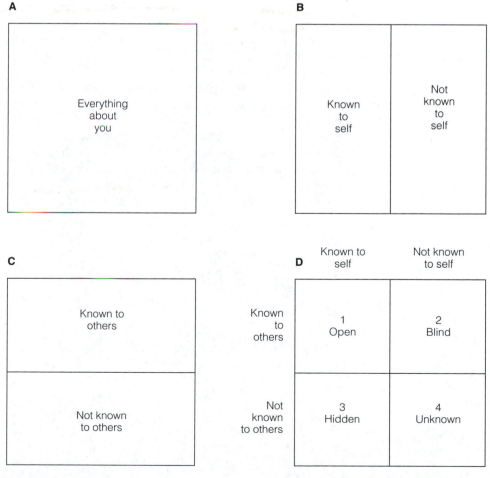

Figure 5.4
A Johari Window

what others know about you and what others do not know about you. This is shown in Figure 5.4(C).

By combining parts B and C of Figure 5.4, we get a Johari Window, as illustrated in Figure 5.4(D). A Johari Window divides everything about you into four parts. Quadrant 1 of part D is the *open* area of yourself, the part of which both you and others are aware. This area has been referred to as the "public self," as it represents how one knowingly presents himself. Quadrant 2 is your *blind* area, which represents the part of yourself that others are aware of but that you are not. It has been called the "bad breath" area because while others may know you have bad breath, you do not. Quadrant 3 is the *hidden* area, the part you are aware of but others are not. This part has been called the "secret" area, as you know all kinds of things about yourself that you are not telling to the group. Quadrant 4 is your *unknown* area, which represents that part of you of which neither you nor others are aware. A Johari Window can be individualized by moving the boundaries into the position that best describes a single personality. For example, the Johari Window in Figure 5.5 describes a man who is very aware of himself but who tends to hide much of himself from others.

Communication in a group generally follows certain principles. Initially, group members tend to be guarded and seldom self-disclose; Quadrant 1 of their Johari Window will be small. Members test the rules for behavior by barely speaking, giving short answers, and being careful about what they reveal. But as the group continues, group members usually begin revealing more about themselves. One common characteristic of groups is that an environment is eventually created in which members feel safe and protected. After a feeling of trust develops, members begin to disclose more personal aspects of their lives. As secret, private information is made public, Quadrant 1 is enlarged and Quadrant 3 becomes smaller.

A key characteristic of the Johari Window is that a change in any one quadrant will affect all other quadrants. For example, the more personal information is shared, the larger Quadrant 1 becomes. Quadrant 2 immediately becomes smaller as others know more about an individual from her self-disclosure. Quadrant 3 may become smaller because others offer feedback, which reduces the size of the blind area as the individual gets to know more about herself. Through this self-disclosure and feedback process, parts of an individual that are unknown may be discovered, which will alter the size of Quadrant 4.

The implications of the Johari Window are that the more information is shared, the more others know and the greater the feedback. This feedback often leads to greater self-awareness, more sharing about ourselves, and more sharing on the part of others.

It should be cautioned, however, that self-disclosure is usually best done gradually. If the first bits of self-disclosure are well received and accepted, the individuals can feel

	Known to self	Not known to self
Known to others	1 Open	2 Blind
Not known to others	3 Hidden	4 Unknown

Figure 5.5
A Johari Window showing hidden personality type

that it is safe to reveal more. It is generally a mistake to try to build a relationship by immediately divulging all the secrets and private details about oneself. Besides the risk of the divulged information being used against the self-discloser, there is also the danger that hasty "undressing" of oneself may scare others away.

Exercise 5.5: Johari Windows

GOAL: This exercise is designed to assist you in learning how to draw Johari Windows.

1. **Reread the material on Johari Windows. Draw a Window for someone you know quite well.**

2. **Draw a Johari Window that represents you.**

3. **Summarize what each of these windows depicts.**

■ HOW TO COMMUNICATE EFFECTIVELY

Given all the factors that can lead to garbled messages, it is important that everyone attempt to send messages effectively. A number of suggestions are given in the following sections for improving communication for both a sender and a receiver.

Sender

If nonverbal and verbal messages match, a receiver can better interpret the information. Double and often contradictory messages are sent when nonverbal and verbal messages do not agree. Messages should be complete and specific. If you have to request a special favor of someone, it is usually desirable to explain why. Also, it is important to specify your request. Vague or incomplete messages are often misinterpreted.

"Own" your messages by using personal pronouns such as "I" to show that you are clearly taking responsibility for your thoughts and feelings. When group members "disown" messages by saying "someone said" or "most people would feel," it is difficult to determine whether *they* think and feel this way, or whether they are simply repeating the thoughts and feelings of others.

Each message should be phrased in a way that is appropriate to the receiver's frame of reference. The words you use in explaining the Johari Window to a child should be quite different from those you use with classmates. Also, supporting verbal messages with handouts, pictures, and written messages will help the receiver understand them. Always ask for feedback when you are unsure whether the receiver has accurately perceived the message.

Express your concerns to others in nonblaming rather than judgmental or evaluative terms. Judgmental or evaluative words make others defensive. Note the immense difference between "I feel put down by what you just said" and "I'm really getting tired of your running me into the ground—watch it." The first is apt to foster communication, the second, defensiveness.

Physical factors that interfere with effective communication include chairs in a row rather than in a circle, poor acoustics, loud outside noises, an unacceptable room temperature, ineffective lighting, uncomfortable chairs, and too little time allotted to discuss issues. Reducing the effects of these barriers to communication generally increases the accuracy of the communication between senders and receivers.

Receiver

Communication is often halted when the receiver takes a message personally. Instead of jumping to the wrong conclusions, a receiver should ask questions that will clarify the sender's intentions and reasoning. Clarification can be ascertained by paraphrasing the sender's message in a question: "Are you saying . . . ?" or "Are you feeling . . . ?" If the receiver immediately disagrees, then the sender may become cautious and defensive, which will interfere with open and honest communication. It is important to remember that communication is fostered if you speak up for yourself *only after* you are accurately aware of the sender's message. In resolving an argument, a group leader can use the principle of *role reversal*. The receiver restates the ideas and feelings of the sender accurately and to the sender's satisfaction before proceeding to present his own views. The receiver should express the sender's feelings and ideas in his own words rather than parroting or mimicking the words of the sender. Before indicating approval or disapproval, a receiver should place himself or herself in the sender's shoes in order to understand what the sender is thinking and feeling.

Social workers should be aware that a sender may not have communicated his or her feelings or meaning accurately or fully. The sender may have chosen the wrong words or used words that were ambiguous. For example, the phrase "I care about you" has meanings ranging from "I care about you as much as I care about any human being" to "I'm in love with you." In such situations, it is extremely important to seek clarification by asking questions in a nonblaming, nonevaluative fashion.

Listening Skills

To communicate effectively it is essential to develop good listening skills. Unfortunately, many people are caught up in their own interests and concerns, and they are distracted by those thoughts when someone is speaking to them. Kadushin explains why it is difficult for an interviewer to develop good listening skills:

> The nature of spoken communication presents a special hazard, seducing the interviewer into an easy nonlistening. The hazard lies in the great discrepancy between the number of words that are normally spoken in one minute and the number of words that can be absorbed in that time. Thought is much more rapid than speech. The average rate of spoken speech is about 125 words per minute. We can read and understand an average of 300–500 words per minute. There is, then, a considerable amount of dead time in spoken communication, during which the listener's mind can easily become distracted. The listener starts talking to herself to take up the slack in time. Listening to the internal monologue may go on side by side with listening to the external dialogue. More often, however, it goes on at the expense of listening to the external dialogue. The interviewer becomes lost in some private reverie—planning, musing, dreaming.[14]

Kadushin gives the following suggestions on how to listen effectively:

> Rather than becoming preoccupied as a consequence of the availability of the spare time between the slow spoken words, the good interviewer exploits this time in the service of more effective listening. The listener keeps focused on the interviewee but uses the time made available to the mind by slowness of speech to move rapidly back and forth along the path of the interview, testing, connecting, questioning: How does what I am hearing now relate to what I heard before? How does it modify what I heard before? How does it conflict with it, support it, make it more understandable? What can I anticipate hearing next? What do I miss hearing that needs asking about? What is he trying to tell me? What other meanings can the message have? What are his motives in telling me this?[15]

Active Listening

Thomas Gordon has developed four techniques that are designed to improve communication: active listening, I-messages, collisions of values, and no-lose problem solving.[16] No-lose problem solving is described in Chapter 6.

Active listening is recommended when listening to a problem. A member in a therapy group says, "I'm fat and ugly—all my friends have boyfriends and not me." For such

---

◼ Active Listening Example in a Group Session at a Runaway Center

Sixteen-year-old youth: I hate school. I'm no longer going to go.

Counselor: You're so unhappy with what's happening at school that you're thinking about dropping out.

Youth: Yes, my home life is a shambles, and school isn't going well either.

Counselor: It's real depressing to have both your home life and school not going well.

Youth: Sometimes, like now, I feel like giving up. I've tried pretty hard to make things better at home and at school.

Counselor: You're feeling bad because the things you've done haven't worked out the way you'd like.

Youth: Yes, I got an F on the English paper I got back yesterday.

Counselor: You're feeling especially bad because of the grade you got on your English paper.

Youth: Since the commotion at home, my grades have started to fall.

Counselor: You're thinking that your problems at home may be affecting your schoolwork.

Youth: I don't really want to admit it to myself, but I guess it's true. For the several weeks it's been harder for me to concentrate on school.

Counselor: You feel your grades are slipping because you haven't been able to concentrate because of what is happening at home.

Youth: I guess when I'm at school I have to focus more on my schoolwork. Maybe if I talked to some of my teachers and let them know what I'm going through, they might be more understanding. I guess I really don't want to drop out of school.

situations Gordon recommends that the group leader (or another member) use active listening. The steps involved in active listening are the receiver of a message tries to understand what the sender's message means or what the sender is feeling, and then the receiver puts this understanding into her own words and restates it for the sender's verification. An active listening response to the previous statement might be, "You want very much to have a boyfriend and think the reason you don't is related to your physical appearance." An active listening response involves either *reflecting feelings* or *restating content*.

Gordon lists a number of advantages of active listening. It facilitates problem solving by the person with the problem, which fosters the development of responsibility. By talking a problem through instead of only thinking about it, a person is more apt to identify the root and arrive at a solution. When a person feels that others are listening, he or she will be more likely to listen to them in the future. In addition, the relationships between group members will probably improve, because when individuals feel they are heard and understood, positive emotions toward others increase. Finally, active listening helps a person with a problem to explore, recognize, and express feelings.

When first using the technique, receivers may make some mistakes. One is to use the technique to guide the person with the problem to a solution preferred by the receiver. The sender will usually then feel manipulated, and the approach may be counterproductive. A second mistake is to parrot back the words rather than paraphrase the intended meanings or feelings. For instance, if a member shouts at a group leader, "You stupid jerk," an appropriate response would be "You're angry with me," not "You think I'm a jerk."

I-Messages

Active listening is used when someone else has a problem. Many occasions arise when another group member causes a problem for you. For example, another group member may irritate or criticize you. You may remain silent and irritated or send a "you-message." There are two types of you-messages: a *solution* message and a *put-down* message. A solution message orders, directs, commands, warns, threatens, preaches, moralizes, or advises. A put-down message blames, judges, criticizes, ridicules, or name-calls. Examples of you-messages include, "You stop that," "Don't do that," "Why don't you be good," "I hate you," and "You should know better."

Gordon asserts that I-messages are better. For example, if a member is loudly tapping a pencil on a table, an I-message might be, "The tapping of the pencil is irritating to me." This example also shows that it is possible to send an I-message without using the word "I."

I-messages, in essence, are nonblaming messages that simply communicate how the sender of the message believes the receiver is affecting the sender. I-messages do not provide a solution, and they do not criticize. The following simple format illustrates how to phrase an I-message: The sender says to the receiver, "When you _____ (sender identifies the irritating behavior), I feel _____ (sender describes his or her feelings)."

You-messages are generally counterproductive because people do not like to be ordered or criticized. You-messages frequently result in an ongoing struggle between the two people involved.

In contrast, I-messages communicate the effect of behavior much more honestly. I-messages tend to be more effective because they help the other group member assume responsibility for his or her behavior. An I-message says that you trust the group member to respect your needs and to handle the situation constructively. I-messages are much less likely to produce an argument. They tend to facilitate honesty, openness, and more cordial relationships within the group.

It should be noted that I-messages will work only if the receiver does not want his actions to adversely affect the sender of the message. If the receiver does not want to cause discomfort to the sender, the receiver is apt to seek to change his adversive behavior when informed by an I-message of how he is adversely affecting the sender. However, if the receiver enjoys causing discomfort to the sender, then the use of an I-message by the sender is apt to result in an *increase* in the receiver's adversive behavior as the receiver is now more fully aware of how to create discomfort in the sender. (An I-message is an invitation by the sending to the receiver for a dialogue.)

Exercise 5.6: Learning to Use I-Messages

GOAL: This exercise is designed to assist you in learning to phrase I-messages. Note: For this exercise it is highly desirable to later discuss in class whether your attempts at phrasing I-messages meet the guidelines for stating an I-message.

Describe an I-message you would use when someone does the following:

a. **You are in a car driving with someone who lights up a cigarette. You do not like to be exposed to secondhand smoke for health reasons.**

b. **You are riding in a car with someone who is speeding and driving recklessly. You fear an accident may occur.**

c. **You are trying to sleep. It is 3:00 A.M. and you have two exams in the morning. In a neighboring apartment someone turns on his or her stereo loudly.**

Collisions of Values

Collisions of values between group members are common. Likely areas of conflict include values about abortion, sexual behavior, clothing, religion, use of drugs, hairstyles, and conscientiousness in carrying out assigned group tasks.

Gordon asserts that there are three constructive ways to resolve value conflicts. The first is to model the values you hold as important. If you value honesty, be honest. If you value openness, be open. If you are not living according to the values you profess, then you need to change either your values or your behavior. Congruence between behavior and values is important if you want to be an effective role model.

The second way is to attempt to be a consultant to the members with whom you are in conflict. There are some dos and don'ts for a good consultant. First of all, a good consultant inquires whether the other person would like to hear his or her views. If the answer is no, then do not proceed to consult because the other group member will react negatively. If the answer is yes, be sure you have all the pertinent facts. Then share these facts once so the other person understands them. Let the other group member have the responsibility of deciding whether to follow the suggestions. To continue consulting, a person must be neither uninformed nor a nag.

The third way to reduce tensions over a values issue is to modify your values. By examining the values held by the other group member, you may realize they have merit, and you may move toward those values or increase your understanding of why the person holds his or her values.

Exercise 5.7: Resolving Collisions of Values

GOAL: This exercise is designed to assist you in learning to identify and resolve collisions of values.

1. Describe a situation in your life where you had a serious collision of values with someone.

2. Describe how this situation was resolved. (If it has not been resolved, describe the issues that still need to be resolved.)

3. Review that material on collision of values in this text. Does this material suggest a better way of resolving the collision of values that you experienced? If it does, please indicate which approach you believe would have been more beneficial for you to use.

NONVERBAL COMMUNICATION

It is impossible not to communicate. No matter what we do, we transmit information about ourselves. Even an expressionless face at a funeral communicates something. As you are reading this, stop for a minute and analyze what nonverbal messages you would be sending if someone were observing you. Are your eyes wide open or are they half closed? Is your posture relaxed or tense? What are your facial expressions communicating? Are you occasionally gesturing? What would an observer deduce you are feeling from these nonverbal cues?

Nonverbal cues often reveal feelings a person is intentionally trying to hide. Bodily reactions such as sweating, stammering, blushing, and frowning often reveal the presence of emotions—fear, embarrassment, or discomfort—that people would rather hide from others. By developing skills in reading nonverbal cues, group leaders can become more aware of what others are feeling and how to interact with them more effectively. Since feelings stem from thoughts, nonverbal cues that reveal what people are feeling also transmit information about what people are thinking.

In literature, perhaps the greatest reader of nonverbal cues was Sherlock Holmes. In this exchange Holmes deduces the following about his friend Watson:

> "How do I know that you have been getting yourself very wet lately, and that you have a most clumsy and careless servant girl?" . . .
>
> "It is simplicity itself," said he; "my eyes tell me that on the inside of your left shoe, just where the firelight strikes it, the leather is scored by six almost parallel cuts. Obviously they have been caused by someone who has very carelessly scraped round the edges of the sole in order to remove crusted mud from it. Hence, you see, my double deduction that you had been out in vile weather, and that you had a particularly malignant boot-slitting specimen of the London slavey."[17]

FUNCTIONS OF NONVERBAL COMMUNICATION

Nonverbal communication interacts with verbal communication and can repeat, substitute for, accent, regulate, or contradict what is spoken.

Repetition

Nonverbal messages may *repeat* verbal messages. A husband may say he is really looking forward to becoming a father and repeat this happy anticipation with glowing facial expressions.

Substitution

Nonverbal messages may *substitute* for verbal messages. If you know a close friend has just failed an important exam, even though she may not talk about it, you can get a fairly good idea of what she is thinking and feeling by watching her.

Accentuation

Nonverbal messages may *accent* verbal messages. If someone you are dating says she is angry and upset with something you did, she may emphasize the depth of these feelings by pounding a fist and pointing an accusing finger. (Accentuation and repetition are closely related, although accentuation usually involves greater emphasis.)

Regulation

Nonverbal messages may serve to *regulate* verbal behavior. Looking away from someone who is talking to you indicates that you are not interested in talking.

Contradiction

Nonverbal messages may *contradict* verbal messages. An example is someone with a red face, bulging veins, and a frown yelling, "Angry! Hell no, what makes you think I'm angry?" When nonverbal messages contradict verbal messages, the nonverbal messages are often more accurate. When receivers perceive a contradiction between nonverbal and verbal messages, they usually believe the nonverbal.[18]

The Risk of Misinterpretation

While nonverbal messages can be revealing, they can also be unintentionally misleading. Think of the times when people have misinterpreted your nonverbal messages. Perhaps you tend to say little when you first wake up, and others have interpreted this as meaning that you are angry or troubled. Perhaps you have been quiet on a date because you were tired or because you were thinking about something that happened recently—has your date at times misinterpreted your behavior to mean you are bored or unhappy with the relationship? While deep in thought, have you had an expression on your face that others have interpreted as a frown? Nonverbal behavior is often ambiguous. A frown, for example, may represent a variety of emotions: anger, rejection, confusion, unhappiness, fatigue, or boredom. *Nonverbal messages should be interpreted not as facts but as clues to be checked out verbally to determine what the sender is thinking and feeling.*

Exercise 5.8: Interpreting Nonverbal Cues

GOAL: This exercise demonstrates that nonverbal cues may be correctly interpreted as well as misinterpreted.

1. **Describe a situation where you correctly interpreted the nonverbal cues of someone.**

2. **Describe a situation where you misinterpreted the nonverbal cues of someone.**

3. When nonverbal cues contradict the verbal message of someone, which message (the verbal or the nonverbal) are you apt to believe?

FORMS OF NONVERBAL COMMUNICATION

Nonverbal communication may take many forms. We communicate by the way we move, the expressions we make, the clothes we wear, even by the way we arrange our homes and offices. The following discussion examines the different avenues of nonverbal expression, including posture and body orientation, gesture, touch, choice of clothing, control of personal space and setting of boundaries, facial expression, voice tone and level, personal appearance, and design of personal environments.

Posture

An indication of how much posture can communicate is the large number of phrases that have posture as a metaphor:

"He can stand on his own two feet."
"I've got a heavy burden to carry."
"She's got a lot of backbone."
"Stand tall."

In picking up nonverbal cues from posture, it is important to note both the overall posture of a person and changes in posture. People tend to be relaxed in nonthreatening situations and to tighten up when under stress. Some people never relax, and their rigid posture shows it.

The degree of physical tenseness can reveal status differences. In interactions between a higher- and a lower-status person, the higher-status person is usually more relaxed, the lower-status person more rigid and tense.[19] For example, note the positions that are usually assumed when a faculty member and a student are conversing in the faculty member's office.

Teachers and public speakers often watch the posture of students or people in the audience to gauge how a presentation is being received. If people in the audience are leaning forward in their chairs, it is a sign the presentation is going well. If the audience members are slumping in their chairs, the presentation is probably beginning to bomb.

Body Orientation

Body orientation is the extent to which we face toward or away from someone with our head, body, and feet. Facing someone signals an interest in starting or continuing a conversation, while facing away signals a desire to end or avoid conversation. The phrase "turning your back" concisely summarizes the message that is sent when you turn away from someone. Can you remember the last time someone signaled a wish to end a conversation with you by turning away?

Facial Expressions

The face and eyes are generally selected as the primary source of nonverbal communication because facial expressions often are mirrors that reflect thoughts and feelings. Ekman and Friesen have identified six basic emotions that facial expressions reflect—

Nonverbal Behavior among Poker Players

Oswald Jacoby has noted that poker players use nonverbal messages extensively and has divided poker players into three classes: naive players, tricky players, and unreadable players.

Naive players are usually beginning players who possess few skills. When they look worried, they probably are. When they have a mediocre hand, they take a long time to bet. They bet quickly on a good hand but frown and scowl and look like bad luck has bitten them if they are dealt poor cards. A bluff is accompanied by a guilty look; when they raise a bet, everyone else folds. Naive players reveal their hands by body language that is seldom apparent in veteran poker buffs. Players of this type usually quit poker at an early stage because of their "bad luck."

Most poker players are "tricky" players and act exactly the opposite of the way they really feel. When they have a poor hand they exude confidence, and when they have a good hand they tremble a little and look nervous as they bet. Sometimes they do a triple cross, by acting the way they really feel.

Unreadable players show no consistency in their behavior. They will randomly exude confidence or look nervous, and these nonverbal messages will give no clue as to the nature of their hand. Unreadable players are the most successful.

_____

Source: Adapted from Oswald Jacoby, *Oswald Jacoby on Poker* (New York: Doubleday, 1974).

---

fear, surprise, anger, happiness, disgust, and sadness.[20] These expressions appear to be recognizable in all cultures; people seeing photos of such expressions are quite accurate in identifying the emotions behind them.

Yet, facial expressions are a complex source of information. They can change rapidly; slow-motion films have found that a fleeting expression can come and go in a fifth of a second. In addition, there are at least eight distinguishable positions of the eyes and lids, at least eight positions for the eyebrows and forehead, and at least ten for the lower face.[21] Multiplying these different combinations leads to several hundred possible combinations. Therefore, it is almost impossible to compile a directory of facial expressions and their corresponding emotions.

Because people are generally aware that their facial expressions reflect what they are feeling and thinking, they may mask them. For example, a person who is angry and does not want others to see the anger may hide this feeling by smiling. In using facial expressions to interpret feelings, social workers must be aware that the sender may be concealing his or her real thoughts and feelings.

Eye Contact

When you want to end a conversation, or avoid a conversation, you look away from the other person's eyes. If you want to start a conversation, you often seek out the receiver's eyes. You may wait until the receiver looks at you: when he does, it is a signal that he is ready to begin talking.

The eyes can also communicate dominance or submission. When a high-status person and a low-status person are looking at each other, the low-status person tends to look away first. Downcast eyes often signal submission or giving in. Of course, downcast eyes may also signal sadness, boredom, fatigue, remorse, or disgust.

Good salespeople are aware that eye contact is a sign of involvement and often manage to catch our eyes. Then they begin their pitch and maintain "courteous" eye contact. They know social norms require a receiver to hear what a person has to say once the person is allowed to begin speaking. These social norms trap us into listening to the sales pitch once eye contact has been made. Salespeople in stores utilize eye contact in another way. They determine which items a customer is looking at most and then emphasize these items in their sales pitch.

The importance of eyes in communication is reflected in these common phrases:

"He could look right through you."
"She has an icy stare."

"He's got shifty eyes."
"Did you see the gleam in her eye?"

Eye expressions suggest a wide range of human feelings. Wide-open eyes imply wonder, terror, frankness, or naiveté. Lowered eyelids may mean displeasure. A constant stare connotes coldness; eyes rolled upward suggest the person believes another's behavior is strange or unusual.

When we become emotionally aroused or interested in something, the pupils of our eyes dilate. Some counselors are sufficiently skilled in reading pupil dilation to tell when they touch a sensitive area by watching a client's eyes. Hess and Polt measured the amount of pupil dilation while showing men and women various kinds of pictures.[22] The greater the subject's interest in the pictures, the more the eyes dilated. Women's eyes dilated an average of 20 percent when looking at pictures of nude men. Men's eyes dilated an average of 18 percent when looking at pictures of nude women. Surprisingly, the greatest increase in pupil size occurred when women looked at a picture of an infant and mother.

Gestures

Most of us are aware that our facial expressions convey our feelings. When we want to hide our true feelings, we concentrate on controlling our facial expressions. We are less aware that our gestures also reveal our feelings, however, and as a result, gestures are sometimes better indicators of feelings.

People who are nervous tend to fidget. They may bite their fingernails, tap their fingers, rub their eyes or other parts of their body, bend paper clips, or tap a pencil. They may cross and uncross their legs, rhythmically swing a crossed leg back and forth, or rhythmically move a foot up and down.

There are many other gestures that provide clues to a person's thoughts and feelings. Clenched fists, whitened knuckles, and pointing fingers signal anger. When people want to express friendship or attraction, they tend to move closer to each other. Hugs can represent a variety of feelings: physical attraction, "good to see you," "best wishes in the future," and friendship. Shaking hands is a signal of friendship and a way of saying hello or goodbye.

Scheflen notes that a person's sexual feelings can be signaled through gestures. He describes "preening behavior," which sends a message that the sender is attracted to the receiver. Preening includes rearranging one's clothing, combing or stroking one's hair, and glancing in a mirror. Scheflen cites a number of invitational preening gestures that he asserts are specific to women: exposing a thigh, protruding a breast, placing a hand on a hip, exhibiting a wrist or palm, or stroking a thigh.[23] Naturally these gestures do not always suggest sexual interest. (It is interesting that comparable research has not been conducted on males. Conducting this research only on women may indicate a sexist bias.)

Gestures are used in relation to verbal messages to repeat, substitute, accent, contradict, and regulate. Some people literally speak with their hands, arms, and head movements. Their gestures may be so automatic that they are surprised when they see themselves on videotape and observe the number of gestures they use.

Touching

Spitz has demonstrated that young children need direct physical contact, such as being cuddled, held, and soothed. Without direct physical contact, the emotional, social, intellectual, and physical development of children will be severely stunted.[24] Spitz observed that in the 19th century high proportions of children died in orphanages and other child-care institutions. The deaths were not found to be caused by poor nutrition or inadequate medical care but by lack of physical contact with parents or nurses. From this research came the practice of "nurturing" children in institutions—picking babies up, holding them close, playing with them, and carrying them around several times a day. With this practice, the infant mortality rate in institutions dropped sharply. Montagu describes research findings that suggest that eczema, allergies, and certain other medical problems are in part caused by a person's lack of physical contact with a parent during infancy.[25]

Adults also need physical contact. People need to know that they are loved, recognized, and appreciated. Touching (through holding hands, hugging, pats on the back) is a way of communicating warmth and caring. Unfortunately, most American men and some American women have been socialized to refrain from touching, except in sexual contexts. Sidney Simon has noted:

> In our now more than slightly cockeyed world, there seems to be little provision for someone to get touched without having to go to bed with whoever does the touching. And that's something to think about. We have mixed up simple, healing, warm touching with sexual advances. So much so, that it often seems as if there is no middle way between "Don't you dare touch me!" and "Okay, you touched me, so now we should make love!"[26]

Our language is a mirror of our culture. Common phrases suggest that more importance is placed on the senses of sight and hearing than on touch:

> "Seeing is believing."
> "It's good to see you again."
> "It's really good to hear from you."
> "I've got my eye on you."

We have coined few phrases that include words for touch. For example, when leaving someone we say, "See you again soon," rather than "Touch you again soon." If we should say the latter, it would be apt to be interpreted as having sexual connotations.

But touching someone is in fact an excellent way of conveying a variety of messages, depending on the context. A hug at a funeral will connote sympathy, while a hug when meeting someone says, "It's good to see you." A hug between parent and child means, "I love you," while a hug on a date may have sexual meanings. A number of therapists have noted that *communication and human relationships would be vastly improved if people reached out and touched others more—with hugs, squeezes of the hand, kisses, and pats on the back.* Touch is crucial for the survival and development of children, and touch is just as crucial for adults to assure them that they are worthwhile and loved.

There is a danger that a hug by someone who wants to send a message of nonsexual love and support may be misinterpreted by the receiver as being an incident of sexual harassment. One way of avoiding this predicament is for the person who wants to give a hug to ask the receiver: "Would you like a hug?"

Clothing

Clothes keep us warm, protect us from illness, and cover certain areas of our body so we are not arrested for indecency. But clothes have many other functions. Uniforms such as those worn by police officers or firefighters tell us what a person does and what services he or she can render. People intentionally and unintentionally send messages about themselves by what they wear. Clothes give messages about occupations, personalities, interests, group norms, social philosophies, religious beliefs, status, values, mood, age, nationality, and personal attitudes. There are numerous "wardrobe engineers" (tailors, manufacturers, sellers of clothes) who assert that a person can obtain what he wants by improving his wardrobe, and there is some truth to the phrase "clothes make the person."

The importance of clothes in determining judgments that people make about strangers was demonstrated in a study by Hoult. Hoult began by having 254 female students rate the photos of male models on qualities such as "best-looking," "most likely to succeed," "most intelligent," "most likely to date or double date with," and "best personality." For these photos, Hoult obtained independent ratings of clothes and models' heads. Hoult then placed higher-ranked outfits on models with lower-ranked heads. Lower-ranked clothing was placed on models with higher-ranked heads. He found that, regardless of how the model's head was ranked, higher-ranked clothing was associated with an increase in rank while lower-ranked clothing was associated with loss of rank.[27]

Adler and Towne have described an experiment in which a student spent a week hitchhiking back and forth from Los Angeles to Santa Barbara, a distance of 100 miles. On Tuesday, Thursday, and Saturday, the student wore stay-pressed slacks, well-shined leather shoes, and an ironed shirt; on Monday, Wednesday, and Friday, he wore old blue jeans, sandals, and a tie-dyed sweatshirt. Other than the clothes, the student kept other factors constant, such as where he stood and at what time of day. The student described the results:

> It was incredible! On my three grubby days I got rides from people who looked just like I did. Two of them drove old VW buses, and the third had a '55 Ford pickup truck. They all wore Levis, boots, et cetera, and all had pretty much the same life style. On the days when I dressed up, I got rides in shiny new Oldsmobiles and Cadillacs from people who were completely opposite from the ones I'd driven with the day before.[28]

Any given item of clothing can convey several different meanings. For example, the tie a person selects to wear may reflect "sophistication" or "nonconformity." In addition, the way the tie is worn (loosened, tightly knotted, thrown over one's shoulder, soiled and wrinkled) may provide additional information.

Clothes also affect our self-image. If a person feels appropriately dressed, she is usually more self-confident, assertive, and outgoing. If not, she becomes more reserved, less confident, and less assertive.

With clothes (as with other forms of nonverbal communication), there is a real danger of misreading nonverbal messages. We often judge others on the basis of skimpy information, and frequently these interpretations are in error. Sometimes we get "burned" by our misinterpretations. Several years ago I had a client who for the previous 10 years had lived elegantly, traveling all over Europe and North America, staying in the finest hotels. He financed his lifestyle by writing bad checks. When he needed money he would dress in an expensive suit because, he explained, people took his check much more readily when he was well dressed.

Personal Boundaries

Each of us wears a kind of invisible "bubble" of personal space wherever we go. The area inside this bubble is strictly private; only people who are emotionally close to us are allowed inside. You can sometimes tell how people are feeling toward each other by noting the physical distance between them. In fact, Hall has identified four distinct distances, or zones, in people's daily interactions that guide their relations with others. These zones are intimate, personal, social, and public.[29] The particular zone chosen depends upon the context of the interaction, feelings toward the person, and interpersonal goals. Boundary behavior, like other nonverbal signals, provides group leaders with important information. For example, the distance maintained by group members should indicate to the group leader the members' personal preferences in individual interactions. These preferences, which may change considerably as the group progresses toward its goals, should be respected; otherwise, leaders are likely to encounter problems, such as resistance or distrust.

Intimate Zone

This zone begins with skin contact and extends out about 18 inches. Only people who are very close emotionally enter this zone, primarily in private situations—comforting, conveying caring, making love, and showing love and affection. When a person voluntarily allows someone to enter this distance, it is a sign of trust because defenses are lowered. On the other hand, if a person maintains a "safe" distance of 2 or more feet, it probably means that the person is still sorting out the relationship.

When an uninvited intruder moves into this intimate zone, a person usually feels invaded and threatened. His posture becomes more upright, his muscles tense, and he may move back and avoid eye contact as a way of signaling he wants a less intimate relationship. When people are forced to stand close to strangers on crowded buses and elevators, they generally avoid eye contact and try not to rub against others, probably to say "I'm sorry I'm forced to invade your territory—I'll try not to bother you."

Personal Zone

This zone, which ranges from approximately 18 inches to 4 feet, is the distance at which a couple stands apart from each other in public. Interestingly, if someone of the opposite sex stands close to someone we are dating or married to, we tend to wonder whether this person is trying to "move in" on us. If we see our spouse or date move close to someone of the opposite sex, we may become suspicious and jealous.

The far range of the personal zone (from about two and a half to four feet) is a distance at "arm's length," just beyond the other person's reach. Interactions occurring at this distance may still be reasonably close, but they are much less personal than those at the near range of the personal zone. Sometimes, communication at "arm's length" represents a test by people to determine whether they want the relationship to become emotionally closer.

Social Zone

This zone, which ranges from about 4 feet to 12 feet, usually encompasses business communications. The nearer part of this zone (from about 4 to 7 feet) is the distance at which coworkers usually converse and at which salespeople and customers usually interact. Hall indicates that the 7- to 12-foot range is used for more impersonal and formal situations. For example, this is the distance at which your boss talks to you when seated behind a desk. If you were to pull your chair around to the side of the boss's desk, a different kind of relationship would be signaled. The way furniture is arranged and the plants and wall hangings that people have in an office also convey signals about their values and interests and the type of relationship they want to establish. If the desk is placed between the office owner and the customer, client, or student, the desk acts as a barrier and suggests that the office owner wants formal and impersonal interaction. An office in which a desk is not used as a barrier and that has plants suggests the office owner wants warmer, less formal interactions.

Public Zone

This zone extends outward from 12 feet. Teachers and public speakers generally use the nearer range of public distance. In the farther range (beyond 25 feet), two-way communication is very difficult. Any speaker who voluntarily places considerable distance between himself and the audience is not interested in having a dialogue.

Territoriality

Territoriality is behavior characterized by identification with an area in a way that indicates ownership and a willingness to defend it against those who may invade it.[30] Many birds and small animals (including dogs, geese, snakes, and skunks) will strike out at much larger animals if they feel their territory is being invaded.

Territoriality also exists in human interactions. Traditionally, Dad and Mom have their chairs, and each child has a separate bedroom. The feeling of territorial ownership is sometimes extended to objects that are not really owned. Students in a class tend to select a certain seat to sit in. If someone else should happen to sit in that seat, the first student may feel that ownership rights are being violated, even though clearly the school campus owns the chairs.

Acquired properties—cars, homes, leisure-time equipment, plants, and clothes—are strong indicators of interests and values and often become topics of conversation. Material objects also communicate status messages, since wealthy people own more property than the poor. Generally, more personal space and greater privacy is granted to people of higher status. Before entering your boss's office, for example, you knock and then wait for an invitation. With people of an equal or lower status, you frequently walk right in.

Voice

Depending on emphasis, a word or phrase may carry many meanings. For example, look at how the meanings of the following sentences are changed by changing the word that is emphasized:

> *He's* giving this money to Herbie.
> (HE is the one giving the money; no one else.)
> He's *giving* this money to Herbie.
> (He is GIVING, not lending, the money.)
> He's giving *this* money to Herbie.
> (The money being exchanged is not from any other source; it is THIS money.)
> He's giving this *money* to Herbie.
> (MONEY is the unit of exchange, not a check.)
> He's giving this money to *Herbie*.
> (The recipient is HERBIE, not Eric or Bill or Rod.)[31]

Usually a person raises her voice at the end of a question and lowers it at the end of a declarative statement. Sometimes an individual intentionally manipulates her voice to contradict the verbal message.

In addition to emphasizing particular words, our voices communicate in other ways. These include length of pauses, tone, pitch, speed, volume, and disfluencies (such as stammering or saying "uh," "um," and "er"). Taken together, these factors have been called paralanguage, which deals with *how* something is said and not with what is said.[32]

By using paralanguage, group members can contradict their verbal messages. For example, by simply changing the tone or inflection in his or her voice, a person can convey the following messages literally or sarcastically:

> "I really like you."
> "I'm having a perfectly wonderful time."
> "You're really terrific."
> "There's nothing that I like better than liver sausage."

Mehrabian has found that when the paralanguage and the verbal message are contradictory, the paralanguage carries more meaning.[33] When there is a contradiction between words and the way something is said, receivers usually interpret the message by the way it was said.

An excellent way to learn more about how a group uses paralanguage is to videotape a meeting and then watch the replay. This process also provides valuable feedback about group members' use of other forms of nonverbal communication.

Physical Appearance

While it is common to hear people say that it is only inner beauty that really counts, research shows that outer beauty (physical attractiveness) influences responses for a broad range of interpersonal interactions. Singer found that male college professors tended to give higher grades to female students who were physically attractive than to those who were less attractive.[34] According to Mills and Aronson, attractive females could modify attitudes of male students more than less attractive females could.[35] Widgery and Webster have determined that attractive people, regardless of sex, will be rated high on credibility, which greatly increases their ultimate persuasiveness in a variety of areas—sales, public speaking, changing attitudes, being recognized as a credible counselor, and so on.[36] An attractive applicant for a position is much more apt to receive an employment offer than an unattractive applicant.

Unattractive defendants are more likely to be judged guilty in courtrooms and to receive longer sentences.[37] The evidence is clear that *initially* we respond much more favorably to physically attractive people. Attractiveness serves to open doors and create greater opportunities.

Physically attractive people outstrip less attractive people on a wide range of socially desirable evaluations, including personality, popularity, success, sociability, persuasiveness, sexuality, and often happiness.[38] Attractive women, for example, are more apt to be helped and less likely to be the objects of aggressive acts.[39] Less attractive people are at a disadvantage from early childhood. Teachers, for example, interact less (and less positively) with unattractive children.[40] Physical attractiveness is also a crucial factor in determining the number of personal interactions. Practically everyone prefers the most attractive date regardless of his or her own attractiveness and regardless of rejection by the most attractive date.[41]

Interestingly, unattractive men seen with attractive women are judged higher in a number of areas than attractive men seen with attractive women.[42] They are considered to make more money, be more successful, and have more intelligence. Apparently, the evaluators reasoned that unattractive males must compensate for their appearance in other areas to obtain dates with attractive women.

Our weight suggests certain stereotypes, which may or may not be accurate. People who are overweight are judged to be older, more old-fashioned, less strong physically, more talkative, less good-looking, more agreeable and good-natured, more sympathetic, more trusting, more dependent, and more warmhearted. Muscular individuals are rated as being stronger, better-looking, younger, more adventurous, more self-reliant, more mature in behavior, and more masculine. A person with a thin physique is rated as younger, more suspicious of others, more tense and nervous, less masculine, more pessimistic, quieter, more stubborn, and more inclined to be difficult.[43] Overweight and very thin people have been discriminated against when attempting to obtain jobs, purchase life insurance, adopt children, or enter college.[44] There are stereotypes (which may be erroneous) that people who are severely overweight or underweight have a low self-image. The important point here is that even our body weight communicates messages.

Being physically attractive does not mean that a person will be more intelligent, more successful, better adjusted, and happier than less attractive people. Attractiveness initially opens more doors to success, but after a door is opened, it is performance that determines outcome. It should also be noted that everyone has the ability to improve his or her physical appearance. Dieting, exercising, managing stress, learning to be assertive, adequate sleep, and good grooming habits will substantially improve a person's physical appearance.

Exercise 5.9: Reading Nonverbal Cues

GOAL: This exercise is designed to help you apply the material in this chapter on nonverbal cues to a real-life situation.

1. Go to a restaurant (a dining hall on campus is fine) and observe two strangers who are dining. For about 10 to 15 minutes record information about the nonverbal communication cues of both individuals.

	Person A	Person B
Posture		
Body Orientation		
Facial Expressions		
Eye Contact		
Gestures		
Touching		
Clothing		
Personal Boundaries		
Physical Appearance		

2. **Review the material you wrote down. Speculate about the following for each of these people: What is the socioeconomic status of each? Is either one stressed, happy, upset, and so on? What appears to be the nature of the relationship between these two individuals?**

Environment

Perhaps all of us have been in immaculate homes that have "unliving rooms" with furniture coverings, plastic lamp coverings, and spotless ashtrays that send nonverbal messages of "Do not get me dirty," "Do not touch," "Do not put your feet up," and "Stay alert to avoid a mistake." Owners of these homes wonder why guests cannot relax and have a good time. They are unaware that the environment is communicating messages that lead guests to feel uncomfortable.

A study by Maslow and Mintz found that the attractiveness of a room shapes the kind of communication that takes place and influences the happiness and energy of people working in it.[45] The researchers used an "ugly" room, which looked like a janitor's closet, and a "beautiful" room, which was furnished with drapes, carpeting, and comfortable furniture. To gauge the subjects' energy levels and feelings of well-being, researchers asked them to rate a series of pictures of models' faces. When subjects were in the ugly room, they became tired and bored sooner, taking longer to complete their task. They described the room as producing fatigue, headaches, monotony, and irritability. When the subjects moved to the beautiful room, they displayed a greater desire to work. They also rated the faces they were judging higher and communicated many more feelings of comfort, importance, and enjoyment. This experiment provides evidence supporting the commonsense notion that workers do a better job and generally feel better when they are in an attractive environment.

Wall decorations, types of furniture, and placement of furniture in a meeting area convey messages as to whether the group leader wants informal, relaxed communications, or formal, to-the-point communications. A round table, for example, suggests egalitarian communication, while a rectangular table suggests status and power differences. At a rectangular table, high-status people generally sit at one end of the table, while low-status individuals sit at the other. If sides of equal strength hold a meeting around a rectangular table, each side sits at opposite ends, rather than intermingling. A classroom in which the chairs are in a circle suggests the instructor wants to create an informal atmosphere. A classroom with the chairs in rows suggests the instructor wants to create a formal atmosphere.

When clients come into the offices of helping professionals, the offices communicate messages. A clean, neat waiting room with comfortable chairs, plants, and soft background music communicates warmth, caring, and a professional approach. Negative messages are sent by an unclean room, hard chairs, few wall decorations, and loose paint on walls. A messy office may suggest to a client that the worker is overwhelmed, perhaps burning out, and therefore is unlikely to be of much help. A worker can *tell* his clients he wants them to feel comfortable by providing comfortable padded chairs instead of hard wooden ones, by providing tissues, by having plants and wall decorations that suggest the worker really likes his job, and by arranging the furniture to facilitate communication.

Other Nonverbal Cues

Social workers need to be aware of other nonverbal cues. When people become anxious, angry, embarrassed, or otherwise emotionally excited, they have a pronounced facial blush or extensive reddening of the chest and neck. In therapy, such a cue may signal that the client is focusing on emotionally charged material, which often needs to be explored.

The breathing pattern of a group member is another cue. When a member is anxious or emotionally excited, breathing rate increases, which can be observed by watching the person's chest.

Another nonverbal cue commonly observed by psychotherapists, educators, and others is a change in muscle tension. When you become acquainted with someone, a common cue that you often use (and frequently are not aware of) to tell whether that person is relaxed or tense (or emotionally excited) is the degree of tenseness of muscles in that person's face, neck, and arms.

When a person is relaxed, the temperature on the surface of his or her hands is normally 10 to 15 degrees warmer than when the person is tense. As part of the reaction to stress, blood flows inward. When a person is relaxed, blood flows outward and warms the hands and skin. When you shake hands with someone, you are apt to receive information about whether that person is relaxed or under stress. (It should be noted that variables other than stress may cause a person's hand to feel colder. For example, the person may have been outside in cold weather or recently held a cold drink.)

■ GROUP EXERCISES

Exercise A: The Johari Window

GOAL: To introduce the Johari Window and demonstrate how it can be used to further self-awareness.
NOTE: The instructor should lead this exercise, and students should be told **not to disclose personal information.**

Step 1. The group leader describes what the Johari Window is and how increased self-disclosure generally leads to greater self-awareness and more meaningful relationships. The group leader may also describe why group members are initially reluctant to self-disclose but gradually begin to do so. With appropriate self-disclosure in groups, cohesion and group morale generally increase. The group leader should note that personal information should *not be* disclosed during this exercise.

Step 2. The members pair up into subgroups. Each member draws a Johari Window representing himself or herself and then his or her partner. These drawings should be made privately.

Step 3. The partners share their drawings with each other. Each describes the reasons for drawing the window in the form that is displayed. The two partners discuss the similarities and differences in their drawings; for example, why did A draw himself or herself as not being very open while B drew A as being a very open person?

Step 4. The class discusses thoughts about the merits and shortcomings of the Johari Window and what they learned from the exercise.

Exercise B: Defense Mechanisms

GOAL: To become more aware of the use of defense mechanisms.

Step 1. The group leader begins by stating the purpose of the exercise and giving brief descriptions of common defense mechanisms (see "Defense Mechanisms" in this chapter).

Step 2. Each member lists on a sheet of paper the three defense mechanisms a *friend* uses most often and then describes one or two examples of each. The leader explains that students will be asked to share what they write with two other students.

Step 3. After Step 2 is completed, the class forms subgroups of three students, and each member is asked to share what he or she wrote. The two listeners should provide feedback on whether the defense mechanisms have desirable or undesirable consequences. For the undesirable, the members discuss more effective approaches.

Step 4. The class discusses what they learned from the exercise and how they feel about it.

Exercise C: Distortions in Transmitting Information

GOAL: To demonstrate the effects of transmitting information through a series of one-way and two-way communications among group members.

Step 1. The leader explains the purpose of the exercise, asks 10 students to step outside, and informs them that their task will be to repeat to someone else what they hear. The remaining students are observers. The first 5 students will use one-way communication, and the second 5 will use two-way communication. A copy of the following story is distributed to the observers, who are asked to record what each participant adds to the communication and what each participant leaves out of the communication.

Step 2. The first participant returns, and the leader slowly reads the following story to him.

> A farmer in western Kansas put a tin roof on his barn. Then a small tornado blew the roof off, and when the farmer found it two counties away, it was twisted and mangled beyond repair.
>
> A friend and lawyer advised him that the Ford Motor Company would pay him a good price for the scrap tin, and the farmer decided he would ship the roof up to the company to see how much he could get for it. He crated it up in a very big wooden box and sent it off to Dearborn, Michigan, marking it plainly with his return address so that the Ford Company would know where to send the check.
>
> Twelve weeks passed, and the farmer didn't hear from the Ford Company. Finally, he was just on the verge of writing them to find out what was the matter, when he received an envelope from them. It said, "We don't know what hit your car, mister, but we'll have it fixed for you by the fifteenth of next month."[46]

The story is read once and no questions are allowed. The second participant enters, the first repeats the story to the second, and so on. The fifth participant should repeat the story to the observers, *and this fifth repetition should be tape-recorded to play back later.*

Step 3. The sixth participant enters and is told that he or she may ask questions about the story he or she is about to hear. The story is read and questions answered. The process is repeated until the tenth participant repeats the story to the observers. The tenth repetition should be tape-recorded to play back later.

Step 4. The group leader explains the effects of leveling, sharpening, and assimilation on the transmission of information. Some observers summarize verbally what each participant added to and left out of the story.

Step 5. The group leader describes why two-way communication is generally superior to one-way communication. The group leader should then play back the fifth and tenth participants' descriptions of the story. A discussion should then follow as to which version was closer to the original story.

Exercise D: The Intruder

GOAL: To present a model for communication and to demonstrate that there are fairly wide variations in what students perceive.

Step 1. Prior to the meeting the group leader arranges for a friend or acquaintance to barge into the class and create a scene. This accomplice should not be known to anyone in class.

Step 2. The group is informed that the purpose of this exercise is to become aware of factors that reduce or prevent effective communication. The group leader describes the communication model presented at the beginning of this chapter. When the group leader is nearly finished, the leader should *unobtrusively* signal the accomplice to enter. The accomplice should barge in, create a ruckus, say some disparaging things about the group leader, threaten the group leader, and then leave angrily.

Step 3. The leader explains that the purpose of this exercise is to see how closely the students' perceptions match. Ask each student to write down on a sheet of paper the following information:
   1. The intruder's height and weight
   2. What the intruder was wearing
   3. What the intruder looked like
   4. What the intruder said and did

Step 4. Several descriptions are read aloud and differences discussed. If there are sharp differences, why did they occur? The leader explains that perceptual differences between people are a major barrier to effective communication.

Exercise E: Active Listening

GOAL: To develop active-listening skills.

Step 1. The leader explains the purpose of the exercise and describes what active listening is and what it is designed to accomplish. The leader indicates that active listening involves using two types of statements—reflecting feelings and restating content.

Step 2. Students pair off. (If there is someone without a partner, the leader should participate.) One member of each pair selects a topic to discuss for about 10 minutes. The topic may involve (1) a philosophical or moral issue such as abortion, (2) a problem with a friend or a relative, or (3) a problem at school.

Step 3. The member who selects a topic discusses the issue for about 10 minutes. The listener should try to respond solely with active-listening statements.

Step 4. After the discussion, the presenter should discuss with the listener the quality of the active-listening statements. Did the listener make the mistake of making suggestions, asking questions, or beginning to talk about personal experiences? Did active listening motivate the presenter to continue talking? Did the presenter perceive the active-listening statements to be primarily "natural" or "artificial"?

The listener should then discuss with the presenter his or her thoughts and feelings about using active-listening statements. Did the listener want to make other types of statements? If so, what?

Step 5. The roles should then be reversed and the process repeated.

Step 6. Students form a circle and discuss the merits and shortcomings of active listening. Did any unique or unusual events occur?

Exercise F: Chairs, Stickpins, and Coat Hangers

GOAL: To identify and observe nonverbal messages that people respond to and to give feedback on the ways in which nonverbal messages are used constructively.

Step 1. The leader describes the purpose of the exercise. She asks the class to identify various types of nonverbal behaviors on the blackboard. A partial list would include:

Muscle tension	Breathing patterns
Eye contact	Clothes
Smiles	Distance between people
Eyebrow movements	communicating
Gestures	Touch
Voice tone	Silence and pauses
Facial color	Facial expressions

Step 2. The class forms groups of three students each. Each subgroup member picks an unimportant topic out of a hat or box. Possible topics include a chair, a stickpin, a coat hanger, or a bar of soap. Insignificant topics are suggested so that the focus will be on nonverbal communication.

Step 3. Each group member talks for a minute and a half to his or her small group on the selected topic. The two who are observing in each group should note the speaker's nonverbal signals. The leader should inform the subgroups when it is time for each member to start and to stop talking.

Step 4. After all three group members have spoken, group members share what they liked about the way each communicated nonverbally.

Step 5. Group members are then asked to think about their nonverbal communication *privately* and about what they could change to communicate more effectively nonverbally.

Exercise G: Nonverbal Cues

GOAL: To learn the kinds of nonverbal cues that should be used to obtain social work employment and establish a relaxed nonthreatening atmosphere for clients.

Step 1. The group leader states the goals of the exercise. The first task for each member of the class is to assume that he or she is a director of a social service agency interviewing applicants for a social work position. As director, which nonverbal cues might enter into the decision as to which applicant to hire? (Responses should be listed on the blackboard.)

Step 2. The second task for each student is to assume the role of a client who is emotionally upset and has painful decisions to make, such as whether to get a divorce. As a client, which nonverbal cues by a counselor would establish a relaxed, nonthreatening atmosphere that would increase the chances of the client fully sharing concerns? As responses are given, they are also listed on the blackboard.

Step 3. The similarities and differences between the two lists are discussed. For the differences, the possible reasons for these discrepancies are also discussed.

Exercise H: A Popular Faculty Member

GOAL: To become more aware of using nonverbal communication in assessing human behavior.

Step 1. The group leader selects a popular faculty member with whom the students are familiar. The class indicates the specific nonverbal cues used by this instructor to increase his or her effectiveness. The following clues should be considered: clothing, eyes, facial expressions, posture, physical appearance, gestures and other body movements, and paralanguage.

Step 2. With this same instructor in mind, the class focuses on the appearance of this faculty member's office and imagines that this is the only information they have about the instructor. The class then discusses the nonverbal messages sent by the types of objects, arrangement of objects, and general conditions of the office. Next, the class discusses which of these nonverbal messages give an impression different from what the instructor is like. Which are consistent? Finally, the class discusses the types of interaction the office atmosphere suggests should take place—for example, whether the communication is expected to be formal and businesslike, or relaxed and informal.

Exercise I: Double Messages

GOAL: To understand how verbal messages can contradict nonverbal messages.

Step 1. The class divides into two groups of equal size and is informed that this is an exercise in keeping conversations going. One group leaves for a separate room or the hallway.

Step 2. The remaining, or first, group is told that this is really an exercise in learning more about how people react when someone seems to be saying one thing verbally and another nonverbally. Each member's task is to pick a topic to discuss with another person in the other group for 10 minutes. The topic may be anything, such as politics, movies, or sports. While discussing the topic, each person should periodically *nonverbally* contradict his or her verbal message by using facial expressions, gestures, laughter, and voice fluctuations. Furthermore, each person should note and observe the partner's nonverbal reactions to these double messages.

Step 3. The second group is told that each person will be paired with someone in the first group. The partner in the first group will start a conversation on a topic. The task of each person in this second group is to keep the discussion going and to inject controversial topics into the conversation.

Step 4. The room should be large enough to allow individuals to spread out and carry on conversations. Perhaps two rooms can be used. Individuals from both groups pair off, and discuss the topic for approximately 10 minutes.

Step 5. The real purpose of the exercise is now explained to the second group. The first group discusses the following questions with the second group listening. What nonverbal cues did they use to contradict their verbal messages? Was sending a double message hard to do? What were the reactions to these double messages?

Then, the second group discusses the following: How did they feel about their partners during this exercise? Did they believe what their partners were saying verbally? How did they cope with the double messages they were receiving? When nonverbal messages conflicted with verbal messages, which were they more likely to believe?

Exercise J: The Flat Tire

GOAL: To become more aware of individual differences and skills in using nonverbal cues to relay messages.

Step 1. The leader explains that the exercise involves students relaying messages nonverbally. Four students volunteer to leave the room. Then, the following is read to a fifth volunteer who must try to remember and communicate it nonverbally to the first student who returns. That student will then nonverbally communicate it to the second student, and so on.

> You are driving a car and your right front tire goes flat. You get out and kick the tire. You go to the trunk, open it, and there's no spare. You angrily slam the trunk shut. You then attempt to hitchhike to a gas station you recently passed. A motorcyclist stops to give you a ride to the gas station.

The volunteers receiving the message may ask questions, but the senders must communicate their answers nonverbally.

While these five volunteers are acting out this exercise, the remainder of the class responds to the following questions on paper each time the message is relayed: What did the relayer add to or delete from the message? If there was a communication breakdown as a result of a weakness in a nonverbal cue, how could this have been avoided by using a better one?

Step 2. The person who receives the final message states it verbally. This message is compared to the original and the whole class discusses the two questions in Step 1.

Exercise K: Communicating While Blindfolded

GOAL: To better understand how communication is affected when the sense of sight is not used.

Step 1. The leader explains that nonverbal communication is heavily dependent on the sense of sight. We watch other people's facial expressions, eyes, posture, hand gestures, and body movements. The leader describes the goal of the exercise and asks for five or six volunteers. These volunteers sit in a circle in the middle of the class. The volunteers are given a controversial topic to discuss (for example, whether the elderly who have a terminal illness and are in severe pain have a right to take their own lives). All volunteers are either blindfolded or asked to keep their eyes tightly shut while discussing the topic. The topic is discussed for 10 to 15 minutes.

Step 2. At the end of 10 or 15 minutes, the discussion ends. The volunteers remove their blindfolds or open their eyes, and discuss the following questions:
1. How did it feel to be blindfolded?
2. How did not being able to see affect the communications?
3. Did having a blindfold on interfere with being able to concentrate on what was said?
4. Was it difficult to hear?
5. Do they think they gestured more or less than they usually do?
6. During this exercise, did they become aware of anything they had not noticed before?
7. Does not being able to see the people you are talking to substantially hamper communication? If yes, in what ways?

Step 3. As an additional optional step, this exercise may be repeated with a new group of volunteers.

Exercise L: Giving and Receiving Feedback about Nonverbal Communication

GOAL: To observe nonverbal communication in others and receive feedback about nonverbal communication.

Step 1. The group leader states the purpose of the exercise and divides the class into two groups of equal size. If there is an uneven number, the group leader can participate. Each member in one group should pair up with someone in the other group.

Step 2. One group sits in an inner circle, and the other group members sit in an outer circle to observe the nonverbal communication of their partners. The inner circle discusses a controversial topic that will arouse strong emotions. The topic can be abortion or whether a male and female who are both severely retarded should legally be permitted to marry and to have children. The discussion should continue for 10 to 20 minutes. People in the outer circle observe the nonverbal communication of their partners—gestures, body movements, eye behavior, paralanguage, facial expressions, and so on.

Step 3. After the discussion, the observing partner informs his or her partner as to what nonverbal cues were used and what messages were communicated. After the observing partner is finished, the partner who was observed should have an opportunity to discuss his or her degree of agreement with the observer's interpretations.

Step 4. The roles of the partners are reversed and Steps 2 and 3 repeated.

Step 5. The class discusses what they learned from this exercise.

Exercise M: Zones of Personal Space

GOAL: To observe how the distance between communicators affects what people are thinking and feeling.

Step 1. The leader explains the purpose of the exercise. Two people volunteer for an exercise to illustrate these effects.

Step 2. The volunteers stand at the farthest corners of the room, away from each other. Their task is to slowly, very slowly, move toward each other. As they are slowly moving toward each other, they engage in small talk about topics of their choosing. They should continue slowly walking and conversing until they touch. When they touch they should slowly start moving away from each other but continue to converse. At the point when they are most comfortable in conversing, they should stop.

Step 3. Other volunteers may be selected to repeat the exercise until interest wanes.

Step 4. The volunteers involved in this exercise should then determine the distances between partners that were most comfortable and least comfortable for conversing. The leader of the exercise should note the points at which the various pairs were most comfortable in conversing, and then make some statements about the extent of the congruence between these "most comfortable points" and the theoretical material in the chapter as to the "most comfortable point" for conversing in this type of situation.

CHAPTER SIX

Task Groups

GOALS

Social workers and other helping professionals are often called upon to chair committees, focus groups, teams, and other task groups. This chapter presents guidelines for leading task groups, and describes the two main purposes of task groups: problem solving and decision making.

■ A VARIETY OF TASK GROUPS

Task groups are used to generate new ideas, to make decisions, and to find solutions to organizational problems. Task groups have three primary purposes: (1) meeting clients needs, (2) meeting organizational needs, and (3) meeting community needs.

Task groups to meet client needs include treatment teams. A few examples will illustrate treatment teams. A group of professionals who deliver home-based hospice care may meet weekly to review the services being provided to patients. Professionals at a county mental health center may meet weekly to review the services being provided to clients who are living in the community. Professionals at a rehabilitation center may meet weekly to review services to clients at that facility. Often, at such meetings a second focus is on *team building;* time is devoted to improving how members function as a group. At times, treatment teams meet for the purpose of developing, monitoring, and coordinating treatment plans for a particular client—for example, professionals at a mental health center may meet to develop a treatment plan for a very depressed elderly man whose wife has recently died.

Task groups to meet organizational needs include committees and boards of directors. The most common type of task group is the committee. Members of a committee may be appointed or elected. A committee is "charged" with completing one or more tasks. Committees may be temporary creations (ad hoc committees) or be more permanent parts of the structure of an organization (standing committees). A board of directors is a governing board charged with responsibility for setting the policies governing the agency. Members of the board provide guidance to the management of an organization.

There are a variety of task groups to meet community needs. There are social action groups that empower members to engage in collective, planned change efforts to improve some aspect of the community's social or physical environment. For example, nontraditional students at a campus may organize and advocate for a child-care center being established at the campus. *Coalitions* (sometimes called alliances) are groups of organizations or social action groups that come together to exert influence by sharing expertise and resources. Coalition members believe their common goals have a greater chance of being achieved by united action than by members acting alone. For example, several organizations, local government leaders, and civil leaders may form a coalition to explore ways to reduce racial tensions in a community. *Delegate councils* are formed for the purpose of facilitating interagency cooperation and communication, and studying community-wide social issues. Members of delegate councils are elected or appointed by a variety of sponsoring units. For example, a representative from each of the human service agencies in a community may have monthly meetings to share information, discuss ways to improve interagency communication, and study emerging issues (such as increases in family violence).

GUIDELINES FOR LEADING TASK GROUPS

A number of guidelines will be given. These guidelines are not mandates as some circumstances will result in the desirability of deviating from these guidelines.

Establishing the Group's Purpose

The first and critically important question is "What is the group's purpose?" Toseland and Rivas state: "A statement of purpose should be broad enough to encompass different goals, yet specific enough to define the common nature of the group's purpose. A clear statement of purpose helps members answer the question 'What are we doing together?'"[1]

A variety of sources may generate the group's purpose. A social worker may seek to form a task group to study an emerging social issue. An agency director, or agency staff may identify the need for the establishment of an ad hoc committee. Recipients of services may request that a task force be established to advocate against government proposed cuts in services. A group of ministers may advocate for the establishment of a delegate council of community agencies and civic leaders to study the need for an expansion of church-affiliated child-care centers.

Potential Sponsorship of the Task Group

In assessing an organization as sponsor for the proposed group, the organizer(s) of the group should pay careful attention to the purpose of the group and the organization's policies and goals. A delegate council of ministers, rabbis, and priests may be a good fit for sponsoring a task force to study the need for an expansion of church-affiliated child-care centers in a community. On the other hand, the local Hooter's restaurant may not be a good fit for sponsoring a task force to study the sociopolitical environment for women in the community.

Selecting Potential Members

Potential members should be selected for their expertise, their interest in the task, and their position and power (including their political influence) to help the group accomplish its purpose. It is also important to seek diversity in membership (including ethnicity, gender, age, and sociocultural factors). Representation of consumers and potential consumers of services under review should also be included.

Recruiting Members

Recruiting can be accomplished in a variety of ways. Directors of organizations and agencies may be asked (by phone, mail, or direct contact) to appoint a representative. If an organizer of a group has a list of potential members, announcements can be mailed directly to them. Announcements may be posted in public places. There may be television, newspaper, and radio announcements.

For ad hoc committees and standing committees within agencies, membership is usually determined by the director, by an executive committee of the agency, or in staff meetings. For many task groups, direct contact with desired group members is often the most effective recruitment approach.

Size of the Group

The organizer needs to make decisions regarding how many members are needed to accomplish the tasks effectively and efficiently. There is no optimal size for task groups. Larger groups are better for accomplishing complex tasks, partly because of the increase in expertise and resources of a larger membership. In larger groups, fewer difficulties arise when one or more members are absent. Larger groups also have disadvantages. Each member has less of an opportunity to speak, and each member will receive less individualized attention. There is also a greater danger of competing alliances being formed. Larger groups are also more difficult for the leader to manage. They frequently require more formalized procedures (such as parliamentary procedures) to accomplish their meeting agendas. They also have greater difficulty achieving cohesiveness and reaching consensus.

Orienting Members to the Group

The purpose needs to be carefully explained. Members' views about the importance of the purpose need to be attended to. Members may be oriented by the organizer of the group prior to the first meeting. During the first meeting the purpose of the group should again be reviewed, and perhaps attention should be given to establishing more specific goals for the group. Individual goals of members may need to be discussed. Prior to the first meeting it may be desirable to send background material to the members. At the first meeting, if questions arise about how the group will conduct its business, discussions should occur, leading to the establishing of routine procedures. Task groups often adopt the following routine procedure: reviewing and approving the minutes from the previous meeting, making announcements, discussing old business, and bringing up and discussing new business.

Meeting Place and Room

The setting for the group has a profound effect on the conduct of group meetings and on the behavior of group members. Room size, chair comfort, acoustics, seating arrangements, furnishings, refreshments, and atmosphere should all be considered. Too large a room can put too much distance between members and result in some members tuning out. Too small a room can lead to discomfort and is especially challenging for anyone who tends to be claustrophobic. People in a wheelchair will need wheelchair access. Carpeting, lighting, work tables, and other furnishings need to be considered in order to create an informal, comfortable atmosphere. Some people physically react to lighting that is too bright. Overly dim lighting is annoying to many people.

First Meeting

If the members are not already familiar with one another, introduction of members by the leader needs to be facilitated. For example, the leader may first introduce himself or herself and give a brief description of his or her background experiences that are related to the group's purpose. Group members may then be asked to do the same, often in round-robin fashion. Usually it is advantageous to then use an appropriate ice breaker, such as "Tell me something personal about you that we would find surprising."

The purpose and function of the group needs to be discussed as it is perceived by the leader, other members, and the sponsoring organization(s). The task and socioemotional aspects of the group need to be attended to and balanced by the leader. Group goals need to be set. The leader should attend to facilitating the members' motivation to work in the group. Perhaps obstacles to achieving individual and group goals may need to be discussed.

It is very helpful to have an agenda for the first, and future, meetings. Often, it is desirable to send the agenda to members prior to the first meeting.

Working with Resistive and Disruptive Members

Resistance is to be expected. Ambivalent feelings about change are common, as it is rare for changes to be proposed and worked on without ambivalent feelings. Acknowledging members' ambivalence is a helpful way to get members to recognize their reactions to change. An open discussion of members' ambivalence issues and their questions about the capacity of a group to achieve a goal helps all members to problem solve and arrive at creative approaches for achieving desired changes and goals. Leaders should treat members' suggestions and ideas about how to proceed with respect. (Additional material on working with disruptive members is presented in Chapter 4.)

Although task groups are usually successful and useful, they can be a source of frustration for members when they function ineffectively. This writer remembers a college promotions committee meeting he attended that lasted for eight hours (from 4 P.M. to midnight), dragging along simply because some committee members must "not have had a life" as they enjoyed the opportunity to talk about topics unrelated to promotions. Meetings that are not run well are boring and unsatisfying. The leader has an obligation to keep the members focused on the task and to move the meeting along to progress in completing the agenda items. Toseland and Risas state:

> . . . well-run meetings can be a positive experience. They have draw people together by creating effective teamwork in which ideas are shared, feelings are expressed, and support is developed for group members and for the decisions made by the group. There are few experiences in the workplace to equal the sense of cohesion, commitment, and satisfaction that members feel when their ideas have been heard, appreciated, and used in resolving a difficult issue and arriving at a decision.[2]

The Middle Stages

The primary purpose of task groups are problem solving and decision making. Members, including the leader, often need to complete a number of tasks related to accomplishing group goals prior to meetings. (Some members are conscientious about doing this, while some drive a group "crazy" by promising to do certain tasks and never completing them.) When the latter happens and such people are identified the group is probably better off not assigning essential tasks to such members. In certain task groups parliamentary procedures are used to conduct business. Most people learn parliamentary procedures through "modeling." They observe a group using parliamentary procedures and learn to use such procedures themselves (including making motions, seconding motions, having a discussion, amending the motion, calling the questions, and voting on the motion or on the amended motion.)

Adjourning a Meeting

When a meeting is near the ending time it is often desirable for the leader to summarize what has been accomplished during the meeting. It may be constructive to praise members for their work. Future agenda items should be specified and recorded. Perhaps a statement needs to be made about the progress that has been made in terms of the overall schedule. It is also often desirable to summarize as clearly as possible the tasks that members agreed to accomplish before the next meeting. The date, time, and place of the next meeting should be established.

Evaluating and Terminating

It is essential for a group to evaluate the extent to which the group has accomplished its goals during the middle phases and when the group is nearing the time when it plans to terminate. Evaluation methods and approaches are described at some length in Chapter 13.

The ending of a group is often a bittersweet experience for members. They are pleased about their accomplishments (which may be celebrated with a get-together, perhaps at a restaurant). The ending of a group may also have unpleasant aspects. Members may be somewhat sad if the goals that were set have not been fully accomplished. (This writer remembers a committee he worked on that involved writing a great proposal; the members looked forward to doing the project if the grant was approved. Sadly, it was not.) Some members may also experience sadness as they have enjoyed the camaraderie of working with others and realize it is ending. Some members may have enjoyed the excitement that is generated when a group continues to creatively problem solve. Considerable material is provided on the process of terminating a task group in Chapter 13.

Exercise 6.1: Successful and Unsuccessful Group Experiences

GOAL: This exercise is designed to have you reflect about how you felt when you participated in a successful group, and also when you participated in an unsuccessful group.

1. **Describe a successful group in which you participated. Indicate why you defined this group as successful—perhaps the goals were accomplished or perhaps you enjoyed the camaraderie, and so on.**

2. **What were the feelings you experienced about participating in this group?**

3. **Describe an unsuccessful group in which you participated. Indicate why you defined this group as unsuccessful—perhaps the goals were not accomplished, you disliked certain members, or you were asked to leave, and so on.**

4. **What were the feelings you experienced about participating in this group?**

■ PROBLEM-SOLVING APPROACH

In a nutshell, practically all of the work done by social work practitioners involves problem solving. Social workers use a problem-solving approach extensively to help individuals, families, small groups, organizations, and community groups. Problem solving has been defined by Johnson and Johnson:

> *Problem solving* is the process of resolving the unsettled matters, of finding an answer to a difficulty; it is a process that results in a solution to a problem, and it involves changing the actual state of affairs until it is identical with the desired state of affairs.[3]

Problem solving can be broken down into six steps: (1) identifying and defining the problem, (2) assessing the size and causes of the problem, (3) developing alternative strategies or plans for solving it, (4) assessing the merits and shortcomings of these alternative strategies, (5) selecting and implementing the most desirable strategy or strategies, and (6) evaluating the success of the strategies used.

Identification and Definition

The more precisely and accurately a problem is defined, the easier it is to solve. Contrast the following two statements describing problems: "Fifty-seven young children in a six-block-square area of this city are in need of care during the daytime because their parents are working." Here the terms of the problem are defined concretely. Because the problem group, its locale, and a time period are specified, the problem can be easily addressed. Now consider another example: "Some children in some school systems in this city seem to be becoming more apathetic about the way their lives are going, and something should be done about it." Since no particular group and no clear symptoms have been identified, there is no way to determine a solution.

When using the problem-solving approach, a group should initially (1) determine the actual or current state of affairs and (2) specify the desired state of affairs. The differences between the actual and desired state of affairs should be thoroughly discussed and agreed upon. If the group concludes that there are serious negative consequences associated with the actual state of affairs, then members' commitment to reach the desired state of affairs is apt to be high.

Arriving at a group definition of a workable problem can be difficult. Brainstorming, which is described in this chapter, can help to develop descriptions of the problem. These descriptions are then rephrased until an agreed-upon definition, including a precise statement of both the actual and the desired state of affairs, is reached.

Assessment of Size and Causes

Once the workable problem is defined, the group next gathers information to help it assess the magnitude and causes of the problem. In assessing the magnitude, the following questions arise: Who is affected? How many people are affected? How seriously? Where are they located?

Often, identifying the causes of a problem will suggest strategies for resolving it. If high unemployment is a problem in a state and most of the unemployed are untrained for available jobs, this suggests that programs to train the unemployed for available jobs will help alleviate unemployment. Only rarely is it possible to resolve a problem without knowing its causes. For example, some urban renewal projects have rebuilt blighted areas without knowing all the causes that led to the deterioration of housing and living conditions.

Development of Alternative Strategies

The third problem-solving step is to formulate alternative ways to solve the problem. Brainstorming is a useful technique for generating a wide range of strategies. Sometimes, the wildest suggestions may stimulate other members to come up with one or more pragmatic alternatives. If group members cannot produce workable strategies, outside experts may be consulted as an alternative to brainstorming.

Assessment of Strategies

Next, the merits and shortcomings of each strategy must be assessed, and often a cost-benefit analysis of each strategy is done. Costs include time, material resources, and professional fees. Although the actual costs and benefits of each strategy are often difficult to assess objectively, reasoned assessments must be made as to what resources will be needed and what the outcomes of applying these resources will be. For example, if racial segregation is a problem in a large city, judgments must be made as to whether the costs of school busing to achieve school integration (such as transportation costs and movement away from the benefits of the neighborhood school concept) justify this type of busing.

Selection and Implementation

The fifth step involves two separate processes. The first is *decision making*, in which the group selects one of the proposed alternatives. (Decision making in a group can be done in a variety of ways. Many of these approaches are described later in this chapter.) After a strategy is selected, the group must *implement* the strategy. Generally, the more solid the group support for the selected strategy, the greater the chances for its successful implementation. Required tasks must be identified, jobs assigned, and deadlines set for starting and completing each task.

Evaluation

Once implementation is complete, evaluating the strategy's success in two areas is necessary: Was the strategy fully implemented, and what were its effects? The main criterion is the extent to which the strategy has narrowed the discrepancy between the actual and desired state of affairs. This is why precise descriptions of each problem are necessary.

If the strategy was not fully implemented, then additional efforts may be required. If the strategy has been fully implemented without achieving the desired state of affairs, perhaps new strategies are in order. In addition, implementation of a strategy may expose other problems. For example, the 1960s Civil Rights movement focused on reducing racial discrimination. But it also generated awareness that many other groups are discriminated against: women, homosexuals, and people with a disability.

The evaluation phase should demonstrate the extent to which the problem has been resolved, what remains to be resolved, and what new problems have been identified. Not surprisingly, the evaluation phase often leads to another problem-solving effort. The old problem is redefined or another problem is identified. The steps of the problem-solving approach are then repeated.

■ BARRIERS TO EFFECTIVE PROBLEM SOLVING

There are several barriers to effective problem solving: inadequate definitions; invalid hypotheses; poor communication; and lack of skills, resources, and motivation within the group.

Inadequate Definitions

If a problem is stated imprecisely, individual group members are apt to vary in their interpretations of the problem. For example, take the following problem statement: "Children are under too much pressure in our school systems." Possible interpretations of "too much pressure" include academic pressure, pressure to use alcohol and drugs, religious pressure, pressure from teachers and parents, pressure resulting from racial tensions, pressure to have sexual experiences, and pressure to break the law. Unless the problem is defined more precisely, group members will probably disagree on how to solve it.

Invalid Hypotheses

Closely related to inadequate definitions, invalid hypotheses and theories about the causes of a problem also erect a formidable barrier. Emotionally disturbed people were once thought to be possessed by demons, for example, and in the early 1900s, criminals were considered to be mentally retarded.[4] Two hundred years ago physicians thought that bloodletting (through using leeches) would help heal people who were physically ill. If a group has faulty theories about the causes of a problem, the members are apt to develop ineffective strategies to solve it. For example, we know today that seeking to drive demons out of someone who has emotional problems will not alleviate emotional trauma, and bloodletting does not heal.

Poor Communication

Poor communication in the group may exist for a variety of reasons. Group members may not possess well-developed communication skills, or some may withhold information in an attempt to manipulate others in the group. Interpersonal conflict between group members may inhibit them from participating effectively. With poor communication, a group will generate fewer alternative strategies and inadequately assess their potential consequences. In addition, enthusiasm and commitment to implement the proposed group strategy will be diminished.

Lack of Skills

A group may lack the skills to define and solve a problem. A group may not have the expertise to design and conduct a necessary research study, for instance, or the skills to write a grant proposal to obtain needed resources. When the group lacks an essential skill, the group must acquire the skill by recruiting appropriate new members or retaining an outside consultant.

Lack of Resources

There never seem to be sufficient financial resources to accomplish everything that is desired. A planning group to combat the homeless problem, for example, may be partially stifled by lack of funds to build a sufficient number of low-cost housing units for the homeless.

Lack of Motivation

Some groups fail to solve problems because their members are not motivated to do so. By creating a supportive, trusting, cooperative atmosphere, a leader can encourage unmotivated members to participate. Unmotivated members can be asked to share their reasons for not participating, and perhaps changes can be made to encourage their input. The motivated members can also carry the group to some initial successes in the hope that the unmotivated members would be inspired to participate more. Relatively easy tasks could be delegated to these individuals, who should be complimented for their efforts.

■ BRAINSTORMING

Brainstorming is a procedure designed to generate ideas in quantity through the full participation of all group members. The procedure helps individuals share their ideas without the interruption of discussion or evaluation. By allowing members to present any idea that comes to mind, more and often better ideas are generated than if the same people had worked independently. Brainstorming was developed by Osborn, who outlined the following ground rules nearly half a century ago.[5] Brainstorming can last anywhere from one minute to half an hour. The session continues as long as ideas are being generated. Each session is to be freewheeling and open. The wilder and more absurd the ideas the better, as these ideas may lead to a breakthrough or a new course of action. Criticism or evaluation of any idea is not allowed. The ideas are simply listed for the group as rapidly as possible without comment, discussion, or clarification.

In this case the quantity of ideas counts, not quality. A greater number of ideas will increase the likelihood of usable ideas. Members are encouraged to build on the ideas of other group members whenever possible, so that thoughts are expanded and new combinations of ideas are formulated. The focus is always on a single issue or problem. Members should not skip from problem to problem, or try to brainstorm a multiproblem situation.

A relaxed, congenial, cooperative atmosphere should be promoted, and all members, no matter how shy and reluctant to participate, should be encouraged to contribute. It is often advisable to limit members to one idea at a time so that less vocal individuals will feel encouraged to express their ideas. For new members unfamiliar with brainstorming, the rationale and rules for brainstorming should be explained. If groups are being formed specifically for brainstorming, the membership should include a diversity of opinions and backgrounds. After the brainstorming session is over, the group selects the best ideas (or a synthesis of these ideas) related to the issue or problem.

Brainstorming has a number of advantages because it increases involvement of all members, reduces a group's dependency upon a single authority figure, and provides a procedure for obtaining a large number of ideas in a relatively short period of time.

The pressure to say the "right things" to impress others in the group is reduced, and the process is interesting, fun, and stimulating. An open sharing of ideas within a nonevaluative climate allows each group member to build upon the ideas of others to create unique combinations.

If group members find brainstorming a strange experience, however, it can lead initially to a sense of discomfort.[6] In a restricted, self-conscious group, brainstorming may actually hinder participation, because it forces members into patterns of behavior that are felt to be "uncomfortable."[7]

In other situations, brainstorming may be effective as an ice breaker to open up a stuffy and inhibited group.[8] What effect brainstorming will have on the group depends partially on the group leader's skills and timing in using the approach.

■ CONFLICT

Conflict is an antagonistic state of action involving divergent ideas or interests and is inevitable in groups. Johnson and Johnson summarize the potential merits and dangers of a conflict in a group:

> A conflict among group members is a moment of truth in group effectiveness, a test of the group's health, a crisis that can weaken or strengthen the group, a critical event that may bring creative insight and closer relationships among members—or lasting resentment, smoldering hostility, and psychological scars. Conflicts can push members away from one another or pull them into closer and more cooperative relationships. Conflicts may contain the seeds of group destruction or the seeds of a more unified and cooperative unit. . . . They have the potential for producing both highly constructive and highly destructive consequences for group functioning.[9]

Many people in our society erroneously believe that conflicts only produce negative results and should be avoided. Conflict is seen as a cause of divorce, low work morale, deterioration of friendships, psychological trauma, violence, and social disorder. In reality, the cause of these destructive events is the ineffective and harmful management of conflicts. Because people have divergent interests, beliefs, values, and goals, it is inevitable that conflicts will occur in interpersonal relationships.

Conflicts are not only a natural part of any relationship within a group; they are also desirable because, when handled effectively, they have a number of payoffs. Without conflict, members may become bored, and disagreements often spark the interest and curiosity of group members and produce lively discussions. Conflicts motivate members to define issues more sharply, search harder for resolution strategies, and work harder in implementing solutions. Conflicts can also lead to greater commitment, cohesion, communication, and cooperation and can revitalize stagnant groups. By expressing and working out their dissatisfactions, group members can assess their beliefs, values, and opinions. Therefore, verbal conflicts can also lead to personal growth and encourage innovation and creativity.

Exercise 6.2: My Tolerance for Conflicts

GOAL: This exercise is designed to assist you in assessing whether you need to become more assertive in confronting interpersonal conflicts.

1. Do you shy away (by usually giving in) from interpersonal conflicts? If "yes," explain your reasons.

2. If you shy away from interpersonal conflicts, do you feel when you give in that the other person is "trodding" on your personal rights?

3. Do you believe that you need to more assertively confront your interpersonal conflicts? If "yes," what do you intend to do in order to become more assertive in confronting conflicts?

■ TECHNIQUES FOR RESOLVING CONFLICTS

There are a variety of strategies for resolving conflicts. These strategies will be summarized in the following sections.

Win-Lose Approach

In ineffective groups, resolutions of conflict between opposing positions become win-lose situations. In many competitive fields, such as sports, business, and politics, individuals or teams are pitted against each other. In groups, conflicts are often cast in the same competitive mold. Because each side denies the legitimacy of the other's interests and concerns, members attempt to sell their position without really listening to the other side. Power blocks are formed to support one position against another. The original goals and objectives of the group may fade into the background as a "win" on issues becomes the only objective of the warring sides.

In win-lose situations, the group as a whole loses because it fails to achieve its long-range goals and objectives. The losing side is not motivated to carry out the winning decision. The losers resent the winners and may attempt to reverse the decision or impede its implementation. In such an atmosphere distrust increases between opposing sides, communication becomes more limited and inaccurate, and group cohesion decreases. Members' unresolved feelings often result in biased judgments and actions; members will frequently refuse to vote for a good idea simply because they dislike the person who suggested it.

Obviously, communication is severely hampered in groups that handle conflict in a win-lose fashion. Conflict in win-lose situations leads to the denial or distortion of unpleasant facts and information, as each side is apt to deny, hide, or distort information inconsistent with its position in an effort to win.[10] Members misinterpret the ideas and actions of those perceived as opponents, causing "blind spots" in communication. A win-lose approach leads to deceitful expression of ideas and feelings because winning sometimes receives higher priority than honesty. Disagreement tends to be interpreted as personal rejection on the part of opposing group members, and the group's future decisions are generally poor.

No-Lose Problem Solving

The no-lose problem-solving approach asserts that it is almost always possible for both sides to have their needs met in a conflict situation. This approach, which is a variation of the problem-solving approach described earlier in this chapter, was developed by Gordon and is based on two basic premises: (1) all people have the right to have their needs met, and (2) what is in conflict between the two sides is almost never their *needs* but their *solutions* to those needs.[11]

The distinction between needs and solutions is all-important. For example, assume that a student social work club is arguing over whether to fund a graduation party for seniors or a campus daycare center in danger of being closed. An analysis of needs and solutions in this discussion would reveal that the club is arguing over solutions rather than needs. There is a need to honor the graduating seniors and a need for the daycare center to receive operating funds. However, there are a variety of ways of meeting both needs. The club may spend its current funds on a graduation party and then hold a fundraiser for the daycare center; or fund the center and hold a graduation party by having members donate food, refreshments, and a few dollars at the party. Half of the club's funds could go to the center and the remainder to a reduced-cost graduation party. In addition, many other solutions could be generated to meet these needs.

The six steps to the *no-lose problem-solving approach* are

1. Identify and define the needs of each opposing side.
2. Generate possible alternative solutions.
3. Evaluate the alternative solutions.
4. Decide on the best acceptable solution.
5. Work out ways of implementing the solution.
6. Evaluate how it worked.[12]

The first step is by far the most difficult because group members often view conflicts in terms of win-lose and attempt to identify and meet primarily their own needs. When each side's needs in a conflict are identified, however, what usually is in conflict are not the *needs* of each side but their *solutions*. No-lose problem solving will generally lead to creative solutions, after *all six steps* are followed. (Readers will note the "no-lose problem-solving process" is identical to the "problem-solving process" described earlier in this chapter.)

The advantages of this no-lose approach are that both sides fulfill their needs, and group harmony and cohesion are increased. The resentment, hostility, and subversive actions of a win-lose situation are also eliminated. Actually, it is in each group member's best interest to resolve conflicts in a way that will help all members achieve their short-term goals and needs and increase the long-term effectiveness of the group, so that the long-term goals and needs of *all* members have a better chance of being achieved. Frequently, with groups that function in terms of win-lose, the winning side may win some battles, but the effectiveness of the group may diminish. All members may thus fail to accomplish their long-term goals and satisfy their needs.

With a problem-solving approach, members tend to listen to one another, recognize the legitimacy of another's interests, and influence one another with rational arguments.

Instead of a competitive environment, problem solving encourages an atmosphere of cooperation.

The differences between a win-lose strategy and a problem-solving strategy can be summarized as follows:

WIN-LOSE STRATEGY	PROBLEM-SOLVING STRATEGY
The conflict is defined as a win-lose situation.	The conflict is viewed as a problem.
Each side seeks solutions to meet only its needs.	Each person seeks to find solutions to meet the needs of all members.
Each side attempts to force the other side into submission.	Each person cooperates with others to find mutually acceptable compromises.
Each side increases its power by emphasizing its independence from the other, and the other's dependence upon itself.	Each person equalizes power by emphasizing interdependence.
Each side inaccurately, deceitfully, and misleadingly communicates its goals, needs, and ideas; information inconsistent or harmful to one's position is not shared.	Each person honestly and openly communicates goals, needs, and ideas.
No expression of empathy or understanding is made of the views, values, and opinions of the other side.	Efforts are made to convey empathy and understanding of the views, values, and opinions of others.
Threats are used to attempt to force the other side into submission.	Threats are avoided to reduce the defensiveness of others.
Rigid adherence to one's position is expressed.	A willingness to be flexible is expressed.
Changes in position are made very slowly in an effort to force concessions from the other side.	Positions are changed readily to help in problem solving.
No suggestions are sought from third parties as the focus is on forcing the other side to give in.	Third parties are sought to help in problem solving.

A cooperative problem-solving approach in a group also promotes *creativity*. Creativity is a process of bringing something new into existence; it results from productive controversy. Because a problem is viewed from new perspectives, new alternatives can be suggested and formulated for resolving the problem.

Deutsch has identified three means of fostering creativity in a group:[13] (1) an appropriate level of motivation for finding a viable solution must be aroused, (2) there must be a cooperative problem-solving atmosphere in the group that allows members to reformulate the problem once an impasse has been reached, (3) diverse ideas must be suggested or available that can be flexibly put together into new and varied solutions.

Groups are most creative when the motivational level is high enough for members to maintain problem-solving efforts despite frustrations and dead ends. However, this level should not be so high that it overwhelms the group by causing members to become too tense to concentrate. Excessive tension leads to defensiveness and reduces receptiveness to innovative approaches. Too much anxiety inhibits members from fully expressing their views, interferes with their listening to the views of others, and often leads to closed-mindedness.

Creative group members seek out different ways of looking at the problem and innovative ways of resolving it in an open-minded way. That is, a member assesses relevant information based on its *own* merits, not on how it resembles or differs from his or her own ideas, opinions, and assumptions. When conflict occurs between two members, each can listen to the other's criticisms, judge their validity fairly, and suggest new strategies that take into account both members' concerns. This leads to a creative solution to the problem.

In contrast, a closed-minded person views relevant information from his own assumptions, beliefs, and frame of reference.[14] Closed-minded members emphasize the differences between what they believe and do not believe, ignoring or denying information contrary to their value system. They tend to have contradictory beliefs that they fail to question, and in their efforts to defend these beliefs, they stifle creativity.

Exercise 6.3: Creativity Inspired by Conflict

GOAL: This exercise is designed to help you understand how conflict often inspires creativity.

Describe a conflict that you had with someone that inspired a creative solution that was satisfying to you and to the other person.

Role Reversal

A useful strategy in resolving both intragroup and intergroup conflict is role reversal. The basic rule for role reversal is this: *Each person expresses his or her opinions or views only after restating the ideas and feelings of the opposing person.* These ideas and feelings should be restated in one's own words rather than parroted or mimicked in the exact words of the other person. It is advisable to begin the restatement with words such as "Your position is . . . ," "You seem to be saying . . . ," or "You apparently feel . . ." Approval or disapproval, blaming, giving advice, interpreting, or persuading should be avoided.

In addition, nonverbal messages should be consistent with the verbal paraphrasing and convey interest, openness, and attentiveness to the opposition's ideas and feelings. Above all, role reversal should be the expression of a sincere interest in understanding the other person's feelings, ideas, and position.

Role reversal can result in a reevaluation and a change of attitude concerning the issue by both parties because the group members involved are apt to be perceived as people who are understanding, willing to compromise, cooperative, and trustworthy.[15] The approach has also been found to increase cooperative behavior between role reversers, to clarify misunderstandings, to change win-lose situations into problem-solving situations, and most important, to allow the issue to be perceived from the opponent's frame of reference.

A shortcoming of this approach is that some people do not like being forced to repeat the words spoken by the person they are in conflict with. Other people do not like hearing the words they have just spoken repeated. For both of these types of people, the following technique is often more acceptable and more effective.

Empathy

A technique closely related to role reversal is the expression of empathy. Empathy involves putting yourself in the shoes of the person you are in conflict with and expressing your understanding of what she is thinking and saying. Some examples of phrases that are useful in helping you express empathy are

> "What you seem to be saying is. . . ."
> "I take it that you think. . . ."
> "I sense that you feel _____ about this issue."

When expressing empathy it is essential to mirror what was said in a nonjudgmental way that will help you grasp the essence of what the other person is thinking or feeling.

Similar to role reversal, empathy is used to facilitate open communication, assist in clarifying misunderstandings, increase cooperative behavior, and facilitate the process of no-lose problem solving.

Inquiry

If you are in conflict with someone and you are confused regarding his thoughts and feelings, the inquiry technique may be useful. This technique involves using gentle, probing questions to learn more about what the other person is thinking and feeling. Tone of voice is very crucial in inquiry because asking a question sarcastically or defensively is apt to draw defensive responses from the person you are in conflict with.

I-Messages

As described in Chapter 5, the technique of using I-messages also facilitates more open and honest communication between parties in conflict. In contrast, you-messages tend to increase defensiveness between parties in conflict.

Disarming

When you are in conflict with someone, using the disarming technique is frequently an effective strategy in resolving the conflict. The disarming technique involves finding some truth in what the other person (or side) is saying and then expressing your "agreement"—even if you feel that the other person is largely wrong, unreasonable, irrational, or unfair. There is always a grain of truth in what the other person says, even if it sounds obnoxious and insulting. When you disarm the other person with this technique, she will recognize that you respect her. Once disarmed, the other person will not feel so dogmatic and will be less likely to insist that she is entirely right and you are entirely wrong. As a result, she is apt to be more willing to examine the merits of your point of view. If you want respect, *give* respect first. If you want to be listened to, disarming helps you listen to the other person first and facilitates open (rather than defensive) communication. Friendly responses facilitate open communication, while hostile responses usually produce defensive communication.

In using the disarming technique, it is important to be genuine in what you say and to express your agreement sincerely.

Stroking

Closely related to disarming, stroking is saying something genuinely positive to the person (or side) you are in conflict with, even in the heat of battle. Stroking tells the other person that you respect him, even though both of you may be angry. During an argument or conflict, you are apt to feel the need to reject the other person before you get rejected (to "save face"). Often, people overreact and differences of opinion are blown out of proportion. To prevent this rejection, simply let the other person know that, although you are at odds, you still think highly of him. This makes it easier for him to open up and to listen because he will feel less threatened.

Exercise 6.4: Disarming and Stroking

GOAL: This exercise is designed to assist you in understanding and applying disarming and stroking to resolve conflict.

1. **Describe an experience where two people were having a conflict (one of those people may have been you) and the conflict was resolved (at least partially) by one of the people using disarming or stroking.**

2. **Summarize your thoughts on the merits and shortcomings of disarming and stroking in resolving conflict.**

Mediation

In the past two decades, mediation has increasingly been used to resolve conflicts between disputing groups. The federal government as far back as 1913 established federal mediators to help resolve issues between employers and employees.[16] It was expected that mediated settlements would prevent costly strikes or lockouts for workers and employers alike, and that the welfare and safety of Americans would be protected. Federal use of mediation in labor disputes set a precedent for many states to pass laws and train a cadre of mediators to handle intrastate labor conflicts.

The Civil Rights Act of 1964 created the Community Relations Service of the U.S. Department of Justice to use mediation to resolve disputes relating to discriminatory practices based on race, color, or national origin.[17] Diverse private agencies, civil rights commissions, and state agencies now use mediation to handle charges of sex, race, and ethnic discrimination. The federal government funds neighborhood justice centers that provide free or low-cost mediation services to the public to resolve disputes, informally, inexpensively, and efficiently.[18] Disputes settled through mediation are resolved much more efficiently and creatively than those resolved in court. Mediation is also used in schools and colleges to settle disputes between students, between students and faculty, between faculty members, and between faculty and administration. The criminal justice system uses mediation to resolve disputes in correctional facilities, for example, prison riots, hostage negotiations, and institutionalized grievance procedures.

Mediation is also used extensively in family disputes involving child custody and divorce proceedings, disputes between parents and children, conflicts involving adoption and the termination of parental rights, and domestic violence situations. Moore states "In family disputes, mediated and consensual settlements are often more appropriate and satisfying than litigated or imposed court outcomes."[19]

Mediation is used to settle disputes between business partners, private individuals, governmental agencies and individuals, landlords and tenants, businesses and customers, and in personal injury cases.

Many professionals now occasionally act as mediators to help people or groups in conflict to resolve their concerns. Such professionals include attorneys, social workers, psychologists, and guidance counselors. A few social workers, attorneys, and other professionals are working full time as mediators—often in public or private mediation agencies.

Moore defines mediation as follows:

> Mediation involves the intervention of an acceptable, impartial, and neutral third party who has no authoritative decision-making power to assist contending parties in voluntarily reaching their own mutually acceptable settlement of issues in dispute. . . . Mediation leaves the decision-making power in the hands of the people in conflict. Mediation is a voluntary process in that the participants must be willing to accept the assistance of the intervenor if the dispute is to be resolved. Mediation is usually initiated when the partners no longer believe that they can handle the conflict on their own and when the only means of resolution appears to involve impartial third-party assistance.[20]

There are various models of the mediation process.[21] As an illustration, the model developed by Blades will be summarized.[22] According to Blades, the mediation process involves five stages:

1. *Introduction/Commitment:* This first stage usually is accomplished in a one- to two-hour session. The mediator sets ground rules, describes mediation, answers questions, discusses fees, and seeks to gain a commitment to the process from the two parties. The mediator also seeks to develop an understanding of the more pressing issues, gains a sense of the personal dynamics of the two parties, and tries to ascertain whether they are ready and willing to mediate. If one or both of the parties are not willing to mediate, then the mediation probably should not proceed. If one or both of the parties are hesitant to proceed, the mediator usually describes the alternatives to mediation—such as a lengthy and expensive court battle.

2. *Definition:* The two parties, with the mediator's assistance, define the areas in which they already agree and disagree. Certain disputes, such as division of property issues in divorce mediation, are apt at this stage to require a considerable amount of information.

3. *Negotiation:* Once the two parties agree on the issues in conflict and relevant factual information on these issues is obtained, the two parties are ready to begin negotiating. At this stage the mediator seeks to have the parties focus on one issue at a time. A problem-solving approach is used in which the needs of each party are first identified and alternatives are generated. The mediator recedes into the background when discussions are proceeding well and steps in when emotions intensify or when the two parties are overlooking creative solutions that will meet their needs.

4. *Agreement:* Once alternatives are generated and related facts are evaluated, the two parties are ready to begin making agreements on the issues. The role of the mediator is to maintain a cooperative atmosphere and to keep the two parties focused on a manageable number of issues. The mediator summarizes areas of agreement and provides legal or other information necessary to a discussion. The mediator helps the two parties examine the merits and shortcomings of the options. During this stage the mediator praises the parties for the progress they are making and gets them to praise themselves for progress made. A mediator seeks to create a positive atmosphere.

5. *Contracting:* In this final stage of mediation the two parties review the agreements and clarify any ambiguities. The agreements are almost always written in the form of a contract, which is available for future reference. Either party, the mediator, or everyone together may do the actual writing of the contract. The contract expresses what each party agrees to do and may set deadlines for the diverse tasks to be completed. It also specifies consequences if either party fails to meet the terms of the contract. Mediators seek to have specific agreements stated in concrete form to prevent future controversies. The ultimate goal of mediation is a contract in which no one is a loser and which both parties willingly abide by.

One of the major techniques a mediator uses is a caucus.[23] At times a mediator or either party may stop the mediation and request a caucus. In a caucus the two parties are physically separated from each other, and there is no direct communication between them. The mediator meets with one of the parties or with both parties individually. There are a wide variety of reasons for calling a caucus. A caucus may be used to vent intense emotions privately, to clarify misperceptions, to reduce unproductive or repetitive negative behavior, to seek clarification of a party's interests, to provide a pause for each party to consider an alternative, to convince an uncompromising party that the mediation process is better than going to court, to uncover confidential information, to educate an inexperienced disputant about the processes of mediation, or to design alternatives that will later be brought to a joint session.

Some parties are willing, in a caucus, to privately express possible concessions. Usually such concessions are conditional upon the other party making certain concessions. By the use of caucuses, a mediator can go back and forth relaying information from one party to the other and seek to develop a consensus.

What If These Strategies Do Not Work?

If used appropriately, these strategies will help resolve interpersonal conflicts in the vast majority of cases. When these strategies fail to work, you can probably correctly conclude that the person you are in conflict with does not really want to resolve the conflict. Perhaps the other person is a very hostile person who wants to generate conflicts to meet his or her personal needs of wanting conflicts in order to vent his or her anger and hostility. Or, perhaps the other person really wants to be in conflict with you in order to make your life uncomfortable.

What can you do when you become aware that the other person really wants to sustain the conflict with you? Using the Law of Requisite Variety is an option. This law states that if you continue to creatively come up with new ways of responding to the daggers being thrown at you, that eventually the other person will grow tired of the turmoil and will finally decide to bury the hatchet. Two examples are presented.

Janice and Pete Palmer were married about a year ago. Unknown to Janice, Pete was having lunch about once a month with a former partner (Paula) that he dated over a three-year period. Seven months ago Janice walked into a restaurant at noon and saw her husband with Paula. In a fit of rage, Janice stomped out. That evening she and Pete had a major uproar about this. Pete claimed Paula was just a friend, and that nothing romantic was occurring. Janice yelled and screamed. Pete indicated he would stop having lunch with Paula. But he did not keep his promise. About once a month he continued to see Paula, and when Janice found out, there was a major argument. Janice suggested a number of resolution options, including marriage counseling. Pete refused to go to counseling and also indicated he had decided (the win-lose approach) that he was going to continue having lunch with Paula. Then one day Janice ran into one of her former partners—Dave. Dave invited Janice for lunch or dinner. A light bulb went on for Janice—she accepted the invitation and made plans for dinner. She went home and gleefully told Pete she ran into Dave (who Pete knew had dated Janice in the past). Pete became very jealous and tried to talk Janice out of having dinner with Dave. Janice said "No way. If it's OK for you to see Paula, then it follows that it's OK for me to see Dave."

Pete was in anguish during the time Janice and Dave were having dinner. When Janice came home, Pete politely said he had called Paula that evening to inform her he was canceling their next scheduled lunch and that he felt it was best that they no longer meet for lunch. Pete then asked Janice if she also would no longer get together with Dave—she said "Yes." Through this experience, Pete and Janice learned to respect and appreciate each other to a greater extent.

Vicki Stewart was a secretary for an attorney, Randy Fuller, who frequently criticized her and never complimented her. The harder she sought to perform well, the more it seemed she was criticized. She tried a variety of resolution strategies—discussing the conflict with him, discussing it with his supervisor, and making a point of complimenting him to set a good example. Nothing worked. Finally, she decided upon a new approach. Mr. Fuller's grammar and spelling were atrocious. Ms. Stewart always improved the spelling and grammar when given rough drafts from Mr. Fuller and the other attorneys in the office. When Mr. Fuller gave her a rough draft of a legal brief to the state supreme court, Ms. Stewart typed it as is and sent it after Mr. Fuller signed it (he frequently signed such documents without proofreading them). When Mr. Fuller finally read the brief three weeks later, he was first angry and then discussed the matter with his supervisor. His supervisor at first laughed and then informed Mr. Fuller that in order to avoid a similar situation in the future, he needed to show appreciation to Ms. Stewart. After a few more days of reflecting about it, Mr. Fuller decided it was in his personal interest to display more respect and appreciation to Ms. Stewart.

Exercise 6.5: Resolving Your Conflicts Effectively

GOAL: This exercise is designed to assist you in learning how to resolve interpersonal conflicts more effectively.

1. Describe a serious interpersonal conflict that you had with someone who was important to you.

2. What conflict resolution strategies did you use to attempt to resolve the conflict?

3. What conflict resolution strategies did the other person seek to use?

4. Has the conflict been successfully resolved? If "yes," describe what led to the resolution. If "no," specify why it has not been resolved.

5. Review the conflict resolution techniques described in this chapter. Specify those that you believe might have been effective in more rapidly resolving the conflict. Provide an explanation for your views.

6. Which of the conflict resolution techniques do you intend to use in the future?

■ INTERGROUP CONFLICT

Just as there is conflict within groups, conflicts often arise *between* groups. Within a single organization, various groups are often forced to vie for funding, human resources, and power. For example, in a university, members of different department faculties (e.g., sociology, psychology, social work) may have conflicts over which department will receive authorization to add a new course (such as human sexuality), which department will be given a new faculty position, what will be the budget allocation for each department, and which department will use what human service agencies for field placements for students.

As with intragroup conflict, the sides involved in intergroup (or between-group) conflict can use either a win-lose approach or a no-lose problem-solving approach to attempt to resolve the conflict. The same advantages and disadvantages described for intragroup conflicts hold true for intergroup conflicts.

When the conflicts are formulated in terms of win-lose situations, the results are both predictable and destructive.[24] Each group becomes much more cohesive as members join together to defend their group against attack; members will close ranks and frequently put aside intragroup conflicts. Group members become more willing to accept autocratic leadership since rapid, consistent decisions must be made and "a solid front" presented. The groups in conflict tend to become more polarized as each perceives its position as right and moral, while the opposing groups are belittled and devalued. Members' satisfaction with the group increases because they feel an increased sense of identity with their group and an increased sense of belonging.

Hostility increases between the two groups. Distortions in perceptions increase as each group highlights the best parts of itself and the worst parts of the other group. Communication and interaction between the groups decrease as each group assigns inaccurate and uncomplimentary stereotypes to the opposing group and views it as distinctly inferior.

Because group members often misinterpret the other side's position, distrust is heightened, and negotiators are often selected from each group to work out differences. These negotiators tend to be the most militant leaders of each group and tend to assert only their group's position rather than work toward a creative agreement that will meet the needs of all sides. They want at any cost to avoid giving in so that they are not branded as losers or traitors. If a third party is brought in to decide the dispute, the winning side will view the third party as fair and objective, while the losing side will view the third party as biased, thoughtless, and irrational.

There are two usual outcomes when intergroup conflict is cast in a win-lose mold. One outcome is a stalemate, in which the opposing groups continue battling and remain deadlocked, perhaps for years. In the other outcome, one side wins and the other side loses.

The side that loses initially loses cohesiveness and may even disband. Members analyze the reasons for losing, often place blame, and then quarrel among themselves. Previous unresolved conflicts surface and tension increases. The group often finds a scapegoat, such as the leader, the third-party negotiator, or the least conforming members of the group. If an "ineffective" leader is blamed for the defeat, he may be replaced. Through a reassessment of the loss, the group reshapes some of its goals and reexamines its positive stereotypes of itself and its negative stereotypes of the opposing groups. This, in effect, may lead to a more realistic assessment of itself and of the opposing groups. Once a loss has been accepted, a losing group that sees hope of victories in the future may reorganize and again become effective. If future victories appear impossible, members may become so demoralized, depressed, and apathetic that they drift away from the group, or become uninvolved and nonproductive.

The group that wins generally celebrates and feels a strong sense of cohesion. It becomes self-satisfied, loses its fighting spirit, and members tend to relax, perhaps even becoming playful, while putting forth little effort for group work. Consequently, the winning group makes few changes—it is content.

In contrast to the win-lose approach, a problem-solving strategy can be used to resolve intergroup conflict through a variety of structural arrangements. One arrangement is for the leaders or representatives of each group to meet, or, if the groups are small enough, a meeting of *all* the members involved can be scheduled. If necessary, a mediator can be chosen to call a meeting of representatives from the groups, or an ongoing committee of representatives from each group can be selected to work on present conflicts and new issues.

Calling a meeting is the easy part; the hard part is to convince each side that it is in the best interest of everyone to use a problem-solving approach. The benefits of using a problem-solving approach for intergroup conflict are the same as those described for intragroup conflict in this chapter. One way of pointing the conflicting groups in this direction is to (1) briefly summarize the disadvantages and likely future problems in using a win-lose approach, (2) indicate the potential benefits to all sides in using a problem-solving approach, and (3) ask the groups in conflict to try the problem-solving approach.

The most important point about intergroup conflict is that it is much better if each side uses a cooperative, problem-solving approach rather than a win-lose approach. Group leaders must be aware that it is very difficult to undo the negative feelings and resentments that result from a competitive win-lose situation. If need be, third-party mediators or arbitrators should be brought in early in a win-lose conflict to turn the situation around.

The win-lose strategy and the no-lose problem-solving strategy are frequently mutually exclusive. If two groups are in conflict, negotiators for each side cannot be both honest and deceitful. They cannot simultaneously convey and withhold empathy and understanding or use threats to win and avoid threats in order to reduce defensiveness. Moreover, these negotiators cannot simultaneously be flexible and rigid.

Although the problem-solving approach is by far the most desirable, a win-lose approach may be necessary when an opposing side refuses to use a problem-solving strategy. Being open, flexible, and willing to make concessions to a group using a win-lose strategy may increase the chances of being exploited and of losing.

■ DECISION MAKING

The effectiveness of a group largely depends on its ability to make good, sound decisions on such issues as when to meet, how meetings will be conducted, why the group is meeting, and what it will do. Decisions almost always involve choosing among several different options and reaching a consensus. Members of some groups are only vaguely aware of how decisions are made, while others spend hours debating how decisions will be made. Seldom is the same procedure used for arriving at all decisions in a group, since different circumstances warrant varied decision-making processes. In our society, important decisions are usually made by groups rather than individuals. If a problem or issue is complex, a group usually makes a better decision than an individual.[25]

■ THE BASES OF DECISIONS

Most people tend to believe that decisions are made primarily on the basis of objective facts and figures. In fact, values and assumptions form the bases of most decisions, and facts and figures are used only in relation to these subjective, learned experiences. Consider the following list of questions. What do they indicate about how we make our most important decisions?

1. Should abortions be permitted or prohibited during the first weeks following conception?

2. Should homosexuality be viewed as a natural expression of sexuality?
3. When does harsh disciplining of a child become child abuse?
4. When should confidentiality be violated?
5. Should the primary objective of imprisonment be rehabilitation or retribution?

Answers to these questions are not usually based on data uncovered after careful research; they are based on individual beliefs about the value of life, personal freedom, and protective social standards. Even everyday decisions are based largely on *values*.

Practically every decision is also based on certain *assumptions*. Without assumptions, nothing can be proven. Assumptions are made in every research study to test any hypothesis. In a market survey, for example, analysts assume that the instruments they use (such as a questionnaire) will be valid and reliable. It cannot even be proven the sun will rise in the east tomorrow without assuming that its history provides that proof. The same holds true for groups involved in decision making. For example, if a local group decides that busing should be used to facilitate racial integration, it probably assumes busing will have certain benefits. On the other hand, if a group decides not to use school busing, it is assuming the probable costs will outweigh the predicted benefits. In either case, the assumption cannot be proven beforehand. Proof comes only when the decision is implemented and its effects are evaluated.

The purpose of statistical information and research studies is to test assumptions, hypotheses, and beliefs. All of the following are beliefs held by many Americans:

- The death penalty has a deterrent effect on people who are considering committing serious crimes such as homicide.
- Most welfare recipients are able to work but would rather live it up on welfare.
- Mental patients are more likely to commit a crime than other people.
- Gay men are apt to display effeminate mannerisms.
- Crimes committed by the lower class are the most costly in our society.

That each of these beliefs has been invalidated by research shows the importance of scientifically testing beliefs. Research demonstrates that a country's adoption of a death penalty generally does not result in a decrease in homicide rates or in rates of other serious crimes.[26] Only a small fraction of welfare recipients are able to work—the vast majority cannot work because they are children, are elderly, have a disability, or are homebound mothers with young children.[27] People labeled as mentally ill are no more likely to commit crimes than people considered sane.[28] Gay males are no more apt to be effeminate than male heterosexuals,[29] and white-collar crime appears to be the most costly in our society.[30]

APPROACHES TO DECISION MAKING

Before discussing an issue leading to a decision, a group must know what decision-making approach it will use because different approaches lead to diverse consequences for the future operation of the group. An effective group is aware of these consequences and must choose the best approach considering the amount of time available, the nature of the decision to be made, and the kind of atmosphere the group wants to create. The nature of the task, the history of the group, and the kind of setting in which the group is working must also be considered. Six decision-making approaches will be discussed:

1. Consensus of the group
2. Simple majority vote
3. Two-thirds or three-fourths majority vote
4. Delegated decisions
5. Multiple voting
6. Averaging individual opinions

Consensus

This approach is the ==most effective for motivating all group members to support and work for the decision because everyone comes to agree with the final decision. This approach is also the most time consuming,== as the concerns of each member have to be recognized. Johnson and Johnson describe consensus as follows:

> Consensus is more commonly defined as a collective opinion arrived at by a group of people working together under conditions that permit communications to be sufficiently open—and the group climate to be sufficiently supportive—so that everyone in the group feels he has had his fair chance to influence the decision. When a decision is made by consensus, all members understand the decision and are prepared to support it. Operationally, consensus means that all members can rephrase the decision to show that they understand it, that all members have had a chance to tell how they feel about the decision, and that those members who continue to disagree or have doubts will, nevertheless, say publicly that they are willing to give the decision an experimental try for a period of time.[31]

To use consensus effectively, the group must have a trusting, cooperative atmosphere. Members must feel free to present their views but must do so as clearly and logically as possible. They must refrain from blindly arguing their own individual views and listen to and respect the views of other members. Members should also *avoid* going along with the group if they believe the majority opinion is a mistake. It is dangerous to yield to the majority if the only reason is to avoid conflict and to appear united. This type of conforming can lead to dangerous groupthink, described later in this chapter. Members, however, should yield to the majority opinion if that position appears to have merit and has a fair chance for positive outcomes.

Differences of opinion should be sought and dealt with respectfully. Divergent views increase the chances of reviewing all crucial aspects of an issue, building upon the views of others, and making viable decisions.

The participation of all members is encouraged, with emphasis placed on finding the best solution that everyone can agree on and support. If a group becomes stalemated over two alternatives, a third alternative is often sought to incorporate the major desires of both subgroups. In this way, the group avoids the kind of divisiveness that can occur with other types of decision making, such as voting.

Consensus is difficult to achieve because it requires that members be flexible. They must also understand that the thorough discussion of divergent points of view should lead to a synthesis of ideas, resulting in an innovative, creative, and high-quality decision. Active participation, equally distributed power, and a substantial amount of time are necessary to analyze divergent views and cooperatively synthesize ideas that will be agreeable to everyone.

Because consensus resolves controversies and conflicts, it increases the group's ability to make high-quality decisions in the future. Other forms of decision making do not resolve conflicts and controversies. When group members feel they have participated in the decision and support it, they may contribute more of their resources to implement the decision. Consensus is useful in making important, serious, and complex decisions in which the success of the decision depends upon all members being committed to it.

Simple Majority Vote

Most groups use a simple-majority vote approach. Issues are discussed until they are clarified and a vote is then taken.

There are several advantages to this type of decision making. Decisions are arrived at much faster. Most decisions do not warrant the full support of all members. Even groups in which members have little trust in one another can become operational by using a simple-majority vote approach. This approach will also work in groups in which communication among members lacks openness and in groups in which some members are unwilling to give up their favorite positions.

However, shortcomings of the simple majority approach are numerous. Minority opinions are not always safeguarded. Racial groups, women, certain ethnic groups, gays and lesbians, and people with a disability have received the brunt of many adverse decisions made by simple majority voting. Majority voting frequently splits a group into winners and losers, and sometimes, the number of losers is nearly as great as the number of winners, who can represent as much as 49 percent of the vote. These losers may feel their concerns are not receiving attention, refuse to support group efforts, and work to subvert or overturn the decision. Obviously, if voting alienates a minority, the future effectiveness of the group is diminished. There is a danger that a majority rule may be interpreted by a minority as being an unfair means of control and manipulation. Therefore, to maintain its effectiveness, groups that use majority voting should create a climate in which members feel they have had their day in court and feel an obligation to support the final group decision.

Two-Thirds or Three-Fourths Majority Vote

A high-percentage majority vote, such as two-thirds or three-fourths, is used primarily for decisions of substantial consequence, such as enacting amendments to the U.S. Constitution or changing the bylaws and constitution of an organization. A high-percentage majority vote is also often used by governmental decision-making units to pass emergency requests for special funds.

This type of vote is a compromise between the consensus and simple majority approaches. A high-percentage majority vote takes more time than a simple majority because more votes are needed but less time than consensus because not everyone must agree. A strong minority can block a decision, so a small majority cannot force its views on them. However, a small minority may still feel controlled and manipulated by a majority rule. A high-percentage majority vote will generally draw stronger support from group members than a simple majority, but it will not generate as much support as consensus. Psychologically, the losing side on a 76 to 24 percent vote under a three-fourths majority system is more apt to go along with the winning side than if the winning side won by 51 percent under a simple majority system.

For crucial decisions that require the support of practically all members, it is advisable to reach as strong a majority agreement as possible. A decision not to grant a faculty member tenure, for example, is less likely to be appealed if the vote in a department is twenty to one rather than eleven to ten.

Delegated Decisions

Because large groups cannot carefully debate and make all daily decisions, many groups delegate less important decisions to an expert, the group leader, or a subgroup. Subgroups include executive, temporary, or standing committees. However, the types of decisions to be delegated must be well defined to avoid potential conflicts and to limit the authority of group members selected to make less important decisions. In many groups, conflicts and disagreements arise when these limits are not clarified. It is common for group members and leaders to differ on which decisions should be made by the leader and which should be made by the group as a whole. When a leader's decision-making authority is in doubt, the group as a whole should deal with the question. Otherwise, the leader may be criticized for overextending his authority.

Expert

Authority can be delegated to the person in the group with the most expertise in a particular area. The expert can review the issues and inform the group of the decision. A major problem is that it is often difficult to determine which member has the most expertise. Personal popularity and power often interfere with the accurate selection of the most expert member. Since the group is leaving the decision to a single member, there is often little or no discussion of options. This may limit the number of viable options that the expert considers. Finally, a decision made by one person may not receive the support of other members to implement it.

Group Leader

A group may allow the leader to make certain decisions. Before making some of these decisions, however, the leader may call a meeting of the group, describe the issues, and use the discussion to arrive at a decision. A chancellor or president of a university often uses this approach by seeking the advice and suggestions of various subgroups. The most time-efficient method is when the leader makes a decision without any group discussion. This procedure works best for uncomplicated, less important issues. Although efficient, it may not be effective. Since the group may not understand the issues, members may disagree with the decision and withhold resources to implement it. If members feel that the leader is overstepping her authority, they may retaliate by limiting her authority or by replacing her. In addition, without input from the group, a leader is less likely to be fully aware of all the viable courses of action. By involving the group, the leader will hear a variety of options and give group members an opportunity to express their views. Still, if the leader's decision is unpopular, support for implementation will be limited.

Subgroup

Another approach to delegating decisions is to allow a subgroup, such as an executive committee or a temporary committee, to make certain decisions. When a subgroup makes a decision, it should consider the views of the larger group because unpopular decisions are generally not supported. If the subgroup continually makes unpopular decisions, the larger group can retaliate by reviewing the decisions, changing the membership of the subgroup, reducing its decision-making powers, or disbanding it. Subgroups are especially effective when a group has a large number of minor decisions to make and limited time.

Multiple Voting

If an organization has a number of alternatives before it, a series of ballots may be taken until one alternative receives the required number of winning votes. Multiple voting may be done in a variety of ways. In selecting a presidential candidate, both the Republican and Democratic conventions ballot until one candidate receives a majority. Another approach is to keep narrowing the number of choices. For example, if there are 50 options, each member may first vote for 5 options. The 10 options receiving the most votes are considered in the second round, with members voting for 3 options. In the third round the top 4 options are considered with members voting for 2 options each. In the fourth and final round, the top 2 options are considered, and members vote for 1 option. With this type of multiple voting, it is essential that the members agree on the voting rules prior to voting. Otherwise, those who want a choice that is not selected may charge, *after* reviewing the results of the voting, that the group leader is arbitrarily and capriciously excluding their favorite choices.

Averaging Individual Opinions

In an emergency, it may not be possible to assemble the members for a meeting. In this situation the group leader may contact each individual member to obtain his vote. The alternative chosen is the one receiving the most votes. Fewer than 50 percent of the votes could pass the motion, since the other votes may be spread over a variety of options. This approach may also be used for making decisions the leader does not believe are important enough for a group meeting.

However, there are a number of disadvantages to this approach. Without group discussion, many of the members may not be fully aware of all the issues, alternatives, or consequences of the proposal. A poor decision may result because the votes of the least informed members may cancel out the votes of the most knowledgeable. With little involvement, members are unlikely to have much commitment toward implementing the decision. There is also a danger that a subgroup opposed to the decision may feel it has been left out and may work hard to overturn the decision or impede its implementation. Another danger is that the person conducting the vote may influence the members to vote for his position.

GROUP VERSUS INDIVIDUAL DECISION MAKING

In theory, the task of making a decision within a group should follow a rational problem-solving process—identify the problem, generate proposed solutions, weigh the merits and shortcomings of proposed solutions, and select the alternative with the fewest risks and the greatest chance of success. In practice, however, subjective influences can impede this process.

We have all heard our share of amusing, yet halfway serious anecdotes about "runaround meetings," "inconclusive conclusions," and "slower-than-snails committees." While group-made decisions have the advantage of being based on a wider variety of information and a greater variety of expertise, they are also susceptible to subjective influences in the group. Without awareness of these subjective obstacles, groups will not necessarily make better decisions than individuals.

Each group member brings not only his or her objective knowledge and expertise to the decision-making process but also his or her subjective experience: unique attitudes, feelings, biases, and vested interests. These will probably not be expressed at the start of a meeting but will be triggered in the course of the ensuing discussion. As the decision-making process continues, there is an increasing tendency for individuals to allow their reactions to one another to interfere with objective thought.

Is group decision making inferior or superior to individual decision making? Individual decision making occurs when decisions are made without group interaction. A leader, an expert, or a poll of individuals make a decision that must be implemented by the group. There is overwhelming evidence that group decision making is usually superior.[32] This conclusion applies even when the individual decision is made by an expert.

There appear to be several reasons why group decision making is usually superior.[33] Through group interaction, the knowledge, abilities, and resources of each member are pooled. An individual acting alone often lacks information, skills, or resources needed to arrive at the best decision. Also, working in the presence of others motivates a person to put forth more effort, be more careful, and increase the quality of his or her work. Having more people working on a problem increases the probability that someone in the group will suggest a viable solution. Through group interaction, the members can build on each other's ideas, develop a decision based on this building-block approach, and identify the positive and negative consequences of each alternative. Since it is always easier to identify other people's mistakes than our own, the problem areas in the favorite alternatives of others can be identified and analyzed. In addition, different ways of looking at problems and tasks are more likely to result when different individuals are contributing. Also, when group members have participated in making a decision, they will be more likely to accept and support it.

It should be noted, however, that subjective influences can substantially reduce the quality of group decision making. Some group members may alter their actual opinions or hold back relevant information because they do not want to displease others in the group. One or several members may begin to contribute so much to the discussion, or state their opinions so forcefully, that others begin to resign themselves to being inactive. Arguments that are not pertinent to the issue at hand may take on major significance. For some group members, winning such arguments becomes more important than reaching a decision. Interpersonal attractions and repulsions among group members also influence decision making; some members are inclined to support alternatives of lower quality that are advocated by members they are attracted to, and they are inclined to reject higher quality alternatives advocated by group members that they dislike. Sometimes a combination of subjective influences results in the development of *groupthink*.

Groupthink

Janis first identified groupthink as a result of a study done on groups of U.S. presidential advisors.[34] During this study, he found that powerful social pressures were often exerted when a dissident began to voice objections to what otherwise appeared to be a group consensus. Groupthink is a problem-solving process in which proposals are accepted without a critical, careful review of the pros and cons of the alternatives, and in which considerable social pressure is brought to bear against those expressing opposing points of view. Groupthink occurs partially because the norms of the group hold that it is more important to bolster group morale than to evaluate all alternatives critically. Another group norm that increases groupthink is that members should remain loyal by sticking with the policies to which the group is already committed, even when those policies are not working.

Janis has listed a number of factors that promote groupthink:

1. Members have an illusion of being invulnerable, which leads them to become overly optimistic about their selected courses of action. This illusion also leads them to take extraordinary risks and causes them to fail to respond to clear warnings of danger.
2. Members have an unquestioning belief in the moral rightness of their group, which leads them to ignore the ethical consequences of their decisions.
3. The group applies social pressures to display disapproval toward any member who momentarily questions the basic policies of the group or who raises questions about a policy alternative favored by the majority.
4. The group constructs rationalizations to discount warnings and other forms of negative feedback that would, if taken seriously, lead the members to rethink basic assumptions about policies that are not working.
5. Group members hold stereotyped views of the leaders of opposing groups. Opposing group leaders are viewed either as so evil that it would be a mistake to try to negotiate differences or as so stupid or so weak that they will not be able to prevent this group from attaining its objectives.
6. Members sometimes assume "mind guard" roles in which they attempt to protect their leader and the group from negative information that might lead them to question the morality and effectiveness of past decisions.
7. Members keep quiet about their misgivings and even minimize to themselves the importance of these misgivings. Through self-censorship members avoid deviating from what appears to be group consensus.
8. The members believe practically everyone in the group fully agrees on the policies and programs of the group.

Groupthink spawns a number of poor decision-making practices. The group limits its discussion to those courses of action consistent with past decisions and policies; as a result, more divergent strategies (some of which are viable) are not considered. The group fails to reexamine a selected course of action, even when risks, drawbacks, and unintended consequences become clear. The group makes little effort to get cost-benefit information on possible strategies from appropriate experts. Members seek primarily to obtain facts and listen to opinions that support their preferred policy and tend to ignore facts and opinions that do not. The group fails to work out contingency plans to cope with foreseeable setbacks, and it spends little time considering how the chosen strategy might be sabotaged by political opponents or hampered by bureaucratic red tape.

In order to prevent the development of groupthink, a group has to be "on guard" about its dangers. Members must realize their selected courses of action may fail and be aware of the ethical consequences of their decisions. The group should welcome the questioning of basic policies by members and realistically assess the merits and short-comings of the views being expressed by opposing groups. Members should feel free to express their misgivings about basic policies and strategies of their group. The group should welcome the advancement of new and novel strategies for resolving the problems that it is combating. Finally, the group needs to consistently apply the problem-solving approach in assessing problems, in generating alternatives, in evaluating these alternatives, and in selecting and implementing strategies.

Exercise 6.6: My Groupthink Experience

GOAL: This exercise is designed to assist you in understanding and applying the theoretical material on groupthink.

1. **Describe a group experience that you had where you believe the group was going in the wrong direction and you failed to express your thoughts or opinions.**

2. Specify why you failed to express your thoughts or opinions.

3. **Do you believe your reasons for not expressing your thoughts or opinions are consistent or inconsistent with groupthink? Explain your views.**

■ GROUP EXERCISES

Exercise A: Suspended from High School

GOAL: To learn how to use the problem-solving approach in a group.

Step 1. The group leader describes the stages of the problem-solving approach:
1. Identify and define the problem
2. Assess the size and causes of the problem
3. Develop alternative strategies or plans for solving it
4. Assess the merits and shortcomings of these alternative strategies
5. Select and implement the most desirable strategy or strategies
6. Evaluate the success of the strategies used

Step 2. The class divides into subgroups of four or five students each. Each subgroup is to apply the problem-solving approach to the following situation.

Five students have been suspended for a four-day period for drinking alcoholic beverages at their high school, which is located in a small city of 5,400. It has been the policy of the school board to suspend any student caught drinking at school. In the past five months a total of 16 students have been suspended. The police department is unhappy with the suspensions because when the students are suspended they usually loiter on the city streets during school hours. The school social worker contacted the parents of the 5 suspended students, and only one couple indicated an interest in receiving counseling for their daughter. The other parents stated they were not sufficiently concerned to talk further about the suspensions.

The task of each subgroup is to arrive at answers (and reasons for their answers) to each of the following five questions:
1. What do you see as the most serious problem to deal with?
2. What do you believe are the causes of this problem?
3. What possible strategies could combat this problem?
4. What do you see as the merits and shortcomings of each of these strategies?
5. Which of these strategies would you select to combat the problem you have identified?

Step 3. Each subgroup shares its answers and reasoning with the class. After all of the subgroups have presented their answers, the class discusses why different problems and strategies were defined and selected by the subgroups.

Exercise B: Brainstorming

GOAL: To show how to use brainstorming.

Step 1. The leader describes the purpose of brainstorming and its ground rules, as explained in this chapter.

Step 2. The leader gives the class an issue or problem to brainstorm. If the class is very large, subgroups of 10 to 15 students may be formed. The issue or problem should be one that the class has some awareness of and background on. One possible topic: "What do you see as the major problem (without naming any person) in our social work program?"

Step 3. The most important problem should be singled out after the brainstorming is completed. For example, each class member could list his or her choices for the five most serious problems on a notecard. A tally could then be made, and the problem receiving the most votes would then be declared the most serious problem.

Step 4. After the most serious problem is determined, a second brainstorming exercise is conducted to generate a list of strategies to resolve it. Following this brainstorming, the most viable strategies should be identified.

Step 5. A discussion elicits the view of the class as to the strengths and shortcomings of brainstorming.

Exercise C: Busing to Achieve Racial Integration

GOAL: To observe and negotiate intergroup conflict.

Step 1. The group leader provides the following background information:

All of you live in a middle-class suburb of Middletown, which has had no racial problems. Your suburb is located next to the big city of Skyscraper. A recent study by the federal government has found that four public schools in the inner city of Skyscraper are racially segregated, as 98 percent of the students are African American. This inner-city school district is spending only half as much money per child on education as is your suburb of Middletown. The dropout rate in these inner-city schools is 55 percent compared to 10 percent in Middletown. Only 15 percent of the graduates from the inner-city schools in Skyscraper go on to college, while 65 percent of the graduates from Middletown go on to college. The federal government has ruled that the school districts in Middletown and Skyscraper must become racially integrated through busing between the systems. Three groups—concerned parents, civil rights activists, and school staff—have been asked by the Middletown school board to arrive at some recommendations to present to the school board on how to integrate the school districts. The school board of Middletown will act on these recommendations and then propose them to the Skyscraper School Board as a way of implementing the federal government's declaration that the school districts in the two communities must become racially integrated.

Step 2. The class is randomly divided into the three groups. Each group receives a handout that describes the group's views and tasks. (No group should be informed of the views of the other two groups.) The views and tasks are further described in the following material:

Concerned parents: You want what is best for your child. You do not want your child to associate with children from inner-city areas. You are vehemently opposed to a busing system that would send your children to an inner-city school. You are less opposed to students being bused from Skyscraper to Middletown, but you want to keep the number of children who are bused to Middletown as small as possible. You are also concerned that your taxes will increase because of busing. Your group tasks are (1) to develop two to four proposals for possible presentation to the Middletown School Board that will get the federal government off your back while minimizing any possible changes in your child's education, and (2) to select a negotiator who will represent your group in negotiations with the other two groups in arriving at a set of proposals to present to the school board.

School staff: Your group is composed of teachers, school administrators, and school social workers. Value-wise, you are in favor of racial integration. You are also in favor of the neighborhood school concept in which the school is a center that serves students and parents in the neighborhood. Therefore, you are unsure whether to support school busing. Some of your staff members fear that juvenile crime, vandalism, and racial clashes will increase if busing occurs. Your tasks are (1) to develop two to four proposals for possible presentation to the Middletown School Board that will creatively further racial integration while interfering very little with the neighborhood-school concept in Middletown, and (2) to select a negotiator who will represent your group in negotiations with the other two groups in arriving at a set of proposals to present to the school board.

Civil rights activists: Your group is delighted that the federal government has declared that the school districts in Skyscraper and Middletown must become racially integrated. You believe such integration will be highly valuable in reducing racial prejudice and racial discrimination in the future. You are ambivalent about using school busing, but you are unaware of other strategies to integrate schools. Your group is composed of a number of community leaders, generally with a liberal orientation. Members of your group include clergy, social workers, directors of social service agencies, and concerned business leaders. You fear that members of the other two groups may seek to minimize efforts to integrate the school systems. Your tasks are (1) to develop two to four proposals that will fully integrate the school systems, and (2) to select a negotiator who will represent your group in negotiations with the other two groups in arriving at a set of proposals to present to the school board.

Step 3. After each group has prepared a set of proposals, the negotiators for the three groups meet to arrive at a consistent set of proposals to present to the Middletown School Board. The other class members observe the negotiations.

Step 4. The group leader defines the win-lose and problem-solving strategies and describes the following techniques that are useful in resolving conflicts: role reversal, stroking, disarming, empathy, I-messages, and inquiry. The class then discusses the following five questions:

1. Did the negotiators arrive at a consistent set of proposals? Why or why not?
2. Did the negotiators use primarily a win-lose or a problem-solving strategy?
3. Did any of the negotiators use the techniques of role reversal, stroking, empathy, I-messages, disarming, or inquiry?
4. How creative were the proposals arrived at by the three groups and the three negotiators?
5. What did the students learn from this exercise?

Exercise D: Creative Thinking

GOAL: To gain experience in coming up with answers that require creative thinking.
NOTE: In doing these exercises on creativity, the group leader is encouraged to add or substitute exercises of his or her own.

Step 1. The group leader explains that questions will be asked that require innovative thinking. The leader may want to create competition and a gamelike atmosphere by dividing the class into two or more subgroups and recording a tally mark on the blackboard when a subgroup shouts out the correct response. (The correct answers are given in Appendix 2.)

1. In counting from 0 to 100, how many 9's do you come across?
2. Two women are playing checkers. They play five games, and each woman wins the same number of games. How come?
3. You are told to take five pills, one every half hour. How many hours will they last?
4. A yacht in the harbor has a 10-foot ladder hanging over the side. If the tide rises 2 feet an hour, how many hours will it take for the water to reach the top of the ladder?
5. Do they have a Fourth of July in England?
6. Why can't someone living in Washington, D.C., be buried west of the Mississippi River?
7. How many outs are there in a baseball inning?
8. A man builds a rectangular house with all four exposures facing south. Then he goes outside and kills a bear. What color is the bear? Where is the house located? (Award a correct response for each answer.)
9. If it takes three minutes to boil an egg, how long will it take to boil seven eggs?
10. Assume two cars start to travel toward each other from a distance of 2,000 miles. If car A travels at a rate of 150 mph and car B at 100 mph, how far will each car be from its origin when they meet?
11. A farmer had three two-thirds size haystacks in one field and six three-fifths size haystacks in another field. He put them all together. How many did he have then?
12. "Jill is my niece," said Paul to his sister Karen. "She is not my niece," said Karen. Explain this.
13. If you had 12 dollars and spent all but 4 dollars, how much would you have left?

Exercise E: The Manhattan Glass

GOAL: To interact in small groups to solve problems that require creativity.

Step 1. The class divides into subgroups of three students each and receives the necessary material (such as matches and handouts) for solving the problems. After one subgroup completes the problem, it is declared a winner and all subgroups receive another problem. A tally of which subgroup arrives at the correct answer first for each problem is kept on the blackboard.

Task 1. These 12 matches are positioned to form 1 large square and 4 small squares. By changing the position of exactly 3 matches, reduce the number of squares to 3 small squares.

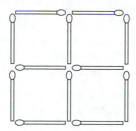

Task 2. These four full-sized matches form a Manhattan glass. The half-match is a cherry. By moving just two matches, make another Manhattan glass of the same shape and size with the cherry on the outside. Do not move the cherry.

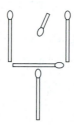

Task 3. Connect all nine dots with only four straight lines without lifting your pencil from the paper.

Task 4. By drawing only two straight lines, divide this shape into four equal parts with two dots in each part.

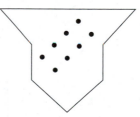

Task 5. Place the numbers 1 through 11 in the 11 circles shown so that every 3 numbers in a straight line add up to 18.

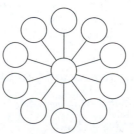

Exercise F: Brainteasers

GOAL: To creatively arrive at answers to 25 brainteasers.

Step 1. The group leader gives the following 25 brainteasers to each student. The class divides into subgroups of about 5 people. The groups have 20 minutes to arrive at answers. The leader starts by indicating that the first answer is "sandbox" and instructs each subgroup to write its answers on a sheet of paper.

Step 2. The subgroups exchange papers for grading. The leader reads the right answers and then asks each subgroup how many correct answers it produced.

1	2	3	4	5
┌─────┐ │SAND │ └─────┘	MAN ───── BOARD	STAND ───── I	R /E/A/D/I/N/G	WEAR ───── LONG
6	**7**	**8**	**9**	**10**
R ROADS A D S	T O W N	CYCLE CYCLE CYCLE	LE VEL	0 ───── M.D. Ph.D. B.S.
11	**12**	**13**	**14**	**15**
KNEE ───── LIGHTS	II III ───── OO	CHAIR	DICE DICE	T O U C H
16	**17**	**18**	**19**	**20**
GROUND ───── feet feet feet feet feet feet	MIND ───── MATTER	He's /Himself	ECNALG	DEATH /LIFE
21	**22**	**23**	**24**	**25**
G.I. ───── CCC CC	─────── Program	B L C O U S E	J YouUMe S T	mt

Exercise G: Resolving Conflicts

GOAL: To practice using techniques to resolve conflicts in real-life situations.

Step 1. The leader describes each of the following techniques that are useful in resolving conflicts: role reversal, stroking, no-lose problem solving, disarming, empathy, I-messages, inquiry, and the law of requisite variety. The students are then instructed to try to use one or more of these techniques to resolve interpersonal conflicts that arise in their daily lives during the next seven days. (To facilitate remembering details of their efforts to use these techniques in conflict situations, students are instructed to record the details of the incidents in a journal.)

Step 2. After a week or so, the leader asks in class for volunteers to (1) describe which techniques they used, (2) briefly summarize the details of the conflict they encountered, and (3) reveal the extent to which the techniques were useful in resolving the conflict. (If no one volunteers, the leader should cite one or two examples of how she used these techniques to resolve interpersonal conflicts in the recent past. Such sharing by the leader may lead others to share their experiences.)

Exercise H: Hard Choices—Funding Social Programs

GOAL: To analyze how decisions are made, to understand that most decisions are based on values and assumptions, and to realize that setting budgets for social programs involves hard choices because of scarce resources.

Step 1. The group leader states that funding sources (such as the federal, state, and local governments, and United Way) have to make difficult choices about how much money to allocate to diverse social programs. Financial resources to fund all social programs are simply unavailable, and some people suffer greatly because they do not receive the needed services and funds.

Step 2. The group divides into subgroups of five or six students. A person from each subgroup volunteers to be an observer for that group. The observer's role is to record information during the exercise related to the following four questions:

1. Which decision-making procedures were used by the group? Possible procedures include consensus, simple majority voting, two-thirds or three-fourths majority voting, and multiple voting. (These procedures should be briefly defined for the observers; the definitions may be given on a handout.)
2. What values and assumptions were expressed as reasons for the decision the subgroup made?
3. Which members appeared to have the most influence in arriving at a decision?
4. What did the influential members say or do to influence the subgroup?

After the exercise is over, the observers will be asked to share this information with the class. The observers should not vote or participate in the discussion of the subgroup.

Step 3. Each subgroup is informed that it is the funding source for a local community and that it has $10 million to allocate for the following social programs, which need a total of $15 million. Each subgroup has the task of deciding how much money to allocate to each agency. No subgroup can go over the $10-million limit. (The group leader should distribute the following information on a handout.)

The Center for Developmental Disabilities needs $1.5 million to care for individuals who have severe cognitive disabilities. All of these individuals are so intellectually impacted that they are unable to walk. It costs $160,000 a year to care for each individual. If the center does not receive its requested funds, there is a danger that some of these clients may not receive the necessary medical care and may die.

The Anti-Poverty Agency needs $3.5 million to maintain families at an income level of only 80 percent of that defined as the poverty line. It costs $14,000 per year to maintain a family of three (generally a single parent with two children). If the agency does not receive its requested funds, there is a danger that many of these families will go hungry, have inadequate shelter, and lack essential clothing for winter.

Protective Services needs $1 million to combat abuse, neglect, and incest. If the agency does not receive all of its needed funds, there is the danger that a number of children will continue to be exposed to abuse, neglect, or incest, which could severely affect them for the rest of their lives.

The Mental Health Center needs $2.5 million to help clients with severe emotional problems, some of whom are so depressed they are suicidal. If the center does not receive all of its needed funds, inadequate services will be provided to clients, and there is a danger that the problems of many clients will intensify. A few may even take their own lives.

The Alcohol and Drug Abuse Treatment Center needs $2 million to help chemically dependent clients and their families. If the center does not receive all of its needed funds, inadequate services will mean the problems experienced by the clients and their families are apt to intensify. Since alcohol and drug abuse are contributing factors to many other problems (such as poverty, mental illness, and family violence), there is a danger these problems will also intensify.

The Shelter for Battered Women, which is located in a house in a residential area, is requesting $500,000. If funds are cut back, the shelter staff assert they will have to turn away some of the battered women and their children who need shelter and other services.

Group Homes for Youths runs four group homes—two for young women and two for young men. It needs $500,000. If needed funds are cut back, this agency will have to reduce the number of youths it is serving. Some will be transferred to more expensive residential treatment programs, some returned to an unhealthy home environment, and some will simply run away.

The Red Cross needs $1 million for its blood bank and for disaster relief. If funds are cut back, there is a danger there will be an insufficient supply of blood available for transfusions, and many of the families who are hit by disasters (such as tornadoes and floods) will not be served.

The Rehabilitation Center provides work training and sheltered work to clients with a variety of physical or mental disabilities. It needs $2 million, or it will be forced to turn away clients. If clients are turned away, they will lose hope of becoming productive and perhaps self-supporting, and will end up requesting assistance from the Mental Health Center and the Anti-Poverty Agency.

Equal Rights is an agency providing a wide range of services to racial minorities in the area—work training, job placement, and housing location. It also investigates and takes legal action against employers and landlords charged with racial discrimination. The agency needs $500,000. If funds are cut back, there is a danger that discrimination against racial minorities will increase.

Step 4. Each subgroup shares with the class its decisions for allocating funds and the reasons behind them. (The cuts that are made can be summarized on the blackboard by having the leader list the names of the agencies, and then having a representative from each subgroup list the amount of money that was cut—totaling $5 million—from the requested allocations.) Ask the subgroup members to share their feelings about the exercise. After each subgroup finishes, the observer for that subgroup should inform the class of the answers to the four questions listed in Step 2. The leader should ask if anyone noted that the Shelter for Battered Women, which has one house, was requesting the same amount of money as Group Homes for Adolescent Youth, which runs four group homes.

Exercise I: Consensus

GOAL: To learn about the complexities of arriving at a consensus on an issue when people hold strongly divergent views.

Step 1. The group leader defines a consensus and describes the group atmosphere necessary to reach a consensus.

Step 2. The class is given a controversial issue to discuss and bring to a consensus. For example, the class may be asked whether it supports legalized abortions during the first several weeks following conception.

Step 3. After the exercise is over, the students discuss their feelings about the pressure to arrive at a consensus in the face of strongly divergent views and why the class was, or was not, able to arrive at a consensus.

Exercise J: Subjective Influences on Merit Raises

GOAL: To demonstrate that group decisions are often substantially affected by subjective influences.

Step 1. Six students volunteer to play the roles of social work faculty members on a merit committee at a university. The department has 18 faculty members, and six of these members have applied for "superior" merit increases. The committee has a total of $12,000, all of which must be distributed to these 6 applicants. The 3 areas of recognizing merit increases are teaching excellence, research and publishing, and services to the campus and the community.

The decision on how much money to distribute to each applicant rests entirely with this committee. The committee may recommend that all, or nearly all, of the $12,000 be distributed to one or two applicants, with the others receiving little or none, or the committee may distribute the money fairly evenly among the applicants. The committee is provided with the information in Table 6.1 about the meritorious activities of the applicants. (This information may be displayed on the chalkboard or on individual sheets distributed to the class.)

Step 2. The leader hands out an individual "additional information card" to each role player. Each card has a one-sentence description of one of the applicants. The other role players are not allowed to see the information on the card. (These cards should be prepared in advance.) Each card provides information likely to foster a strong personal reaction toward the respective faculty member. The role players are told they are free to bring up the information on their cards during the role playing or to disregard the information. The leader is free to be creative in writing the additional information on the cards. The following are some appropriate examples:

> "Garcia is planning to retire next year, so a significant merit increase would not only recognize his years of public service to the community, but would also substantially increase the pension he will receive after retirement since monthly payments from the pension plan are based on a teacher's last three earning years."
>
> "Pagel, single mother with three young children, is working on her doctorate and is by far the lowest-paid member of the department; in fact, she's barely able to financially provide for her family."

■ TABLE 6.1

Faculty Member	Summary of Meritorious Activities	Teacher Rating[1]
Juan Garcia	Served on university budget committee. Is president of the Board of Directors of the United Way in the community.	4.1
Karen Pagel	Attended two professional conferences. Is the faculty advisor to the Student Social Work Club.	4.2
Dale Riesen	Published a social work textbook and two articles in professional journals.	3.5
Jean Duvey	Is chair of the department and did the bulk of the work needed to achieve reaccreditation of the social work program by the Council on Social Work Education.	4.0
Kevin Aaron	Wrote and received a grant on "Long Distance Social Work Education" that brought $150,000 to the program for using communication technology to provide social work education classes to other communities in the state.	3.9
Joyce Jackson	Presented three papers on child abuse intervention at national conferences.	4.3

[1]Based on student course evaluations (5 = highest, 1 = lowest)

"Riesen is married but is also secretly dating one of the female students in the social work program; he refuses to advise students or to serve on departmental committees."

"Duvey works many more hours for the department than any other faculty member, but much of the work that she does (paperwork and advising of prospective students) goes unnoticed by the other faculty members."

"Aaron is addicted to alcohol (he was recently involved in a drunk-driving accident and left the scene of the accident in which someone was injured); he refuses to acknowledge his alcohol abuse, and has hidden the drunk-driving incident from the other social work faculty members and the university administration."

"Jackson has been extremely helpful to you and the other young instructors in the department, but her mentoring of young faculty members has not been recognized financially by the campus."

Step 3. The role players discuss the applicants for merit awards. The role players are given an opportunity to share their additional information about one faculty member. Also, if they desire, they can fabricate and share additional information (which may be positive or negative in nature) about the faculty member listed on their card. The role players then end up making decisions about how much money to assign to each of the six applicants.

Step 4. The role players and the class then process the decisions that were arrived at by discussing the following kinds of questions:

1.   Did the additional information—and/or any other subjective information that was fabricated—play an important role in determining the amount of the merit raises assigned to the six applicants?

2.   Did the role players reveal the additional information on their cards in the group discussions? Why, or why not?

3.   What were the key values (such as quality teaching or family values) that contributed to the decisions that were made?

4.   In making group decisions, such as this one, which tends to have greater weight— objective information or subjective information?

Exercise K: Midterm Exam Using Jigsaw Puzzles*

GOAL: To evaluate the extent to which students are able to apply group concepts/theories to a real situation.

NOTE: The instructor of the class should lead this exercise.

Step 1. The instructor should acquire identical jigsaw puzzles. Enough puzzles should be acquired so that each subgroup of six to eight students in class has a jigsaw puzzle. There should be a table (such as a card table) for each jigsaw. The jigsaw puzzles should each have at least two hundred pieces and should not be too difficult, nor too easy. The instructor should also have a hand-held video camera.

Step 2. Students should be informed early in the semester that the midterm exam will be a combination of an in-class activity and take home exam. Prior to the exam, students should have read at least the first six chapters in the text, and also have read the instructions for this exam.

Step 3. On the day of the exam, the instructor should place each puzzle (with the pieces still in the box) on a table, prior to the students arriving. Tables should be spaced far enough apart so that group members may move around freely, and there should be enough room to allow videotaping of each individual student. Chairs should be accessible but not placed around the tables. In this way each group will have to make decisions concerning seating arrangements. A towel should cover each puzzle, so that students cannot study the puzzles when they enter the classroom.

Step 4. Instructions to Students: Upon arrival:

1.   Remind students that the exercise will take the entire class period, typically one hour and fifteen minutes. Divide the class into subgroups or teams by counting off

*This exercise was written by Michael Wallace, MSW, instructor at the University of Wisconsin-Whitewater.

by A-B-A-B or 1-2-1-2, etc. If there are three tables the count should go A-B-C-A, etc. Groups must be identical in size of six to eight members each. Send students to their respective tables.

2. Remove towels, uncovering the jigsaw puzzles.

3. Inform students that the purpose of the exercise will become clear after completion of the task at hand.

4. Inform the class that the teams are in competition with one another, and that the team to finish first wins. (Bonus points may be given by the instructor to each member of the winning team.)

5. The only rule is that students may not talk to members of the opposing team or switch teams.

6. Inform students that the instructor will videotape both teams in action during the puzzle competition. Students must not ask any questions of the instructor during taping.

7. Finally, remind the class that in order to accomplish the task, utilizing problem-solving and communication skills is required.

Step 5. Videotaping tips for the instructor:

1. Position yourself for videotaping. Make sure the camera is turned on, lens cap removed. Begin recording as you tell the class to start working on their jigsaw puzzles.

2. During the first five minutes of recording, switch focus fairly often between the tables. Find out who takes initial leadership roles such as holding the cover of the puzzle box on which the completed puzzle is depicted.

3. After the first five minutes, focus on a single table for five minutes before switching to the opposing team. Note: complete the jigsaw puzzle typically takes between fifteen and twenty-five minutes.

4. Be aware of when a team is about to complete its puzzle so that you can tape the winning moment, then switch to taping the other team's reactions.

Step 6. Class Discussion and Group Observation:

1. After one team has completed their jigsaw puzzle, have students take their seats. As the instructor rewinds the videotape, the opportunity for a brief discussion and general question and answer period may arise. Appropriate questions the instructor may pose include: what was the activity like for you, or did anyone in your group assume a leadership role, or how well did you communicate with one another?

2. After rewinding the tape and brief discussion, distribute Part I of the exam. Instruct the class to take out a blank sheet of paper and list each member of their respective group on the page. This is used as an aid while viewing the tape for specific communication patterns, who assume which roles, and nothing other aspects of group dynamics.

3. Remind students to watch and listen attentively since the videotape will only be shown once. Play the video.

4. After viewing the video, distribute Part II of the exam, the take home portion. Again review areas of focus and answer any final questions from students.

Step 7. The instructor informs the students that their answers to the exam are due at a specified date. The exams are turned in, and graded by the instructor. The exams are later returned to the students, and then discussed.

PART I OF EXAM

Group Observation

Before viewing the videotape of the group exercise, PLEASE READ CAREFULLY.

The first part of this Exam utilizes your observation skills in viewing the videotape of the group puzzle exercise. When doing so, focus only on the group you participated in. Take notes on a separate sheet of paper.

When observing, please pay attention to the following:

> Group Development
> Leadership
> Roles
> Power
> Norms
> Conformity

Specifically pay attention to:

Verbal Communication—Who spoke to whom? Who talked? How often did she/he talk? Was everyone listened to? Who interrupted whom? How often? Who encouraged others to speak? Use the observation sheet as a guide.

Nonverbal Communication—Who held the cover of the box with the completed puzzle picture? Was the picture displayed for all to see? Did members pass the cover to one another? How often, and to whom? Did anyone work alone? If so, who? Did members stay seated, or standing in the same position? Did people move around the table? Or visit the other table? Did some members focus on one section of the puzzle? Any other nonverbals, facial expressions, paralanguage, tone on voice, gestures?

Pay attention to your own nonverbals.

PART II OF EXAM

Group Process Analysis—Take Home

Using your notes from observing the videotape, your own experience as a participant in the group puzzle exercise, class handouts, and the text, please answer the following questions:

Group Development
Did you experience any of the stages of group development as described in the text (Garland, Jones, and Kolodny; Tuckman, etc.)? If so, identify and describe the stage(s). Say why these fit.

Leadership
Did anyone take leadership of the group? Did she/he fit into any of the approaches to leadership as described in the text (trait, charismatic, etc.)? If so, which one? Justify your answer. If you took a leadership role, answer the same. Which approach? Justify your answer.

Roles
The texts describe both task and maintenance roles. Which role(s) did you assume? Define the role(s). Describe why this fit your participation in the group.

Power
Was there any member (or members) including yourself in the group who influenced other participants? If so, what type of power was exerted as described in text (French and Raven)? Please describe why this fits.

Group Norms/Conformity
Was pressure exerted upon any member to conform to the group? If so, did it change the member's behavior? If you felt pressure to conform, what was that like? Any positive or negative reinforcement? Please describe.

Did you, or any members, engage in any disruptive behavior? If so, what type (as defined in the text: clown, bear, etc.)? Support your answer. If disruptive behavior occurred, how was this handled by the group?

Verbal Communication

What were the patterns of communication within the group? One way? Two way? Who spoke to whom? Who talked? How often did she/he talk? Was everyone listened to? If not, any reasons why not? Who interrupted whom? How often did you speak? To whom? Did you use "I statements?" Did you use active listening skills? Did you encourage others to speak?

Nonverbal Communication

Who held the cover of the box with the completed puzzle picture? Was the picture displayed for all to see? Did members pass the cover to one another? How often, and to whom? Did anyone work alone? If so, who? Did members stay seated, or standing in the same position? Did people move around the table? Or visit the other table? Did some members focus on one section of the puzzle? What were your nonverbals like? Facial expressions, paralanguage, tone of voice, gestures?

Goal Achievement

Did the group you participated in complete the task (finish the puzzle)? If yes, what factors do you think contributed to its success? If not, what factors do you think contributed to the task not being completed? Was the atmosphere of the group competitive or cooperative? Use text to explain.

Group Analysis

Did group members share information appropriately? Request information as needed? Did you feel that the group created an atmosphere in which information could be shared comfortably? Did all members participate? If not, why not? What could have been done to gain wider participation? Was everyone listened to? If not, why not? How cooperative or competitive were your group members? How did the group make decisions? What problems did the group have in working together?

Personal Analysis

How active were you, or how much did you contribute to the group process? Were you willing, and were you able to express your opinion? If not, why not? Did you find yourself working with others or alone? Did you feel you assumed a leadership role, or followed the group? Explain how this happened. What was the group experience like for you? What did you learn about yourself?

PLEASE NOTE: Your group process analysis should be typed, double-spaced, and 5 to 10 pages in length. The notes that you wrote in class in response to Part I of the exam should be attached to your group process analysis paper.

CHAPTER SEVEN

Working with Diverse Groups

GOALS

Social work practice, whether it includes working with individuals or groups, must take into account the enormous diversity of clients and consumers of social services. The goal of this chapter is to present some ideas and information regarding various diverse groups that is useful for group workers and should enhance their ability to work with people whose backgrounds and experiences are substantially different from their own. Material is presented on: ethnic sensitive practice, empowerment, strengths perspective, culturally competent practice, and feminist intervention.

The profession of social work has had a long tradition of seeking to protect the rights of populations at risk and advocating equal opportunities for their members. For example, the Code of Ethics of the National Association of Social Workers states:

> Social workers should act to prevent and eliminate domination, exploitation, and discrimination against any person, group, or class on the basis of race, ethnicity, national origin, color, age, religion, sex, sexual orientation, marital status, political belief, mental or physical disability, or any other preference, personal characteristic, or status.[1]

The code also states:

> Social workers should act to expand choice and opportunity for all persons, with special regard for vulnerable, disadvantaged, oppressed, and exploited persons and groups.
>
> Social workers should promote conditions that encourage respect for the diversity of cultures and social diversity within the United States and globally.[2]

■ DEFINITIONS OF KEY TERMS

Unfortunately, there has been a long history of prejudice, discrimination, and oppression against populations at risk in our culture. Some definitions may be useful.

Prejudice means prejudging, making a judgment in advance of due examination. Prejudice is a combination of stereotyped beliefs and negative attitudes, so that prejudiced individuals think about members of a minority group in a predetermined, usually negative, categorical way.

Discrimination involves taking action against people because they belong to a category. Discriminatory behavior often derives from prejudiced attitudes.

Merton, however, notes that prejudice and discrimination can occur independently of each other. Merton describes four different "types" of people:

1. The *unprejudiced nondiscriminator,* in both belief and practice, upholds American ideals of freedom and equality. This person is not prejudiced against other groups and, on principle, will not discriminate against them.

2. The *unprejudiced discriminator* is not personally prejudiced but may sometimes, reluctantly, discriminate against other groups because it seems socially or financially convenient to do so.

3. The *prejudiced nondiscriminator* feels hostile to other groups but recognizes that law and social pressures are opposed to overt discrimination. This person does not translate prejudice into action.

4. The *prejudiced discriminator* does not believe in the values of freedom and equality and consistently discriminates against other groups in both word and deed.[3]

An example of an unprejudiced discriminator is the owner of a condominium complex in an all-white, middle-class suburb who refuses to sell a condominium to an African American family because he fears that doing so will reduce the value of the remaining units. An example of a prejudiced nondiscriminator is a personnel director of a fire department who believes Hispanics are unreliable and poor firefighters yet complies with affirmative action efforts to hire and train Hispanic firefighters.

It should be noted that it is difficult to keep personal prejudices from eventually leading to some form of discrimination. Strong laws and firm informal social norms are necessary to break the causal relationship between prejudice and discrimination.

Two types of discrimination exist—*de jure* and *de facto*. De jure discrimination is legal discrimination. The so-called Jim Crow laws in the South in the last century gave force of law to many discriminatory practices against blacks, including denial of the right to trial, prohibition against voting, and prohibition against interracial marriage. Today, in the United States, there is practically no de jure discrimination, as these laws have been declared unconstitutional and have been removed.

De facto discrimination refers to discrimination that actually exists, whether legal or not. Housing patterns in many cities are an example of de facto discrimination. Wealthy whites tend to live in affluent suburbs, nonwhites in inner-city areas. The effects of such segregation tend to carry over to other arenas; for example, clear discrepancies in the quality of educational systems between affluent suburbs and inner-city areas.

Oppression is the unjust or cruel exercise of authority or power. Members of populations at risk in our society are frequently victimized by oppression from segments of the white power structure. Oppression and discrimination are closely related, as all acts of oppression are also acts of discrimination.

A *minority group* is a group that has a subordinate status and is subjected to discrimination. It is not size that is critical in defining a group as a minority but rather lack of power. Women comprise the majority in our society but are a minority according to this definition.

Populations at risk are diverse populations currently victimized (or in danger of being victimized in the future) by discrimination, economic deprivation, or oppression. Chapter 2 also indicates that social workers have an obligation to advance social and economic conditions for populations at risk.

Diverse groups are groups with characteristics that are distinct from the dominant group in a society. Many diverse groups in our society are also populations at risk.

Professional social work education is committed to understand and appreciate human diversity.[4] The population groups that compose human diversity, according to the Educational Policy and Accreditation Standards of the Council on Social Work Education, include, but are not limited to, those groups distinguished by "age, class, color, disability, ethnicity, family structure, gender, marital status, national origin, race, religion, sex, and sexual orientation."[5]

Social justice is an ideal condition in which all members of a society have the same basic rights, protection, opportunities, obligations, and social benefits.[6] Economic justice is also an ideal condition in which all members of a society have the same opportunities for attaining material goods, income, and wealth.

Stereotypes are fixed mental images of a group that are applied to all its members. Stereotyping is the attribution of a fixed and usually inaccurate and unfavorable conception to a category of people.

In working with diverse groups, a social worker needs (1) to be aware of personal stereotypes and preconceptions about diverse groups, (2) to have a knowledge about the diverse groups that he or she is working with and the special needs of those groups, and (3) to be aware of which intervention techniques are apt to be effective with those groups and which will not.

Exercise 7.1: Some of My Stereotypes

GOAL: This exercise is designed to identify some of your personal stereotypes that you need to be aware of in order to develop an objective approach to social work practice with diverse groups.

1. **Assume that you are single. Place an *X* by the name of each group into which you would hesitate to marry.**

   _____ Russian

   _____ Cuban

   _____ French

   _____ Mexican

   _____ African American

   _____ White American

   _____ Native American

   _____ Puerto Rican

   _____ Italian

   _____ German

   _____ Polish

   _____ Norwegian

   _____ Samoan

   _____ Arab

   _____ Israeli

   _____ Chinese

   _____ Japanese

   _____ Filipino

   _____ Eskimo

   _____ Brazilian

   _____ Hungarian

   _____ Vietnamese

   _____ Pakistani

   _____ Korean

2. **As specifically as possible, state (next to each group that you checked) the reasons for the groups you checked.**

3. **Do you hold stereotypes about the groups you checked?**

■ YOUR STEREOTYPES AND PRECONCEPTIONS

Our society has had a long history of discriminating against populations at risk. The extent of the discrimination has changed with time for some diverse groups. Italian Americans and Chinese Americans, for example, were victimized by discrimination to a greater extent during the last century than now.

All of us have some prejudices against populations at risk because we were socialized among others where prejudices abound. Abraham Lincoln is recognized as the person who was most responsible in our society for ending slavery. But Lincoln had prejudices against African Americans, as illustrated in the following statement:

> I will say, then, that I am not, nor ever have been in favor of bringing about in any way the social and political equality of the white and black races; that I am not, nor ever have been, in favor of making voters or jurors of Negroes, nor of qualifying them to hold office, nor to intermarry with White people . . . and in as much as they cannot so live, while they do remain together there must be the position of superior and inferior, and I as much as any other man am in favor of having the superior position assigned to the White race.[7]

As social workers it is critically important for each of us to recognize our personal prejudices and stereotypes against populations at risk. Social workers have taken a professional value position to combat discrimination as stated in the NASW Code of Ethics. In working with populations at risk it is important to be aware of our stereotypes and prejudices so that we do not subtly discriminate against them. By being aware of our prejudices and stereotypes, we can work on reducing and eliminating them.

Exercise 7.2: Questionnaire about Gays and Lesbians

GOAL: This exercise is designed to assess your views about gays and lesbians.

1. **Answer the following questionnaire in terms of your current views.**
   1. Gay men are effeminate; they have a "swishy" walk, talk with a lisp, and are limp-wristed.
      a. True   b. False

   2. Most lesbians are masculine; they have short hair, dress mainly in men's clothes, and appear manly.
      a. True   b. False

   3. Gay men desired to be women.
      a. True   b. False

   4. Lesbians desire to be men.
      a. True   b. False

   5. In a gay or lesbian couple, one partner will assume the dominant (sometimes called masculine) role and the other will assume the submissive (sometimes called feminine) role.
      a. True   b. False

   6. Most gay men are child molesters.
      a. True   b. False

7. People are either homosexual or heterosexual.
   a. True   b. False

8. Most gays and lesbians are mentally ill.
   a. True   b. False

9. Gays and lesbians are to blame for the AIDS epidemic.
   a. True   b. False

10. People choose to be gay or lesbian.
    a. True   b. False

2. **Read the material in this chapter on myths and facts about gays and lesbians. Did this material lead you to want to change any of your answers to these questions? If yes, specify which answers you would change.**

Currently there are a number of commonly accepted myths and stereotypes about gays and lesbians. Some of these myths will be summarized and then followed with factual information. As you read these myths, consider whether or not you believe any of them.

Myth 1—Appearance and Mannerisms. All gay men are effeminate; they have a "swishy" walk, talk with a lisp, and are limp-wristed. Correspondingly, all lesbians are masculine; they have short hair, dress mainly in men's clothes, and appear manly.

Fact. Because of these stereotypes, many people erroneously believe it is easy to identify gays and lesbians. The fact is that most gays and lesbians dress, look, and behave just like everyone else. Except for a small percentage of individuals, it is impossible to recognize a gay or lesbian simply by his or her appearance or mannerisms.[8]

Myth 2—Gender Identity. Gay men desire to be women, and lesbians desire to be men.
Fact. This myth confuses gender identity (masculine or feminine) with choice of sexual partner (homosexual or heterosexual). The fact is that while gays and lesbians generally choose a sexual partner of the same sex, their gender identity is identical to that of heterosexuals. A gay man views himself as male and does not desire to be female. A lesbian views herself as female and does not desire to be male.[9]

Myth 3—Sexual Roles. In a gay or lesbian couple, one partner will assume the dominant (sometimes called masculine) role and the other will assume the submissive (sometimes called feminine) role.
Fact. Such role playing occurs infrequently as most gays and lesbians engage in many forms of behavior and do not restrict themselves to one or another role. Gay or lesbian partners often switch roles during the sexual act or engage in mutual oral-genital stimulation. In regard to role playing outside the sexual act itself, the vast majority of gay men do not attempt to play the female role, and the vast majority of lesbians reject the entire practice of male-female role playing.[10]

Myth 4—Child Molesters. Gay men are child molesters.

Fact. The vast majority of child molesting is done by heterosexual men to young girls.[11] Parents should be more fearful that heterosexual male teachers will try to seduce their young daughters than that the gay male teachers will molest their young sons. There is no reason to assume that a homosexual is more apt to be a child molester than is a heterosexual.

Myth 5—Homosexual or Heterosexual. People are either homosexual or heterosexual.

Fact. Kinsey and his colleagues demonstrated that it is a mistake to conceptualize homosexuality and heterosexuality as comprising two separate categories. Instead, these researchers found that many people have had some heterosexual and some homosexual experiences, to varying degrees.[12] Their seven-point continuum is shown in Figure 7.1. Probably a majority of adults either have had a gay or lesbian experience or have fantasized about having one.

Myth 6—Mental Illness. Gay and lesbians are mentally ill.

Fact. Research has found no evidence that homosexuals are less well-adjusted than heterosexuals. Personality tests reveal no differences (except for sexual orientations) between gays and lesbians and heterosexuals.[13] In 1973, the American Psychiatric Association voted to remove homosexuality from its list of mental disorders, and thus homosexuality is no longer officially classified as a psychiatric disorder.

Myth 7—AIDS. Gays and lesbians are to blame for the AIDS epidemic.

Fact. Although gay men are a high-risk group for the AIDS virus in our society, very few cases have been reported among lesbians. (Gay men are at high risk for acquiring AIDS due to the transfer of bodily fluids that occurs during anal intercourse.) AIDS is a life-threatening disease for anyone (gay/lesbian or heterosexual) who is HIV-infected. In many African countries, the majority of people afflicted with AIDS are heterosexuals.

Gay men are not the cause of AIDS. Blaming a deadly disease on the group who, in the United States, have suffered and died disproportionately from AIDS is a classic case of blaming the victim. While it is true that the largest single risk group of persons with AIDS is gay men, it is ludicrous to conclude that this group caused this health crisis. AIDS is caused by a virus. It is also ludicrous to assert that gay men want to deliver the disease to the world after first delivering it to themselves. Quite the contrary, the gay male community in the United States has been in the forefront of educating people about behavior that minimizes the transmission of the disease. Gay men have radically altered their sexual behavior patterns, as evidenced by a substantial drop in the rate of transmission of the disease among this group in the past few years.

Myth 8—Sexual Preference. People choose to be gay or lesbian.

Fact. Research shows that sexual orientation is established early in life, perhaps long before adolescence.[14] While every person has the potential to behave sexually in

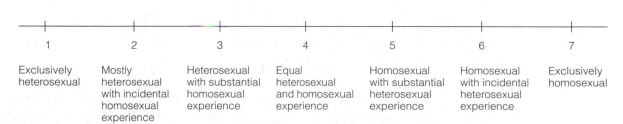

1	2	3	4	5	6	7
Exclusively heterosexual	Mostly heterosexual with incidental homosexual experience	Heterosexual with substantial homosexual experience	Equal heterosexual and homosexual experience	Homosexual with substantial heterosexual experience	Homosexual with incidental heterosexual experience	Exclusively homosexual

Figure 7.1
Sexual orientation

the manner he or she may choose, one's true sexual orientation may be set before birth or at a very early age, and then no longer influenced by the environment. Many homosexually oriented persons behave as if they are heterosexual in this society because there are so many sanctions against homosexuality. However, their true sexual orientation and preferred sexual partner, in the absence of these negative sanctions, would be someone of the same gender. Human beings certainly have the ability to respond sexually to people who are not their preferred sexual partners, but to do so requires going against the current of their innermost inclinations. The question of what causes a person's sexual orientation to be set (either as homosexual or heterosexual) has not as yet been answered. It appears that some people are naturally heterosexual in orientation and others are naturally homosexual, just as some people are naturally left-handed and others are naturally right-handed.

■ KNOWLEDGE ABOUT DIVERSE GROUPS

Social workers sometimes make the mistake of using their own social, cultural, or economic values as the norm. The following example illustrates this mistake by an adult services worker for a public welfare department. (Names and other identifying information have been changed.)

> Bill Ridder received an anonymous call that a 79-year-old male, Vern Broadcort, was living in abysmal conditions. Ridder made a home visit. Vern Broadcort lived alone in a rural area in northern Minnesota. The house was a mess. There was nearly an inch of dirt and newspapers on the floor. The house had no running water or toilet facilities, and Broadcort's clothes were filthy. He had not taken a bath for over a year. The house was heated, even in winter, by only a small wood stove in the kitchen. The refrigerator had a rancid odor because some of the food had spoiled. There were no clean dishes; a green mold was growing on some that had been used but not washed. Broadcort mentioned he occasionally washed his dishes in rainwater. The dishwater that was in a large bowl had a muddy, dark brown color to it.
>
> Ridder also visited some of Broadcort's neighbors, who expected the house to catch fire one of these days. They said Broadcort frequently drank himself into a stupor and then would smoke cigarettes. When he coughed, which he often did (according to the neighbors), hot ashes from the cigarette would be blown several feet away. Broadcort did appear mentally alert, however, and he stated his doctor felt he was in fair health. He did suffer from emphysema, arthritis, and an occasional occurrence of gout.
>
> Ridder decided that the best place for Broadcort to live was in a nursing home and found one with an available bed. He then asked Broadcort if he would be interested in moving there. The reply from Broadcort shocked Ridder. "No way am I moving to a nursing home," he said. "This is my home. I was born and raised here, and I intend to die here. If you should get a court order to send me to a nursing home, I'll give up the will to live and soon die there. I personally don't believe you can get a court order to make me move out of here. I own this place, and I'm mentally alert and not hurting anyone. Who do you think you are that you can come in here and tell me where to live!"
>
> Ridder went back to his supervisor to discuss the case. The supervisor informed Ridder that Broadcort, if mentally competent, had the right to live where he chose, as long as he was not hurting anyone else in the process. The supervisor then tactfully asked Ridder to think about whether he was seeking to force his values onto Broadcort, who obviously was content with his living environment. Ridder thought a while and agreed that he probably was.

If a social worker has experienced the prejudices that a client is exposed to and was raised in an environment similar to a client's, that worker may be more perceptive about and empathetic to that client. An African American social worker, for example, may better understand what African American clients are saying and experiencing than a white social worker would. Similarly, a worker with a disability may be more perceptive to what a client with a disability is thinking and feeling. Conversely, clients who are members of a population at risk may initially feel they are being better understood when the worker is a member of the same group.

On the other hand, a social worker does not need to be a member of the client's minority group in order to work effectively with that client. The problematic nature of cross-cultural social work does not preclude its effectiveness. Mizio has noted, for example, that effective white workers can establish viable working relationships with non-white clients and that some nonwhite workers are less effective with others of the same race or culture than white workers.[15] The following example illustrates this point:

> In answering the question of whether a white middle-class psychiatrist can treat a black family, I cannot help but think back over my own experiences. When I first came to New York and decided to go into psychotherapy I had two main thoughts: (1) that my problems were culturally determined, and (2) that they were related to my Catholic upbringing. I had grown up in an environment in which the Catholic Church had tremendous influence. With these factors in mind, I began to think in terms of the kind of therapist I could best relate to. In addition to being warm and sensitive, he had to be black and Catholic. Needless to say, that was like looking for a needle in a haystack. But after inquiring around, I was finally referred to a black Catholic psychiatrist.
>
> Without going into too much detail, let me say that he turned out to be not so sensitive and not so warm. I terminated my treatment with him and began to see another therapist who was warm, friendly, sensitive, understanding and very much involved with me. Interestingly enough, he was neither black nor Catholic. As a result of that personal experience, I have come to believe that it is not so much a question of whether the therapist is black or white but whether he is competent, warm and understanding. Feelings, after all, are neither black nor white.[16]

Perhaps it is helpful to state the obvious. We are all human, and we all have some uniquenesses and differences. But being human, we also have a lot in common. As with any client, the social worker who is working with a client who is a member of a population at risk needs the skills that will lead to positive changes. Such skills include listening, relationship building, competence, empathy, and problem solving. A worker's effectiveness is also increased substantially by knowledge of a client's minority group and its unique characteristics.

There are an *immense* number of different minority groups in our society—several racial groups, numerous ethnic groups, women, gays and lesbians, many religious groups, people with mental or physical disabilities, the elderly, and others. It is beyond the scope of this chapter to describe the unique characteristics of these diverse groups. Instead, a few characteristics of some minority groups will be summarized to illustrate the importance of learning about the minority group of a client.

When working with Native Americans (American Indians) it is considered rude—an attempt to intimidate, in fact—to maintain direct eye contact.[17] Social workers and other professionals need to respect this cultural pattern by seeking to substantially reduce direct eye contact with Native Americans.

If a male client begins talking about his partner, it is a mistake to assume the partner is a woman and refer to the person as "she" or "her."[18] The client may be gay. Such an erroneous assumption could lead the client to terminate the interview and further contact. Obviously, this caution applies to female clients as well. Most helping professionals have also come to realize that attempts to change a client's sexual orientation are usually unsuccessful. In the past, some heterosexual therapists attempted to change homosexual orientation, with poor results. As explained previously, sexual orientation appears to be established early in life.

Chicano men, in contrast to Anglo men, have been described as exhibiting greater pride in their maleness.[19] Machismo—a male's sense of personal virility—is highly valued among Chicano men and is displayed by males to portray dominance and superiority. Machismo is demonstrated differently by different people. Some may seek to be irresistible to women and to have a number of sexual partners. Some resort to weapons or fighting. Others boast of their achievements, even those that never occurred. Recent writers have noted that the feminist movement, urbanization, upward mobility, and acculturation are contributing to the decline of machismo.[20] Chicanos also tend to be more familistic than Anglos. Familism is the belief that the family takes precedence over the individual. Schaefer notes:

Familism is generally regarded as good because an extended family provides emotional strength at times of family crisis. . . . The many significant aspects of familism include: (1) importance of the *compadrazo* (godparent–godchild relationship); (2) benefits of financial dependency of kin; (3) availability of relatives as a source of advice; and (4) active involvement of the elderly within the family.[21]

On the negative side, familism may discourage youth from pursuing opportunities that will take them away from the family. It should be noted that the differences between Chicanos and Anglos with regard to machismo and familism are differences of degree, not of kind. Later in this chapter we will examine how the concept of familism can be utilized in providing services to Chicanos.

Our culture places a high value on physical beauty. Americans spend large proportions of their budgets on clothes, cosmetics, exercise programs, and special diets to look more attractive. Beauty is identified with goodness and ugliness with evil. Movies, television, and books portray heroes and heroines as physically attractive and villains as ugly. Snow White, for example, was beautiful, while the evil witch was ugly. Unfortunately, this emphasis on the body beautiful has caused those with a disability to be the object of cruel jokes and has occasionally resulted in people with a disability being shunned or treated as inferior. Wright has noted that the emphasis on the body beautiful has also led society to believe that those with a disability "ought" to feel inferior.[22] Wright has coined the term *the requirement of mourning* for this expectation of society.[23] An able-bodied person who spends a great deal of time, money, and effort to be physically attractive psychologically wants a person with a disability to mourn the absence of physical perfection. The able-bodied person needs feedback that it is worthwhile and important to strive to have an attractive physique.

Another consequence of the body-beautiful cult is that people with a disability are sometimes pitied. Most resent such pity and the accompanying condescension. They want to be treated as equals. Our society also tends to equate a specific disability with general incompetence. Weinberg has noted that people talk louder in the presence of someone who is blind, assuming that people who cannot see cannot hear either.[24] People with a physical disability at times are assumed to be mentally and socially retarded.[25]

In seeking to participate fully in our society, people with a disability must face not only the obstacles created by their disabilities but also the additional obstacles created by society's reaction to disability. When working with people with a disability, helping professionals need to provide assistance in both areas. Social workers also need to advocate for eradicating prejudices and discrimination against people with a disability to ensure equal rights and opportunities for them.

There are many ways for social workers to learn about the values, beliefs, and culture of diverse individuals and groups. The approaches include reading books and articles, watching videos and films, joining clubs and organizations that have numerous diverse members, socializing with people of diverse backgrounds, taking courses in diversity, attending workshops on diversity, living in communities with diversity, and so on.

■ POSTURE OF RECIPROCITY

Kalyanpur and Harry assert that a key approach for social workers in providing culturally responsive services is a "posture of reciprocity."[26] With the posture of reciprocity, a worker establishes a relationship with diverse clients in which both the worker and the clients not only feel free but also are expected to share their relevant beliefs and values about key service issues.

To illustrate the importance of the posture of reciprocity, Kalyanpur and Harry describe a court case involving white social workers and a Hmong family—a court case in which the social workers failed to take a posture-of-reciprocity approach. While the social workers were providing services to this Hmong family, they knew that one of the children (seven-year-old Kou) had two club feet and wanted Kou to have corrective surgery. The social workers were aware that in the United States a club foot is considered a deformity and therefore a stigmatizing condition. When Kou's parents refused surgery, the social workers did not ask the parents for an explanation. Inquiring along with explaining their own views on this situation would have been consistent with the posture of reciprocity. Instead of taking this approach, the social workers petitioned a court to order the surgery to be performed.

In court, Kou's parents stated that Kou's club feet were "a sign of good luck" and that Kou was born with club feet so that a "warrior ancestor whose own feet were wounded in battle could be released from a sort of spiritual entrapment."[27] They opposed the operation because they believed a superior being had made it possible for the warrior ancestor to escape his spiritual entrapment by Kou's being created with two club feet. To defy the superior being by having the surgery, the Hmong family argued, would result in the superior being's taking out wrath on this Hmong family, and probably on the larger Hmong community. The judge ruled in favor of the parents and did not order surgery.

Some important questions arise from this case. Does the Hmong family's refusal of surgery for their son's club feet because of a belief that the condition is a blessing to the family constitute abuse? Whose views are best for the child—the parents' or the social workers'? Is the child better off living his life with two club feet, which are seen as a blessing in the Hmong community, or having corrective surgery, which is viewed in the Hmong community as defying the superior being? In any case, would not a frank and open sharing of beliefs and values between the social workers and the Hmong family have been a better approach? Perhaps such an approach would have prevented an adversarial relationship developing as a result of the social workers' charging the parents with abuse when they refused surgery.

■ WHICH INTERVENTION TECHNIQUES WORK?

Exercise 7.3: Victimized in Iran

GOAL: This exercise is designed to assist you in understanding the fears and trepidations of certain ethnic and racial groups when they seek help from a social service agency in this country.

1. Imagine that you and a friend are traveling in Iran. In a medium-size city in central Iran, your knapsacks are stolen, and they contain your passports, other forms of identification, travelers checks, and money. What are your fears and trepidations?

2. If you decide to go to a social service agency for help, would you be wary of how you will be treated? Would you be worried the agency may not believe your story and perhaps will turn you over to the police—who may throw you in jail?

3. **Because you do not speak the national language, would you be worried about how you will communicate your predicament?**

The feelings you stated in Exercise 7.3 are similar to those of many members of racial and ethnic groups when they seek help from a social service agency in this country. They probably have been victimized by Anglo prejudice and discrimination in the past. Perhaps they have even been victimized by entire systems—education, law enforcement, and health care, for example. When they seek help they may display their fears and concerns through anxiety, fear, and visible stress. Some may appear depressed, nonassertive, and passive because they feel overwhelmed and seek to be compliant. Others may be extremely sensitive to the slightest evidence of unjust treatment and may respond aggressively to such normal procedures as waiting or filling out forms.

White workers with nonwhite clients need to be aware that the emotional reactions displayed by clients will probably be a combination of their reactions to their problems and to their distrust of agencies they view as part of the white power structure. If clients are highly anxious and fearful, workers need initially to focus on putting them at ease by conveying warmth, competence, calmness, and interest. They need to listen carefully to clients, convey understanding, and identify specific fears so those fears can be alleviated.

Anger Management

Social workers should generally not personalize the outbursts of anger from clients. Clients may display anger for a variety of reasons over which the individual worker has little or no control. Ventilation can sometimes reduce anger, and the worker can be available for that process. Often it is helpful for the worker to identify the source of the anger and attempt to deal with that. Sometimes anger can be dissipated simply by conveying warmth and understanding, and helping the client solve a problem. If a worker believes the client may become violent, he or she should invite one or more coworkers to participate in the sessions. If a worker is making a home visit and senses danger, it may be advisable to say something such as "I think we need some time to cool off in order to take a more objective look at this. I'll be back tomorrow at this same time." If the visit involves investigation of child abuse or some other potentially volatile situation, a police officer might be asked along for the return visit.

There is a limit to the verbal abuse that a worker should take from a client. To maintain credibility the worker must have the respect of the client and that means limiting verbal abuse. A variety of statements can be used. For example: "I realize you are angry. But I've reached the limit of listening to your verbal abuse. Either we are going to discuss this calmly, or I'm going to have to ask you to leave. Which do you prefer?"

Cultural Communication

In working with adult clients who are not fluent in English, it is better to avoid using the client's bilingual children as interpreters.[28] Using the children as interpreters embarrasses parents because it makes them partially dependent on their children and suggests they are ignorant of essential communication skills. In addition, children probably will not communicate well because of their limited vocabulary and experience. When an interpreter is used, another important guideline is that the worker should talk to the client, not to the interpreter. Talking to the translator places the client in the position of bystander rather than central figure in the relationship.

Workers should always use their own patterns of communication and avoid the temptation to adopt the client's accent, vocabulary, or speech.[29] Mistakes in pronunciation or usage may be offensive or make the worker appear insincere.

Space limitations here do not permit a complete listing of which intervention techniques work with specific minority groups. The following examples, however, demonstrate the need for a worker to learn the techniques appropriate to a particular client or group.

As mentioned earlier, Chicanos tend to have a strong sense of familism. Delgado and Humm-Delgado suggest that natural support systems are a useful resource in providing assistance to Chicanos.[30] These support systems include extended family, folk healers, religious institutions, and merchant and social clubs. The extended family includes the family of origin, nuclear family members, other relatives, godparents, and those considered to be like family. Folk healers are prominent in Chicano communities. Some use treatments that blend natural healing methods with religious or spiritual beliefs. Religious institutions (especially the Roman Catholic Church) provide such services as pastoral counseling, emergency money, job locating, housing assistance, and some specialized programs, such as drug-abuse treatment and prevention. Merchant and social clubs can provide items such as native foods, herbs, referral to other resources, credit and information, prayer books, recreation, and the services of healers. The reluctance of Chicano clients to seek help from a social welfare agency can be reduced by greater use of these natural support systems. Outreach can be done through churches and community groups. If a social welfare agency gains a reputation for utilizing such natural support systems in the intervention process, Chicanos will have greater trust in the agency and be much more apt to seek help. Utilizing such natural support systems also increases the effectiveness of the intervention process.

Religious organizations that are predominantly African American usually have a social and spiritual mission. They are apt to be highly active in efforts to combat racial discrimination. Many prominent African American leaders, such as the late Martin Luther King, Jr., and Jesse Jackson, have been members of the clergy. African American churches have served to develop leadership skills. They have also served as social welfare organizations to meet such basic needs as food, clothing, and shelter. African American churches are natural support systems that workers need to utilize to serve troubled African American individuals and families.

A worker with an urban background employed in a small rural community needs to live a life consistent with community values and standards. Someone who violates community norms will not be effective in a small community because he or she will not have the necessary credibility. A worker in a small community needs to identify community values regarding religious beliefs and patterns of expression, dating and marriage patterns, values related to domestic and wild animals (for example, opposing deer hunting in rural communities may run counter to strong local values), drug usage, political beliefs and values, and sexual mores. Once such values are identified, the worker should attempt to achieve a balance between the kind of lifestyle he or she wants and the kind of lifestyle the community expects.

Kadushin recommends that workers in initial meetings with adult clients of diverse racial and ethnic groups should observe all formalities.[31] Such usage would include a formal title (Mr., Miss, Mrs., Ms.), the client's proper full name, greeting with a handshake, and other common courtesies. In initial contacts workers should also show their agency identification and state the reasons for the meeting. In addition, agencies and workers should establish working hours that coincide with the needs of the groups being served. Doing so might mean evening and weekend hours to accommodate working clients.

In the area of group services to racially diverse clients, Davis recommends that membership be selected in such a manner that no one race vastly outnumbers the others.[32] Sometimes it is necessary to educate clients about the processes of individual or group counseling. Using words common to general conversation is much better than using sophisticated technical jargon that clients are not likely to comprehend.

Native Americans place a high value on the principle of self-determination.[33] This sometimes presents a perplexing dilemma for a worker who wonders "How can I help if I can't intervene?" Native Americans will request intervention infrequently, and the worker needs to have the patience to wait for the request. How long this will take varies. During the waiting period the non-Native American worker should be available and may offer assistance as long as there is no hint of coercion. Once help is accepted, the worker will be tested. If the client believes the worker has been helpful, the word will spread and the worker is likely to have more requests for help. If the worker is not helpful, this assessment will also spread and the worker will face increased difficulties.

To establish rapport with African Americans, Hispanics, Native Americans, or clients of other groups who have suffered from racial oppression, a peer relationship should be sought in which there is mutual respect and mutual sharing of information. An attitude of superiority is offensive and should be avoided.

When working with gays or lesbians, it is not uncommon for workers to experience homophobia—the irrational fear of homosexuality—because homosexuality has traditionally been viewed negatively as an illness, an emotional disturbance, a deviance, a criminal act, a sin. Personal homophobia must be confronted and resolved, however. One way is to apply social work values to gay clients. It is a serious mistake for a worker to convey a negative evaluation of a client's homosexuality because it contradicts the basic social work value of the client's right to self-determination. Another suggestion is for a worker to become familiar with the gay lifestyle and gay community. Such knowledge is essential in helping gay clients identify and evaluate the various alternatives available.[34] Knowing resource people within the gay community will also enable a worker to be more aware of available services, activities, and events. Many services that focus on specific aspects of gay life are needed by gays and lesbians. These include support groups for gay men who are in the process of recognizing their homosexuality, legal advice for gay parents seeking child custody, counseling for gay couples, information on safer sex practices to avoid acquiring AIDS, and lesbian support groups.

Social workers have an obligation to help protect the civil rights of gays and lesbians through education and advocacy. Sexual orientation should be respected instead of criticized. Political candidates who are advocates of gay rights should be supported. Agencies that discriminate against gays and lesbians need to be confronted and educated to provide their services in a fair and just manner. Social workers should encourage the development of local support groups, if such groups have not been developed in the community. Gramick has suggested that social workers need to refuse to accept homophobic behavior from colleagues and states that such actions should be pointed out as a violation of the NASW Code of Ethics.[35] As stated earlier, social workers have an obligation to advance social and economic justice for all populations at risk. The social work concept of ethnic-sensitive practice highlights the major emphases in this section.

Ethnic-Sensitive Practice

Traditionally, professional social work practice has used the medical model for the delivery of services. The medical model is a deficit model that focuses on identifying problems or deficits within a person (see Chapter 2). The medical model largely ignores environmental factors that impact the person-in-situation. A major shortcoming of a deficit model is that it focuses on the deficits of a person or a group while ignoring strengths and resources. (When one emphasizes only the shortcomings of a person, that person's self-esteem is apt to be severely affected negatively; that person may define himself or herself in terms of shortcomings and, in the process, overlook strengths and resources.)

Ethnic-sensitive practice seeks to incorporate understanding of diverse ethnic, cultural, and minority groups into the theories and principles that guide social work practice.[36] Ethnic-sensitive practice is based on the view that practice must be attuned to the values and dispositions related to clients' ethnic group membership and social-class position. Ethnic-sensitive practice requires that social workers have an in-depth understanding of the effects of oppression on racial and ethnic groups.

Another important segment of the conceptual framework is the concept of the "dual perspective."[37]

This concept is derived from the view that all people are a part of two systems: (1) the dominant or sustaining system (the society that one lives in), which is the source of power and economic resources, and (2) the nurturing system, composed of the physical and social environment of family and community. The dual perspective concept asserts that the adverse consequences of an oppressive society on the self-concept of a person of color or of any minority group can be partially offset by the nurturing system.

Ethnic-sensitive practice requires that social workers have a special obligation to be aware of and seek to redress the oppression experienced by ethnic groups. Ethnic-sensitive practice assumes that each ethnic group's members have a history that has a bearing on the members' perceptions of current problems. For example, the individual and collective history of many African Americans leads to the expectation that family resources will be available in times of trouble.[38] Ethnic-sensitive practice, however, assumes that the present is most important. For example, many Mexican American and Puerto Rican women currently feel tension as they attempt to move beyond traditionally defined gender roles into the mainstream as students and paid employees.[39]

Ethnic-sensitive practice does not introduce new practice principles or approaches.

Instead, it urges the adaptation of prevailing therapies, social work principles, and skills to take account of ethnic reality. Regardless of which practice approach is used, two concepts and perspectives that are emphasized are empowerment and the strengths perspective.

Empowerment

Empowerment has been defined as "the process of helping individuals, families, groups, and communities increase their personal, interpersonal, socioeconomic, and political strength and influence toward improving their circumstances."[40]

In working with an ethnic or racial group, empowerment counters the negative image or stereotype of the group (which has been established through a long history of discrimination) with a positive value or image and an emphasis on the ability of each group member to influence the conditions of his or her life. Empowerment counters hopelessness and powerlessness with an emphasis on the ability of each person to address problems competently, beginning with a positive view of the self. Empowerment counters oppression and poverty by helping ethnic groups and their members to increase their ability to make and implement basic life decisions.

Strengths Perspective

The strengths perspective is closely related to empowerment. The strengths perspective seeks to identify, use, build, and reinforce the abilities and strengths that people have in contrast to the pathological perspective, which focuses on their deficiencies (see Chapter 2). It emphasizes people's abilities, interests, aspirations, resources, beliefs, and accomplishments. For example, strengths of African Americans in the United States are found in more than 100 predominantly African American colleges and universities; fraternal and women's organizations; and social, political, and professional organizations. Many of the schools, businesses, churches, and organizations that are predominantly African American have developed social service programs—such as family support services, mentoring programs, food and shelter services, transportation services, and educational and scholarship programs. Through individual and organized efforts, self-help approaches and mutual aid traditions continue among African Americans. African Americans tend to have strong ties to immediate, extended family. They tend to have a strong religious orientation, a strong work and achievement orientation, and egalitarian role sharing.[41]

According to Saleebey,[42] five principles underlie the guiding assumptions of the strengths perspective:

1. *Every individual, group, family, and community has strengths.* The strengths perspective is about discerning these resources. Saleebey notes:

   > In the end, clients want to know that you actually care about them, that how they fare makes a difference to you, that you will listen to them, that you will respect them no matter what their history, and that you believe that they can build something of value with the resources within and around them. But most of all, clients want to know that you believe they can surmount adversity and begin the climb toward transformation and growth. (p. 12)[43]

2. *Trauma, abuse, illness, and struggle may be injurious, but they may also be sources of challenge and opportunity.* Clients who have been victimized are seen as active and developing individuals who, through their traumas, learn skills and develop personal attributes that assist them in coping with future struggles. There is dignity to be found in having prevailed over obstacles. We often grow more from crises that we find ways to handle effectively than from periods of time in our lives when we are content and comfortable.

3. *Assume that you do not know the upper limits of the capacity to grow and change, and take individual, group, and community aspirations seriously.* This principle means workers need to hold high their expectations of clients and form alliances with their visions, hopes, and values. Individuals, families, and communities have the capacity for restoration and rebounding. When workers connect with the hopes and dreams of clients, clients are apt to have greater faith in themselves. Then they are able to put forth the effort needed for their hopes and dreams to become self-fulfilling prophecies.

4. *We best serve clients by collaborating with them.* A worker is more effective when seen by the client as a collaborator or consultant rather than as an expert or a professional. A collaborative stance by a worker makes her or him less vulnerable to many of the adverse effects of an expert-inferior relationship, including paternalism, victim-blaming, and preemption of client views.

5. *Every environment is full of resources.* In every environment (no matter how harsh) there are individuals, groups, associations, and institutions with something to give, and with something that others may desperately need. The strengths perspective seeks to identify these resources and make them available to benefit individuals, families, and groups in a community.

Exercise 7.4: The Strengths Perspective Applied to a Homeless Family

GOAL: This exercise is designed to assist you in applying the strengths perspective to a case.

1. **Read the following case scenario:**
   Ms. Hull was recently evicted from her two-bedroom apartment. She had been working at a small business that did not offer health insurance coverage to her. She is a single mother with three children, ages 7, 9, and 10. She developed pneumonia that hung on because she could not pay to see a physician. The small business experienced financial problems, and her employment was terminated. She has been seeking another job but has not found one. She wants a job that has health benefits. Unable to pay rent, she was evicted from her apartment. She cares a lot for her children, and they display respect for her. The children are all doing well in school. Ms. Hull and her children lived on the street for three days and nights but then located a homeless shelter at the Salvation Army. They have been at the homeless shelter for the past two and a half weeks. The children are fairly healthy and are respectful of the services they are receiving from the shelter. Ms. Hull has largely recovered from her pneumonia, partly because of the physician's visit she asked the Salvation Army to arrange for her.

2. **List the strengths that you identify in this family.**

Culturally Competent Practice*

Projections indicate that by the middle of the 21st century nearly half the population of the United States will be people of color.[44] Social workers will be dealing with people who are increasingly diverse, politically more active, and more aware of their rights. It is therefore incumbent upon social workers to become increasingly culturally competent. In order to become culturally competent social workers need to: (1) become aware of culture and its pervasive influence, (2) learn about their own cultures, (3) recognize their own ethnocentricity, (4) learn about other cultures, (5) acquire cultural knowledge about their clients, and (6) adapt social work skills and intervention approaches accordingly.[45]

In 2001, the National Association of Social Workers approved the following 10 standards for cultural competence in social work practice:

1. *Ethics and Values*—Social workers shall function in accordance with the values, ethics, and standards of the profession, recognizing how personal and professional values may conflict with or accommodate the needs of diverse clients.
2. *Self-Awareness*—Social workers shall seek to develop an understanding of their own personal, cultural values and beliefs as one way of appreciating the importance of multicultural identities in the lives of people.
3. *Cross-Cultural Knowledge*—Social workers shall have and continue to develop specialized knowledge and understanding about the history, traditions, values, family systems, and artistic expressions of major client groups that they serve.
4. *Cross-Cultural Skills*—Social workers shall use appropriate methodological approaches, skills, and techniques that reflect the workers' understanding of the role of culture in the helping process.
5. *Service Delivery*—Social workers shall be knowledgeable about and skillful in the use of services available in the community and broader society and be able to make appropriate referrals for their diverse clients.
6. *Empowerment and Advocacy*—Social workers shall be aware of the effect of social policies and programs on diverse client populations, advocating for and with clients whenever appropriate.

---

*Material in this section is adapted from *Introduction to Social Work and Social Welfare,* 8th ed. by Zastrow. © 2004. Reprinted with permission of Brooks/Cole, a division of Thomson Learning, Inc.

7. *Diverse Workforce*—Social workers shall support and advocate for recruitment, admissions and hiring, and retention efforts in social work programs and agencies that ensure diversity within the profession.

8. *Professional Education*—Social workers shall advocate for and participate in educational and training programs that help advance cultural competence within the profession.

9. *Language Diversity*—Social workers shall seek to provide or advocate for the provision of information, referrals, and services in the language appropriate to the client, which may include use of interpreters.

10. *Cross-Cultural Leadership*—Social workers shall be able to communicate information about diverse client groups to other professionals.*

Exercise 7.5: Culturally Competent Standards

GOAL: This exercise is designed to assist you in assessing standards of cultural competence that you need to work on.

Review the 10 standards for cultural competence. Specify those standards that you believe you need to work on in order to become more culturally competent.

It is a mistake for a social workers to conclude that working effectively with a different cultural group presents insurmountable barriers and obstacles. In actuality, the similarities between worker and clients almost always outweigh the dissimilarities.

The major professional social work organizations have in the past few decades taken strong positions to work toward ending racial discrimination and oppression. The National Association of Social Workers, for example, has lobbied for the passage of civil rights legislation. The NASW Code of Ethics has an explicit statement that:

> Social workers should act to prevent and eliminate domination, exploitation, and discrimination against any person, group or class on the basis of race, ethnicity, national origin, color, age, religion, sex, sexual orientation, marital status, political belief, mental or physical disability, or any other preference, personal characteristic, or status.[46]

The Council on Social Work Education (CSWE) in Educational Policy and Accreditation Standards (EPAS) requires that baccalaureate and master's programs in social work include content on racism. EPAS also requires that accredited programs also provide considerable content on populations at risk, diversity, and the promotion of social and economic justice.[47] Professional social work education is committed to preparing social

---

*Reprinted with permission from *NASW Standards for Cultural Competence in Social Work Practice.* Copyright 2001, National Association of Social Workers, Inc.

work students to understand and appreciate cultural and social diversity. Students are taught to understand the dynamics and consequences of oppression, and they learn to use intervention strategies to combat social injustice, oppression, and their effects. The Association of Black Social Workers also has been very active in combating racial prejudice and discrimination.

Social workers have an obligation to work vigorously toward ending racial and ethnic discrimination and advancing social justice. The social work professional needs to recognize the reality of practice in a culturally diverse environment. Social workers do have many of the prejudices and misperceptions of the general society, and the tendency to use one's own prejudices and stereotypes poses dangers for the well-meaning practitioner.

THE RAP FRAMEWORK FOR LEADING MULTIRACIAL GROUPS

Whenever people of different races interact in a group, the leader should assume that race is an issue but not necessarily a problem. Race is an issue in a multiracial group because it is a very apparent difference among participants and one that is laden with considerable social meaning. The leader of a multiracial group should not attempt to be color-blind because being color-blind leads to ignoring important dynamics related to race.

In leading a multiracial group, Davis, Galinsky, and Schopler urge that the leader use the RAP framework.[48] RAP stands for: *recognize, anticipate,* and *problem solve.* Each element will be briefly described in the sections that follow.

Recognize

Recognizing crucial ethnic, cultural, and racial differences in any group requires the leader to be both self-aware and aware of the racial dynamics of the group. A leader of a multiracial group needs to

- Be aware of personal values and stereotypes.
- Recognize racial, ethnic, and cultural differences among the members.
- Respect the norms, customs, and cultures of the populations represented in the group.
- Become familiar with resources (community leaders, professionals, agencies) in the community that are responsive to the needs of the racial components of the group. These resources can be used as consultants by the leader when racial issues arise and may also be used as referral resources for special needs of particular members.
- Be aware of various forms of institutional discrimination in the community and of their impact on various population groups.
- Be aware of racial tensions in the community that may concern members of the group. Such tensions may directly impact interactions among members of different races in the group.

Anticipate

Anticipating how individual members will be affected by racial issues prepares the leader to respond preventively and interventively when racial issues arise. The leader should anticipate potential sources of racial tension in the group when the members formulate their group goals and when the leader structures the group's work. Because relationships between members and race-laden outside issues (i.e., outside of the group) change over time, anticipating racial tensions is an ongoing leadership responsibility. To anticipate tensions and help members deal effectively with them, the leader should

- Seek to include more than one member of any given race. If the group has a solo member, the leader should acknowledge the difficulty of this situation for that member and should make it clear that that member is not expected to serve as the representative of his or her race.

- Develop a leadership style that is culturally appropriate to the group's specific racial configuration. This requires that the leader become knowledgeable about the beliefs, values, and cultures of the various racial components of the group.
- Treat all members with respect and equality in both verbal and nonverbal communications.
- Help the group formulate goals responsive to the concerns and needs expressed by all the members.
- Seek to empower members to obtain their rights, particularly if they are being victimized by institutional discrimination or other forms of racism in the community.
- Acknowledge in initial contacts with members and in initial sessions that racial and ethnic differences do exist in the group and that any issues that arise in the group regarding race must be openly discussed—even if discussing such issues and differences is uncomfortable.
- Encourage the development of norms of mutual respect and appreciation of diversity.
- Announce in initial sessions that at times people do and say things that are racially inappropriate. When this occurs, these comments and actions will be thoroughly discussed in order to resolve the issues and to work toward appreciation of differences.

Problem Solve

When incidents related to racial issues do arise, the leader must intervene to resolve the issues. The leader should

- Use a problem-solving approach (described in Chapter 6). Briefly, this approach involves identifying the issues and needs of each party, generating alternatives to meet those needs, evaluating the merits of each of these alternatives, and selecting and implementing the most promising alternative.
- Use conflict-resolution approaches (described in Chapter 6). These approaches include role reversal, empathy, inquiry, I-messages, disarming, stroking, and mediation.
- Use interventions and goals that are culturally acceptable and appropriate for all members of the group.
- Provide some rules when involving members in problem solving and conflict resolution (for example, no name calling).
- Assist members in being assertive in confronting and dealing with problems related to race.
- Be prepared to advocate outside the group on a member's behalf when that member is being victimized by discrimination and oppression in the community.

◼ FEMINIST INTERVENTION*

The feminist perspective on social work intervention has been developed by a number of authors; no one is specifically recognized as its founder. However, authors Van Den Bergh and Cooper have made extensive contributions.[49]

Feminism is a multifaceted concept that is difficult to define accurately. In *The Social Work Dictionary*, Barker defines *feminism* as "the social movement and doctrine advocat-

---

*Material in this section is adapted from *The Practice of Social Work*, 7th ed., by Zastrow. © 2003. Reprinted with permission of Brooks/Cole, a division of Thomson Learning, Inc.

ing legal and socioeconomic equality for women. The movement originated in Great Britain in the eighteenth century."[50] Barker then defines *feminist social work* as "the integration of the *values*, skills, and knowledge of social work with a feminist orientation to help individuals and society overcome the emotional and social problems that result from *sex discrimination*"[51] [italics added].

Barker further defines *feminist therapy* as follows:

> A psychosocial treatment orientation in which the professional (usually a woman) helps the client (usually a woman) in individual or group settings to overcome the psychological and social problems largely encountered as a result of *sex discrimination* and sex-role stereotyping. Feminist therapists help clients maximize potential, especially through *consciousness-raising*, eliminating sex stereotyping, and helping them become aware of the commonalities shared by all women[52] [italics added].

Kirst-Ashman and Hull define *feminism* as follows:

> . . . the *philosophy of equality* between women and men that involves *both attitudes* and *actions*, which infiltrates virtually *all aspects of life,* which often necessitates providing *education and advocacy* on the behalf of women, and which appreciates the existence of *individual differences* and personal accomplishments regardless of gender[53] [italics added].

Let us examine the five emphasized components of this definition. The *philosophy of equality* between men and women does not mean that women should adopt behaviors that are typically masculine. It means that women and men should have equal or identical rights to opportunities and choices and that neither women nor men should be discriminated against on the basis of gender.

The second component embodies *both attitudes and actions.* In regard to attitudes, feminism emphasizes the importance of viewing other people in a fair, objective perspective and of avoiding stereotyping. In regard to actions, feminism involves a commitment to act on one's beliefs involving gender equality. For example, a supervisor (male or female) who asserts that he or she believes in feminism has an obligation to confront a male supervisee who tells sexist jokes or who treats women according to traditional gender-based stereotypes (for example, making demeaning comments about female social workers being too emotionally involved with their clients).

In the third component, *all aspects of life,* equality does not apply just to equal opportunity to attain a specific job or promotion, it involves many other aspects of life, such as freedom to have opinions on political, social, and religious issues; freedom to ask another person out for a date; freedom to decide what to do with leisure time; freedom to attend, or not to attend, college; freedom to choose to become involved in competitive sports; and freedom to choose to have a sexual encounter.

The fourth component is the frequent need to *provide education and advocacy* on behalf of women. Feminism involves valuing equal opportunities for women as well as for men. Since women have been subjected to sex-role stereotyping and gender-based discrimination, a person who values feminism has an obligation to provide education and advocacy on behalf of women. For example, the male employee who is telling sexist jokes at work needs to be educated about sexual harassment. He also needs to be informed about the negative impact such jokes have on women and that adverse consequences will result if he continues to make sexist remarks. Feminist advocacy involves speaking out for (or championing the rights of) those women who need help. These women are usually in positions of lesser power and opportunity.

The fifth component is the appreciation of *individual differences*. The feminist perspective places a high value on empowering women by emphasizing individual qualities and strengths.

Principles of Feminist Therapy

Nine principles of feminist intervention have been identified.[54]

1. A client's problems should be viewed "within a sociopolitical framework."[55] Feminist intervention is concerned with the inequitable power relationship

between women and men and is opposed to all "power-over" relationships, regardless of gender, race, class, age, and so on. Such relationships lead to oppression and domination. Feminism is concerned with changing all social, economic, and political structures based on the relationships between the haves and the have-nots. The problems of the have-nots are often rooted in a sexist social and political structure. Another way of stating this principle is that "personal is political." According to Van Den Bergh:

> This principle maintains that what a woman experiences in her personal life is directly related to societal dynamics that affect other women. In other words, an individual woman's experiences of pejorative comments based on sex are directly related to societal sexism. For ethnic minority women, racism and classism also are factors that affect well-being.[56]

A primary distinguishing characteristic of feminist treatment is to help the client analyze how her problems are related to systematic difficulties experienced by women in a sexist, classist, and racist society.

2. Traditional sex roles are pathological and clients need encouragement to free themselves from traditional gender-role bonds. Women are put in a double bind due to *femininity achievement incompatibility*. There is a traditional view in our society that a woman cannot be both feminine and an achiever. Achievement, erroneously, is thought to reduce a woman's femininity, and the truly feminine woman is thought to be someone who does not seek to be an achiever. Traditionally, women have been socialized to fill a "learned helplessness" role. Van Den Bergh describes the effects of such sex-role stereotyping:

> Sex-role stereotypes suggest that women should be submissive, docile, receptive, and dependent. The message is one of helplessness; that women cannot take care of themselves and are dependent upon others for their well-being. This sets up a dynamic in which a woman's locus of control is external to her self, preventing her from believing that she can acquire what she needs on her own in order to develop and self-actualize. In other words, oversubscription to sex-role stereotypes engenders a state of powerlessness in which a woman is likely to become involved in situations where she becomes victimized. . . . For example, because young girls are socialized to be helpless, when they become women they tend to have a limited repertoire of responses when under stress; e.g., they respond passively.[57]

In feminist treatment, clients are helped to see how their difficulties may be related to oversubscription to traditional sex-role stereotypes. They are shown that by internalizing traditional sex roles, women are inevitably set up to play passive, submissive roles and experience low self-esteem and self-hatred. The feminist approach asserts that clients need encouragement to make their own choices and pursue the tasks and achievements they desire, rather than be constrained by traditional sex roles.

3. Intervention should focus on client empowerment. Van Den Bergh describes the empowerment process:

> Helping women to acquire a sense of power, or the ability to affect outcome in their lives, is a crucial component of feminist practice. Empowerment means acquiring knowledge, skills, and resources that enhance an individual's ability to control her own life and to influence others. Traditionally women have used indirect, covert techniques to get what they want, such as helplessness, dependency, coyness, and demureness.[58]

Empowerment is fostered in a variety of ways: (1) by helping the client define her own needs and clarify her personal goals so she can derive a sense of purposefulness; (2) by providing the client with education and access to resources; (3) by helping the client see that the direction and ability to change lie within herself (that is, alterations in her life will result only from her own undertakings); and

(4) by focusing on the identification and enhancement of the client's strengths rather than on her pathologies. Women need to be empowered so they can increase their ability to control their environments in order to get what they need.

4. Clients' self-esteem should be enhanced. Self-esteem and self-confidence are essential for empowerment. Self-esteem can be enhanced in a variety of ways. The worker should try to be an encouraging person. The worker should help clients identify and recognize their unique qualities and strengths. Many clients with low self-esteem tend to blame themselves for everything that is wrong. For example, a battered woman typically tends to blame herself for being battered. These clients need to look more realistically at those areas in which they are blaming themselves and feeling guilt. They need to distinguish where their responsibility for dysfunctional interactions ends and other individuals' responsibility begins.

5. Clients should be encouraged to develop their identity (sense of self) on the basis of their own strengths, attributes, qualities, and achievements. It is a serious mistake for a woman to develop her identity in terms of her spouse or dating partner. Women need to develop an independent identity that is not based on their relationships with others.

6. Clients need to value and develop social support systems with other women. In a society that devalues women, it is all too easy for some women to view other women as insignificant. With social support systems, women can ventilate their concerns and share their experiences and the solutions they have found to similar problems. They can serve as brokers in identifying resources and can provide emotional support and nurturance to one another.

7. Clients need to find an effective balance between work and personal relationships. Feminist intervention encourages both women and men to share in the nurturant aspects of their lives and in providing economic resources.

8. The nature of the relationship between practitioner and client should approach equality as much as possible. Feminist practitioners do not view themselves as experts in resolving clients' problems, but as catalysts whose role is helping clients empower themselves. Feminist practitioners try to eliminate dominant/submissive relationships. In regard to an egalitarian relationship, Van Den Bergh notes:

> Obviously, there is an innate power differential between practitioner and client because the former has expertise and training as an "authority." However, the feminist admonition is to avoid abusing that status; "abuse" in this sense might be, for example, taking all credit for client change, or using terminology and nomenclature that are difficult for the client to understand.[59]

9. Many clients can benefit from learning to express themselves assertively. The steps in assertiveness training are described in Appendix 1: Module 2. As indicated earlier, many women are socialized to be passive and nonassertive, and as a result, they have difficulty expressing themselves assertively. Clients can be helped through individual and group counseling.

Clients who learn to express themselves assertively will experience increased self-confidence and self-esteem. They will be better able to communicate their thoughts, feelings, and opinions. Also, learning to express oneself assertively is an important component of empowerment.

Many women feel considerable anger over being victimized by sex discrimination and gender stereotyping. Some of these women turn these feelings inward, resulting in depression. Assertiveness training can help women recognize their right to be angry and also help them identify and practice constructive ways to express their anger assertively, rather than aggressively.

Exercise 7.6: Feminist Intervention

GOAL: This exercise is designed to further your understanding of feminist issues and feminist intervention.

1. **Describe the plight of a female who you know would benefit from feminist intervention. Do not give identifying information (such as last name) of this person in your description.**

2. **Speculate how a social worker could use the principles of feminist therapy to counsel this person.**

Using Feminist Intervention in Groups

The feminist perspective on therapy can be, and usually is, used in conjunction with other theoretical approaches. Group therapists who have a feminist perspective almost always have training in and use other psychotherapeutic approaches—such as behavior therapy, reality therapy, rational therapy, and transactional analysis. They also often use a number of specific treatment approaches—such as assertiveness training, parent effectiveness training, mediation, meditation, sex therapy, and relaxation techniques.

Feminist intervention is particularly applicable in group therapy with women who have been victimized by sex discrimination and sex-role stereotyping. By sharing their experiences, such women can help each other identify the problems encountered in inequitable power relationships between women and men. Such sharing facilitates their recognizing that many of their blocked opportunities are directly related to societal sexism. Such sharing also helps them recognize how their difficulties may be related to traditional sex-role stereotypes. The group approach facilitates members to pursue the tasks and achievements they desire, rather than be constrained by traditional sex roles.

The group setting also is conducive to empowering members to increase their capacities to control their environment in order to get what they want. Members in such a setting are also encouraged to develop an independent identity. Social support systems for women are almost always developed in such a setting, as women are encouraged to share their experiences and the solutions they have found to similar problems. These women often serve as brokers to one another in identifying resources. In addition, the group setting is conducive to members' learning to express themselves assertively, including learning ways to express their anger assertively.

A case example of feminist intervention follows:

> Marcia is the mother of three children and has lived with her abusive husband, Dennis, for years. The abuse was particularly violent when Dennis was intoxicated—which he was several times a month. Over the years Dennis had succeeded in isolating Marcia from her family and friends, in lowering her self-esteem, and in making Marcia financially dependent on him (i.e., he prevented her from working outside the home).
>
> One evening while intoxicated, Dennis smashed Marcia in the face and chest with his fists, breaking her nose and three ribs. The oldest child called 911 and an ambulance came, along with two police officers. Dennis was jailed for the evening for domestic abuse, and Marcia received emergency care at a hospital. The hospital social worker persuaded Marcia to take her children with her to a battered women's shelter, where they stayed for 44 days.
>
> During this time she had daily group counseling with other battered women. The group was led by a social worker with a feminist perspective, who applied many of the principles of that perspective. Marcia came to realize that she and many of the other women in the group were being victimized by men who held traditional gender-role stereotypes. The women were given educational material and were led in exercises that helped Marcia become more assertive, express her anger about being dominated by her husband, recognize that she had a right to end an abusive relationship, and realize she was a person worthy of respect. She received help from the shelter's staff in applying and being accepted for public assistance, receiving job training as a dental technician, obtaining a job in this field, finding an apartment for herself and her children, filing for divorce, and obtaining a restraining order against her soon-to-be-ex-husband who had continued to harass her.
>
> Now, two years later, caring for her three children (both financially and emotionally) continues to be a challenge. But, she is much happier with her life and with the kind of person she is becoming. She also is pleased that her children are slowly but surely gaining pride in her and respect for her.

■ EVALUATION OF FEMINIST THERAPY

Since the feminist perspective is almost always used in conjunction with other therapeutic approaches, it is extremely difficult to conduct evaluative studies that test its effectiveness.

Van Den Bergh and Cooper emphasize that the feminist perspective is consistent with the core values of social work practice, including equality, respect for individuals, and promotion of social and economic justice for populations at risk.[60] They conclude that "a feminist social work practice is a viable way to accomplish the unique mission of social work, to improve the quality of life by facilitating social change."[61]

While most contemporary approaches to psychotherapy look for the causes of a client's problems inside the client (for example, internal conflicts, repressed feelings, and early childhood traumas), the feminist perspective emphasizes viewing a client's problems in terms of the social, political, and economic systems that impact the client. This perspective is consistent with social work's emphasis on the person-in-environment, a systems approach, and an ecological approach.

The feminist perspective has also been helpful in identifying and conceptualizing numerous structural problems in our society. For example, feminists who practiced in the mental health field in the early 1970s began to view traditional psychotherapy as an agent of social control that maintained traditional sex roles by encouraging women to "adapt."[62] Feminists have asserted that women need to be recognized as having the right to their reproductive capacities (including the right to choose to terminate a pregnancy); otherwise their lives would be largely controlled by the men who impregnate them, since raising a child requires a commitment of at least two decades. Feminists have also drawn attention to the sociopolitical forces that have led to an increase in the feminization of poverty in our society.

An extremely positive aspect of the feminist perspective is the view that all social workers have an obligation to identify inequalities in our social, economic, and political systems and then use macropractice techniques to confront these inequalities. Sometimes feminist social workers may involve clients in changing systems. Van Den Bergh notes:

> The social worker should model her concern for changed societal conditions that elimi-
> nate institutionalized inequalities by working on some social change projects, such as
> abortion rights, comparable worth, anti-apartheid activism, or environmental protection.
> Clients can be encouraged to engage in social activism themselves, as the experience of
> collective action can help to validate one's sense of self, personal worth, and power to
> change. However, judgment will have to be used as to whether this is appropriate, based
> on the client's current level of functioning and willingness to take risks.[63]

Feminism is concerned with ending oppression and discrimination in our society and throughout the world.

The women's movement is bringing about a gender-role revolution in our society. Men and women are becoming aware of the negative effects of gender-role distinctions. More and more women are entering the labor force. Women are becoming more involved in athletics and pursuing a number of professions and careers that previously were all male. Changes are also occurring in human interactions; more women are being assertive and seeking out egalitarian relationships with men. To some extent, men are (more slowly) beginning to realize the negative effects of gender-role distinctions. They are gradually realizing that the stereotypical male role limits their opportunities in terms of emotional expression, interpersonal relationships, occupations, and domestic activities.

One limitation of the feminist perspective is that a number of uninformed people reject feminism in reaction to stereotypes. Apparently feminism has had some difficulties in informing segments of the general public about its basic tenets and principles. In this regard, Kirst-Ashman and Hull state:

> Some people have extremely negative reactions to the word "feminism." The emotional
> barriers they forge and the resulting resistance they foster makes it very difficult even to
> approach the concept with them. Others consider feminism a radical ideology which
> emphasizes separatism and fanaticism. In other words, they think feminism involves the
> philosophy adopted by women who spurn men, resent past iniquities, and strive violent-
> ly to overthrow male supremacists. Still others think of feminism as an outmoded tradi-
> tion that is no longer relevant.[64]

Group Development Stages in Women's Groups*

Schiller believes that groups go through distinctive developmental stages. (See, for example, the models described in Chapter 1.) However, she proposes a modified version of developmental stages in women's groups.[65] This model is based on a feminist perspective of women's psychological development and the relational model with particular emphasis placed on issues of status, power, and conflict. The differences between women and men in groups regarding these issues are reflected in the developmental stages identified for women's groups. Schiller's perspective is significant to social workers leading women's groups since it states the need for groups leaders to have an understanding of the "particular and unique patterns of growth and development" so they can "intervene more effectively and in a style that best meets the differential needs of the group and its members."[66]

The relational model proposed for women in groups is structured much like the five-stage model presented by Garland, Jones and Kolodny (described in Chapter 1). In fact, Schiller concurs with them regarding preaffiliation (stage 1) and termination (stage 5) and views these two stages as universal to all groups. The difference is in the middle three stages of development in women's groups:

---

*The description of this model was written by Michael Wallace, MSW, instructor at the University of Wisconsin–Whitewater.

2. Establishing a relational base
3. Mutuality and interpersonal empathy
4. Challenge and change[67]

Second Stage—Establishing a Relational Base

The second stage of Schiller's model differs significantly from most models of group development. The emphasis here is not on power and control. Rather, focus is on "establishing a common ground and a sense of connection with each other and with the facilitator."[68] In women's groups at this stage, members find similarities in their experiences and seek approval from one another and the group leaders. The relational base is the establishment of a sense of safety within the group.

Third Stage—Mutuality and Interpersonal Empathy

The third stage corresponds with what other theorists have termed the work stage.[69] At this stage of development in women's groups, members move beyond making connections and recognize their similarities. They are now at a place of increased trust and self-disclosure. This allows group members to respect differences without losing their connection with one another. If the group has been able to successfully negotiate the second stage, then the relational base will allow for both respect for differences and empathetic connection.

Fourth Stage—Challenge and Change

In order for growth and change to happen, group members must be able to challenge themselves and each other. This can be accomplished by confronting issues of how one views oneself, his or her world, and/or his or her interpersonal relationships. How this occurs in women's groups is uniquely different compared to men's groups. This is because of the different values placed on power by women as opposed to men. For example, power in men's groups seems to come from their individual power. Power in women's groups seems to evolve from a sense of community. Therefore, in order for this stage to develop women must "have sufficiently experienced connection, empathic attunement, and respect for differences." Then women are "free to challenge themselves, each other, and the facilitators."[70] If this can be established, it allows women's group members to challenge one another, take risks, and express disagreements without fearing the loss of valued connections made with one another.

■ GROUP EXERCISES

Exercise A: Whom Wouldn't You Marry?

GOAL: To identify personal stereotypes and prejudices.

Step 1. The following questionnaire is distributed to the students.

MARRIAGE QUESTIONNAIRE
Assume that you are single. Place an X by the description of anyone you would be hesitant to marry. To maintain anonymity, do not write your name on this sheet.

___ Person who is bisexual	___ a Native American
___ Person who is blind	___ a Puerto Rican
___ Person who is deaf	___ an Italian
___ Person who has cerebral palsy	___ a German
___ Person who is elderly	___ a Yugoslav
___ Person who has genital herpes	___ a Norwegian
___ Person who is mildly retarded	___ a Samoan
___ Person who has been hospitalized for an emotional problem	___ an Arab
	___ an Israeli
	___ a Chinese

___ a Russian	___ a Japanese
___ an American	___ a Filipino
___ a Cuban	___ an Eskimo
___ a French person	___ a Brazilian
___ a Mexican	___ a Hungarian
___ a White Protestant	___ a Vietnamese
___ a Roman Catholic	___ a Pakistani
___ a Jew	___ a Korean
___ a Muslim	___ a White American
___ an African American	

Step 2. After completing the first step, the students write the reasons they would hesitate to marry the indicated people. The instructor explains that this part of the exercise is very important because it helps students clarify their values. The explanations should be complete and specific. Statements such as "It wouldn't work out," for example, or "My parents would object" are not acceptable without elaboration.

Step 3. The students hand in their responses anonymously, and the instructor reads many of them. (If a member of a group represented on the list is present, the instructor must use discretion in deciding which responses are read aloud.) A discussion of how to maintain objectivity in the face of personal prejudice should then be initiated. The instructor may conclude the exercise with the following question: "If you checked one or more of these groups, does it suggest that you hold negative stereotypes and prejudices toward these groups?"

Exercise B: Coming Out of the Closet

GOAL: To identify stereotypes and myths that you may hold about gays and lesbians.

Step 1. The students assume they have a gay or lesbian orientation, which they have been hiding. Each student then writes a letter to his or her parents revealing this sexual orientation and asking for acceptance and support.

Step 2. As the students are writing their letters, the leader observes their verbal and nonverbal communication and makes notes on apparent stereotypes. (Students are apt to express stereotypes in conversations with students seated next to them.) A few volunteers are asked to read their letters to the class.

Step 3. After a few letters are read, the leader summarizes apparent stereotypes he or she observed.

Step 4. As an optional step, the myths and facts about homosexuality may be summarized. A summary of this material appears earlier in the chapter.

Step 5. If negative stereotypes are expressed, the leader should seek to initiate a discussion of how a heterosexual worker who has negative stereotypes about homosexuality can seek to be objective in working with clients who are homosexual.

Exercise C: Spaceship to Futura

GOAL: To clarify your feelings about groups that have been discriminated against.

Step 1. The group leader indicates that one purpose of this exercise is to help students clarify their values related to the continuation of the human race after a nuclear war. The class forms subgroups of five or six, and the following vignette is read to the students:

The United States has discovered in another galaxy a planet, Futura, whose environment is very similar to Earth's. There is every indication that the planet will be able to support human life, although no human life has been detected on Futura. The United States has just completed a spaceship that will be able to travel to Futura. The spaceship is being built on a remote island in the Pacific Ocean and will hold only a total of seven people. Your subgroup has been appointed by the government to select the first 7 people to go to Futura. Your subgroup is in frequent contact with the chief scientist for this project. The spaceship is remarkable in that it has a new computer system that has already been programmed to automatically guide the spaceship to Futura without requiring a pilot.

Suddenly, a nuclear war breaks out between the world powers. It is New Year's Eve. Russia, China, the United States, and Israel are already launching their nuclear warheads. It looks like the nuclear destruction may eliminate human civilization on this planet. The chief scientist frantically calls. The spaceship must take off in 15 minutes to Futura, or it will be destroyed. She and your subgroup believe that the 7 people who go may be the only people left to start the human race again.

There are 13 people at the spaceship. Your subgroup must decide who will be selected. (If the 13 people themselves decide, they are likely to become irrational and begin fighting.) Your subgroup has only 15 minutes to make a decision. If a decision is not made in 15 minutes, a nuclear warhead is apt to hit the island and destroy the spaceship. All you know about the 13 people is the following:

1. The chief scientist, female, 47 years old
2. A Hispanic peasant, female, four months pregnant
3. An African American male, third-year medical student
4. A white female, prostitute, 27 years old, a Communist
5. A white male, homosexual, Olympic athlete, 24 years old
6. A white biology professor, 67 years old
7. A rabbi, 27 years old
8. A white female, on public assistance, 28 years old, has been arrested for several felonies, has never been employed
9. A female home economist, 24 years old, white, has cerebral palsy
10. A Korean child, male, 8 years old
11. A white male, moderately retarded due to a lack of oxygen at birth, 33 years old
12. A white female elementary schoolteacher, 27 years old, has genital herpes
13. A 28-year-old white farmer, has had a vasectomy

Step 2. The group leader distributes copies of this list to the students and the subgroups begin their discussions. The group leader informs the subgroups when 10, 5, 3, and 1 minutes remain. At the end of 15 minutes, the discussions end.

Step 3. Each subgroup shares its selections and reasoning. The leader then conducts a discussion that explores what values underlie the selections, why certain individuals were rejected, how a social worker can be objective when faced with personal prejudice or stereotypes, and what students think they have learned.

Exercise D: Feminist Intervention in Counseling

GOAL: Assist students in applying the feminist perspective to counseling.

Step 1. Either describe the principles of the feminist perspective to therapy or have the students read the material in this chapter.

Step 2. Ask for a volunteer to role-play being a counselor who uses the feminist perspective in a simulated counseling situation. Ask for a second volunteer (probably a female) to role-play a situation in which the feminist perspective might be useful. Possible examples include:

1. A woman discovers her partner has had three affairs since they began dating four years ago.
2. A woman is frequently verbally abused by her partner.
3. A woman is physically abused by an alcoholic husband; she feels she cannot leave him because she has three young children and is not employed outside the home.
4. A female employee is being sexually harassed by her male employer; for financial reasons, she needs to continue working.

Step 3. Instruct the two volunteers to role-play this simulated counseling situation. After the role-playing, ask the class to discuss (1) what the "counselor" did well in applying the feminist perspective to counseling, and (2) what else the "counselor" might have done to apply the feminist perspective to this counseling situation.

Step 4. If time permits, repeat Steps 2 and 3 with a different client problem.

Exercise E: Are You a Feminist?

GOAL: Help students assess the extent to which they have a feminist perspective and identify some key tenets of the feminist perspective.

Step 1. Instruct the students to answer "true" or "false" to each of the following statements on a sheet of paper. Inform them that their responses will remain anonymous and that they should not write their name on the paper. Read each statement slowly, giving the students an opportunity to answer.

STATEMENTS

1. Men make better supervisors than women.
2. Men make better leaders than women.
3. A woman would not do as good a job as a man in being president of this country.
4. Women should have the primary responsibility for raising children in our society.
5. In a heterosexual couple, the man should be the head of the household.
6. A male and a female living together should share the housework equally (for example, cleaning the bathroom, washing dishes, cooking, doing the laundry, vacuuming, grocery shopping, taking out the garbage).
7. Women and men living together tend to share housework equally in our society.
8. Women should have the same access to jobs and social status as men.
9. A man who frequently relates jokes that are degrading to women in a work setting where women are present is guilty of sexual harassment.
10. I am willing to advocate on behalf of women (for instance, poor women or women who have been sexually assaulted).
11. Our society is generally structured politically, socially, and economically by and for men.
12. In heterosexual couples, the male has the obligation to be the primary breadwinner.
13. It is generally inappropriate for a woman to ask a man out on a date.
14. A male has a right to expect sexual gratification after dating a woman several times.

Step 2. Write the numbers of the statements on the blackboard. Ask the students to hand in their responses. Ask for volunteers to tally the responses on the board.

Step 3. After the responses are tallied, reread each statement. Discuss the results, encouraging students to make comments or raise questions about the issues.

Step 4. End the exercise by indicating that those students who answered true to statements 6, 8, 9, 10, 11 and false to statements 1, 2, 3, 4, 5, 7, 12, 13, 14 probably have a belief system that is consistent with the feminist perspective.

Exercise F: Double Standards

GOAL: Help students identify and examine double standards for male and female interactions.

Step 1. Ask the males to form subgroups of four or five people, and the females to form subgroups of four or five people. Ask each subgroup to identify double standards in dating relationships, marital relationships, and sexual behaviors between males and females. For example, society generally allows males to be more aggressive and to use more vulgar language; and males are expected to ask females for dates, but females traditionally have been raised to believe they should not ask males for dates. For each double standard, the subgroup should decide whether the double standard is desirable or undesirable. (Males are separated from females in this exercise because they may have differing views about the desirability of the double standards that are identified.)

Step 2. After the subgroups have completed their work, ask a representative from each subgroup to summarize the double standards the group identified and its views on the desirability of these double standards. Class discussion may well ensue. End the exercise by summarizing the items identified and the differences between males and females regarding the desirability of such double standards.

CHAPTER EIGHT

Self-Help Groups

GOALS

Self-help groups constitute one alternative to coping alone by assisting members to meet their specific needs through the understanding and help of others who have had similar experiences. This chapter describes the objectives of self-help groups, outlines some of the therapeutic principles they use, and discusses the reasons self-help groups are effective.

MENDED HEARTS: AN EXAMPLE

Founded by four patients recovering from heart surgery in a Boston hospital in 1951, Mended Hearts is now a national organization for heart surgery patients and their families.[1] The four patients shared their concerns about their uncertain future, and the pain and changes in lifestyle they faced. They also focused on the positives—new feelings of well-being, their plans and hopes for the future, and the happiness they experienced from having "mended hearts." From these experiences, they concluded such conversations would be immensely helpful to others facing heart surgery. With the assistance of a heart surgeon, Dr. Dwight Harken, they formed the first Mended Hearts group. They adopted the slogan, "It's great to be alive and to help others." Mended Hearts was formally incorporated in 1955, and a constitution and bylaws were adopted. As hospitals began performing heart surgeries in other regions in the country in the 1960s, chapters of Mended Hearts were formed in these regions. With the number of heart surgeries sharply increasing since the 1960s, the number of chapters and members has grown dramatically.

Meetings are typically held in the hospitals where heart surgeries are performed. At a typical meeting, a physician or medical expert will speak on an aspect of heart disease, surgery, and the recovery process. Other meetings will feature other topics and speakers on exercise, social security, nutrition, insurance, employment, or related topics. A question-and-answer period usually follows. The meetings are open to heart patients, their spouses, and professionals.

Local chapters generally have a monthly newsletter with a variety of information on advances in heart surgery, inspirational material, anniversaries of members' heart surgeries, and announcements of the activities of the local and national organizations.

An important service provided by Mended Hearts is accredited visitors who visit heart patients before and after surgery to offer support, information, and encouragement. To become accredited, the visitors, who have all had heart surgery, attend a series of seminars (8 to 10 hours of training) that consist of lectures, role plays, and discussions of visitor guidelines. They are then tested on their knowledge of functions of the heart, various heart problems, and the corresponding treatment approaches. Before making visits by themselves, prospective visitors accompany accredited visitors on their hospital rounds. This process screens potential visitors to ensure an effective, high-quality program.

In a study of the impact of Mended Hearts, Borman and Lieberman conclude:

> Our findings with Mended Hearts . . . indicate that those patients who are forced into early retirement seem to benefit the most from their service responsibilities as Mended Heart visitors. At the same time, from the perspective of those about to undergo heart surgery, such visits from those who have had the experience seem to be most welcome.[2]

■ DEFINITION AND CHARACTERISTICS

Self-help groups are diverse. Some are small, grassroots affiliations unrelated to external structures. Others are part of large, well-organized, national organizations. The diversity of self-help groups has been summarized by Lieberman and Borman:

> Self-help groups have been seen as support systems; as social movements; as spiritual movements and secular religions; as systems of consumer participation; as alternative care-giving systems adjunct to professional helping systems; as intentional communities; as subcultural entities that represent a way of life; as supplementary communities; as expressive-social influence groups; and as organizations of the deviant and stigmatized.[3]

Hepworth and Larsen define self-help groups this way:

> Self-help groups consist of people who share common conditions, experiences, or problematic situations (e.g., obesity, alcoholism, child abuse, minority status, history of mental disorders, parents of developmentally disabled children, or single parents) and mutually seek to assist each other to enhance their coping capacities related to their common factors. The help these groups provide is available without charge and is based on the experiences of members rather than professional expertise. Largely self-governing and self-regulating, self-help groups generally have effective communication networks among members that, in addition to regular group meetings, provide opportunities for both telephone and face-to-face contacts.[4]

Self-help groups emphasize peer solidarity rather than hierarchical governance. They tend to disregard in their organizational structure the usual institutional distinctions between board of directors, professionals, and consumers, as members (at various times) give and receive help and share responsibility for performing leadership tasks and for accomplishing the goals of the group. Self-help groups tend to be self-supporting and thrive largely on donations from friends and relatives rather than on government funds, foundation grants, or fees from the public.

Riessman summarizes the distinctive characteristics of self-help groups as follows:

- Noncompetitive, cooperative orientation
- Anti-elite, antibureaucratic focus
- Emphasis on the indigenous—people who have the problem and know a lot about it from the inside, from experiencing it
- Attitude of do what you can, one day at a time. You can't solve everything at once.
- Shared, often revolving leadership
- Attitude of being helped through helping (the helper-therapy principle) . . .
- Understanding that helping is not a commodity to be bought and sold
- Strong optimism regarding the ability to change
- Understanding that although small may not necessarily be beautiful, it is the place to begin and the unit to build on
- Critical stance toward professionalism, which is often seen as pretentious, purist, distant, and mystifying. Self-helpers like simplicity and informality.
- Emphasis on the consumer, or, in Alvin Toffler's term, the "prosumer." The consumer is a producer of help and services.

- Understanding that helping is at the center—knowing how to receive help, give help, and help yourself . . .
- Emphasis on empowerment[5]

When people help each other in self-help groups, they tend to feel empowered, as they are able to control important aspects of their lives. When help is given from the outside (from an expert or a professional), there is a danger that dependency may develop, which is the opposite effect of empowerment. Empowerment increases motivation, energy, personal growth, and an ability to help that goes beyond helping oneself or receiving help.

CLASSIFICATION OF SELF-HELP GROUPS

Two different classifications of self-help groups will be summarized in order to convey the varieties and focuses of self-help groups that now exist. The first classification is by Katz and Bender, and the second, by Powell.

Katz and Bender Classification

Katz and Bender have formulated the following classification of self-help groups:[6]

1. Groups that focus on self-fulfillment or personal growth; examples are Alcoholics Anonymous, Recovery, Inc. (for former mental patients); Gamblers Anonymous; and Weight Watchers.
2. Groups that focus on social advocacy; examples are welfare rights organizations, MADD (Mothers Against Drunk Drivers), and The Committee for the Rights of the Disabled. Katz and Bender note that the advocacy "can be both on behalf of broad issues, such as legislation, the creation of new services, change in the policies of existing institutions and so on; or it can be on behalf of individuals, families, or other small groups."[7]
3. Groups whose focus is to create alternative patterns for living; examples are gay liberation and certain religious cults, such as the Moonies.
4. "Outcast haven" or "rock-bottom" groups. Katz and Bender define this type as follows:

   These groups provide a refuge for the desperate, who are attempting to secure personal protection from the pressures of life and society, or to save themselves from mental or physical decline. This type of group usually involves a total commitment, a living-in arrangement or sheltered environment, with close supervision by peers or persons who have successfully grappled with similar problems of their own.[8]

   Ex-drug addict organizations are one example.
5. Groups of mixed types that have characteristics of two or more categories; an example is Parents Without Partners, which focuses on personal growth, advocacy, and providing social events.

Powell Classification

Powell classifies self-help groups into the following five categories:[9]

1. *Habit disturbance organizations:* These organizations focus on a specific and concrete problem. Examples of this category include Alcoholics Anonymous, SmokeStoppers, Overeaters Anonymous, Gamblers Anonymous, Take Off Pounds Sensibly (TOPS), Women for Sobriety, Narcotics Anonymous, and Weight Watchers.
2. *General purpose organizations:* In contrast to habit disturbance organizations, general purpose organizations address a wider range of problems and predicaments.

Examples of this category are Parents Anonymous (for parents of abused children), Emotions Anonymous (for people with emotional problems), the Compassionate Friends (for people who have experienced a loss through death), and GROW, an organization that works to prevent the hospitalization of mental patients through a comprehensive program of mutual aid.

3. *Lifestyle organizations*: These organizations seek to provide support for, and advocate for, the lifestyles of people whose members are viewed by society as being different (the dominant groups in society are generally indifferent or hostile to that difference). Examples of this category include Widow-to-Widow Programs, Parents Without Partners, ALMA (Adoptees' Liberty Movement Association), Parents/FLAG (Parents and Friends of Lesbians and Gays), National Gay and Lesbian Task Force, and the Gray Panthers, an intergenerational group that advocates for the elderly.

4. *Physical handicap organizations*: These organizations focus on major chronic diseases and conditions. Some are for people with conditions that are relatively stable, some for conditions that are likely to get worse, and some for terminal illnesses. Examples of this category include Make Today Count (for the terminally ill and their families), Emphysema Anonymous, Lost Chord clubs (for those who have had laryngectomies), stroke clubs, Mended Hearts, the Spina Bifida Association, and Self-Help for Hard of Hearing People.

5. *Significant other organizations*: The members of these organizations are parents, spouses, and close relatives of troubled and troubling people. Very often, members of significant other groups are last-resort caregivers. Significant others contend with dysfunctional behavior. Through sharing their feelings, they obtain a measure of relief. In the course of sharing, they may also learn about new resources or new approaches. Examples of such organizations include Al-Anon, Gam-Anon, Toughlove, and the National Alliance for the Mentally Ill.

■ BENEFITS OF SELF-HELP GROUPS

Many direct service self-help groups emphasize (1) a confession to the group that they have a problem; (2) a testimony to the group recounting their past experiences with the problem and their plans for handling the problem in the future; (3) the requirement that when a member feels an intense urge of a recurrence (such as to drink or abuse a child), the member calls another member of the group who comes over to stay with the person until the urge subsides.

There appear to be several reasons self-help groups are successful. The members have an internal understanding of the problem, which helps them to help others. Having experienced the misery and consequences of the problem, they are highly motivated and dedicated to finding ways to help themselves and their fellow sufferers. The participants also benefit from the helper-therapy principle; that is, the helper gains psychological rewards by helping others.[10] Helping others makes a person feel "good" and worthwhile, and enables the helper to put his or her own problems into perspective. Other members have problems that may be as serious or more serious.

Some self-help groups (such as parents of children and adults with a cognitive disability) raise funds and operate community programs. Many people with a personal problem use self-help groups in the same way that others use social agencies. An additional advantage of self-help groups is that they generally operate with a minimal budget. As discussed earlier, self-help groups often empower their members. Hundreds of self-help groups are now in existence.

Many people who have problematic behaviors (such as abusing their children) have few friends and relatives they can turn to for help and are thus socially isolated. Those who join a self-help group soon become aware that associating with caring others who have experienced similar problems is a source of immense support. Hepworth and Larsen summarize some of the benefits of a self-help group for members:

1. Having a reference group wherein one shares common problems or concerns with others and is accepted by them.
2. Gaining hope based on the knowledge that other members have experienced similar difficulties and are coping (or have coped) successfully with them.
3. Confronting problems head-on and accepting responsibility for them as a result of confrontations by other members.
4. Putting their problems in perspective and applying knowledge and skill derived from the experiences shared by others.[11]

Borman found five therapeutic factors of direct service self-help groups:

1. *Cognitive restructuring:* Members develop a new perspective on themselves and their problems.
2. *Hope:* Members develop hope that their life will get better as they see the lives of others with similar problems improve.
3. *Altruism:* Members feel good about themselves for helping others.
4. *Acceptance:* Members feel they will not be rejected or blamed for their problems.
5. *Universality:* Members become aware that they are not alone in having the problems they face.[12]

Kurtz summarizes the results of some of the findings of outcome research on self-help groups:

> Useful outcomes of self-help participation included reduced psychiatric symptomatology, reduced use of professional services, increased coping skills, increased life satisfaction, and shorter hospital stays. Members of health-related groups reported better adjustment, better coping, higher self-esteem, and improved acceptance of the illness.[13]

Exercise 8.1: Merits and Shortcomings of a Self-Help Group

GOAL: This exercise is designed to assist you in having a better understanding of the merits and shortcomings of self-help groups.

1. **Interview someone who has participated in a self-help group. (If you have participated yourself, you may answer the questions in this exercise by sharing your personal experiences.) Most campuses have several self-help groups on campus, such as an eating disorder group, a gay/lesbian group, and groups combating substance abuse. The student counseling center is usually a good resource for identifying contact people for the available self-help groups. Describe the goals of the self-help group that you investigate.**

2. **Describe the activities of this self-help group.**

3. **Ask the person you interview to summarize the merits and shortcomings of this self-help group and then record this information here.**

■ LINKAGE WITH SOCIAL WORKERS

Because self-help groups are often more effective than one-to-one counseling or group therapy in treating problematic behaviors, it is vitally important that social workers relate to them constructively. Social workers need to be aware of the self-help groups available in their community so they can function as brokers or case managers in making appropriate referrals for clients. Social workers also need to be knowledgeable about how self-help groups function so that they work in synergy, rather than in competition, with such programs.

Another major function that social workers can perform with self-help groups is to work as consultants. There is a myth that self-help groups are antiprofessional. In reality, many were started with the help of one or more professionals, and most continue to receive professional consultation. Professionals can provide support and consultation on organizational issues, resources for members in unique circumstances, fundraising activities, efforts to enact or change legislation, and social advocacy efforts to change the service policies of one or more agencies. Maguire has provided a partial list of the ways in which a professional can assist a self-help group:

1. Help arrange a meeting place.
2. Help locate funds.
3. Refer members to the group.
4. Arrange or provide training of members and leaders.
5. Accept referrals from the group.
6. Help provide credibility of the group within the professional community and within the community.[14]

Another important function that social workers can serve is to help form needed self-help groups in a community. Hepworth and Larsen note:

Practitioners can also serve as organizers where resources are sparse and appropriate self-help groups do not exist. By working with clients who demonstrate leadership potential, a practitioner may stimulate them, assisting them as needed, to contact a national or regional self-help organization for the purpose of establishing a local chapter. If a national organization does not exist, the practitioner may serve as a catalyst and consultant in organizing a local group, which necessitates working with selected lay leaders in recruiting members, developing objectives and bylaws (if needed), arranging facilities, planning refreshments, and developing an organizational meeting.[15]

■ STARTING A SELF-HELP GROUP

Starting a self-help group is similar to starting any group. If there is a national organization, it is essential to contact this organization to get material on guidelines for establishing a local chapter. If a national organization does not exist, then it may be necessary to start from "scratch." The following kinds of questions need to be answered:

1. What are the goals of the group?
2. What kinds of services should be provided to meet the goals?
3. What are the criteria for membership?
4. What are the costs; for example, will dues be charged?
5. Where will the group meet?
6. How will potential members be contacted?
7. What are the procedures for joining and leaving the group?
8. What kind of organizational structure should the group have?

These questions should not be answered by the professional alone. Self-help groups tend to work best when concerned and motivated individuals who are facing a problem meet and arrive at answers to these questions. Most self-help groups have evolved as circumstances warrant rather than being carefully planned from the start.

■ Examples of Self-Help Groups

ORGANIZATION	SERVICE FOCUS
Abused Parents of America	For parents who are abused by their adult children
Adoptees' Liberty Movement Association	For adoptees searching for their natural parents
Alcoholics Anonymous	For adult alcoholics
American Diabetes Association	Clubs for diabetics, their families, and friends
American Sleep Apnea Association	For persons with sleep apnea and their families
Burns United Support Group	For burn victims
Candlelighters Childhood Cancer Foundation	For parents of young children with cancer
Conjoined Twins International	For families of conjoined twins
CROHNS	For persons with Crohns disease and their families
Concerned United Birthparents (CUB)	For parents who have surrendered children for adoption
Depressed Anonymous	For depressed persons
Divorce Care	For divorced persons
Emotions Anonymous	For persons with emotional problems
Encephalitis Support Group	For those with encephalitis and their families
Families Anonymous	For relatives and friends of drug abusers
Fortune Society	For ex-offenders and their families
Gam-Anon	For families of gamblers
Gray Panthers	An intergenerational group
Herpes Anonymous	For persons with herpes and their families and friends
High Risk Moms, Inc.	For women experiencing a high-risk or problem pregnancy
Impotents World Association	For impotent men and their partners
Make Today Count	For persons with cancer and their families
Molesters Anonymous	For men who molest children
National Organization for Women	For women's rights
Overeaters Anonymous	For overweight persons
Parents Anonymous	For parents of abused children
Sexaholics Anonymous	For those with sexually self-destructive behavior
WINGS Foundation, Inc.	For men and women traumatized by incest

Note: Barbara White and Edward J. Madara in *The Self-Help Sourcebook*, 6th ed. (Denville, NJ: American Self-Help Clearinghouse, 1998), describe more than 800 self-help groups.

A few comments will be made about some of these questions. Usually the nature of the problem will determine how to contact potential members. For example, if former heart surgery patients want to start a Mended Hearts chapter, they should first contact heart surgeons to explain the group and to determine if the surgeons would like a local chapter of Mended Hearts at the hospital. The surgeons can be a valuable resource by providing access to new patients facing heart surgery. For other groups, prospective members may be contacted in a variety of ways: radio and television announcements, notices in church buildings and social service agencies, flyers to service providers, door-to-door solicitation, flyers mailed to target groups, and notices in local newspapers.

Generally, it is best to hold meetings at a public agency, business, church, or private agency. If meetings are held in the home of a member, that member may eventually decide that regular meetings are too much of an inconvenience. Rotating meetings in the homes of individual members is generally not a good idea either because members may find it frustrating to continually locate new places. New members may get so discouraged with changes in the meeting place that they drop out.

In the process of starting a self-help group Lieberman and Borman note:

> There is an early zig-zag process of groping, trying out various approaches, dropping some, and developing new ones. Changes occur on a number of fronts . . . : (1) organizational size; (2) organizational structure; (3) program focus; (4) nature of membership; (5) nature of leadership; (6) articulation with professionals and agencies; and (7) sources of financial support.[16]

ONLINE SELF-HELP GROUPS

The personal computer is a tool for overcoming some of the traditional barriers to group participation. Such barriers include: no local self-help group available, lack of time or transportation for travel, limitations of a severe physical disability, and rarity of the condition. Over a thousand self-help groups now connect people with one another through

---

Alcoholics Anonymous: A Self-Help Group

In 1929, Bill Wilson was a stock analyst. When the stock market crashed, he lost most of his money and took to the bottle. A few years later his doctor warned him that his continual drinking was jeopardizing his health and his life. Bill W. underwent what he perceived was a spiritual experience, and he made a commitment to stop drinking. He had discovered that discussing his drinking problem with other alcoholics helped him to remain sober. One of the people he discussed his problem with was Robert Smith, an Ohio doctor and an alcoholic. Together they formed Alcoholics Anonymous (AA), a self-help group composed of recovering alcoholics.

AA stresses (1) an admission to the group that the member has a drinking problem, (2) a testimony to the group recounting past experiences with the drinking problem and plans for handling the problem in the future, and (3) support from another member of the group, who will even stay with a person who feels an intense urge to drink until the urge subsides. Today, AA has chapters in over one hundred countries.

The term "recovering" is used because AA believes there is no such thing as a permanently recovered alcoholic. The local chapters (usually from ten to thirty persons per chapter) meet once or twice a week for discussion sessions. These groups resemble traditional group therapy meetings without the presence of a trained professional leader.

Bill W. and Dr. Bob, as they are known within AA, remained anonymous until their deaths. Local chapters still follow the treatment procedures they initiated—the sharing of similar experiences in order to abstain from the first drink that is too many and the thousand drinks that are not enough.

AA is still widely regarded as the treatment approach that has the best chance of helping an alcoholic. In testimony to its value are hundreds of other self-help groups with treatment programs based on the AA model—Weight Watchers, Prison Families Anonymous, Parents Without Partners, Debtors Anonymous, Gamblers Anonymous, Emotions Anonymous, Emphysema Anonymous, and many more.

Source: Alan Gartner and Frank Riessman, *Help: A Working Guide to Self-Help Groups* (New York: Franklin-Watts, 1980), p. 8.

An AA Meeting

Alcoholics Anonymous (AA) is a remarkable human organization. Its chapters now cover every part of the United States and most of the world. There is more caring and concern among the members for one another than in most other organizations. Group members work together to save each other's lives and restore self-respect and sense of worth. AA has helped more people overcome their drinking problems than all other therapies and methods combined.

AA is supported entirely by voluntary donations from the members at meetings. There are no dues or fees. Each chapter is autonomous, free of any outside control by the AA headquarters in New York City or by any other body. There is no hierarchy in the chapters. The only office is that of group secretary. This person chooses a chairperson for each meeting, makes the arrangements for meetings, and sees that the building is opened, the chairs set up, and the tea and coffee put on. The group secretary holds office for only a limited time period; after a month or two the secretary's responsibilities are transferred to another member.

The only requirement for membership in AA is a desire to stop drinking. All other variables (such as economic status, social status, race, religion) do not count. Members can even attend meetings while drunk, as long as they do not disturb the meeting.

AA meetings are held in a variety of physical locations—churches, temples, private homes, business offices, schools, libraries, or banquet rooms of restaurants. The physical location is unimportant.

When a newcomer first arrives, he or she will usually find people setting up chairs, placing ashtrays, putting free literature on a table, and making coffee. Other members will be socializing in small groups. Someone is apt to introduce himself or herself and other members to the newcomer. If someone is shy about attending the first meeting alone, he or she can call AA and someone will take the person to the meeting and introduce him or her to the other members.

When the meeting starts, everyone sits down around tables or in rows of chairs. The secretary and/or chairperson and one or more speakers sit at the head of a table or on a platform if the meeting is in a hall.

The chairperson opens with a moment of silence, which is followed by a group recitation of a prayer that is nondenominational. The chairperson then reads or gives a brief description of Alcoholics Anonymous and may read or refer to a section of the book *Alcoholics Anonymous* (a book that describes the principles of AA and gives a number of case examples).

Then, the chairperson usually asks if anyone is attending for the first, second, or third time. The new people are asked to introduce themselves according to the following: "Hello, my name is (first name), and this is my first (second, third) meeting." Those who do not want to introduce themselves are not pressured to do so. New members are the lifeblood of AA, and the most important people at the meeting in the members' eyes.

(All the longer-term members remember their first meeting and how frightened and inhibited they felt.)

If the group is small, the chairperson usually then asks the longer-term members to introduce themselves and say a few words. If the group is large, the chairperson asks volunteers among the longer-term members to introduce themselves by saying a few words. Each member usually begins by saying, "My name is (first name); I am an alcoholic" and then discloses a few thoughts or feelings. (The members do not have to say they are alcoholic unless they choose to do so.) Each member sooner or later generally chooses to say this, to remind himself that he is an addictive drinker who is recovering and that alcoholism is a lifelong disease, which he must battle daily. Those who introduce themselves usually say whatever they feel will be most helpful to the newcomers. They may talk about their first meeting, or their first week without drinking, or something designed to make the newcomers more comfortable. Common advice for the newcomers is to get the phone numbers of other members after the meeting so that they can call them when they feel a strong urge to drink. AA considers such help as vital in recovering. The organization believes members can remain sober only through receiving the help of people who care about them and who understand what they are struggling with.

AA members want newcomers to call when they have the urge to drink, at any time day or night. The members sincerely believe that by helping others they are helping themselves to stay sober and grow. Members indicate such calling is the newcomer's ace in the hole against the first drink, if everything else fails. They also inform newcomers that it is good to call others when lonely, just to chat.

In his own words, a newcomer explains how AA began to help him:

> Here's what happened to me. When I finally hit bottom and called AA for help, a U.S. Air Force officer came to tell me about AA. For the first time in my life, I was talking to someone who obviously really understood my problem, as four psychiatrists had not, and he took me to my first meeting, sober but none too steady. It was amazing. I went home afterward and didn't have a drink. I went again the next night, still dry, and the miracle happened a second time. The third morning my wife went off to work, my boys to school, and I was alone. Suddenly I wanted a drink more than I had ever wanted one in my life. I tried walking for a while. No good. The feeling was getting worse. I tried reading. Couldn't concentrate. Then I became really desperate, and although I wasn't used to calling strangers for help, I called Fred, an AA-er who had said that he was retired and would welcome a call at any time. We talked a bit; he could see that talking on the phone wasn't going to be enough.

(continued)

■ An AA Meeting (*continued*)

He said, "Look, I've got an idea. Let me make a phone call, and I'll call you back in ten minutes. Can you hold on that long?" I said I could. He called back in eight, asking me to come over to his house. We talked endlessly, went out for a sandwich together, and finally my craving for a drink went away. We went to a meeting. Next morning I was fine again, and now I had gone four days without a drink.[1]

After such discussion, speakers may describe their life of drinking, how drinking almost destroyed their life, how they were introduced to AA, their struggles to remain sober one day at a time, how AA has helped them, and what their life is now like.

At the end of a meeting the chairperson may ask the newcomers if they wish to say anything. If they do not wish to say much, that is okay. No one is pressured to self-disclose what they do not want to reveal.

Meetings usually end after the chairperson makes announcements. (The collection basket for donations is also passed around. New members are not expected, and frequently not allowed, to donate any money until after their third meeting. If someone cannot afford to make a donation, none is expected.) The group then stands, usually holding hands, and repeats in unison the Lord's Prayer. Those who do not want to join in this prayer are not pressured to do so. After a meeting the members socialize. This is a time for newcomers to meet new friends and to get phone numbers.

AA is a cross-section of people from all walks of life. Anonymity is emphasized. It is the duty of every member to respect the anonymity of every person who attends. Concern for anonymity is a major reason for two kinds of meetings in AA, open and closed. Anyone is welcome at open meetings. Only people with drinking problems are allowed at closed meetings. Therefore, if a person feels uncomfortable going to an open meeting and has a drinking problem, closed meetings are an alternative.

Members do not have to believe in God to get help from AA. Many members have lost, or never had, a faith in God. AA does, however, assert that faith in some Higher Power is a tremendous help in recovery because such a belief offers a source of limitless power, hope, and support whenever one feels she has come to the end of her resources.

How does AA help? New members, after years of deteriorating feelings of rejection, loneliness, misunderstanding, guilt, and embarrassment, find they are not alone. They feel understood by others who are in similar predicaments. Instead of being rejected, they are welcomed. They see that others who had serious drinking problems are now sober, apparently happy that way, and are in the process of recovering. It gives them hope that they do not need alcohol to get through the day and that they can learn to enjoy life without alcohol. They find that others sincerely care about them, want to help them, and have the knowledge to do so.

At meetings they see every sort of personal problem brought up and discussed openly, with suggestions for solutions being offered by others who have encountered similar problems. They can observe that group members bring up "unspeakable" problems without apparent embarrassment, and that others listen and treat them with respect and consideration. Such acceptance gradually leads newcomers to share their personal problems and to receive constructive suggestions for solutions. Such disclosure leads individuals to look more deeply into themselves and to ventilate deep personal feelings. With the support of other members, newcomers gradually learn how to counter strong desires to drink, through such processes as calling other members.

Newcomers learn that AA is the means of staying away from that first drink. AA also serves to reduce the stress that compels people to drink by (1) providing a comfortable and relaxed environment, and (2) having members help each other to find ways to reduce the stresses encountered in daily living. AA meetings and members become a safe port that is always there when storms start raging. AA helps members to be programmed from negative thinking to positive thinking. The more positive a member's thinking becomes and the more stress is relieved, the better he begins to feel about himself, the more the compulsion to drink decreases, and the more often and more effectively the person begins to take positive actions to solve his problems.

---

[1]Clark Vaughan, *Addictive Drinking* (New York: Penguin Books, 1984), pp. 75–76.

e-mail, chat rooms, and websites on the Internet.[17] The personal computer can be a source of education about disabilities by providing information to both sufferers and interested professionals. A frequently forgotten population, homebound caregivers, can use a computer to find specific information and prompt support.

Some self-help groups (such as the Alzheimer's Association) offer World Wide Web homepages that provide hypertext links to an immense variety of literature. (*Hypertext* refers to highlighted words or images that, when selected by mouse click or keyboard arrow, connect directly with another resource without the necessity of typing or even knowing its web address.)

There are four primary forms of online self-help support networks: (1) chat rooms, (2) bulletin boards, (3) email, and (4) listservs. Chat rooms are virtual spaces, opened during specified time periods, where individuals can post messages and receive feedback interactively in a short time frame. In contrast, bulletin boards are usually open 24 hours a day. They enable individuals to post messages that can be answered at any time. Email allows an individual to write messages to particular individuals who can respond at any time. Listservs allow a large group of individuals to present and receive information and news. Thus, some computer-assisted group meetings occur in real time; that is, everyone participates at a specific time and the discussion in interactive. Other group meetings require members to post messages to which other members can respond at any time.

Computer-mediated services have a number of advantages. They offer a variety and diversity of support. They can provide services to homebound people for whom transportation to the offices of professionals is a major challenge. They can provide services to individuals in geographic areas that have few, or almost no, human services. They also offer anonymity to those who do not like to share the details of their concerns in face-to-face settings. Online services, after the initial purchase of a computer, are relatively inexpensive.

Computer-mediated services also have some shortcomings. Computer-mediated services often lack clear and accountable leadership—which can lead to misinformation or even potentially harmful interactions; for example, some vulnerable people have been victimized by sexual predators whom they met over the Internet.

Exercise 8.2: Checking Out Online Self-Help Groups

GOAL: This exercise is designed to familiarize you with online self-help groups.

Using the Internet, check out the web pages of three online self-help groups. Some suggested websites are the following:

Alcoholics Anonymous: www.alcoholicsanonymous.org
Adult Children of Alcoholics: www.adultchildren.org
American Foundation for Suicide Prevention: www.afsp.org
Gamblers Anonymous: www.gamblersanonymous.org
Overeaters Anonymous: www.overeatersanonymous.org
Sexaholics Anonymous: www.sa.org

Summarize the information you found for the three online self-help groups

■ GROUP EXERCISES

Exercise A: Alcoholics Anonymous

GOAL: To increase awareness of how a self-help group functions.

Step 1. Local chapters of Alcoholics Anonymous usually hold some open meetings that anyone may attend. The leader contacts a local chapter, inquires whether the class may attend, and makes the necessary arrangements—including time, date, and place. If these arrangements cannot be made with AA, the leader contacts other self-help groups in the community.

Step 2. At the class period following the meeting of the self-help group, the leader leads a discussion of the students' thoughts about the meeting they attended. The class also discusses the merits and shortcomings of this self-help group.

Exercise B: Combating Terrorism

GOAL: To increase awareness of how a social action self-help group functions.

Step 1. The leader explains the purpose of the exercise and indicates that terrorism is one of the most serious problems currently facing all nations. The students are told that their function is to serve as a social action self-help group. The class forms subgroups of five or six people. Each subgroup has the task of developing recommendations that this self-help group will then advocate to confront worldwide terrorism. (If the leader thinks it advisable, some other topic may be chosen.)

Step 2. Each subgroup selects its top three recommendations for confronting worldwide terrorism.

Step 3. The class reassembles. Each subgroup presents its three recommendations and lists them on the blackboard. The students then select the top five recommendations their self-help group ought to advocate for. A discussion should then follow on how this self-help group can realistically seek to implement these recommendations.

Social Work with Families*

GOALS

This chapter begins with an overview of social work with families. The assessment techniques of an eco-map and a genogram are described. The chapter also summarizes three prominent approaches to family therapy, targets some basic group work concepts, applies these concepts to family groups, and relates them to a simulated family situation.

A family is one category out of a number of categories of small groups. The focus of social work services is often the family, an interacting, interdependent system. The problems faced by people are usually influenced by the dynamics within the family, and dynamics within the family are, in turn, influenced by the wider social and cultural environment. Because a family is an interacting system, change in any member will affect all others. Tensions between a husband and wife, for example, will be felt by their children, who may then respond with disturbed behavior. Treating the children's behavior alone will not get to the root of the family problem.[1]

Another reason for the focus on the family rather than the individual is that other family members are often needed in the treatment process. They can help identify family patterns. In addition, the whole family, once members perceive the relationships among their various behaviors, can form a powerful team in reestablishing healthier patterns.[2] For example, family members can pressure their alcoholic mother to acknowledge her problem. They may provide important emotional support for her efforts to stop drinking. They may also need counseling themselves (or support from a self-help group) to assist in coping with them when she is drinking.

◼ DIVERSITY OF FAMILY FORMS

The family is a social institution that is found in every culture and has been defined by Coleman and Cressey as "a group of people related by marriage, ancestry, or adoption who live together in a common household."[3] This definition does not cover a number of living arrangements whose members consider themselves a family, such as these:

- A husband and wife raising two foster children who have been in the household for several years
- Two women, lesbians in a loving relationship, raising children born to one of the partners while in a heterosexual marriage that ended in divorce

---

*Material in the first part of this chapter, up to the section on Family Therapy is adapted from *The Practice of Social Work*, 7th ed., by Zastrow. © 2003. Reprinted with permission of Brooks/Cole, a division of Thomson Learning, Inc.

- Grandparents raising grandchildren due to illness or addiction of the parents
- A family with one spouse living away from home—perhaps because of military service in a foreign country or because of incarceration
- A family with one child who has a severe and profound cognitive disability living in a residential treatment facility
- A man and a woman who have been living together for years in a loving relationship but who have never legally married

A wide diversity of family patterns exists in the world. Families in different cultures take a variety of forms. In some societies, husband and wife live in separate buildings. In others, they live apart for several years after the birth of a child. In some societies, husbands are permitted to have more than one wife. In a few countries, wives are allowed to have more than one husband. Some cultures permit (and a few encourage) premarital and extramarital intercourse.

Some societies have large communes where adults and children live together. There are communes in which the children are raised separately from adults. In some cultures, surrogate parents (rather than the natural parents) raise the children. Some societies encourage certain types of gay/lesbian relationship, and a few recognize gay/lesbian, as well as heterosexual, marriages.

In many cultures, marriages are still arranged by the parents. In a few societies, an infant may be "married" before birth (if the baby is of the wrong sex, the marriage is dissolved). Some societies do not recognize romantic love. Some cultures expect older men to marry young girls. Others expect older women to marry young boys. Most societies prohibit the marriage of close relatives, but a few subcultures encourage marriage between brothers and sisters or between first cousins. Some expect a man to marry his father's brother's daughter, whereas others insist that he marry his mother's sister's daughter. In some societies, a man, on marrying, makes a substantial gift to the bride's father, whereas in others the bride's father gives a substantial gift to the new husband.

These are indeed substantial variations in family patterns. People in each of these societies feel strongly that their particular pattern is normal and proper, and many feel the pattern is divinely ordained. Suggested changes in their particular form are viewed with suspicion and defensiveness and are often sharply criticized as being unnatural, immoral, and a threat to the survival of the family.

In spite of these variations, sociologists note that most family systems can be classified into two basic forms: The extended family and the nuclear family. An *extended family* consists of a number of relatives living together, such as parents, children, grandparents, great-grandparents, aunts, uncles, in-laws, and cousins. The extended family is the predominant pattern in preindustrial societies. The members divide various agricultural, domestic, and other duties among themselves.

A *nuclear family* consists of a married couple and their children living together. The nuclear family type emerged from the extended family. Extended families tend to be more functional in agricultural societies where many "hands" are needed; the nuclear family is more suited to the demands of complex, industrialized societies, as its smaller size and potential geographic mobility enable it to adapt more easily to changing conditions—such as the need to relocate to obtain a better job.

Although the nuclear family is still the predominant family form in the United States, Canada, and many other industrialized countries, it is a serious mistake for social workers and other helping professionals to use the nuclear family as the ideal model that individuals in our society should strive to form. Many other family forms are functioning in our society, such as the following:

- A married couple without children who are the primary caregivers for the wife's mother, who has Alzheimer's disease and who resides with the couple
- Two gay men in a committed relationship, each of whom has joint custody of two children with his former wife
- A childless married couple who have decided not to conceive children

- A single parent with three young children
- A blended family in which the husband and wife have children in the current marriage, plus children from earlier marriages, all of whom live in the household
- An unmarried young couple living together in what amounts to a trial marriage

In the past few decades there has been a trend in the United States for greater diversity in marital arrangements and family forms. There are increasing numbers of transracial marriages, marriages between spouses of diverse ages and cultural backgrounds, transracial adoptions, single-parent families, and blended families. Although some social workers may personally judge a few of these types to be "wrong," it is essential that they not allow their personal beliefs to reduce the quality or quantity of professional services that are provided to these family units. It is also essential that social workers who work with families of diverse cultural backgrounds learn about those backgrounds and understand the customary norms for family functioning.

Some family forms have been discriminated against, such as a single-parent household, and a gay or lesbian couple with children.

Exercise 9.1: Composition and Strengths of My Family

GOAL: This exercise is designed to assist you in identifying your "core" family members and also the strengths of your family.

1. Specify the names and approximate ages of your "core" family members. (These may, or may not, include aunts, uncles, grandparents, foster children, etc.) Also, briefly describe each member. (Example: Jim Ryberg is my dad. He is 47, a truck driver, and a devout Catholic.)

2. Specify the strengths of your family. (Do not identify current family challenges, which will be focused on in a later exercise.) Consider such strengths as reputation in the community, health of members, exercise patterns, caring for one another, educational levels, financial resources, support from others, religious values, fun activities the family does together, rituals for family holidays, and so on.

■ SOCIETAL FUNCTIONS OF FAMILIES

Families in modern industrial societies perform the following essential functions that help maintain the continuity and stability of society:

1. *Replacement of the population.* Every society has some system for replacing its members. Practically all societies consider the family as the unit in which children are to be produced. Societies define the rights and responsibilities of the reproductive partners within the family unit. These rights and responsibilities help maintain the stability of society, although they are defined differently from one society to another.

2. *Care of the young.* Children require care and protection until at least the age of puberty. The family is a primary institution for the rearing of children. Modern societies have generally developed supportive institutions to help in caring for the young—for example, medical services, daycare centers, parent training programs, and residential treatment centers.

3. *Socialization of new members.* To become productive members of society, children have to be socialized into the culture. Children are expected to acquire a language, learn social values and mores, and dress and behave within the norms of society. The family plays a major role in this socialization process. In modern societies, a number of other groups and resources are involved in this socialization process. Schools, the mass media, peer groups, the police, movies, and books and other written material are important influences. (Sometimes these different influences clash by advocating opposing values and attitudes.)

4. *Regulation of sexual behavior.* Failure to regulate sexual behavior results in clashes between individuals due to jealousy and exploitation. Every society has rules that regulate sexual behavior within family units. Most societies, for example, have incest taboos, and most disapprove of extramarital sex.

5. *Source of affection.* Humans need affection, emotional support, and positive recognition from others (including approval, smiles, encouragement, and reinforcement for accomplishments). Without such affection and recognition, our emotional, intellectual, physical, and social growth would be stunted. The family is an important source for obtaining affection and recognition, because family members generally regard each other as among the most important people in their lives and gain emotional and social satisfaction from family relationships.

■ FAMILY PROBLEMS AND THE NATURE OF SOCIAL WORK

An infinite number of problems occurs in families. The box, "A Sampling of Family Problems," lists a few of them.

When problems arise in a family, social services are often needed. The types and forms of services that social workers provide to troubled families are extremely varied. We can group them into two major categories: in-home services and out-of-home services.

In-home services are preventive. Although not all are offered literally within the home itself, they are specifically designed to help families stay together. They include financial aid; protective services (services to safeguard children or frail older adults from abuse and neglect); family preservation services (intensive crises intervention within the home setting where children are so seriously at risk that removal to foster care would otherwise be required); family therapy (intensive counseling to improve family relationships); day care (caretaking services for children or older adults to provide respite for caregivers who might otherwise be overwhelmed or to permit them to work outside the home); homemaker services (for the same purpose); and family life education (classes, often offered at traditional family service agencies, that cover such topics as child development, parenting skills, communication issues, etc.). Obviously, not all of these

A Sampling of Family Problems

Divorce	Unemployment of wage earners
Alcohol or drug abuse	Money management difficulties
Unwanted pregnancy	Injury from serious automobile accident involving one or
Bankruptcy	more members
Poverty	A child with a severe cognitive disability
Terminal illness	Incarceration or institutionalization of one or more members
Chronic illness	Compulsive gambling by one or more members
Death	Victim of a crime
Desertion	Force retirement of a wage earner
"Empty-shell" marriage	Caregiver for an elderly relative
Emotional problems of one or more members	Involvement of a child in delinquent and criminal activities
Behavioral problems of one or more members	Illness of a member who acquires AIDS
Child abuse	A runaway teenager
Child neglect	Sexual dysfunctions of one or more members
Sexual abuse	Infidelity
Spouse abuse	Infertility
Elder abuse	

services can be provided by social workers, but workers must know where to find them and how to help the family obtain them when needed.[4]

Out-of-home services, on the other hand, are those services that must be operationalized when the family can no longer remain intact. They are a manifestation that something has gone seriously wrong, since the breakup of any family amounts to a tragedy that will have ramifications beyond family boundaries. While family members usually receive the blame, the larger system (social environment, and the level of support it provides to troubled families) may be called into question. Out-of-home services include foster care, adoption, group homes, institutional care (for example, residential treatment centers), and the judicial system (which provides a different kind of institutional care, prison or jail, for family members who have run into difficulty with the law).

To perform these services, social workers engage in a variety of roles (for example, broker, educator, advocate, supporter, mediator). The following examples illustrate many common services and important roles.

- Mark Schwanke, age 32, has AIDS. Ms. Seely, a social worker with the AIDS Support Network in the community, serves as a case manager in providing a variety of services to Mark, his wife (who is HIV-positive), and their two children. These services include medical information and care, housing, counseling, emotional support services, and financial assistance. Because of frequent discrimination against people with AIDS and people with the AIDS virus, Ms. Seely often must advocate on the family's behalf to ensure that they receive the services they need.
- Beth Roessler, age 15, has been convicted of committing six burglaries. Steve Padek, a juvenile probation officer and social worker, is her juvenile probation officer. Mr. Padek provides the following services to Beth and her mother, who is divorced: He holds weekly supervision meetings with Beth to monitor her school performance and leisure activities, links Beth's mother with a Parents Without Partners group, and conducts several counseling sessions with Beth and her mother to mediate conflicts in their relationship.
- The aunt of Amy Sund, a 3-year-old child, has contacted Protective Services about Amy's mother (Pat) and her lover's physical abuse of Amy. Investigators

confirm the abuse; Amy has bruises and rope burns on her body. Instead of referring the case to court, Protective Services refers the case to Family Preservation for services. Maria Gomez, social worker at Family Preservation, meets with Pat Sund and Amy a total of 37 times over the next 90 days. Pat Sund terminates her relationship with her abusive lover, is accepted into a financial assistance program through the Social Services Department for a two-year period, and enrolls in a job training program. Ms. Gomez arranges for child care for Amy when Ms. Sund is attending the job training program. Ms. Gomez also arranges for a temporary housekeeper who provides training in cleaning the apartment and in making meals. Ms. Gomez encourages Ms. Sund to join the local chapter of Parents Anonymous, which she does. (Parents Anonymous is described in Chapter 1.) Had family preservation services been unavailable or unsuccessful, Amy would have had to be placed in a foster home.

■   Cindy Rogerson, age 27, has three young children. She is badly battered by her husband and contacts the House of Hope, a shelter for battered women and their children. Sue Frank, a social worker at the shelter, makes arrangements for shelter for Mrs. Rogerson and her children. The oldest child is attending school, so Ms. Frank arranges for him to continue attending school. Ms. Frank at the shelter provides one-to-one counseling to Mrs. Rogerson to help her explore her options and to inform her of potential resources that she may not be aware of. Ms. Frank also leads groups at the shelter for residents and nonresidents, which Mrs. Rogerson is required to attend while at the shelter. After $2\frac{1}{2}$ weeks, Mrs. Rogerson decides she wants to return to her husband. Ms. Frank convinces Mrs. Rogerson to give her husband an ultimatum prior to returning—he must receive family counseling together with her from the Family Service agency in the community and must attend a group for batterers in the community. Mrs. Rogerson reluctantly agrees. Mrs. Rogerson, at the urging of Ms. Frank, only then returns to live with her husband, with the understanding that she will leave immediately if he hits her again or if he drops out of either family counseling or the group for batterers.

■   Katy Hynek, age 76, has Alzheimer's disease. She has been living alone in her house since her husband died three years ago. Her physician contacts Adult Services of the Department of Social Services and requests that an assessment of living arrangements be conducted. Linda Sutton, social worker, does an assessment and determines that Katy Hynek can no longer live lone. Katy's son Mark and his wife Annette agree to have Katy move in with them. During the next 19 months, Ms. Sutton has periodic contact with the Hyneks. As is common with this disease, Katy Hynek's physical and mental condition continue to deteriorate. Ms. Sutton listens to Mark and Annette's concerns and seeks to answer their questions about the disease. She also provides suggestions to help them cope with the changes in Katy's condition. As Katy's condition deteriorates, Ms. Sutton makes arrangements for Katy to attend an adult daycare center during the daytime, partly for respite care for Mark and Annette. At the end of 19 months, Mark and Annette request a meeting with Ms. Sutton to discuss the possibility of placing Katy in a nursing home as her condition has so deteriorated that she now needs 24-hour care. (For example, she gets up in the middle of the night and gets lost in closets; she is also now incontinent.) The pros and cons of placing Katy in a nursing home are identified and discussed. Making the decision is exceedingly emotional and agonizing for Mark and Annette. With a careful discussion of the entire situation with Ms. Sutton, Mark and Annette decide they have no choice but to seek a nursing home placement.

Ms. Sutton gives them the names of three nursing homes, which they visit, and then they proceed to select one.

FAMILY ASSESSMENT

The two areas in family social work practice that have received the most attention are family assessment and family therapy. In this section we focus on family assessment.

There are a variety of ways to assess families. Conducting a social history of a family and its members is a widely used approach. With regard to family assessment, however, two techniques have received considerable discussion in recent years: eco-maps and genograms.

The Eco-Map

The eco-map (Figure 9.1) is a paper-and-pencil assessment tool used to assess specific troubles and plan interventions for clients. The eco-map, a drawing of the client family in its social environment, is usually drawn jointly by the social worker and the client. It helps both parties achieve a holistic or ecological view of the client's family life and the nature of the family's relationships with groups, associations, organizations, and other families and individuals. The eco-map has been used in a variety of situations, including marriage and family counseling, and adoption and foster-care home studies. It has also been used to supplement traditional social histories and case records. The eco-map is a shorthand method for recording basic social information. The technique helps clients and workers gain insight into the clients' problems by providing a "snapshot view" of important interactions at a particular point in time. Ann Hartman is the primary developer of this tool.[5]

A typical eco-map consists of a family diagram surrounded by a set of circles and lines used to describe the family within an environmental context. Eco-map users can create their own abbreviations and symbols, but the most commonly used symbols are shown in Figure 9.1.

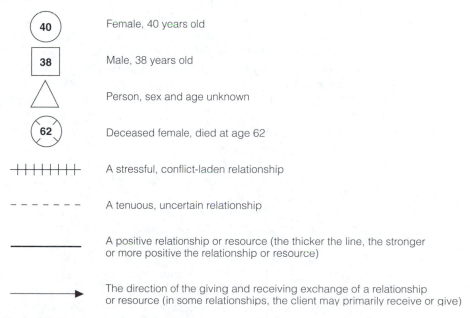

Figure 9.1
Commonly used symbols in an eco-map

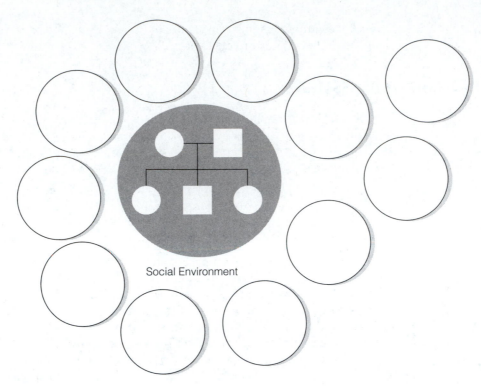

Figure 9.2
Setting up an eco-map

First, a circle (representing the client's family) is drawn in the center of a large blank sheet of paper (see Figure 9.2). The composition of the family is indicated in the circle. Other circles are then drawn around the family circle. These circles represent other systems—that is, the groups, other families, individuals, and organizations—with which the family ordinarily interacts.

Lines are drawn to describe the relationships that members of the client family have with these systems. Arrows show the flow of energy (giving or receiving resources, and communication between family members and significant systems). Figure 9.3 shows the eco-map for the Wilbur family case example (see box on p. 246).

A major value of an eco-map is that it helps both worker and client view the client's family from a system and ecological perspective. Sometimes, as happened in the Wilbur case example, clients and workers gain greater insight into the social dynamics of a problematic situation.

In summary, eco-maps are useful to both workers and clients. For the workers, a completed eco-map graphically displays important interactions of a client family with other systems (that is, the groups, other families, individuals, and organizations) that the family ordinarily interacts with at a particular point in time. Such a diagram allows the worker to better understand the environmental factors impacting the family. It then helps the worker generate hypotheses of problematic dynamics in the family-environmental system, which the worker can then further explore by questioning the family members. Once problematic dynamics are identified, the worker can focus attention on helping family members generate strategies to resolve the problematic dynamics.

Similarly, for the client family members, an eco-map helps them identify and understand problematic dynamics in their family-environmental system. Once identified, family members are then in a position to generate strategies (together with their worker) to resolve the dynamics.

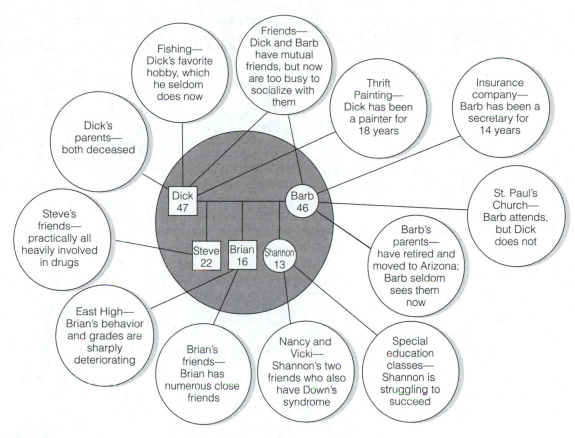

Figure 9.3
Sample eco-map: The Wilbur family

Exercise 9.2: An Eco-Map of My Family

GOAL: This exercise is designed to assist you in learning how to construct an eco-map.

1. **Draw an eco-map of a significant day in the life of your family. The event may be a happy event (perhaps a wedding) or a crisis.**

■ Case Example of Using an Eco-Map: The Wilbur Family

Barb and Dick Wilbur are contacted by Mary Timm, School Social Worker at East High School. The Wilbers' second-oldest son, Brian (age 16), had a knife in his jacket at school and liquor on his breath. The Wilburs are shocked. They agree to meet with Ms. Timm the next day to discuss these incidents. Brian will also be present.

At the meeting Ms. Timm asks Brian why he brought a knife to school. At first, he refuses to respond. Ms. Timm also notes that records show he used to receive mainly B's, but now his grades are primarily D's and F's. Mr. and Mrs. Wilbur also sternly ask Brian what is happening. They add that the school system has informed them that he apparently has been drinking during school hours. Gradually tears come to Brian's eyes. He says no one cares about him. He asserts his parents are too busy at work and too busy looking after his older brother, Steve, and his younger sister, Shannon.

At first, Mr. and Mrs. Wilbur are surprised. They indicate they love Brian very much. Gradually they disclose they have been so involved with the demands of their other two children that they may have been "shortchanging" Brian in recent months. Shannon, age 13, has Down's syndrome and requires considerable individual attention, especially with her coursework. (Shannon is enrolled in special education courses.)

Brian is asked where he obtained the knife. He hesitantly indicates his older brother, Steve, gave it to him for "protection." Brian adds that he sees nothing wrong with carrying a knife; Steve frequently carries a pistol. In addition, Brian says Steve urged him to take the knife to school because some people who are unhappy with Steve have said they may come after Brian. Ms. Timm asks Mr. and Mrs. Wilbur if they know anything about this. Barb and Dick suggest it may be best if Brian is excused at this point. Ms. Timm sets up a later meeting with Brian, and he leaves.

Both Barb and Dick then become teary-eyed. They indicate they are nearing their wit's end. Both work full time, and in recent years Steve and Shannon have required so much of their attention that they now no longer are able to spend any time with their former friends. In addition, they have been arguing more and more. They feel that their family is disintegrating and that they are "failing" as parents. They also disclose that Steve is addicted to both alcohol and cocaine and has been for several years. He has been in for inpatient treatment three times but always goes back to using soon after leaving treatment. They don't know where Steve is getting the money for his cocaine habit. They fear he may be dealing. He hasn't been able to hold a full-time job. He is usually terminated because he shows up for work while under the influence. Currently, he is working part-time as a bartender.

Mr. and Mrs. Wilbur fear that unless something is done soon, Brian may follow in Steve's footsteps. They add they have contemplated asking Steve to leave but are reluctant to do so because they feel it is their parental obligation to provide a house for their children as long as the children want to stay.

At this point Ms. Timm suggests it may be helpful to diagram their present dilemma. Together the Wilburs and Ms. Timm draw the eco-map shown in Figure 9.3 (see p. 245).

While drawing the map, Ms. Timm asks whether providing housing for Steve is helping him or whether it may be a factor in enabling him to continue his drug use and his irresponsible behavior. The eco-map helps the Wilburs see that as a result of working full time and spending the remainder of their waking hours caring for Shannon, Steve, and Brian, they are gradually becoming too emotionally and physically exhausted to cope. During the past few years, they have stopped socializing. The Wilburs ask Ms. Timm to explain what she means by "enabling" Steve to continue his drug use and his irresponsible behavior. Ms. Timm explains enabling and indicates that a "tough love" approach may be an option. (In this case, a tough love approach would involve the Wilburs' demanding that Steve live elsewhere if he continues to abuse alcohol and cocaine.) Ms. Timm also gives them pamphlets that describe enabling and tough love. They make an appointment for the next week.

For the next several weeks Ms. Timm continues to meet weekly with the Wilburs and individually with Brian. The Wilburs eventually decide to use a tough love approach with Steve. Steve leaves but continues to use alcohol and cocaine. However, living on his own does appear to be somewhat beneficial as he now works full time at a maintenance job to pay his bills. With Steve out of the house, Barb and Dick are able to spend more time with Brian and Shannon, and they begin to socialize again with some of their former friends.

2. **Briefly describe the significant event represented in your eco-map and the roles played by the people and other significant factors you identified.**

The Genogram

The genogram is a graphic way of investigating the origins of a client's or client family's presenting problem by diagramming the family over at least three generations. The client and worker usually jointly construct the family genogram, which is essentially a family tree. Bowen is the primary developer of this technique.[6] The genogram helps the worker and family members examine problematic emotional and behavioral patterns in an intergenerational context. Patterns tend to repeat themselves; what happens in one generation often occurs in the next. Genograms help family members identify and understand family relationship patterns.

Commonly used genogram symbols are shown in Figure 9.4. Together, the symbols provide a visual picture of a family tree, for at least three generations, including the following: who the members are; their names, ages, and gender; marital status; sibling positions; and so on. When relevant, additional items of information are included, such as emotional difficulties, behavioral problems, religious affiliation, ethnic origins, geographic locations, occupations, socioeconomic status, and significant life events. The use of the genogram is illustrated in the Kull family case example in Figure 9.5. (For full case example, see p. 250.)

In summary, genograms are useful to both worker and clients. For the worker, a completed genogram graphically points out intergenerational family dynamics. Such a diagram allows the worker to better understand the intergenerational patterns impacting a client family. It then helps the worker generate hypotheses of problematic patterns from prior generations, which the worker can further explore by questioning family members. Once problematic dynamics are identified, the worker can then focus attention on helping family members to generate strategies to resolve the patterns. A strengths perspective should also be used by workers—that is, they should also focus on helping family members identify intergenerational patterns that are *resources* that will help the family confront challenges. (Such resources include longevity, high educational achievement levels, valuing and practicing good health patterns, low rates of divorce, and high levels of constructive community participation.)

Similarly, for the client family, a genogram helps them identify and understand problematic intergenerational patterns and resources. Once such patterns are identified, family members can begin to generate strategies (together with their worker) to break these patterns.

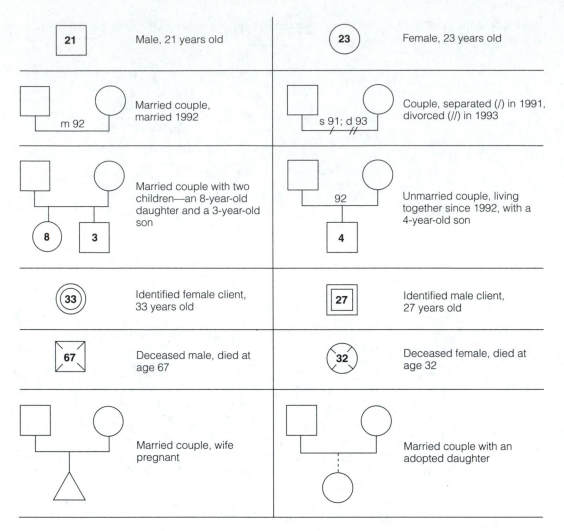

Figure 9.4
Commonly used genogram symbols

The eco-map and the genogram have a number of similarities. With both techniques, users gain insight into family dynamics. Some of the symbols used in the two approaches are identical. There are differences, however. The eco-map focuses attention on the family's interactions with groups, resources, organizations, associations, other families, and other individuals. The genogram focuses attention on intergenerational patterns, particularly those that are problematic or dysfunctional.

Exercise 9.3: A Genogram of My Family

GOAL: This exercise is designed to assist you in learning how to construct a genogram.

1. Draw a genogram of your family.

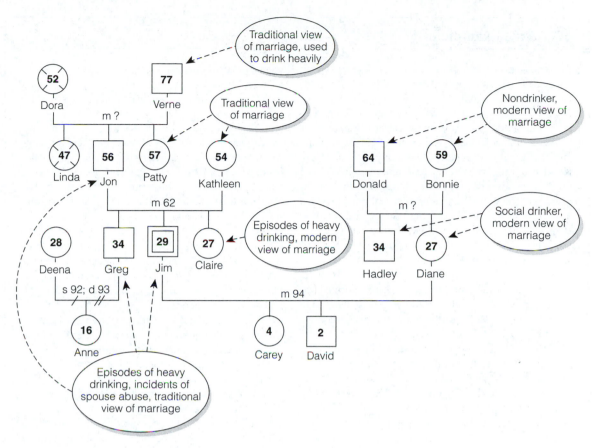

Figure 9.5
Sample genogram: The Jim and Diane Kull family

2. **Specify significant patterns that tend to repeat themselves in your family.**

Case Example of Using a Genogram: The Kull Family

Jim Kull is referred by Rock County District Attorney's Office to the Rock County Domestic Violence Program. He was arrested two nights ago for an incident in which his wife, Diane, received several severe bruises on her body and her face. Kris Koeffler, a social worker, has an intake interview with Mr. Kull. Mr. Kull is an involuntary client and is reluctant to discuss the incident. Ms. Koeffler informs Mr. Kull he has a right not to discuss it, but if he chooses not to, she is obligated to inform the district attorney that he refused services. She adds that in such cases the district attorney usually files a battery charge with the court, which may lead to jail time.

Mr. Kull reluctantly states he and his wife had a disagreement, which ended with her slapping him and him defending himself by throwing a few punches. He adds that yesterday, when he was in jail, he was informed she left home with the children and is now staying at a women's shelter. He is further worried she may contact an attorney and seek a divorce.

Ms. Koeffler inquires about the specifics of the "disagreement." Mr. Kull indicates he came home after having a few beers, his dinner was cold, and he "got on" Mrs. Kull for not cleaning the house. He adds that Mrs. Kull then started "mouthing off," which eventually escalated into them pushing and hitting each other. Ms. Koeffler then inquires whether such incidents had occurred in the past. Mr. Kull indicates "a few times," and then adds that getting physical with his wife is the only way for him to "make her shape up." He indicates he works all day long as a carpenter while his wife sits home watching soap operas. He feels she is not doing her "fair share"; he states the house usually looks like a "pigpen."

Ms. Koeffler asks Mr. Kull if he feels getting physical with his wife is justifiable. He responds with "sure," and adds that his dad frequently told him "spare the rod and spoil both the wife and the kids." Ms. Koeffler asks if his father was at times abusive to him when he was a child. He indicates that he was and adds that to this day he detests his dad for being abusive to him and to his mother.

Ms. Koeffler then suggests that together they draw a "family tree," focusing on three areas: episodes of heavy drinking, episodes of physical abuse, and traditional versus modern gender stereotypes. Ms. Koeffler explains that a traditional gender stereotype includes the husband as the primary decision maker and the wife as submissive to him and primarily responsible for domestic tasks. The modern gender stereotype involves an equalitarian relationship between husband and wife. After an initial reluctance (related to his expressing confusion as to how such a "tree" would help get his wife back), Mr. Kull agrees to cooperate in drawing such a "tree." The resulting genogram is presented in Figure 9.5.

The genogram helps Mr. Kull see that he and his wife are products of family systems that have strikingly different values and customs. In his family the males drink heavily, have a traditional view of marriage, and use physical force in interactions with their spouse. Mr. Kull further adds his father also physically abused his brother and sister when they were younger.) On questioning, Mr. Kull mentions he frequently spanks his children and has struck them "once or twice." Ms. Koeffler asks Mr. Kull how he feels about repeating the same patterns of abuse with his wife and children that he despises his father for using. Tears come to his eyes, and he says "not good."

Ms. Koeffler and Mr. Kull then discuss courses of action that he might take to change his family interactions and how he might best approach his wife in requesting that she and the children return. Mr. Kull agrees to attend Alcoholics Anonymous (AA) meetings as well as a therapy group for batterers. After a month of attending these weekly meetings, he contacts his wife and asks her to return. Mrs. Kull agrees to return *if* he stops drinking (since most of the abuse occurred when he was intoxicated, *if* he agrees to continue to attend group therapy and AA meetings, and *if* he agrees to go to counseling with her. Mr. Kull readily agrees. (Mrs. Kull's parents, who have never liked her husband, express their disapproval.)

For the first few months, Mr. Kull is on his best behavior and there is considerable harmony in the family. Then one day, on his birthday, he decides to stop for a few beers after work. He drinks until he is intoxicated. When he finally arrives home, he starts to verbally and physically abuse Mrs. Kull and the children. For Mrs. Kull, this is the last straw. She takes the children to her parents' house, where they stay for several days until they are able to find and move into an apartment. She also files for divorce and follows through in obtaining one.

At first glance, this case is not a "success." In reality, many social work cases are not successful. However, Mr. Kull now realizes that he has acquired, and acts out, certain dysfunctional family patterns. Unfortunately, he is not ready to make lasting changes. Perhaps in the future he will be more committed. At the present time he has returned to drinking heavily. Mrs. Kull and the children are safer and can now start to break the cycle of abuse.

3. **Identify any dysfunctional patterns in your family that tend to be repeated. For each identified dysfunctional pattern, seek to specify courses of action that may stop these patterns from being repeated.**

■ FAMILY THERAPY

One of the many social services provided to families is family therapy (also called family counseling). A substantial amount of literature about family therapy has been developed in social work. The remainder of this chapter focuses on family therapy. Although social work with families involves many approaches and services in addition to family therapy, the importance of family therapy in social work practice necessitates an extended discussion of this approach.

Family therapy—what is it? Strictly speaking, it is a subset of the broader classification of group therapy that is aimed at helping families with whatever interactional, behavioral, and emotional problems arise in the course of everyday living. Problems include marital conflicts, parent–child interactional problems, and conflicts with grandparents or other relatives. A wide variety of problems are dealt with in family therapy: domestic violence, communication problems, disagreements between family members on drug use and abuse, curfew hours, school performance, money management, sexual values and behavior, performance of domestic tasks, and methods of disciplining the children. The following is a typical scenario.*

George and Martha Sitzke were fed up. They just didn't know what to do with their 16-year-old daughter, Sharon, anymore. She wouldn't cooperate on anything. She had cropped her hair close to her head and dyed the remainder a rainbow of colors, was flunking most of her subjects at school, and was staying out until all hours of the night regardless of what they told her. Who knows what she might be doing—alcohol, drugs, sex, or worse. Not only that, but she was a terror to live with at home. They felt she was sarcastic, argumentative, and hostile.

The Sitzkes finally admitted that Sharon was out of their control. They didn't understand what was happening, but they knew they needed help. They brought her to the local mental health clinic and asked for counseling. Something had to be done.

The story of the Sitzke family is an example of one of the many types of family situations in which social workers are called upon for assistance. The context is frequently one in which the family as a group has a problem. A social worker applies intervention knowledge and skills to help this family or one like it solve its problems. A family therapy perspective involves seeing any problem within the family as a family group problem, not as a problem on the part of any *one* individual member.[7] This reinforces the idea that a group orientation applies when working with families.

---

*The remainder of this chapter was written by Karen K. Kirst-Ashman, PhD, professor, Social Work Department, University of Wisconsin–Whitewater.

Several relevant aspects of families as groups have been targeted here for discussion. The first is verbal communication, including a variety of avenues of communication. The second is nonverbal communication. The importance of congruence between verbal and nonverbal communication is also stressed. The third aspect of families addressed here involves family group norms, and the fourth aspect is the roles family members often assume. Setting goals, both personal and group, is the fifth aspect of working with families. Identification of some common group conflicts, problems, and strategies for resolution is the sixth. Finally, three specific family therapy approaches will be highlighted and two specific techniques explained.

We will begin our focus on family therapy by concentrating on the assessment phase because this is where family dynamics and interactions are discovered and most easily examined.

■ VERBAL COMMUNICATION

Communication, both verbal and nonverbal, is critical in group functioning. Chapter 7 describes how information is translated from thoughts into words and sent to a receiver, who then interprets its meaning. Effective communication implies the mutual understanding of information conveyed. Satir summarizes the meaning of effective communication. It includes being able to firmly state your case, clarify it, and ask for and be receptive to feedback.[8] This is very difficult to accomplish since there are many possibilities for interference and misinterpretation both in families and in other groups. The sender may be vague or inaccurate with his or her message. Interruptions and distractions may detract from the communication process. Also, the receiver may not be attentive, fail to understand, or distort what has been said.

One focus of family treatment is the communication patterns within the family.[9] Scherz reflects that "communication in the family is the channel through which the rules and roles, the processes of identification and differentiation, the management of tasks, conflicts, and resolutions—in short, the business of life—is conducted."[10] Verbal communication patterns inside the family include who talks a lot and who talks only rarely. They involve who talks to whom and who defers to whom. They also reflect the subtle and not so subtle qualities involved in family members' relationships.

For example, a 17-year-old son asks his father, "Dad, can I have the car next Saturday night?" Dad, who's in the middle of writing up his tax returns, which are due in two days, replies, "No, Harry." Harry interprets this to mean that his father is an authoritarian tyrant who does not trust him with the family car. Harry stomps off in a huff. However, what Dad really meant was that he and Mom need the car this Saturday because they're taking their best friends, the Jamesons, out for their 20th wedding anniversary. Dad was also thinking that perhaps the Jamesons wouldn't mind driving. Or maybe he and Harry could work something out to share the car. At any rate, Dad really meant that he was much too involved with the tax forms to talk about it and would rather discuss it during dinner.

This is a good example of ineffective communication. The information was vague and incomplete. Neither person clarified his thoughts or gave feedback to the other. There are endless variations to the types of ineffective communication that can take place in families. At any rate, it's up to the social worker to help clarify, untangle, and reconstruct communication patterns.

Avenues of Communication

Perez cites "five avenues of communication," any or all of which family members may use in a given day. They include consonance, condemnation, submission, intellectualization, and indifference.[11] Evaluating how a family communicates using these avenues provides clear clues regarding where change is needed.

Consonance

Consonance refers to the extent to which the receiver of a communication accurately hears and understands the sender. In other words, the sender's *intent* closely resembles the receiver's *impact*. Healthy families are likely to have high levels of consonance in their communications; family members understand each other well.

Condemnation

Condemnation involves family members severely criticizing, blaming, negatively judging, or nagging others in a consistent manner. More than occurring only once or twice, such interaction instead forms a regular pattern. This pattern may involve any number of the family members. One person may typically condemn a particular individual. Or one person may typically condemn all the others. Likewise, all family members may condemn one person in particular. Or two, or three members may condemn one or more.

People who form patterns of condemnation frequently do it to enhance their self-esteem.[12] Blaming or criticizing another person makes one's qualities and behaviors appear better or superior. For instance, take the 80-year-old woman who constantly condemned her husband of 55 years. He was 84. She regularly harped on how he was an alcoholic who couldn't keep a job. However, he hadn't touched a drop of liquor in over 40 years. Additionally, he had worked regularly as a carpenter for most of those years. When the woman criticized her husband for behavior that had occurred over 40 years earlier, she made herself feel better. If he was so bad, then she looked good by comparison.

Submission

Submission occurs when a person feels so downtrodden, guilt-ridden, or incapable that he or she succumbs completely to another's will. The person doesn't feel valuable or worthwhile enough to be assertive about his or her own rights and needs. Perez sums up situations involving submission by saying, "The submissive person, like the condemner, is difficult to live with. His or her feelings of ineptness and inadequacy put family members under constant pressure to support, to guide, to direct, to lead him. And again, when the dependency pressure becomes too demanding, the family members may well respond via condemnation."[13]

Intellectualization

Intellectualization refers to the process of putting all communication on a strictly logical, rational realm. The existence of any emotion is denied or suppressed. A person who intellectualizes likes to evaluate a problem rationally and establish a solution as soon as possible. This person does not want illogical emotions to interfere with the process of dealing with and controlling reality. The problem usually faced by the intellectualizer, however, is that *everyone* has emotions. Emotions that are constantly suppressed may build up and explode uncontrollably at inopportune times. Explosions may even result in violence.

Another problem with intellectualization occurs when the intellectualizer is unable to meet the needs of other family members. A person who intellectualizes can seem to be cold and unloving. Traditional gender-role stereotypes that direct men to be strong, unemotional decision makers encourage intellectualization. This often becomes a problem in relationships for those women who have been raised to express emotions. A typical scenario involves a woman who seeks expression of love and emotion from a spouse who intellectualizes.

Take, for instance, a man who stated point-blank that he has no emotions; he said he was always happy. His wife responded with the question, "Well, then, what are you when you're yelling at me?"

The man replied hesitantly, "Then . . . I'm mad." At this, the woman smiled to herself. She had made some progress. She had just doubled her mate's emotional repertoire.

Indifference

Indifference involves remaining apparently unconcerned, not caring one way or the other, and appearing aloof. Two common ways indifference is manifested in families is through "science" and "ignoring behaviors."[14] One or more family members may not talk or respond to one or more other family members.

Indifference can be a powerful and manipulative means of communicating. A mother who ignores her teenage daughter may convey a number of messages to her. Perhaps the daughter feels her mother doesn't care enough about her to expend the energy. Or maybe the mother is angry at her for some reason.

Being ignored can be either painful or annoying. For example, take a newlywed woman who was very emotionally insecure. During the first few weeks of marriage, she asked her husband a dozen times a day if he really loved her. At first, he answered, "Yes, dear, I do." However, he soon tired of her constant need for reassurance. He began simply to "turn her off" and ignore her. She was devastated. She needed to learn that her consistent questioning had the opposite effect of that which she desired. In her desire to feel more secure, she was driving her husband away from her.

Exercise 9.4: Problematic Verbal Communication Patterns in My Family

GOAL: This exercise is designed to assist you in identifying problematic verbal communication patterns in your family.

Reread the material in the preceding section and then summarize problematic verbal communication patterns in your family.

■ NONVERBAL COMMUNICATION

Nonverbal communication is just as important as verbal communication. It includes the facial expressions, voice inflections, and body positions that convey information about a person's thoughts and feelings. Chapter 5 elaborates on the importance of nonverbal communication in groups, and family groups are no exception. Nonverbal behavior provides a major means of conveying information, so effective communication is based just as much on appropriate and accurate nonverbal messages as on verbal ones.

One especially important aspect of assessing messages is whether they are congruent or incongruent. Satir states that communication is incongruent when two or more messages contradict each other's meaning.[15] In other words, the messages are confusing. Contradictory messages within families disturb effective family functioning.

Chapter 5 describes how nonverbal messages can contradict verbal messages. These double messages can also occur in families. For example, a recently widowed woman says, "I'm sorry Frank passed away," with a big grin on her face. The information expressed by the words indicates that she is sad. However, her accompanying physical expressions show that she is happy. Her words are considered socially appropriate for the situation. However, in this particular case, she is relieved to get rid of "the old buzzard" and happy to be the beneficiary of a large life insurance policy.

The double message reflected by the widow's verbal and nonverbal behavior provides a relatively simple, clear-cut illustration of potential problem communication within families. However, congruence is certainly not the only important aspect of nonverbal communications. All of the principles of nonverbal communication can be applied to communication within families.

Exercise 9.5: Problematic Nonverbal Communication Patterns in My Family

GOAL: This exercise is designed to assist you in identifying problematic nonverbal communication patterns in your family.

Reread the material in the preceding section and then summarize problematic nonverbal communication patterns in your family.

▪ FAMILY GROUP NORMS

Chapter 4 defines norms as rules that specify proper behavior in a group. It also discusses the explicit and implicit norms or rules that all groups have. Families also have rules. Janzen and Harris define these rules as "relationship agreements which influence family behavior."[16] They note that frequently the most powerful rules are those that are not clearly and verbally stated but rather those that are implicit. These implicit rules are repeated family transactions that all family group members understand but never discuss.

As in other groups, it's important to establish norms in families that allow the entire family and each individual member to function effectively and productively. Each family differs in its individual set of norms or rules. For example, Family A has a relatively conservative set of norms governing communication and interpersonal behavior. Although the norms allow frequent pleasant talk among family members, it is always on a superficial level. The snowy winter weather or the status of the new variety of squash grown in the garden is fair game for conversation. However, nothing more personal is ever mentioned. Taboo subjects include anything to do with feelings, interpersonal relationships, or opinions about careers or jobs. On one occasion, for example, a friend asked the family matriarch what her son and daughter-in-law would name their soon-to-be-born first baby. With a shocked expression on her face, she replied, "Oh, my heavens, I haven't asked. I don't want to interfere."

Family B, on the other hand, has a vastly different set of norms governing communication and behavior. Virtually everything is discussed and debated, not only among the nuclear family members but also among several generations. Personal methods of birth control, stances on abortion, opinions on capital punishment, and politics number among the emotionally heated issues discussed. Family members frequently talk about their personal relationships, including who is the favorite grandchild and who tends to fight all the time with rich, old Aunt Harriet. The family is so open that price tags are left on Christmas gifts.

The rules of behavior that govern Family B are very different from those of Family A. Yet, in each family, all the members consider their family's behavior to be normal and are comfortable with these rules. Members of each family may find it inconceivable that families could be any other way.

In families with problems, however, most frequently the family rules do not allow the family or the individual members to function effectively and productively. Group work principles state that only group norms that help the group function effectively should be developed and allowed. The case is the same with families. Ineffective norms need to be identified and changed. Positive, beneficial norms need to be developed and fostered.

The following is an example of a family in which there was an implicit, invalid, and ineffective norm functioning. The norm was that no one in the family would smoke cigarettes. A husband, wife, four children, and two sets of grandparents composed this family. Although never discussed, the understanding was that no one had ever or would ever smoke. One day the husband found several cigarette butts in the ashtray of the car typically used by his wife. He thought this odd but said nothing. Over the next six months, he frequently found cigarette butts in the same ashtray. Because no one in the family smoked, he deduced that these butts must belong to someone else. He assumed that his wife was having an affair with another man, which devastated him. However, he said nothing about it and suffered in silence. His relationship with his wife began to deteriorate. He became sullen, and spats and conflicts became more frequent. Finally, in a heated conflict, he revealed his thoughts and feelings about the cigarette butts and her affair. His wife expressed shocked disbelief. The reality was that it was she who smoked the cigarettes but only when no one else was around. Her major time to be alone was when she was driving to and from work. She took advantage of this time to smoke but occasionally forgot to empty the ashtray. She told him the entire story, and he was tremendously relieved. Their relationship improved and prospered.

This example illustrates how an inappropriate norm almost ruined a family relationship. Such a simple thing as the wife being a "closet smoker" had the potential for destroying a marital relationship. In this instance, a simple correction in communication solved the problem. The interesting thing is that eventually the entire family learned of this incident. The wife still smokes but still insists on doing it privately. The family now functions effectively with an amended family rule that accepts smoking.

Norms are as important to families as they are to other groups. A group worker needs to attend to group norms, monitor them, and make certain they are beneficial for group functioning. Likewise, a social worker providing treatment for a family needs to identify the family norms, assess them, and initiate changes when necessary to enhance family functioning.

Exercise 9.6: Functional and Problematic Norms in My Family

GOAL: This exercise is designed to assist you in identifying the functional and problematic norms in your family.

1. Specify the functional norms in your family.

2. Specify the problematic norms in your family.

FAMILY ROLES

A role is "a culturally determined pattern of behavior that is prescribed for an individual who occupies a specific status" or rank in relation to others.[17] In a family, these rules usually involve behaviors that work for the benefit of the family. For instance, the parental role prescribes behaviors helpful in supporting, directing, and raising children. Likewise, parents might assume worker roles by being employed outside of the home to earn financial sustenance for the family. Children, on the other hand, might assume the role of "student" in school and "helper" in household tasks.[18]

In addition to these formal socially acceptable roles, family members may hold a variety of informal roles, often related to the individual personalities and interactional patterns among family members. For instance, such roles may include the troublemaker, the oppressed one, the illustrious star, the one to blame for everything (scapegoat), the perfect loner, the old battle ax, or the black sheep.

A broad range of roles can be found in families. One family comes to mind that has a white sheep within its flock. The nuclear family consists of two parents and three children, two females and one male, who is also the youngest. All family members are now adults. All members of this family except for the youngest male like to drink, party, and do their share of swearing. None except the youngest is involved in any organized religion. The youngest, on the other hand, is a fundamentalist preacher—the white sheep.

Because each person and each family is unique, there is no formula for what roles are best. Each family must be evaluated on how its unique configuration of roles functions to the family's advantage or disadvantage.

Holman stresses that "the worker must examine how roles are performed and whether or not they meet the needs of the family"[19] and proposes a series of questions to explore:

What specific roles does each family member occupy?
Do the various roles played work well together for the family's benefit?
Are any of the roles ambiguous, redundant, or left empty?
Is there flexibility among family roles so that the family is better able to adjust to crisis situations?
Do the family's roles conform with basic social norms? (For example, society does not condone a criminal role.)
Do the family's roles function to enhance the family's feelings of self-worth and well-being or detract from these feelings?

Exercise 9.7: Functional Roles and Problematic Roles of My Family Members

GOAL: This exercise is designed to assist you in identifying the functional roles and problematic roles that members of your family play.

1. **Reread the preceding section. Specify the functional roles that members of your family play.**

2. **Specify problematic roles that some members of your family may play.**

■ PERSONAL AND GROUP GOALS

It's important for any group to establish goals in order to give itself direction and motivate members (see Chapter 4). The same rationale applies to families. Minuchin emphasizes the importance of a family therapist assessing a family and, on the basis of this assessment, establishing therapeutic goals. He continues that the primary thrust is helping the entire family function better. He states, "Although individuals must not be ignored, the therapist's focus is on enhancing the operation of the family system."[20]

Janzen and Harris also emphasize the importance of working toward a problem consensus in family treatment; a problem consensus involves the family member and the therapist arriving at a general agreement about what problems are to be dealt with in therapy. Janzen and Harris stress that social workers should make strong efforts to elicit information from all family members during the initial assessment.[21] Family members may see the problem differently, and each individual may have a different personal goal in mind. If these individual views are not clearly understood and incorporated into the family goals, some members may be excluded from treatment. The more congruence there is between the personal goals of family members and the goals of the family group, the more attracted to the therapy the members are likely to be. In order to be motivated to participate in treatment, each member needs to feel that family goals are personally relevant.

For example, a couple came to a university diagnostic training center to have their four-year-old son Jimmy, who has a developmental disability, evaluated for future education and therapy. The diagnostic center evaluated the whole family on the basis of physical, emotional, and psychological needs. Therefore, as part of the overall assessment, other family members and their relationships were also examined.

The mother was a slender, pretty, extremely quiet woman of 28. She seemed to be cooperative and eager to do whatever she could to help her son deal with his disability. The father, a tall, handsome, personable man of 30, also expressed strong desires to cooperate. As he was very outgoing and she very quiet, he did virtually all of the talking. The social worker began to talk about the parents' relationship as part of the overall assessment and treatment planning process. Much of Jimmy's extensive physical and psychological assessment had already been completed. Jimmy's father dismissed all talk about the marital relationship as an unimportant procedural matter.

The father, in essence, was saying that he appreciated all the efforts of the center's staff and that everything else was fine. As usual, he was doing all of the talking. The social worker made a point of asking Jimmy's mother to describe her feelings about their relationship, but her husband began to answer for her. The social worker gently broke in and asked if she could please answer the question herself. The woman hesitated and looked down at the floor. Then she blurted out, "I can't stand it anymore, I want a divorce!" Her husband's jaw dropped, and the social worker looked stunned. Neither had had any inkling of her strong feelings before this.

Upon further exploration, several problems in the couple's relationship were uncovered. Jimmy's mother felt suffocated by what she considered to be her husband's overbearing, dogmatic attitude. Through their eight years of married life, she felt she could never voice her opinion or function as an individual. She was also sick of having sole responsibility for the housework. For years she had secret ambitions of becoming a legal librarian. However, because of her own quiet personality and her insecurity, she never felt confident enough to express her feelings.

Her husband, on the other hand, felt that she needed protection and direction. Many times he had become tired of the burden of assuming responsibility for making all of the family decisions. He had often wished his wife would be more assertive, but he didn't feel it was in her nature to do so. In one way, he felt relieved when she finally expressed her true feelings.

Further discussion revealed that they both were relieved to get their feelings out in the open and hear what each other really felt. Treatment sessions helped to establish new patterns of communication and behavior. With feedback, the husband became aware of how it had become a habit to answer questions for his wife. His wife also became aware that she needed to be more assertive and not rely on her husband to answer for her. They began to establish a more equal relationship and discussed how to divide household chores and child-care tasks more evenly. When his wife began training to become a legal librarian, the husband gave her his genuine support. Not only was he proud of her for developing her individuality, but he also appreciated the extra income she would be bringing into the household.

This experience exemplifies how important it is to make sure each family member has personal input into the goal-setting process. Otherwise, family group goals might miss the point entirely. If Jimmy's mother had not been asked her opinion and actively encouraged to express it, the real family problem might have remained hidden. Appropriate goals might not have been set concerning communication and behavior patterns. In view of the strong feelings expressed, it seemed very likely that the family would not have functioned effectively, and Jimmy's treatment plan would have suffered.

Hidden Agendas

This example also can be used to illustrate a concept related to goal-setting called the hidden agenda. A hidden agenda is a personal goal held by a group member that is unknown to the other group members and that interferes with the accomplishment of group goals. Such unknown personal goals can be destructive both to the group and to the group process. In the previous example, the wife had a hidden agenda that included her secret wishes to be more independent and to pursue a career. For the family to function effectively, this hidden agenda had to be brought to the surface and resolved.

Exercise 9.8:　Personal Goals, Group Goals, and Hidden Agendas in My Family

GOAL: This exercise is designed to assist you in recognizing the importance of personal goals, group goals, and hidden agendas.

1. Briefly summarize the personal goals of each member of your family.

2. Specify the group goals of your family.

3. Do some members of your family have hidden agendas? If "yes," specify the ones you are aware of.

■ FAMILY CONFLICTS, PROBLEMS, AND RESOLUTIONS

Chapter 6 defines conflict as "an antagonistic state or action involving divergent ideas or interests." It indicates that conflicts are inevitable in any group and that many times they are positive and desirable. Groups, including families, are made up of unique individuals, each with individual opinions and ideals. Conflict can represent the open sharing of these ideas and can serve as a mechanism for improving communication, enhancing the closeness of relationships, and working out dissatisfactions.

Thorman points out that although each family is unique, conflicts and problems within families tend to be clustered in four major categories.[22] First, there are marital problems between the husband and wife. Second, there are difficulties existing between parents and children. Third are the personal problems of individual family members. Finally, there are stresses imposed on the family by the external environment.

Family problems do not necessarily fall neatly into any one of these categories. Frequently, families experience more than one category of problems. Nor are these problem categories mutually exclusive. Many times one problem will be closely related to another. Consider, for instance, the wife and mother who is a department store manager and the primary breadwinner for her family. The store at which she has been working for the past 11 years suddenly goes bankrupt and out of business. Despite massive efforts, she is unable to find another job with similar responsibilities and salary. This can be considered a family problem caused by stresses in the environment. However, this is also a personal problem for the wife and mother. Her sense of self-worth is seriously diminished by her job loss and inability to find another position. As a result, she becomes cranky, short-tempered, and difficult to live with. The environmental stress she is experiencing causes her to have difficulties relating to both children and spouse. The entire family system becomes disturbed.

The following section will examine each of the four problem categories and offer some treatment directions.

Marital Difficulties

Communication difficulties surface as one of the major causes of conflict in marital relationships.[23] Other major sources of conflict include disagreements over children, sexual problems, conflicts over recreational time and money, and unfaithfulness. This study provides some clues concerning the areas practitioners need to address when assessing a marital couple's relationship within the family.

For instance, Bill and Linda, both in their mid-thirties, had a communication problem. They had been married one year. The marriage occurred after a lengthy dating period filled with strife. A primary source of stress was Linda's desire for a permanent commitment of marriage and Bill's unwillingness to make such a commitment. In view of Linda's threats to leave him, Bill finally decided to get married.

Before the marriage another source of difficulty was the amount of time that Bill and Linda spent together. They each owned a condominium and lived separately. Bill was involved in a physical fitness program, working out at a health club four nights a week, including Fridays. Bill also had numerous close friends at the club with whom he enjoyed spending his time. Linda was infuriated that Bill restricted the time he spent with her to some of the days when he didn't work out at the club. Her major concern, however, remained Bill's inability to make a commitment. Linda felt that things would change once they got married.

After marriage, things did not change very much. Although Linda and Bill now lived together, he still worked out at the club with his friends four nights a week, and Linda was still infuriated. In a discussion the two expressed their feelings. Linda said, "I hate all the time Bill spends at the club. I resent having him designate the time he thinks he can spend with me. I feel like he's putting my time into little boxes."

Bill responded, "My physical health is very important to me. I love to work out at the club. What should I do—stay home every night and become a couch potato watching television?"

One way of assessing this couple's communication is evaluating the intent (what the speaker wants to communicate to the receiver) and the actual impact of the communication (what the listener actually hears).[24] Many times the intent and impact of communication are different. One therapeutic goal is to improve the accuracy of communication, that is, the extent to which the intent of the speaker and the impact upon the listener resemble each other.

Although other difficulties existed in the relationship that are too lengthy to describe here, we will address some of the issues involved in this simple communication. After further meetings and discussion, the following scenario developed. Linda verbally stated that she is intensely unhappy that Bill goes to the health club. The impact on Bill is that he feels Linda is trying to tell him what to do. He loves Linda but is wary of losing his independence and what he sees as his identity. When Linda places demands on him, he becomes even more protective of his time.

Linda's intent in her communication is very different from her impact; she feels Bill thinks the club and his friends are more important than she is. This is related to her basic lack of self-esteem and self-confidence.

Bill's response to Linda's statement also has serious discrepancies between its intent and impact. Bill states that he loves to work out. The impact on Linda (that is, what she is hearing Bill say) is that he likes the club and his friends more than he likes her. Bill's actual intent is to tell Linda his physical health and appearance are important to him. He also wants to communicate that his sense of independence is also important to him. He loves her and wants to be committed to her. Yet, his long-term fear of commitment is related to his actual fear that he will lose his identity in someone else's. He's afraid of losing his right to make choices and decisions. He fears being told what to do.

One treatment goal here is to enhance the congruence of each person's intent and impact. A practitioner can help each spouse communicate more effectively by giving suggestions about how to rephrase statements in words to reflect more clearly what the speaker really means. Another suggestion is to encourage feedback, that is, having the listener tell the speaker what impact a message had.[25] For instance, instead of responding to Linda's demands defensively, Bill might be encouraged to tell her, "I love you very much, Linda. I need to keep in shape, and I need some time to myself. How can we work this out?"

Eventually, Bill and Linda used a problem-solving approach (see Chapter 6) to resolve this issue. Through counseling, the accuracy of their communication gradually improved. Each learned how to communicate personal needs. Instead of their old stand-off, they began to identify and evaluate alternatives. Their final solution involved several facets. First, Bill would continue to go to the club to work out three nights a week. Fridays, however, would be spent with Linda; it became clear that she was particularly annoyed at not being able to go out with Bill on Friday nights. Linda, who also was an avid believer in physical fitness, would occasionally go with Bill to the health club to work out. This gave her a sense of freedom to join him when she chose to. The important thing was that she no longer felt restricted. In reality, she rarely went with him to the club. Linda also chose to take some post-graduate courses in her field on those evenings when Bill visited the club. She enjoyed such activities, and they enhanced her sense of professional competence. The personal issues of Bill's need to feel free and Linda's lack of self-esteem demanded ongoing efforts by both spouses. Enhanced communication skills helped them communicate their ongoing needs.

Parent/Child Relationship Difficulties

The second major type of family problem involves relationships between parents and children, including parents' difficulties in controlling their children and, especially as children reach adolescence, communication problems. There are many perspectives on child management and parent/child communication techniques. Two major approaches are application of learning theory and Parent Effectiveness Training (PET) developed by Gordon.[26]

Practitioners can help parents improve their control of children by assessing the individual family situations and teaching parents some basic behavior modification techniques.[27] Behavior modification involves the application of learning theory principles to real-life situations. For instance, it's easy for parents to get into a punishment rut with a misbehaving child. For example, four-year-old Freddie spills the contents of drawers and cabinets in the kitchen area whenever he is unobserved. His parents have seen enough flour, honey, silverware, and plastic bags in heaps on the floor to last them several lifetimes. In their frustration, they typically respond by swatting Freddie on the rump. He cries a little bit. But the next time he has the opportunity to be in the kitchen alone, he repeats the unwanted behavior.

In family counseling Freddie's parents were taught several new behavior management techniques (that is, behavior modification techniques applied to specific child management situations). First, they were taught the value of positive reinforcement. These are "positive events or consequences that follow a behavior and act to strengthen that behavior."[28] Instead of relying solely on punishment, the parents were taught to react more positively to Freddie during those times when he was playing appropriately and not emptying drawers. By closely examining Freddie's behaviors and the circumstances surrounding them, the parents gradually learned to view Freddie in a different way. They learned that he felt he was not getting enough attention in general. To get the attention he needed, he resorted to the destructive drawer-emptying behavior. Providing Freddie with structured positive play times when they gave Freddie their sole attention and commenting positively about his good behavior helped to diminish Freddie's need for getting attention in inappropriate ways. Freddie's parents learned that their punishment was having an effect opposite of what they intended. That is, instead of stopping his bad behavior, the punishment encouraged it. Punishing Freddie was actually positive reinforcement because it provided the attention he wanted.

As an alternative, Freddie's parents were taught the time-out technique. Time out involves a procedure in which "previous reinforcement is withdrawn with the intended result being a decrease in the frequency of a particular behavior."[29] Instead of swatting Freddie when he emptied drawers, his parents placed him in a corner with his eyes to the wall for five minutes. (Five minutes should be the maximum duration of a time out because effectiveness diminishes after this period.) They administered the time out immediately after Freddie misbehaved so that he related it to his misbehavior. Time outs provided Freddie's parents with a way to deprive their son of attention without hurting him. Since attention was what Freddie really wanted, this behavior control technique worked well. It should be emphasized, however, that Freddie needed continued attention and positive reinforcement for appropriate behavior. Had he not been seeking needed attention he would not have misbehaved in the first place.

Parent Effectiveness Training is a second method frequently used when parent/child relationship problems occur. Two principles involved in this approach include active listening and the sending of I-messages.[30] Active listening resembles the intent-impact communication approach described earlier and involves two basic steps. First, the receiver of the message tries earnestly to understand what the sender really means. In the second step, the receiver puts this understanding into her own words and returns this understanding for the sender's verification.[31] For instance, 13-year-old Tyrone says to his mother, "Dances are boring. I'm not going to that boring old dance on Friday." His mother has learned to use active listening and tries to see the situation from Tyrone's perspective. She replies, "You mean you'd really like to go but you don't think you can dance very well." Tyrone responds, "Yep." His mother has accurately heard his real concerns.

A second technique used in Parent Effectiveness Training is the use of I-messages, nonblaming messages that communicate only how the sender of the message believes the receiver is adversely affecting the sender. I-messages do not provide a solution, nor are they put-down messages. It is possible to send an I-message without using the word "I," as the essence of I-messages involves sending a nonblaming message of how the parent feels the child's behavior is affecting the parent.[32]

For example, Mr. and Mrs. Boushon have just finished shampooing the carpet in the family room. Their nine-year-old son comes into the house with considerable mud on his tennis shoes and is about to walk into the family room. Mrs. Boushon could choose to say "If you walk into the family room with those muddy shoes, I'll ground you for a week. I'm so tired of having to clean up your messes." This is a blaming, threatening statement. Instead, she chooses to say, "We just finished shampooing the carpet and want to keep it clean from now on." Her son sits down and takes off his tennis shoes. In this illustration, the mother takes responsibility for her own feelings without placing blame on her son.

Personal Problems of Individual Family Members

Sometimes a family will come to a practitioner for help and identify one family member as being "the problem." However, a basic principle of family therapy is that the entire family "owns" the problem.[33] Sometimes one family member becomes the scapegoat for a malfunction of the entire family system. A scapegoat is a person others blame for some problem, regardless of whether she or he is really at fault. The practitioner is responsible for helping the family define the problem as a group rather than blame an individual. Treatment goals will most likely involve restructuring various family relationships.

For example, a family of five came in for treatment. The family consisted of a 48-year-old husband and father, a 45-year-old wife and mother, and three children: Bob, age 19, Ralph, 16, and Rosie, 12. The family lived in a rural Wisconsin town of 8,000 people. The father was a successful businessman involved in local politics. The mother was a homemaker who did not work outside the home. Bob was a freshman at the University of Wisconsin–Madison. The identified client was Ralph. For the past year, Ralph had been stealing neighbors' cars and running down mailboxes. To say the least, this behavior annoyed the townspeople. The family came to counseling as a last resort.

After several sessions in which family members pointed blaming fingers at Ralph, Rosie quietly commented to her parents, "Well, you never say anything about *his* problem" and proceeded to point at Bob. Suddenly, as if a floodgate had been opened, the entire family situation came pouring out. Rosie was referring to her parents' difficulties in accepting Bob's recent announcement that he was gay. Bob was going through a difficult period as he was "coming out"—making lifestyle decisions and relating to old friends and family members. His father was terrified that the local townspeople, who were severely homophobic, would find out. He feared he would lose his social status and, that his political career would be damaged. The mother turned out to be an alcoholic, a secret the family kept well guarded. The parents had not had a sexual relationship for 10 years and slept in separate bedrooms. The father was a harsh, stern man who felt it necessary to maintain what he considered absolute control over family members, including his wife. Highly critical of his family, he never risked sharing his own feelings. Finally, Rosie was having serious problems with both her grades and her attendance in school. She was also sexually active with a variety of young men. Both she and her parents lived in constant fear that she would become pregnant.

As it turned out, Ralph was one of the better adjusted individuals in the family. He attended school regularly, had a B average, and was active in sports before being suspended for his delinquent behavior. This family provides a good illustration of a family-owned problem. The entire family system was showing disturbances. Ralph was the scapegoat, the identified client, largely because his behavior was more public. All Ralph was doing was calling attention to the family's deeper problems.

External Environmental Stresses

The fourth category of problems frequently found in families is problems caused by factors outside the family. These problems can include inadequate income, unemployment, poor housing, inadequate access to means of transportation and places for recreation, and lack of job opportunities.[34] Included in the multitude of other potential problems are poor health, inadequate schools, and dangerous neighborhoods.

To begin addressing these problems, practitioners need effective brokering skills. They need to know what services are available and how to make a connection between families in need and these services.

Many times appropriate services are unavailable or nonexistent. Practitioners need to advocate, support, or even help to develop appropriate resources for their clients.[35] Services that do not exist, for example, will need development. Unresponsive agency administrations will need to be confronted. Legal assistance may be required. There are no easy solutions to solving such nationwide problems as poverty or poor health care. This is a constant, ongoing process, and political involvement may be necessary. Such environmental stresses pose serious problems for families, and practitioners cannot ignore them.

Exercise 9.9: Challenges Faced by My Family

GOAL: This exercise is designed to assist you in identifying challenges your family is currently facing and to begin problem solving these challenges.

1. **Specify the challenges/difficulties that one or more members of your family are currently facing. (You have the right to not reveal challenges you do not wish to reveal.)**

2. **For each of these challenges, what actions are being taken to confront these challenges?**

3. **If one or more challenges are currently not being effectively confronted, specify other options for each that might be tried. (Feel free to consult with others about identifying other options.)**

■ THREE APPROACHES TO FAMILY THERAPY

There are many approaches to family therapy. Three prominent examples are those focusing on family communication, family structure, and family function.

All examples presented here are similar in that all concentrate on various aspects of the ongoing interaction and relationships in families. Likewise, they all involve focusing on how family members communicate. However, the approaches differ in their emphases, core concepts, and perspectives on how practitioners can help families effect positive change.

A Communication Pattern Approach

Virginia Satir is a communications theorist. She stresses the clarification of family communication patterns that, in troubled families, tend to be vague and indirect. The husband and wife tend to avoid talking with one another about their needs and desires, or they talk via their children, which unfortunately places the children in the position of holding the family together. A competitive atmosphere is often created as each parent attempts to form an alliance with each child.[36]

Why does faulty communication develop in families? Satir believes one reason is that both the husband and the wife have a low self-worth. Since they try to hide their feelings of inferiority by acting confident and strong, neither reveals what he or she really wants or talks about feelings of worthlessness for fear of driving the other away. Another reason is that people who have low self-esteem marry in order to have another meet their needs. They marry "to get," expecting their spouses to read their minds and to then meet their needs. A spouse is viewed as having an *obligation* to meet their needs, and these individuals are frustrated, angry, and irritated when the spouses fail. Partners in a troubled relationship also tend to view each other as a possession rather than as a distinct, unique person. Instead of furthering each other's growth, the spouses restrict and stifle each other. In these troubled relationships, faulty communication patterns gradually evolve. Three types of communications problems can arise: use of vague, indirect statements; incongruent messages; and double binds.

In a strained relationship, the husband and wife are generally afraid to risk a clear statement, such as "I would like to get a dog." Because they don't want to drive the other person away, they express their wants and needs vaguely. Observe the following interaction:

Husband: Uncle Harry just got a cocker spaniel and really likes it.
Wife: Dogs are too much trouble to take care of.

The interaction ends. The husband is left with angry feelings because he feels he won't be able to get a dog. The wife senses from his nonverbal messages that her husband is upset and angry but does not understand why. She's afraid to deal with the conflict and therefore does not ask, "why?"

With an incongruent message, the nonverbal communication contradicts the verbal. For example, a person may state he is not angry (for a variety of reasons) when his nonverbal communication—clenched fists, stern look, white knuckles, reddened cheeks—suggests otherwise. (Some authorities define an incongruent message to be one type of double-bind message.)

With double-bind messages, the sender gives contradictory messages. For example, a father may firmly maintain that "All real children should keep their toys picked up" yet tell his son that "All real boys are messy." In this situation, the son is unable to figure out whether he can please his father by picking up toys or by not picking them up. Or a wife may ask her husband for help in disciplining the children. When he does, she criticizes him for disciplining the children for something that is inconsequential. The victim in a double bind may respond in a variety of ways: withdrawing, not listening at all, aggressively fighting back, or developing emotional difficulties.

Satir's goals in family therapy are to improve communication patterns, to increase the self-worth and self-esteem of each member, and to end possessiveness. By improving communication patterns, each member can learn to express needs and desires. Toward this end, Satir seeks to help members learn to send direct and congruent messages. She instructs family members in using: I-messages rather than you-messages (see Chapter 5); the role reversal technique (see Chapter 6); the problem-solving approach rather than the win-lose approach (see Chapter 6); and active listening (see Chapter 5). She helps members identify which family rules are constructive and which are destructive. While rules may be bad, the people setting them are not. Destructive family rules are discarded, and new ones are negotiated. Vague messages, incongruent messages, and double binds are identified, and family members often role play using more effective communication patterns.

Satir's family therapy approach is also noted for its positive atmosphere. By modeling respect toward others, she fosters the growth of each member and increases each member's self-worth and self-esteem. Communication that is disrespectful is pointed out, and family members are encouraged to learn how to be more respectful. To help members improve their low self-esteem, she uses a variety of approaches, such as challenging negative statements about self. Satir's approach involves ending feelings of possessiveness and helping family members see each other as unique, distinct people with individual needs, desires, and self-worth.

A Family Subsystem Approach

Structural family therapy as espoused by Minuchin uses a systems approach to family therapy. The primary emphasis is on restructuring the major family subsystems so that each subsystem interacts appropriately and accomplishes its major duties.[37]

Minuchin notes that every family has multiple interacting subsystems. In families with children, there are three major types of subsystems: spouse, parent, and sibling. Thus, a family subsystem might include two spouses or all of the siblings within a family. Likewise, a family subsystem might involve the oldest daughter and youngest son in a family of 12 because of their special, caring relationship with each other. Subsystems usually are formed on the basis of common roles or special relationships among family members.

A spouse subsystem is healthy and functional if both the husband's and wife's needs for companionship, emotional and sexual fulfillment, and financial support are being met. An example of a dysfunctional spouse subsystem is one in which the wife wants to seek employment to fulfill herself and help the family out financially, while the husband wants her to stay home to care for the children and do the domestic tasks.

A healthy parent subsystem involves parents who meet the emotional and physical needs of their children without placing undue stress upon themselves. A dysfunctional system results in disputes and stress among family members. For example, parents may have conflicting philosophies about how to raise and discipline children that result in family fighting and dysfunction.

A healthy sibling subsystem exists when siblings get along fairly well and learn and interact with each other. An example of a dysfunctional sibling subsystem is one in which siblings bicker constantly, preventing each other from completing required tasks such as assigned homework or housework.

Each family subsystem has major functions that must be fulfilled if the family is to survive as a healthy unit. In therapy, Minuchin analyzes the functions and dysfunctions of each subsystem to determine where interaction is healthy and where it is not. His main goal is to enhance the effective interaction of the spouse, parent, and sibling subsystems. Healthy functioning in each of these subsystems is not precisely defined, since a type of interaction that works well in one family system may work terribly in another. For example, spending money on a lavish vacation to Hawaii may be very beneficial for a family that can easily afford it but very unhealthy for a family deeply in debt.

According to structural family therapy, typical dysfunctions found in families include disengagement and enmeshment.[38] These reflect the extreme opposites of how family boundaries might be formed. Disengagement concerns relationships among family members that are exceedingly distant. Communication is usually strained, aloof, and ineffective. In some disengaged families, members communicate rarely, if at all. Emotional interaction is virtually nonexistent. For example, a family's teenage son might become so involved in a street gang that he disengages from his family of origin. To him the gang becomes a replacement for his original family. Another example involves an intact two-parent family whose husband and father, assuming the traditional role of primary breadwinner, is hardly ever home. He involves himself so intensively in his work that he disengages almost totally from interaction with other family members.

Enmeshment is the opposite of disengagement. Enmeshment involves relationships among family members that are too close and probably stifling. Enmeshed boundaries within a family system become blurred and poorly defined. For example, a healthy spousal subsystem may be disrupted if one parent bonds too closely with a newborn child and neglects the needs of the other spouse. The identified parent's relationship with the newborn might become enmeshed at the same time that the spousal subsystem becomes disengaged. Another example involves a father and 13-year-old daughter who become enmeshed in an incestuous relationship. The boundaries between parent and child become blurred and ineffective. They require clarification for effective family functioning.

A technique Minuchin employs in family therapy involves drawing a number of structural diagrams. In this way he can illustrate the functional and dysfunctional aspects of these subsystems and help members clarify boundaries with these subsystems. If an older daughter is sharing responsibility for caring for younger children when both parents are working, for example, Minuchin wants the family members to clarify when the older daughter is to have parental responsibilities and when she is to interact as an older sibling.

Minuchin encourages the use of many of the same communication techniques as Satir, such as I-messages, role reversal, and the problem-solving approach. At times, Minuchin may bypass direct cognitive understanding by a family of its dysfunctions in order to restructure the family subsystems. He may, for example, use a paradoxical suggestion in cases where direct exploration of family communication patterns and behavior has failed to change the dysfunctional aspects. For example, in a family where a husband wants his wife to stay at home while the wife wants to seek employment, Minuchin may use a paradoxical suggestion like, "Yup, it's best, Mary, if you stay at home and be submissive to your husband. It's your job in life to keep your husband happy. You should not attempt to grow as a person. Your primary interests and satisfactions in life should be in cleaning toilets and washing your husband's dirty shorts. So, who cares if the bills don't get paid and you wind up being a brainless servant?" Such a suggestion is designed to push the wife into asserting her interest in having an equal relationship and to help the husband understand the consequences of controlling his wife's life.

A Functional Approach

Alexander and Parsons describe functional family therapy as focusing on how individual family members function within the family context.[39] The idea is to examine carefully how family members interact with respect to each other. It is not as important how any individual behaves as how other family members' reactions to that behavior affect the overall family functioning. Interaction among family members then is considered neither good nor bad but rather effective or ineffective within the family context. For example, consider a family consisting of a mother, father, and two teenage daughters. The father in such a family cannot be "overbearing" and "pushy" unless other family members resent his actions and interpret his behavior in this manner. His actions can be considered assertive or aggressive depending on how other family members perceive them.

According to Alexander and Parsons, there are three primary classifications of interpersonal functions: merging, which reflects close contact; separating, which reflects independence and distance; and midpointing, which lies somewhere between the first two. Alexander and Parsons explain:

> Behaviors and interpersonal styles that produce contact/closeness in a relationship tend to increase psychological intensity, enhance the opportunities for interaction, and maintain or strengthen contacts that would otherwise decrease. Typically (but not always) non-problematic behaviors that function to increase contact/closeness include asking for or giving friendly help, crying, remaining close physically, and verbally and physically expressing tenderness ("I love you").[40]

Functional family therapists would assume *merging* was neither good nor bad until they assessed the effects of any particular merging situation on a family's internal functioning. For example, consider a six-year-old daughter who was determined to remain by her mother's side constantly whenever both of them were home. This behavior would be considered functional if it satisfied the needs of both, and if both could continue to function well independently when not with each other. However, the same behavior by the daughter would be considered dysfunctional if neither mother nor daughter could tolerate being without each other for more than a moment at a time.

The second major category of interpersonal functions, called *separating*, includes those behaviors and interactions that emphasize interpersonal distance and independence from each other. For example, consider parents, each working two full-time jobs in order "to get ahead," who must leave their three small children in daycare and with babysitters. They are essentially separating from their children. A functional family therapist would make no assumptions as to whether this situation was good or bad. Rather, such a therapist would evaluate the effects of this separating behavior on family interaction. In the event that day care and babysitting are both excellent and consistent for the children and the parents are satisfied with their situation, the parents' behavior is considered functional. However, if the children begin acting out from insecurity and a need for parental attention, the parents' identical behavior would be dysfunctional within that particular family context.

The third classification of interpersonal family functions is *midpointing*. This type of interaction involves neither merging nor separating. Rather, there are some aspects of both concepts involved in the family's functioning. An example of a functional family employing midpointing is a family made up of a single mother and two sons, ages 13 and 16. Each member of this particular triad feels comfortable in coming to each other and relying on each other when help, care, or attention is needed. Yet, each member can also back away and rely on his or her respective wits when other family members are not available. This family is functional if its mode of interaction works for all the family members involved. If, on the other hand, the 13-year-old son required more merging with his mother and brother than he was getting, the same family would be considered dysfunctional.

As with the communication pattern approach developed by Satir and the structural approach established by Minuchin, functional family therapy as portrayed by Alexander and Parsons considers communication an important aspect of family functioning and a common target of change. A typical approach used by a functional family therapist is to identify alternative means of communication that would improve the family functioning beyond what it had achieved in the past.

After assessing the effectiveness of family functioning among family members, a functional family therapist would most likely provide intricate feedback to family members about their interaction. Feedback would focus on family members' thoughts, feelings, and behaviors. The old ways of family functioning would be questioned and evaluated. In some ways, such challenging can thrust the family into confusion. However, this confusion sets the stage for improvement. A functional family therapist subsequently helps the family initiate and develop new means of interaction to improve family functioning.

Alexander and Parsons describe two techniques that are frequently used in functional family therapy. They include "nonblaming" and "relabeling."[41] Nonblaming involves helping family members reconceptualize the problem. Instead of blaming specific family members for what's wrong, the members reconceptualize the problem as one belonging to the entire family. Finger-pointing is discouraged while, at the same time, assuming responsibility for improving the family's interaction is encouraged.

Relabeling concerns helping family members view the same behavior, issue, or problem from a different perspective or understand it in a new way. It is also referred to as reframing (see Appendix 1: Module 2). Within the family treatment context, this usually means helping one family member change negative thinking about another family member to new positive thinking. Relabeling or reframing often helps one person empathize with another or understand more clearly the other person's perspective. For instance, consider a husband who regularly criticizes his wife for her obesity. The wife views her husband's verbal behavior as critical and ineffective in helping her lose weight. A functional family therapist might relabel the husband's behavior as his means of showing his concern for his wife's health. She has extremely high blood pressure, and he is desperately worried that she may have a stroke.

The following are some examples of a client's statement followed by a therapist's relabeling or reframing of the client's thought:

Client A's Statement: Johnny hates me. All he does is scream at me. I don't even want to go near him anymore.

Therapist's Reframing: You sound upset and hurt at how Johnny yells at you so much. Maybe he's upset and hurt, too. Maybe he feels you're avoiding him. If he didn't care about you, he wouldn't expend so much energy yelling at you and trying to get your attention.

Client B's Statement: My dad says I'm much too close to my grandmother. He says it's a sick relationship, that all she does is manipulate me.

Therapist's Reframing: It's interesting that he's so concerned about that relationship. Maybe he's jealous that you two are so close. Maybe he'd like to feel closer to you, too. After all, you visit your grandmother whenever you have the chance. Yet you never visit him. Also, you know how he resents his own mother and how she tried to manipulate him when he was small.

Client B's Statement: All my parents do is try to control me. They're like two little dictators. They ask me who I'm going out with everytime I'm getting ready to go out. They tell me I'm supposed to have a 10:00 P.M. curfew. If I'm two seconds late, they're waiting for me at the door to ask me where I've been. They're driving me crazy.

Therapist's Reframing: You sound like you're feeling suffocated by your parents. It sounds to me like they're very concerned about you. If they didn't really care what happened to you, they wouldn't care what you did. Maybe they don't see their behavior as controlling. Maybe they see it as being good parents and trying to keep you out of trouble.

At least one other aspect of functional family therapy merits mention here, namely, the importance of education. Alexander and Parsons explain:

Education in functional family therapy is the process of providing a context for people to learn specific skills that they can use to maintain positive change. Therapy doesn't help people learn new skills; it merely helps people become receptive to learning them.[42]

Thus, specific skill training is considered extremely important. This includes more effective communication skills such as the use of "I" language and active listening. A functional family therapist might also incorporate any of a wide range of specific techniques for improving family functioning. Since such improvement in functioning is the ultimate goal of family treatment, any activities that actively move the family toward that goal might be employed. For example, a functional family therapist might teach parents how to use behavior modification techniques such as a token economy or time-out strategies in order to manage their children's behavior more effectively. Likewise, specific homework may be assigned to various family members. For instance, a functional family therapist might instruct family members to involve themselves in a range of conflict management exercises or even undertake a family outing together before the next therapy session.

Exercise 9.10: Applying Family Therapy Concepts to My Family

GOAL: This exercise is designed to assist you in understanding how the three family therapy approaches may be applied to families facing challenges.

Reread the preceding section on family therapy approaches. Do any of these three approaches have merit in confronting the challenges/difficulties that your family is currently facing? If "yes," summarize what you believe may be useful.

■ GROUP EXERCISES

Exercise A: The Sitzke Family

GOAL: To examine some basic group concepts operating within families and apply these concepts to a simulated family treatment situation.

Step 1. The leader presents the introductory material describing family group treatment to the class and describes the concepts of verbal communication, hidden agendas, nonverbal communication, group norms, personal and group goal-setting, and congruent and double messages.

Step 2. The Sitzke family is introduced as follows:
> This family treatment session involves a family of four including a mother, father, and two daughters. The family has been referred to the local family treatment clinic because of one of the daughters' behavioral problems. Her school was the referral agent. To avoid wasting time gathering the following initial information, this meeting will be considered the second meeting between the two social workers and the family. This agency uses cocounseling (that is, two therapists) when working with families. The meeting's primary purpose will be to assess the family's problems.

Step 3. On four separate notecards, type the following descriptions of the four members of the hypothetical Sitzke family. The "description" and "hidden agenda" sections should be clearly separated. Read only the "description" section of each card aloud to the class.

SHARON SITZKE

Description: Sharon, the 16-year-old daughter, is considered the family troublemaker. She smokes, drinks, occasionally uses drugs, is frequently truant, and associates with a peer group having a similar reputation.

Hidden agenda: Sharon is actually a very bright, sensitive, caring person who has a very poor self-concept. She genuinely wants to be loved and accepted by her parents but feels she doesn't know how. She is terribly worried about her parents' fighting and their threats of divorce. Although she loves her sister, Delores, she is terribly jealous of her. To make everything worse, she's afraid that she's pregnant.

GEORGE SITZKE

Description: George, a 40-year-old husband and father, is a quiet, relatively shy person who considers himself fairly intelligent. He owns and runs a small cheese factory that consumes a lot of his time. He is very worried about Sharon because all she seems to do is to get into trouble. He's indicated that he's eager to do anything he can to help.

Hidden agenda: George is simply very confused about what's happening because it seems his whole personal life is falling apart. It's very difficult for him to express his feelings and emotions. All Sharon seems to do is get into trouble. His wife Martha is so irritable lately that it seems all they do is fight. He's so upset that he can't even remember what they fight about. It seems all he can do is withdraw and bury himself in work and in television sports. He loves his family and really just wants things to go back to normal.

MARTHA SITZKE

Description: Martha, the 38-year-old wife and mother of the family, is outgoing and energetic, and considers herself to be a nice person. She is terribly disgusted with Sharon, who seems to do everything she can to cause trouble. She is tired of the whole situation because she feels she has done everything she can to help Sharon.

Hidden agenda: There are many other things that are also bothering her. Her children are getting older and will be leaving home soon. Although she finished two years of college, she's never worked outside the home. She's afraid of the future. It seems she and George have been drifting apart over the years. All they do is fight lately. He's even mentioned divorce. She thinks she still loves him and wants to stay together, but she doesn't know what to do about it. He's always been the quiet type. However, lately it seems whenever they're together as a couple with other people, she has to do all the talking.

DELORES SITZKE

Description: Delores, the 12-year-old daughter, is a pleasant, outgoing, seemingly happy person who gets straight A's in school.

Hidden agenda: Delores is terribly worried about her family. She feels guilty and fearful that somehow the problems are all her fault. If it weren't for her, she feels her mother would be a happy, independent career woman. Delores is angry at her sister for causing so many problems.

Step 4. Students volunteer to play the role of each family member and take the appropriate notecard. They are to behave on the basis of all the information available on the card. They may share their hidden agendas with the rest of the class when they see fit, and they may make up any additional facts as needed.

Step 5. Two students volunteer to play the roles of co-social workers. Two students should be used in order to diffuse the responsibility of keeping the session going. When one is at a loss for words, the other may jump in and take over. The students should keep in mind that the social workers' goal during this session is to assess or define the family's problems. *The leader must remember that the social workers and the remainder of the class are unaware of the family members' hidden agendas.* The student social workers should follow these guidelines:

1. Encourage the family members to discuss the problem and talk to each other.
2. Observe their verbal and nonverbal communication patterns.
3. Ask family members to talk about the values and norms operating within the family.
4. Explore possible hidden agendas.
5. Make certain to ask each family member how he or she defines the problem. Also, ask each person what goals he or she would like the family to work toward.

Step 6. The simulation is performed with the remainder of the class observing and takes approximately 15 to 20 minutes.

Step 7. The leader arbitrarily halts the role play and involves the entire class in discussion, focusing on the following questions:

1. What were some of the communicative patterns evident within the family?
2. Was verbal communication congruent with nonverbal communication or were double messages being sent?
3. What family group norms seemed to be operating within the family?
4. How did each family member define the problem?
5. Were there differences in problem definition among family members?
6. What were the personal goals of each family member?
7. Was a group goal apparent?
8. Were any hidden agendas operating within this family? If so, what were they?

Step 8. Upon completion of this discussion, each "family member" reads his or her hidden agenda aloud. Briefly, the class discusses how obvious each person's hidden agenda was, and the leader stresses the importance of discovering agendas as part of the family treatment process.

Exercise B: You and Your Family

GOAL: To identify and relate some basic group concepts to dynamics occurring in your own family. The group concepts include verbal and nonverbal communication and family group norms.

Note: *Students should be urged* **not** *to divulge sensitive personal information.*

Step 1. Using the information presented in this chapter and in Chapters 7 and 8, the leader asks students to identify the verbal and nonverbal communication patterns operating within their own families and to write down their ideas. Writing down thoughts helps make students think more deeply about their own families and commit themselves to an opinion.

Step 2. The students divide into groups of four to six people to discuss the following questions among themselves:

1. What are the verbal and nonverbal communication patterns in your family?
2. What are the similarities among the group's families in their verbal and nonverbal communication patterns?
3. What are the differences among the families in their verbal and nonverbal communication patterns?

Step 3. One student from each group summarizes the group's conclusions for the entire class.

Step 4. The leader directs the group's attention to the concept of group norms, and each individual writes down a summary of the norms operating in his or her own family.

Step 5. Once again, the students share their feelings in the small groups and discuss the following questions:

1. What are the family norms in your family?
2. What are the similarities in norms among the group's families?
3. What are the differences in norms among the group's families?

Step 6. A volunteer summarizes what each group discovered and shares this information with the entire class.

Step 7. The leader summarizes how communication patterns and family norms differed among families by verbally recapping the information developed in specific groups.

Exercise C: Analyzing Your Family in Terms of Group Concepts

GOAL: To analyze your family in terms of the group concepts described in this text.
Note: It is expected students will gain a better understanding of how their family is structured and how it functions from this exercise.

Step 1. The leader explains the purpose of the exercise, indicates it is a visualization exercise, and states the following, pausing briefly after each question.

I want you to get in a comfortable position, and close your eyes. . . . Take a couple of deep breaths, and relax. . . . Keep your eyes closed during this exercise. . . . I want you to think of your family as I ask you a number of questions. . . . Who is the primary leader in your family? . . . Who makes most of the major decisions in your family? . . . Is the primary leader autocratic, democratic, or laissez faire? . . . Is leadership distributed among different family members in different areas as suggested by the distributed functions theory? . . . Who is generally the task specialist? . . . Who is generally the social-emotional specialist? . . . Who has the most power in your family? . . . For this power person, what is the basis of this power. Is it reward power, coercive power, legitimate power, expert power, or referent power? . . .

What are the rules or norms that exist in your family about: dating, drug and alcohol use, acceptable sexual behaviors, the way you dress, religious expectations, expectations about going to college? . . . Who set these rules or norms, and how were they set? . . . What is your role in your family? . . .

How are disputes usually settled in your family? . . . Is a win-lose approach used or is a problem-solving approach generally used? . . . Are major decisions made by consensus, by simple majority voting, or are they made autocratically? . . . Do members use active listening to further communications? . . . Is the role reversal technique used to foster communication and to settle disputes? . . . When your father is angry, how does he communicate his anger nonverbally? . . . When your mother is angry, how does she communicate her anger nonverbally? . . . Do members seek to express their irritations to others or do members seek to hide their irritations in order to attempt to avoid conflict? . . . Does your family have a cooperative atmosphere or a competitive atmosphere? . . . One person can destroy the morale in a family—has this occurred in your family? . . . Think about each family member—who is generally nonassertive, who is usually aggressive, and who is generally assertive?

What are the major sources of stress in your family at the present time? . . . What different stress management techniques are used in your family—such as meditation, positive thinking, exercising, taking vacations, rewarding yourself with personal goodies, taking mental health days, using support groups, talking problems out with others, seeking to change distressing events, seeking to challenge and change negative and irrational thinking? . . . Do certain members of your family tend to procrastinate? . . . For those who procrastinate, what do you think would help them stop procrastinating? . . . How well do members of your family manage time? . . .

Probably every person is grieving about something; what are the members of your family grieving about? . . . What are the usual ways of handling grief in your family? . . .

Are some members of your family presently chemically dependent? . . . If so, how are other members of your family reacting to the dependency—for example, are they enablers, are they trying to ignore the problem, are they fighting about it? . . . What can realistically be done to help to reduce problems in this area? . . .

Do the different members of your family have a fairly well thought-out sense of who they are? . . . Do the different members have generally a positive sense of self? . . . For those who have a low self-concept, what might realistically be done to improve their sense of self? . . .

What are the family values about religion, sexual behavior, chemical use, going to college, smoking, whom you associate with, racial integration, politics, majoring in social work?

Do members of your family generally communicate openly with each other? . . . Do some members send vague, indirect messages? . . . Do some members send incongruent messages? . . . Do some members send double-bind messages? . . . Are some members afraid to express their needs and desires? . . . How can communication be improved in your family? . . . What are the dysfunctional aspects of the parent subsystem in your family? . . . What are the dysfunctional aspects of the spouse subsystem in your family? . . . What are the dysfunctional aspects of the sibling subsystem in your family? . . . How might these dysfunctions be improved? . . . My questions have ended. Take a minute or two to relax, and then open your eyes.

Step 2. The students discuss whether such concepts are useful in helping them to analyze and better understand their families. Students are invited to share a family situation—such as seeking ideas on how to deal with parents who are autocratic, or how to handle the problems created by someone who is chemically dependent. The students discuss the merits of this exercise.

CHAPTER TEN

Organizations, Communities, and Groups

GOALS

This chapter provides an introduction to social work practice with organizations and communities. The close relationships between the terms *group* and *organization*, and between *group* and *community* are examined. Several models of organizations are presented. The chapter presents guidelines for helping professionals to survive and thrive in a bureaucracy. A framework for analyzing a community is presented, along with three models a social worker can use in seeking constructive community changes.

An organization is defined here as a collectivity of individuals gathered together to serve a particular purpose. The types of purposes (or goals) that people organize to achieve are infinite in number, ranging from obtaining basic necessities to eliminating the threat of worldwide terrorism or attaining world peace. In each case an organization exists because people working together can better accomplish tasks and achieve goals than one individual can.

Etzioni described the importance of organizations in our lives:

> We are born in organizations, educated by organizations, and most of us spend much of our lives working for organizations. We spend much of our leisure time paying, playing, and praying in organizations. Most of us will die in an organization, and when the time comes for burial, the largest organization of all—the state—must grant official permission.[1]

The importance of organizations for social work practice has been summarized by Netting, Kettner, and McMurtry:

> As social workers, our roles within, interactions with, and attempts to manipulate organizations define much of what we do. Clients often come to us seeking help because they are not able to obtain help from organizations that are critical to their survival or quality of life. In turn, the resources we attempt to gain for these clients usually come from still other organizations. . . . Social workers with little or no idea of how organizations operate, how they interact, or how they can be influenced and changed from both outside and inside are likely to be severely limited in their effectiveness.[2]

Many disciplines (including business, psychology, political science, and sociology) have produced a prodigious amount of theory and research on organizations. However, in spite of the importance of organizations to social work practice, the amount of social work literature devoted to organizations is limited.

THE RELATIONSHIP BETWEEN A GROUP AND AN ORGANIZATION

In Chapter 1 a group is defined as

> two or more individuals in face-to-face interaction, each aware of his or her membership in the group, each aware of the others who belong to the group, and each aware of their positive interdependence as they strive to achieve mutual goals.[3]

An organization, as previously stated, is a collectivity of individuals gathered together to serve a purpose. How do these two terms relate?

There is considerable overlap between these two terms. Some organizations can also be considered groups and vice versa. For example, a social work student club can be considered to be both an organization and a group. Another example of both a group and an organization is a parent–teacher association at an elementary school.

However, a large organization is generally not considered a group. For example, the General Motors Corporation is considered an organization but not a group. One reason it is not referred to as a group is that its employees and owners (including stockholders) are so large in number that no one has personal contact with all the other members of the organization. In a similar manner, most other large organizations (such as the National Rifle Association and the American Medical Association) are not considered groups. Such associations are "gathered together" for a specific purpose. However, the term *gathered together* does not mean that everyone has personal contact with everyone else as do the members of a group.

Most small, informal groups with no specific purpose are not considered organizations. For example, a group of neighborhood children who occasionally meet to play with one another is not considered an organization.

Exercise 10.1: Refuting Our Organizational Myths

GOAL: Many students erroneously believe they have had very little involvement in an organization. This exercise is designed to demonstrate that you have participated in many organizations.

1. **Make a list of the organizations you have participated in. These would include organizations such as the Boys and Girls Club, Girl Scouts, church groups, athletic organizations and teams, organizations you have volunteered for, organizations you have worked for, school organizations, student social work clubs, and daycare centers you attended.**

2. **Select one organization that you particularly enjoyed participating in. Describe the goals of this organization. Also describe what you learned from participating in this organization and also why you enjoyed participating in this organization.**

3. **Many students erroneously believe that organizational involvement is "distasteful." Now that you realize that you have already enjoyed participating in a variety of organizations, do you now look forward (more positively) to participating with organizations in the future?**

■ MODELS OF ORGANIZATIONS*

The Autocratic Model

The autocratic model has been in existence for thousands of years. During the Industrial Revolution, this model was the prominent model of how an organization should function. The model depends on *power.* Those who are in power act autocratically. The message to employees is "You do this—or else," meaning that an employee who does not follow orders is penalized, often severely.

An autocratic model uses one-way communication—from the top to the workers. Management believes that it knows what is best. The employee's obligation is to follow orders. Employees have to be persuaded, directed, and pushed into performance, and this is management's task. Management does the thinking, and the workers obey the directives. Under autocratic conditions, the workers' role is *obedience* to management.

The autocratic model does work in some settings. Most military organizations throughout the world are formulated on this model. The model was also used successfully during the Industrial Revolution, for example, in building great railroad systems and in operating giant steel mills.

The autocratic model has a number of disadvantages. Workers are often in the best position to identify shortcomings in the structure and technology of the organizational system, but one-way communication prevents feedback to management. The model also fails to generate much of a commitment among the workers to accomplish organizational goals. Finally, the model fails to motivate workers to put forth effort to further develop their skills (skills that often would be highly beneficial to the employer).

Exercise 10.2: Working for an Autocratic Boss

GOAL: This exercise is designed to have you reflect on the merits and shortcomings of someone who is autocratic.

1. **Briefly describe a job you held in which you worked for someone who was autocratic. (In essence, an autocratic boss uses one-way communication—does not want the workers' input on how to do the job.) If you have not worked for an autocratic boss, interview someone who has and then answer these questions.**

---

*Material in this section is adapted from *The Practice of Social Work,* 7th ed., by Zastrow. © 2003. Reprinted with permission of Brooks/Cole, a division of Thomson Learning, Inc.

2. **How did you feel about working for someone who was autocratic—that is, someone who told you what to do and would not listen to your thoughts and concerns?**

3. **Were you motivated to do your best work? Why, or why not?**

4. **Research has found that two-way communication is superior to one-way communication. Why do you believe that so many bosses, even today, use one-way communication?**

The Custodial Model

Many decades ago when the autocratic model was the predominant model of organizational behavior, some progressive managers began to study their employees and soon found that the autocratic model often caused the employees to be filled with insecurity, frustration, and feelings of aggression toward management. Since the employees could not directly express their discontent, it was expressed indirectly. Some employees vented their anger on their families and neighbors, and the entire community suffered. Others sabotaged production. Davis and Newstrom described sabotage in a wood-processing plant.

> Managers treated workers crudely, sometimes even to the point of physical abuse. Since employees could not strike back directly for fear of losing their jobs, they found another way to do it. They *symbolically* fed their supervisor to a log-shredding machine! They did this by purposely destroying good sheets of veneer, which made the supervisor look bad when monthly efficiency reports were prepared.[4]

In the 1890s and 1900s some progressive employers thought that if these feelings could be alleviated, employees might feel more like working, which would increase productivity. To satisfy the employees' security needs, a number of companies began to provide welfare programs; examples include pension programs, child-care centers at the workplace, health insurance, and life insurance.

The custodial approach leads to employee dependence on the organization. According to Davis and Newstrom, "If employees have ten years of seniority under the union contract and a good pension program, they cannot afford to quit even if the grass looks greener somewhere else!"[5]

Employees working under a custodial model tend to focus on their economic rewards and benefits. They are happier and more content than working under the autocratic model, but they do not have a high commitment to helping the organization accomplish its goals. They tend to give *passive cooperation* to their employer. The model's most evident flaw is that most employees are producing substantially below their capacities. They are not motivated to advance to higher capacities. Most such employees do not feel fulfilled or motivated at their place of work. In summary, contented employees (which the custodial model is designed to generate) are not necessarily the most productive employees.

The Scientific Management Model

One of the earliest and most important schools of thought on the management of functions and tasks in the workplace was based on the work of Frederick Taylor.[6] Taylor was a mechanical engineer, an American industrialist, and an educator. He focused primarily on management techniques that would lead to increased productivity. He asserted that many organizational problems in the workplace involved misunderstandings between managers and workers. Managers erroneously thought that workers were lazy and unemotional, and they mistakenly believed they understood workers' jobs. Workers mistakenly thought that managers cared most about exploiting them.

To solve these problems, Taylor developed the *scientific management model,* which focused on the need for managers to conduct scientific analyses of the workplace. One of the first steps was to conduct a careful study of how each job could best be accomplished. An excellent way to do this, according to Taylor, was to identify the best worker for each job and then carefully study how he or she effectively and efficiently did the work. The goal of this analysis was to discover the optimal way of doing the job—in Taylor's words, the "one best way." Once this best way was identified, tools could be modified to better complete the work, workers' abilities and interests could be fitted to particular job assignments, and the level of production that the average worker could sustain could be gauged.

Once the level of production for the average worker was determined, Taylor indicated the next step was to provide incentives to increase productivity. His favorite strategy for doing this was the piece-rate wage, in which workers were paid for each unit they produced. The goals were to produce more units, reduce unit cost, increase organizational productivity and profitability, and provide incentives for workers to produce more.

Taylor's work has been criticized as having a technicist bias, since it tends to treat workers as little more than cogs in a wheel. No two workers are exactly alike, so the "one best way" of doing a job is often unique to the person doing it. In fact, forcing the same work approach on different workers may actually decrease both productivity and worker satisfaction. In addition, Taylor's approach has limited application to human services. Since each client is unique—with unique needs, unique environmental impact factors, and unique strengths and capacities—each human services case has to be individualized, and therefore it is difficult (if not impossible) to specify the "one best way" to proceed.

The Human Relations Model

In 1927 the Hawthorne Works of the Western Electric Company in Chicago began a series of experiments designed to discover ways to increase worker satisfaction and worker productivity.[7]

Hawthorne Works manufactured telephones on an assembly-line basis. Workers needed no special skills and performed simple, repetitive tasks. The workers were not unionized, and management sought to find ways to increase productivity. If job satisfaction could be increased, employees would work more efficiently and productivity would increase.

The company tested the effects on productivity of a number of factors: rest breaks, better lighting, changes in the number of work hours, changes in the wages paid, improved food facilities, and so on. The results were surprising. Productivity increased, as expected, with improved working conditions, but it also increased when working conditions worsened. This latter finding was unexpected and led to additional study.

The investigators discovered that participation in the experiments was extremely attractive to the workers. They felt they had been selected by the management for their individual abilities, and so they worked harder, even when working conditions became less favorable. In addition, the workers' morale and general attitude toward work improved, since they felt they were receiving special attention. By participating in this study, the workers were able to work in smaller groups and became involved in making decisions. Working in smaller groups allowed them to develop a stronger sense of solidarity with their fellow workers. Being involved in decision making decreased their feelings of meaninglessness and powerlessness about their work.

In sociological and psychological research, the results of this study have become known as the Hawthorne effect. In essence, when subjects know they are participants in a study, this awareness may lead them to behave differently and substantially influence the results.

The results of this study, and of other similar studies, led some researchers to conclude that the key variables impacting productivity are social factors. Etzioni summarized some of the basic tenets of the human relations approach:

- The level of production is set by social norms, not by physiological capacities.
- Noneconomic rewards and sanctions significantly affect the behavior of the workers and largely limit the effect of economic incentive plans.
- Workers do not act or react as individuals but as members of groups.
- The role of leadership is important in understanding social factors in organizations and this leadership may be either formal or informal.[8]

Numerous studies have provided evidence to support these tenets.[9] Workers who are capable of greater productivity often will not excel because they are unwilling to exceed the "average" level set by the norms of the group, even if this means earning less. These studies have also found that attempts by management to influence workers' behavior are often more successful if targeted at the group as a whole, rather than at individuals. Finally, the studies have documented the importance of informal leadership in influencing workers' behavior in ways that can either amplify or negate formal leadership directives. This model asserts that managers who succeed in increasing productivity are most likely responsive to the workers' social needs.

One criticism of the human relations model is (surprisingly) that it tends to manipulate, dehumanize, oppress, and exploit workers. The model leads to the conclusion that management can increase productivity by helping workers become content, rather than by increasing economic rewards for higher productivity. The human relations model allows for concentrated power and decision making at the top. It is not intended to empower employees in the decision-making process or to assist them in acquiring genuine participation in the running of the organization. The practice of dealing with people on the basis of their perceived social relationships within the workplace may also be a factor in perpetuating the "good old boys" network; this network has disadvantaged women and people of color over the years. Another criticism of the human relations approach is that a happy work force is not necessarily a productive work force, because the norms for worker production may be set well below the workers' levels of capability.

Theory X and Theory Y

McGregor developed two theories of management.[10] He theorized that management thinking and behavior are based on two different sets of assumptions, which he labeled Theory X and Theory Y.

Theory X managers view employees as incapable of much growth. Employees are perceived as having an inherent dislike for work and attempting to evade work whenever possible. Therefore, X-type managers believe they must control, direct, force, or threaten employees to make them work. Employees are also viewed as having relatively little ambition, wishing to avoid responsibilities, and preferring to be directed. Theory X managers therefore spell out job responsibilities carefully, set work goals without employee input, use external rewards (such as money) to force employees to work, and punish those who deviate from established rules. Because Theory X managers reduce responsibilities to a level at which few mistakes can be made, work usually becomes so structured that it is monotonous and distasteful. These assumptions, of course, are inconsistent with what behavioral scientists assert are effective principles for directing, influencing, and motivating people. (Theory X managers are, in essence, adhering to an autocratic model of organizational behavior.)

In contrast, *Theory Y managers* view employees as wanting to grow and develop by exerting physical and mental effort to accomplish work objectives to which they are committed. These managers believe that the promise of internal rewards, such as self-respect and personal improvement, are stronger motivators than external rewards (money) and punishment. They also believe that under proper conditions, employees will not only accept responsibility but seek it. Most employees are assumed to have considerable ingenuity, creativity, and imagination for problem solving. Therefore, they are given considerable responsibility to test the limits of their capabilities. Mistakes and errors are viewed as necessary phases of the learning process, and work is structured so employees have a sense of accomplishment and growth.

Employees who work for Y-type managers are generally more creative and productive, experience greater work satisfaction, and are more highly motivated than employees who work for X-type managers. Under both management styles, expectations often become self-fulfilling prophecies.

Exercise 10.3: Working for Theory X versus Theory Y Managers

GOAL: This exercise is designed to assist you in understanding the merits and shortcomings of each of these two management styles.

1. Describe a job you had in which you worked for someone who used a Theory X style of management. Why would you categorize this person as having a Theory X style?

2. Describe a job you had in which you worked for someone who used a Theory Y style of management. Why would you categorize this person as having a Theory Y style. (If you have not worked for a Theory X or Theory Y manager, interview someone who has and then answer these questions.)

3. Compare your feelings about working for a Theory X versus Theory Y manager.

4. For which manager were you more motivated to do your best work? Indicate your reasons for this choice.

The Collegial Model

A useful extension of Theory Y is the collegial model, which emphasizes the team concept. It involves employees working closely together and feeling a commitment to achieve a common purpose. Some organizations—such as university departments, research laboratories, and most human services organizations—have a goal of creating a collegial atmosphere to facilitate achieving their purposes. (Sadly, many such organizations are unsuccessful in creating such an atmosphere.)

Creating a collegial atmosphere is highly dependent on management building a feeling of partnership with employees. When such a partnership develops, employees feel needed and useful. Managers are then viewed as joint contributors rather than as bosses. Management is the *coach* who builds a better team. Davis and Newstrom described some of the approaches to developing a team concept:

> The feeling of partnerships can be built in many ways. Some organizations have abolished the use of reserved parking spaces for executives, so every employee has an equal chance of finding one close to the workplace. Some firms have tried to eliminate the use of terms like "bosses" and "subordinates," feeling that those terms simply create perceptions of psychological distance between managers and nonmanagers. Other employers have removed time clocks, set up "fun committees," sponsored company canoe trips, or required managers to spend a week or two annually working in field or factory locations. All of these approaches are designed to build a spirit of mutuality, in which every person makes contributions and appreciates those of others.[11]

If the sense of partnership is developed, employees produce quality work and seek to cooperate with coworkers, not because management directs them to do so but because they feel an internal obligation to produce high-quality work. The collegial approach thus leads to a sense of *self-discipline*. In this environment, employees are more apt to have a sense of fulfillment, to feel self-actualized, and to produce higher-quality work.

Theory Z

William Ouchi described the Japanese style of management in his 1981 best seller *Theory Z*.[12] In the late 1970s and early 1980s, attention in the U.S. business world became focused on the Japanese approach to management, as markets long dominated by U.S. firms (such as the automobile industry) were being challenged for dominance by Japanese industries. Japanese industrial organizations had rapidly overcome their earlier reputation for poor quality work and were setting worldwide standards for quality and durability.

Theory Z asserted that the theoretical principles underlying Japanese management went beyond Theory Y. According to Theory Z, a business organization in Japan is more than the profitability oriented entity that it is in the United States. It is a way of life. It provides lifetime employment. It is enmeshed with the nation's political, social, and economic network. Furthermore, its influence spills over into many other organizations, such as nursery schools, elementary and secondary schools, and universities.

The basic philosophy of Theory Z is that involved and committed workers are the key to increased productivity. Ideas and suggestions about how to improve the organization are routinely solicited and implemented, where feasible. One strategy for accomplishing this is the *quality circle,* where employees and management routinely meet to brainstorm about ways to improve productivity and quality.

In contrast to U.S. organizations, Japanese organizations tend not to have written objectives or organizational charts. Most work is done in teams and decisions are made by consensus. The teams tend to function without a designated leader. Cooperation within units and between units, loyalty to the organization, and organizational loyalty to the employee are all emphasized.

Experiments designed to transplant Japanese-style management to the United States have resulted in mixed success. In most cases U.S. organizations have concluded that Theory Z probably works quite well in a homogeneous culture that has Japan's societal values, but some components do not fit well with the more heterogeneous and individualistic character of the United States. In addition, some firms in volatile industries (such as electronics) have difficulty balancing their desire to provide lifetime employment with the need to adjust their work forces to meet rapidly changing market demands.

Management by Objectives

Fundamental to the core of an organization is its purpose, that is, the commonly shared understanding of the reason for its existence.

Management theorist Peter Drucker proposed a strategy for making organizational goals and objectives the central construct around which organizational life is designed to function.[13] In other words, instead of focusing on employee needs and wants or on organizational structure as the ways to increase efficiency and productivity, Drucker proposed beginning with the desired outcome and working backward. The strategy is first to identify the organizational objectives or goals and then to adapt the organizational tasks, resources, and structure to meet those objectives. This management by objectives (MBO) approach is designed to focus the organization's efforts on meeting these objectives. Success is determined, then, by the degree to which stated objectives are reached.

This approach can be applied to the organization as a whole, as well as to internal divisions or departments. When the MBO approach is applied to internal divisions, the objectives set for each division should be consistent and supportive of the overall organizational objectives.

In many areas, including human services, the MBO approach can also be applied to the cases serviced by each employee. Goals are set with each client, tasks to meet these goals are then determined, and deadlines are set for the completion of these tasks. The degree of success of each case is then determined at a later date (often when a case is closed) by the extent to which stated goals were achieved.

An adaptation of the MBO approach, called strategic planning and budgeting (SPB), became popular in the 1990s and still is widely used. The process involves first specifying the overall vision or mission of an organization, then identifying a variety of more specific objectives or plans for achieving that vision, and finally adapting the resources to meet the specific high-priority objectives or plans. Organizations often hire outside consultants to assist in conducting the SPB process.

One major advantage of the MBO approach for an organization (or its divisions) is that it produces clear statements (made available to all employees) about the objectives and the tasks that are expected to be accomplished in specified time periods. This type of activity tends to improve cooperation and collaboration. The MBO approach is also useful because it provides a guide for allocating resources and a focus for monitoring and evaluating organizational efforts.

An additional benefit of the MBO approach is that it creates diversity in the workplace. Prior to this approach, those responsible for hiring failed to employ women and people of color in significant numbers. As affirmative action programs were developed within organizations, the MBO approach was widely used to set specific hiring goals and objectives. The result has been significant changes in recruitment approaches that have enabled a number of women and other minorities to secure employment.

Total Quality Management

Total quality management (TQM) has been defined as

> the integration of all functions and processes within an organization in order to achieve continuous improvement of the quality of goods and services. The goal is customer satisfaction.[14]

TQM is based on a number of ideas. It means thinking about quality in terms of all functions of the enterprise and is a start-to-finish process that integrates interrelated functions at all levels. It is a systems approach that considers every interaction among the various elements of the organization. TQM asserts that management, in many businesses and organizations, makes the mistake of blaming what goes wrong in an organization as the fault of individual people, not of the system. TQM, instead, believes in the 85/15 Rule, which asserts that 85 percent of the problems can be corrected only by changing systems (structures, rules, practices, expectations, and traditions that are largely determined by management), and fewer than 15 percent of the problems can be solved by individual workers. When problems arise, TQM asserts that management should look for causes in the system and work to remove them before casting blame on workers.

TQM asserts that quality includes continuously improving all the organization's processes that lead to customer satisfaction. Customer satisfaction is the main purpose of the organization. The customer is not the "point of sale." The customer is part of the design and production process, as the customer's needs must continually be monitored.

In recent years numerous organizations have adopted a TQM approach to seeking to improve their goods and services. One reason that quality is being emphasized more is that consumers are increasingly shunning mass-produced, poorly made, disposable products. Companies are realizing that in order to remain competitive in global markets, high quality is essential in their products and services. Ford's motto of "Quality Is Job One" symbolizes this emphasis on quality.

There are a variety of approaches to TQM, because numerous theoreticians have advanced their own diverse approaches. A summary of these approaches is contained in *Principles of Total Quality*.[15] A description of all these approaches is beyond the scope of this text. However, Hower provides a summary of many of the basic principles of TQM:

- Employees asking their external and internal customers what they need and providing more of it
- Instilling pride into every employee
- Concentrating on information and data (a common language) to solve problems, instead of concentrating on opinions and egos
- Developing leaders, not managers, and knowing the difference
- Improving every process (everyone is in a process), checking this improvement at predetermined times, then improving it again if necessary
- Helping every employee enjoy his or her work while the organization continues to become more productive
- Providing a forum or open atmosphere so that employees at all levels feel free to voice their opinions when they think they have good ideas
- Receiving a continuous increase in those suggestions and accepting and implementing the best ones
- Utilizing the teamwork concept, since teams often make better decisions than individuals
- Empowering these teams to implement their recommended solutions and learn from their failures
- Reducing the number of layers of authority to enhance this empowerment
- Recognizing complaints as opportunities for improvement[16]

These principles indicate the "flavor" of TQM.

Exercise 10.4: Applying Concepts of Models of Organizations

GOAL: This exercise is designed to assist you in understanding models of organizations and then applying some of their theoretical concepts.

1. **Review the material in this chapter on the following models of organizations:**
   - The Autocratic Model
   - The Custodial Model
   - The Scientific Management Model
   - The Human Relations Model
   - Theory X
   - Theory Y
   - The Collegial Model
   - Theory Z
   - Management by Objectives
   - Total Quality Management

Select an organization that you have worked for and describe the goals of this organization.

2. List the models that provide some useful concepts that assist you in understanding the behavior of the "boss/leader" and the "workers." Also summarize the theoretical concepts of these models that you found useful.

■ SURVIVING IN A BUREAUCRACY*

A bureaucracy is a subcategory (or type) of organization. A bureaucracy can be defined as a form of social organization whose distinctive characteristics include a vertical hierarchy with power centered at the top; a task-specific division of labor; clearly defined rules; formalized channels of communication; and selection, compensation, promotion, and retention based on technical competence.

There are basic structural conflicts between helping professionals and the bureaucratic systems in which they work. Helping professionals place a high value on creativeness and changing the system to serve clients. Bureaucracies resist change and are most efficient when no one is "rocking the boat." Helping professionals seek to personalize services by conveying to each client that "you count as a person." Bureaucracies are highly depersonalized, emotionally detached systems that view every employee and every client as a tiny component of a large system. In a large bureaucracy employees *don't* count as "people" but only as functional parts of a system. Additional conflicting value orientations between a helping professional and bureaucratic systems are listed in the box, "Value Conflicts between a Helping Professional and Bureaucracies."

---

*Material in this section is adapted from *The Practice of Social Work*, 7th ed., by Zastrow. © 2003. Reprinted with permission of Brooks/Cole, a division of Thomson Learning, Inc.

Value Conflicts between a Helping Professional and Bureaucracies

ORIENTATIONS OF A HELPING PROFESSIONAL	ORIENTATIONS OF BUREAUCRATIC SYSTEMS
Desires democratic system for decision making.	Most decisions are made autocratically.
Desires that power be distributed equally among employees (horizontal structure).	Power is distributed vertically.
Desires that clients have considerable power in the system.	Power is held primarily by top executives.
Desires a flexible, changing system.	System is rigid and stable.
Desires that creativity and growth be emphasized.	Emphasis is on structure and the status quo.
Desires that focus be client-oriented.	System is organization-centered.
Desires that communication be on a personalized level from person to person.	Communication is from level to level.
Desires shared decision making and shared responsibility structure.	A hierarchical decision-making structure and a hierarchical responsibility structure are characteristic.
Desires that decisions be made by those having the most knowledge.	Decisions are made in terms of the decision-making authority assigned to each position in the hierarchy.
Desires shared leadership.	System uses autocratic leadership.
Believes feelings of clients and employees should be highly valued by the system.	Procedures and processes are highly valued.

Exercise 10.5: Your Orientation toward Bureaucratic Systems

GOAL: This exercise is designed to assist you in arriving at a realistic view of bureaucratic systems.

1. Examine the "orientations of a helping professional," and "orientations of bureaucratic systems" in Exhibit 10.1. Which set of orientations did you have prior to reading this material?

2. If you listed "orientations of a helping professional," do you now believe you need to view bureaucratic systems in terms of "orientations of bureaucratic systems"? Explain your views on this issue.

Any of these differences in value orientations can become an arena of conflict between helping professionals and the bureaucracies in which they work. Knopf summarized the potential areas of conflict between bureaucracies and helping professionals:

> The trademarks of a BS (bureaucratic system) are power, hierarchy, and specialization; that is, rules and roles. In essence, the result is depersonalization. The system itself is neither "good" nor "bad"; it is a system. I believe it to be amoral. It is efficient and effective, but in order to be so it must be impersonal in all of its functionings. This then is the location of the stress. The hallmark of the helping professional is a highly individualized, democratic, humanized, relationship-oriented service aimed at self-motivation. The hallmark of a bureaucratic system is a highly impersonalized, valueless (amoral), emotionally detached, hierarchical structure of organization. The dilemma of the HP (helping person) is how to give a personalized service to a client through a delivery system that is not set up in any way to do that.[17]

Numerous helping professionals respond to these orientation conflicts by erroneously projecting a "personality" onto the bureaucracy. The bureaucracy is viewed as being red tape, officialism, uncaring, cruel, the enemy. A negative personality is sometimes also projected onto the officials, who may be viewed as being paper shufflers, rigid, deadwood, inefficient, and unproductive. Knopf states:

> The HP (helping person) . . . may deal with the impersonal nature of the system by projecting values onto it and thereby give the BS (bureaucratic system) a "personality." In this way, we fool ourselves into thinking that we can deal with it in a personal way. Unfortunately, projection is almost always negative and reflects the dark or negative aspects of ourselves. The BS then becomes a screen onto which we vent our anger, sadness, or fright, and while a lot of energy is generated, very little is accomplished. Since the BS is amoral, it is unproductive to place a personality on it.[18]

A bureaucratic system is neither good nor bad. It has neither a personality nor a value system of its own. It is simply a structure developed to carry out various tasks.

A helping person may have various emotional reactions to these conflicts in orientation with bureaucratic systems.[19] Common reactions are anger at the system, self-blame ("It's all my fault"), sadness and depression ("Poor me," "Nobody appreciates all I've done"), and fright and paranoia ("They're out to get me," "If I mess up I'm gone").

Knopf identified several types of behavior patterns that helping professionals choose in dealing with bureaucracies.[20]

The *warrior* leads open campaigns to destroy and malign the system. A warrior discounts the value of the system and often enters into a win–lose conflict. The warrior generally loses and is dismissed.

The *gossip* is a covert warrior who complains to others (including clients, politicians, and the news media) how terrible the system is. A gossip frequently singles out a few officials for criticism. Bureaucratic systems often make life very difficult for the gossip by assigning distasteful tasks, refusing to promote, giving very low salary increases, and perhaps even dismissing.

The *complainer* resembles a gossip but confines complaints to other helping people, to in-house staff, and to family members. A complainer wants people to agree in order to find comfort in shared misery. Complainers desire to stay with the system, and generally do.

The *dancer* is skillful at ignoring rules and procedures. Dancers are frequently lonely, often reprimanded for incorrectly filling out forms, and have low investment in the system or in helping clients.

The *defender* is scared, dislikes conflict, and therefore defends the rules, the system, and bureaucratic officials. Defenders are often supervisors and are viewed by others as bureaucrats.

The *machine* is a bureaucrat who takes on the orientation of the bureaucracy. Often a machine has not been involved in providing direct services for years. Machines are frequently named to head study committees and policy groups and to chair boards.

The *executioner* attacks people within an organization with enthusiasm and vigor. An executioner usually has a high energy level and is impulsive. An executioner abuses power by indiscriminately attacking and dismissing not only employees but also services and programs. Executioners have power and are angry (although the anger is disguised, denied). They are not committed to either the value orientation of helping professionals or the bureaucracy.

Knopf listed 66 tips on how to survive in a bureaucracy.[21] The most useful suggestions are summarized here:

1. Whenever your needs, or the needs of your clients, are not met by the bureaucracy, use the following problem-solving approach: (1) Precisely identify your needs (or the needs of clients) that are in conflict with the bureaucracy; this step is defining the problem. (2) Generate a list of possible solutions. Be creative in generating a wide range of solutions. (3) Evaluate the merits and shortcomings of the possible solutions. (4) Select a solution. (5) Implement the solution. (6) Evaluate the solution.

2. Obtain a knowledge of how your bureaucracy is structured and how it functions. This knowledge will reduce fear of the unknown, make the system more predictable, and help in identifying rational ways to best meet your needs and those of your clients.

3. Remember that bureaucrats are people who have feelings. Communication gaps are often most effectively reduced if you treat them with as much respect and interest as you treat clients.

4. If you are at war with the bureaucracy, declare a truce. The system will find a way to dismiss you if you remain at war. With a truce, you can identify and use the strengths of the bureaucracy as an ally, rather than having the strengths be used against you as an enemy.

5. Know your work contract and job expectations. If the expectations are unclear, seek clarity.

6. Continue to develop your knowledge and awareness of specific helping skills. Take advantage of continuing education opportunities (for example, workshops, conferences, courses). Among other advantages, your continued professional development will assist you in being able to contract from a position of competency and skill.

7. Seek to identify your professional strengths and limitations. Knowing your limitations will increase your ability to avoid undertaking responsibilities that are beyond your competencies.

8. Be aware that you can't change everything, so stop trying. In a bureaucracy, focus your change efforts on those aspects that most need change and that you have a fair chance of changing. Stop thinking and complaining about those aspects you cannot change. It is irrational to complain about things that you cannot change or to complain about those things that you do not intend to make an effort to change.

9. Learn how to control your emotions in your interactions with the bureaucracy. Emotions that are counterproductive (such as most angry outbursts) particularly need to be controlled. Doing a rational self-analysis of unwanted emotions (see Appendix 1: Module 1) is one way of gaining control of your unwanted emotions. Learning how to respond to stress in your personal life will also prepare you to handle stress at work better.

10. Develop and use a sense of humor. Humor takes the edge off adverse conditions and reduces negative feelings.

11. Learn to accept your mistakes and perhaps even to laugh at some of them. No one is perfect.

12. Take time to enjoy and develop a support system with your coworkers.

13. Acknowledge your mistakes and give in sometimes on minor matters. You may not be right, and giving in sometimes allows other people to do the same.

14. Keep yourself physically fit and mentally alert. Learn to use approaches that will reduce stress and prevent burnout (see Chapter 11).

15. Leave your work at the office. If you have urgent unfinished bureaucratic business, do it before leaving work or don't leave.

16. Occasionally take your supervisor and other administrators to lunch. Socializing prevents isolation and facilitates your involvement with and understanding of the system.

17. Do not seek self-actualization or ego satisfaction from the bureaucracy. A depersonalized system is incapable of providing this. Only you can satisfy your ego and become self-actualized.

18. Make speeches to community groups that accentuate the positives about your agency. Do not hesitate to ask after speeches that a thank-you letter be sent to your supervisor or agency director.

19. If you have a problem involving the bureaucracy, discuss it with other employees; focus on problem solving rather than on complaining. Groups are much more powerful and productive than an individual working alone to make changes in a system.

20. No matter how high you rise in a hierarchy, maintain direct service contact. Direct contact keeps you abreast of changing client needs, prevents you from getting stale, and keeps you attuned to the concerns of employees in lower levels of the hierarchy.

21. Do not try to change everything in the system at once. Attacking too much will overextend you and lead to burnout. Start small and be selective and specific. Double-check your facts to make certain they accurately prove your position before confronting bureaucratic officials.

22. Identify your career goals and determine whether they can be met in this system. If the answer is no, then (1) change your goals, (2) change the bureaucracy, or (3) seek a position elsewhere in which your goals can be met.

◼ COMMUNITIES, ORGANIZATIONS, AND GROUPS

A community has been defined as, "a group of individuals or families that share certain values, services, institutions, interests or geographic proximity."[22] The term *institution* in this definition is sometimes rather difficult to comprehend. Barker has defined institution as "an organization established for some public purpose and the physical facility in which its work occurs, such as a prison."[23]

The reader will note that the terms *organization* and *community* are closely related. An organization was defined earlier in this chapter as a collectivity of individuals gathered together to serve a particular purpose. Some communities are also organizations. A nursing home can be considered both an organization (the residents and staff form a collectivity of individuals having a specific purpose) and a community (the residents and staff share certain values, services, physical facilities, interests, and geographic proximity).

But not all communities are institutions, and vice versa. The residents of a large city form a community, as they share certain services and institutions, and have geographic proximity; but a large city is not an organization, as its residents are not gathered together to serve a particular purpose.

The owners and employees of a large multinational corporation (such as Philip Morris Corporation, which has offices in many countries and sells a variety of products including tobacco and groceries) form an organization. However, the Philip Morris Corporation is not considered a community because the corporation is so large that its vast number of owners and employees do not engage sufficiently in "sharing" with one another to be considered a community.

Exercise 10.6: Enjoying and Appreciating a Community

GOAL: Some students erroneously believe social work practice with communities is not rewarding. This exercise is designed to show students that community involvement has numerous rewards.

1. Describe a community that you have enjoyed participating in. This may be a sorority, a fraternity, the community you live in, a community you visited during a trip or vacation, a church group you are involved with, a residence hall that has become a community for you at this campus, and so on. In your description, seek to highlight the unique aspects of this community.

2. Specify the aspects of this community that you have enjoyed and appreciated.

3. Has this exercise moved you, at least a little, to conclude that community involvement (and yes, social work practice with communities) may be something you want to continue to pursue?

THE RELATIONSHIP BETWEEN A GROUP AND A COMMUNITY

The terms *community* and *group* are closely related. As noted in Chapter 1, a group is:

> . . . two or more individuals in face-to-face interaction, each aware of his or her membership in the group, each aware of the others who belong to the group, and each aware of their positive interdependence as they strive to achieve mutual goals.[24]

A distinguishing characteristic of a group is that its members have personal contact with one another. A community, as stated earlier in this chapter, is "a group of individuals or families that share certain values, services, institutions, interests, or geographic proximity."[25]

In many cases a group and a community overlap and the group can also be considered a community. The congregation of St. Peter's Catholic Church in Madison, Wisconsin, is both a group and a community. The members have personal contact with one another (characteristic of a group) and share the religious values of the Catholic Church (characteristic of a community).

There are a number of other examples in which a group is also a community. The small unincorporated village of Little Chicago, Wisconsin, is composed of one bank, three stores, one tavern, a restaurant, and five residential homes. The village is a community (its residents share geographic proximity, services, values, and interests) and have personal contact with one another (a key characteristic of a group). Some of the interests and values that are shared are hard work, helping neighbors out in times of trouble, a belief in Christianity, and the cherishing of country living in rural America.

Many communities are so large that their members do not have personal contact with one another and therefore are not a group. For example, Roman Catholics throughout the world have a common set of values and therefore can be considered to be a community. However, no one has personal contact with everyone else, so they are not considered a group. The residents of New York City form a community, as they share geographic proximity (in fact, distinct geographic boundaries). But this community is not a group since no resident has personal contact with everyone else.

ANALYZING A COMMUNITY

A variety of frameworks have been developed for analyzing a community. The following framework presents an elementary approach:

1. *Community Members:* Who are the members of this community? How many members are there? What unique or distinct characteristics do these members have? What is their ethnic or racial composition? What is the age composition? Do the members have pride in their community? If "yes," what aspects do the residents have pride in?

2. *Economic Characteristics:* What are the principal economic characteristics of the community? What are the principal types of employment? What are the major industries? Have there been recent changes in the economic base? What is the unemployment rate?

3. *Community Values:* Does the community have a distinct set of values? If "yes," what are these values? Who set these values and why were they selected, or how did they develop? Have there been changes in these values over time? If "yes," what changes have occurred and for what reasons?

4. *Needs and Social Problems:* What do the members perceive as their most critical needs? Why are these needs perceived as critical? How effectively do the members perceive that their community is responding to their needs? Closely related to the previous questions are the following: What major social problems affect the members? Are subgroups of the population experiencing social problems of

critical proportions? What data is available on these identified social problems, and what are the sources of this data?

5. *Oppression and Discrimination:* Are some subgroups of the population being victimized by oppression and discrimination? (Oppression can be defined as the unjust or cruel use of authority or power.) If "yes," the following questions are important: Why are oppression and discrimination occurring? How is the power structure in the community responding to the oppression and discrimination? What efforts are being made to combat this oppression and discrimination? Who are the leaders in these efforts?

6. *Power Structure:* Who holds the power in the community? What is the nature of the power—such as financial, military or police strength, election processes? How does the power structure maintain its power? Is the power fairly evenly distributed among the members, or is the power in the hands of a small segment of the members? What are the attitudes of the power structure toward those in the community with little or no power?

7. *Human Services:* What existing human service agencies and organizations are seen as the major service providers in the community? What primary human services are provided? Who are the major beneficiaries of these services? Are subgroups with critical needs being ignored? If "yes," why are their needs being ignored? What is the image of the social work profession in the community?

8. *Educational Services:* What are the major educational resources in the community? What educational services are being provided? Who are the major beneficiaries of these services? Are there subgroups whose educational needs are being ignored? If "yes," why are these needs being ignored?

Exercise 10.7: Analyzing Your Home Community

GOAL: This exercise is designed to assist you in learning how to apply a framework for analyzing a community.

1. **Using the framework described in "Analyzing a Community," answer as many questions as you can about the community you live in at home. (There is no need to do much research—just answer in terms of what you now know about your home community.)**

2. **Summarize your thoughts about the merits and shortcomings of this framework for analyzing a community.**

MODELS OF COMMUNITY PRACTICE*

A variety of approaches have been developed for community practitioners to bring about community change. In reviewing these approaches, Rothman and Tropman have categorized them into three models: locality development, social planning, and social action.[26] It should be noted that these models are "ideal types." Actual approaches to community change have tendencies or emphases that categorize them in one of the previous models, yet most approaches also have components characteristic of one or both of the other models. Advocates of the social planning model, for example, may at times use community change techniques (such as wide discussion and participation by a variety of groups) that are characteristic of the other two models. At this point we will not attempt to deal with the mixed forms but for analytical purposes will instead view the three models as "pure" forms.

Locality Development Model

Locality development (also called community development) asserts that community change can best be brought about through broad participation of a wide spectrum of people at the local community level. The model seeks to involve a broad cross section of people (including the disadvantaged and the power structure) in identifying and solving their problems. Some themes emphasized in this model are democratic procedures, a consensus approach, voluntary cooperation, development of indigenous leadership, and self-help.

The roles of the community practitioner in this approach include enabler, catalyst, coordinator, and teacher of problem-solving skills and ethical values. The approach assumes that conflicts that arise between various interest groups can be creatively and constructively handled. It encourages people to express their differences freely but assumes people will put aside their self-interests in order to further the interests of their community. The approach assumes people will put aside their self-interests through appeals to altruism. The basic theme of this approach is "Together we can figure out what to do and do it." The approach seeks to use discussion and communication between different factions to reach consensus about the problems to focus on and the

---

*This section is adapted from *The Practice of Social Work*, 7th ed., by Zastrow. © 2003. Reprinted with permission of Brooks/Cole, a division of Thomson Learning, Inc.

▨ Case Example of the Locality Development Model

Robert McKearn, a social worker for a juvenile probation department, noticed in 1995 that an increasing number of school-age children were being referred to his office by the police department, school system, and parents from a small city of 11,000 people in the county served by his agency. The charges included status offenses (such as truancy from school) and delinquent offenses (such as shoplifting and burglary). Mr. McKearn noted that most of these children were from single-parent families.

Mr. McKearn contacted the community mental health center, the self-help organization Parents Without Partners, the pupil services department of the public school system, the county social services department, some members of the clergy, and the community mental health center in the area. Nearly everyone he contacted saw an emerging need to better serve children in single-parent families. The pupil services department mentioned that such children were performing less well academically in school and tended to display more serious disciplinary problems.

Mr. McKearn arranged a meeting of representatives from the groups and organizations that were contacted.

At the initial meeting a number of concerns were expressed about the problematic behaviors being displayed by children who had single parents. The school system considered these children to be "at risk" for higher rates of truancy, dropping out of school, delinquent activities, suicide, emotional problems, and unwanted pregnancies. Although a number of problems were identified, no one at this initial meeting was able to suggest a viable strategy to better serve single parents and their children. The community was undergoing an economic recession; therefore, funds were unavailable for an expensive new program.

Three more meetings were held. At the first two a number of suggestions for providing services were discussed, but all were viewed as either too expensive or impractical. At the fourth meeting of the group, a single parent representing Parents Without Partners mentioned that she was aware that Big Brothers and Big Sisters programs in some communities were of substantial benefit to children who were raised in single-parent families. This idea seemed to energize the group. Suggestions began to "piggy back." The group, however, determined that funds were unavailable to hire staff to run a Big Brothers and Big Sisters program. However, Rhona Quinn, a social worker in the pupil services department, noted that she was willing to identify at-risk younger children in single-parent families and that she would be willing to supervise qualified volunteers in a "Big Buddy" program.

Mr. McKearn mentioned that he was currently supervising a student in an undergraduate field placement for an accredited social work program from a college in a nearby community. He noted that perhaps arrangements could be made for undergraduate social work students to be "Big Buddies" for their required volunteer experience. Rhona Quinn said she would approve of the suggestion if she could have the freedom to screen interested applicants for being "Big Buddies." Arrangements were made over the next two months for social work students to be "Big Buddies" for at-risk younger children from single-parent families. After a two-year experimental period, the school system found the program sufficiently successful that it assigned Ms. Quinn half-time to supervise the program, which included selecting at-risk children, screening volunteer applicants, matching children with Big Buddies, monitoring the progress of each matched pair, and conducting follow-up to ascertain the outcome of each pairing.

strategies or actions to resolve these problems. A few examples of locality development efforts include neighborhood work programs conducted by community-based agencies; Volunteers in Service to America; village-level work in some overseas community development programs, including the Peace Corps; and a variety of activities performed by self-help groups. A case example of the locality development model is presented in the box "Case Example of the Locality Development Model."

Social Planning Model

The social planning approach emphasizes a technical process of problem solving. The approach assumes that community change in a complex industrial environment requires highly trained and skilled planners who can guide complex change processes. The role of the expert is stressed in this approach to identifying and resolving social problems. The expert or planner is generally employed by a segment of the power structure, such as area planning agency, city or county planning department, mental health center, United Way board, Community Welfare Council, and so on. Because the social planner is employed by a segment of the power structure, there is a tendency for the

Case Example of the Social Planning Model

In 1995 the board of directors of Lincoln County Social Planning Agency authorized its staff to conduct a feasibility study on establishing a centralized information and referral (I&R) center. Donald Levi (a social planner on the staff) was assigned to direct the study. Mr. Levi collected data showing the following:

- There were over 350 community service agencies and organizations in this largely metropolitan county of one-half million people. Not only clients but also service providers were confused about what services were available from this array of agencies.

- There was a confusing array of specialized I&R services being developed. (Specialized information and referral services provided I&R services in only one or two areas.) Specialized I&R services were developing in suicide prevention, mental health, cognitive disabilities, day care, adoption services, and alcohol and drug treatment.

Mr. Levi then designed a program model for a centralized information and referral service. The model described a service that would provide I&R services on all human and community services in the county. For example, I&R would provide information not only on what daycare services were available but also on where to find public tennis courts and whom to call to remove a stray cat killed in front of your house. The centralized information and referral service number would be widely publicized on television, radio, and billboards and in newspapers and telephone directories. A budget was developed by Mr. Levi for the program costs.

The board of directors of the Lincoln County Social Planning Agency concluded that such a centralized information and referral service would be more efficient and economical than the confusing array that had been developing. The board therefore authorized Mr. Levi to pursue the development of this centralized service.

Mr. Levi conducted a questionnaire survey of all the human service agencies and all the clergy in the county. The results showed that both groups strongly supported the development of a centralized I&R service. In addition, the Easter Seal Society felt so strongly that such a service was needed that they contacted Mr. Levi to indicate that they were willing to donate funds for the new program. Mr. Levi was delighted, and an arrangement was worked out for the Easter Seal Society to fund the program for a 3-year demonstration period.

Only one barrier remained. The proposal for this new service needed to be approved by the county board of supervisors, as the proposal required the county to fund the program (beginning 3 years in the future) if the service proved to be effective during the 3-year demonstration phase. Mr. Levi and two members of the board of the Lincoln County Social Planning Agency presented the program proposal to the county board of supervisors. The presentation included graphs showing the savings of a centralized I&R service over specialized I&R services and contained written statements of support from a variety of sources, including city council members, the United Way, human service agencies, and members of the clergy. It was also indicated that there would be no cost to the county for a 3-year demonstration period. At the end of that time, there would be an evaluative study of the merits and shortcomings of the program. Mr. Levi fully expected approval and was speechless when the county board of supervisors said "no." They turned the proposal down because they felt a centralized I&R meant that more people would be referred to county social service agencies, which would raise costs to the county, and because this board was opposed to making a commitment to funding any new social welfare program in the future.

The county continues to be served by less effective specialized I&R services. This case example realistically illustrates that some planning efforts are unsuccessful.

planner to serve the interests of the power structure. Facilitating radical social change is generally not an emphasis in this approach.

The planner's roles in this approach include gathering facts, analyzing data, and serving as program designer, implementer, and facilitator. Community participation may vary from little to substantial with this approach, depending on the community's attitudes toward the problems being addressed. For example, an effort to design and obtain funding for a community center for the elderly may or may not result in substantial involvement by interested community groups, depending on the politics surrounding such a center. Much of the focus of the social planning approach is on identifying needs and on arranging and delivering goods and services to people who need them. The change focus of this approach is "Let's get the facts and take the next rational steps." A case example of this approach is presented in the box "Case Example of the Social Planning Model."

Social Action Model

The social action approach assumes there is a disadvantaged (often oppressed) segment of the population that needs to be organized, perhaps in alliance with others, to pressure the power structure for increased resources or for treatment more in accordance with democracy or social justice. Social action approaches at times seek basic changes in major institutions or seek changes in basic policies of formal organizations. Such approaches often seek redistribution of power and resources. Whereas locality developers envision a unified community, social action advocates see the power structure as the opposition—the target of action. Perhaps the best-known social activist was Saul Alinsky, who advised, "Pick the target, freeze it, personalize it, and polarize it."[27]

The roles of the community practitioner in this approach include advocate, agitator, activist, partisan, broker, and negotiator. Tactics used in social action projects include protests, boycotts, confrontation, and negotiation. The change strategy is one of "Let's organize to overpower our oppressor."[28] The client population is viewed as being a "victim" of the oppressive power structure. Examples of the social action approach include boycotts during the civil rights movement of the 1960s, strikes by unions, protests by antiabortion groups, and protests by African American and Native American groups.

The social action model is not widely used by social workers at present. Many workers find that being involved in social action activities may lead their employing agencies to penalize them with unpleasant work assignments, low merit increases, and denial of promotions. Many agencies will accept minor and moderate changes in their service delivery systems but are threatened by the prospect of radical changes that are often advocated by the social action approach.

An example of the social action approach is presented in the box "Case Example of the Social Action Model." Table 10.1 presents a summary of the three models that have been discussed—locality development, social planning, and social action.

■ BUILDING AND SUSTAINING COMMUNITY ASSETS

Many communities have major social problems, such as high levels of poverty, homeless people, divorce, child abuse, battered spouses, unemployment, deteriorated housing, cancer and other health problems, crime, alcoholism and other drug abuse, school drop outs, and births outside of marriage. If we focus on these deficiencies and problems in a community, we are using the half-empty glass approach. When we view the

---

■ Case Example of the Social Action Model

Saul Alinsky, a nationally noted social action strategist, provides an example of a creative social action effort. The example also shows that social action efforts are often enjoyable.

I was lecturing at a college run by a very conservative, almost fundamentalist Protestant denomination. Afterward some of the students came to my motel to talk to me. Their problem was that they couldn't have any fun on campus. They weren't permitted to dance or smoke or have a can of beer. I had been talking about the strategy of effecting change in a society and they wanted to know what tactics they could use to change their situation. I reminded them that a tactic is doing what you can with what you've got. "Now, what have you got?" I asked. "What do they permit you to do?"

"Practically nothing," they said, "except—you know—we can chew gum." I said, "Fine. Gum becomes the weapon. You get 200 or 300 students to get two packs of gum each, which is quite a wad. Then you have them drop it on the campus walks. This will cause absolute chaos. Why, with 500 wads of gum I could paralyze Chicago, stop all the traffic in the Loop." They looked at me as though I was some kind of nut. But about two weeks later I got an ecstatic letter saying, "It worked! It worked! Now we can do just about anything so long as we don't chew gum."

Source: Saul Alinsky, *Rules for Radicals* (New York: Random House, 1972), pp. 145–146.

■ **TABLE 10.1 Characteristics of Three Models of Community Planning**

Characteristic	Locality Development	Social Planning	Social Action
1. Goals	Self-help; improve community living; emphasis on process goals	Use problem-solving approach to resolve community problems; emphasis on task goals	Shifts power relationships and resources to an oppressed group; create basic institutional change; emphasize task and process goals
2. Assumptions concerning community	Everyone wants community living to improve and is willing to contribute to that improvement	Social problems in the community can be resolved through the efforts of planning experts	Community has a power structure and one or more oppressed groups, so social injustice is a major problem
3. Basic change strategy	Broad cross section of people involved in identifying and solving problems	Experts using fact-gathering and problem-solving approach	Members of oppressed groups organizing to take action against the power structure—i.e., the enemy
4. Characteristic change tactics and techniques	Consensus: communication among community groups and interests; group discussion	Consensus or conflict	Conflict or contest: confrontation, direct action, negotiation
5. Practitioner roles	Catalyst; facilitator; coordinator; teacher of problem-solving skills	Expert planner; fact gatherer; analyst; program developer; and implementor	Activist; advocate agitator; broker; negotiator; partisan
6. Views of power structure	Members of power structure are collaborators in a common venture	Power structure is employers and sponsors	Power structure is external target of action, oppressors to be coerced or overturned
7. Views of client population	Citizens	Consumers	Victims
8. Views of client role	Participant in a problem-solving process	Consumer or recipient	Employer or constituent

glass as half-empty, we focus on the negative aspects of life, and we are apt to become consumed with negativity and overcome with despair. Furthermore, if the focus is on problems and deficiencies, most members of that community will begin to despair. Despair becomes a self-fulfilling prophecy; members of the community will put little effort into developing themselves and little effort into developing the community.

Of critical importance, therefore, is to see the glass as half-full—that is, to focus on the positive elements in our life and the positive elements in the community in which we live. Perception is reality. What we believe to be true often becomes the center of our thoughts so much that it really becomes true. By viewing the glass as half-full, we see the depth of the human spirit and the richness of the creative potential that exists in every community. We identify people who are talented and experienced in a variety of areas. The rate of unemployment in some communities may be high; let's say it's 17 percent—which means 83 percent of able-bodied adults are employed! There are strong social networks and associations in every community. There are many successful people in every community. There are beautiful landscapes where nature can be enjoyed. There are people getting things done that need to be done by using what is available. In other words, a focus on strengths and assets leads to vitality and positive actions. Every citizen has capacities that can be tapped to make life in the community better.

Social work has had a long tradition of practice focused strengths and assets. For example, Dennis Saleeby and his colleagues at the University of Kansas School of Social Welfare have spent much of the last two decades developing, testing, and promoting a strengths perspective for social work practice.[29] The strengths perspective provides an

Case Example of an Asset Approach: Cochran Gardens*

Cochran Gardens was once a low-income housing project typical of many deteriorating housing projects in large urban areas. It was filled with rubbish, graffiti, and broken windows, and its residents were plagued by frequent shootings, crime, and drug trafficking.

Bertha Gilkey grew up in this housing project. Had it not been for her, this neighborhood might have continued to deteriorate. As a youngster, Gilkey believed the neighborhood could improve if residents worked together. As a teenager, she attended tenant meetings in a neighborhood church. When she was 20 years old, she was elected to chair this tenants' association. The neighborhood has since undergone gradual, yet dramatically positive, changes.

Gilkey and her group started with small projects. They asked tenants what realistically achievable things they really wanted. There was a consensus that the housing project needed a usable laundry room. The project's previous laundry rooms had all been vandalized, and the only working laundry room in the project had no locks. In fact, the entry door had been stolen. Bertha and her group requested and received a door from the city housing authority. The organization then held a successful fund-raiser for a lock. Next the group held a fund-raiser for paint, and that too was a success. The organization then painted the laundry room. The residents were pleased to have an attractive, working facility, and its presence increased their interest in joining and supporting the tenants' association. The group then organized to paint the hallways, floor by floor, of the housing project. Everyone who lived on a floor was responsible for being involved in painting their hallway. Gilkey states:

> Kids who lived on the floor that hadn't been painted would come and look at the painted hallways and then go back and hassle their parents. The elderly who couldn't paint prepared lunch, so they could feel like they were a part of it too.[a]

The organization continued to initiate and successfully complete new projects to spruce up the neighborhood. Each success inspired more and more residents to take pride in their neighborhood and to work toward making improvements. In the process, Gilkey and the tenants' organization also reintroduced a conduct code for the project. A committee formulated rules of behavior and elected monitors on each floor. The rules specified no loud disruptions, no throwing garbage out of the windows, and no fights. Slowly, residents got the message, and living conditions improved, one small step at a time.

The building was renamed Dr. Martin Luther King, Jr., Building. (Symbols are important in community development efforts.) The organization also held a party and a celebration for each successfully completed project.

Another focus of Gilkey's efforts was to reach out to children and adolescents. Positive behaviors were highlighted. The young people wrote papers in school on "what I like about living here." In art class, they built a cardboard model of the housing project that included the buildings, streets, and playground. These efforts were designed to build the self-esteem of the young people and to instill a sense of pride in their community.

Today Cochran Gardens is a public housing project with flower-lined paths, trees, and grass—a beautiful and clean neighborhood filled with trusting people who have a sense of pride in their community. The high-rise buildings have been completely renovated. There is a community center, and there are tennis courts, playgrounds, and townhouse apartments to reduce density in the complex. Cochran Gardens is managed by the tenants. The association (now named Tenant Management Council) has ventured into owning and operating certain businesses: a catering service, day-care centers, health clinics, and a vocational training program.

The Cochran Gardens success story has been based on the principles of self-help, the strengths perspective, empowerment, responsibility, and dignity. Gilkey states:

> This goes against the grain, doesn't it? Poor people are to be managed. What we've done is cut through all the bullshit and said it doesn't take all that. People with degrees and credentials got us in this mess. All it takes is some basic skills. . . . if we can do it in public housing, it can happen anywhere.[b]

---

*This case example was adapted from *Introduction to Social Work and Social Welfare*, 8th ed., by Zastrow. © 2004. Reprinted with permission of Brooks/Cole, a division of Thomson Learning, Inc.

[a] Quoted in Harry C. Boyte, "People Power Transforms a St. Louis Housing Project." *Occasional Papers* (Chicago: Community Renewable Society, Jan. 1989), p. 5.
[b] Ibid.

Sources: Harry C. Boyte, "People Power Transforms a St. Louis Housing Project," *Occasional Papers* (Chicago: Community Renewable Society, Jan 1989), pp. 1–5; "The New Urban Renewal: St. Louis, Missouri," available at www.pbs.org/newurban/stlouis.html (accessed Feb. 10, 2003).

---

orientation to practice that seeks to uncover and reaffirm people's talents, abilities, survivor skills, and aspirations. A focus on the strengths found in individuals, families, groups, and communities increases the likelihood that people will reach the goals they set for themselves. An asset approach is illustrated in the box "Case Example of an Asset Approach: Cochran Gardens."

■ GROUP EXERCISES

Exercise A: Analyzing a Human Services Organization

GOAL: This exercise is designed to give students a framework for analyzing organizations.

Step 1. The leader divides the class into subgroups of five or six students. Each subgroup has to select a human services agency to analyze. (Each subgroup should select a different agency.) Each subgroup will gather information through interviews at its agency and then give a report at a future class session covering the following questions:

1.   What is the agency's mission statement?
2.   What are its clients' major problems?
3.   What services does the agency provide?
4.   How are client needs determined?
5.   What percentage of clients are people of color, women, gays or lesbians, elderly, or members of other at-risk populations?
6.   What was the total cost of services for the past year?
7.   How much money is spent on each program?
8.   What are the agency's funding sources?
9.   How much and what percentage of funds are received from each source?
10. What eligibility criteria must prospective clients meet before services will be provided?
11. What other agencies provide the same services in the community?
12. What is the organizational structure of the agency? For example, is there a formal chain of command?
13. Is there an informal organization (that is, people who exert a greater amount of influence on decision making than would be expected for their formal position in the bureaucracy)?
14. How much decision-making input do the direct service providers have on major policy decisions?
15. Does the agency have a board that oversees its operations? If yes, what are the backgrounds of the board members?
16. Do employees at every level feel valued?
17. What is the morale among employees?
18. What are the major unmet needs of the agency?
19. Does the agency have a handbook of personnel policies and procedures?
20. What is the public image of the agency in the community?
21. In recent years what has been the rate of turnover among staff at the agency? What were the major reasons for leaving?
22. Does the agency have a process for evaluating the outcomes of its services? If yes, what is the process, and what are the outcome results?
23. What is the subgroup's overall impression of the agency? For example, if members of the subgroup needed services that this agency provides, would they want to apply at this agency? Why, or why not?

Exercise B: Understanding and Applying Models of Organizations

GOAL: This exercise is designed to increase students' knowledge of organizational models and to teach them how to apply the models.

Step 1. The leader should summarize the models of organizations described in this chapter: the autocratic model, the custodial model, the scientific management model, the human relations model, Theory X, Theory Y, the collegial model, Theory Z, management by objectives, and total quality management. (As an alternative, assign the students to read this material in the text.)

Step 2. Ask the students to form subgroups of about five members. Ask each subgroup to decide which models are currently most applicable to describing organizational behavior within the organization of social work faculty in the program. (If the number of social work faculty members is very small, the class may instead be asked to decide which models are currently most applicable to describing the organizational behavior of the departmental faculty of which the social work program is a component.)

Step 3. Have the members of each subgroup state their views on which models are most applicable and the reasons for their decisions. Seek to have a class discussion among the subgroups, because there are apt to be differences of opinion.

Exercise C: Theory X and Theory Y

GOAL: To become more aware of Theory X and Theory Y styles of management.

Step 1. The leader explains the purpose of this exercise and describes both theories of management, providing personal examples of employment under a manager who used one or the other style.

Step 2. Class members describe examples of their own employment held under these styles of management and then discuss their feelings about working under each system.

Step 3. Since Theory Y is apparently superior to Theory X in motivating employees to be creative and productive, students should discuss why Theory X is used by so many managers.

Exercise D: Appreciating Communities

GOAL: To have a greater appreciation of communities.

Step 1. The leader explains that at the next class session each student will be asked to briefly describe a community that she or he has lived in or visited. Each student should focus on the unique aspects of this community, as well as the positive aspects of this community. The leader may give an example of what is desired by describing a community.

Step 2. At the next class session, each student takes a turn in briefly describing his or her selected community.

Step 3. The leader may choose to end the exercise by summarizing positive aspects about the communities that the students described.

Exercise E: Analyzing a Community

GOAL: This exercise is designed to instruct students in understanding and analyzing communities.

Step 1. The leader begins by defining the term *community*. Subgroups of three or four students are then formed. Each subgroup selects a different community to analyze.

Step 2. Using the framework presented in this chapter in the section entitled "Analyzing a Community" (or some other framework chosen by the subgroup), each subgroup gathers information on the community it selected. At future class sessions, each subgroup makes a presentation to the class on its selected community.

Exercise F: Analyzing Community Change

GOAL: This exercise is designed to have students learn how to analyze community change efforts.

Step 1. The leader should describe the three models of community change developed by Rothman and Tropman. These models are locality development, social planning, and social action. In addition to describing these approaches, the leader should instruct the students to read the related material in this chapter.

Step 2. Have the class form subgroups of about three students each. Each subgroup should select a different community change or community planning effort to report on to the class. An example of a planning effort is a project by the social work student organization to plan an educational conference or workshop on a topic such as AIDS. Another example is the efforts of a community group to establish a homeless shelter.

Step 3. Each subgroup should gather information to answer the following questions about its selected community change effort. One way to gather the information is for the subgroup to interview the planners. In future class sessions each subgroup should give a presentation to the class on its selected planning effort.

QUESTIONS

1. What are the goals of the planning effort? How many planners are involved? Who are the planners, and what are their planning credentials? Why is this planning effort being undertaken?
2. Which of the three community change models is this planning group primarily using? What characteristics of this model (see Table 10.1) are being displayed by the planners? Does this planning effort have any characteristics of these other two models? If "yes," what characteristics of the other two models are being displayed?
3. What are the results of this planning effort—that is, to what extent are the goals being accomplished? What are the strengths and shortcomings of this planning effort?

CHAPTER ELEVEN

Educational Groups: Stress Management and Time Management as Examples

GOALS

Educational groups led by social workers are an important component of social work with groups. This chapter illustrates material in this area by highlighting material on stress management and time management.

Stress is considered to be a contributing factor or cause of most physical illnesses and many emotional and behavioral problems. This chapter presents material on the nature, causes, and effects of stress and describes burn-out as one of the reactions to stress. A variety of ways to manage stress and prevent burn-out are included. Time is the most valuable commodity we have. It cannot be renewed, recycled, or otherwise recovered. This chapter describes the principles of time management, presents time-saver tips, and summarizes suggestions for overcoming procrastination.

■ EDUCATIONAL GROUPS

Educational groups usually have a classroom atmosphere, involving considerable group interaction and discussion; a professional person with expertise in the area, often a social worker, assumes the role of teacher. While the topics covered vary widely, all education groups teach specialized skills and knowledge such as classes on child-rearing, stress management, parenting, English as a foreign language, and assertiveness training. Orientations offered by social service organizations to train volunteers fall into this category as well.

This chapter will illustrate material on educational groups by highlighting two types of educational groups: stress management and time management.

Stress Management

It is essential that students, social workers, and other helping professionals learn to manage stress in themselves and to help their clients manage stress. Stress is a contributing factor in a wide variety of *emotional and behavioral problems,* including anxiety, child abuse, spouse abuse, temper tantrums, feelings of inadequacy, physical assaults, explosive expressions of anger, feelings of hostility, impatience, stuttering, suicide attempts, and depression.[1]

Stress is also a contributing factor in most physical illnesses. These illnesses include hypertension, heart attacks, migraine and tension headaches, colitis, ulcers, diarrhea, constipation, arrhythmia, angina, diabetes, hay fever, backaches, arthritis, cancer, colds, flu, insomnia, hyperthyroidism, dermatitis, emphysema, Raynaud's disease, alcoholism, bronchitis, infections, allergies, and enuresis. Stress-related disorders have now been recognized as our number-one health problem.[2]

Becoming skillful at relaxation is important in treating and facilitating recovery from both emotional and physical disorders. The therapeutic value of learning to manage stress has been dramatically demonstrated by Simonton and Simonton, who have reported success in treating terminal cancer patients by instructing them on stress management.[3] People who have AIDS tend to live longer if they utilize stress management techniques.[4]

In fact, the increased recognition of the importance of stress management in treating physical and emotional disorders is gradually altering the traditional physician-patient relationship. Instead of being passive participants in treatment, patients are increasingly being taught (by social workers and other health professionals) how to prevent illness and how to speed up recovery by learning stress management strategies. People who are successful in managing stress have a life expectancy several years longer than those who are continually at high stress levels.[5] Moreover, effective stress management is a major factor that enables people to live fulfilling, healthy, satisfying, and productive lives.[6]

■ CONCEPTUALIZING STRESS

Stress can be defined as the physiological and emotional reactions to stressors. A *stressor* is a demand, situation, or circumstance that disrupts a person's equilibrium (internal balance) and initiates the stress response. Every moment people are alive their bodies are responding to stressors that call for adaptation or adjustment. Their bodily reactions are continually striving for *homeostasis,* or balance. There are an infinite variety of possible stressors: loss of a job, loud noise, toxic substances, value conflicts, arguments, death of a friend, getting engaged, getting married, heat, cold, pollutants, serious illness, moving away from home, or lack of purpose in life.

Reactions to Stress

Hans Selye, one of the foremost authorities on stress, found that a person's body reacts to stressors in the same way regardless of the source of stress.[7] This means an individual's body reacts to positive stressors (e.g., a romantic kiss) in the same way it reacts to negative stressors (e.g., an electric shock).

Selye found a three-stage physical reaction to stress—an alarm phase, a resistance phase, and an exhaustion phase.[8] Selye called this three-phase response the General Adaptation Syndrome.

In the *alarm phase* the body recognizes the stressor and responds by preparing for fight or flight. The body's reactions are numerous and complex, and will be only briefly summarized here.[9] The hypothalamus (located in the brain) sends a message to the pituitary gland to release its hormones. These hormones trigger the adrenal glands to release adrenaline. The release of adrenaline and other hormones results in the following physical reactions:

1. Increased breathing and heartbeat rates
2. A rise in blood pressure
3. Increased coagulation of blood, which minimizes potential loss of blood in case of physical injury
4. Diversion of blood from the skin to the brain, the heart, and contracting muscles
5. A rise in serum cholesterol and blood fat

6. Decreased mobility of the gastrointestinal tract
7. Dilated pupils

These changes result in a huge burst of energy, improved vision and hearing, and increased muscular strength—all changes that increase a person's capacity to fight or to flee. A major problem of the fight-or-flight reaction is that a threat cannot always be dealt with by fighting or fleeing. In our complex civilized society, fighting or fleeing generally violates sophisticated codes of acceptable behavior. The fight-or-flight response, appropriate and functional for humans in primitive societies who often had only these two courses of action when attacked by animals or other humans, is now seldom needed.

Exercise 11.1: My Physiological Reactions to High Levels of Stress

GOAL: This exercise is designed to assist you in recognizing how you physiologically react to high levels of stress.

1. **Specify two events that were very stressful to you—where you physiologically were in the alarm phase—in the past week.**

2. **What physiological reactions do you remember having? Review the preceding material on reactions to stress, then specify the physiological reactions that you remember having.**

In the *resistance phase,* bodily processes attempt to return to homeostasis, and the body tries to repair any damage caused by the stressors. In handling most stressors, the body generally goes through only the two phases of alarm and repair. During a lifetime these two phases are repeated thousands of times.

The third phase of *exhaustion* occurs only when the body remains in a state of high stress for an extended period of time and is unable to repair damage. If exhaustion continues, a stress-related illness, such as high blood pressure, ulcers, or migraine headaches, may develop.

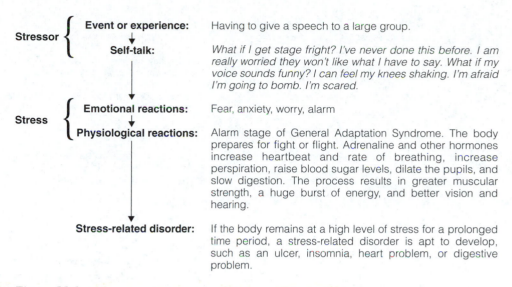

Figure 11.1
A model of stress response

Exercise 11.2: My Stress-Related Illnesses

GOAL: This exercise is designed to highlight the importance of learning and using stress management techniques.

1. Specify the stress-related illnesses that you have experienced. Also indicate (as best you can) the starting and ending times for these illnesses.

2. Rate the importance (1–5) for you of learning and using stress management strategies:

_____	_____	_____	_____	_____
Not important	Somewhat important	Fairly important	Very important	Absolutely essential

Stressors

A stressor has two components: (1) the experience or event encountered, and (2) our self-talk about the event.[10] Figure 11.1 presents a model of a stress response indicating both a sequence of events and reactions as they occur.

The following example shows how a person's thinking can turn a potentially positive event into a source of negative stress.

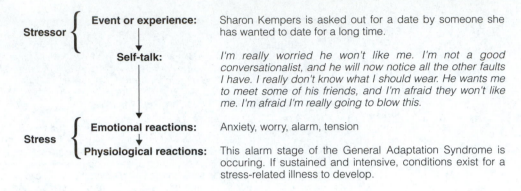

The model in Figure 11.1 suggests two broad approaches for reducing stress: (1) either change the distressing event, or (2) change the self-talk about the event. (These two approaches will be discussed at greater length in a later section.)

It should certainly be noted that not all stress is bad. Life without it would be boring. Selye indicates that stress is often "the spice of life" and that it is impossible to live without experiencing stress.[11] Even dreaming produces stress. At times stress is beneficial because it stimulates and prepares individuals to perform tasks.

Optimal Levels of Stress

Virtually every task or activity requires some response from the alarm stage of the General Adaptation Syndrome, and for each task there is an optimal level of response. Students, for example, sometimes find that they need to be under moderate stress to study effectively for an exam. At too low a level of alarm stage response, they may have trouble concentrating and may even fall asleep. At too high a level of alarm stage response, they become anxious—which also interferes with concentration. Maximum levels of alarm stage response are needed only during emergencies when great physical strength is required—for example, when a heavy object has fallen on someone. At the opposite extreme, falling asleep requires relaxation—that is, an almost-zero level of

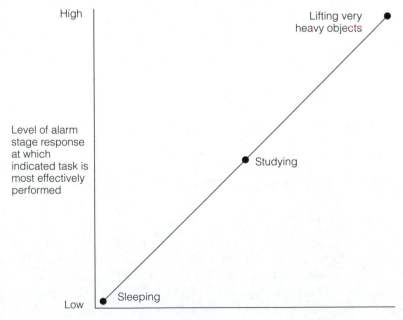

Figure 11.2
Levels of alarm stage response and efficiency in performing tasks

alarm stage response. People who suffer from insomnia are not relaxed. They are still thinking about things which generate a moderate level of alarm stage response and keep them from dozing off. For a graphic illustration of this concept, see Figure 11.2.

Grasping this concept is important because self-talk can be altered and thereby increase or decrease levels of alarm stage response in order to bring it to an optimal level.

■ LONG-TERM DISTRESS

Selye calls harmful stress "distress."[12] Long-term distress generally results in a stress-related physical illness. Distress occurs when the stressors are prolonged so that a person enters the exhaustion phase of the General Adaptation Syndrome. There are a number of signals, presented in Table 11.1, that we can use to measure our level of stress. Most of us use the signals identified in Table 11.1 to judge whether our friends are under too much stress. But most of us fail to use these same signals to determine when

■ TABLE 11.1 Indicators of Stress Level

Positive Level	Level Too High
1. Behaviors	
Creative, making good decisions	High-pitched nervous laughter
Friendly	Not creative
Generally successful	Poor work quality
Able to listen to others	Overdrink or overeat
Productive, getting a lot done	Smoke to excess
Appreciate others, sensitive to others, and	Stutter
recognize contributions of others	Unable to concentrate
Smile, laugh, joke	Easily startled by small noises
	Impatient
	Let little things bother you
	Unpleasant to be around
	Put others down, irritable
	Engage in wasteful activity
2. Feelings	
Confident	Resentful, bitter, dissatisfied, angry
Calm, relaxed	Timid, tense, anxious, fearful
Pleasure and enjoyment	Paranoid
Excitement and exhilaration	Weary, depressed, fed up
	Feeling inadequate
	Confused, swamped, overwhelmed
	Feeling powerless or helpless
3. Body Signals	
Able to sleep well	Loss of appetite, diarrhea, or vomiting
Absence of aches and pains	Accident proneness
Coordinated body reactions	Sweating, frequent need to urinate
Unselfconsciousness about body functioning	Trembling, nervous tics
In good health, stress-related illnesses absent	Feeling dizzy or weak
	Frequent colds and flu
	High blood pressure
	Tight or tense muscles
	Asthma or breathing irregularities
	Skin irritations, itches, and rashes
	Problems sleeping
	Upset stomach or ulcers
	Various aches and pains—muscle aches, backaches, neck aches, and headaches

Note: You have to use your own judgment based on these signals to determine whether a stress level is too high.

our own stress level is too high. For our emotional and physical health, we need to give more attention to monitoring these signals in ourselves.

Long-term distress occurs when we continue to think negatively about events that have happened to us. When unpleasant events occur, we always have a choice to react negatively or positively. If we continue to think negatively about the situation, our thinking keeps our body under a high level of stress—which can then lead to a stress-related illness. On the other hand, if we think positively about the situation, our thinking enables the body to relax and repair any damage that was done. In addition, when we are relaxed, our natural immune system is much more effective in combating potential illnesses. There is substantial evidence that our self-talk (that is, our thinking process) has immense interaction with the functioning of our immune system. Our self-talk can function as both a slayer and a healer. If we *awfulize* (that is, think negative thoughts), we set off the alarm stage of the General Adaptation Syndrome. When we are in the alarm stage, our immune systems are depressed and do not function well. As a result, we are more susceptible to infections and diseases. On the other hand, when we think positive and relaxing thoughts, our bodies are in the resistance stage of the General Adaptation Syndrome. As a result, our immune systems are functioning at their optimal level and can fight off diseases and infections and assist in repairing any damage caused when our bodies were in the alarm stage.

Earlier it was indicated that our bodies react to positive stressors the same way they react to negative stressors. The reason negative stressors are much more likely to result in stress-related disorders is that we tend to stop thinking intensely about positive stressors (such as a romantic kiss) within a few hours after they occur, while we tend to intensify and dwell on negative stressors for several hours (or even days) after they occur. By thinking intensely about negative stressors, we keep our bodies under a moderate or high level of stress.

Exercise 11.3: Events and Self-Talk as Stressors

GOAL: This exercise is designed to assist you in recognizing current stressors and in realizing that stressors consist of distressing events and self-talk associated with those events.

1. Specify the events that are currently stressors in your life.

2. For each stressful event, specify your self-talk associated with the event. (The self-talk may intensify, or decrease, your overall feeling of being under stress.)

3. Which form of a stressor (the event or the associated self-talk) do you believe is the major contributor to the level of stress that you experience? Explain your views on this issue.

■ BURN-OUT

Burn-out is increasingly recognized as a serious problem affecting many people, particularly professionals employed in human services. Several books have been published on this subject.[13] Maslach and Pines have conducted extensive studies of burn-out among social workers, psychiatrists, psychologists, prison personnel, psychiatric nurses, legal-aid attorneys, physicians, child-care workers, teachers, ministers, and counselors, and have summarized a number of symptoms:

> Burn-out involves the loss of concern for the people with whom one is working. In addition to physical exhaustion (and sometimes even illness), burn-out is characterized by an emotional exhaustion in which the professional no longer has any positive feelings, sympathy, or respect for clients or patients. A very cynical and dehumanizing perception of these people often develops, in which they are labeled in derogatory ways and treated accordingly. As a result of this dehumanizing process, these people are viewed as somehow deserving of their problems and are blamed for their own victimization and thus there is a deterioration in the quality of care or service that they receive. The professional who burns out is unable to deal successfully with the overwhelming emotional stresses of the job, and this failure to cope can be manifested in a number of ways, ranging from impaired performance and absenteeism to various types of personal problems (such as alcohol and drug abuse, marital conflict, and mental illness). People who burn out often quit their jobs or even change professions, while some seek psychiatric treatment for what they believe to be their personal failings.[14]

Freudenberger describes the symptoms of burn-out as follows:

> Briefly described, burn-out includes such symptoms as cynicism and negativism and a tendency to be inflexible and almost rigid in thinking, which often leads to a closed mind about change or innovation. The worker may begin to discuss the client in intellectual and jargon terms and thereby distance himself from any emotional involvement. Along with this, a form of paranoia may set in whereby the worker feels that his peers and administration are out to make life more difficult.
>
> Another sign is that the worker takes on a superior "know-it-all" attitude that borders on the condescending. He hardly communicates with others and tends to become a loner or withdrawn. On the other hand, he may go to the other extreme and hardly do any work because he is socializing most of the time. Other workers experiencing burn-out may begin to limit their contact with their clients. They begin to speak of being bored with the work. . . . All is becoming too routine. They may also begin to verbalize a sense of helplessness as well as hopelessness about the clients and begin to speak of them in derogatory or flip terms.[15]

The term *burn-out* has been applied to many different situations. A student who has been writing a term paper for three hours may feel burned out with writing but have plenty of energy to do something else. Some people who abuse their spouses or children may attempt to explain their actions by claiming they are under considerable stress and just burned out. Apathetic and cynical workers dealing with a frustrating job may claim they are burned out, and even some college and professional sports coaches claim the pressure to win is so intense that after several seasons they feel burned out.

Exercise 11.4: A Time When I Burned Out

GOAL: This exercise is designed to demonstrate that we all burn out, and it also helps us recognize what we can do when we experience burn-out.

1. **Describe a time in your life when you experienced burn-out. When you were experiencing burn-out, did you conclude (for awhile)—"I just can't take this anymore"?**

2. **If you have recovered from feeling burned out, describe what helped you to recover. If you are still feeling a sense of being burned out, speculate about what you need to do to make progress in recovering.**

Structural Causes of Burn-Out

In order to understand the nature of burn-out, it is useful to conceptualize it as one of several possible reactions to continuing high levels of stress. As suggested in Figure 11.3, burn-out is caused *not only* by experiences that people encounter but by what people tell themselves about these experiences. Examples of this kind of thinking are "I've had it"; "What's the use? Whatever I try won't work"; "I'm going to give up—I'm no longer going to make an effort." Other people encountering the same events will not burn out if they do not have such self-defeating thoughts.

As indicated in Figure 11.4, events, or structural factors, are one of the causes of high stress levels and burn-out. Edelwich has identified a number of these structural factors associated with work:[16]

too many work hours	not enough money
too much paperwork	no support for important decisions
not sufficiently trained for job	powerlessness
not appreciated by clients	destructive office politics
not appreciated by supervisor	isolation from peers

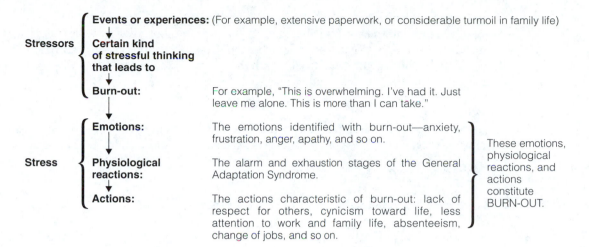

Figure 11.3
Burn-out as a reaction to high stress level

The Helping Professions

Edelwich adds that people who seek a career in the helping professions are particularly vulnerable to burn-out, as many enter this field with unrealistic expectations. Such expectations include the beliefs that (1) the services they provide will decisively improve the lives of their clients, (2) they will be highly appreciated by the employing agency and clients, (3) they will be able to substantially change bureaucracies to be more responsive to clients' needs, and (4) there will be many opportunities for rapid advancement and high status. In addition, Maslach has found that high case loads in the helping professions are a major cause of stress and may lead to burn-out:

> Burn-out often becomes inevitable when the professional is forced to provide care for too many people. As the ratio increases, the result is higher and higher emotional overload until, like a wire that has too much electricity flowing through it, the worker just burns out and emotionally disconnects.[17]

The frustrations experienced at work and the gradual recognition that many expectations are unrealistic contribute to stress and burn-out.

Lack of Time Out

A lack of approved "time out" at work is another source of stress and may be a factor leading to burn-out. Time out does not merely involve short coffee breaks but also opportunities for professionals to switch to less stressful tasks when they are having a difficult day. Break periods are possible in large agencies that have shared work responsibilities. Maslach notes:

> When institutional policies prevented the use of voluntary time-outs, we found lower staff morale, greater emotional stress and the inevitable consequence of more dissatisfied citizens, frustrated at not getting the care they needed.[18]

Clients

Certain types of clients are more apt to cause high levels of stress, particularly those whose problems are depressing or emotionally draining (such as terminally ill, belligerent, suicidal, and obnoxious clients, as well as incest and severe abuse cases).[19] Working with "chronic" clients who show no improvement (such as an alcoholic family in which the problem drinker denies a drinking problem) also may lead to frustration and high stress levels. Dealing with clients who remind the worker of current personal difficulties—for example, providing marriage counseling services when the worker is also having marital difficulties—is emotionally draining.

Personal Difficulties

Another important factor contributing to high stress and burn-out at work is personal difficulties at home. Home responsibilities (for example, caring for a terminally ill parent, a child who is getting into trouble with the police, or dealing with an unhappy marriage) are stressful and may lead to burn-out.

Other Causes

Additional causes include poor time management, inability to work effectively with other people, lack of purpose or undefined goals in life, and inability to handle emergencies effectively.[20]

■ MANAGING STRESS AND PREVENTING BURN-OUT

The following approaches have been useful for helping group members reduce stress and prevent burn-out. It is up to each individual to select the ones that will be most helpful. Managing stress is similar to dieting: It will work for those who put forth the effort. (For further reading on these approaches, see the notes for this chapter.)

Goal Setting and Time Management

Stress and burn-out can come from the feeling of "too much to do and too little time in which to do it." Often, this feeling is due to not having clear short-term and lifetime goals and not knowing how to manage time effectively to achieve them. Realistic goals and a plan for achieving them lead to increased self-confidence, improved decision making, a greater sense of purpose, and an improved sense of security.

One technique for stress management is to help group members define short-term and lifetime goals and teach them how to prioritize the tasks necessary to achieve them.[21] High-priority tasks should be accomplished first, and low-priority (low-payoff) tasks should generally be ignored because they can interfere with the accomplishment of high-priority tasks. (Time management is more fully discussed later in this chapter.)

Relaxation

Deep-breathing relaxation, imagery relaxation, progressive muscle relaxation, meditation, and biofeedback are effective techniques for reducing stress and inducing the "relaxation response" (becoming relaxed).[22] Each of these techniques is facilitated by sitting in a comfortable position in a quiet place and closing one's eyes.

Deep-breathing relaxation involves stopping thoughts about day-to-day concerns and concentrating on breathing processes. For 5 to 10 minutes, a group member may slowly and gradually inhale deeply and exhale, while thinking something like "I am relaxing, breathing smoother. This is soothing, and I'm feeling calmer, renewed, and refreshed." *Continued practice* of this technique will enable a person to become more relaxed when confronting a tense situation.

By using *imagery relaxation,* a group member can switch his or her thinking from daily concerns to focusing on an ideal relaxation place for 10 to 15 minutes. This ideal setting might include lying on a beach by a scenic lake in the warm sun or relaxing in warm water in a bathtub while reading a magazine. The group member should savor all the pleasantness, the peacefulness, focusing on everything that he or she finds calming, soothing, and relaxing. The member will sense his or her whole body becoming refreshed, revived, and rejuvenated.

Progressive muscle relaxation is based on the principle that a person whose muscles are relaxed cannot be anxious.[23] The group leader instructs members to tighten and then relax a set of muscles. As they relax their muscles, they are asked to concentrate on the relaxed feeling while noting that the muscles are becoming less tense. The following is an excerpt of the first part of rather lengthy instructions to a group for progressive muscle relaxation:

Make a fist with your dominant hand (usually right). Make a fist and tense the muscles of your (right) hand and forearm; tense it until it trembles. Feel the muscles pull across your fingers and the lower part of your forearm. . . . Hold this position for five to seven seconds, then . . . relax. . . . Just let your hand go. Pay attention to the muscles of your (right) hand and forearm as they relax. Note how these muscles feel as relaxation flows through (twenty to thirty seconds).[24]

The procedure of tensing and then relaxing the hand and forearm is repeated three or four times until they are relaxed. Next, other muscle groups are tensed and relaxed in the same manner, one group at a time. In succession, the muscle groups might include: left hand and forearm, right biceps, left biceps, forehead muscles, upper lip and cheek muscles, jaw muscles, chin and throat muscles, chest muscles, abdominal muscles, back muscles between shoulder blades, right and left upper leg muscles, right and left calf muscles, and toes and arches of the feet. With practice, a group member can gradually develop the capacity to relax whenever anxious simply by visualizing the muscles relaxing.

There are a variety of *meditative approaches*—imagery relaxation and deep breathing relaxation are two examples. Benson has identified four basic components in meditative approaches that induce the relaxation response.[25] These components are (1) being in a quiet environment free from external distractions, (2) being in a comfortable position, (3) having an object to dwell on, such as a word, sound, chant, phrase, or imagery of a painting,[26] and (4) assuming a passive attitude and not thinking about day-to-day concerns. This last component Benson asserts is the key element in inducing the relaxation response.

Biofeedback equipment provides mechanical feedback to a person about his or her level of stress. This equipment can inform people about levels of stress they are usually unaware of—until a markedly higher level is reached. For example, a person's hand temperature may vary 10 to 12 degrees in an hour's time, with an increase in temperature indicating increasing calm and relaxation. With biofeedback equipment, numerous physical conditions can be measured and fed back, such as blood pressure, hand temperature, muscle tension, heartbeat rate, and brain waves. With biofeedback training, a client is first instructed in using the equipment to recognize high levels of anxiety or tenseness. Then, he or she is instructed on how to reduce such high levels either by closing the eyes and adopting a passive, "letting go" attitude or by thinking about something pleasant and calming. Often relaxation approaches are combined with biofeedback to elicit the relaxation response.

Exercise

Stress prepares our body to move or become involved in large-muscle activity (including fight or flight). Large-muscle activity refers to the kinds of exercise involving many muscle groups at the same time, such as jumping rope. Through exercise, a group member can use up fuel in the blood, reduce his or her blood pressure and heart rate, and reverse the other physiological changes set off during the alarm stage of the General Adaptation Syndrome. Exercising helps a person keep physically fit and have more physical strength to handle crises. It also reduces stress and relieves tension. For these reasons group members should be encouraged to have a daily exercise program. A key to adhering to a daily exercise schedule is to select an enjoyable program. Many activities are available: walking, stretching, jogging, isometric exercises, jumping rope, swimming, playing tennis, dancing, housework, sex, gardening, or golf.

Taking Care of Your Physical Self

In addition to exercising, it is important to have a nourishing diet, to take appropriate care of oneself, and to get enough sleep. Not only does a nourishing diet help keep people fit to resist stress but research shows there are direct links between what individuals eat and how they feel emotionally. Some foods (such as coffee) produce tension, while overeating causes individuals to feel drowsy and even ill. Staying slim and trim helps a person feel good about himself or herself. Appropriate medical care also is a way to strengthen weak physical links that are vulnerable to stress-related illnesses.

Social Support Groups

Everyone needs to feel close to others. Support groups allow people to share their lives, have fun with others, and let their hair down. These groups are also a resource for help when emergencies and crises arise. There are a variety of possible support groups that center on coworkers, a hobby or sports, a service (such as Rotary), a family, an extended family, a church, a community organization, a social club (such as Parents Without Partners), and so on. Essential characteristics of support groups are (1) the group meets regularly, (2) the same people attend, (3) there is an opportunity for spontaneity and informality, and (4) a feeling of closeness develops among members.[27]

Talking to Others

Every human needs someone with whom to share good times as well as personal difficulties. Sharing concerns with someone helps to vent emotions, and talking a concern through often generates constructive strategies for resolving it. A good listener is someone who conveys caring and understanding, keeps the information confidential, is empathic, helps explore the difficulty in depth, helps arrive at alternatives for resolving the difficulty, and encourages the person to select and try out a resolution strategy.

Positive Thinking

When anticipated and unanticipated events occur, people can choose to take either a positive or negative view of the situation. If they take a negative view, they are apt to experience more stress and alienate friends and acquaintances. If they take a positive view, they are likely to maintain their composure, stay relaxed, and cope with the situation quickly and easily, minimizing negative consequences. (This approach is described in the box "Positive Thinking.")

Akin to positive thinking is having a philosophy of life that allows you to take crises in stride and maintain a relaxed pace. When work is approached in a relaxed fashion, greater creativity is generated and stress is reduced. Leisure time should be enjoyed and used to develop oneself more fully as a person and to find enjoyment in each day.

When distressing events happen to you, it is psychologically therapeutic to view the event with the perspective of "Good luck? Bad luck? Who knows?" This perspective is indicated by the following story related by Anthony de Mello, S.J.:

> There is a Chinese story of an old farmer who had an old horse for tilling his fields. One day the horse escaped into the hills and when all the farmer's neighbors sympathized with the old man over his bad luck, the farmer replied, "Bad luck? Good luck? Who knows?" A week later the horse returned with a herd of wild horses from the hills and this time the neighbors congratulated the farmer on his good luck. His reply was, "Good luck? Bad luck? Who knows?" Then, when the farmer's son was attempting to tame one of the wild horses, he fell off its back and broke his leg. Everyone thought this very bad luck. Not the farmer, whose only reaction was, "Bad luck? Good luck? Who knows?" Some weeks later the army marched into the village and conscripted every able-bodied youth they found there. When they saw the farmer's son with his broken leg they let him off. Now was that good luck? Bad luck? Who knows?[28]

Changing Stress-Producing Thoughts

It is often erroneously believed that emotions, including feelings of tenseness and anxiety, are primarily determined by experiences—that is, by events that occur. However, cognitive therapies have shown the primary source of a person's emotions to be what she tells herself about her experiences.[29] An example will help clarify this important concept:

Positive Thinking

Give a smile to everyone you meet (smile with your eyes)—and you'll smile and receive smiles. . . .

Give a kind word (with a kindly thought behind the word)—you will be kind and receive kind words. . . .

Give appreciation (warmth from the heart)—you will appreciate and be appreciated. . . .

Give honor, credit, and applause (the victor's wreath)—you will be honorable and receive credit and applause. . . .

Give time for a worthy cause (with eagerness)—you will be worthy and richly rewarded. . . .

Give hope (the magic ingredient for success)—you will have hope and be made hopeful. . . .

Give happiness (a most treasured state of mind)—you will be happy and be made happy. . . .

Give cheer (the verbal sunshine)—you'll be cheerful and cheered. . . .

Give encouragement (the incentive to action)—you will have courage and be encouraged. . . .

Give a pleasant response (the neutralizer of irritants)—you will be pleasant and receive pleasant responses. . . .

Give good thoughts (nature's character builder)—you will be good and the world will have good thoughts for you. . . .

Source: W. Clement Stone, "Be Generous," in *A Treasury of Success Unlimited,* edited by Og Mandino (New York: Hawthorne Books, 1966), pp. 9–10.

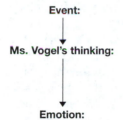

Event: Vicki Vogel is promoted to unit supervisor at a large insurance company.

Ms. Vogel's thinking: *This promotion will make others jealous and lead to conflict with the people with whom I work. I don't believe I'm prepared to handle these new responsibilities. If I fail, I'll be demoted and will be a failure. My career will end.*

Emotion: Worry, alarm, tension, anxiety.

On the other hand, if Ms. Vogel tells herself something else, her emotions will be quite different.

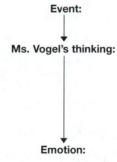

Event: Vicki Vogel is promoted to unit supervisor at a large insurance company.

Ms. Vogel's thinking: *This is really great that the company is recognizing the skills I have. I've been working here for six-and-a-half years and thoroughly know how to do the work in this unit. Supervising people will be a challenge, but I've supervised people before in some of the church's projects I've headed up. This kind of challenge will help me grow in my career and as a person. I have a number of ideas I want to try here to improve what we do.*

Emotion: Excitement, a feeling of self-worth, mild anxiety accompanied by self-confidence.

This example illustrates two important concepts. First, a person's thoughts primarily determine his or her emotions. Second, by challenging and changing negative and irrational thinking, individuals can eliminate an unwanted emotion. Frequently, events cannot be changed, but individuals have the power to view such events rationally and positively, and to control, to a large degree, their emotions.[30] (See Appendix 1: Module 1 for a fuller discussion.)

Changing or Adapting to Distressing Events

There are an infinite number of distressing events: the death of someone close, the breakup of a romantic relationship, being fired, having an unfulfilling job, failing some courses, getting into an argument, or having unresolved religious questions. When distressing events occur, group members should be encouraged to confront them directly to try to improve the situation. If a person is grieving because of the death of someone else, he or she might find it helpful to talk about it within the group or seek professional private counseling. Terminated or fired employees should find out the reasons they were dismissed so they can deal constructively with them and begin to seek another job. If a person has unresolved religious questions, group discussion followed by talking to a member of the clergy or taking a course on the philosophy of religion may help.

Most distressing events can be improved by confronting them head on and taking constructive action to change them. However, a number of events cannot be changed. Group members may not be able to change the irritating habits of others. If a situation cannot be changed, the only constructive alternative is to accept it. It is counter-productive to nag, complain, and become upset. Acceptance of things that cannot be changed will leave an individual more relaxed and calm.

Personal Pleasures

Personal pleasures relieve stress, provide a change of pace, are enjoyable, make us feel good, and are (in reality) personal "therapies." What is pleasurable to one person may not be to another. Common pleasures are being hugged, listening to music, going shopping, taking a hot bath, going to a movie, having a glass of wine, family and religious get-togethers, taking a vacation, singing, and so on. Such "treats" remind individuals that they have worth; they also add spice to life.

Enjoyable activities beyond work and family responsibilities are also pleasures that relieve stress. Research has found that "stress reduces stress"; that is, an appropriate level of stressful activities in one area helps reduce excessive stress in others.[31] Getting involved in enjoyable outside activities switches a person's negative thinking about his or her daily concerns to positive thoughts about the enjoyable activities. Therefore, it is stress reducing to become involved in enjoyable activities such as golf, tennis, swimming, scuba diving, taking flying lessons, traveling, and so on.

Personal pleasures can also be used as "payoffs" to ourselves for jobs well done. Most of us would not shortchange others for doing well; we ought not to short-change ourselves. Such rewards make us feel good and motivate us to move on to new challenges.

"Mental-health time" is an indulgence that should be used when one is under extended stress. When a stress level has been too high for too long, relaxation is crucial to one's physical and emotional health. One should take a day off and do only what is pleasurable. (A number of agencies now allow employees a certain number of paid mental-health days.)

Exercise 11.5: Stress Management Techniques for Me

GOAL: This exercise is designed to familiarize you with available stress management techniques.

1. Review the material in this chapter on stress management techniques. List those techniques that you have used. Also, briefly describe whether each technique was beneficial to you in helping to reduce the level of stress you were experiencing.

2. **Specify the stress management techniques that you are planning to use in the future.**

TIME MANAGEMENT

To waste our time is to waste our life. Time is life. When our time is gone, we are gone. Time management focuses on helping people become more effective. It emphasizes the importance of selecting the best task to do and then doing it in the most productive way. Unfortunately, time is a nonrenewable resource that, as Taylor adds,

> is measured in past accomplishments. Those who look back and see few goals accomplished, few achievements, few times when they felt proud of what they have done—those people feel that life has sped by too quickly. They feel cheated.
>
> But those who look back and are flooded with memory after memory of satisfying activities, achievements, relationships, feel they have lived a long and fruitful life.[32]

When people fail to accomplish important tasks in their lives, it is often because they are not well-organized. As we will see, time management can help group members set goals in their lives and organize their time and resources to reach these goals. However, too much organization is as ineffective as too little. Overly organized people are too busy making "to do" lists, updating, losing, and redoing them.

Time management begins with setting goals. What do you really want from life? Constructive answers to this question are the first step toward having a fulfilling and rewarding life. People who do not set lifetime goals are apt to be bored, unhappy, depressed, confused, and unfulfilled. They haven't figured out what they want out of life, so they really do not know what will be fulfilling and satisfying to them. They "muddle through." Generally, they are followers who let others make decisions and then are frustrated and angry when a decision doesn't work out for them. (When others make decisions for you, they are apt to make the decisions in terms of what they want rather than in terms of what is in your best interest.) Muddlers frequently become complainers and have difficulty making major decisions. When asked to marry, they delay. When a new job presents itself, they vacillate. When an opportunity arises for moving to another geographic area, they hesitate. And when a "big" decision is made, they second-guess themselves—all because they have no meaningful goals to guide them.

SETTING AND PRIORITIZING GOALS AND TASKS

Setting life goals is not an easy task. It requires considerable contemplation, reflection, and sifting through numerous options. But, people who set life goals are generally more comfortable, happy, contented, and fulfilled. They know what brings them enjoyment and fulfillment and therefore can work toward accomplishing those goals. They tend to make decisions for themselves rather than having decisions made for them. When confronted with major decisions (such as marriage, having children, or a new job opportunity), they compare alternatives in terms of their life goals and arrive at a decision that will likely be in their long-term best interests.

Set Goals

The first step in a time-management process is for individual group members to set personal goals. They should answer two questions:

1. What are my long-term goals?
2. What are my goals for the next six months?

Answers to each of these questions should be listed on separate sheets of paper. In identifying these goals, group members should recognize that their short-range and long-range goals will change over time. That is to be expected. Trapping themselves into working toward goals they no longer want is a mistake. As time passes, certain goals will be dropped or altered, and others will be replaced.

In specifying short-range and long-range goals, group members should consider a variety of areas, including career, financial position, marital status, family goals, community involvement, religious goals, education, exercise, stress-reduction, self-improvement, relationships, vacations, retirement, hobbies, and recreation and leisure.

Prioritize Goals

The next step is to prioritize these goals. Lakein recommends using three categories: assigning the letter "A" to high-value goals, "B" to medium-value goals, and "C" to those with low values.[33] Prioritizing should be done separately for both the short-range and the long-range goals. The A, or high-value goals, should be further prioritized by ranking them in order: A-1, A-2, A-3, A-4, and so on. With this process, group members will have identified just what it is they want to do with their lives at this time.

Long-term goals tend to change for a variety of reasons. A person could accomplish a number of them, such as graduating from college, getting married, or finding a career position. Some of the unattained goals may no longer be important or valuable. Therefore, it is advantageous to review and refine long-term goals periodically (perhaps annually). Since short-term goals are generally for six-month periods, they should be reviewed semi-annually.

List Tasks for A Goals

The most important goals are A goals, and these should receive the bulk of attention and time. Since a group member cannot *do* a goal, the next step in the planning process is to list specific tasks that will help him or her move toward each short-range and long-range A goal.

A junior majoring in social work, for example, might have chosen "obtaining a social work job after graduation" as a longer-range goal. Specific tasks for reaching this goal might be listed as follows:

1. Studying carefully for exams and writing quality papers to get good grades
2. Doing volunteer work in social service agencies
3. Writing a resumé
4. Identifying areas in social work where vacancies are located and then taking elective courses related to these areas
5. Actively participating in the social work organization at this campus
6. Asking a social work faculty member that I trust to give me feedback on my strengths and deficiencies for obtaining social work employment and on what I need to work on to improve my chances of getting a job
7. Selecting a field placement that will (1) best help me to develop my social work skills and knowledge, and (2) establish contacts with people who can help me get a job

Prioritize Tasks

If group members were conscientious in listing possible tasks for each goal, they would have too many tasks and not enough time for all of them. Therefore they should prioritize each task into A, high-value tasks; B, medium-value tasks; and C, low-value tasks. A tasks for each A goal should then be further prioritized into A-1, A-2, A-3, A-4, and so on. (Readers will note that the method for prioritizing tasks is the same method that was used to prioritize goals.)

Exercise 11.6: My High Value Goals and Tasks

GOAL: This exercise is designed to assist you in specifying your short-range and long-range goals, and to identify the tasks that will help you achieve these goals.
Note: If this process is conscientiously followed, you will have a clear vision of your goals in life and what you need to do to achieve these goals.

1. **List your goals for the next six months on one sheet of paper and your long-range goals on another.**

2. **Prioritize your goals by assigning "A" to high-value goals, "B" to medium-value goals, and "C" to low-value goals. Next, the A, or high-value goals, are further ranked in order: A-1, A-2, A-3, and so on.**

3. **List tasks needed to achieve the specified A goals.**

4. **Prioritize each task's value in achieving each of your A goals using the A, B, C, and so on approach.**

Schedule Tasks

If group members have faithfully followed the prioritizing process, they will have a clear vision of their important short-range and long-range goals, and of the specific tasks that will help them achieve these goals. Daily work on each A task for each A goal is not possible, so group members need to select one or two (or a few more) daily tasks to focus on. If the A tasks a person selects seem too overwhelming (such as writing quality papers for each of his or her courses), they should be divided into smaller segments (such as doing library research for a policy paper).

In planning a schedule, time to achieve A tasks should be blocked out by designating specific hours or days for each task. Lakein suggests setting aside a special A time each day and banishing all C tasks and interruptions during this time period.[34] A weekly reminder calendar can help to schedule meetings, exam dates, paper due dates, and other important tasks. By using a calendar, group members can block out times to do A tasks in a place free from interruptions and distractions.

Each person has an *internal prime time,* which is when that person is most effective and productive. Each group member should find his or her own internal prime time since it varies considerably among individuals. For some it is the morning; for others it is the afternoon or evening. Group members should schedule their A tasks during their internal prime time.

In scheduling daily time, members may be flexible to accommodate whatever emergencies may arise. Therefore, it is important to leave an hour or so each day uncommitted. Too rigid a schedule will lead to high stress. Built into each daily schedule should be time for exercising, relaxing, and rewards.

In scheduling time, it is crucial to list high-value tasks and to avoid listing low-value tasks. Lakein has adapted the 80/20 rule to time management:

> If all items were arranged in order of value, 80 percent of the value would come from 20 percent of the items, while the remaining 20 percent of the value would come from 80 percent of the items. . . . The 80/20 rule suggests that in a list of ten items, doing two of them will yield most (80 percent) of the value. Find these two, label them A, get them done. Leave most of the other eight undone.[35]

This rule is not carved in stone, Lakein explains, as some items have more or less value than the 80/20 rule suggests. He illustrates the rule with the following examples:

80 percent of sales come from 20 percent of customers.

80 percent of production is in 20 percent of the product line.

80 percent of sick leave is taken by 20 percent of employees.

80 percent of file usage is in 20 percent of files.

80 percent of dinners repeat 20 percent of recipes.

80 percent of dirt is on 20 percent of floor areas that are highly used.

80 percent of dollars is spent on 20 percent of the expensive meat and grocery items.

80 percent of the washing is done on the 20 percent of the wardrobe that is well-used items.

80 percent of TV time is spent on 20 percent of programs most popular with the family.

80 percent of reading time is spent on 20 percent of the pages in the newspaper (front page, sports page, editorials, columnists, feature page).

80 percent of telephone calls come from 20 percent of all callers.

80 percent of eating out is done at 20 percent of favorite restaurants.[36]

■ TIME-SAVER TIPS

A number of time-saver ideas for college students are presented here. Select those of value to you.

Planning Tomorrow

At the end of each day, write down on your calendar the essential tasks you will do tomorrow. Planning in this way organizes tomorrow and enables you to relax today, your mind free from worries about tomorrow. This "to do" list could contain mostly A tasks, discussed earlier, but it can also include B and C tasks, such as "buy tickets for a ball game this weekend."

Concentrated Study

One or two hours of intensive, concentrated study time are more effective than four or five hours of slight concentration, daydreaming, and socializing. Using this approach of intense concentration in my senior year in college, I studied only one-third as much and received better grades. In lectures, I focused intensely on what the instructor was saying, studied intensely for only one or two hours at a time, and accomplished much more.

Best Use of Time

People who use time effectively monitor themselves throughout the day by asking: "What's the best use of my time right now?" Many of us squander our time by doing C tasks instead of A tasks. For example, if we have an important, difficult exam to study for, we may waste our time cleaning our apartment or room and rationalize that that is important, too. Doing C tasks as a way of avoiding doing A tasks has been called "productive avoidance." Ask yourself, "Would anything terrible happen if I didn't do this task?" If the answer is "No," then don't do it.

Writing Papers and Reports

When writing a term paper or a report, complete it in as few planning, research, and writing sessions as possible. Do not switch back and forth from writing a little on the paper and then doing something else. Much time is wasted in getting reoriented when you return to working on a partially completed paper.

When writing letters or answering mail, handle each piece of paper only once. Substantial time is wasted (through getting reoriented) by returning to write partially completed letters.

Physical Environment

Close your door when you do not want to be disturbed. Place your lists of high value goals and tasks where you can see them, so they remind you what you should be working on. Be prepared to carry study material at all times. Then you can take advantage of unexpected delays during a commute, in a physician's office, or waiting for a friend.

Saying "No" Assertively

Learn to say "No" as a time saver when friends and relatives suggest an activity that will interfere with your plans to do an A task. Seek to end unproductive activities as quickly as possible.

Deadlines

Set deadlines and stick to them. Avoid typewritten messages when handwritten messages will suffice. Ideas for how to complete A tasks can be written down with a deadline attached to them, rather than trusting to memory. Meetings started and ended on schedule do not waste people's time.

Avoid "Shoulds"

Avoid running your life by "shoulds." Somehow we never do many of our shoulds, as they are often interpreted as distasteful. Reinterpret the "shoulds" to be items you either will do or won't do. The "won'ts" you no longer have to do, and the "wills" are psychologically much more desirable to do than "shoulds."

Be Optimistic

Be an optimist. Don't waste time regretting or worrying about events that have not turned out well. Give yourself time off and special rewards when you successfully accomplish major projects.

Amount of Sleep

Can you reduce the amount of time you sleep? For most people, sleep takes up the largest single block of time during a day, and many get more than they need. Try reducing your sleep time by half an hour to see if you are as effective as before. In addition, have a light lunch rather than a big meal at noon so you won't become drowsy in the afternoon.

Relaxation

Try not to think of work on weekends. Learn to "let go" of negative events that happened earlier in the day and relax each evening. It is important to "do nothing" now and then to refresh yourself. A person who manages time effectively does not work harder, just smarter. (Relaxation techniques are described earlier in this chapter.)

Other Study Hints

By taking a speed-reading course you will learn to read faster and probably increase your comprehension. Marking the important points in a book with a pen, pencil, or marker during the first or second reading will save you time later during a review for an exam.

Exercise 11.7: My Time Savers

GOAL: This exercise is designed to assist you in being more aware of time savers that may work for you.

1. **Review the material on time-saver tips in this chapter. List the time-saver strategies that you have used, and briefly describe whether each of the strategies you listed were beneficial for you.**

2. **List the time-saver strategies you have not as yet used but you plan to use in the near future.**

■ OVERCOMING PROCRASTINATION

Procrastination is intentionally putting off doing something that should be done now; it is the thief of time. Once we develop the procrastination habit, we find plenty of ways to support it. We know we should be doing a certain A task, but instead we delay getting at it. We often squander our time by doing lesser-value tasks. For example, we know a paper is due in two days, but instead of writing it, we go shopping, spend hours talking to friends, wash clothes, or watch television. Sound familiar?

Procrastination is a major barrier to achieving short-range and long-range goals. The reason most people put off doing an A task is because it seems overwhelming or unpleasant. Overwhelming tasks are viewed as too complex or too time consuming. For example, you put off starting to write a 20-page paper due in one week because it seems that little can be accomplished in the short study time available. Unpleasant tasks, of course, generate negative emotions that may be difficult to deal with. For example, you put off telling your parents that you're failing a course because you fear their reactions and because you dread how you will feel after you inform them.

Swiss Cheese Approach

The key to getting an overwhelming A task under control is to poke holes in it by breaking it down into smaller tasks—the Swiss cheese approach. Completion of the smaller tasks nibbles away at the larger task until it is finally eliminated altogether.

For example, you have a research proposal to write for a class, and you feel overwhelmed because you have never written a proposal before and because you have little idea for the proposal topic. Divide the task into smaller tasks. Begin by making a list of three or four research topics you're interested in. The next step is to formulate a research hypothesis in each of the areas. The third step might be to meet with your instructor to get his or her thoughts about the hypotheses. The fourth step might be to go to the library to examine what research has been done related to your hypotheses and to review what kinds of research designs have been used. Once you have done this, you will be ready to select a topic. And, in reviewing the literature, you will in all probability have come across a design that you can adapt for writing your proposal. At this point, you may want to make a rough outline of your design that you can take to your instructor for feedback. After you make the changes suggested by your instructor, you are ready to sit down and write the research proposal.

Other Suggestions

Begin research: Unpleasant tasks can sometimes be made less unpleasant simply by learning more about them. Library research and interviews with experts or others knowledgeable in the field are good ways to begin.

Isolate parts of a task that can be done immediately: Completing several tasks early in the process provides initial success and motivation.

Set deadlines: Reasonable deadlines are a good way to avoid procrastination and build motivation.

Plan ahead: As parts of the project are completed, know the next step. This will keep the work moving forward.

Change of scene: If the work becomes boring or fatiguing, a change of pace or scene can often help. This approach simply means working for a while in the library, then in a dormitory room or even a student lounge. Such changes add variety and reduce boredom.

Attack fear: Fear of failure or of a specific task can be a deterrent to even beginning work on a project. That fear can be attacked through a rational self-analysis (see Appendix 1: Module 1). This process can effectively neutralize fears and enable the project to proceed.

Consider the consequences: Delaying work can mean missed deadlines, hurried and thus inferior work, and poor grades. It can also mean missed opportunities. Contemplating the consequences of procrastination can be an effective motivator.

Consider the benefits: A personal reward system for completing a task—or parts of a task—is a good way to begin moving forward on a project.

Cut off escape routes: Common escapes from work include socializing, daydreaming, sleeping, and watching television programs. Escape routes can be blocked by removing the temptation or by working in a place or at a time when the temptations will not be available.

Exercise 11.8: Ending My Procrastination

GOAL: This exercise is designed to assist you in ending your procrastination.

1. List the top three items that you are currently procrastinating about.

2. Examine these items and write down next to each one whether you are procrastinating because you view the task as "unpleasant," "overwhelming," or "both unpleasant and overwhelming."

3. For each task that needs to be done, list the strategies that you intend to use to stop procrastinating and to start doing these tasks.

■ ADVANTAGES OF TIME MANAGEMENT

While most of the material on time management in this chapter is directed toward college students, time management and time-saver principles are applicable to work situations throughout life. Time management is a *way* of life. People who are effective time managers are easy to identify. They accomplish major projects with quality and within deadlines. They show little hesitation, indecision, or confusion. They are successful people who have confidence in themselves. They are smooth, calm, appear in control, and display little wasted motion. They have a calming effect on others. They know when and how to relax. They're the kind of people you like to do business with. They don't procrastinate.

Taylor says:

Time management is not a finite skill or a body of knowledge that can be studied for two days, two weeks or two years, learned, and then put into practice. Like time itself, it is never ending. It is a continuing process of managing yourself more and more effectively with respect to time.

Search out ideas, new methods, new techniques, and adapt them to your use. Investigate timesaving products. Wage a campaign against bad habits which rob you of precious time. Form new habits. Keep your goals in mind—and on paper—and refer to them constantly. Review them. Revise them. Make sure everything you do relates to them.[37]

■ GROUP EXERCISES

Exercise A: Resolving Current Stressors

GOAL: To identify and work on resolving current stressors.

Step 1. The leader describes what stressors are and indicates the goal of this exercise. The leader then instructs students to write their answers to the following questions. (These questions may be written on the blackboard.) The leader should inform students to feel free to write responses they want to keep private, as they will not be required to reveal anything they do not want to share.

1.   What are the three most serious, unresolved stressors that you are currently facing?
2.   What attempts have you made to resolve each of these stressors?
3.   Why have you not as yet been able to resolve each of these stressors?

4. Are you currently awfulizing about these stressors?
5. What constructive actions do you think you should now take to resolve each of these stressors?

Step 2. After the students write their answers to these questions, they form subgroups of three persons. In the subgroups each member shares those responses that they are comfortable in sharing. While a member is sharing his or her responses, the other two members focus on suggesting alternatives to resolving the stressors being discussed.

Step 3. After the subgroups finish their discussions, the leader asks if anyone (or any subgroup) has a complicated situation that he or she would like to share with the class. Such situations are discussed, with efforts being made to suggest alternatives to resolve the stressors. (If a distressing event cannot be changed, it is usually possible for the person involved to change his or her cognitions about the distressing event.) The exercise ends when no one has additional complicated situations to share.

Exercise B: Relaxation through Meditation

GOAL: To relax through meditating, thereby reducing stress and preventing burn-out.

Step 1. The leader briefly describes what stress is and its causes and effects. He or she then explains that burn-out is one of the reactions to high levels of stress and summarizes approaches for reducing stress and preventing burn-out. (Preparing a handout that summarizes these approaches would be helpful.) The leader notes that it is important for each person to learn some ways to reduce stress.

Step 2. The leader explains that meditating is one way to reduce stress and then leads the group in the following meditative exercise. (The leader should feel free to modify, and add to, the following material.)

I will now lead you in a meditation exercise. The purpose is to show you that through meditating you can reduce stress and anxiety. You can do this exercise by yourself whenever you are anxious or want to relax. You can do it, for example, before giving a speech in class, taking a crucial exam, or going to bed at night.

Herbert Benson, who wrote the book, *The Relaxation Response,* has identified four key elements common to meditative approaches that help people to relax. These four elements are (1) being in a quiet place; (2) getting in a comfortable position; (3) having an object to dwell on, such as your breathing or a phrase that you continually repeat silently to yourself; and (4) having a passive attitude in which you let go of your day-to-day concerns by no longer thinking about them. Having a passive attitude is the key element in helping you to relax.

Now, I want you to form a circle. (Wait until a circle is formed.) I will lead you in three types of meditation. First, we will do a deep-breathing exercise. Then, we will move into repeating the word *relax* silently to ourselves. Third, I'll have you focus on visualizing your most relaxing place. We will move directly from the first to the second, and then from the second to the third without stopping. When we do this exercise, don't worry about anything unusual happening. There will be no tricks. Concentrate on what I'm telling you to focus on, while taking a passive attitude where you let go of your everyday thoughts and concerns. Everyday thoughts and concerns may occasionally enter your mind, but seek to let go of them when they do.

Before we start, I want each of you to identify one of your most relaxing scenes. It may be lying in the sun on the beach or by a lake. It may be sitting in warm water in a bathtub reading a book. It may be sitting by a warm fireplace. Is there anyone who hasn't identified a relaxing scene? (Wait until everyone has identified one.)

OK, we're ready to start. (If possible, dim the lights, or turn out some of them.) First, I want you to close your eyes and keep them closed for the entire exercise. Next, get in a comfortable position. If you want, you can sit or lie on the floor. (Take 5 or 6 minutes for each of the three meditative exercises. Speak softly and slowly. Pause frequently, sometimes for 20 seconds or more without saying anything. Feel free to add material to the following instructions.)

First, I want you to focus on your breathing. Breathe in and out slowly and deeply. . . . Breathe in and out slowly . . . as you breathe out feel how relaxing it feels. . . . While exhaling, imagine your concerns are leaving you . . . as you're breathing in and out, feel how you're becoming more calm, more relaxed, more refreshed. . . . Just keep focusing on breathing slowly in and out. . . . Don't try to be in sync when I'm talking about breathing in and out. . . . Find a breathing rhythm that's comfortable for you. . . . Breathe in slowly and deeply, and then slowly breathe out. . . . You've got the power within you to get more and more relaxed. . . . All you have to do is focus on your breathing. . . . Breathe in slowly and deeply, and then slowly breathe out. . . . If other thoughts happen to enter your mind, just let them drift away as effortlessly as possible. . . . The key to becoming more relaxed is to let go of your day-to-day concerns. . . . To do this, all you need to do is simply focus on your breathing. . . . Breathe in slowly and deeply, and then breathe out.

Now, we will switch to repeating silently to yourself the word *relax*. Keep your eyes closed . . . just keep repeating to yourself the word *relax*. . . . Keep repeating *relax* to yourself silently and slowly. . . . All of us encounter daily stressors. . . . It is impossible to avoid daily stressors. . . . The important thing to remember about stress management is not to seek to avoid daily stressors but to find ways to relax when we are under high levels of stress. . . . An excellent and very simple way to learn to relax is to sit in a quiet place, in a comfortable position, and silently repeat to yourself the word *relax* . . . *relax* . . . *relax*. . . . By simply repeating the word *relax* to yourself, you have the power within you to become more and more relaxed. . . . Find a nice comfortable pace for repeating the word *relax* to yourself. . . . The pace should be slow enough so that you can relax. . . . But not be so slow that thoughts about your day-to-day concerns enter your mind. . . . Remember, the key to relaxing is letting go of your day-to-day concerns. . . . If such concerns begin to enter your mind, focus more of your attention on repeating *relax* silently and slowly to yourself. . . . By repeating *relax* to yourself, you will find it will appear to have magical powers for you, as you will find yourself becoming more and more relaxed and refreshed. . . . [Have the members repeat *relax* for 5 or 6 minutes.]

Now, we will switch to focusing on your most relaxing scene. Don't open your eyes. . . . Focus on being in your most relaxing place. . . . Feel how good and relaxing it feels. . . . Just dwell on how relaxing it feels. . . . Enjoy everything about how calm and relaxing this place is. . . . Feel yourself becoming calmer, more relaxed. . . . Enjoy the peacefulness of this place. . . . Feel yourself becoming more relaxed, more renewed and refreshed. . . . Enjoy all the sights and sounds of this special place for you. . . . Notice and cherish the pleasant smells and aromas. . . . Feel the warmth, peacefulness, and serenity of this very special place for you. . . . Whenever you want to become more relaxed, all you have to do is close your eyes, sit quietly, and visualize yourself being in this very relaxing place. . . . The more you practice visualizing being in your relaxing place, the quicker you will find yourself becoming relaxed. . . . It will appear to you that your relaxing place has magical, relaxing powers for you, but in reality you are simply relaxing yourself by letting go of your day-to-day concerns and instead focusing on enjoying the peacefulness of your most relaxing place. . . . If you have to give a speech or are facing some other stressful situation, you can learn to reduce your level of anxiety by simply closing your eyes for a short period of time and focusing your thoughts on being in your most relaxing place. . . . You always have the power within you to reduce your level of anxiety. . . . All you have to do is close your eyes and visualize being in your very special relaxing place. . . . Continue to visualize, now, being in this very relaxing place. . . . Feel yourself becoming more relaxed, refreshed, and calm. . . . If you're feeling drowsy, that's fine. . . . Feeling drowsy is an indication that you're becoming more and more relaxed. . . . You're doing fine. . . . Just keep on visualizing being in your very relaxing place. . . . You will become more and more relaxed by simply letting go of your day-to-day concerns and by enjoying this very special relaxing place. . . . (Pause for 5 or 6 minutes, then continue this exercise.)

Unfortunately, in a minute or so it will be time to return to this class. But there is no hurry. I will slowly count backwards from five to one, and then ask you to open your eyes shortly after we reach one. . . . (5) Enjoy how relaxed you feel. You may now feel warmer, drowsy, and so relaxed that you feel you don't even want to move a muscle. . . . Enjoy this very special feeling. . . . It is healthy to become this relaxed, as your immune system functions best when you are relaxed. . . . (4) Slowly begin to return to this class. . . . There is no rush. . . . There is no hurry. . . . Take your time to become more alert. Anytime you want to relax, all you need to do is use one of these three meditative approaches. With practice you will gradually get better at relaxing by using these approaches. . . . (3) You should now focus on returning in a short time to this class. . . . Take your time . . . we still have a half-minute or so. . . . Examine whether you want to make a commitment to use relaxation exercises to reduce the daily stress you encounter. . . . (2) We are nearly at the time to return to this class. . . . You should now work toward becoming more and more alert. . . . (1) Slowly open your eyes. . . . There is no hurry. . . . Take your time to get oriented. A word of caution: if you have to drive someplace soon, please walk around for several minutes before trying to drive a car, as you may be so relaxed now that you may not be alert enough to drive safely.

Step 3. The leader then asks questions such as What do you think of these three approaches? How relaxed did you get? Did any of you have trouble getting relaxed? If yes, why? Which of the three approaches did you like better and why? (If the members are very relaxed and drowsy, they may feel they do not have the energy to respond to these questions. The leader should respect such a "mood," and not pressure members to respond.) *Note:* As an additional relaxation technique, the leader might play a muscle relaxation tape so that the class can experience this relaxation technique as well.

Exercise C: Setting High-Value Goals and Tasks

GOAL: To set short-range and long-range goals and to identify high-value tasks for accomplishing these goals.

Step 1. The leader begins by defining time management and describing the purpose of this exercise.

Step 2. Group members are asked to list their goals for the next six months on one sheet of paper and their long-range goals on another. A variety of areas should be considered, such as career, exercise and health, and education.

Step 3. After Step 2 is completed, group members prioritize their goals by assigning A to high-value goals, B to medium-value goals, and C to low-value goals, further ranking high-value goals in order: A-1, A-2, A-3, and so on.

Step 4. Group members then list the tasks needed to achieve the specific A goals.

Step 5. Group members then prioritize each task's value in achieving their A goals using the A, B, C approach. The leader explains that if this process is conscientiously followed, a person will have a clear vision of his or her important short-range and long-range goals, and of the specific tasks that will help to achieve these goals.

Step 6. The class discusses the merits and shortcomings of this process and what they learned from this process.

Exercise D: Time Diagram

GOAL: To use a time diagram to determine how you are spending your time and whether this is the way you want to spend your time.

Step 1. The group leader explains that the way we spend our time can be viewed as a revolving stage with each setting being a section. These settings can be diagrammed according to the amount of time we invest in each. The following examples should be provided.

Note that the time spent sleeping is usually excluded from such diagrams, unless it is a specific time-management problem.

Step 2. Students prepare diagrams showing how they spent their time for the past month. Each diagram should include the settings in which time was spent and the amount of time spent.

Step 3. The class forms subgroups of three or four to share diagrams and comment on the following information:

1.   Was this a typical month? If not, explain why.
2.   Is this the way you *really want* to spend your time and energies?
3.   Are you primarily directing your life, or is someone else? If someone else is primarily directing your life, who is this person, and what are your feelings about it?
4.   If Exercise C has been done, the class discusses the extent to which the amount of time they are spending on high-value tasks is correlated to their use of time during the past month.

Exercise E: Ending Procrastination

GOAL: To develop strategies for doing the important tasks you are putting off.

Step 1. The group leader defines procrastination and explains that the main reason people procrastinate is that tasks are viewed as overwhelming or unpleasant. The leader then summarizes a number of strategies for ending procrastination. The leader may want to distribute a handout listing these strategies.

Step 2. Each person writes down answers to the following three questions on a sheet of paper.

1.   What important tasks are not getting done because you're procrastinating?
2.   Why are you procrastinating?
3.   What specific strategies do you intend to use to stop procrastinating and to start doing these tasks?

Step 3. The class forms subgroups of three or four to share their responses and to suggest additional strategies for overcoming procrastination.

Step 4. The class discusses what they learned from this exercise.

Exercise F: Internal Prime Time

GOAL: To identify and more effectively utilize internal prime time.

Step 1. The leader explains the concept of internal prime time. The leader instructs each person to take a sheet of paper and draw the following outline for a graph. Members are then instructed to map their daily energy cycle on this graph. In this mapping process, members first place dots, representing their energy levels, at each two-hour interval. (This mapping process should be done separately for weekdays and for weekends.) After dots are placed, lines are drawn to connect the points. A solid line is used to represent a weekday, and a dotted line is used to represent a weekend. The high point on each line is then marked with an X and the low point with an O.

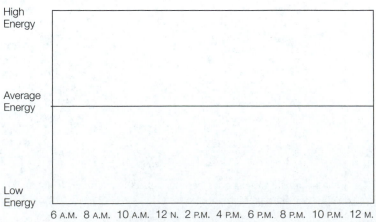

Step 2. Members form subgroups of three or four people. Each member is asked to share his or her graph and respond to the following questions. (These questions may be written on the blackboard.)

1. How does my internal prime time relate to my daily work schedule? Am I doing my most creative and taxing work at my high energy points during the day?
2. How does my weekend cycle differ from my weekday cycle? If there is a difference, why does it exist?
3. What changes do I need to make in my work schedule to more effectively utilize my internal prime time?

Step 3. The exercise may be ended by having members reassemble in a large group and asking them what they learned from this exercise.

CHAPTER TWELVE

Treatment Groups

GOALS

This chapter summarizes a number of guidelines for starting, leading, and ending therapy groups. A number of aspects are covered, including preparation and homework, relaxing before starting a session, cues upon entering the meeting room, seating arrangements, introductions, clarifying roles, building rapport, exploring problems in depth, exploring alternative solutions, stages of development, ending a session, ending a group, cofacilitating a group, legal safeguards for group facilitators, and professional boundaries with clients.

Counseling people with personal problems is neither magical nor mystical. Although training and experience in counseling are beneficial, everyone has the potential to help another by listening and talking through difficulties. This is not to say that everyone will be successful at counseling. Helping professionals (such as social workers, psychiatrists, psychologists, and guidance counselors) have a higher probability of being successful, largely because they have received extensive training in counseling. But competence and empathy, rather than degrees or certificates, are the keys to effective counseling.

This chapter seeks to present a number of suggestions for how to effectively start, lead, and end treatment groups. Since experienced group facilitators may find this material to be rather obvious, the primary intended readers are those facilitators who are planning to lead their first groups and facilitators who have already led some groups but are seeking additional suggestions for improving their group skills.

■ PREPARATION AND HOMEWORK

Extensive preparation is needed for leading treatment groups. The leader should have considerable training in (1) assessing human behavior and human problems; (2) comprehensive therapeutic intervention approaches—such as reality therapy, behavior therapy, rational therapy, and feminist intervention;[1] (3) specialized therapeutic intervention techniques, such as assertiveness training and relaxation techniques;[2] (4) interviewing and counseling; and (5) principles of group dynamics, such as cohesion, task roles, social-emotional roles, and effects of authoritarian versus democratic styles of leadership. Baccalaureate and master's programs in social work generally provide considerable material in these areas.

For any treatment group, the leader also needs to study the literature on the causes of problems that members are experiencing, the most effective intervention strategies for these programs, the prognosis for positive changes, and expectations as to the length of time the intervention strategies need to be applied to induce positive changes.

When leading a group, extensive preparation is key to a successful group experience for the members (including yourself). Even experienced leaders have to carefully prepare for each group and for each time the group meets.

In planning for a new group, answers to the following questions need to be formulated. What are the overall purpose and general goals of the group? What are the ways in which these general goals might be accomplished? What are the characteristics of the members? What are the unique and individual needs of each member? What resources do the members need to have in order to help them better handle their personal problems? What should be the format for the first meeting? What are the individual therapeutic goals for each member? When the group first meets, should an ice-breaker exercise be used? If so, what? Should refreshments be provided? How should the chairs be arranged? What type of group atmosphere will best help the members solve their personal problems? What is the best available meeting place? Why have you been selected to lead the group? What do the members expect you to do?

As you plan for the first meeting, it is very helpful to view the group as a new member would view it. Questions and concerns that a new member may have are the following: Why am I joining? Will my personal goals be met in this group? Will I feel comfortable in this group? Will I be accepted by other members? Will the other members be radically different in terms of background and interests? If I do not like this group, can I get out of attending meetings? Will other members respect what I have to say, or will they laugh and make fun of me? What exactly will be discussed during these meetings? What will I be expected to say and do? Will pressures be put on me to make changes that I do not want to make? Through considering such concerns, the leader can plan the first meeting in a way that will assist the other members to feel comfortable and that will help clarify the members' questions as to the format and activities of the group.

Exercise 12.1: My Concerns about Participating in a Treatment Group

GOAL: This exercise is designed to assist you in understanding the concerns of new members in becoming involved in a treatment group.

1. **Imagine you have a serious emotional concern (such as being depressed) or have a behavioral difficulty (such as being bulimic). Also imagine you will soon be attending your first treatment group meeting. Specify your concerns about participating (and revealing personal details of your issue) in a treatment group.**

2. **What could the leader do or say to help alleviate these concerns?**

When you are going to be a leader, it is *absolutely essential* that you do your home-work prior to the first meeting to identify as precisely as possible what the members' needs and expectations are. The quickest way to fail as a leader is to allow a group to go in a different direction than the members desire.

There are a variety of ways to identify what the members want. It may be possible to discuss with each member, prior to the first meeting, what his or her expectations are and what each member can realistically expect to achieve in the group. If you are asked by someone else to lead the group, it is essential to ask that person what the expecta-tions for the group are. The members should generally be asked at the first meeting to give their views as to what they desire to get out of the group. Another way to deter-mine group members' expectations (which needs to be done for preparatory reasons anyway) is to obtain the following information about the group:

1. How many members are expected?
2. What are their characteristics (personal problems, ages, socioeconomic status, racial and ethnic backgrounds, gender mix, educational and professional back-grounds, and so on)? If you are involved in selecting who will be in the group, you will have to make some judgments regarding whom to include and whom to exclude. Two important criteria for including members in a treatment group are (1) the potential benefit of the group experience for each member, and (2) the degree to which each member's presence is potentially beneficial to the other members in the group.
3. How knowledgeable and informed are the members about the issues the group will be dealing with?
4. What are apt to be the personal goals and agendas of the members?
5. How motivated are the members to accomplish the purposes for which the group is being formed? This can partly be determined by examining how voluntary the membership is. Involuntary members in a group (for example, members who have been court ordered to attend due to a conviction for driving while intoxi-cated) are apt initially to have little motivation to participate and perhaps may even be hostile that they are being forced to attend.
6. What are apt to be the underlying value systems of the members? A group of teenagers who have an eating disorder is apt to differ significantly from a group of adult parents who are mourning the death of a child. (However, it is important to remember to view the members in terms of being unique people rather than in terms of stereotypes.)

In planning for the first (and additional) sessions, it is helpful to visualize (imagine) how you, as leader, want the session to go. For example, at the first session, the follow-ing scenario may be visualized:

The members will arrive at various times. I will be there early to greet them, to introduce myself, to assist them in feeling comfortable, and to engage in small talk. Possible subjects of small talk that are apt to be of interest to these new members are _____, _____, and _____.

I will begin the session by introducing myself and the overall purpose of the group. I will use the following ice-breaker exercise for members to introduce them-selves and to get acquainted with each other. I will ask the group to give me a list of four or five items that they would like to know about the other members. Then members will introduce themselves and give answers to the four or five items. I will also answer these items and encourage the members to ask further questions that they have about me and the group.

After the ice-breaker exercise I will briefly state the overall purpose of the group and ask if the members have questions about this. Possible questions that may arise are _____. If such questions arise, my answer will be _____.

We will then proceed to an introductory exercise that is designed to encourage the members to begin sharing the personal problems they are experiencing. If this exercise fails to elicit much discussion after considerable probing on my part, I will present theoretical material on some of the psychological and societal dynamics of the personal problems they are experiencing.

The kind of group atmosphere I will seek to create is a democratic, egalitarian one. Such an atmosphere is best suited for encouraging members to share and problem solve the issues they are experiencing. I will seek to do this by arranging the chairs in a circle, by drawing out through questions those who are silent, by using humor, and by making sure that I do not dominate the conversation.

I will end the session by summarizing what has been covered and what is planned for future sessions. During this summary I will encourage members to give their suggestions for what should be dealt with in future sessions. We will set a time for the next session. Finally, I will ask if anyone has any additional comments or questions. Throughout the session I will seek to establish a positive atmosphere, partly by complimenting the members on the contributions they make.

If a group has met one or more times, the leader needs to review the following kinds of questions:

- Has the overall format for the group been sufficiently decided upon and clarified? If not, what needs to be done in this clarification process?
- Is each member making adequate progress in problem solving? If not, what obstacles are preventing these members (and perhaps the group) from sufficiently progressing? Do these obstacles need to be confronted?
- Are there more effective courses of action that might be considered that would benefit the group and certain members?
- What should be the format for the next session? What activities should be planned?
- Will successful completion of these activities move the group and the members toward accomplishing their overall goals? If not, perhaps other activities need to be selected.
- Does each member seem sufficiently interested and motivated to work on his or her problems, or are there some members that appear disinterested? If so, why do they appear disinterested, and what might be tried to stimulate their interests?

Guidelines and strategies for working with involuntary clients are presented in the box shown on page 336.

Exercise 12.2: My Concerns about Cofacilitating a Treatment Group

GOAL: This exercise is designed to assist you identifying what you need to work on in order to be able to cofacilitate a treatment group.

1. **Imagine you are an intern in a field placement, and you will soon be cofacilitating a treatment group with an experienced treatment group facilitator. Specify your concerns about being a cofacilitator for a treatment group.**

Strategies for Working with Hostile, Involuntary Members

A significant number of involuntary members are openly hostile in initial (and sometimes later) contacts with their assigned leader. What strategies can leaders use to develop rapport with such members and to motivate them to make positive changes? A number of strategies are summarized here.

1. Treat such members with respect. Leaders need to understand that such members probably do not want to discuss their situation with the group. Modeling respect can help calm members and may then lead members to show respect for the leader and the other group members.

2. Allow members to vent their unhappiness over being forced to join the group. In many cases, it is useful to indicate, "It is understandable that you are upset about having to be here—if the tables were turned and I was in your situation, I wouldn't want to be here either. It may help if we begin by you sharing your concerns about being forced to be here." Venting their concerns can have a calming effect.

3. Allowing members to vent concerns may also generate goals that the leader can help members work toward. For example, if a member is in a group because he physically abused his son while disciplining him, the leader can say, "I know you disciplined your child because you want the best for him—however, hurting a child is not acceptable. I wonder if we could explore some alternatives, like timeouts for Timmy and anger management techniques?" *A key ingredient in working with involuntary members is establishing goals that are personally meaningful to them.* A leader should seek to limit the leader's goals for involuntary members to legal mandates and then seek to add realistic goals that members desire. The strategy here is to search for common ground between the legal mandates and a member's personal goals. Often, redefining the problem in a way that adequately addresses the concerns of both the member and referral source reduces the member's resistance and makes a workable agreement possible.

4. Utilize the "disarming technique" (described in greater detail in Chapter 6), which involves finding some truth in what involuntary members are saying, even when the leader believes they are largely wrong, irrational, unfair, or unreasonable. There is always a grain of truth to be found. When the leader disarms members with this technique the leader is offering respect; this may make them more cooperative. This technique also facilitates open (rather than defensive) communication.

5. Do not subject yourself to extensive verbal abuse. If hostile members become overly verbally abusive, postpone the contact with something like, "Sir, I'm treating you with respect, and in exchange I also have a right to be treated with respect. I see we presently are not getting anywhere. Let's postpone focusing on this issue until our next meeting—by that time we will hopefully be better able to more calmly discuss this."

6. If a member continues to be verbally abusive in subsequent meetings, the leader should meet with her immediate supervisor to discuss available options—such as terminating the member's participation in the group.

2. What can you do at the present time to alleviate some of these concerns?

■ RELAXING BEFORE STARTING A SESSION

Before starting a session, you are apt to be nervous about how the session may go. Some anxiety is helpful in order to be mentally alert and to facilitate your attending to what is being communicated during the session. Some leaders, however, have too high a level of anxiety, which reduces their effectiveness. If your anxiety is too high, you can reduce it by engaging in activities that you find relaxing. Relaxation techniques are highly recommended (see Chapter 11). Other suggestions include taking a walk, jogging, listening to music you find relaxing, and finding a place where you can be alone to clear your mind. Effective group leaders generally learn they can reduce their level of anxiety through using one or more of these techniques. Through practice in leading groups, you will gradually build up your confidence.

■ CUES UPON ENTERING THE MEETING ROOM

It is important for you as leader to be on time—perhaps even a little early. By being early, you can check to see that everything is as you planned. You'll be able to do what needs to be done—such as checking to see that refreshments are available (if refreshments are planned), erasing the blackboard, arranging the chairs in the way you desire, and so on.

Being early will also give you an opportunity to observe the moods of the group members. If it is a group you have not previously met, being early gives you an opportunity to gain information about the interests of the participants from their age, gender, clothes and personal appearance, small talk, and the ways they interact with one another. An effective leader observes such cues and generally finds a way to join such participants.

■ SEATING ARRANGEMENTS

The seating arrangement is important for several reasons. It can affect who talks to whom and have an influence on who will play leadership roles. As a result, it can have an effect on group cohesion and group morale.

It is important in most groups for the members to have eye contact with one another. It is even more important that the group leader be able to make eye contact with everyone in order to obtain nonverbal feedback on what the members are thinking and feeling. A circle is ideal for generating discussion, for encouraging a sense of equal status for each member, and for promoting group openness and group cohesion.

When a group meets for the first time (and often later), members are apt to sit next to friends. If it is important that everyone in the group interact with one another, it may be desirable to ask people to sit next to people they do not know in order to counteract any cliquishness in the group and to encourage all members to get to know each other.

■ INTRODUCTIONS

During the introductions, the leader's credentials should be summarized in such a way that members gain a sense of confidence that he or she can fulfill their expectations. If the leader is introduced by someone, a brief concise summary of the leader's credentials *for the expected role* is desirable. If the leader is introducing himself or herself, important credentials should be summarized in a nonarrogant fashion. The summary should also be delivered in a way that creates the desired atmosphere—informal or formal, fun or serious, and so on. An excellent way in many groups to handle the introductions is to use an ice-breaker exercise.

In meeting with a group, it is highly desirable to learn the members' names as quickly as possible. This requires extra attention on the leader's part. Name tags facilitate this process for everyone. Members appreciate being addressed by name—it helps convey to them that they have importance.

It is generally advantageous for each member to introduce himself or herself, perhaps through using an ice breaker. It is often desirable during introductions that members state their expectations for the group. This helps uncover hidden agendas. If a stated expectation is beyond the scope of the group, the leader tactfully states and discusses it in order to prevent an unrealistic expectation becoming a source of frustration or dissatisfaction for that member.

In treatment groups, as in individual counseling, there are two types of members—voluntary and involuntary. In voluntary groups, the facilitator can take a more casual, less directive approach to begin with. In such groups the facilitator may begin by involving members in small talk. This preliminary chit-chat may be about the weather, parking problems, baseball, something currently in the news, and so on. Casual conversation has the advantage of letting group members become acquainted with the facilitator and the other group members.

In involuntary groups, the facilitator may begin by introducing himself or herself and making a formal statement about the purpose of the group. Then members may be asked to introduce themselves. Generally, in involuntary groups, less is left up to the members themselves, since they have less motivation for being there and less commitment to the group's success.

With both voluntary and involuntary groups, it is sometimes helpful (after introductions) to begin a session with some factual information. This can be done in a brief presentation by the group leader or by showing a short film or videotape. For example, if the group members are involuntary clients who have been convicted of operating a motor vehicle while intoxicated, the leader may choose to show a film that vividly shows that as alcohol consumption increases, reaction times slow and the chance of serious accidents occurring dramatically increases. Such factual information is designed not only to provide educational material, but also to serve as a trigger to start a discussion. After factual information is presented, it is sometimes useful to involve the group members in an exercise related to the factual material.

If the group has met previously, the leader may choose to begin by bringing up for discussion a topic that was not fully discussed at the last meeting. Or, if "homework" assignments were given to some members, the leader may begin by saying, "Jim, at the last meeting you indicated you were going to do (such and such). How did that work out?"

■ CLARIFYING ROLES

As leader of a group, you must understand clearly your roles and responsibilities. In most situations it is a mistake for the leader to do the majority of the work. The group generally is most productive if all members make substantial contributions. The more members contribute to a group, the more they are apt to psychologically feel a part of the group.

The helper therapy principle is generally operative in groups.[3] With this principle, members at times interchange roles and sometimes become the helper for someone else's problems. In the helper role, members receive psychological rewards for helping others. Groups also help members to put their problems into perspective as they realize others have problems as serious as their own.

Exercise 12.3: The Helper Therapy Principle

GOAL: This exercise is designed to assist you in understanding the helper therapy principle.

1. Describe a time when you went out of your way to help someone.

2. Psychologically, how did you feel about yourself after you went out of your way to help someone?

Even if you are fairly clear about what you would like your role to be, the other group members may be confused about what your role is, or may have different expectations of you. If there is a chance that the other members are puzzled about your role, you should explain carefully what you perceive your role to be. If members indicate they have different expectations, time should be devoted to clarifying the roles and responsibilities of the designated leader and other group members.

In explaining what you perceive your role to be, it is generally desirable to be straightforward about your skills and resources. Generally speaking, you want to come across as a knowledgeable person rather than as an authority figure who has all the answers.

Be prepared to explain the reasoning behind the things you do. For example, if you are doing an exercise, inform the group about the goals or objectives of that exercise. (If questions arise about whether the goals for the exercise are consistent with the overall goals for the group, be prepared to provide an explanation.)

The role that the leader assumes in a group will vary somewhat from situation to situation. For example, there are apt to be substantial differences in the responsibilities of the leader in an eating disorders group for teenagers versus an assertiveness group in a shelter for battered women.

Remember that leadership is a shared responsibility. Every member at times will take on leadership roles. Designated leaders should not seek to dominate a group nor should they believe they are responsible for directing the group in all of its task functions and group maintenance functions. In fact, productivity and group cohesion are substantially increased when everyone contributes.

■ BUILDING RAPPORT

The facilitator tries to establish a nonthreatening group atmosphere wherein the members feel accepted and safe enough to communicate their troubles fully. During the initial contacts, the facilitator "sells" himself or herself (but not arrogantly) as a knowledgeable, understanding person who may be able to help and who wants to try. The tone of the facilitator's voice conveys the message that he or she understands and cares about group members' feelings. The facilitator is calm and never expresses shock or laughs when members begin to open up about problems. Emotional reactions, even if subtle, lead group members to believe that the facilitator is not going to understand or accept their difficulties, and they will usually stop discussing them.

A knowledgeable facilitator views group members as equals. New facilitators sometimes make the mistake of thinking that because someone is sharing intimate secrets with them, facilitators must be very important, and end up assuming a superior position vis-à-vis their clients. If members feel that they are being treated as inferiors, they will be less motivated to reveal and discuss personal issues.

The facilitator should use a shared vocabulary with the members. This does not mean that the facilitator should use the same slang and the same accent as group members. If clients perceive that the facilitator is mimicking their speech patterns, they may feel seriously offended. In order to communicate effectively, the facilitator should use words that members understand and do not find offensive.

The facilitator and other group members need to keep what members say confidential. Unfortunately, many people have nearly irresistible urges to share juicy secrets with someone else. If a group member discovers that confidentiality has been violated, that member's trust in the group will be quickly destroyed. It is essential that the facilitator explains the importance of the rule "what is said in the group, remains in the group."

■ EXPLORING PROBLEMS IN DEPTH

While exploring a member's problems in depth, the facilitator and group members examine areas such as the extent of the problem, how long the problem has existed, what the causes are, how the member feels about the problem, and what physical and mental capacities and strengths the member has to cope with the difficulty, prior to exploring alternative solutions. A problem area is often multidimensional; that is, there are usually a number of problems involved. Explore all of them. A good way to decide which problem to handle first is to ask the group member which problem he or she perceives as most pressing. If it is a problem that can be solved, start by exploring it in depth and together develop a solution. Success in solving one problem will increase each group member's confidence in the leader and thereby further improve rapport.

Facilitators should convey *empathy,* not sympathy, and encourage group members to do so, too. Empathy is the capacity to understand and to share in another person's feelings. Sympathy also involves sharing feelings, but it results in offering pity. The difference is subtle. Empathy usually encourages problem solving, while sympathy usually encourages group members to dwell on the problem without taking action to improve the situation. For example, if a leader offers sympathy to a depressed person, that person will keep telling his or her sad story over and over, each time having the emotional outpouring reinforced by the leader's sympathy, without taking any action to improve the situation. Retelling the story only opens old wounds and prolongs the depression.

Facilitators should "trust their guts." The most important resources facilitators have are their own feelings and perceptions. Facilitators should continually strive to place themselves in members' shoes, understanding that members' values and pressures may be different from their own. It probably never happens that a group leader is 100 percent on target in an appraisal of a client's pressures, problems, and perspectives, but 70 to 80 percent is usually sufficient to allow the facilitator to be helpful. Empathizing is very useful in helping the facilitator determine what additional areas to explore, what should be said, and what possible solutions might be effected.

When a facilitator believes that a client has touched on an important area of concern, further communication can be encouraged in a number of ways. Showing interest nonverbally (by making and continuing eye contact, leaning forward, and raising eyebrows slightly) encourages further sharing. Allowing for pauses is important. New facilitators usually become anxious when there is a pause and hasten to say something—anything—to keep the conversation going. This is usually a mistake, especially when it leads to a change in the topic. Although a pause often makes a group member anxious, it provides time to think about what areas of concern are most important and then usually motivates the member to continue the conversation in that area.

Neutral inquiries that do not control the direction of conversation but encourage further communication are helpful. For example, "Could you tell me more about it?" "Why do you feel that way?" and "I'm not sure I understand what you have in mind" all ask for further information, but just what kind is left up to the member. Reflecting feelings—for example, "You seem angry" or "You appear to be depressed about that"—works the same way. In your response, summarizing what a group member is saying shows not only that you are listening but also that you have received the message the group member sent. An example is, "During this past hour, you made a number of critical comments about your spouse; it sounds like you're fairly unhappy about certain aspects of your marriage."

Approach socially unacceptable topics tactfully. Tact is an essential quality of a competent facilitator. Try not to ask a question in such a way that the answer will put the respondent in an embarrassing position.

Exercise 12.4: Using Tact in Treatment Groups

GOAL: This exercise is designed to assist you in tactfully confronting a group member about something she or he needs to be aware of.

A client (George) is a member of a treatment group you are facilitating. George recently received a Master's degree in engineering. He has interviewed for a number of engineering positions, but someone else has always been hired. George has poor grooming habits and related body odor. There are vacant positions for engineers in your community. You and the other group members have exhausted (in treatment with George) all other explanations—it appears George is not being hired because of his grooming habits. Specify the words you would use in confronting George about his grooming habits. Also, would you confront George in the group or do the confronting in private?

When pointing out a limitation that a group member has, also mention and compliment the member on any assets. When a limitation is mentioned, the person will feel that something is being laid bare or taken away. Therefore, compliment him or her in another area to offer encouragement.

A competent leader watches for nonverbal cues and uses them to identify a sensitive subject, as the client will generally display anxiety by a changing tone of voice, fidgeting, yawning, stiff posture, or a flushed face. Some leaders claim that they can tell when a member's pupils dilate.

Facilitators should be honest. An untruth may be discovered. If that happens, the group member's confidence in the facilitator will be seriously damaged and the relationship seriously jeopardized. Being honest goes beyond not telling lies. For example, the facilitator should point out shortcomings that are in the group member's best interest to correct. If a client is fired from jobs because of poor grooming habits, this problem should be brought to the person's attention.

■ EXPLORING ALTERNATIVE SOLUTIONS

After a problem is explored in depth, the next step is to consider alternative solutions. The facilitator begins by asking something like "Have you thought about ways to resolve this?" The merits, shortcomings, and consequences of the alternatives thought of by the member are then tactfully and thoroughly examined. Next, the facilitator seeks to involve other group members by asking them if they are aware of any alternatives that may work for this situation. Those members who do suggest alternatives temporarily assume a "helper" role. In such a role the helper therapy principle operates as the member receives psychological rewards from helping others. If the facilitator has additional viable alternatives to suggest, they should then be mentioned. The merits, shortcomings, and consequences of the alternatives suggested by group members and by the facilitator are then thoroughly explored.

Group members usually have the right to self-determination, that is, to choose one course of action from possible alternatives. The facilitator's role is to help individuals clarify and understand the likely consequences of each available alternative but usually not to give advice or choose the alternative for them. If a facilitator were to select an alternative, there are two possible outcomes: (1) the alternative may prove to be undesirable for the group member, in which case he or she will probably blame the facilitator for the advice and their future relationship will be seriously hampered; or (2) the alternative may prove to be desirable for the person involved. This immediate outcome is advantageous. But the danger is that the group member will become overly dependent on the facilitator seeking the facilitator's advice for nearly every decision in the future and generally being reluctant to make decisions.

The guideline of not giving advice means that the facilitator should suggest, not insist on, alternatives that a client has not considered. It is the facilitator's responsibility to suggest and explore all viable alternatives with a client. A good rule to follow is that when a facilitator believes a client should take a certain course of action, this should be phrased as a suggestion—"Have you thought about . . . ?"—rather than as advice, "I think you should . . ."

Group treatment is done *with* group members, not *to* or *for* them. Each member should take responsibility for doing many of the tasks necessary to improve a situation. A good rule to follow is that each member should do those tasks that he or she has the capacity to carry out. Doing things *for* group members, similar to giving advice, brings with it the risk of creating a dependent relationship. Successful accomplishment of tasks by clients leads to personal growth and better prepares them for taking on future responsibilities.

A group member's right to self-determination should be taken away only if the selected course of action has a high probability of seriously hurting the client or others. For example, if it is highly probable that a group member may attempt to take his or her life, the facilitator should intervene (making arrangements for the member to receive in-patient psychiatric care if the risk of suicide is high) even if the group member objects to the intervention. For most situations, however, the group member should have the right to select a course of action even when the facilitator believes that another alternative is better. Frequently, a client is in a better position to know what is best, and if it turns out not to be the best, he or she will probably learn from the mistake.

When a group member selects an alternative, he or she should clearly understand what the goals are, what tasks need to be carried out, how to accomplish the tasks, and who will carry them out. Frequently, it is desirable to write a contract for future reference, with a time limit set for the accomplishment of each task. (The box "Guidelines on Formulating a Contract" shows how to formulate a contract with a client.)

If a group member fails to meet the terms of the contract, the facilitator should not criticize or accept excuses. Excuses let people off the hook; they provide temporary relief, but they eventually lead to more failure and to a failure identity. Simply ask, "Do you still wish to try to fulfill your commitment?" If the person answers affirmatively, another time deadline acceptable to the member is set.

Perhaps the biggest single factor in determining whether a group member's situation will improve is the motivation to carry out essential tasks. A facilitator tries to motivate apathetic group members. One way to increase a member's motivation is to clarify what will be gained by meeting a goal. When individuals meet commitments, facilitators should reward them, verbally or in other ways. Never criticize members for failing. Criticism usually increases hostility and rarely leads to positive, lasting change. Also, criticism serves only as a temporary means of obtaining different behavior; when a person believes that he or she is no longer under surveillance, that person will usually return to the destructive behavior.

If a group member lacks confidence or experience, it may be helpful to role play a task before the person actually attempts it. For example, if a pregnant single woman

Guidelines on Formulating a Contract

Contracts in social work practice specify goals to be accomplished and the tasks to be performed to accomplish them. In addition, contracts set deadlines for completion of the specified task and identify rewards for successful completion of tasks. Contracts also specify consequences for unsuccessful completion of tasks. A contract is, therefore, an agreement between a facilitator and one or more clients in their joint efforts to achieve specified outcomes. Formulating an explicit contract is directly related to a positive outcome for clients.

A contract, in outline format, should contain the following components:

1. Goals to be accomplished (ranked in order of priority)
2. Tasks to be accomplished by the client and by the facilitator. (These tasks must be directly related to accomplishing the goals, so that accomplishing the tasks will result in successfully meeting the goals.)
3. Time frame for completing the tasks
4. Means of monitoring progress toward accomplishing *the tasks and the goals*
5. Rewards for the client if the terms of the contract are met
6. Adverse consequences to the client upon nonfulfillment of the terms of the contract

Some facilitators prefer written contracts, and others prefer verbal contracts. A written contract has the advantage of emphasizing the commitment to the contract by both the facilitator and the client, and it also minimizes the risks of misunderstandings. A verbal contract has the advantage of avoiding the sterility of a written contract.

A verbal contract is generally as effective as the written contract with regard to the goals being successfully accomplished. If a facilitator chooses to use a verbal contract, the facilitator should still record the essential elements of the contract in his or her notes for future reference.

The most difficult element in formulating an effective contract is for the facilitator and the client to formulate goals. Goals specify what the client wishes to accomplish and should directly relate to the needs, wants, or problems being encountered by the client. Goals serve the following important functions:

1. Goals ensure that the facilitator and the client are in agreement about the objectives to be accomplished.
2. Goals provide direction to the helping process and thereby reduce needless wandering.
3. Goals guide selection of appropriate tasks (and interventions) that are focused on achieving the objectives.
4. Goals serve as outcome criteria in evaluating the extent to which the tasks (and interventions) are being successful.

Useful guidelines when setting goals include:

1. *Goals must relate to the desired end results sought by the client.* The client must believe that accomplishing the selected goals will enhance his or her well-being. Therefore, the therapist needs to integrally involve the client in the process of selecting and specifying the goals.
2. *Goals should be stated in specific and measurable terms.* Nebulous goals (such as "Client gaining increased control over his emotions") are not sufficiently specific and often lead the client to drift or wander in the helping process. A specific goal (such as "The client will express his angry feelings with his mother in an assertive rather than an aggressive manner when they are having conflicts") is substantially more explicit. In addition, it is also measurable, whereas a nebulously stated goal is not. The client's mother (and others) can monitor the number of times, over a specified time period, that the client expresses his or her angry feelings assertively as compared to aggressively. Clients tend to define goals more nebulously, so it is important for the therapist to assist clients in stating their goals in such a way that they are both specific and measurable.
3. *Goals should be feasible.* Unachievable goals set the client up for failure, which is then apt to lead to disappointment, disillusionment, and a sense of defeat. It is vital that the goals chosen can be accomplished by the client. For clients with grandiose tendencies, it is important for the facilitator to assist them (tactfully) in lowering their expectations to the upper level of what can reasonably be attained.

When arriving at feasible goal statements with a client, the facilitator should agree only to assist the client in working toward goals for which the facilitator has the requisite skills and knowledge. If the goal is beyond the facilitator's competence (for example, assisting the client in overcoming a complex sexual dysfunction), the facilitator has the responsibility to refer the client to a more appropriate resource in the community.

Once the client has settled on his or her goals, the final step in the process of negotiating goal statements is to assign priorities to the goals. The purpose of this step is to ensure that the initial change efforts are directed to the goal that is most important to the client.

The following example illustrates formulation of a contract. We begin with background information. Ray and Klareen Norwood have been married for three years. They join a treatment group composed of four married couples and a facilitator—the focus of the group is on improving their marital relationship. Klareen reveals that she is increasingly afraid of Ray's

(continued)

■ Guidelines on Formulating a Contract *(continued)*

angry outbursts at her. Ray is physically and verbally abusive to her when he is angry. He has not hit Klareen yet, but she is afraid that Ray's escalating aggressiveness when they argue will lead to her being battered. Klareen is considering separating from Ray. She has already contacted an attorney to discuss divorce proceedings. Both partners, however, state that they want to maintain the marriage. The therapist and the other group members assist the Norwoods in formulating the following contract:

Goals: (1) Ray will cease being physically abusive to Klareen and will reduce by at least two-thirds the incidents of being verbally abusive to Klareen over the next 30 days. (This goal is rated number one.)

(2) The Norwoods will begin discussing, at some future date, raising a family. (This goal is rated number two.) The Norwoods both agree to put off further discussion of it at this time as Klareen says she first needs to make a decision about whether she wants to remain in the marriage.

Tasks of the participants:

Facilitator: The facilitator will instruct Ray in the following anger control techniques: (1) Ray learning to express his angry feelings to Klareen in an assertive rather than aggressive manner (see Appendix 1: Module 2), (2) Ray learning to reduce the intensity and frequency of his angry outbursts by countering negative and irrational self-talk underlying his anger with rational and positive self-talk (see Appendix 1, Module 1), (3) Ray learning how to counter his feelings of anger with deep-breathing relaxation (see Chapter 11), and (4) Ray learning to blow off steam nondestructively when he is angry through such physical activities as jogging or hitting a pillow (see Chapter 11). (Interestingly, the other group members also express interest in learning these anger control techniques during their group treatment sessions.)

Mr. Norwood: His main task is to use these techniques to cease being physically abusive to Klareen and to substantially reduce the incidents of being verbally abusive to Klareen. After 30 days, if Ray succeeds, a renegotiation of the terms of the contract will occur.

Mrs. Norwood: Klareen will seek to calmly discuss issues she has with Ray (in and outside the therapy sessions) to avoid provoking Ray's anger. Klareen also has the responsibility to record any incidents in which Ray is physically or verbally abusive to her in the next 30 days.

Duration of contract: 30 days

Means of monitoring progress: Klareen will record incidents where Ray expresses his anger toward her in assertive or nondestructive ways. (This is designed to measure positive ways in which Ray is learning to express his anger.) Klareen will also record any incidents in which Ray is verbally or physically abusive to her.

Rewards for Ray and Klareen if contract is met: They will continue their marriage, which is what both partners want.

Consequences for Ray and Klareen if contract is not met: If Ray hits Klareen one time in the next 30 days, she will separate. If Ray does not reduce by two-thirds the number of times he is being verbally abusive in the next month, she will separate. (To get baseline information, Klareen is asked to identify in the past week—taking each day at a time—the number of times Ray has been verbally abusive. Nine incidents are identified. As a result, Ray agrees he will, at most, be verbally aggressive to Klareen no more than 12 times in the next 28 days. If he exceeds this limit, it is agreed that Klareen will move in with her parents.)

---

wants help in telling her partner about the pregnancy, role playing the situation within the group assists the woman in selecting words and developing a strategy for informing him. The facilitator or another group member plays the woman's role and models an approach, letting the woman play the partner's role. Then, the roles are reversed so that the woman practices telling her partner.

■ STAGES OF GROUP DEVELOPMENT

The group leader needs to be aware that treatment groups have stages of development. A useful model for understanding the developmental stages is the Garland, Jones, and Kolodny model that was described in Chapter 1.[4] These stages will briefly be reiterated here.

The central focus of the model is emotional closeness among members, which is reflected in struggles that occur during the following five stages: preaffiliation, power and control, intimacy, differentiation, and separation.

In the first stage, *preaffiliation,* members are ambivalent about joining the group, and interaction is guarded. Members test out whether they want to belong and continue on. They attempt to protect themselves from being hurt or taken advantage of by maintaining a certain amount of distance from other members and by attempting to get what they can from the group without taking many risks. During this first stage the leader should seek to have the group appear as attractive as possible by allowing and supporting distance, using ice breakers, gently inviting trust, and gently indicating the likely benefits of continuing on. This first stage ends when the members gradually feel safe and comfortable within the group and when they realize that the potential rewards from participating are worth a tentative emotional commitment.

In the second stage, *power and control,* the character of the group begins to emerge. Alliances, patterns of communication, and subgroups begin to emerge. Members assume certain responsibilities and roles, norms develop for handling group tasks, and members more openly ask questions. Power struggles are apt to develop in which each member attempts to gain greater control over the rewards to be received from the group. The leader usually becomes a major source of gratification for the other group members as the leader gives and withholds emotional and material rewards. The leader is also attractive to the members as he or she influences the direction of the group. During this phase, group members realize the group is becoming important to them. A variety of power struggles may emerge. Does the group or the leader have primary control? To what extent will the leader use his or her power? Subgroups are apt to struggle with one another. Such struggles result in anxiety and considerable testing by group members—to gauge limits and establish norms for the power and the authority of both the leader and the other group members. Rebellions may occur, and the dropout rate is often highest at this phase. During these struggles the leader should help the members to (1) understand that these struggles are a normal process of group development, (2) give emotional support to help members weather the discomfort, (3) problem solve the issues that are emerging, and (4) assist in establishing norms to resolve the uncertainties. When members gradually trust the leader to maintain a safe balance of shared power and control, the members make a major commitment to become involved.

The third stage is *intimacy.* The group becomes more like a family. The likes and dislikes of intimate relationships are expressed. "Sibling rivalries" are apt to be exhibited, and the leader is sometimes viewed as a parent. Members more openly express and discuss feelings. The group becomes recognized as a place where growth and change are apt to take place. Members feel free to examine and make efforts to problem solve their issues, concerns, and difficulties. There is more of a feeling of cohesiveness and "oneness." Members in the group examine "what this group is all about."

The fourth stage is *differentiation.* Members are freer to experiment with new and alternative behavior patterns. Leadership is more evenly shared, members communicate more effectively, and roles are more functional. Power struggles are now minimal. Decisions are made on a more objective, less emotional basis. The differentiation stage is analogous to a healthy, functioning family in which the children have reached adulthood and are now becoming successful in pursuing their own lives. Relationships are now more egalitarian, and members are mutually supportive and able to relate to each other in more rational and objective ways.

The final stage is *separation.* Group goals have been achieved, and members have learned new behavioral patterns that are more functional for them. Termination is often a bittersweet experience. Some members may be reluctant to move on and may display regressive behavior to seek to prolong the existence of the group. Some members may express anger or may psychologically deny that termination is approaching. The leader in this phase must be able to let go. The leader needs to help members evaluate the merits and shortcomings of the group, problem solve their fears and trepidation about the group ending, identify resources they can turn to when future issues arise, and assist members in recognizing their strengths and capacities to handle future challenges that may arise.

■ ENDING A SESSION

Ending is not always easy. Ideally, the facilitator and group members accept the fact that the session is ending, and subjects being discussed are not "left hanging." Abrupt endings are apt to be perceived by the group members as discourteous and rejecting.

There are some useful guidelines on how to terminate a treatment session. Initiate preparation for ending the session at the beginning of the session. Inform the members explicitly of the time the session will end. Unless an unusual situation develops, the leader assertively seeks to terminate at the scheduled time. When the allotted time is nearly up, the facilitator informs the group members by saying something like "I see our time is just about up. Is there anything you'd like to add before we look at where we've come to, and where we now go from here?"

It is often helpful to summarize what was discussed during the session. If the session focused only on exploring problems that the members have, another session can be set up for fuller exploration and to begin looking at alternatives for resolving the problems.

It is helpful to give members homework assignments between sessions. A couple who are having trouble communicating with each other might be encouraged to set aside a certain amount of time each evening to discuss their thoughts. At the next session this "homework" assignment may be reviewed.

Ideally, the group members are emotionally at ease when the session ends. Therefore, the facilitator should not introduce emotionally charged content at the end of the session. Just as it is sometimes advisable to begin a session with small talk, a short social conversation at the end may provide a transition out of the session. If a group member displays a reluctance to end a session, it is sometimes helpful to directly confront this by saying, "It appears to me that you wish we had more time." The reasons for the person's reluctance can then be discussed.

At times, a group session can be ended with a restatement of the way both the facilitator and group have agreed to proceed. Or, a more explicit summation may be made by the group leader of what was discussed, what decisions were arrived at, what questions remain to be resolved, and what actions will be taken. A somewhat different approach is to ask each group member to state one item that was discussed or learned from the session and/or what he or she now plans to do. Some treatment groups end by each member leaving a bad feeling and taking home a good one to be acted upon during the week.

Sometimes concerns that were alluded to but not fully discussed might be mentioned in closing as topics that will be taken up at the next session. Some members reveal their most serious concerns for the first time at the end of a session, perhaps because they are ambivalent about whether they are ready to fully explore these concerns with the group. In these instances the facilitator has to make a professional judgment about whether to extend the session beyond the allotted time, or to set up an appointment to discuss these concerns privately, or to wait until the next group session.

Sometimes it is helpful to end a group session with a relaxation exercise (described in Chapter 11). A relaxation exercise helps members not only to relax but also to reduce their level of stress so that they can more objectively view and work on resolving their problems after they leave.

Closing is especially important because what occurs during this last phase is likely to determine the members' impressions of the session as a whole. Leave enough time for closing so that the members do not feel rushed, as that might create the impression that they are being evicted.

ENDING A GROUP

The ending phase of a group frequently offers the greatest potential for powerful and important work. Group members may feel a sense of urgency as they realize there is little time left, and this can lead them to reveal their most sensitive and personal concerns. Because the work remaining to be done is usually clearly identified at this point, members can focus their efforts on completing it. However, the relationship dynamics are also heightened in this phase, as the members prepare to move away from each other, and the termination of the group may evoke powerful feelings in members.

If group members have grown emotionally close to each other, the ending of a group will be interpreted as a loss and produce a variety of emotions. Kübler-Ross's stages of emotional reactions that people display when terminally ill resemble the reactions that people have to other important losses, including the ending of a successful and cohesive group.[5] Members may display denial through ignoring the imminent end of the group, anger and rage, or sadness and depression. They may attempt to bargain for an extension of the group in a variety of ways, such as urging that the group deal with additional problems. Ideally, members will ventilate and work through such feelings, and gradually come to accept the ending of the group.

Other emotions may also be displayed. Some members may feel guilty because of adverse comments they made or because they believe they failed to take certain actions that would have benefited themselves or other members in the group. If a member left prematurely, some members may feel the group let him or her down. Members may want to share their feelings about the support system they will lose when the group ends. If certain members want the group to continue, they may interpret the ending of the group as a personal rejection. On the other hand, members who feel that the group was very successful may want to have a celebration to give recognition to the successes and to say goodbye.

In many ways the concluding sessions are the most difficult for the facilitator and the group members. Strong emotions are often generated and should be ventilated and worked through. It is painful to terminate a group when members have formed relationships to share their most personal and important concerns and feelings. Our society has done little to train us to handle such separations; in fact, some segments in our society have a norm of being strong and not expressing feelings.

The facilitator can help members accept the ending of a group in a number of ways. The process of terminating a group should begin during the early stages of the group. This guideline is particularly relevant for time-limited groups. The facilitator should attempt to prevent the formation of dependency relationships between the members and the facilitator. The goal is independence and better functioning, and this should be reiterated whenever appropriate during group sessions.

The facilitator may summarize the emotional reactions that people have to group endings. An appropriate point for a discussion occurs when members display denial, anger, guilt, bargaining, or sadness. When discussing these feelings, the facilitator shares personal feelings and recollections, since the ending of the group has meaning for the facilitator as well. The facilitator can provide a model that may help members to express both their positive and negative concerns about the group ending. A problem-solving approach may be used to alleviate concerns; for example, if a group member is apprehensive about future problems, the facilitator might provide the member with several other counseling resources.

The ending process should provide enough time for the facilitator and the members to sort out their feelings and use the ending productively. A sudden ending cuts short necessary work and may not allow enough time for members to work through feelings and complete the remaining work. Sometimes, members indirectly express their anger by arriving late, appearing apathetic, being sarcastic, or battling over minor issues. In these situations the facilitator should respond directly to the indirect cues by saying something like, "I wonder if your recent critical remarks are related to your anger that this group is ending? I know you have invested a lot in this group and may dislike that our meetings are coming to an end." By helping members to recognize and articulate their feelings, a facilitator can help them express and work through those feelings. Once such feelings are dealt with, members will be more productive during the remaining time.

At or near the end of a group, members may test new skills and do things independently. They may report having tackled a tough problem or dealt with an issue by themselves. The facilitator should acknowledge their independence and make positive remarks about the members' ability to "go it alone."

At times, the facilitator may be the person leaving the group, perhaps to take a job elsewhere. In this situation, the facilitator should create a smooth transition. If appropriate, involve the members in selecting the new leader. It may be helpful for the former leader and the new leader to be coleaders for a brief period of time.

The ending of a group is a transition to something else. The important element during the ending phase of a group is to work with all members to help them develop a game plan so that the transition enables them to work toward new goals. The transition should not stifle members; rather, it should help them to progress. It may be valuable to note that life is full of transitions and passages: from early childhood to kindergarten; from kindergarten to elementary school; from childhood to puberty; from puberty to dating; from school to the work world; from being single to being married; from having responsibility only for oneself to becoming a parent; from working to retirement; and so on. In a transition phase we have the potential to make choices that will affect our future; the choices we make and the efforts we put forth determine whether the transition is constructive or destructive for us. Helping each member to make productive, realistic plans for the future is a goal of the ending phase of many groups.

During the process of terminating a group it is important that the facilitator spend time obtaining feedback on how to improve future groups. Usually this is done by having members fill out a brief evaluation at the last (or next-to-last) session. This evaluation is done anonymously by the members. The following questions apply to a variety of treatment groups. For the first seven questions use the following scale: (1) Strongly disagree, (2) Disagree, (3) Neutral or uncertain, (4) Agree, (5) Strongly agree.

1. I am very satisfied with what this group accomplished.
   1   2   3   4   5
2. My personal goals in this group have been attained.
   1   2   3   4   5
3. I truly enjoyed being a member of this group.
   1   2   3   4   5
4. The facilitator has done a superb job in leading the group.
   1   2   3   4   5
5. This has been one of the most rewarding groups I have participated in.
   1   2   3   4   5
6. I have grown extensively as a person through participating in this group.
   1   2   3   4   5
7. I have made substantial progress in resolving those personal problems that led me to join this group.
   1   2   3   4   5

The next three questions are open-ended:

8. The strengths of this group are:
9. The shortcomings of this group are:
10. My suggestions for changes in this group are:

At the final session it is also desirable for the members to discuss what they got out of the group, the merits of the group, and suggestions for improving it. Members should be given a chance to bring up unfinished business. In some cases an extra session may be held to complete unfinished business items.

One final important suggestion will be given. Occasionally, a facilitator refers an individual to another group or facilitator, or discusses a group member with another professional facilitator. The reason may be (1) the facilitator feels that he or she is unable to empathize with that group member; (2) the facilitator has extreme personal difficulty in accepting the fact that a member is choosing alternatives that the facilitator finds disgusting (such as continuing to abuse a family member); (3) the member's problems are of such a nature that the facilitator feels unable to provide the therapeutic help; and/or (4) a working relationship is not established with the member. A competent facilitator knows that he or she can work with and help some people but not all. It may be in an individual's and a facilitator's best interests to refer a group member to someone else who can help.

■ COFACILITATING GROUPS

Even though many settings do not have the resources to allow two leaders to facilitate a group, some programs can afford this type of group facilitation. Also, many students in internships are given opportunities to cofacilitate groups with either their field instructor or some other professional at their agency. The cofacilitator approach has many advantages, including the following:

- Each facilitator can grow from working with, observing, and learning from the other.
- Group members can benefit from the different life experiences, insights, and perspectives of the two facilitators.
- The two facilitators can complement each other, thereby benefiting the group.
- The two facilitators can provide valuable feedback to each other by discussing what happened in a session and how to approach a complex issue.
- The two facilitators can serve as models for the members with respect to how they relate and communicate to each other and to the group.
- If one of the leaders is female and the other is male, barriers that some members have involving gender can be more effectively confronted, explored, and resolved.
- While one facilitator is working with a particular member, the other facilitator can scan the group to get a sense of how the other members are reacting.
- Cofacilitating offers a certain safety, especially when practitioners are leading a group for the first time, since it is typical for beginning group facilitators to experience self-doubt and anxiety. Facing a group for the first time with a cofacilitator whom you respect and trust can turn what initially seems a frightening task into a delightful learning experience.

It should be noted that major disadvantages to cofacilitating a group occur when the facilitators fail to develop and maintain an effective working relationship. In order to develop such a working relationship, it is essential that the two facilitators respect each other. The two facilitators are likely to have some differences in leadership style and may not always agree or share the same perceptions and interpretations. However, when there is mutual respect, they will generally be able to communicate and discuss these differences, trust each other, and work cooperatively instead of competitively. If trust and respect between the facilitators are lacking, the members are bound to sense disharmony and the group is apt to be negatively affected. Power struggles between two incompatible cofacilitators may divide the group. Friction between the two facilitators can serve as a model for the other members to focus on negatives within the group and to subtly or overtly verbally hurt one another.

It is important for group facilitators to learn whom they can cofacilitate with and whom they cannot. Even secure, competent, and experienced facilitators who respect one another may not be able to work effectively together if their styles clash. For example, a facilitator who believes in leading by giving a great many suggestions aimed at providing quick answers for every problem expressed by group members is likely to clash with a facilitator who believes members best learn and grow by struggling and arriving at their own answers to their personal issues. If two facilitators discover that they cannot effectively work together, it does not necessarily mean that one is right and the other wrong, or that one or both are incompetent. It may simply mean that their styles clash and that each would be better off making arrangements to work with someone who has a similar style.

It is important for cofacilitators to get together regularly (ideally shortly after the end of each session) to discuss where the group has come and where the group needs to go. Additional areas to be discussed include how the facilitators view the group and the individual members, how the facilitators feel about working with each other, and how to approach any complex issues that have arisen related to the group. The facilitators also need to make plans for the next session.

LEGAL SAFEGUARDS FOR GROUP FACILITATORS

Unfortunately, filing lawsuits has become a national pastime. In order to avoid a malpractice suit or to provide a defense if a lawsuit arises, a group facilitator should maintain reasonable, ordinary, and prudent (marked by wisdom or judiciousness) practices. Following are some guidelines for group leaders that are useful in translating the terms *reasonable, ordinary,* and *prudent* into concrete actions:

- Screen candidates for a group experience carefully. Many potential problems can be avoided by effective screening practices. The facilitator should select group members whose needs and goals are compatible with the goals of the group, who will not impede the group process, and whose well-being will not be jeopardized by the group experience.
- Adequately inform the members about the group process. Entrance procedures, time parameters of the group experience, expectations of group participation, goals of the group, intervention methods that will be used, rights of members, responsibilities of members and facilitator, methods of payment (where appropriate), and termination procedures should be explained at the outset of the group.
- Obtain written parental consent when working with minors.
- Obtain written informed-consent procedures at the outset of a group. Contracts signed by both the facilitator and the members are an example of such a procedure.
- Have a clear rationale for the techniques and exercises you employ in group sessions.
- Be prepared to concisely explain and defend the theoretical underpinnings of your techniques and exercises.
- Consult with your supervisor or an attorney on issues involving complex legal and ethical matters.
- Avoid becoming entangled in social relationships with group participants.
- Be aware of those situations in which you are legally required to break confidentiality.
- Carry malpractice insurance.
- Actively engage in keeping up with the theoretical and research developments that have a direct application to group therapy.
- Be knowledgeable about, and abide by, the codes of ethics for social workers. (In the United States, refer to the *NASW Code of Ethics* and in Canada refer to the *Canadian Association of Social Workers' Code of Ethics.*)

- Be aware of when it is appropriate to refer a group member for another form of treatment, and also be aware when group therapy might be inadvisable.
- Instruct members on how to evaluate their progress toward their individual goals. Also, routinely assess the general progress of the group.
- Write and maintain adequate records on the needs and goals of each member and the progress (or lack of it) made by each member in the group.
- Avoid promising members magical cures. Create reasonable expectations about what the group can and cannot achieve.
- Practice within the boundaries of your state and local laws.
- If you work for an agency, have a contract that specifies the agency's legal liability for your professional functioning.
- Abide by the policies of the agency that employs you. If you strongly disagree with agency policies and if they interfere with your ability to do your job, seek first to change these policies. If the policies cannot be changed, consider resigning.
- Define clearly to the members what confidentiality means and why it is important, and emphasize that what the members disclose must be kept confidential—even though the members should be aware that confidentiality cannot be guaranteed because some members may intentionally or unintentionally breach confidentiality.

SETTING PROFESSIONAL BOUNDARIES WITH CLIENTS

Is it appropriate for a social worker to have lunch or dinner with a client? Is it appropriate to attend a party (where alcoholic drinks are being served) where clients may be present? Is it appropriate to hug a client who is experiencing emotional distress? These are examples of boundary questions that arise in interactions with clients. Over the years I have seen a number of social workers and a number of social work interns subjected to severe disciplinary actions for failing to establish and maintain appropriate professional boundaries with clients. For example, a female intern was terminated at her field placement in a halfway house for chemically addicted correctional residents after she began dating one of the residents. A male social worker in a high school was dismissed for relating sexually explicit stories to the female clients he was working with.

Social workers have an obligation to establish appropriate boundaries in professional relationships with clients. The Canadian Association of Social Workers' Code of Ethics contains the following statements on these boundary issues:

> A social worker shall not exploit the relationship with a client for personal benefit, gain or gratification.
>
> A social worker shall not become involved in a client's personal affairs that are not relevant to the service being provided.
>
> The social worker shall distinguish between actions and statements made as a private citizen and actions and statements made as a social worker.
>
> The social worker shall not have a sexual relationship with a client.
>
> The social worker shall not have a business relationship with a client, borrow money from a client, or loan money to a client.[6]

The NASW Code of Ethics contains these statements on boundary issues:

> Social workers should not take unfair advantage of any professional relationship or exploit others to further their personal, religious, political, or business interests.
>
> Social workers should not engage in dual or multiple relationships with clients or former clients in which there is a risk of exploitation or potential harm to the client. In instances when dual or multiple relationships are unavoidable, social workers should take steps to protect clients and are responsible for setting clear, appropriate, and culturally sensitive boundaries. (Dual or multiple relationships occur when social workers relate to clients in more than one

relationship, whether professional, social, or business. Dual or multiple relationships can occur simultaneously or consecutively.)

Social workers should under no circumstances engage in sexual activities or sexual contact with current clients, whether such contact is consensual or forced.

Social workers should not engage in activities or sexual contact with clients' relatives or other individuals with whom clients maintain a close, personal relationship where there is a risk of exploitation or potential harm to the client. Sexual activity or sexual contact with clients' relatives or other individuals with whom clients maintain a personal relationship has the potential to be harmful to the client and may make it difficult for the social worker and client to maintain appropriate professional boundaries. Social workers—not their clients, their clients' relatives, or other individuals with whom the client maintains a professional relationship—assume the full burden for setting clear, appropriate, and culturally sensitive boundaries.

Social workers should not engage in sexual activities or sexual contact with former clients because of the potential for harm to the client.

Social workers should not provide clinical services to individuals with whom they have had a prior sexual relationship.

Social workers should not engage in physical contact with clients where there is a possibility of psychological harm to the client as a result of the contact (such as cradling or caressing clients). Social workers who engage in appropriate physical contact with clients are responsible for setting clear, appropriate, and culturally sensitive boundaries that govern such physical contact.[7]

It is impossible to develop additional guidelines that will answer all the questions that may arise when social workers set boundaries with clients. The following guidelines may be useful in resolving some boundary dilemmas:

- In your professional *and* personal life, try to be a role model for the values and principles of the social work profession.
- In relationships with clients, try to gain their respect and to exemplify the values and principles of the social work profession, rather than establish a friend-to-friend relationship.
- Never try to meet your personal needs or wants in relationships with clients.
- Try to increase your awareness of your own needs, feelings, values, and limitations so you become increasingly aware of how such factors may impact client relationships.
- When questions arise about the appropriateness of certain interactions with a client (such as whether to go to lunch), try to arrive at an answer by gauging whether the interaction will have a constructive impact on the client and your relationship. If a concrete beneficial impact cannot be objectively specified, do not engage in the interaction.
- Constructive professional relationships with clients require a certain amount of distance. If you have questions about whether contemplated social interactions will interfere with the boundaries of a professional relationship, consult your supervisor or a respected colleague.
- In your professional social work role with clients, be aware of any inappropriate behavior, verbal communications, and dress your part. For example, sharing details of your wild parties with teenage clients is probably unprofessional.

Exercise 12.5: Boundaries with Clients

GOAL: This exercise is designed to assist you in determining appropriate boundaries with clients.

1. Is it ever appropriate for a worker to ask a client if she or he would like a hug? If you answer "yes," specify when it would be appropriate.

2. Are there situations where it would be appropriate for a social worker to go to lunch or dinner with a client? If you answer "yes," specify what those situations would be.

3. A social worker who facilitates a treatment group also has rental property. One of the clients in the group makes an offer to rent an apartment from the worker. What should the worker do?

4. You are a social worker at a high school. You are single but have been dating someone for three years. A 16-year-old niece of the person you are sexually involved with is a student at this school and comes to your office asking for counseling assistance for some personal dilemmas she is facing. Should you counsel her?

■ THE THERAPEUTIC FACTORS: WHAT IT IS THAT HEALS

What are the therapeutic factors that lead to positive changes in clients who receive group treatment? The definitive factors are not yet fully known. This section will present two different frameworks, the first formulated by Dr. Albert Ellis, who developed rational therapy, and the second advanced by Dr. Irvin Yalom, a prominent group therapist.

Ellis asserts that any therapy technique that changes unwanted emotions or destructive actions is effective primarily because it changes a person's thinking from self-talk that is negative or irrational to self-talk that is more rational and positive. This approach is described at considerable length in Appendix 1: Module 1.

Yalom lists 12 factors that he thinks lead to positive changes in clients who receive group treatment:[8]

1. *Instillation of hope:* Members are inspired and their expectations raised by contact with other group members who have trod the same path and then improved their lives.
2. *Universality:* Many members enter treatment with the erroneous notion that they are unique in their pain and suffering. Group treatment assists members in discovering that others have similar problems and have made progress in resolving their problems and improving their lives via group treatment.
3. *Imparting information:* Members receive useful information (including advice, suggestions, and direct guidance) from either the group leader or other group members. Members learn about psychic functioning, the meaning of symptoms, interpersonal and group dynamics, the process of treatment, and how to solve their problems more effectively.

4. *Altruism:* This concept is similar to the helper therapy principle described in Chapter 1. Members at times interchange roles and become the helper for someone else, which helps members put their own problems into perspective. Helping others makes a person feel good and worthwhile. Another more subtle benefit of the altruistic act is that it gives additional meaning to life, particularly for those who complain of meaninglessness.

5. *The corrective recapitulation of the primary family group:* Many members in group treatment have a highly unsatisfactory experience in their primary family. Group treatment facilitates members' gaining a better understanding of traumatic family experiences that occurred in the past. Members can interact with leaders and other members in ways reminiscent of how they once interacted with parents and siblings. Group treatment provides an opportunity for early familial conflicts to be relived and healed.

6. *Development of socializing techniques:* Social learning occurs in all treatment groups. Members receive social feedback from other members about their strengths and the challenges they need to work on. There are opportunities to try out more functional behaviors, for example, to be assertive instead of aggressive or nonassertive, or to be more communicative of one's thoughts and feelings, which is particularly beneficial for those having a pattern of being noncommunicative. Members also learn how to listen more effectively and to respond more helpfully to others. Many members learn methods of conflict resolution. Opportunities also exist for members to experience and express empathy.

7. *Imitative behavior:* Group leaders and other group members model constructive behavior (such as problem-solving skills, being assertive, being empathetic, being supportive) that is often imitated by members having issues in these areas. This phenomenon is sometimes referred to as *vicarious* or *spectator* treatment.

8. *Catharsis:* Group treatment provides members with an opportunity to ventilate. Through venting their feelings, fears, past traumatic events, and concerns, members gain a release of anxiety or tension, which often improves functioning. In groups, strong expression of emotions almost always enhances the development of group cohesiveness.

9. *Existential factors:* Members learn that there is a limit to the guidance they can get from others and that they bear the ultimate responsibility for their lives. They learn that everyone is thrown into the world alone and must die alone. Such isolation is partially countered through learning there is deep comfort (and meaning to life) through relating intimately to fellow travelers in the world.

10. *Group cohesiveness:* Considerable research indicates that positive changes in members are much more likely to occur when the treatment atmosphere creates trust, warmth, empathic understanding, and acceptance. In order for members to feel comfortable in revealing (and solving) their problems, it is essential that they trust other group members not to reveal their disclosures outside the group.

11. *Interpersonal learning:* The need to relate closely to others is as basic as any biological need and is equally necessary for survival. Many members have treatment goals of improving their interpersonal relationships. Group treatment often facilitates learning to communicate more effectively with others, to be more trusting and honest with others, and to learn to love.

12. *The group as social microcosm:* The group gradually becomes a microcosm of the world the participant members live in. Over time, group members begin to be themselves. They gradually interact with the other group members as they interact with others in their social sphere. Members will inevitably begin to display their maladaptive interpersonal behavior in the treatment group, presenting an opportunity presented for the leader and other group members to help that member acknowledge the maladaptive behavior. Furthermore, the other group members and the leader can assist that member to problem solve and explore interacting with others in more functional ways.

Exercise 12.6: What Causes Positive Changes through Counseling?

GOAL: This exercise is designed to assist you in arriving at your conclusions as to what causes people with emotional issues or behavioral issues to make positive changes through counseling.

It is critical that social workers have an awareness of what causes positive changes in clients through counseling. We need to know the "components" that cause positive changes in counseling so that we will be certain to apply these "components" when we are counseling someone. Rational therapy, developed by Ellis (see Appendix 1: Module 1), presents one explanation. Yalom, in the preceding material, presents another. Review these two explanations and then specify what you believe causes people with emotional or behavioral issues to make positive changes through counseling.

◼ GROUP EXERCISES

Exercise A: Developing Counseling Skills with Role Playing

GOAL: To develop counseling skills through role playing.

Step 1. The leader summarizes the following five phases of group counseling: (1) starting the meeting; (2) building a relationship; (3) exploring problems in depth; (4) exploring alternative solutions with clients and then trying one or more of the alternatives; and (5) ending the meeting. The purpose of the exercise is explained.

Step 2. Two students volunteer to play the role of clients with personal problems. These two students may be allowed to come up with their own contrived problem or be given one. An infinite number of personal problems are possible, for example:

1. Two siblings are concerned about their dad living alone. Dad's wife recently died, and he has difficulty in getting around because of his arthritis. He tends to be gruff and not easy to live with.
2. A married couple has three children and is fairly content. The wife, however, wants to be a surrogate mother for a couple who wants a child. The husband does not want his wife to be a surrogate.
3. Two males or females have become sexually involved with each other. They do not know what the future will hold for their relationship and wonder whether they should inform their close friends and relatives.
4. A wife sometimes becomes so irritated at her two children that she physically abuses them. The husband wants the abuse to stop but does not know why the abuse is occurring or what he can do to prevent it.
5. One person who does not drink is concerned that his friend has a drinking problem. The second person denies a problem exists. Both are seeking counseling to resolve this conflict.

6. A 16-year-old girl has informed her mother that sexual relations have been occurring frequently for the past three years with her stepfather. The mother is shocked; the teenager is embarrassed and afraid. Both are seeking counseling on how they can emotionally cope and what they should do.

Step 3. The group leader may do the counseling or ask one or two students to role play the counselor. (If the group leader does the counseling, she or he should not be told what situation is being role played prior to the interview.) It is useful to have two counselors for the role play, so that one counselor isn't "stuck" not knowing what to say.

Step 4. Role-play the interview.

Step 5. The class discusses the merits and shortcomings of the counseling. The counseling may be analyzed in terms of the guidelines presented in the chapter.

Step 6. Additional situations may be role-played and then discussed.

Exercise B: Group Treatment in Action

GOAL: To give an experiential awareness of being in a group treatment session.

Step 1. The leader announces that at the next class period a simulated group treatment session will be conducted and states the goal of the exercise. Each student is given the homework assignment of identifying one or two personal problems that a friend or relative currently has. Students are told that they should not reveal the identity of the person having the problem and that the personal problem should be that of a friend or relative *and not of themselves.*

Step 2. At the next class period, the leader begins by stating ground rules:

Today, we will have a simulated group treatment session in order to give you an experiential awareness of being in group treatment. Because this is a class, I strongly request that you do not reveal any personal information about any dilemmas or difficulties you are experiencing. Instead, describe one or two complicated personal dilemmas that a friend or relative is currently facing. For confidentiality reasons, please do not reveal the identity of the person whose problems you talk about. Remember, for reasons of confidentiality, what is said here stays here. Are there any questions about what we are going to do, or about the ground rules?
    If there are questions, try to answer them.

Step 3. Ask students to begin sharing concerns being faced by a friend or relative. If the class is reluctant to start, the leader initiates the process by specifically asking a normally vocal student to begin. When a student is sharing, the leader encourages the other students to probe with questions in order to further explore the problem and then encourages them to suggest realistic and creative courses of action to resolve the problem. (In group treatment sessions, each member will at times takes on the role of facilitator.)

Step 4. After the dilemma revealed by one student is fully discussed and problem solved, other students share dilemmas that are currently being experienced by their friends and relatives. The exercise continues until the end of the class period or until no one has anything further to share. At the end of the exercise, students are asked their thoughts about the benefits and shortcomings of the exercise, and their suggestions for changes in the format of the exercise when it is again used. During the exercise, one or more of the students may begin talking about a personal problem he or she is facing. The leader at this point has to make a judgment as to whether to let the student continue. The leader should not allow students to divulge personal information that they are apt to later regret sharing.

Exercise C: Facilitating an Intervention Group

GOAL: To have each student in class develop skills at leading intervention groups.

Step 1. The instructor states the purpose of the exercise and indicates that a component of most class sessions will be the students taking turns in facilitating an intervention group. The instructor demonstrates an approach to doing this by sharing a personal issue that she is currently dealing with or has dealt with in the past. Possible topics are infinite: depression, grief management, ending a relationship, creative financing, stress management, assertiveness, resolving an interpersonal dispute, and so on. The instructor then asks if anyone in the group has experienced a similar issue and encourages volunteers to share. The instructor then asks the group for ideas (strategies) on how to resolve dilemmas that have been raised. The merits and shortcomings of these strategies are then discussed. The instructor ends the exercise by summarizing important points that were made during the exercise.

Step 2. The instructor passes out a sign-up sheet where each student selects a date in class to lead the group in a similar fashion to the previous example. Each student should take 15–20 minutes to lead the group. Each student is graded on a pass/fail basis by the instructor. Those students who do not pass at first are given additional opportunities to lead a group in later class sessions. The instructor should inform those students who have to lead another session of what they need to work on to improve. When students facilitate such intervention groups, it is advisable for the instructor to sit outside the circle of students, so that the students attend to the facilitator rather than to the instructor. When sitting outside the circle, the instructor should evaluate the facilitator's strengths, note areas needing attention, and provide suggestions for changes. The instructor also informs the facilitator whether she or he has passed or whether another session has to be led. If someone should continue not to receive a passing grade after several tries, the student and the instructor should meet privately to explore options. (Because it is important for social work students to be able to facilitate intervention groups, the instructor may choose to require that students receive a passing grade on this exercise in order to receive a passing grade in the class.)

Note: During these intervention exercises, two ground rules must be strictly followed:

1. Confidentiality—"What is said here, stays here" and should not be revealed outside the class.
2. Emotional safety—If someone begins to share and feels his or her disclosure is becoming too personal, the student should say, "This is becoming too personal," and there should be no group pressure for that person to say more.

Exercise D: Who Am I?

GOAL: Do develop an improved sense of who you are and what you want out of life. (This exercise is sometimes used in treatment groups.)

Step 1. The leader indicates that the question "Who am I?" and "What do I want out of life?" are probably the most important we will ever have to answer. Identity is the most important psychological need of an individual. While the past has brought us to where we currently are, what we want out of the future, along with our motivation to achieve our goals, is more important than our past experiences in determining what our future will be.

Forming an identity essentially involves *thinking* about, and arriving at, answers to the following questions:

1. What do I want out of life?
2. What kind of person do I want to be?
3. Who am I?

These questions are not easily answered because they require considerable conscious contemplation and trial and error. However, the answers are important to the person who wants to lead a gratifying, fulfilling life based on direction and meaning. Without answers, individuals may muddle through life being passive responders to situations that arise, rather than continual achievers of their life's goals. To assist an individual in arriving at a sense of who she is and what she wants out of life, a series of more specific questions follow. As a person arrives at answers to these specific questions, she will simultaneously be arriving at an increased sense of who she is.

Step 2. The leader distributes the following questions on a handout, with space for the students to write down their answers. The students take 20 to 30 minutes to outline their answers.

1. What do I find satisfying/meaningful/enjoyable? (Only after you identify what is meaningful and gratifying will you be able to be consciously involved in activities that will make your life fulfilling and avoid those activities that are meaningless or stifling.)
2. What is my moral code? (One possible code is to attempt to fulfill your needs and to find enjoyable experiences, as long as you do so in a way that does not deprive others of the ability to fulfill their needs.)
3. What are my religious beliefs?

4. What kind of career do I desire? (Ideally, such a career should be stimulating and satisfying to you and provide you with enough money to support your chosen lifestyle.) Also, what do I enjoy doing during my leisure time?

5. What are my sexual mores? (All of us should develop a consistent "comfortable" code that meets our needs without exploiting others. There is no one right code—what works for one may not work for another because of differences in lifestyles, life goals, and personal values.)

6. Do I wish to marry? (If yes, to what type of person and when? How consistent are your answers here with your other life goals?)

7. Do I want to have children? (If yes, how many and when? How congruent are these answers with other life goals?)

8. What area of the country or world do I want to live in? (Variables to be considered are climate, geography, type of dwelling, rural or urban setting, closeness to relatives or friends, and characteristics of the neighborhood.)

9. What kind of image do I want to project to others? (A person's image will be projected by style of clothes, grooming habits, emotions, personality, degree of assertiveness, capacity to communicate, material possessions, moral code, physical features, and voice patterns. Strengths and shortcomings should be assessed honestly in this area and improvements made.)

10. What type of people do I enjoy being with, and why?

11. Do I hope to improve the quality of my life and that of others? If yes, in what ways? How can these goals be achieved?

12. What type of relationships do I want to have with relatives, friends, neighbors, and people I meet for the first time?

13. What are my thoughts about death and dying?

14. What do I hope to be doing 5 years, 10 years, 20 years from now?

Step 3. The leader asks for volunteers to summarize what they wrote down.

Step 4. The leader may end this exercise by summarizing the following. To establish a fairly well-developed sense of identity, group members need to have answers to most of these questions. Although few individuals have rational, consistent answers to every question, having answers to most of them will provide a reference for arriving at answers to questions that are as yet unanswered.

Honest, well-thought-out answers to these questions will assist members in defining their identity. Again, leaders should remind members that what a person wants out of life, along with his or her motivation to achieve these goals, will primarily determine his or her future. The foregoing questions are simple to state, but arriving at answers is a complicated, ongoing process. In addition, changes in life goals should be expected periodically. Just as group goals have to be continually reevaluated, an individual's identity has to be reassessed as short-term and long-term goals are reached. Environmental influences such as changes in working conditions and personal growth alter an individual's beliefs, attitudes, and values. If changes are accepted and a person's identity remains intact, life goals can be redefined so that continued direction predominates.

Exercise E: The Miracle Workers

GOAL: To identify physical and material characteristics that are important to you. (This exercise may be used in a treatment group.)

Step 1. The leader explains the purpose of the exercise, distributes on a handout the descriptions that follow, and explains to the students that their first task is to choose four miracle workers whose miracles they would most like to have.

THE MIRACLE WORKERS
The following group of miracle workers have gotten together and graciously decided to provide four of the following services to you. Whichever services you select, you are guaranteed to be 100 percent satisfied with them. It is up to you to select the four authorities whose services you most desire.

1. *Dr. Jean Olympic:* A famous athlete, she can make you an outstanding athlete in any one sport that you choose. If you select a well-paying sport, you will be guaranteed fame and fortune.

2. *Dr. Jane Adams:* A well-known social worker, she will train you to become a highly competent social worker, and you will gain a national reputation for your outstanding work.

3. *Dr. Joshua Methuselah:* This renowned gerontologist guarantees you a long life (beyond the age of 300) with the aging process slowed way down. For example, at age 100 you will look and feel like 25.

4. *Dr. Will Masters:* An expert in sexuality, he will guarantee you a perfectly happy sexual life. Every day or two, or as often as you wish, you will be in sexual heaven, without criticisms, without hassles, and without fear of a venereal disease.

5. *Dr. "Pop" U. Larity:* This charming gentleman guarantees that you will always have close friends who are honest and sincere and whom you will always enjoy being with.

6. *Dr. Ben Spock:* A family therapist, Spock guarantees you a happy family life, both with your parents and your children.

7. *Dr. Mary Monroe:* This acting coach guarantees you a famous film career. You will win an Academy Award and will also have a long-term series on television.

8. *Dr. Abe Lincoln:* The political guru guarantees you that you will become president of the United States. Although you will have some political hassles, you will go down in history as one of our best presidents.

9. *Dr. Gore Geous:* A famous plastic surgeon will guarantee you that you will look the way you want to as long as you live. You can have the weight, height, color and kind of hair, and physical appearance that you want.

10. *Dr. Act U. Puncture:* A medical expert, he will guarantee you perfect health and protection from physical injury as long as you live.

11. *Dr. Al Einstein:* A famous scientist, he will guarantee you creativity and very high intelligence. You will eventually make some scientific discoveries that will benefit all humankind.

12. *Dr. H. Hughes:* A billionaire will give you the skills to earn fantastic sums of money. You will become one of the richest people in the world.

13. *Dr. Sig Freud:* A famous psychiatrist will guarantee you freedom from emotional problems and a positive self-concept.

14. *Dr. John Paul:* A famous religious leader will guarantee you a life in which you follow moral and religious values. Also, if a heaven exists, you will be guaranteed a reservation.

15. *Dr. Jon Dewey:* A famous educator will guarantee that you will graduate with highest academic honors from college. After graduating from college you will be guaranteed a high-paying job and will always have the capacity to think rationally.

Step 2. After the students have made their choices, they form subgroups of four or five people and each subgroup selects the four miracles it most desires.

Step 3. After the subgroups have reached their decisions, a representative from each subgroup states the miracles his or her subgroup wants and the reasons they selected the miracles.

Step 4. The students discuss their feelings about this exercise. Did the students have strong feelings about a subgroup choosing some miracles that were not their personal choices? Did this exercise help them to determine what is really important in their lives?

CHAPTER THIRTEEN

Termination and Evaluation of a Group

GOALS

Termination and evaluation are among the most important phases of a group. This chapter begins by briefly summarizing what students should have learned after reading and doing the exercises in this text. The chapter then discusses several ways to terminate a group. The chapter ends by describing research approaches to process evaluation and to outcome evaluation in groups.

Through reading this text, participating in the exercises, and leading some of the exercises, it is hoped that you have developed the skills needed to become an effective group leader and member. Your verbal and nonverbal communication in groups and active listening skills should have improved. Having gained an understanding of why controversy is desirable for groups, you should be able to use problem-solving and decision-making approaches to foster group effectiveness. You should be able to lead a brainstorming group and a nominal group, and have some familiarity with parliamentary procedure.

Groups can be used to help members control unwanted emotions, manage grief, become more comfortable with death, become more assertive, manage stress, treat chemical dependency, prevent burn-out, improve time management, develop a positive self-identity, and improve close relationships. At the end of this class, you should be better able to lead a variety of social work groups. Effective functioning in groups helps us accomplish our personal goals, furthers our personal growth, and improves our interpersonal relationships. Acquiring group skills and knowledge facilitates our capacities to function effectively in organizations, communities, families, and society. Now that we have reached the end of this class and the end of this text, we need to focus on how to end a group.

■ TERMINATION

The process of ending a treatment group has already been described in Chapter 12. This section will describe the process of termination for a broad array of groups.

Inherent in termination is separation from the group and from group members. Separation typically involves mixed feelings that vary in intensity according to a number of factors, several of which will be discussed here. The more emotionally close and emotionally invested a member is to a group, the greater will be that member's feeling of loss. The greater the feeling of success of members in accomplishing their goals via the group, the greater will be their feelings of "sweet sorrow"—sweetness from feeling that they have grown and had success, and sorrow because of separation from the group that has come to be an important and meaningful part of their lives.

The more emotionally dependent a member has become on a group, the more he or she is apt to feel anger, rejection, and depression over termination. The more a member has experienced difficulties in separating in the past from significant others, the more likely it is that the separation will be experienced as difficult, as the pattern of reacting to separations is apt to be repeated.

Exercise 13.1: The Emotions Involved in Leaving a Group Important to You

GOAL: This exercise is designed to assist you in understanding the emotions involved when members leave a group that has become emotionally important to them.

1. **The emotions that members experience when leaving a group important to them are comparable to the emotions you experienced when you ended participation in something that was emotionally important to you. Describe an experience that you had in which you ended participation in something that was emotionally important to you. It might be leaving a group (such as Girl Scouts or a baseball team), or moving from your family and friends to go to college, or leaving high school, and so on.**

2. Describe your feelings about leaving and "moving on." Specify both positive and negative feelings. Perhaps this experience of leaving was "bittersweet"—sadness about leaving but sweetness about positive memories and positive feelings about moving on to another phase in your life.

3. If you felt really sad (or other negative emotions) about leaving, have you let go of these feelings? If "yes," what helped you to let go? If "no," what do you still need to work on, and what is your strategy to assist in letting go?

There are a variety of types of termination, which include:

1. Termination of a successful group
2. Termination of an unsuccessful group
3. A member dropping out
4. Transfer of a member
5. The leader leaving

Each of these types will be briefly described.

Termination of a Successful Group

A successful group is one in which the group and its members have generally accomplished their goals. Termination of such a group is apt to generate the "sweet sorrow" reaction. The members are apt to be delighted with their accomplishments. The accomplishments are apt to increase their levels of self-confidence and self-esteem. Members are also apt to experience a feeling of loss (varying in intensity) due to separating from a group in which they have become emotionally invested. Such a group may desire to dine or have some other ceremony to commemorate and recognize the group and its accomplishments.

In terminating a successful group it is essential that formal termination begin one or more meetings before the final meeting. Ideally, the date of the last meeting should be discussed and agreed upon by the members well in advance of the final meetings. (For some groups the final meeting is scheduled even before the group begins to meet.) Sufficient time has to be allowed in terminating a successful group so that (1) progress made in accomplishing the tasks and goals of the group and its members can be evaluated; (2) plans can be made for continued work by the members on remaining problems; (3) work can be done on unresolved, last-minute issues that are identified by members; (4) emotional reactions of members to terminating can be handled; and (5) members have time to discuss whether they want to plan for a special social event for the group's ending.

While goodbyes are often sad, the negative feelings can be offset by emphasizing what members have given and received, the ways they have grown, the skills they have learned, and what the group has accomplished. In some cases, an extra session could be held to complete unfinished business items. The members may decide to have "class reunions" periodically or social get-togethers in the future.

Termination of an Unsuccessful Group

An unsuccessful group is one in which most or all of the goals of the group and its members are largely unmet. The reactions of members to the lack of progress may vary considerably: anger, frustration, disappointment, despair, guilt (for unproductive efforts or over lack of effort), scapegoating, blaming, and apathy. In rarer cases, it is possible for an unsuccessful group to be fairly pleased and accepting of its efforts. For example, a group that is formed to write a grant (when there is limited hope of funding) from the federal government may be pleased with its efforts and with the new relationships with others that were formulated and only mildly disappointed when they learn they were not funded.

In planning the termination of an unsuccessful group it is essential that formal termination be as well-planned as with successful groups. The date of the last meeting should be discussed and agreed upon by the members well in advance of the final meeting. Sufficient time has to be allowed in terminating an unsuccessful group so that (1) reasons for the lack of progress of the group can be assessed and analyzed; (2) discussions can be held of alternatives for the group and its members to reach their goals (such alternatives may involve changing the format of the present group, referral of members to other groups, and alternatives involving individual actions rather than group efforts); (3) emotional reactions of members to terminating and their reactions to the lack of progress made by the group can be handled; (4) members have time to work on unresolved, last-minute issues; and (5) members have time to discuss whether they want to plan for a special social event for the group's ending.

At times the ending of an unsuccessful group is chaotic and abrupt. For example, a group that has been appointed to write a grant may be nearly finished when they are informed the funding organization has had a financial shortfall and is therefore withdrawing its request for funding proposals. Such a group may end abruptly in despair. Or, in a group of involuntary members (such as at a prison or at an adolescent residential treatment facility), the leader may decide it is counterproductive to continue a group in which the members are continually "goofing off" and not putting effort into achieving the goals of the group. In every case, the reasons for the group's ending should be fully explained, and time should be given to dealing with the reactions of the members to the closing. If there is insufficient time at the final meeting to dealing with the tasks involved in ending a group, it is sometimes advisable either to have another session or for the leader to meet individually with each member to discuss their reactions to goals being unmet, alternatives for reaching their goals, reactions to the group ending, and unresolved concerns they may have.

When an unsuccessful group ends abruptly, some group members may be highly critical of the leader, of other group members, or of experiences that occurred in the group. If the leader contacts members to gain their thoughts about the group, he or she needs to be prepared to respond to highly critical feedback. One way the leader can prepare is to "visualize" possible criticisms and then formulate a positive and realistic response to each anticipated criticism.

A Member Dropping Out

When a member drops out, that person no longer attends, even though the group continues. A member may drop out for a variety of reasons. The member may become disenchanted with the group and feel that the group will not accomplish the goals that have been set. The member may have a disagreement with or dislike another group member. The member may be a parent who has to provide child care at the time the group meets. The member may start a new job with work hours that conflict with the meeting time. And there are numerous other reasons.

When a group member drops out without informing the group as to the reasons, the leader should contact the person to ascertain the reasons for terminating. In some instances it is desirable for the leader to explain that deciding to leave is a major decision that should not be made abruptly and that the leader would like the opportunity to explore the reasons that led to the decision. If the member has a conflict with another group member, perhaps the conflict can be resolved so that the member decides to return. Perhaps action can be taken to enable the member to return. For example, if child care is a problem for a parent, child-care arrangements can be made.

If the member decides not to return, the reasons for leaving should be explored. Perhaps the member may raise legitimate concerns that need to be dealt with so that other members do not also become discouraged and leave. If a person drops out of a treatment group, a sensitivity group, or an educational group and still has unresolved personal concerns, a referral to another group or to one-to-one professional help may be advisable.

Whenever a member drops out, the leader needs to inform that member of his or her positive contributions to the group. Dropping out of a group is often viewed as a personal failure, and therefore the person needs to be thanked for positive contributions to soothe the sense of personal failure.

When a member drops out, the remaining members may experience a variety of emotions. Some may feel they failed this member. Some may feel guilt for what they said or did—or feel guilt for failing to do or say what they believe would have led the person to stay. Some may feel relief or joy over the member leaving, as they may view the member as unworthy of the group or as an obstacle in the group's efforts to accomplish its goals. Some may feel sadness for the member dropping out and be concerned that something tragic has happened to that member. Some members may experience anger toward the person for leaving, as they feel he or she is abandoning the group. A few may feel personally rejected. Often, when a member drops out, rumors begin to circulate as to the reasons. Therefore, it is essential that the group be informed about the reasons for the person's decision to leave. A member's leaving can be devastating to group morale. If several members depart, the group's survival may be jeopardized.

Ideally, the person who leaves should inform the group about the reasons, either in person or in writing. If the member does not do this, the leader or some other group member should contact the person to ascertain the reasons for leaving and then inform the group.

Exercise 13.2: The Experience of Being Rejected

GOAL: This exercise is designed to give you increased awareness of what a member of a group is apt to feel when he or she is asked to leave a group that is emotionally important.

1. Describe an event when you were rejected. The rejected event should be something that was emotionally important to you.

2. What feelings did you experience? (Such feelings are perhaps comparable to those of a group member when she or he is asked to leave an important group.)

3. Have you successfully dealt with your negative feelings over being rejected? If "yes," what helped you let go? If "no," what is your strategy to emotionally let go?

Transfer of a Member

A transfer of a group member to another group or to some other type of professional services generally involves a planned arrangement between the group leader and the member. The transfer may occur for a variety of reasons. In a problem-solving group, the employing agency may decide the group member's talents and skills could be better used in some other capacity. In a therapy group, the leader and group members may jointly decide the member would be better served by receiving more specialized services in some other therapeutic format. A group member may transfer from any kind of a group because of a conflict that cannot be resolved between that group member and other group members. The conflict may severely interfere with goal accomplishment within the group. (For example, there may be a serious and insurmountable gap in mutual understanding and communication caused by differences in religious beliefs, values, or language.)

When a transfer occurs, the leader does everything possible to keep the transfer from being unexpected or abrupt. The member being transferred should clearly understand the reasons for the transfer and be accepting of the transfer. In addition, the group should receive an explanation as to the reasons for the transfer. Ideally, the member should explain to the group why he or she is transferring. This allows the other group members an opportunity to wish the member well and to gain a sense of closure to the member leaving the group.

The Leader's Leaving

Sometimes a group leader must terminate work with a group because of reassignment, change of employment, health reasons, or family crises. Such a termination is difficult for both the group leader and the members. Emotional reactions may be intense, and adequate time for working through these reactions may not be available. Members who feel vulnerable and dependent upon the leader may feel devastated. Some may personalize the leader's leaving as due to something they said or did. Some may feel angry and betrayed because they made a commitment to the group, confided in and trusted the leader, and then the leader left when their goals and the group's goals were only partially accomplished.

The leader, too, may experience intense emotions, including guilt for not following through on the implicit commitment to lead the group until its goals were accomplished.

When a leader leaves, he or she should encourage the members to express their feelings. The leader may want to initiate this expression by fully explaining why he or she is leaving, listing a number of positive things about the group, and expressing feelings of sadness and guilt over leaving. Before leaving, the leader (or group) should select a new leader. If the new leader is not a member of the group, the leader who is leaving should inform (outside a group meeting) the new leader about the goals, characteristics of members, current tasks and difficulties, and progress toward goals that the group has made. This new leader should be introduced to the group by the leader who is leaving. As much as possible, a smooth transition is the goal in shifting responsibilities from the former leader to the new leader.

Exercise 13.3: The Experience of a Significant Person Leaving

GOAL: This exercise is designed to assist you in being aware of what group members emotionally feel when a valued leader leaves the group.

1. **Describe an experience where a valued person did not reject you but geographically moved away from you.**

2. How did you feel about this person leaving?

■ EVALUATION

In the past few decades, accountability has become a major emphasis in social welfare. Funding sources demand research evidence that funds allocated are having a beneficial effect. An essential component of accountability is evaluation.

In broad terms, evaluation is designed to assess whether services provided were effective and efficient. Services provided in which goals and objectives are unmet are neither effective nor efficient. In evaluating the services provided by a group, there are two dimensions of evaluation—process evaluation and outcome evaluation.

Process Evaluation

Process evaluation is an assessment, generally by group members, as to the aspects of the group that were useful or detrimental. Feedback about techniques and incidents that blocked or enhanced process is of immense value to the group leader. With this information, the leader can hone certain skills, eliminate some materials, and give direction for approaches and materials to add. Such feedback can aid confidence. If the feedback is highly critical, it can be humbling and even devastating. It is far better to make changes suggested by the evaluation than to reject and "deny" the feedback and repeat the same mistakes in future groups. Group leaders need to welcome criticism and be prepared to respond to it constructively, which is the way that social workers expect clients to take constructive criticism.

Process evaluation can be conducted orally by asking the group members to discuss the aspects, techniques, materials, and incidents that were constructive and those that were counterproductive. An advantage of such an oral evaluation is that most members enjoy a verbal discussion. A disadvantage is that some may be inhibited from giving negative feedback verbally as there is a social norm in such situations to focus on the positives.

Process evaluation can also be accomplished by a brief questionnaire. Three key questions follow:

1. Summarize the strengths of this group. (Cite specific materials and incidents. Also cite skills and techniques used by the leader.)
2. Summarize the shortcomings of this group. (Cite specific materials and incidents. Also cite skills and techniques used by the leader.)
3. Briefly outline your specific suggestions for changes.

In process evaluations, group members typically cite positive factors more than negative ones.[1] Such positive feedback not only has a "stroking value" but also enables leaders to be more aware of their strengths so that they are apt to increase the use of these strengths in the future.

Negative feedback is as valuable as, and often more valuable than, positive feedback. It informs the leader of aspects that need improvement, which the leader can then attend to. Hepworth and Larsen note, "As with clients, awareness precedes change."[2]

Another way of evaluating process is by *peer review,* a form of quality control. Peer review is conducted by having one or more "peers" (usually other group leaders) periodically sit in on a group. (Some agencies have one-way mirrors so that the group can be unobtrusively observed.) Prior to a peer review, the agency or organization should agree upon a set of principles or criteria that reflect quality group leadership. A peer review is a review of a small portion of the total functioning of the group. That small portion may be typical or atypical of the total functioning of the group. (Many colleges and universities use a peer-review process in which tenured faculty in a department sit in on some of the classes of recently hired faculty.)

A variation of the peer-review process is taping (either audio or video) a meeting. That tape is played back and reviewed by the leader and a peer (or by the leader's supervisor). Prior to taping a meeting, the leader should explain the reasons for wanting to tape the meeting, indicate who will view the tape, and then ask the members for their permission to tape the session.

Exercise 13.4: Your Process Evaluation of a Group

GOAL: This exercise is designed to familiarize you with process evaluation.

1. **Describe a group that you participated in, which has now ended.**

2. **Summarize the following:**
   a) **Strengths of this group:**

   b) **Shortcomings of this group:**

   c) **Suggestions for how this group could have been improved:**

Outcome Evaluation

Outcome evaluation involves assessing the extent to which the goals have been accomplished that were formulated when the group began. Specific approaches to measure goal attainment are single-subject design, task achievement scaling, and satisfaction questionnaire.

Single-Subject Design

Single-subject design has become increasingly popular in the helping professions in the past two decades. There are more than a dozen variations of single-subject design, some of which are very complex and rigorous.[3] Fortunately, the simpler designs can be used by entry-level social workers in many direct practice situations. The basic elements of the design are described here.

Single-subject design has been identified by several other terms—single-system design, single N or N = 1 research, intensive or ideographic research, single case-study design, single-organism research, time-series research or design, and single-case experimental design.[4] The phrase *single-subject* indicates a focus of research attention on a single client—which is usually an individual but can be a small group or a family.

In a single-subject design, the client becomes the control group. For this reason, the approach is relatively easy to incorporate into a practitioner's usual services.

The steps in the research process involve:

1. Specifying the outcome
2. Selecting a suitable measure
3. Recording baseline data
4. Implementing intervention and monitoring the outcome
5. Assessing change
6. Inferring effectiveness[5]

The first step in single-subject design is to specify the outcome of interest. The selected outcome should reflect the needs of the client and what is realistic to achieve. It also must be an outcome that can be defined specifically and measured. For a bulimic client who is binging and purging, an appropriate outcome may be cessation of purging. For a family in which there are frequent heated arguments, an appropriate outcome may be a sharp reduction in heated arguments.

The second step in the design process is to select a suitable measure. The target behavior that the practitioner and client hope to change (such as reduction in heated arguments) must be specified in such a way that it can be measured in some reliable way. There are a variety of ways for measuring client outcomes, including direct observation, self-reports from the client, and standardized measures. Standardized measures include tests, questionnaires, rating scales, inventories, and checklists. A variety of standardized measures have been developed to measure variables such as self-esteem, level of assertiveness, level of depression, anxiety level, degree of marital satisfaction, burnout, amount of stress, potential for suicide, and generalized contentment.

The third step is to record baseline data. Baselining involves collecting data for a period of time before implementing the intervention. The objective of baselining is to establish the base rate of the outcome measure before intervention occurs. This baselining rate can then be used to provide a basis of comparison for the occurrence of the target behavior (behavior to be changed) before, during, and after intervention.

The fourth step is to implement intervention and monitor the outcomes. For example, for a client who is generally nonassertive, the intervention may be to have the client participate in an assertiveness training group.

The fifth step is to assess change. This step involves a comparison of the occurrence of the target behavior before, during, and after treatment. Often the occurrence of the target behavior during these three time periods can be displayed on a graph, as shown in Figure 13.1.

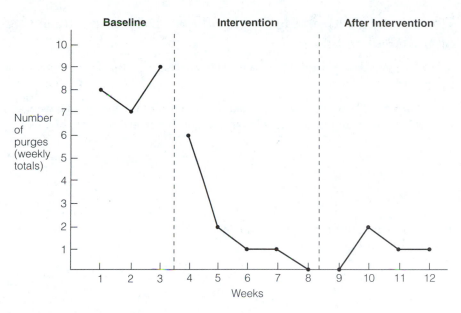

Figure 13.1

Intervention results for a client with bulimia

The sixth step in the process is to infer effectiveness. This step involves demonstrating logically and empirically that the intervention is the only reasonable explanation for the observed change in client outcome. In essence, this stage involves ruling out other possible explanations for the observed change. The primary criterion for inferring causality is concomitant variation; that is, the observed change in the outcome must occur at (or soon after) the time the intervention is implemented. If positive changes begin during the baseline period, then logically we have to conclude that something other than the intervention may have contributed to the positive changes. Likewise, if change occurs too long after intervention, then other possible factors may be responsible for the change. If we examine the chart for the Intervention Results for a Bulimic Client (Figure 13.1), we can logically conclude that the intervention had a positive effect, as the number of purges per week declined sharply during and after intervention. However, the usual goal with bulimic clients is complete cessation of purging. Since the client is still purging periodically, additional interventions may be advisable.

In some situations in single-subject research it is necessary to use a multiple baseline, which indicates the use of more than one baseline as a means of measuring change. Sheafor, Horejsi, and Horejsi summarize an example of where a multiple baseline might be used:

> In work with a child having trouble in school, one baseline might focus on frequency of school attendance, a second on grades received for weekly assignments, and a third on a teacher's weekly rating of the student's level of cooperation in the classroom. Unless the target behavior is highly specific, multiple baselines are usually necessary in order to capture the impact of an intervention.[6]

There are a couple of ways to use single-subject design in therapeutic, sensitivity, and educational groups. One way is to construct a single-subject design for each member. If the group is living together (for example, in a group home) and members have interpersonal problems (such as heated arguments), a single-subject design can be constructed on the group as the client. For example, if decreasing the number of heated arguments is the target behavior, the number of heated arguments per week among group members can be counted by the staff members during the three time periods of baseline, intervention, and after intervention.

Exercise 13.5: Applying Single-Subject Design to Alleviating One of Your Bad Habits

GOAL: This exercise is designed to assist you in understanding and applying single-subject design.

1. Identify a bad habit that you have and that you want to reduce in frequency or eliminate entirely. It might be, for example, drinking fewer alcoholic beverages or quitting smoking.

2. For alleviating this habit, specify the following:
   a) Your outcome:

   b) A suitable measure to determine progress:

   c) Your baseline data:

   d) Implementing intervention and monitoring the outcome:

e) Assessing change:

f) Inferring effectiveness:

3. Being realistic, after completing this evaluation, do you have a commitment to alleviating your undesired habit?

Task Achievement Scaling

The objective of this approach is to gauge the degree to which group members and/or the leader have completed agreed-upon intervention tasks. In this approach, the work toward the goals of the members and of the group is broken down into many separate actions or tasks. The tasks are selected by mutual agreement of the members, and each member is assigned or selects specific tasks to reach his or her goal and the overall goal of the group. Usually, a deadline is set for the completion of each task. Task Achievement Scaling refers to a procedure for rating the degree to which each agreed-upon task has, in fact, been achieved.

Reid and Epstein, in using this approach, utilize a four-point scale to record progress on each task:[7]

4 = Completely achieved
3 = Substantially achieved, action is still necessary
2 = Partially achieved, considerable work needs to be done
1 = Minimally achieved or not achieved

Where appropriate, they have a fifth rating: "No" for "No opportunity to work on task." With this approach, only results are rated—not effort, motivation, or good intentions. The appealing features of this approach are its simplicity and the fact that it can be used when more rigorous procedures are not feasible because of insufficient time, insufficient data, or difficulties in finding a suitable way to measure changes in the target behavior. The approach also has limitations. For example, if the tasks are erroneously conceptualized to be constructive in resolving the client's problems, then completing the tasks may have little effect on resolving the client's problems.

Satisfaction Questionnaire

Still another way to assess the outcome of a group is to have group members fill out a questionnaire that measures level of satisfaction. An example of such a questionnaire is the Group Member Satisfaction Questionnaire shown in Figure 13.2.

Such a questionnaire is a relatively simple and inexpensive way to measure the members' satisfaction level with the group. The questionnaire can be filled out at the last meeting of the group or can be mailed to members some time after the last meeting. Questions that evaluate process (described earlier in this chapter) can be added to this questionnaire.

Exercise 13.6: Applying a Satisfaction Questionnaire to a Group You Participated In

GOAL: This exercise is designed to assist you in applying a satisfaction questionnaire.

1. **Describe a group that you participated in that has now ended.**

Thank you for taking a few minutes to evaluate your experiences in our group. Your answers to this brief questionnaire will help us to improve future groups. Feel free to offer your comments. To assure anonymity, please do not sign your name.

1. Did you accomplish what you expected when you joined the group?
   _____ Yes, completely
   _____ Mostly
   _____ No real progress
   _____ Worse off now than before

   Comments _____

2. Do you feel the group accomplished its goals?
   _____ Yes, completely
   _____ Mostly
   _____ No real progress
   _____ The group was an utter failure

   Comments _____

3. How do you feel about the group leader?
   _____ Very satisfied
   _____ Satisfied
   _____ No feelings one way or another
   _____ Dissatisfied
   _____ Very dissatisfied

   Comments _____

4. How do you feel about the other members in the group?
   _____ Satisfied with everyone
   _____ Satisfied with some, and dissatisfied with others
   _____ No feelings one way or another
   _____ Dissatisfied with most of the other members
   _____ Dissatisfied with all of the other members
   _____ Very dissatisfied with all of the other members

   Comments _____

Figure 13.2
Group member satisfaction questionnaire

2. **Answer the questions from the Satisfaction Questionnaire that appears in Figure 13.2 for the group you identified.**

■ GROUP EXERCISE

Exercise A: Evaluating and Ending the Class

GOAL: To bring closure to a group.
Note: The instructor of the course should lead this exercise.

Step 1. The instructor begins by expressing a number of positive thoughts and feelings that she or he has about the group. The instructor may also mention a few memorable experiences.

Step 2. The group sits in a circle and the instructor asks: "Is there anything that anyone wants to express before the class ends? Is there any unfinished business that we should deal with?"

Step 3. The instructor leads a discussion in which the group reflects upon the course through questions such as: "Do you believe this course has helped prepare you to lead groups in social work?" "What else might have been done to better prepare you to lead groups?" "What exercises or materials have helped you grow as a person?" "What do you see as the strengths of this course?" "What do you see as the shortcomings of this course?" "How might this course be improved?" (An alternative to a verbal discussion of the questions in this step is to have the students record their responses anonymously on a sheet of paper and then hand them in.)

Step 4. The members express what they will most remember about this course and/or what they feel they have learned. Each member should be given an opportunity to express this.

Step 5. Each member expresses nonverbally how she or he felt about being in this class at the first session and how she or he now feels about having been in the class. (This step is optional.)

Step 6. The leader asks each member to give an imaginary gift to the person on his or her right. Each person should take a turn so everyone can hear what the gifts are. When giving or receiving the gift the members extend their hands to symbolize the giving or receiving of the gift. Examples of such gifts are the time-management key to ending procrastination, a warm sun for a smiling personality, a heart for happier relationships, positive and rational thinking for handling unwanted emotions, and the gift of meditation for reducing stress. (This step is optional.)

Step 7. The instructor may end the class by administering a student course evaluation, by saying some final words, or in some other appropriate way.

Group Treatment Theories Resource Manual (GTTRM)

In this manual you will find three prominent theories of group treatment intervention. Use it as a reference guide in your future practice and as a primer in your current coursework.

An effective group treatment leader needs a knowledge of prominent group treatment theories. An effective group treatment leader generally knows several treatment approaches and, depending on the problems being presented by group members, is able to pick and choose from a "bag of tricks" an intervention strategy likely to have the highest probability of success. The material in the GTTRM summarizes three prominent group treatment theories (rational therapy, behavior therapy, and reality therapy) that group treatment leaders commonly use. Case examples illustrate how each is used.

■ MODULE 1: RATIONAL THERAPY IN GROUPS

GOALS

Rational therapy asserts that unwanted emotions and dysfunctional behaviors are primarily determined by our thought processes rather than by external events. This chapter summarizes rational therapy and describes how to use rational therapy in groups.

Albert Ellis*

The founder of rational therapy, Albert Ellis (1913–   ) practiced psychoanalytic approaches to therapy during the late 1940s and early 1950s but became disenchanted with both the results and the approach. Ellis observed that even when patients achieved incredible insight into their childhood and unconscious processes, they continued to experience emotional difficulties.

Ellis developed a new approach, *rational therapy* (also called *rational-emotive therapy*), in which he treated clients by challenging and changing their irrational beliefs.[1]

In 1959 Ellis established the Institute for Rational Living in New York City, which provides adult education courses in rational living and a moderate-cost psychotherapy clinic for clients. In 1968 Ellis founded the Institute for Advanced Study in Rational

---

*This history is adapted from *The Practice of Social Work*, 7th ed., by Zastrow. © 2003, Brooks/Cole, a division of Thomson Learning, Inc.

Psychotherapy, which provides helping professionals with extensive training in rational therapy and also provides seminars and workshops throughout the country. Ellis is also recognized nationally as an authority on sexuality.

In addition to running workshops and seminars and being a practicing psychotherapist, he has written 54 books and over 600 articles!

Rational therapy has had an enormous impact on both professionals and the public. The principles of rational therapy have been applied to such areas as an assertiveness training, sexuality, adolescence, law and criminality, religion, executive leadership, children's literature, music, feminism, philosophy, personal problems, alcoholism, marriage and the family, and sex adjustment and therapy.

The approach has the potential to enable those who become skillful in rationally analyzing their self-talk to control or get rid of their undesirable emotions and dysfunctional behaviors.

Theory of Rational Therapy

Most people erroneously believe that our emotions and our actions are primarily determined by our experiences (that is, by events that happen to us). On the contrary, rational therapy has demonstrated that the primary cause of all our emotions and actions is what we tell ourselves about events that happen to us.

All feelings and actions occur according to the following format:

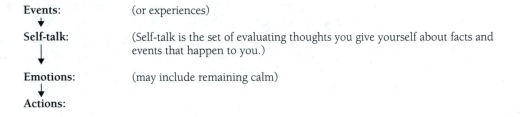

Events: (or experiences)

Self-talk: (Self-talk is the set of evaluating thoughts you give yourself about facts and events that happen to you.)

Emotions: (may include remaining calm)

Actions:

An example will illustrate the above process.

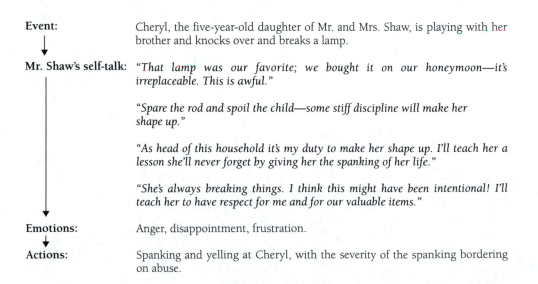

Event: Cheryl, the five-year-old daughter of Mr. and Mrs. Shaw, is playing with her brother and knocks over and breaks a lamp.

Mr. Shaw's self-talk: *"That lamp was our favorite; we bought it on our honeymoon—it's irreplaceable. This is awful."*

"Spare the rod and spoil the child—some stiff discipline will make her shape up."

"As head of this household it's my duty to make her shape up. I'll teach her a lesson she'll never forget by giving her the spanking of her life."

"She's always breaking things. I think this might have been intentional! I'll teach her to have respect for me and for our valuable items."

Emotions: Anger, disappointment, frustration.

Actions: Spanking and yelling at Cheryl, with the severity of the spanking bordering on abuse.

If, on the other hand, Mr. Shaw gives himself a different set of self-talk, his emotions and actions will be quite different.

Event:	Cheryl, the five-year-old daughter of Mr. and Mrs. Shaw, is playing with her brother and knocks over and breaks a lamp.
Mr. Shaw's self-talk:	*"This was a lamp we cherished, but I know she didn't break it intentionally. It was an accident. My getting angry at this point won't help."*
	"I might have prevented this accident by informing Cheryl and our son that they can horse around in the house only in the rec room and in their their bedrooms."
	"With young children some accidents are bound to happen."
	"The most constructive thing I can do at this point is to say that I understand that it was an accident, that all of us are disappointed that the lamp broke, and tell them in the future their horsing around should be limited to the rec room and the bedrooms."
Emotions:	Some disappointment but generally remaining calm.
Actions:	Talking to the children in an understanding fashion and expressing his thoughts in line with his self-talk.

The most important point about this process is that our self-talk determines how we feel and act; by changing our self-talk, we can change how we feel and act. Generally, we cannot control events that happen to us, but we have the power to think rationally and thereby change *all* of our unwanted emotions and ineffective actions.

The rehabilitative aspect of this conceptualization of self-talk is that any unwanted emotion and any ineffective behavior can be changed by identifying and then changing the underlying self-talk.

The self-talk we give ourselves about specific events that happen to us is often based on a variety of factors, including our beliefs, attitudes, values, wants, motives, goals, and desires.[2] For example, the self-talk a married woman might give herself on being informed by her husband that he wants a divorce would be influenced by her desire (or lack of desire) to remain married, by her values and beliefs about being a divorcée, by her attitudes toward her husband, by how she believes getting a divorce would be consistent or inconsistent with her present goals, and by her beliefs about the reasons why her husband says he wants a divorce.

Another important thing about self-talk is that with repeated occurrences of an event, a person's emotional reaction becomes nearly automatic because the person rapidly gives himself or herself a large set of self-talk gradually acquired through past experiences. For example, a few years ago I counseled a woman who became intensely upset and depressed every time her husband came home intoxicated. In examining her emotional reactions it became clear that because of the repeated occurrences she would rapidly tell herself the following on seeing him inebriated:

"He's making a fool of himself and of me."
"He's foolishly spending money we desperately need."
"For the next few hours I'm going to have to put up with his drunken talk and behavior—this is awful."
"He loves drinking more than he loves me because he knows I do not want him to get drunk."
"Woe is me."

Exercise M1.1*: Our Self-Talk Causes Our Emotions

GOAL: This exercise is designed to illustrate that it is primarily our self-talk (rather than the event) that causes our emotions.

1. **Specify a negative emotion that you recently experienced.**

2. **Describe the event associated with this emotion.**

3. **Specify your self-talk associated with this event.**

4. **Review the material on self-talk being the primary source of our emotions. Is it not true that if you had given yourself a different set of self-talk about this event, you would have felt differently?**

5. **Do you now believe that self-talk is the primary source of our emotions? Explain your views.**

---

*The M1.1 in this exercise designates this as the first exercise for Module 1. Similar designations will be used for additional exercises in these modules.

Changing Unwanted Emotions

Rational therapy is increasingly being used to change unwanted emotions. Because this is a primary focus of rational therapy, the methods used to change unwanted emotions will be specified in this section.

Rational therapy asserts that all emotions are primarily determined by self-talk, even the emotion of love. Individuals often believe that love is a feeling beyond their control. The language of love reinforces this erroneous belief: "I just *couldn't help it,* he swept me off my feet," "*I fell* in love," and "*It was* love at first sight." In reality, even the emotion of love is based primarily on self-talk. The following format illustrates this process.

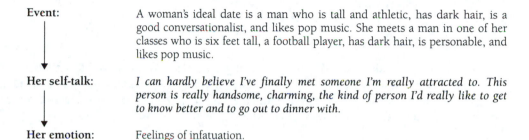

Event: A woman's ideal date is a man who is tall and athletic, has dark hair, is a good conversationalist, and likes pop music. She meets a man in one of her classes who is six feet tall, a football player, has dark hair, is personable, and likes pop music.

Her self-talk: *I can hardly believe I've finally met someone I'm really attracted to. This person is really handsome, charming, the kind of person I'd really like to get to know better and to go out to dinner with.*

Her emotion: Feelings of infatuation.

There are five ways to change an unwanted emotion. Three are constructive: getting involved in a meaningful activity, changing the negative and irrational thinking underlying the unwanted emotion, and changing the distressing event. Each can be learned and practiced within a group setting. Two are destructive: abuse of alcohol, drugs, and food; and suicide. We will discuss each of the five in turn.

Meaningful Activity

Practically everyone encounters day-to-day frustrations and irritations—having a class or two that aren't going well, working at a job that's unpleasant, or coping with a dull social life. Dwelling on such irritations will spawn such unwanted emotions as depression, anger, frustration, despair, or feelings of failure. Which of these emotions a person has will directly depend upon the person's self-talk.

Meaningful, enjoyable activity, however, produces satisfaction and a healthful distraction from unwanted emotions. Group members can learn the value of meaningful activity by writing an "escape" list of activities they find motivating, energizing, and enjoyable—taking a walk, playing golf or tennis, going to a movie, shopping, doing needlework, visiting friends, and so on. By having an "escape" list of things they enjoy doing, group members can nip unwanted emotions in the bud. By getting involved in things they enjoy, they can use enjoyable activities to take their minds off their day-to-day concerns and irritations. The positive emotions they experience will stem directly from the things they tell themselves about the enjoyable things they are doing.

In urging group members to compile and use an escape list, rational therapy is not suggesting that members avoid doing something about unpleasant events. If something can be done to change a distressing event, all constructive efforts should be tried. However, we often do not have control over unpleasant events and cannot change them. Although we cannot change unpleasant events, we always have the capacity to control and change what we tell ourselves about the unpleasant events. It is this latter focus that is often helpful in learning to change our unwanted emotions.

Exercise M1.2: Using Meaningful Activities to Change Unwanted Emotions

GOAL: This exercise demonstrates that when we are awfulizing about something and thereby feeling bad, we can alleviate the unwanted emotions by getting involved in meaningful activities.

1. **Describe a time when you were awfulizing about something and thereby, feeling bad, and then alleviated the unwanted emotions by getting involved in something you enjoyed doing.**

2. **Reflect on this experience. Is it not true that getting involved in enjoyable activities stopped you from awfulizing (that is, you stopped thinking about an unpleasant event and instead switched to thinking about an activity you were enjoying)? Also, is it not true that when you stopped awfulizing, you then alleviated your unwanted emotions?**

Changing Self-Talk

A second approach to changing unwanted emotions is to identify and then alter the negative and irrational thinking that leads to them. Maultsby has developed an approach entitled Rational Self-Analysis (RSA) that is useful for learning to challenge and change irrational thinking.[3] An RSA has six parts, as shown in Figure M1.1.

The goal in doing an RSA is to change an unwanted emotion (anger, love, guilt, depression, hate) by recording the event and one's self-talk on paper. Under Part A (facts and events), group members state the facts or events that occurred. Under Part B (self-talk), they write all of their thoughts about the events in Part A. Group members num-

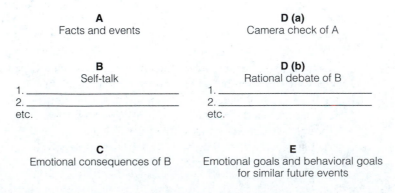

Figure M1.1
Format for Rational Self-Analysis (RSA)

ber each statement in order (1, 2, 3, 4, and so on), and write "good," "bad," or "neutral" after each self-talk statement to show themselves how they believe each Part B statement reflects on themselves as individuals. Under Part C (emotional consequences), they write simple statements describing their gut reactions/emotions stemming from the self-talk in Part B.

Part D(a) is to be written *only* after Parts A, B, and C have been completed; Part D(a) is a "camera check" of Part A. Group members reread Part A and ask themselves, "If I had taken a moving picture of what I wrote was happening, would the camera verify what I have written as fact?" A moving picture would probably have recorded the facts but not personal beliefs or opinions. Personal beliefs or opinions belong in Part B. A common example of a personal opinion mistaken as a fact is: "Karen made me look like a fool when she laughed at me while I was trying to make a serious point." Under D(a), camera check of A, group members correct any opinions by stating only the factual part: "I was attempting to make a serious point when Karen began laughing at what I was saying." Then, the personal opinion part of the statement should be added to B (that is, "Karen made me look like a fool").

Part D(b) determines whether the self-talk statements in B are rational. Each B statement should be taken separately. Group members read B-1 first and ask themselves if it is consistent with rational thinking. It is *irrational* if it does one or more of the following:

1. *Does not fit the facts:* For example, when a person *feels* unloved after a lover has ended their relationship, even though several close friends and relatives love that person
2. *Endangers one's life:* For example, when someone takes drugs to escape from a problem
3. *Keeps one from achieving short- and long-term goals:* For example, when a person wants to do well in college but decides to go out socializing instead of studying before exams
4. *Causes significant trouble with other people:* For example, when a person challenges others to a fight when feeling insulted
5. *Leads one to feel emotions that one does not want to feel*

If the self-talk statement is rational, group members should merely write "that's rational." If, on the other hand, the self-talk statement is irrational, group members should then think of an alternative self-talk to that B statement. This new self-talk statement is of crucial importance in changing an undesirable emotion (and dysfunctional behavior that is associated with the unwanted emotion) and needs to be (1) rational, and (2) a self-talk statement a group member is willing to accept as a new opinion for himself. After jotting down this D(b)-1 self-talk in Part D(b), group members consider B-2, B-3, and so on in the same way.

Under Part E, the new emotions group members desire in similar, future A situations should be noted. In listing these new emotions, members should keep in mind that they will follow from their self-talk statements in Part D(b). This part may also contain a description of specific actions they intend to take to help them achieve their emotional goals when they encounter future A events.

To make a rational self-analysis work, group members must challenge their negative and irrational thinking with rational debates. With effort, they can learn to change any unwanted emotion, and this capacity is one of the most important abilities a person can have. (Once members become adept in RSA, they will be able to do the process without having to write it out.)

Challenging negative and irrational thinking *will* change unwanted emotions if members put the needed effort into it. Just as dieting is guaranteed to result in a loss of weight, so this approach is guaranteed to change unwanted emotions. Both, however, require effort and a commitment to use the processes in order to make them work.

Example of a Rational Self-Analysis: Combating Unwanted Emotions following the Ending of a Romantic Relationship

A.   Facts and Events

A.   For two months I steadily dated a guy that I really thought I liked. I knew something was not quite right with our relationship. I was unable to figure out what it was until he finally said that he had been dating another girl for two years and was still seeing her. However, he promised that they would break up soon and urged me to "hang on" for a little while. Three weeks passed, and then I saw them speaking to each other one night. When she left, I went over to talk to him and he seemed to be in a bad mood. I tried to get out of him what was the matter. Then, we began to talk about the other girl, and he said he could not break up with her for a while and we were not going to see each other at all for a while. Then, I started to yell at him for various things, and the crying began.

D(a).   Camera Check of A

D(a).   All of this is factual.

B.   Self-Talk

B 1.   I hate him! (bad)

B 2.   How could I be such a sucker for the last two months? (bad)

B 3.   All guys are jerks. (bad)

B 4.   I'll never date anyone else again. (bad)

B 5.   I'm glad I know now where I stand for sure. (good)

B 6.   What did I ever do to him to be treated like this? (bad)

B 7.   No one loves me. (bad)

D(b).   My Rational Debates of B

1.   I don't really hate him. He was good to me, and we did enjoy the times we had together.

2.   I should not feel as if I was a sucker because I did not know about the other girl until he finally told me.

3.   Guys are not all jerks. I have many male friends who are far from being jerks. In fact, I do not even know what a "jerk" is. I've never seen a jerk. Guys are humans, not jerks. It is irrational to label someone a "jerk" and then to relate to that person as if the label were real.

4.   I know I will date again, since I always have after other breakups

5.   That's rational.

6.   He told me I never did anything to have this happen. It was just a situation he got himself into and now he needs time to work things out.

7.   How can I say that! I have a lot of close friends and relatives, and I know several guys that think highly of me.

B 8. I'm a failure. (bad)

B 9. I'll never find anyone I loved as much as him to date. My life is ruined. (bad)

B 10. This guy just used me and took what he could get. (bad)

B 11. My life is over. I'll never find happiness again. (bad)

B 12. This is awful! This is the worst thing that could happen to me. (bad)

C.   My Emotions
Outward emotions were crying and yelling. Inner emotions were feeling angry, hurt, depressed, embarrassed, a failure, and unloved.

D(b). My Rational Debates of B (*continued*)

8.   I'm not a failure. I'm doing well in college and at my part-time job.

9.   My life is certainly not ruined. I'm accomplishing many of my goals in life. With two million eligible guys in the world there are certainly many other worthy guys to form a relationship with. I told myself the same erroneous things a few years ago when I broke up with someone else. I will eventually get involved in another relationship with someone else I love. I need to think positively and dwell on the positive things I've learned in this relationship.

10.   Neither of us "used" the other. I'm even uncertain what "used" means. We enjoyed being together and had a lot of good times. He told me he has a lot of positive feelings toward me. He was forced to make a choice between two people, both of whom he enjoyed being with.

11.   My life is certainly not over. I have many positive things happening to me right now, and there are many things I enjoy doing. I also have a number of close relatives and friends who'll be there when I need them.

12.   Life is full of ups and downs. It is a mistake to "awfulize" and to exaggerate how this breakup will affect my future. There are many other more dreadful things that could happen—such as a terminal illness.

E.   My Emotional and Behavioral Goals
To be able to change my unwanted emotions so that I no longer am angry, depressed, and hurt about this breakup. Also, I would like to talk to him in private and apologize for my behavior. After I become more comfortable with this breakup, I will gradually be interested in dating someone else in the future.

Exercise M1.3: Changing Unwanted Emotions with a Rational Self-Analysis

GOAL: This exercise demonstrates that writing (and then using the rational debates) will change unwanted emotions.

1. **Review the material on a Rational Self-Analysis. Write a Rational Self-Analysis on an unwanted emotion you recently experienced.**

2. **Do you believe that if you apply the rational debates to your negative and irrational self-talk, you will be able to change unwanted emotions? Explain your views.**

Changing the Distressing Event

A third way to change unwanted emotions is to change the distressing event. There are an infinite number of distressing events: losing a job, the breakup of a romantic relationship, receiving failing grades, being in an automobile accident, and so on. In some cases, constructive action can be taken to change the distressing event. For example, if a man is terminated from a job, he can seek another; when he finds one he will feel better. If a student is getting failing grades, a conference with the instructor may give the student some ideas about how to improve the grades. If the suggestions appear practical and have merit, the student will feel better.

Not all distressing events can be changed. For example, a woman may have a job that she needs and be forced to interact with other employees who display behaviors she dislikes. If that individual cannot change the behaviors of the others, the only other constructive option is to "bite the bullet" and adapt to the circumstances. However, when it is practical to change distressing events, they should be changed. When constructive changes in events are made, a person is then apt to feel better because he or she will then (in all likelihood) be having more positive self-talk related to the constructive changes that have been made.

Exercise M1.4: Changing Unwanted Emotions by Changing Events

GOAL: This exercise demonstrates that unwanted emotions can be changed by changing the event that is associated with your unwanted emotion.

1. Describe a time in your life when you were awfulizing about something and thereby feeling bad, and you then changed the event—which resulted in your stopping to awfulize. For example, you may have had an unpleasant job, which you then changed. Or, you may have been in an abusive relationship, which you then ended.

2. Is it not true that you stopped feeling bad after changing the unpleasant event because you stopped awfulizing and then had more positive self-talk related to the constructive changes that you made? Explain your views on this.

Destructive Ways of Dealing with Unwanted Emotions

There are two destructive ways to deal with unwanted emotions that, unfortunately, some people use. (I want to make it clear that I strongly discourage using either of the following two ways. I present them only in order to complete the list of ways to deal with unwanted emotions.) One method is to temporarily relieve intense unwanted emotions through the use of alcohol, other drugs, or food. When the effects of the drug wear off, the person's problems and unwanted emotions remain, and there is a danger that through repeated use the person will become dependent on the drug. Some people overeat for the same reasons—loneliness, insecurity, boredom, and frustration. The process of eating and the feeling of having a full stomach provide temporary relief from intense unwanted emotions. Such people are apt to become overweight or bulimic—or both.

The other destructive way to relieve unwanted emotions is suicide. This is the ultimate destructive approach to dealing with unwanted emotions. If you know of someone who is contemplating suicide, you have a legal right and an ethical obligation to seek to connect that person with professional help—even when the suicidal person requests that you do not inform anyone else of his or her intentions.

Exercise M1.5: Changing Unwanted Emotions by Abusing Alcohol, Other Drugs, or Food

GOAL: This exercise demonstrates that unwanted emotions can temporarily be changed through the abusive use of alcohol, other drugs, or food.

1. Describe someone you know who emotionally was feeling bad and turned to abusive use of alcohol, other drugs, or food. If you do not know anyone who did this, describe a time in your life where you were feeling bad and resorted to the abusive use of alcohol, other drugs, or food.

2. Is it not accurate that the abusive use of alcohol, other drugs, or food only provides temporary relief? Give a short explanation of your views on this question.

Assessing and Changing Dysfunctional Behavior

Our self-talk is the primary determinant not only of our emotions, but also of our actions, as illustrated in the following diagram:

Events
↓
Self-talk
↓
Emotions
↓
Actions

In a nutshell, our actions are primarily determined by our self-talk (cognitions). Our thoughts determine our actions. To demonstrate this principle, reflect on the last time you did something bizarre or unusual. What self-talk statements were you giving yourself (that is, what were you thinking) prior to and during the time when you did what you did?

Rational therapy maintains that the reasons for any dysfunctional act (including crime) can be determined by examining what the offender was telling himself or herself prior to and during the time when the act was being committed. Two examples of cognitions that lead to dysfunctional behavior are the following:

Cognition: A 16-year-old sees an unlocked Firebird and thinks, "Hey, this is the ultimate car to drive. Let me cross the starting wires and take it for a ride."

Behavior: Car theft.

Cognition: A 23-year-old male is on his third date with the same woman. He brings her to his apartment and thinks, "She is really sexy. Since I've wined and dined her three times, now it's time for her to show her appreciation. I'll bet she wants it as much as I do. I'll show her what a great lover I am. If she says, 'Don't,' I know she really means 'Don't stop.' I'll use a little force if I have to. When it's over, she'll really love me."

Behavior: Date rape.

It should be noted that the cognitions underlying each dysfunctional behavior may vary considerably among perpetrators. For example, possible cognitions for shoplifting a shirt might be the following. "This shirt would look really nice for the wedding I'm going to on Saturday. Since I'm buying a number of other items from this store, they still will make a profit from me even if I take this without paying for it." Another may be: "This will be a challenge to see if I can get away with taking this shirt. I'll put it on in the fitting room and put my own shirt and coat on over it, and no one will even see me walk out of the store with it. Since I've taken a number of things in the past, I'll act real casual as I walk out of the store." Or: "My son really needs a decent shirt. He doesn't have any nice ones to wear. I don't get enough money from public assistance to buy my children what they need. I know my son is embarrassed to wear the rags that he has. I'll just stick this shirt under my coat and walk out with it."

Assessing human behavior is largely a process of identifying the cognitions that underlie unwanted emotions or dysfunctional behavior. The stages of this process are as follows:

1. Identify as precisely as possible the unwanted emotions and/or dysfunctional behavior that a client has.
2. Identify the cognitions or thinking patterns that the client has during the time when the client is having unwanted emotions or is displaying dysfunctional behavior. There are two primary ways of identifying these cognitions. One way is to ask the client what he was thinking prior to and during the time when the client was having unwanted emotions or displaying dysfunctional behavior. If this approach does not work (perhaps because the client refuses to divulge what he was thinking), a second approach is to obtain information about the client's life circumstances at that time. Once these life circumstances are identified, the professional conducting the assessment needs to place herself mentally into the life circumstances of the perpetrator, and then reflect on the kinds of cognitions that would lead this client to have his specific unwanted emotions or dysfunctional behavior. For example, if the client is a 16-year-old female who has run away from home and is unemployed, it is fairly easy to identify (to some extent) the kinds of cognitions that would lead such a person to turn to prostitution.

A deduction of the principle that thinking processes determine dysfunctional behaviors and unwanted emotions is that *in order to change dysfunctional behaviors or*

Our Thinking Determines Our Behaviors and Our Emotions

A few years ago I was describing to a class the concept that our thinking primarily causes our emotions and our actions. A male student voluntarily self-disclosed the following:

> What you're saying makes a lot of sense. It really applies to something that happened to me. I was living with a female student whom I really cared about. I thought, though, that she was going out on me. When I confronted her about it, she always said I was paranoid and denied it.
>
> Then one night I walked into a bar in this town and I saw her in a corner in a "clutch" position with this guy. I told myself things like "She really is cheating on me. Both of them are playing me for a fool." Such thinking led me to be angry.

> I also told myself "I'm going to set this straight. I'm going to get even with them. I'll break the bottoms off these two empty beer bottles and then jab each of them with the jagged edges." I proceeded to knock off the bottoms on the bar, and then started walking toward them. I got to within 8 feet of them and they were still arm in arm and didn't see me. I began, though, to change my thinking. I thought that if I jabbed them, the end result would be that I would get 8 to 10 years in prison, and I concluded she isn't worth that. Based on this thinking I decided to drop the beer bottles, walk out, and end my relationship with her—which is what I did.

unwanted emotions it is necessary for the affected person to change his or her thinking patterns. These concepts are illustrated in the box. "Our Thinking Determines Our Behaviors and Our Emotions"

Exercise M1.6: Our Actions Are Determined by Our Thoughts

GOAL: This exercise demonstrates that most of our actions are determined by what we think.

1. Describe something quite embarrassing that you did.

2. Describe what you were thinking that led you to do the embarrassing thing that you described.

3. Can you identify any actions that you engaged in that were not partially influenced by what you were thinking? If "yes," specify such actions.

4. In criminal court proceedings, prosecuting attorneys are expected to identify the motive as to why the defendant committed the alleged crime. Is not the search for the motive, in actuality, a search to identify the thinking patterns that led the defendant to commit the alleged crime? Explain your views.

5. Is it not true that in order to stop someone from engaging in dysfunctional or deviant behavior, that person needs to change the thought patterns underlying the dysfunctional behaviors? Explain your views.

6. As an example, what intervention might be used to change the abusive behavior of a husband who abuses his wife?

What Really Causes Psychological Changes via Psychotherapy?

Client-centered therapy, psychoanalysis, rational therapy, feminist intervention, behavior therapy, transactional analysis, reality therapy, hypnosis, meditation, and crisis intervention have all been used to treat a wide range of emotional and behavioral problems. Practically all of these approaches have been used to treat people who are depressed or lonely; have marital or other interpersonal relationship problems; have disabling fears and phobias; are overly aggressive; have drinking problems; or suffer from grief, shame, or guilt. Each of the therapies differs substantially from every other in treatment techniques and in terms of explaining why therapeutic change occurs. Yet, each approach is used by various practitioners who are able to provide case examples that each of these approaches leads to positive changes.

How can all these distinct and diverse psychotherapeutic approaches produce positive changes in clients? What is it that produces positive changes in therapy? Is there a single explanation that will describe psychotherapy changes that are produced by diverse therapies? (The explanation presented here is one that is advanced by rational therapists. This explanation has not as yet been universally accepted.)

Rational therapy asserts that unwanted emotions and dysfunctional actions arise primarily from our self-talk, generally self-talk that is negative or irrational. If this conceptualization is accurate, an important corollary is that *any therapy technique that is successful in changing emotions or actions is effective primarily because it changes a person's thinking from self-talk that is negative or irrational to self-talk that is more rational and positive.* In other words, self-talk appears to be the key therapeutic agent in all approaches that produce positive changes in our emotions and our behaviors.

Exercise M1.7: The Key Therapeutic Change Agent

GOAL: This exercise is designed to have you reflect about whether the key therapeutic change agent, common to any psychotherapy technique that is effective, is changing the client's thinking from self-talk that is negative or irrational to self-talk that is more rational and positive.

1. Summarize your thoughts on what causes unwanted emotions.

2. Summarize your thoughts on what causes dysfunctional behaviors.

3. How can unwanted emotions be changed?

4. How can dysfunctional behaviors be effectively changed?

5. Do you believe the key therapeutic change agent, common to any psychotherapy technique that is effective, is changing the client's thinking from self-talk that is negative or irrational to self-talk that is more rational and positive? Explain your thoughts.

Using Rational Therapy in Groups

Rational therapy asserts that learning how to think rationally (and thereby countering unwanted emotions and dysfunctional behaviors) is an educational process. Clients can learn how to analyze and change irrational self-talk in a variety of ways: instructions by the therapist; viewing videotapes and films on rational therapy; reading books and pamphlets; and attending workshops or seminars on rational therapy.

In group therapy, the therapist first teaches clients the basic concepts of rational therapy. Group members are then assisted in identifying their unwanted emotions and dysfunctional behaviors, identifying the irrational and negative self-talk that causes their unwanted emotions and dysfunctional behaviors, and developing more rational and positive thinking processes to counter their negative and irrational self-talk. Group members also are assisted in other ways to change their unwanted emotions and dysfunctional behaviors—for example, by getting involved in meaningful activities and by changing distressing events. One common strategy in rational therapy groups is to give each member the homework assignment of writing a Rational Self-Analysis (RSA) on an unwanted emotion or dysfunctional behavior that he or she wants to change. At future group sessions, these RSAs are shared and discussed.

■ GROUP EXERCISES

Exercise A: Changing Unwanted Emotions with Self-Talk

GOAL: To learn that unwanted emotions stem primarily from negative and irrational self-talk and that they can be relieved by positive, rational self-talk.

Note: It is advised that the instructor be the designated leader for the exercises in this chapter, as the exercises may generate strong emotions in the participants. Students should not divulge sensitive personal information.

Step 1. Ask the students to think about the last time they were depressed or angry and then to relate what made them depressed or angry. List three or four responses on a blackboard under the two headings "Angry" and "Depressed." (I've run the exercise over 50 times, and people will always provide events or experiences that they believe cause their unwanted emotions.) After making the list, point out that events cannot generate an emotion; instead a person's thoughts about these events cause the unwanted emotions.

Elaborate on this by suggesting certain self-talk statements that may have led students to be angry or depressed. For example, if someone says "I became depressed because my boyfriend didn't send me flowers on Valentine's Day," you might say, "Was your self-talk something like, 'He really doesn't love me. He didn't even remember me on Valentine's Day. This is the pits. This is awful. I feel so hurt. I put so much time into this relationship and it appears he doesn't think very much of me'?" (As an alternative to guessing at self-talk, you can ask students to tell the class what their thoughts were about the events.) Diagram the self-talk process to the class, illustrating that unwanted emotions arise from our self-talk about events.

Step 2. Ask the students what their self-talk would be if the following event occurred: Someone they have been dating for three years says the relationship is over. This event is listed on the blackboard under the heading "A-Event." List each of the self-talk statements given by the students on the blackboard under a B section (B-1, B-2, etc.). For each self-talk statement, the students discuss what emotions would result. (For example, if a student says, "I'll never find anyone else," the resulting emotions might be depression and despair.) Write the emotions on the blackboard under a C section (C-1, C-2, etc.).

Step 3. Explain that all unwanted emotions can be changed by challenging each negative and irrational self-talk statement with a rational debate. Ask the students to give a rational debate for each of the negative and irrational self-talk statements listed in the B section.

Exercise B: Writing a Rational Self-Analysis

GOAL: To demonstrate how to write a Rational Self-Analysis.

Step 1. Explain that all emotions arise primarily from self-talk and that unwanted emotions can be changed by identifying the negative and irrational self-talk and then challenging this self-talk with rational debates. Distribute a handout of a Rational Self-Analysis (the example in this chapter will work) to show how an RSA is written. Have each person in the class write an RSA on an unwanted emotion they have experienced in the recent past. Then, complete the exercise by having the students discuss the merits and shortcomings of writing a Rational Self-Analysis.

Exercise C: Using Positive Affirmations

GOAL: To provide another way to change negative and irrational thinking.

Step 1. Indicate that some people find writing a Rational Self-Analysis to be too time consuming and cumbersome. An alternative is to use a positive affirmation, a positive assertion that helps one achieve emotional and behavioral goals. The process of writing a positive affirmation also enables a person to identify negative and irrational thinking that the person may not be aware of.

Step 2. Each student selects a realistic emotional or behavioral goal that he or she wants to achieve. The following are examples:

"I believe I am a person of worth."
"I will no longer be depressed about _____."
"I will no longer get angry and aggressive when _____ occurs."
"I will lose 15 pounds in two months."
"I will stop smoking today."
"I will limit my drinking of alcohol to two drinks when I go out."
"I will no longer feel guilty about _____."
"I believe I am an attractive person."
"I will assertively express myself when _____ occurs."

Step 3. Have each student start writing (on a sheet of paper) one positive affirmation over and over. When negative thoughts enter their minds, have them record those thoughts and then continue writing the positive affirmation according to the following format:

POSITIVE AFFIRMATIONS	NEGATIVE THOUGHTS
I will lose 15 pounds in two months.	
I will lose 15 pounds in two months.	
I will lose 15 pounds in two months.	I overeat when I'm bored, depressed, or lonely.
I will lose 15 pounds in two months.	
I will lose 15 pounds in two months.	I will need to develop an exercise program, which I hate to do.
I will lose 15 pounds in two months.	One reason I'm fat is that I snack between meals.
I will lose 15 pounds in two months.	I will have to limit the number of beers - that I have when I go out—beer is putting a lot of weight on me.
I will lose 15 pounds in two months.	I wonder if I really want to make all the - changes that I will have to make to lose 15 pounds.
I will lose 15 pounds in two months.	
I will lose 15 pounds in two months.	
I will lose 15 pounds in two months.	

Step 4. Allow the students to write for 10 to 15 minutes. Ask for volunteers to share what they wrote. Have the class discuss the merits and shortcomings of writing positive affirmations. One advantage of repeated writing of the affirmation, for example, is that it trains the mind to more readily accept the positive affirmation.

Exercise D: Assessing and Changing Dysfunctional Behavior

GOAL: To facilitate students' learning how to assess and change dysfunctional behavior.

Step 1. The leader indicates that rational therapy asserts that thinking processes primarily determine behavior. This approach maintains that the reasons for unusual or dysfunctional behavior can always be identified by determining what the perpetrator was thinking prior to and during the time when the act was being committed. Divide the class into subgroups of about four people. Hand each subgroup a card that identifies a perpetrator who has engaged in dysfunctional behavior. Each subgroup should have a different dysfunctional behavior to focus on. Examples of character types to distribute to students include:

1. Alcoholic
2. Spouse abuser
3. Child abuser
4. Bulimic
5. Anorexic
6. Date rapist
7. Compulsive gambler
8. Embezzler
9. Adulterer
10. Arsonist

Step 2. Each subgroup seeks to specify the cognitions that would lead its assigned perpetrator to engage in the indicated dysfunctional behavior. After the subgroups identify the cognitions through a discussion, each subgroup is instructed to specify the interventions that it believes would be most effective in changing the thinking patterns of its assigned perpetrator and curbing the dysfunctional behavior. (Examples of interventions include individual and group therapy, support groups, legal intervention, and family therapy.) The subgroup then selects a spokesperson to summarize the cognitions and list of interventions for the class.

Step 3. Each subgroup specifies to the whole class the type of perpetrator it was assigned to focus on, and the spokesperson then summarizes the cognitions and interventions listed. After each subgroup presents this information, the remainder of the class has an opportunity to suggest cognitions and interventions that the subgroup may have overlooked.

Step 4. The exercise is ended by the class discussing the merits and shortcomings of the assertion by rational therapy that cognitions determine behavior, and changing negative and irrational cognitions in a positive and rational direction is the key psychotherapeutic agent in changing dysfunctional behavior.

Exercise E: Improving Self-Concepts

GOAL: To improve your self-concepts.

Step 1. The leader explains that a negative self-concept stems from negative and irrational self-talk that people give themselves. One way to improve a negative self-concept is to identify the underlying negative self-talk and then challenge this self-talk with rational self-challenges. The leader describes how to write a Rational Self-Analysis. (An example is given in the chapter.)

Step 2. Prior to the next session, students are instructed to write a Rational Self-Analysis (RSA) on the negative thinking that underlies negative components of their self-concepts. The leader answers questions about this assignment and asks that they bring their RSAs to the next session.

Step 3. At the next session the leader asks the students if they had any problems in writing a Rational Self-Analysis, and what they learned from it. A discussion should ensue.

■ MODULE 2: BEHAVIOR THERAPY IN GROUPS

GOALS

Behavior therapy approaches are based on learning theories. This chapter begins by describing three learning processes and then summarizes the following behavior intervention techniques that are used by social workers in groups: assertiveness training, token economies, behavioral contracting, and cognitive behavior techniques.

No one person is credited with the development of behavioral approaches to psychotherapy. Behavior therapists vary considerably in both theory and technique. The main assumption of this therapy system is that maladaptive behaviors are primarily acquired through learning and can be modified through additional learning.

Historically, learning theory has been the philosophical foundation for behavior therapy, even though there has never been agreement as to which learning theory is the core of behavior therapy. A number of authorities have advanced somewhat different theories of how people learn. Pavlov, a Russian who lived between 1849 and 1936, was one of the earliest. Other prominent learning theorists include Edward Thorndike, E. R. Guthrie, C. L. Hull, E. C. Tolman, and B. F. Skinner.[4]

A large number of behavior therapists have achieved international recognition for developing therapy approaches based on learning principles. Some of these therapists include R. E. Alberti and M. L. Emmons, A. Bandura, B. F. Skinner, J. B. Watson and R. Rayner, and J. Wolpe.[5]

In spite of the wide variation in behavioral therapy approaches and techniques, there are some common emphases. One is that the maladaptive behavior (such as bed-wetting) is the problem and needs to be changed. This approach is in sharp contrast to the psychoanalytic approach that views the problematic behavior as being a *symptom* of some underlying, subconscious causes. While psychoanalysts assert the underlying, subconscious causes must be treated to prevent the substitution of new symptoms or the return of old symptoms, behavior therapists assert that treating the problematic behavior will not result in symptom substitution.

Another common emphasis of behavior therapists is the assertion that therapy approaches must be tested and validated by rigorous experimental procedures. Such a focus requires that the goals of therapy be articulated in behavioral terms that can be measured. Baseline levels of problematic behaviors are established prior to therapy in order to measure whether the therapy approach is producing the desired change in the rate or intensity of responding.

Types of Learning Processes

The three major types of learning processes postulated by learning theory are operant conditioning, respondent conditioning, and modeling. These three learning processes are briefly described in the following sections.

Operant Conditioning

Much of human behavior, according to learning theory, is determined by positive and negative reinforcers. A *positive reinforcer* is any stimulus that, when applied following a behavior, increases or strengthens that behavior. Common examples of such stimuli are food, water, sex, attention, affection, and approval. The list of positive reinforcers is inexhaustible and highly individualized. Praise, for example, is a positive reinforcer when, and only when, it maintains or increases the behavior with which it is associated (for example, efforts to improve one's writing skills).

A synonym for negative reinforcer is aversive stimulus. A *negative reinforcer* (or aversive stimulus) is any stimulus that a person will terminate or avoid if given the opportunity. Common examples of negative reinforcers are frowns, electric shock, and criticism. (It should be noted that the same stimulus—for example, the smell of Limburger cheese—can be a positive reinforcer for one person, while it may be a negative reinforcer for another.)

There are four basic learning principles involving positive reinforcers and aversive stimuli:

1. If a positive reinforcer (for example, food) is presented to a person following a response, the result is positive reinforcement. With positive reinforcement that occurrence of a given behavior is strengthened or increased.
2. If a positive reinforcer is withdrawn following a person's response, the result is punishment.
3. If an aversive stimulus (for example, an electric shock) is presented to a person following a response, the result is punishment. (As can be seen, there are two types of punishment.)
4. If an aversive stimulus is withdrawn following a person's response, the result is negative reinforcement. In negative reinforcement, a response (behavior) is increased through removing an aversive stimulus (for example, fastening one's seat belt in a car to turn off the obnoxiously loud and annoying buzzer).

In sum, positive and negative reinforcement increase behavior, and punishment decreases behavior. Principles of operant conditioning are used in three behavioral techniques that are described in this chapter (assertiveness training, token economies, and contingency contracting). Operant conditioning principles are also used in aversive techniques (such as administering an electric shock when a client engages in maladaptive behavior). Aversive techniques will not be described in this chapter, as they are seldom, if ever, used by social workers. *Positive reinforcement (reward) approaches are generally more effective than those based on punishment. Punishment is often counterproductive as it can lead to the client becoming hostile about the treatment procedures.* Also, punishment may have only temporary effects. When the client realizes she is no longer under surveillance, she may return to exhibiting the maladaptive behavior.

Exercise M2.1: Operant Conditioning

GOAL: This exercise is designed to assist you in understanding and applying operant conditioning.

1. Describe an experience where a behavior of yours was increased by a positive reinforcer.

2. Describe an experience where a behavior of yours was decreased by a negative reinforcer.

Respondent Conditioning

Respondent learning has also been called classical or Pavlovian conditioning. A wide range of everyday behaviors are considered to be respondent behaviors—including many anxieties, fears, and phobias. A key concept in respondent learning is "pairing"; that is, behaviors are learned by being consistently and over time paired with other behaviors or events. In order to explain respondent conditioning, we will begin by defining the following key terms:

Neutral stimulus (NS): A stimulus that elicits little or no response
Unconditioned stimulus (UCS): A stimulus that elicits an unlearned or innate response
Unlearned or innate response (UR): A response that is innate; for example, the response of salivating to having food in the mouth
Conditioned response (CR): A new response that has been learned
Conditioned stimulus (CS): An originally neutral stimulus that through pairing with an unconditioned stimulus now begins to elicit a conditioned response

Respondent learning asserts that when a neutral stimulus (*NS*) is paired with an unconditioned stimulus (*UCS*), the neutral stimulus will also come to elicit a response similar to that being elicited by the UCS. That new response is called a *conditioned response (CR)* because it has been learned; the originally neutral stimulus, once it begins to elicit the response, becomes the conditioned stimulus (CS). Thus, it is possible for an event that originally elicited no fear whatsoever (for example, being in the dark) to come to elicit fear when it is paired with a stimulus that does elicit fear (for example, horrifying stories about being in the dark). This learning process is indicated in the following paradigm:

1. *UCS* (horrifying stories about being in the dark) ⟶ elicits *UR* (fear)
2. *NS* (being in the dark)
   ↓
   (paired with)
   UCS ⟶ elicits ⟶ *CR* (fear)
3. *NS* becomes *CS* ⟶ elicits *CR* (fear)

The *CS* ⟶ *CR* bond can be broken by *respondent extinction* or by *counterconditioning.* Respondent extinction involves continuing presentation of the conditioned stimulus without any further pairing with the unconditioned stimulus. Respondent extinction gradually weakens, and eventually eliminates, the CS-CR bond.

Counterconditioning is based on the principle that the CS-CR bond can be broken by using new responses that are stronger than and incompatible with old responses that are elicited by the same stimulus. For example, it is possible to teach a person to relax (new response) instead of becoming anxious (old response) when confronted with a particular stimulus (for example, the prospect of flying in a small plane).

Exercise M2.2: Pavlovian Conditioning

GOAL: This exercise is designed to assist you in understanding and applying respondent conditioning.

Describe an experience where a behavior of yours was shaped by respondent conditioning.

Modeling

Modeling refers to a change in behavior as a result of the observation of someone else's behavior; that is, learning by vicarious experience or imitation. Much of everyday learning is thought to take place through modeling—using both live models and symbolic models (such as films). Modeling has been used in behavior modification to develop new behaviors that are not in a person's repertoire; for example, showing a youngster how to swing a bat. Modeling has also been used to eliminate anxieties and fears; for example, through using a model in assertiveness training. Anxieties and fears are reduced or eliminated through modeling in assertiveness training by exposing fearful observers to modeled events in which the model performs feared activity without experiencing any adverse effects and even enjoys the process.

Exercise M2.3: Modeling

GOAL: This exercise is designed to assist you in understanding and applying the principles of modeling.

Describe an experience where you learned a new behavior by modeling.

Theory of Behavior Therapy

Behavior therapy is based on the assumption that all behavior occurs in response to stimulation, internal or external. The first task of the behavior therapist is to identify the probable stimulus-response (S-R) connections that are occurring for the client. This part of the therapy process is called the behavioral or functional analysis. The following is an illustration of an S-R connection: For a person who has a fear of heights, the stimulus (S) of flying in a small plane would have the response (R) of intense anxiety and seeking to avoid the stimulus.

Prior to, and during the time when the therapist is doing the behavioral analysis, the therapist is also attempting to establish a working relationship. During the behavioral analysis, the therapist attempts to determine the stimuli that are associated with the maladaptive responses. Through this analysis both the client and the therapist arrive at an understanding of the problem and generally how it developed. This insight, although it does not treat the problem, is useful because it reduces some of the client's anxiety and the client no longer feels possessed or overwhelmed by unknown, mysterious forces. It should be noted that errors about hypothesized S-R connections at this diagnostic stage usually lead to ineffective treatment, as the treatment will then be focused on treating S-R connections that are *not* involved in perpetuating the maladaptive behavior.

The therapist begins a behavioral analysis by taking a detailed history of the presenting problem, its course, and particularly of its association with current experiences. In making such an analysis it is crucial to obtain specific, concrete details about the circumstances in which the presenting problem arises. If, for example, a client is shy in some situations, it is important to identify the specific interactions in which the client is shy. Furthermore, it is important to determine the reasons why the client is shy: Is it because the person does not know how to express himself or herself, or is it because the person has certain fears? The treatment chosen depends on such information.

If the clients do not know how to express themselves, a *modeling* approach through role-playing might be used. On the other hand, if clients have the response potential but are inhibited because they do not think they have the right to assertively express themselves, reframing (described later in this chapter) might be used to change their thinking processes so that they realize that everyone has the right to express thoughts and feelings.

The objective in doing a behavioral analysis is to identify the antecedent stimuli that are generating the maladaptive responses. Once these connections are identified, they are discussed with the client to help the client gain insight and to obtain the client's feedback on possible erroneous connections. The client and the therapist then agree upon the goals for the treatment. The process of how therapy will proceed (along with the techniques to be used) are described to the client. This provides the client with an idea of his or her role in treatment, and Orne and Wender have found that this knowledge fosters positive outcomes and reduces the dropout rate.[6]

Chambless and Goldstein describe the sources of information for making a behavioral analysis:

> The behavior therapist may base the functional analysis on interviews with the client and important people in the client's life or on information gained by having the client keep a journal. Questionnaire data are often useful. Interpersonal problems may be more clearly defined if the therapist and client role play interactions with which the client reports difficulty. When the therapist has a difficult time making the analysis, observing the client in the situation where the problem occurs may lead to a wealth of information. Obviously, there are times when this would be impossible or in poor taste, but direct observation is used much less frequently than it should be.[7]

The remainder of this chapter is focused on presenting behavior therapy techniques that are commonly used by social workers. These techniques include assertiveness training, token economies, behavioral contracting, and cognitive behavior techniques.

Assertiveness Training

Assertiveness training has become the most frequently used method in modifying unadaptive interpersonal behavior. It is particularly effective in changing both timid behavior and aggressive behavior. Wolpe originally developed this approach,[8] and it has been further developed by a variety of authors, including Alberti and Emmons, and Fensterheim and Baer.[9]

Assertiveness problems range from extreme shyness, introversion, and withdrawal to inappropriate rages that can alienate others. A nonassertive person is often acquiescent, fearful, and afraid of expressing his real feelings spontaneously. Frequently, resentment and anxiety build up, which may result in general discomfort, feelings of low self-esteem, tension headaches, fatigue, and perhaps a destructive explosion of anger and aggression. Some people are overly shy and timid in nearly all interactions; however, most encounter occasional problems in isolated areas where it would be to their benefit to be more assertive. For example, a young man might be quite effective and assertive in his job as a store manager but still be awkward and timid in a social situation.

Nonassertive, Aggressive, and Assertive Behaviors

There are three basic styles of interacting with others—nonassertive, aggressive, and assertive—and they have been summarized by Alberti and Emmons as follows:

> In the *nonassertive* style, you are likely to hesitate, speak softly, look away, avoid the issue, agree regardless of your own feelings, not express opinions, value yourself "below" others, and hurt yourself to avoid any chance of hurting others.
>
> In the *aggressive style,* you typically answer before the other person is through talking, speak loudly and abusively, glare at the other person, speak "past" the issue (accusing, blaming, demeaning), vehemently expound your feelings and opinions, value yourself "above" others, and hurt others to avoid hurting yourself.
>
> In the *assertive style,* you will answer spontaneously, speak with a conversational tone and volume, look at the other person, speak to the issue, openly express your personal feelings and opinions (anger, love, disagreement, sorrow), value yourself equal to others, and hurt neither yourself nor others.[10]

The following examples describe two typical situations in which an assertive response could be used effectively. In the first situation, the level of intimacy is low since the situation occurs with a business associate. However, in the second instance, the social situation involves a husband and wife and a much more intimate relationship. Group leaders should note that just as it is more difficult to say "no" to a friend than to a stranger who wants to borrow $50, it is more difficult to deal with assertive behavior on an intimate than on a superficial level.

1. You are driving with a business associate to a distant city for a conference. The associate lights up a pipe; you soon find the smoke irritating and the odor somewhat stifling. What are your choices?

    Nonassertive response: You attempt to carry on a cheery conversation for the three-hour trip without commenting about the smoke.

    Aggressive response: You become increasingly irritated until you explode, "Either you put out that pipe or I'll put it out for you—the odor is sickening."

    Assertive response: In a firm, conversational tone, you look directly at the associate and state, "The smoke from your pipe is irritating me. I'd appreciate it if you would put it away."

2. At a party with friends, your husband subtly puts you down by stating, "Wives always talk too much." What do you do?

    Nonassertive response: You don't say anything, but feel hurt and become quiet.

    Aggressive response: You glare at him and angrily ask, "John, why are you always criticizing me?"

Assertive response: You carry on as usual, waiting until the drive home to calmly look at him and say, "When we were at the party tonight, you said that wives always talk too much. I felt you were putting me down when you said that. What did you mean by that comment?"

Assertiveness training is designed to lead one to realize, feel, and act on the assumption that one has the right to be oneself and express one's feelings freely. Assertive responses are generally not aggressive responses, and the distinction between these two types of interactions is important. If, for example, a woman has an overly critical mother-in-law, the woman may intentionally do things that will upset her (not visiting, serving food she dislikes, not cleaning the house), urging her husband to tell his mother to "shut up," and getting into loud arguments with her. On the other hand, an effective assertive response would be to counter criticism by saying: "Jane, your criticism deeply hurts me. I know you're trying to help when you give advice, but I feel that you're criticizing me. I know you don't want me to make mistakes, but to grow, I need to make my own errors and learn from them. If you want to help me, let me do it myself and be responsible for the consequences. The type of relationship I'd like to have with you is a close adult relationship and not a mother–child relationship."

Assertiveness Training in Groups

All of us are nonassertive in some situations where it would be to our benefit to be assertive. Many of us are aggressive in some situations in which it would be more constructive to be assertive. Assertiveness training groups are ideal settings to learn to be more assertive, for they allow members to test new assertive behaviors through interactions with others. Assertiveness training groups also allow members to learn new assertive strategies through observing effective assertive responses that are modeled by other group members. The following material summarizes a step-by-step approach for facilitating an assertiveness training program within a group setting.[11]

Examining Group Interactions: The first step to implementing assertiveness training in a group is for each member to examine his or her interactions. Aggressive, assertive, and nonassertive behavior are defined by the group leader, and examples are provided. Then, group members are asked by the leader to silently and privately arrive at answers to the following questions:

1. Are there situations that you would like to handle more assertively?
2. Are there situations in which you habitually withhold opinions and feelings that you want to express?
3. Are there situations in which you habitually become angry and lash out at others, only to regret your aggression later?

Selecting Areas for Improvement: Group members individually and privately select interactions (identified in the preceding step) in which it would be to their benefit to be more assertive. These may include situations in which they were overpolite, too apologetic, timid, or allowed others to take advantage of them while inwardly harboring feelings of resentment, anger, embarrassment, fear, or self-criticism for not having the courage to express themselves; and overly aggressive interactions in which they exploded in anger or walked over others. For *each* set of nonassertive or aggressive interactions, group members can become more assertive, as shown in the next steps. The group leader should add at this point that the members will not be required to reveal the situations in which they have habitually been nonassertive or aggressive.

Visualizing an Incident: Group members are instructed to concentrate on a specific incident involving their problematic interactions. They close their eyes for several minutes and vividly imagine the details, including specific conversations and feelings. As part of this visualization process, the leader indicates that nonverbal communication is as important as verbal communication. The leader then asks the members to silently arrive at answers to the following questions:

1. *Eye contact:* "Did you look directly at the other person in a relaxed, steady manner? Looking down or away suggests a lack of self-confidence. Glaring is an aggressive response."

2. *Gestures:* "Were your gestures appropriate, free-flowing, relaxed, and used to emphasize your message effectively? Awkward stiffness suggests nervousness; other gestures, such as an angry fist, signal an aggressive reaction."

3. *Body posture:* "Did you show the importance of your message by facing the other person, leaning forward, holding your head up, and sitting or standing appropriately close?"

4. *Facial expression:* "Did your facial expression show the firmness of purpose and self-confidence consistent with an assertive response?"

5. *Voice tone and volume:* "Was your response stated in a firm, conversational tone? Shouting may suggest anger. Speaking softly suggests shyness, a cracking voice nervousness."

6. *Speech fluency:* "Did your speech flow smoothly, clearly, and slowly? Rapid speech or hesitation in speaking suggests nervousness."

7. *Timing:* "Were your verbal reactions to a problem stated at the appropriate time? Generally, spontaneous expressions are the best, but certain situations should be handled at a later time—for example, challenging some of your boss's erroneous statements in private rather than in front of the group he is addressing."

8. *Message content:* "Which of your statements were aggressive, which assertive, and which nonassertive? Why do you believe you responded nonassertively or aggressively? Have you habitually responded nonassertively or aggressively in this situation?"

Visualizing an Assertive Model: The leader instructs the group members to continue to keep their eyes closed. The leader states: "We will now focus on coming up with some alternative approaches for being assertive that you can use in your problematic situation. One way to do this is to visualize how someone you view as being fairly assertive would handle this situation. What would this assertive model say? How would this person be assertive nonverbally in this situation?" (Pause)

Alternative Assertive Approaches: The leader continues the visualization exercise by asking group members to come up with several alternative approaches for being assertive in this situation. Members then are instructed to visualize using each of these approaches. For each approach, members should think through what the full set of interactions would be, along with the consequences. (The leader pauses frequently while group members are visualizing these alternatives.) The leader then instructs members to select an approach, or combination of approaches, that each believes will work best in his or her situation. Through imagery, members should continue practicing this approach until they feel comfortable with it.

If anyone has difficulty in thinking of a strategy to use, the leader indicates that it may be helpful after this visualization exercise ends to have someone else in the class role-play an assertive approach for this situation. Group members continue, through imagery, to practice their chosen strategy until they feel ready to use it when their problematic situation occurs again. The leader informs the members that when a real-life situation occurs they should expect to be somewhat anxious when they first try to be assertive. Members are also informed that after trying out their assertive strategy in a real-life situation, they should reflect on its effectiveness by asking themselves the following questions:

1. Considering the nonverbal and verbal guidelines for being assertive, which components of your responses were assertive, which were aggressive, and which were nonassertive?

2.   What were the consequences of your effort?

3.   How do you feel after trying out this new set of interactions?

The leader explains that some success is to be expected but not complete personal satisfaction with these initial efforts. Learning to be more assertive is a continuing process. Also, group members should be told: "Pat yourself on your back for the progress you made in being more assertive—you've earned it! Learning to be more assertive is an exhilarating experience. But you should also identify the areas where you need to improve and continue to use the process." Finally, members should be informed that the visualization exercise is drawing to a close and should now open their eyes.

Role Playing: The leader distributes note cards and asks members to write down anonymously one or two problematic situations they would like others in the class to role-play. After the cards are handed in the leader selects an interesting situation and asks volunteers to role-play it. Generally, there are two people in the situation, and one role involves using an assertive strategy. After the situation is role-played, the class discusses what was done well and what else might have been done. Another role-play situation is then selected, and the process continues.

The Assertiveness Model: After several situations are role-played, the leader summarizes how one becomes more assertive:

1.   Identify a problematic situation in which you are habitually nonassertive or aggressive.

2.   Visualize a problematic incident and identify your nonverbal and verbal communication.

3.   Develop alternative approaches for being assertive in this situation. A few approaches may be arrived at by visualizing how an assertive model would act.

4.   Select an assertive strategy and continue to practice it through imagery.

5.   Role-play an assertive strategy to gain confidence or watch someone else role-play the strategy. After watching someone else, role-play the approach yourself.

6.   Try out the assertive strategy in a real-life situation.

7.   Analyze what you did well and what you still need to work on to become more assertive.

Comments: The leader may want to supplement the previous material by showing one or more films or videotapes on assertiveness training. If a group member is still afraid of attempting assertive behavior, he or she should repeat the modeling, visualizing, and role-playing steps. For those few individuals who fail to develop the needed confidence to try out being assertive, seeking professional private counseling is advised, since being able to express oneself and have effective interactions with others is essential for personal happiness.

The leader should add that it is a mistake to seek to be assertive in all situations. There are some situations in which it is best to be nonassertive. For example, if two large muscular people are physically fighting, it may be a mistake for a small person to assertively intervene. There are also some situations where it is best to be aggressive. For example, if you observe someone being sexually assaulted, it may be advantageous to intervene by aggressively seeking to stop the perpetrator.

The format of the technique in assertiveness training is relatively simple to comprehend. Considerable skill (common sense and ingenuity), however, is needed to determine what will be an effective assertive strategy when a real-life situation arises. The joy and pride obtained from being able fully to express oneself assertively is nearly unequaled.

Exercise M2.4: Becoming Assertive

GOAL: This exercise is designed to assist you in understanding and applying the principles of assertiveness training.

1. Describe a behavior of yours where you are routinely nonassertive and you instead want to be more assertive.

2. Review the material on assertiveness training. Visualize yourself being assertive in this situation. Describe what you will say, and describe what you want to communicate with your nonverbal behavior.

3. Describe a behavior of yours where you are routinely aggressive and you instead want to be more assertive.

4. Visualize yourself being assertive in this situation. Describe what you will say, and describe what you want to communicate with your nonverbal behavior.

5. **When these problematic situations again arise where you have either been nonassertive or aggressive, are you committed to now seeking to be assertive?**

Token Economies

Tokens are symbolic reinforcers, such as poker chips or points on a tally sheet, which can later be exchanged for items that constitute direct forms of reinforcement, such as candy or increased privileges (for example, an adolescent in a group home being allowed to go to movies). An economy involves an exchange system that specifies exactly what the tokens can be exchanged for, and how many tokens it takes to get particular items or privileges. The economy also specifies the target behaviors (such as going to school or making a bed) that can earn tokens and the rate of responding that is required to earn a particular number of tokens. For example, attending school every day for two weeks earns 10 tokens at an adolescent group home, and 10 tokens can be exchanged for attending a sports event.

Token economies have been successfully used in a wide variety of institutional settings, including mental hospitals, training schools for delinquents, classrooms for students with emotional problems, schools for people with a cognitive disability, rehabilitation centers for people with a physical or cognitive disability, and group homes for adolescents. There is more evidence to support the effectiveness of token economies than for almost any other behavioral technique.[12] Token economies have been used to effect positive changes in a wide variety of behaviors, including personal hygiene, social interactions, job attendance and performance, academic performance, domestic tasks such as cleaning, and personal appearance. At times, clients not only earn tokens for desired behaviors but also lose tokens for undesired behaviors (for example, instigating a fight).

Effective token economies are much more difficult to establish than it appears at first glance. Prochaska summarizes some of the most important factors that need to be given attention in establishing a token economy:

> Some of the more important considerations include staff cooperation and coordination, since the staff must be more observant and more systematic in their responses to clients than in a noncontingent system. A variety of attempts at establishing token economies have failed because the staff did not cooperate adequately in monitoring the behavior of residents. Effective token economies must also have adequate control over reinforcements, since an economy becomes ineffective if residents have access to reinforcements by having money from home or being able to bum a cigarette from a less cooperative staff member. Problems must be clearly defined in terms of specific behaviors to be changed in order to avoid conflicts among staff or patients. Improving personal hygiene, for example, is too open to interpretation by individuals, and patients may insist that they are improving their hygiene even though staff members may disagree. There is much less room for misunderstandings if personal hygiene is defined as clean fingernails, no evidence of body odor, clean underwear, and other clear-cut rules. Specifying behaviors that are positive alternatives to problem behavior is very critical in teaching residents what positive actions they can take to help themselves, rather than relying on just a negative set of eliminating responses. Perhaps most important for more lasting effectiveness of token economies is that they be gradually phased out as problem behaviors are reduced and more adaptive responses become well established. Obviously the outside world does not run according to an institution's internal economy, and it is important that clients be prepared to make the transition to the larger society. Using an abundance of social reinforcers along with token reinforcers helps prepare clients for the fading out of tokens, so that positive behaviors can be maintained by praise or recognition rather than by tokens. Also encouraging patients to reinforce themselves, such as by learning to take pride in their appearance, is an important step in fading out tokens. Some institutions use transitional wards where clients go from token economies and learn to maintain adaptive behaviors through more

naturalistic contingencies, such as praise from a fellow patient. In such transitional settings, backup reinforcers are available if needed, but they are used much more sparingly than in the token economies. Without the use of fading, token economies can become nothing more than hospital management procedures that make the care of patients more efficient without preparing patients to live effectively in the larger society.[13]

Exercise M2.5: Token Economy

GOAL: This exercise is designed to assist you in understanding a token economy.

Describe a token economy that you participated in. Perhaps it was a token economy that a former teacher used with the class. Perhaps it was a system that your parents used to pay you for you doing work that they wanted completed.

Behavioral Contracting

Closely related to token economies is behavioral contracting. Behavioral contracts provide the client with a set of rules that govern the change process. Contracts may be unilateral; that is, a client may make a contract with himself or herself. For example, a woman with a weight problem may limit herself to a certain calorie intake, with a system of rewards being established for staying within the calorie limit. Contracts may also be bilateral and specify the obligations and the mutual reinforcements for each of the parties.

Helping professionals are finding it very useful to develop behavioral contracts with clients. Formulating contracts with clients in both one-to-one settings and group settings has a number of advantages. The contracts serve as guides to clients as to the specific actions they need to take in order to improve their problematic situations. Contracts tend to have a motivational effect because when people commit to the terms of a contract, they usually feel a moral obligation to follow through on the commitments they make. In addition, reviewing whether or not commitments made in contracts are being met provides therapists and clients with one method for measuring progress. If a client's commitments are usually fulfilled, positive changes are probably occurring. If commitments are generally unfulfilled, it suggests that positive changes are not occurring.

Contracts in social work practice specify goals to be accomplished and the tasks to be performed to accomplish them. In addition, contracts set deadlines for completion of the specified task and identify rewards for successful completion of tasks. Contracts also specify consequences for unsuccessful completion of tasks. A contract is, therefore, an agreement between a social worker and one or more clients in their joint efforts to achieve specified outcomes. Formulating an explicit contract is directly related to a positive outcome for clients.[14]

A contract, in outline format, should contain the following components:

1. Goals to be accomplished (ranked in order of priority)
2. Tasks to be accomplished by the client and by the worker (These tasks must be directly related to accomplishing the goals, so that accomplishing the tasks will result in successfully meeting the goals.)
3. Time frame for completing the tasks
4. Means of monitoring progress toward accomplishing the tasks and the goals
5. Rewards for the client if the terms of the contract are met
6. Adverse consequences to the client upon nonfulfillment of the terms of the contract

Some workers prefer written contracts, and others prefer verbal contracts. A written contract has the advantage of emphasizing the commitment to the contract by both the worker and the client, and it minimizes the risks of misunderstandings. A verbal contract has the advantage of avoiding the sterility of a written contract. Research comparing the effectiveness of written versus verbal contracts shows that the verbal contract is generally as effective as the written contract with regard to the goals being successfully accomplished.[15] If a worker chooses to use a verbal contract, the worker should still record the essential elements of the contract in his or her notes for future reference.

The most difficult element in formulating an effective contract is for the worker and the client to formulate goals. Goals specify what the client wishes to accomplish and should directly relate to the needs, wants, or problems being encountered by the client. Goals serve the following important functions:

1. Goals ensure that the worker and the client are in agreement about the objectives to be accomplished.
2. Goals provide direction to the helping process and thereby reduce needless wandering.
3. Goals guide selection of appropriate tasks (and interventions) that are focused on achieving the objectives.
4. Goals serve as outcome criteria in evaluating the extent to which the tasks (and interventions) are being successful.

Useful guidelines when setting goals include

1. *Goals must relate to the desired end results sought by the client:* The client must believe that accomplishing the selected goals will enhance his or her well-being. Therefore, the worker needs to integrally involve the client in the process of selecting and specifying the goals.
2. *Goals should be stated in specific and measurable terms:* Nebulous goals (such as "Client gaining increased control over his emotions") are not sufficiently specific and often lead the client to "drift" or wander in the helping process. A specific goal (such as "The client will express his angry feelings with his mother in an assertive rather than an aggressive manner when they are having conflicts") is substantially more explicit. In addition, it is also measurable, whereas a nebulously stated goal is not. The client's mother (and others) can monitor the number of times, over a specified time period, that the client expresses his angry feelings assertively as compared to aggressively. Clients tend to define goals more nebulously, so it is important for the worker to assist clients in stating their goals in such a way that they are both specific and measurable.
3. *Goals should be feasible:* Unachievable goals set the client up for failure, which is then apt to lead to disappointment, disillusionment, and a sense of defeat. It is vital that the goals chosen can be accomplished by the client. For clients with grandiose tendencies, it is important for the worker to assist them (tactfully) in lowering their expectations to the upper level of what can reasonably be attained.

When arriving at feasible goal statements with a client, the worker should agree only to assist the client in working toward goals for which the worker has the requisite skills and knowledge. If the goal is beyond the worker's competence (for example, assisting the client in overcoming a complex sexual dysfunction), the worker has the responsibility to refer the client to a more appropriate resource in the community.

Once the client has settled on his or her goals, the final step in the process of negotiating goal statements is to assign priorities to the goals. The purpose of this step is to ensure that the initial change efforts are directed to the goal that is most important to the client. The example presented earlier in Chapter 12 illustrates the formulation of a behavioral contract.

Exercise M2.6: Contingency Contracting

GOAL: This exercise is designed to assist you in understanding and applying contingency contracting (which is a type of a behavioral contract).

1. **Identify a behavior of yours that you want to change (such as quitting smoking, stopping procrastination on a project, or only having two alcoholic beverages when you go out).**

2. **State your behavioral goal.**

3. **Specify what you need to do to accomplish your goal.**

4. State your time frame for accomplishing the tasks.

5. Specify the means of monitoring progress toward accomplishing the tasks and goals.

6. Specify how you will reward yourself if you accomplish your goal.

7. Specify what you will do whenever you engage in behavior inconsistent with your goal (such as donating $5 to a charity).

Cognitive Behavior Techniques

A major trend in behavior therapy in the past two decades has been recognition of the role of cognition (thinking processes) in human behavior. Following the observations of cognitive therapists such as Ellis and Beck, cognitive behavior therapists have accepted the notion that changing one's thoughts will often change one's feelings and behavior.[16]

The traditional paradigm of behavior therapy has been S (stimulus) → R (response). Cognitive behavior therapists insert an additional step in this paradigm:

$$S \text{ (stimulus)} \rightarrow O \text{ (cognitions of organism)} \rightarrow R \text{ (response)}[17]$$

This section summarizes the following techniques that have been developed to change cognitions—thought stopping and covert assertion, diversion techniques, and reframing.

Thought Stopping and Covert Assertion

Thought stopping is used by clients whose major problems involve obsessive thinking and ruminations about events which are very unlikely to occur (such as worrying that a plane they will be taking in two weeks will crash, or worrying that they are becoming mentally ill).

In thought stopping, the client is first asked to concentrate on and express out loud obsessive, anxiety-inducing thoughts. As the client begins to express those thoughts, the therapist suddenly and emphatically shouts "Stop." This procedure is repeated several times until the client reports that the thoughts are being successfully interrupted. Then the responsibility for the intervention is shifted to the client, so that the client now says "Stop" out loud when he or she begins to think about the troubling thoughts. Once the overt shouting is effective in stopping the troubling thoughts, the client then begins to practice saying "Stop" silently whenever the troubling thoughts begin.

Rimm and Masters supplemented the thought-stopping technique with a *covert assertion* procedure.[18] In addition to interrupting obsessive thoughts by saying "Stop," the client is encouraged to produce a positive, assertive statement that is incompatible with the content of the obsession. For example, a client who worries about becoming mentally ill (when there is no basis for such thinking) may be encouraged to add the covert assertion "I'm perfectly normal" whenever he or she interrupts the obsessive thinking with "Stop."

Mahoney successfully used thought stopping and covert assertion as part of a comprehensive program for overweight clients.[19] Mahoney first instructed clients to become aware of such self-statements as, "I just don't have the will power" and "I sure can taste eating a strawberry sundae." The clients were then trained to use thought stopping and covert assertion to combat these thoughts.

Exercise M2.7: Applying Thought Stopping and Covert Assertion

GOAL: This exercise is designed to demonstrate how to use thought stopping and covert assertion.

1. This may sound strange, but start awfulizing about a current problem in your life. Awfulize for about five minutes about this problem.

2. After five minutes yell "stop" to yourself (either out loud or silently). Also think of a positive, assertive statement that is incompatible with the content of the obsession. Now, whenever you start awfulizing about your problem, yell "stop" and also use your covert assertion.

3. Specify what you were awfulizing about.

4. Specify the covert assertion you used.

5. Indicate whether the thought stopping and covert assertion approach worked for you.

6. If the technique did not work very well, indicate why you believe it did not work very well for you.

Diversion Techniques

Diversion techniques are used with clients who have strong, unwanted emotions—such as loneliness, bitterness, depression, frustration, and anger. As indicated in Module 1, unwanted emotions stem primarily from negative and irrational thinking. By becoming involved in physical activity, work, social interactions, or play, these clients will usually switch their negative cognitions to cognitions related to the diversion activities they are involved in. Once they focus their thinking on the diversion activities that they find meaningful and enjoyable, they will experience more pleasing emotions.

Diversion techniques are used in both rational therapy (see Module 1) and cognitive behavior therapy. Rational therapy and cognitive behavior therapy are closely related. In fact, rational therapy is sometimes classified as a cognitive-behavioral approach.

Exercise M2.8: Applying the Diversion Technique

GOAL: This exercise is designed to demonstrate that most people can change an unwanted emotion by the diversion technique.

1. Think about a situation in your past where you tended to awfulize extensively about and then used a diversion technique to stop the awfulizing—and thereby changed an unwanted emotion related to the awfulizing. (For example, you may have awfulized about someone breaking up with you.)

2. Specify what you were awfulizing about. Also indicate your resulting unwanted emotion(s).

3. Describe the diversion technique that you used.

4. Describe the results of using your diversion technique.

5. Are you willing to try the diversion technique the next time you start awfulizing?

Reframing

Reframing involves helping a client change those cognitions that cause unwanted emotions or dysfunctional behaviors. As the following material describes, there are a variety of categories of cognitions that may be reframed.

One focus of reframing is on *positive thinking*. When unpleasant events occur (such as receiving a lower grade on an exam than anticipated), we can choose to think positively or to think negatively. If we take a positive view and focus on problem solving, we are apt to identify and initiate actions to improve the circumstances. On the other hand, if we think negatively, we develop unwanted emotions (such as depression and frustration) and fail to focus on problem solving. With negative thinking, we generally do not do anything constructive and may even engage in destructive behavior.

When a client is thinking negatively, a therapist can use reframing to assist the client in realizing that he or she is thinking negatively. At times it is helpful to say to the client that both negative and positive thinking often become self-fulfilling prophecies, then, through asking the client to name some positive aspects of the situation, the therapist seeks to assist the client in thinking more positively. (If the client is unable to identify any positives, the therapist may suggest some positive aspects.) The client may be encouraged to tell himself or herself to "stop" whenever negative thinking occurs and instead to focus on self-talk about positive aspects of the situation.

Some people take a negative view of most events that happen to them; for such people, reframing through using positive cognitions is more difficult and time consuming. However, if they are successful in learning to think positively, they often make substantial gains.

A second closely related way in which reframing is used is "*deawfulizing*." When distressing events occur, most of us tend to awfulize—we exaggerate the negatives. Think about how you reacted when someone with whom you were romantically involved broke up with you or when you received a parking or speeding citation. Did you awfulize the situation and as a result feel angry, hurt, or depressed? When we awfulize, we focus only on the negatives and do not identify constructive actions to improve the situation. When a client is awfulizing, a therapist can usually help the client identify such thought processes by simply inquiring, "I wonder if you're awfulizing?" The therapist can then assist the client, as described in the material on reframing with positive thinking, to give cognitions that are more positive and oriented toward problem solving.

A third reframing focus involves *decatastrophizing*.[20] Decatastrophizing is used when clients are worrying about anticipated feared events. Decatastrophizing involves continually asking clients "what if" an anticipated, undesired consequence occurs. For example, the following is a dialogue with a 21-year-old college student who feared expressing his thoughts and feelings in class:

Therapist: What do you think will happen if you begin expressing your views in your classes?

Client: My voice may crack, and the others may laugh at me.

Therapist: It is unlikely that your voice will crack. But even if it does and the students happen to laugh a little, is that really worse than your anger and frustration over not sharing your thoughts?

Client: I don't know.

Therapist: Which is worse when you're asked a question in class: Shrugging your shoulders and appearing tongue-tied, or responding as best as you can even though your voice may crack?

Client: I hear what you're saying.

Therapist: What other negative consequences might occur if you begin expressing yourself in class?

Client: (pause) None that I can think of.

Therapist: What positives may come from your speaking up in class?

Client: I'd probably get more out of the class and feel better about myself. Enough of this. I get the message loud and clear. I will commit myself to speaking up at least once a week in each of my classes.

People who catastrophize usually exaggerate the anticipated feared consequences. Decatastrophizing is designed to demonstrate to clients that even if feared consequences occur (which they seldom do), those consequences are not as severe as feared.

A fourth focus of reframing is to assist clients in *separating positive intents from negative behaviors,* so that the positive intents become linked to new, positive behaviors. A parent who is physically abusive to a child has the positive intent of raising the child well, but when the parent is under stress and the child is misbehaving, that parent may not be aware that there are other options that are much more constructive than physically beating the child. A therapist can assist such a parent by helping him to reframe thoughts so that when the child misbehaves the parent can focus his thinking processes on alternative responses. For example, the stressed parent can ask his spouse to handle the child's misbehavior or punish the child with a time-out. An example of this type of reframing is given in the box "Case Example: Reframing Cognitions That Cause Dysfunctional Behaviors."

Redefining is a fifth focus of reframing that is used for clients who believe a problem is beyond their personal control.[21] For example, a bored person who believes "Life is boring" may be encouraged to think, "The reasons I'm bored are I don't have special interests and I'm not initiating activities. It's not life that is boring, it's my thinking processes that are leading me to feel bored. What I'm going to do is get involved in activities I enjoy and initiate interactions with people I like to be with." Redefining is accomplished by the therapist first demonstrating that emotions, such as being bored, primarily stem from self-talk (see Module 1). The therapist demonstrates that if the client thinks more positively and realistically, she will feel better. Together, the client and the therapist identify the client's negative thinking patterns that cause her to believe the problem is beyond personal control. Finally, they identify new cognitions that the client can make a commitment to use to counter the cognitions that are (in actuality) causing the unwanted emotions and ineffective behaviors.

Decentering is a sixth focus of reframing that is used with anxious clients who erroneously believe that they are the focus of everyone's attention.[22] Decentering occurs by having such clients observe the behaviors of others rather than focusing on their own anxiety; thereby, they come to realize they are not the center of attention. Beck and Weishaar give an example:

■ Case Example: Reframing Cognitions That Cause Dysfunctional Behaviors

A 28-year-old woman came into treatment because she wanted her husband to stop drinking so much. She indicated that one or two nights a week her husband would stop off at a bar with other construction workers. She indicated he would usually be two or three hours late for dinner and would be quite intoxicated when he arrived home. She would then chastise him for being late, for spending their scarce money on alcohol, and for ruining her evening by his "foolish talk." Her husband generally reacted with name-calling and by verbally abusing his wife in other ways. The woman added that generally there were problems in the marriage only when her husband was drinking. She also stated that her husband denies he has a drinking problem and refuses to join her in counseling. The counselor reframed the positive intent of her behavior in the following manner:

It appears you and your husband get along well, except when he's been drinking. When he comes home drunk, you definitely want to make the best of the situation. Up until now your wanting to make the best of the situation has led you to respond by verbally getting on his case for drinking. At that point he probably feels a need to defend himself, and a 'blow-up' occurs. Since you want to avoid the heated exchanges with him when he's drunk, I'm wondering if there aren't other actions you can take—such as taking a walk by yourself, going shopping, or going to visit someone when he is intoxicated?

The woman thought about this for a while and concluded that such suggestions might well work. In the next session a month later she reported that the strategy of leaving home when her husband came home intoxicated was working out well. Since she realized she did not have the capacity to stop her husband from drinking, she stated that reducing the difficulties the drinking created was her next best choice.

One student who was reluctant to speak in class believed his classmates watched him constantly and noticed his anxiety. By observing them instead of focusing on his own discomfort, he saw some students taking notes, some looking at the professor, and some daydreaming. He concluded his classmates had other concerns.[23]

Exercise M2.9: Applying Reframing

GOAL: This exercise is designed to assist you in understanding and applying reframing.

1. **Specify an unwanted emotion you are currently (occasionally) experiencing, or a dysfunctional behavior you sometimes engage in.**

2. **Specify the cognitions that underlie your unwanted emotion or dysfunctional behavior.**

3. **Specify a "reframe" for each of these cognitions.**

4. **When you have this unwanted emotion in the future or are tempted to engage in your dysfunctional behavior, do you think it will be useful to focus your thinking on using your specified "reframes"? Explain your views.**

■ GROUP EXERCISES

Exercise A: Role-Playing Assertive Behavior

GOAL: To provide practice in being assertive.

The leader asks the group if there is a situation involving assertiveness they would like to see others in the class role-play. If members suggest some situations, volunteers role-play these. If no situations are suggested, volunteers role-play some of the following:

1. Someone is smoking near you, and you find the smoke very annoying. Request the smoker to put out the cigarette.
2. Ask someone to turn down a stereo that is too loud.
3. Ask for a date or refuse a request for a date.
4. Inform your parents you want to be treated as an equal, rather than as a child, continually being told what to do.
5. Refuse to lend an item that someone is trying to borrow. (Before doing this one, ask the "refuser" to identify the possession he or she does not want to lend.)
6. You are a female, and a male is making derogatory sexist comments. Assertively request that he stop.

Another approach is for group members to write down (anonymously on note cards) a situation they would like others in class to role-play. The members should place their note-cards in a container in such a way that anonymity is maintained.

After each situation is role-played, the class discusses the strengths of the approach and what else could have been done.

Exercise B: Giving and Receiving Compliments

GOAL: To learn to give and receive compliments assertively.

Step 1. The group leader begins by stating the following:

The purpose of this exercise is to learn how to give and receive compliments assertively. We all seek to receive compliments and very much appreciate it when we do receive them. Yet, when we receive a compliment, we often say things that discourage the giver of the compliment from giving us additional compliments. For example, if someone compliments you by saying "That's a good-looking sweater that you're wearing," you may discourage future compliments by saying something like, "Oh really? I've had the thing for years. I don't really like it." Or future compliments may be discouraged by a comment like, "Of course it looks good on me. I look good in everything." Now, I'd like to begin the exercise by having you tell me some other negative things people have said that would discourage the giver of the compliment from giving another compliment.

These negative statements are written on the blackboard and then discussed.

Step 2. The leader states:

While people are frequently seeking positive compliments and recognition from others, they often fail to give them. Also, compliments are sometimes offered in less than a positive fashion. For example, "Most people may not like that coat that you have, but I do." Now, as the second part of this exercise, I'd like to hear statements you've heard that were intended as compliments but that came out sounding critical.

The group leader then lists these statements on the blackboard; class discussion follows.

Step 3. The class sits with name cards visible if the members do not know each other's names. The leader states the following:

Now, let's practice giving and receiving sincere and assertive compliments. I'll start by giving a compliment to someone in the group. That person should assertively receive the compliment by saying something like "Well, thank you, I really appreciate your saying that." Each time, the receiver should vary his or her response to the compliment given. After the receiver acknowledges the compliment, the receiver gives a compliment to someone else—who acknowledges it, and then gives a compliment to someone else. We'll just keep going at this until I say "Stop."

Step 4. After Step 3, the group discusses the positive ways in which compliments were given and received.

Exercise C: Expressing Anger Constructively

GOAL: To learn how to express anger constructively.

Step 1. The leader states the following:

Many of us have been taught that getting angry is bad and that anger should not be expressed. It is true that violent and aggressive expressions of anger are generally dangerous and destructive. Yet, feeling angry is not evil. All of us get angry at times, and anger is a normal human emotion. We have a right to get angry, but unfortunately, some people tell us we should not. How many times have you been told not to get angry by a parent, teacher, or authority figure? Others may try to convince us that we should not be angry when we are, but even if we try to comply, the unexpressed angry feelings will still exist. When angry feelings are not expressed assertively, they tend to be expressed indirectly in destructive ways. Turning anger inward can lead to depression. Being angry, but failing to express it, can lead to anxiety. It can also lead to guilt (punishing ourselves for getting angry when we erroneously believe we should not). Some people seek to relieve their angry feelings through self-destructive excessive drinking or overeating. So, the question should not be, "Is anger acceptable?" The question should be, "How can we express anger constructively?"

Step 2. The leader explains that there are constructive ways to express anger. These ways include the following:

1. Taking responsibility for your angry feelings by admitting when you are angry. Only you can make yourself angry; do not blame getting angry on someone else. Remember, you have a right to your emotions, including anger.
2. Expressing your anger at the time you become angry so that you do not "stew" about it. If you delay expressing anger, the hostility may build up until you explode.
3. Expressing your angry feelings assertively so that no one is hurt in the process. Seek to use "I" statements in which you nonblamingly communicate your feelings. For example,

"When you make comments like that, I become angry because I feel I don't have your respect." Expressing anger in a nonblaming way does not put the other person on the defensive. Instead, it gives the other person a chance to understand why you are upset, and provides that person with an opportunity to voluntarily change those actions that he or she now realizes are upsetting you. (I-messages are further described in Chapter 5.)

4. Attempting to blow off steam nondestructively through such physical activity as running, hitting a punching bag or pillow, or tearing up paper, especially if your anger is intense and you feel like you are going to explode.
5. Analyzing your rational and irrational self-talk by writing out a rational self-analysis (see Module 1).

Step 3. The leader requests that each student write out answers to the following three questions on a sheet of paper:

1. Three things that make me angry are:
2. When I am angry, I usually:
3. Things I can do to express anger more constructively are:

The class has 5 or 10 minutes to complete the answers.

Step 4. The class divides into groups of three people to share what they wrote and to receive suggestions on how they could express anger more constructively. If someone does not want to share what she or he wrote, that is acceptable.

Step 5. The class shares the constructive approaches to expressing anger that they came up with and discusses what they learned or discovered from this exercise.

Exercise D: Identifying and Accepting Personal Rights

GOAL: To learn to identify and accept one's personal rights.

Step 1. The leader states the following:

Often, people are not assertive because they are unclear about what rights they have and what rights others have. The basic interpersonal right that individuals have is the right to express and act upon their beliefs, opinions, needs, and feelings as long as they do not violate the rights of others. For example, we have the right to express our opinions here, but we do not have the right to tell others to "shut up."

Step 2. The class lists the personal rights they can think of on a blackboard. The leader might begin by giving a few examples from the following list:

RIGHTS

to get angry	to change one's mind
to make requests	to try and to fail
to refuse requests—the right to say no	to pursue one's own goals
	to make mistakes
to be treated with respect	to choose not to assert oneself
to disagree	to decide what happens to one's body

Step 3. Each student silently selects one of the rights he or she feels most uncomfortable accepting (or a right that he or she has experienced problems with in the past) in preparation for a visualization exercise. The leader gives the following instructions:

Close your eyes . . . take a couple deep breaths . . . Breathe in and out slowly . . . Get as comfortable as possible . . . there are no surprises in this exercise. . . . Now imagine that you have the right that you chose from the list. . . . What situations or circumstances in the past were troublesome for you because you did not know that you had this right? . . . Vividly imagine all the details of these situations. . . . If you really believed you had this right, what would you now do or say differently? . . . If you assert yourself in having this right, how will you feel about yourself? . . . How would life change for you if you accepted this right?

This visualization continues for about two minutes. The leader pauses and then says:

> Now let's do a switch. . . . Imagine that you do not have this right. . . . How would your interactions with others change if you could not express this right? . . . What would be the consequences to you if you could not express this right? . . . How would you feel about yourself? . . . How would you feel about other people? . . . OK, gradually open your eyes.

Step 4. The leader explains that it is acceptable not to share a visualization. The class members divide into groups of three people to discuss the following questions:

1. What right did you choose?
2. What situations in the past have been troublesome for you because you were uncertain you had this right?
3. How did you feel when you visualized yourself having this right?
4. What do you intend to say or do differently in the future because you now know you have this right?
5. How did you feel when you visualized that this right was taken away from you?

(If someone does not want to share what she or he wrote, that is acceptable.)

Step 5. The class discusses what they learned from this exercise, and the leader asks if members have questions about the personal rights listed on the blackboard. The leader asks if anyone would like to see a situation related to personal rights role-played.

Exercise E: Behavioral Contracting

GOAL: To demonstrate the principles of behavioral contracting by applying the principles to one's own behavior.

Step 1. Describe the goal of this exercise and explain the principles of behavioral contracting.

Step 2. Ask each student to prepare a contract about an area of behavior he or she would like to change. The behavior may involve an area such as eating less, drinking less, exercising more, ending procrastination, studying more, or increasing contact with parents and other relatives. In preparing the contract ask the students to write on a sheet of paper answers to the following questions. (Indicate that the students will not be required to reveal what they wrote.)

1. What behavior do you want to change? (Be as specific as possible.)
2. What is your behavior goal?
3. What specifically will you do to achieve this goal?
4. What are your deadlines for doing these tasks?
5. How will you reward yourself for doing the tasks necessary to reach this goal?
6. What adverse consequences will you apply to yourself if you fail to do the tasks?

Step 3. Ask for volunteers to share what they wrote. Have the class discuss the merits and shortcomings of writing such a behavioral contract.

Step 4. As an added component of the exercise, students may discuss whether they want to attempt to fulfill the conditions they have written into their contracts. If the class decides to do this, a future date (such as four weeks later) may be set for the students to describe their successes and failures in fulfilling the conditions of their contract.

Exercise F: Reframing

GOAL: To demonstrate how to reframe cognitions involving awfulizing.

Step 1. Describe the concepts of reframing and awfulizing. To illustrate the process of awfulizing, the leader indicates a few examples in which he or she has awfulized in the past.

Step 2. Instruct each student to record his or her responses to the following questions and instructions on a sheet of paper. Students will not be required to reveal their responses.

1. Briefly describe a distressing event that occurred to you and that you awfulized over.
2. Specify the awfulizing cognitions that you gave yourself about this distressing event.
3. For each awfulizing cognition, specify a more positive and realistic cognition that you could give yourself about this event. (Ideally, many of these countering cognitions should also facilitate problem solving.)
4. Indicate the approximate length of time that you awfulized over this event.
5. Are you still awfulizing about this event?
6. Do you believe countering the awfulizing cognitions with more positive and realistic cognitions would have shortened the time you spent awfulizing?

Step 3. Ask for volunteers to share their responses to these questions. The exercise can be ended by asking students to indicate their thoughts on the merits and shortcomings of using reframing in therapy.

■ MODULE 3: REALITY THERAPY IN GROUPS

GOALS

Reality therapy is based on choice theory. The approach emphasizes the importance of relationships and also asserts that there are dynamic interactions between our thoughts, emotions, actions, and physiology. This chapter summarizes reality therapy and describes how to use reality therapy in groups.

William Glasser

The founder of reality therapy is William Glasser (1925–   ). Glasser has developed two variations of reality therapy. The first was developed in the 1960s and was based on identity theory.[24] The second has been developed in the past two decades and is based on choice theory.[25] This second version will be described in this module.

William Glasser is an internationally recognized psychiatrist. He graduated from Case Western Reserve Medical School in Cleveland, Ohio, in 1953. In 1956 he became a consulting psychiatrist to the Ventura School for Girls, a California state institution for the treatment of delinquent girls.

Glasser had grown skeptical of the value of orthodox psychoanalysis. At the Ventura School for Girls, he set up a new treatment program based on the principles of his *reality therapy*. The program showed promise, and participants expressed enthusiasm.

In 1966 Glasser began consulting in the California school system and applied the concepts of reality therapy to education. His emphasis on the need for schools to highlight involvement, relevance, and thinking continues to have a profound impact on the education system.

Glasser does not believe in the concept of mental illness. He has written over 20 books. In 1967, he founded the Institute for Reality Therapy, which has trained over 60,000 people worldwide in reality therapy.

In recent years Glasser's major focus has been to teach the world his views on choice theory, a new psychology that is described in this chapter.

Choice Theory

A major thrust of choice theory is that we carry around pictures in our heads, both of what reality is like and of how we would like to be. Glasser asserts, "All our behavior is our constant attempt to reduce the difference between what we want (the pictures in our heads) and what we have (the way we see situations in the world.)"[26]

Some examples will illustrate this idea. Each of us has a detailed idea of the type of person we would like to date or form a relationship with; when we find someone who closely matches these characteristics, we seek to form a relationship. Each of us carries around a picture album of our favorite foods; when we're hungry, we select an item and go about obtaining that food.

How do we develop these pictures/albums/ideas that we believe will satisfy our needs? Glasser asserts that we begin to create our albums at an early age (perhaps even before birth) and that we spend our whole life enlarging them. Essentially, whenever what we do gets us something that satisfies a need, we store the picture of it in our personal albums. Glasser gives the following example of this process by describing how a hungry child added chocolate-chip cookies to his picture album:

> Suppose you had a grandson and your daughter left you in charge while he was taking a nap. She said she would be right back, because he would be ravenous when he awoke and she knew you had no idea what to feed an eleven-month-old child. She was right. As soon as she left, he awoke screaming his head off, obvious starved. You tried a bottle, but he rejected it—he had something more substantial in mind. But what? Being unused to a howling baby, and desperate, you tried a chocolate-chip cookie and it worked wonders. At first, he did not seem to know what it was, but he was a quick learner. He quickly polished off three cookies. She returned and almost polished you off for being so stupid as to give a baby chocolate. "Now," she said, "he will be yelling all day for those cookies." She was right. If he is like most of us, he will probably have chocolate on his mind for the rest of his life.[27]

When this child learned how satisfying chocolate-chip cookies are, he placed the picture of these cookies in his personal picture album.

By the term *pictures,* Glasser means *perceptions* from our five senses of sight, hearing, touch, smell, and taste. The pictures in our albums do not have to be rational. Anorexics picture themselves as too fat and starve themselves to come closer to their irrational picture of unhealthy thinness. Rapists have pictures of satisfying their power needs, and perhaps sexual needs, through sexual assault. To change a picture, we must replace it with one that will at least reasonably satisfy the need in question. People who are unable to replace a picture may endure a lifetime of misery. Some battered women, for example, endure brutal beatings and humiliations in marriage because they cannot picture themselves as worthy of a loving relationship.

Glasser notes that whenever the picture we see and the one we want to see differ, a *signal* generated by this difference leads us to behave in a way that will obtain the picture we want. We examine our behaviors and select one or more than we believe will help us reduce this difference. These behaviors not only include straightforward problem-solving efforts but also manipulative strategies like anger, pouting, and guilt. People who act irresponsibly or ineffectually have either failed to select responsible behaviors from their repertoires or have not yet learned responsible courses of action.

Glasser believes we are driven by five basic, innate needs. As soon as one need is satisfied, another need (or perhaps more than one acting together) pushes for satisfaction. Our first need is *survival.* This includes such vital functions as breathing, digesting food, sweating, regulating blood pressure, and meeting the demands of hunger, thirst, and sex.

Our second need is *love and belonging.* We generally meet this need through family, friends, pets, plans, and material possessions.

Our third need is *power.* Glasser says this need involves getting others to obey us and to then receive the esteem and recognition that accompanies power. Our drive for power is sometimes in conflict with our need to belong. Two people in a relationship may struggle to control it rather than create an equalitarian relationship.

Our fourth need is *freedom.* People want the freedom to choose how they live their lives, to express themselves, to read and write what they choose, to associate with whom they select, and to worship or not worship as they believe.

Our fifth need is *fun*. Glasser believes learning is often fun; this gives us a great incentive to assimilate what we require to satisfy our needs. Classes that are grim and boring are major failings of our educational system. Laughing and humor help fulfill our needs for fun. Fun is such a vital part of living that most of us have trouble conceiving of life without it.

Choice is an *internal control psychology*; it explains why and how we make the choices that determine the course of our lives. By internal control psychology, Glasser asserts we choose everything we do.[28]

Axioms of Choice Theory

1. The only person whose behavior we can control is our own. No one can make us do anything we do not want to do as long as we are willing to endure the consequences—punishment for not doing what others want us to do. If we choose to do what others want us to do under the threat of severe punishment, we tend to be passive-aggressive by not performing very well. When we try to force others to do what they do not want to do, they may choose not to do it—or choose to also be passive-aggressive by not performing well.

Exercise M3.1: Seeking to Change Someone and Being Controlled by Someone

GOAL: This exercise is designed to illustrate that we are prone to attempting to change others and that others sometimes attempt to control us. The consequences of attempting to control others, and of others attempting to control us are also examined.

Note: Isn't it interesting? We think we have a right to attempt to change irritating behavior of people we are dating, but we don't like to have others attempt to change us!

1. **Describe a situation where you attempted to change the behavior of someone else. (It might be your attempting to change irritating actions of someone you were dating.)**

2. **Were you successful in changing the behavior of this person? Also, what were the emotional reactions of this person to your attempting to change him or her?**

3. If the person did change the behavior that you found irritating, do you think this person changed because you forced him or her to change or because this person "chose" to change?

4. Describe a situation where someone (perhaps a parent or someone you were dating) sought to change your behavior (that he or she found irritating.)

5. Did you change your behavior? Also, how did you feel about someone trying to change (or control) you?

6. **If you did change your behavior, did you change because someone forced you to change or because you "chose" to change?**

2. All we can give or get from other people is information. How we deal with that information is our, or their, choice. A teacher, for example, can assign readings to students but is not responsible if some students chose not to do the readings. The teacher therefore should not feel personally responsible for those students who choose not to do the readings. The teacher can choose, of course, to give consequences to those students who fail to follow the reading instructions—such as giving a lower grade to those students.

3. All we can do from birth to death, according to Glasser is "behave." Glasser indicates all behavior is "total behavior" and is made up of four inseparable components: acting, thinking, feeling, and physiology. Each of these components interacts and affects the three other components. (The next two axioms elaborate on this interaction.)

4. All long-lasting psychological problems are relationship problems. Relationship problems are also a partial cause of many other problems, such as fatigue, pain, weakness, and autoimmune diseases (such as fibromyalgia and rheumatoid arthritis). Glasser states:

> Most doctors believe that adult rheumatoid arthritis is caused by the victims' immune systems attacking their own joints as if these joints were foreign bodies. Another way of putting it is that their own creative systems are trying to protect these people from a perceived harm. If we could figure out a way to stop this misguided creativity, millions of people who suffer from this disease and a host of other relentless diseases, called autoimmune diseases, could be helped.[29]

> Our usual way of dealing with an important relationship that is not working out the way we want it to is to choose misery—emotional misery and physical misery.

5. Human brains are very creative. A woman who has frequently been sexually abused as a child may develop a dissociative identity disorder to psychologically shield herself from the emotional pain of the abuse. Glasser asserts that almost all medical problems for which physicians are unable to identify the cause are partially created by the ill person's brain to deal with unhappiness that she or he is experiencing. Unhappiness is the force that inspires the creativity inherent in the brain to be a partial cause of symptoms describe in the American Psychiatric Association's *DSM-IV*: aches and pains (such as migraine headaches), and physical illnesses (such as heart disease, cancer, adult asthma, and eczema).[30]

In regard to the brain creating the symptoms in the *DSM-IV*, Glasser describes how unhappiness may lead the brain to create hallucinations:

> Suppose, instead of your creativity presenting an idea to you as a thought, it created a voice uttering a threat or any other message directly into the auditory cortex of your brain. You would hear an actual voice or voices; it could be a stranger or you might recognize whose voice it was. It would be impossible, just by hearing it, for you to tell it from an actual voice or voices.[31]

Because we can hear voices, our brain can create voices that we hear when no one else is around. Because we can see, it can create visual hallucinations. Because we can feel pain, it can create pain—perhaps in greater severity and duration than what we experience from an injury or illness. Since we are able to fear, it can and does create disabling phobias.

Exercise M3.2: The Creativity in Our Brains

GOAL: This exercise is designed to assist you in understanding that our mental thoughts are a factor in causing our somatic problems, emotional difficulties, and behavioral dysfunctions.

1. **Identify a somatic problem (such as migraine headaches) of unknown physical cause that you have or someone close to you has. Speculate on the way mental thoughts may be a factor in causing the somatic problem.**

2. **Identify an emotional or behavioral problem that you have or that someone close to you has. Speculate on how this person's mental thoughts contributed to this emotional or behavioral problem.**

6. Barring untreatable physical illnesses or severe poverty, unsatisfying relationships are the primary source of crimes, addictions, and emotional and behavioral disorders.

7. It is a serious mistake (and irrational) to seek to control others by nagging, preaching, punishing, or threatening or punish them. As indicated earlier, the only person we can effectively control is ourself. In order to progress in improving human relationships, we need to give up seeking to control others through nagging, preaching, putting down, or threatening punishment.

Exercise M3.3: The Effects of Nagging and Preaching

GOAL: This exercise is designed to increase your awareness of the effects of nagging, preaching, putting down, or threatening punishment.

1. **Describe a situation where someone tried to control you by nagging, preaching, putting down, or threatening punishment.**

2. **How did you feel about someone else attempting to control you with these external control strategies?**

3. **Did you change your behavior? If you did change, was it because you were forced to change or because you "chose" to change?**

4. **Describe a situation where you attempted to change someone by nagging, preaching, putting down, or threatening punishment.**

5. How did that person emotionally react to your external control attempts?

6. Did that person change his or her behavior? If the person did change, was it because you forced him or her to change or because he or she "chose" to change?

8. The unsatisfying (problematic) relationship is always a current one. We cannot live happily without at least one satisfying relationship. In a quality relationship between two people, each person seeks to meet his or her needs and wants, and those of the other person.

9. The *solving circle* is a good strategy for two people who know choice theory to use in redefining their freedom and improving their relationship. Glasser advocates its use in marital and dating relationships. Each person pictures the relationship inside a large circle, called the solving circle. An imaginary circle is drawn on the floor. Both people take a seat on a chair within the circle. The two people are told there are three entities in the solving circle: The two people and the relationship. The two people are asked to agree that maintaining the relationship takes precedence over what each person wants. In the circle, each person tells the other what he or she will agree to do to help the relationship. Within those limits, the two people must reach a compromise on their conflicts.

10. Painful events that happened in the past have a great deal to do with what we are today, but dwelling on the painful past can contribute little or nothing to what we need to do now—which is to improve an important, present relationship.

Exercise M3.4: Improving an Unhappy Relationship

GOAL: This exercise is designed to assist you in improving, through problem solving, a significant relationship in your life.

1. Identify and briefly describe a significant relationship in your life that you would like to improve.

2. Do you believe the unhappy components in this relationship may be having an adverse impact on your physical or mental well-being? Please explain. (If you cannot identify a problematic current relationship, describe a past unhappy relationship and indicate how it negatively impacted your physical and mental well-being.)

3. Speculate on what you might do to improve a current problematic relationship.

11. It is not necessary to know our past before we can deal with the present. It is good to revisit the parts of our past that were satisfying, but it is even better to leave what was unhappy alone.

Exercise M3.5: Letting Go of Grudges

GOAL: This exercise is designed to assist you in letting go of severe feelings of being wronged by others in the past.

1. Describe a situation in which you felt that someone severely wronged you and about which you currently still awfulize.

2. Does it do you any good to continue to awfulize about this? Research shows hostility toward others is a major factor in heart disease and other stress-related illnesses.[32] By holding a grudge, are you not adversely impacting your physical and mental well-being? Speculate on how holding a grudge may currently be affecting you.

3. Speculate on what you can do to let go of this grudge.

12. We can satisfy our basic needs only by satisfying one or more pictures in our quality world. Our quality world consists of three kinds of need-satisfying pictures: (1) people (such as parents); (2) things (such as a car and clothes); and (3) beliefs (such as our religious and political beliefs). The most freedom we ever experience is when we are able to satisfy one or more pictures in our quality world. We are giving up part of our freedom when we put pictures into our quality world that we cannot satisfy.

13. When we have difficulty in getting along with other people, we usually make the mistake of choosing to employ *external control psychology* in which we attempt to coerce or control others by nagging, preaching, moralizing, criticizing, or by using put-down messages.

14. Since relationships are central to human happiness, improving our emotional and physical well-being involves exploring how we relate to others and looking for ways of improving how we relate to others (particularly those people who we feel closest to.)

15. It is therapeutic to view our "total behavior" in terms of verbs. For example, it is much more accurate to say to oneself "I am choosing to depress" instead of thinking "I am suffering from depression" or "I am depressed." When we say "I am

choosing to depress," we are immediately aware that we are actively choosing to depress and have the choice to do and feel something else (such as "I will go golfing and enjoy the day"). People who instead say "I am depressed" mistakenly tend to believe the depressing is beyond their control. (In addition, they are apt to mistakenly believe the depressing has been caused by what someone else has done to them. To recognize that we have power to choose to stop depressing (or to stop angering or frustrating, etc.) is a wonderful freedom that people who adhere to the view that they are largely controlled by others will never have.

Exercise M3.6: Expressing Our Negative Emotions in Terms of Verbs

GOAL: This exercise is designed to demonstrate that expressing our negative emotions in terms of verbs assists us in recognizing that we are *choosing* to feel this way and that we can *choose* to feel positive emotions instead.

1. **List all of the negative emotions you have felt in the past week.**

2. **Rephrase all of these negative emotions in terms of verbs (for example, "I am depressing" instead of "depressed").**

3. Does this exercise help you to understand that we *choose* to feel negative emotions and that we have the choice to feel positive emotions instead? Explain your thoughts on this.

16. All total behavior (thinking, feeling, acting, and physiology) is chosen, but we have direct control over only the acting and thinking components. We do, however, control our physiology and our feelings through how we choose to act and think. It is not easy to change our actions and thoughts, but it is all we can do. When we succeed in coming up with more satisfying actions and thoughts, we gain a great deal of personal freedom.

Exercise M3.7: Changing Our Feelings and Improving Somatic Problems

GOAL: This exercise is designed to demonstrate that our negative emotions can be changed, and some of our somatic problems can be improved, by changing our thoughts and actions.

1. Describe how you changed a negative emotion by changing your thoughts or actions.

2. Describe how you improved on a somatic problem (perhaps a headache) by changing your thoughts or actions.

17. Whenever you feel as if you don't have the freedom you want in a relationship, it is because you, your partner, or both of you are unwilling to accept a key axiom of choice theory: *You can only control your own life.* The more both you, and your partner, learn choice theory, the better you will get along with one another. Choice theory supports the golden rule (do unto others as you would have them do unto you).

18. People choose (although some are unaware of their choice) to play the mentally ill roles that are described in the *DSM-IV.*[33] These people have the symptoms described in the *DSM-IV,* but they are not mentally ill (if mental illness is defined as a disease of the mind). These people do not have an untreatable or incurable mental illness. The symptoms are only an indication that these people are not as healthy as they could learn to be. (See boxes "Does Mental Illness Exist?" and "Case Example: Reality Therapy.")

▪ Does Mental Illness Exist?

Thomas Szasz, in the 1960s, was one of the first authorities to assert that mental illness is a myth—that it does not exist. Beginning with the assumption that the term *mental illness* implies a "disease in the mind," Szasz categorizes all of the so-called mental illnesses into three types of emotional disorders and discusses the inappropriateness of calling such human difficulties "mental illnesses":

1. *Personal disabilities,* such as excessive anxiety, depression, fears, and feelings of inadequacy. (Another term for personal disabilities is "unwanted emotions.") Szasz says such so-called mental illnesses may appropriately be considered "mental" (in the sense that thinking and feeling are considered "mental" activities), but he asserts they are not diseases.

2. *Antisocial acts,* such as bizarre homicides and other social deviations. Homosexuality used to be in this category but was removed from the American Psychiatric Association's list of mental illnesses in 1974. Szasz says such antisocial acts are only social deviations, and he asserts they are neither "mental" nor "diseases."

3. *Deterioration of the brain with associated personality changes.* This category includes the "mental illnesses" in which personality changes result following brain deterioration from such causes as arteriosclerosis, chronic alcoholism, Alzheimer's disease, general paresis, or serious brain damage due to an accident. Common symptoms are loss of memory, listlessness, apathy, and deterioration of personal grooming habits. Szasz says these disorders can appropriately be considered "diseases" but are diseases of the *brain* (that is, brain deterioration specifies the nature of the problem) rather than being diseases of the *mind.*

Szasz, in "The Myth of Mental Illness," asserts that the notion that people with emotional problems are mentally ill is as absurd as the belief that the emotionally disturbed are possessed by demons:

> The belief in mental illness as something other than man's trouble in getting along with his fellow man, is the proper heir to the belief in demonology and witchcraft. Mental illness exists or is real in exactly the same sense in which witches existed or were real. (p. 67)

The point that Szasz and many other writers are striving to make is that people do have emotional and behavioral problems, but they do not have a mystical mental illness. These writers believe that terms that describe unwanted emotions and dysfunctional behaviors are very useful: for example, *depression, anxiety, obsession, compulsion, excessive fear, hallucinations, and feelings of being a failure.* Such terms describe personal problems that people have. But mental illness terms (such as schizophrenia and psychosis), they assert, are not useful because there is no distinguishing symptom that would indicate whether a person has, or does not have, the "illness."

Source: Thomas Szasz, "The Myth of Mental Illness," in *Clinical Psychology in Transition,* ed. John R. Braun (Cleveland, OH: Howard Allen, 1961).

Case Example: Reality Therapy

A number of years ago when I [the author] was employed as a social worker at a maximum security hospital for the criminally insane, my supervisor asked me to develop and lead a therapy group. When I wondered aloud who should be in the group and what its objectives should be, my supervisor indicated those decisions would be mine. He added that no one else was doing group therapy at the hospital and that the hospital administration thought it would be desirable to develop such a program.

Being newly employed at the hospital and wary because I had never been a group leader before, I asked myself, "Who is in the greatest need of group therapy?" and "If the group members do not improve, or even deteriorate, how will I be able to explain this—that is, cover my tracks?" I concluded that I should select those identified as being most ill (those labeled as chronic schizophrenics). Because such patients are generally expected to show little improvement, I felt I would not be blamed if group members did not improve. However, if they did improve, I thought it would be viewed as a substantial accomplishment.

First I read the case records of all the residents (11) who were diagnosed as chronic schizophrenics. I then met individually with each of these residents to invite them to join the group. (To my surprise, each of the residents appeared to be very different from the impressions I received from reading the case records.) I explained the purpose of the group and the probable topics to be covered. Eight of the 11 who were contacted decided to join; some frankly stated they would join primarily because it would look good on their records and increase their chances for an early release.

In counseling these group members, the approach I used was based on reality therapy. I began the first group meeting by stating I knew what the "key" was to their being discharged from the hospital and asked if *they* knew what that might be. This statement got their attention. I indicated that the key was very simple—they had to learn to "act sane" so that the medical staff would think they had recovered. At the first meeting the purpose and the focus of the group was presented and described. Our purpose was not to review the past but to make life in the present more enjoyable and meaningful and to plan for the future. Various topics would be covered: how group members could convince the hospital staff they no longer needed hospitalization; how they could prepare for returning to their home community (for example, learning an employable skill while at the institution); and what to do when they felt depression or some other unwanted emotion or had an urge to do something that would get them into trouble again after their release. Also to be covered were discussions on how to improve relationships with people who were important to them. Occasionally films covering some of these topics would be shown and discussed. The group would meet for about one hour each week for 12 weeks.

This focus on improving the current circumstances of the group members stimulated their interest, but soon they found it uncomfortable and anxiety-producing to examine what the future might hold for them. They also became uncomfortable after being told they had considerable control over their future. They reacted to this discomfort by stating that they were "mentally ill" and therefore had some internal condition that was causing their strange behavior. Further, since no cure for their schizophrenia had yet been found, they believed they could do little to improve.

I told them that their excuses were "garbage" (stronger terms were used) and spent a few sessions convincing them that the term "chronic schizophrenic" was a meaningless label. I spent considerable time in explaining the myth of mental illness: that people do not have a "disease of the mind," though they may have emotional problems. I went on to explain that what had gotten them locked up was their deviant behavior. The only way for them to get out was to stop such behavior and convince the staff that they would not exhibit it if released.

The next excuse they tried was that the broken homes or inferior schools or broken romances or other misfortunes had "messed up" their lives for good, and they could do little about their situation. "Garbage," I told them. True, their past experiences were important. But, I emphasized, what they *wanted* out of their future and the motivation they had to achieve their goals were more important in determining the future.

Finally, after working through a number of excuses we focused on how they could better handle specific problems: how to handle being depressed, how to stop exhibiting behavior considered "strange," how to present themselves as being "sane" in order to increase their chances of an early release, and how to adjust to returning to their home communities. We also focused on what kind of work or career they desired upon their release and how they could prepare themselves for their selected careers by learning a skill or trade while at the institution. Another focus was to help them examine what they wanted out of the future and the specific steps they would have to take to achieve their goals. Also discussed was how they could improve relationships important to them.

The results of this approach were encouraging. Instead of idly spending much of the time brooding about their situation, group members became motivated to take action. At the end of the 12 weeks, the 8 members spontaneously stated that the meetings were making a positive change in their lives and requested that another social worker from the hospital be assigned to continue the group after I left to return to school. This was arranged. Three years later on a return visit to the hospital, I was informed that 5 of the 8 group members had been released to their home communities and two of the others had shown improvement. One group member's condition was described as "unchanged."

19. Glasser asserts that prescribed drugs by psychiatrists and doctors may make you feel better—temporarily. In doing so, these drugs are no different from any legal drug you may use on your own, such as alcohol, nicotine, or caffeine. Unless you solve the personal problems bothering you, the initial lift from prescribed drugs will wear off and you may need a higher dose. The misguided psychiatric effort has created an epidemic of drug-treated "mental illness."

There is considerable evidence that all brain drugs used to treat nonexistent mental illnesses act on the brain in ways that harm its normal function.[34] Many people who take "brain drugs" develop mental and physical illnesses that cannot be distinguished from Parkinson's disease.

Manufactuers of brain drugs spend millions on public relations campaigns to sell the brain drugs they make to "cure" it.

Exercise M3.8: The Use of Psychotropic Drugs

GOAL: This exercise is designed to assist you in assessing the merits and shortcomings of psychotropic drugs.

1. Psychotropic drugs are drugs used by psychiatrists and other physicians to help their patients achieve psychological or emotional changes. These drugs include *antidepressant medications* (such as Prozac, Elavil, Norpramin, Pertofrane, Sinequan, Aventl, and Vivactil), *antianxiety drugs* (such as Valium, Librium, Tranxene, Ativan, Serax, and various barbiturates), *antipsychotic medications* (such as Thorazine, Haldol, Compazine, Selazine, Navane, Mellaril, Serentil, Trilafon, and Prolixin), and *antimanic medications* (lithium carbonate—that is, Eskalith, Lithane, or Lithonate).[35] Have you or are you aware of any family members or friends who have used psychotropic drugs? If "yes," specify, if you can, the name of the drug or drugs.

2. Specify your thoughts on the benefits and side effects of these drugs for the person taking them.

3. Do you agree with Glasser that psychotropic drugs are over-prescribed and overused? Explain your thoughts.

20. A mentally healthy person enjoys being with most of the people he or she knows—especially the important people such as family and friends. A mentally healthy person likes people and is more than willing to help an unhappy friend, colleague, or family member to feel better. A mentally healthy person laughs a lot and leads a mostly tension-free life. He or she enjoys life and has no trouble accepting others who are different. He or she does not focus on criticizing others nor tries to change others. He or she is creative. A mentally healthy person, when unhappy (no one can be happy all the time), knows why she or he is unhappy and will attempt to do something about it.

Exercise M3.9: A Mentally Healthy Person

GOAL: This exercise is designed to help you identify what you need to work on to improve your mental well-being.

1. Review Glasser's definition of a mentally healthy person. Describe components of your current life that are consistent with mental well-being.

2. Identify components in your life that you need to work on in order to improve your mental well-being.

3. For the components that you need to work on, speculate about courses of action that you should take in order to improve your mental well-being.

Principles of Reality Therapy

1.   It is what you choose to do in a relationship, not what others choose to do, that is the focus of reality therapy.
2.   People choose the behaviors that have led them into therapy because it is always perceived by them as being their best effort to deal with either an unsatisfying relationship, or with no relationship at all.
3.   The task of the counselor is to help unhappy clients choose new relationship-improving behaviors. These new behaviors will also help clients satisfy one or more of their five basic needs: love and belonging, power, freedom, fun, and survival.
4.   Satisfying the need for love and belonging is the key to satisfying the other four needs, as the five basic needs can only be satisfied when we have good relationships with other people.
5.   Because love and belonging (like all of the basic five needs) can be satisfied only in the present, reality therapy focuses almost entirely on the here and now.
6.   Although most of us have been traumatized in the past, we are only victims of our past if we currently choose to be. The solution to our problems is rarely found in explorations of the past; one exception may be a focus on past successes.
7.   The symptoms or the pain that clients choose (because of their unhappiness) is not important to the counseling process. The focus in counseling needs to be on improving present relationships. (It is usually a fruitless endeavor to seek to determine why one discontented person may choose to depress, another to drink, a third to obsesses, and a fourth to go crazy).

8. A continuing goal of reality therapy is to create a choice theory relationship between the counselor and the client. By experiencing a satisfying relationship, the client can learn a lot about a model relationship and how to improve the troubled relationship that brought him or her into counseling.

9. As long as clients continue to use the choice theory concepts they've learned in counseling, the therapy never ends.

10. With marriage or couple counseling, Glasser urges that *structured reality therapy* be used.[36] This approach emphasizes that marriage is a partnership and the only way to help a troubled couple is to focus on what's best for their marriage, not on what may be best for one or the other. Any marital counseling that allows one partner to blame the other will only harm the marriage. Couples are urged to never say or do anything in a relationship that experience indicates will drive the two further apart. They are urged to only say and do what will bring them closer, or keep them close. Couples are also instructed to extensively use the solving circle (which was described earlier).

Exercise M3.10: The Solving Circle

GOAL: This exercise is designed to have you speculate about the merits and shortcomings of the solving circle.

1. **Specify difficulties you are currently having in a relationship that is significant to you.**

2. **Review the material on a solving circle. Do you believe that using a solving circle with the person you are currently having difficulties with would be useful? (If possible, try to become involved in an actual solving circle with this person.) Speculate about the merits and shortcomings of the solving circle.**

11. Reality therapy is a "doing" approach. Clients are guided in the direction of actually doing something about their problems.

12. In this newer approach to reality therapy, the original term "responsibility" (in the first version of reality therapy) is now replaced with the more explicit idea that we choose all our behaviors because we can't be anything but responsible for all we choose to do. In this way, the possible argument over what is responsible, and what is not, is avoided.

13. The therapist looks for every opportunity to teach choice therapy to clients and their families so that everyone involved can begin the process of replacing external control psychology with choice theory.

14. A symptom is a cry for help. People use symptoms to avoid situations that they fear will increase their frustration.

15. Good or bad, happy or sad, people choose everything they do all day long.

Exercise M3.11: Symptoms as a Cry for Help

GOAL: This exercise is designed to assist you in recognizing that emotional difficulties, dysfunctional behaviors, somatic problems, and relationship problems are cries for help.

Describe how someone you know is demonstrating that their emotional difficulties, relationship problems, dysfunctional behaviors, or somatic problems are cries for help.

Using Reality Therapy in Groups

Reality therapy has been found to be effective with clients in one-to-one situations and in groups. Reality therapy focuses on the importance of improving relationships with people who are significant to us. The approach emphasizes the importance of the interactions between our thoughts, actions, emotions, and physiology. By changing our negative thoughts and dysfunctional behaviors, we can improve our emotions and alleviate some somatic problems.

Various approaches can be used to apply reality therapy to groups. Members can read about the concepts of the approach prior to group meetings and then discuss the concepts in groups. Members can do the exercises in this module (either prior to group meetings or during group meetings) and then share and discuss what they wrote. The leader can assist members in treatment sessions by first having members specify the emotional, behavior, relationship, or somatic problems they are facing, and then assisting them in identifying specific courses of action they can take to attempt to alleviate these difficulties.

An example of the use of reality therapy is presented in the box "Case Example: Reality Therapy" found earlier in this module. Reality therapy is an approach that is rich in psychodynamic concepts. It has the potential to assist people in improving their physical and emotional well-being, and helping people to eliminate their ineffective and dysfunctional behaviors.

■ GROUP EXERCISE

Exercise A: Mental Illness Debate

GOAL: To identify the arguments as to whether mental illness exists.

Step 1. At a class session some students in the class form two panels—one that will argue that mental illness exists, and the other that will argue that mental illness is a myth. Panel members are given a few days to gather information and prepare their arguments. Panel members may interview counselors and therapists in the community and read reference materials.

Step 2. At the selected class date, a debate is held. At the end of the debate, the students uninvolved in the debate summarize the strong points made by the debaters.

Answers to Group Exercises D–F in Chapter 6

Exercise D

1. Twenty; 9, 19, 29, 39, 49, 59, 69, 79, 89, 90, 91, 92, 93, 94, 95, 96, 97, 98, 99.
2. They're playing with different partners.
3. Two hours.
4. The water will never reach the top of the ladder because the boat keeps rising with the tide.
5. Of course.
6. He's still alive.
7. Six.
8. The bear is white because it is a polar bear. The house is located at the North Pole.
9. Three minutes.
10. Car A travels 1,200 miles, Car B travels 800 miles from the point of origin.
11. One haystack.
12. Karen is Jill's mother.
13. Four dollars.

Exercise E

Task 1:

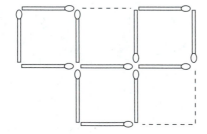

Task 2:

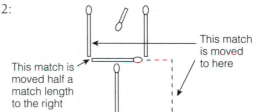

This match is moved half a match length to the right

This match is moved to here

Task 3:

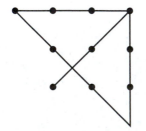

Task 4:

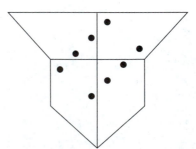

Task 5:

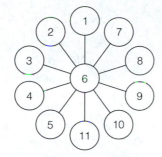

Exercise F

1. Sandbox
2. Man overboard
3. I understand
4. Reading between the lines
5. Long underwear
6. Crossroads
7. Downtown
8. Tricycle
9. Split level
10. Three degrees below zero
11. Neon lights
12. Circles under the eyes
13. High chair
14. Paradise
15. Touchdown
16. Six feet underground
17. Mind over matter
18. He's beside himself
19. Backward glance
20. Life after death
21. G.I. overseas
22. Space program
23. See-through blouse
24. Just between you and me
25. Empty

NOTES

CHAPTER 1:
GROUPS: TYPES AND STAGES OF DEVELOPMENT

1. Gerald L. Euster, "Group Work," in *Contemporary Social Work,* 2d ed., ed. Donald Brieland et al. (New York: McGraw-Hill, 1980), p. 100.
2. Ibid., p. 100.
3. Herbert Stroup, *Social Welfare Pioneers* (Chicago: Nelson-Hall, 1986), p. 9.
4. Dorothy G. Becker, "Social Welfare Leaders as Spokesmen for the Poor," *Social Casework* 49, No. 2 (Feb. 1968): 85.
5. Stroup, *Social Welfare Pioneers,* pp. 1–29.
6. Ibid., pp. 255–80.
7. Ibid., p. 297.
8. Euster, "Group Work," p. 100.
9. David W. Johnson and Frank P. Johnson, *Joining Together: Group Theory and Group Skills,* 8th ed. (Boston: Allyn and Bacon, 2003), p. 19.
10. Robert L. Barker, *The Social Work Dictionary,* 5th ed. (Washington DC: NASW Press, 2003), p. 165.
11. Alfred H. Katz and Eugene I. Bender, *The Strength in Us: Self-Help Groups in the Modern World* (New York: Franklin Watts, 1976), p. 9.
12. Thomas J. Powell, *Self-Help Organizations and Professional Practice* (Silver Spring, MD: National Association of Social Workers, 1987).
13. Frank Riessman, "The 'Helper Therapy' Principle," *Journal of Social Work* 10 (1965): 27–34.
14. Euster, "Group Work," p. 103.
15. Kurt Lewin, "Group Decision and Social Change," in *Readings in Social Psychology,* eds. G. E. Swanson, T. M. Newcomb, and E. L. Hartley (New York: Holt, 1952), pp. 459–73.
16. Barker, *The Social Work Dictionary,* p. 390.
17. Steward L. Tubbs and John W. Baird, The *Open Person . . . Self-Disclosure and Personal Growth* (Columbus, OH: Charles E. Merrill, 1976), pp. 48–50.
18. Ibid., p. 48.
19. Carl Rogers, *Carl Rogers on Encounter Groups* (New York: Harper & Row, 1970), pp. 40–41.
20. E. L. Shostrom, "Group Therapy: Let the Buyer Beware," *Psychology Today* 2, No. 12 (May 1969): 38–39.
21. Morton A. Lieberman, Ervin D. Yalom, and Matthew B. Miles, "Encounter: The Leader Makes the Difference," *Psychology Today* 6 (Mar. 1973): 11.
22. A. Paul Hare, *Handbook of Small Group Research* (New York: Free Press, 1962).
23. P. E. Slater, "Contrasting Correlates of Group Size," *Sociometry* 21 (1958): 137–38.
24. Ibid., p. 135.
25. James C. Hansen, Richard W. Warner, and Elsie M. Smith, *Group Counseling: Theory and Process,* 2d ed. (Chicago: Rand McNally College Publishing, 1980).
26. Ibid., pp. 57–69.
27. H. J. Bertcher and Frank Maple, "Elements and Issues in Group Composition," in *Individual Change Through Small Groups,* eds. Paul Glasser, Rosemary Sarri, and Robert Vinter (New York: Free Press, 1974), pp. 186–208.
28. Ibid., pp. 187–204.
29. James A. Garland, Hubert Jones, and Ralph Kolodny, "A Model for Stages of Development in Social Work Groups," in *Explorations in Group Work,* ed. Saul Bernstein (Boston: Milford House, 1965), pp. 12–53.
30. James A. Garland and Louise A. Frey, "Applications of Stages of Group Development to Groups in Psychiatric Settings," in *Further Explorations in Group Work,* ed. Saul Bernstein (Boston: Milford House, 1973), p. 3.
31. Ibid., p. 5.
32. Ibid., p. 6.
33. B. Tuckman, "Developmental Sequence in Small Groups," *Psychological Bulletin* 63, 1965: 384–99.
34. Helen Northen and Roselle Kurland, *Social Work with Groups,* 3d ed. (New York: Columbia University Press, 2001).
35. Ibid., p. 288.
36. Robert F. Bales, "The Equilibrium Problem in Small Groups," in *Small Groups: Studies in Social Interaction,* eds. A. Hare, E. Borgatta, and R. Bales (New York: Knopf, 1965), pp. 444–76.

CHAPTER 2: SOCIAL GROUP WORK AND SOCIAL WORK PRACTICE

1. For a summary see Charles Zastrow, *The Practice of Social Work,* 7th ed. (Pacific Grove, CA: Brooks/Cole, 2003).
2. Published 1982. National Association of Social Workers, Inc. Reprinted with permission, from *Standards for the Classification of Social Work Practice,*

Policy Statement 4, p. 5. Copyright National Association of Social Workers, Inc.

3. A. Pincus and A. Minahan, *Social Work Practice: Model and Method* (Itasca, IL: Peacock, 1973), p. 54.

4. Robert L. Barker, *The Social Work Dictionary*, 5th ed. (Washington, DC: NASW Press, 2003), p. 408.

5. Published 1982. National Association of Social Workers, Inc. Reprinted with permission, from *Standards for the Classification of Social Work Practice,* Policy Statement 4, p. 5. Copyright National Association of Social Workers, Inc.

6. J. Anderson, *Social Work Methods and Processes* (Belmont, CA: Wadsworth, 1981).

7. D. Brieland, L. B. Costin, and C. R. Atherton, *Contemporary Social Work: An Introduction to Social Work and Social Welfare,* 3d ed. (New York: McGraw-Hill, 1985), pp. 120–21.

8. Grafton Hull, Jr., *Social Work Internship Manual* (Eau Claire, WI: University of Wisconsin–Eau Claire, 1990), p. 7.

9. Council on Social Work Education, *Educational Policy and Accreditation Standards* (Alexandria, VA: Council on Social Work Education, 2001).

10. W. H. Masters and V. E. Johnson, *Human Sexual Inadequacy* (Boston: Little, Brown, 1970).

11. D. D. Jackson, "The Study of the Family," *Family Process* 4 (1965), p. 1–20.

12. D. L. Rosenhan and M. E. Seligman, *Abnormal Psychology,* 3d ed. (New York: Norton, 1995), p. 54.

13. Ibid., p. 54.

14. Richard B. Stuart, *Trick or Treatment* (Champaign, IL: Research Press, 1970).

15. National Association of Social Workers, *Standards for the Classification of Social Work Practice* (Washington, DC: National Association of Social Workers, 1982), p. 17.

16. Reprinted with permission from *Educational Policy and Accreditation Standards* (EPAS), Alexandria, VA: Council on Social Work Education, 2001.

17. D. H. Hepworth and J. Larsen, *Direct Social Work Practice: Theory and Skills,* 2d ed. (Pacific Grove, CA: Brooks/Cole, 1986), p. 563.

18. Barker, *The Social Work Dictionary,* p. 58.

19. F. Riessman, "The 'Helper Therapy' Principle" *Journal of Social Work* 2 (April 1965): 27–34.

20. Barker, *The Social Work Dictionary,* pp. 84.

21. Reprinted with permission from *Educational Policy and Accreditation Standards* (EPAS), Alexandria, VA: Council on Social Work Education, 2001.

22. Reprinted with permission from *Educational Policy and Accreditation Standards* (EPAS), Alexandria, VA: Council on Social Work Education, 2001.

23. Betty L. Baer, "Developing a New Curriculum for Social Work Education," in *The Pursuit of Competence in Social Work,* eds. F. Clark and M. Arkava (San Francisco: Jossey-Bass, 1979), p. 106.

24. Published 1982, National Association of Social Workers, Inc. Reprinted with permission, from *Standards for the Classification of Social Work Practice,* Policy Statement 4, pp. 17–18. Copyright National Association of Social Workers, Inc.

25. Published 1982. National Association of Social Workers, Inc. Reprinted with permission, from *Standards for the Classification of Social Work Practice,* Policy Statement 4, p. 18. Copyright National Association of Social Workers, Inc.

26. Reprinted with permission from *Educational Policy and Accreditation Standards* (EPAS), Alexandria, VA: Council on Social Work Education, 2001.

27. Reprinted with permission from *Educational Policy and Accreditation Standards* (EPAS), Alexandria, VA: Council on Social Work Education, 2001.

28. Reprinted with permission from *Educational Policy and Accreditation Standards* (EPAS), Alexandria, VA: Council on Social Work Education, 2001.

29. Reprinted with permission from *Educational Policy and Accreditation Standards* (EPAS), Alexandria, VA: Council on Social Work Education, 2001.

■ CHAPTER 3: GROUP DYNAMICS: LEADERSHIP

1. David Krech, Richard S. Crutchfield, and Egerton L. Ballachey, *Individual in Society* (New York: McGraw-Hill, 1962), pp. 428–31.

2. A. Paul Hare, *Handbook of Small Group Research* (New York: Free Press, 1962), pp. 292–93.

3. J. S. Davis and A. P. Hare, "Button-Down Collar Culture: A Study of Undergraduate Life at a Men's College," *Human Organization* 14 (1956): 13–20.

4. J. G. March, "Influence Measurement in Experimental and Semi-experimental Groups," *Sociometry* 19 (1956): 260–71.

5. David W. Johnson and Frank P. Johnson, *Joining Together: Group Theory and Group Skills,* 3d ed. (Englewood Cliffs, NJ: Prentice-Hall, 1987), p. 43.

6. Ibid., p. 44.

7. R. Christie and F. Geis, *Studies in Machiavellianism* (New York: Academic Press, 1970).

8. K. Lewin, R. Lippitt, and R. K. White, "Patterns of Aggressive Behavior in Experimentally Created Social Climates," *Journal of Social Psychology* 10 (1939): 271–99.

9. Hare, *Handbook,* p. 309.

10. R. F. Bales, *Interaction Process Analysis: A Method for the Study of Small Groups* (Reading, MA: Addison-Wesley, 1950).

11. David Johnson and Frank P. Johnson, *Joining Together: Group Theory and Group Skills,* pp. 26–27. Published by Allyn and Bacon, Boston, MA. Copyright 1975 by Pearson Education. Reprinted by permission of the publisher.

12. P. Hersey and K. Blanchard, *Management of Organizational Behavior: Utilizing Human Resources,* 3d ed. (Englewood Cliffs, NJ: Prentice-Hall, 1977).

13. J. R. P. French and B. Raven, "The Bases of Social Power," in *Group Dynamics: Research and Theory,* 3d ed., eds. Dorwin Cartwright and Alvin Zander (New York: Harper & Row, 1968), pp. 259–69.

14. E. E. Jones and H. B. Gerard, *Foundations of Social Psychology* (New York: John Wiley and Sons, 1967).

15. L. J. Halle, "Overestimating the Power of Power," *New Republic* 10 (June 1967): 15–17.

16. Dorwin Cartwright and Alvin Zander, "Power and Influence in Groups," in *Group Dynamics,* 3d ed., eds. Cartwright and Zander (New York: Harper & Row, 1968), pp. 215–35.

17. M. Deutsch, "Conflicts: Productive and Destructive," *Journal of Social Issues* 25 (1969): 7–43.

18. Saul Alinsky, *Rules for Radicals* (New York: Vintage, 1972).

19. Ibid., pp. 143–44.

20. *Standards for Social Work Practice with Groups,* copyright 1999 and 1998, reprinted with permission from the Association for the Advancement of Social Work with Groups, Inc.

■ CHAPTER 4: GROUP DYNAMICS: GOALS AND NORMS

1. David W. Johnson and Frank P. Johnson, *Joining Together: Group Theory and Group Skills* (Englewood Cliffs, NJ: Prentice-Hall, 1975), p. 88.

2. Ibid., p. 103.

3. Ibid., pp. 104–105.

4. Ibid., p. 97.

5. M. Deutsch, "A Theory of Cooperation and Competition," *Human Relations* 2 (1949): 129–52.

6. Johnson and Johnson, *Joining Together,* p. 97.

7. H. H. Kelly and A. J. Stahelski, "Social Interaction Basis of Cooperators' and Competitors' Beliefs about Others," *Journal of Personality and Social Psychology* 16 (1970): 66–91.

8. M. Deutsch, "The Effect of Motivational Orientation upon Trust and Suspicion," *Human Relations* 13 (1960): 123–39.

9. Andre L. Delbecq and Andrew Van de Ven, "A Group Process Model for Problem Identification and Program Planning," *Journal of Applied Behavioral Science* 7 (1971): 466–92.

10. Andrew Van de Ven and Andre L. Delbecq, "Nominal versus Interacting Group Processes for Committee Decision-Making Effectiveness," *Academy of Management Journal* 14 (1971): 205.

11. For an illustration of the nominal group approach in developing social programs, see Charles Zastrow, "The Nominal Group: A New Approach to Designing Programs for Curbing Delinquency," *Canadian Journal of Criminology and Corrections* 15 (1973): 109–17.

12. For an additional discussion of using the nominal group approach to identify course content, see Charles Zastrow and Ralph Navarre, "The Nominal Group: A New Tool for Making Social Work Education Relevant," *Journal of Education for Social Work* 13 (1977): 112–18.

13. Van de Ven and Delbecq, "Nominal versus Interacting Group Processes," p. 205.

14. Ibid.

15. Rodney W. Napier and Matti K. Gershenfeld, *Groups: Theory and Experience,* 2d ed. (Boston: Houghton Mifflin, 1981), p. 134.

16. Muzafer Sherif, "A Study of Some Social Factors in Perception," *Archives of Psychology* 187 (1935): 1–27; M. Sherif, *The Psychology of Social Norms* (New York: Harper, 1936); and M. Sherif, "Conformity—Deviation, Norms and Group Relations," in *Conformity and Deviation,* eds. I. A. Berg and B. M. Bass (New York: Harper, 1961), pp. 159–98.

17. S. E. Asch, "Effects of Group Pressure upon the Modification and Distortion of Judgments," in *Groups, Leadership, and Men,* ed. H. Guetzkow (Pittsburgh: Carnegie, 1951), pp. 177–90; S. E. Asch, "Opinions and Social Pressure," *Scientific American* 193, no. 5 (1955): 31–35; and S. E. Asch, "Studies of Independence and Conformity: A Minority of One Against a Unanimous Majority," *Psychological Monographs* 70, no. 9 (1956): 1–70.

18. Stanley Schachter, *The Psychology of Affiliation* (Palo Alto, CA: Stanford University Press, 1959); and Stanley Schachter and J. Singer, "The Theory of Social Comparison," *Psychological Review* 69 (1962): 379–99.

19. David Krech, Richard S. Crutchfield, and Egerton L. Ballachey, *Individual in Society* (New York: McGraw-Hill, 1962), pp. 509–12.

20. S. Milgram, "Behavioral Study of Obedience," *Journal of Abnormal and Social Psychology* 68 (1963): 371–78.

21. E. P. Hollander, "Conformity, Status, and Idiosyncrasy Credit," *Psychological Review* 65 (1958): 117–27.

22. George R. Bach and Peter Wyden, *The Intimate Enemy* (New York: Avon, 1981).

23. Thomas Gordon, *Parent Effectiveness Training* (New York: Peter H. Wyden, 1970).

■ CHAPTER 5: VERBAL AND NONVERBAL COMMUNICATION

1. Quoted in Ronald B. Adler and Neil Towne, *Looking Out/Looking In,* 3d ed. (New York: Holt, Rinehart and Winston, 1981), p. 253.

2. Gordon W. Allport and L. J. Postman, "The Basic Psychology of Rumor," *Transactions of the New York Academy of Sciences,* 11th ser., vol. 8 (1945): 61–81; and F. C. Bartlett, *Remembering* (Cambridge, England: Cambridge University Press, 1932).

3. Douglas McGregor, *The Professional Manager* (New York: McGraw-Hill, 1967).

4. A. A. Harrison, *Individuals and Groups* (Pacific Grove, CA: Brooks/Cole, 1976), pp. 100–107.

5. Ronald B. Adler and Neil Towne, *Looking Out/Looking In,* 3d ed. (New York: Holt, Rinehart and Winston, 1981), p. 171.

6. Ibid., p. 178.

7. Ibid.

8. Ibid., p. 180.

9. Jack R. Gibb, "Defensive Communication," *Journal of Communication* 11 (1961): 141–48.

10. Adler and Towne, *Looking Out,* p. 38.

11. Sidney M. Jourard, *The Transparent Self* (New York: Van Nostrand Reinhold, 1971).

12. Ibid., pp. 47–63.

13. Joseph Luft, *Of Human Interaction* (Palo Alto, CA: National Press Books, 1969).

14. Alfred Kadushin, *The Social Work Interview* (New York: Columbia University Press), p. 188.

15. Ibid., p. 190.

16. Thomas Gordon, *Parent Effectiveness Training* (New York: Peter H. Wyden, 1970).

17. Sir Arthur Conan Doyle, "A Scandal in Bohemia," in *The Adventures of Sherlock Holmes* (London: John Murray, 1974).

18. Adler and Towne, *Looking Out,* p. 257.

19. Albert Mehrabian, *Silent Messages,* 2d ed. (Belmont, CA: Wadsworth, 1981).

20. Paul Ekman and Wallace V. Friesen, *Unmasking the Face* (Englewood Cliffs, NJ: Prentice-Hall, 1975).

21. Adler and Towne, *Looking Out,* p. 266.

22. E. H. Hess and J. M. Polt, "Pupil Size as Related to Interest Value of Visual Stimuli," *Science* 132 (1960): 349–50.

23. Albert E. Scheflen, *How Behavior Means* (Garden City, NY: Anchor, 1974).

24. Rene Spitz, "Hospitalization: Genesis of Psychiatric Conditions in Early Childhood," in *Psychoanalytic Study of the Child* 1 (1945): 53.

25. Ashley Montagu, *Touching: The Human Significance of the Skin* (New York: Harper & Row, 1971).

26. Quoted in Adler and Towne, *Looking Out,* p. 279.

27. R. Hoult, "Experimental Measurement of Clothing as a Factor in Some Social Ratings of Selected American Men," *American Sociological Review* 19 (1954): 324–28.

28. Adler and Towne, *Looking Out,* p. 281.

29. Edward T. Hall, *The Hidden Dimension* (Garden City, NY: Doubleday, 1969).

30. Mark L. Knapp, *Nonverbal Communication in Human Interaction,* 2d ed. (New York: Holt, Rinehart and Winston, 1978), p. 115.

31. Ibid., p. 323.

32. G. L. Trager, "Paralanguage: A First Approximation," *Studies in Linguistics* 13 (1958): 1–12.

33. Mehrabian, *Silent Messages,* pp. 46–55.

34. J. E. Singer, "The Use of Manipulative Strategies: Machiavellianism and Attractiveness," *Sociometry* 27 (1964): 128–51.

35. J. Mills and E. Aronson, "Opinion Change as a Function of the Communicator's Attractiveness and Desire to Influence," *Journal of Personality and Social Psychology* 1 (1965): 73–77.

36. R. N. Widgery and B. Webster, "The Effects of Physical Attractiveness upon Perceived Initial Credibility," *Michigan Speech Journal* 4 (1969): 9–15.

37. E. K. Solender and E. Solender, "Minimizing the Effect of the Unattractive Client on the Jury: A Study of the Interaction of Physical Appearance with Assertions and Self-experience References," *Human Rights* 5 (1976): 201–14.

38. Knapp, *Nonverbal Communication,* p. 156.

39. E. Berscheid and E. H. Walster, "Physical Attractiveness," in *Advances in Experimental Social Psychology,* ed. L. Berkowitz (New York: Academic Press, 1974), 7: 158–215.

40. R. Algozzine, "What Teachers Perceive—Children Receive," *Communication Quarterly* 24 (1976): 41–47.

41. Knapp, *Nonverbal Communication,* p. 159.

42. D. Bar-Tal and L. Saxe, "Perceptions of Similarity and Dissimilarity of Physically Attractive Couples and Individuals," *Journal of Personality and Social Psychology* 33 (1976): 772–81.

43. R. W. Parnell, *Behavior and Physique: An Introduction to Practical and Applied Somatometry* (London: Edward Arnold, 1958).

44. Knapp, *Nonverbal Communication,* p. 166.

45. A. H. Maslow and N. L. Mintz, "Effects of Esthetic Surroundings. I. Initial Effects of Three Esthetic Conditions upon Perceiving 'Energy' and 'Well-Being' in Faces," *Journal of Psychology* 41(1956): 247–54.

46. This story by Samuel J. Sackett, entitled "Tin Lizzie," appears in David W. Johnson and Frank P. Johnson, *Joining Together: Group Therapy and Group Skills* (Englewood Cliffs, NJ: Prentice-Hall, 1975), pp. 327–28.

CHAPTER 6: TASK GROUPS

1. Ronald W. Toseland and Robert F. Rivas, *An Introduction to Group Work Practice,* 4th ed. (Boston: Allyn and Bacon, 2001), pp. 157–58.

2. Ibid., p. 323.

3. David W. Johnson and Frank P. Johnson, *Joining Together: Group Therapy and Group Skills* (Englewood Cliffs, NJ: Prentice-Hall, 1975), p. 257.

4. William Kornblum and Joseph Julian, *Social Problems,* 10th ed. (Upper Saddle River, NJ: Prentice Hall, 2001).

5. See Rodney W. Napier and Matti K. Gershenfeld, *Groups: Theory and Experience,* 2d ed. (Boston: Houghton Mifflin, 1981), p. 384.

6. See V. H. Vroom, L. D. Grant, and T. S. Cotton, "The Consequences of Social Interaction in Group Problem Solving," *Journal of Organizational Behavior and Human Performance* 4 (1969): 79–95; and R. A. Collaros and L. Anderson, "Effects of Perceived Expertness upon Creativity of Members of Brainstorming Groups," *Journal of Applied Psychology* 53 (1969): 159–64.

7. T. J. Bouchard, "Training, Motivation and Personality as Determinants of the Effectiveness of Brainstorming Groups and Individuals," *Journal of Applied Psychology* 56 (1972): 324–31.

8. Napier and Gershenfeld, *Groups,* p. 385.

9. Johnson and Johnson, *Joining Together,* p. 139.

10. Christopher W. Moore, *The Mediation Process* (San Francisco, CA: Jossey-Bass, 1986), p. 158.

11. Thomas Gordon, *Parent Effectiveness Training* (New York: Peter H. Wyden, 1970).

12. Ibid., p. 237.

13. M. Deutsch, "Conflicts: Productive and Destructive," *Journal of Social Issues* 25 (1969): 7–43.

14. Milton Rokeach, *The Open and Closed Mind* (New York: Basic, 1960).

15. David W. Johnson, "Role Reversal: A Summary and Review of the Research," *International Journal of Group Tensions* 1 (1971): 318–34.

16. Moore, *Mediation Process,* p. 21.

17. Ibid., pp. 21–22.

18. Ibid., p. 22.

19. Ibid., p. 23.

20. Ibid., p. 6.

21. See Moore, *Mediation Process,* for a review.

22. Joan Blades, *Mediate Your Divorce* (Englewood Cliffs, NJ: Prentice-Hall, 1985).

23. Moore, *Mediation Process.*

24. Muzafer Sherif, *In Common Predicament* (Boston: Houghton Mifflin, 1966); G. Watson and David W. Johnson, *Social Psychology: Issues and Insights,* 2d ed. (Philadelphia: Lippincott, 1972); and R. R. Blake and J. S. Mouton, "The Intergroup Dynamics of Win-Lose Conflict and Problem-Solving Collaboration in Union-Management Relations," in *Intergroup Relations and Leadership,* ed. Muzafer Sherif (New York: John Wiley and Sons, 1962), pp. 94–142.

25. David W. Johnson and Frank P. Johnson, *Joining Together: Group Therapy and Group Skills* (Englewood Cliffs, NJ: Prentice-Hall, 1975), p. 55.

26. George F. Cole, *The American System of Criminal Justice,* 6th ed. (Pacific Grove, CA: Brooks/Cole, 1992), p. 534.

27. David Whitman, "Welfare: The Myth of Reform," *U.S. News & World Report* (January 16, 1995): 30–39. James W. Coleman and Donald R. Cressey, *Social Problems,* 5th ed. (New York: HarperCollins, 1993), pp. 202–08.

28. Kornblum and Julian, *Social Problems.*

29. Ibid.

30. Ibid.

31. Johnson and Johnson, *Joining Together,* p. 60.

32. Ibid., p. 75.

33. G. Watson and David W. Johnson, *Social Psychology: Issues and Insights,* 2d ed. (Philadelphia, PA: Lippincott, 1972).

34. Irving L. Janis, "Groupthink," *Psychology Today* (November 1971): 43–46, 74–76.

■ CHAPTER 7: WORKING WITH DIVERSE GROUPS

1. Code of Ethics of the National Association of Social Workers, National Association of Social Workers (Washington, DC: NASW Press, 1996).

2. Ibid.

3. Robert Merton, "Discrimination and the American Creed," in *Discrimination and National Welfare,* ed. Robert M. MacIver (New York: Harper & Row, 1949).

4. Council on Social Work Education, *Educational Policy and Accreditation Standards* (Alexandria, VA: Council on Social Work Education), 2001.

5. Ibid.

6. Robert L. Barker, *The Social Work Dictionary,* 5th ed. (Washington, DC: NASW Press, 2003), p. 404–05.

7. Excerpted from a speech by Abraham Lincoln in Charleston, Illinois, in 1858, as reported in Richard Hofstader, *The American Political Tradition* (New York: Knopf, 1948), p. 116.

8. Janet S. Hyde and John DeLamater, *Understanding Human Sexuality,* 6th ed. (New York: McGraw-Hill, 1997), pp. 371–99.

9. Ibid., pp. 375–86.

10. Ibid., pp. 376–92.

11. Ibid., pp. 382–96.

12. Alfred Kinsey, W. B. Pomeroy, and C. E. Martin, *Sexual Behavior in the Human Male* (Philadelphia, PA: Saunders, 1948).

13. Hyde and DeLamater, *Understanding Human Sexuality,* pp. 386–87.

14. Alan P. Bell, Martin S. Weinberg, and Sue Kiefer Hammersmith, *Sexual Preference* (Bloomington, IN: Indiana University Press, 1981).

15. Mizio Emelicia, "White Worker-Minority Client," *Social Worker* 17 (May 1972): 82–86.

16. Clifford J. Sager, Thomas L. Brayboy, and Barbara R. Waxenberg, *Black Ghetto Family in Therapy: A Laboratory Experience* (New York: Grove Press, 1970), pp. 210–11.

17. Ronald G. Lewis and Man Keung Ho, "Social Work with Native Americans," *Social Work* 20 (Sept. 1975): 378–82.

18. Lloyd G. Sinclair, "Sex Counseling and Therapy," in Charles Zastrow, *The Practice of Social Work,* 7th ed. (Pacific Grove, CA: Brooks/Cole, 2003), p. 492.

19. Richard T. Shaefer, *Racial and Ethnic Groups,* 5th ed. (New York: HarperCollins, 1993), pp. 273–99.

20. Ibid.

21. Ibid., p. 296.

22. Beatrice A. Wright, *Physical Disability: A Psychological Approach* (New York: Harper & Row, 1960), p. 259.

23. Ibid.

24. Nancy Weinberg, "Rehabilitation," in *Contemporary Social Work,* 2d. ed., eds. Donald Brieland, Lela Costin, and Charles Atherton (New York: McGraw-Hill, 1980), p. 310.

25. Ibid.

26. Mary Kalyanpur and Beth Harry, "A Posture of Reciprocity: A Practical Approach to Collaboration Between Professionals and Parents of Culturally Diverse Backgrounds," *Journal of Child and Family Studies,* 6 (Dec. 1997): 487–509.

27. Ibid., p. 493.

28. Dolores G. Norton, "Incorporating Content on Minority Groups into Social Work Practice Courses," in *The Dual Perspective* (New York: Council on Social Work Education, 1978), p. 22.

29. Grafton H. Hull, Jr., "Social Work Practice with Diverse Groups," in Charles Zastrow, *The Practice of Social Work,* 5th ed., (Pacific Grove, CA: Brooks/Cole, 1995), p. 359.

30. Melvin Delgado and Denise Humm-Delgado, "Natural Support Systems: Source of Strength in Hispanic Communities," *Social Work* 27, no. 1 (Jan. 1982): 83–89.

31. Alfred Kadushin, *The Social Work Interview* (New York: Columbia University Press, 1972).

32. Larry E. Davis, "Racial Composition of Groups," *Social Work* 24 (May 1979): 208–13.

33. Jimm G. Good Tracks, "Native American Noninterference," *Social Work* 18 (Nov. 1973): 30–34.

34. A. E. Moses and R. O. Hawkins, *Counseling Lesbian Women and Gay Men: A Life-Issues Approach* (St. Louis, MO: C. V. Mosby, 1982).

35. Jeannine Gramick, "Homophobia: A New Challenge," *Social Work* 28, no. 2 (March-April 1983): 137–41.

36. W. Devore and E. G. Schlesinger, *Ethnic-Sensitive Social Work Practice,* 4th ed. (Needham Heights, MA: Allyn & Bacon, 1996).

37. D. G. Norton, "Incorporating Content on Minority Groups into Social Work Practice Courses," in *The Dual Perspective* (New York: Council on Social Work Education, 1978).

38. Devore and Schlesinger, *Ethnic-Sensitive Social Work Practice.*

39. Ibid.

40. Barker, *The Social Work Dictionary,* p. 142.

41. A. Billingsley, *Climbing Jacob's Ladder: The Enduring Legacy of African-American Families* (New York: Simon & Schuster, 1993).

42. D. Saleeby, *The Strengths Perspective in Social Work Practice,* 2d ed. (New York: Longman, 1997), pp. 12–15.

43. Ibid., p. 12.

44. Surjit S. Dhopper and Sharon E. Moore, *Social Work Practice with Culturally Diverse People* (Thousand Oaks, CA: Sage, 2001).

45. Ibid.

46. National Association of Social Workers, *NASW Code of Ethics,* (Washington, DC: NASW, 1996).

47. Council on Social Work Education, *Educational Policy and Accreditation Standards* (EPAS), (Washington, DC: CSWE, 2001).

48. Larry E. Davis, Maeda J. Galinsky, and Janice H. Schopler, "RAP: A Framework for Leadership of Multiracial Groups," *Social Work* 40, no. 2 (March 1995): 155–65.

49. Nan Van Den Bergh and Lynn B. Cooper, "Feminist Social Work," in *The Encyclopedia of Social Work* (Washington, DC: National Association of Social Workers, 1987), pp. 610–18.

50. Barker, *The Social Work Dictionary,* p. 161.

51. Ibid.

52. Ibid.

53. Karen Kirst-Ashman and Grafton H. Hull, Jr., *Understanding Generalist Practice* (Chicago: Nelson-Hall, 1993), p. 427.

54. Van Den Bergh and Cooper, "Feminist Social Work"; Kirst-Ashman and Hull, *Understanding Generalist Practice;* and Nan Van Den Bergh, "Feminist Treatment for People with Depression," in *Structuring Change,* ed. Kevin Corcoran (Chicago: Lyceum Books, 1992), pp. 95–110.

55. Kirst-Ashman and Hull, *Understanding Generalist Practice,* p. 613.

56. Van Den Bergh, "Feminist Treatment for People with Depression," p. 103.

57. Ibid., p. 101.

58. Ibid., p. 104.

59. Ibid., p. 104.

60. Van Den Bergh and Cooper, "Feminist Social Work," p. 617.

61. Ibid.

62. Van Den Bergh, "Feminist Treatment for People with Depression," pp. 95–110.

63. Ibid., p. 105.

64. Kirst-Ashman and Hull, *Understanding Generalist Practice,* p. 427.

65. Linda Y. Schiller "Stages of Development in Women's Groups: A Relational Model," in *Group Work Practice in a Troubled Society: Problems and Opportunities,* eds. Roselle Kurland and Robert Salmon (Binghamton, NY: Haworth Press, 1995), pp. 117–138.

66. Ibid., p. 117.

67. Ibid., p. 122.

68. Ibid., p. 122.

69. L. Shulman, *The Skills of Helping Individuals and Groups,* (Itasca, IL: Peacock Publishers, 1992).

70. Schiller "Stages of Development in Women's Groups," p. 130.

■ CHAPTER 8: SELF-HELP GROUPS

1. Gary Bonds et al., "Growth of a Medical Self-Help Group," in *Self-Help Groups for Coping with Crisis,* eds. Morton A. Lieberman, Leonard D. Borman, and Associates (San Francisco, CA: Jossey-Bass, 1979), pp. 43–66.

2. Leonard D. Borman and Morton A. Lieberman, "Conclusion: Contributions, Dilemmas, and Implications for Mental Health Policy" in Lieberman et al., *Self-Help Groups for Coping with Crisis: Origins,*

Members, Processes, and Impact. (San Francisco, CA: Jossey-Bass, 1979), p. 408.

3. Morton A. Lieberman and Leonard D. Borman, "Overview: The Nature of Self-Help Groups," in Lieberman et al., *Self-Help Groups for Coping with Crisis,* p. 2.

4. Dean H. Hepworth and Jo Ann Larsen, *Direct Social Work Practice: Theory and Skills* (Homewood, IL: Dorsey Press, 1986), p. 549.

5. Frank Reissman, "Foreword," in Thomas J. Powell, *Self-Help Organizations and Professional Practice* (Silver Spring, MD: National Association of Social Workers, 1987), pp. ix–x.

6. Alfred H. Katz and Eugene I. Bender, *The Strength in Us: Self-Help Groups in the Modern World* (New York: Franklin-Watts, 1976).

7. Ibid., p. 38.

8. Ibid.

9. Thomas J. Powell, *Self-Help Organizations and Professional Practice* (Silver Spring, MD: National Association of Social Workers, 1987).

10. Frank Riessman, "The 'Helper Therapy' Principle," *Journal of Social Work* (April 1965): 27–34.

11. Hepworth and Larsen, *Direct Social Work Practice,* p. 549.

12. L. Borman, "New Self-Help and Support Systems for the Chronically Mentally Ill," paper presented at the Pittsburgh Conference on Neighborhood Support Systems, Pittsburgh, PA, June 15, 1979.

13. Linda F. Kurtz, *Self-Help and Support Groups: A Handbook for Practitioners* (Thousand Oaks, CA: Sage, 1997), p. 13.

14. Lambert Maguire, "Natural Helping Networks and Self-Help Groups," in *Primary Prevention in Mental Health and Social Work,* ed. Milton Nobel (New York: Council on Social Work Education, 1981), p. 41.

15. Hepworth and Larsen, *Direct Social Work Practice,* p. 550.

16. Lieberman and Borman, "Overview," p. 31.

17. Kurtz, *Self-Help and Support Groups,* p. 187.

▪ CHAPTER 9: SOCIAL WORK WITH FAMILIES

1. B. Compton and B. Galaway, *Social Work Processes,* 6th ed. (Pacific Grove, CA: Brooks/Cole, 1999).

2. Carolyn Wells, *Stepping to the Dance, the Training of a Family Therapist* (Pacific Grove, CA: Brooks/Cole, 1998).

3. J. W. Coleman and D. R. Cressey, *Social Problems,* 8th ed. (Englewood Ciffs, NJ: Prentice-Hall, 1995), p. 124.

4. M. A. Suppes and C. Wells, *The Social Work Experience, An Introduction to Social Work and Social Welfare,* 3d ed. (New York: McGraw-Hill, 2000).

5. Ann Hartman, "Diagrammatic Assessment of Family Relationships," *Social Casework* 59 (Oct. 1978): 465–476.

6. M. E. Kerr and M. Bowen, *Family Evaluation: An Approach Based on Brown's Theory* (New York: Norton, 1988).

7. Mark Worden, *Family Therapy Basics,* 2d ed. (Pacific Grove, CA: Brooks/Cole, 1999).

8. Virginia Satir, *Conjoint Family Therapy* (Palo Alto, CA: Science & Behavior Books, 1967), p. 70.

9. National Association of Social Workers, *Encyclopedia of Social Work,* 19th ed. (Washington, DC: NASW Press, 1995), p. 987.

10. Frances H. Scherz, "Theory and Practice of Family Therapy," in *Theories of Social Casework,* eds. Robert W. Roberts and Robert H. Nee (Chicago: University of Chicago Press, 1970), p. 234.

11. Joseph E. Perez, *Family Counseling Theory and Practice* (New York: Van Nostrand, 1979), p. 47.

12. Ibid.

13. Ibid., p. 49.

14. Ibid., p. 51.

15. Satir, *Family Therapy,* p. 82.

16. Curtis Janzen and Oliver Harris, *Family Treatment in Social Work Practice,* 3d ed. (Itasca, IL: F. E. Peacock, 1997), p. 26.

17. Robert L. Barker, *The Social Work Dictionary,* 5th ed. (Washington, DC: NASW Press, 2003), p. 417.

18. Adele M. Holman, *Family Assessment: Tools for Understanding and Intervention* (Beverly Hills, CA: Sage, 1983), p. 29.

19. Ibid., p. 30.

20. Salvador Minuchin, *Families and Family Therapy* (Cambridge, MA: Harvard University Press, 1974), p. 111.

21. Janzen and Harris, *Family Treatment.*

22. George Thorman, *Helping Troubled Families: A Social Work Perspective* (New York: Aldine, 1982), p. 65.

23. Joe H. Brown and Carolyn S. Brown. *Marital Therapy: Concepts and Skills for Effective Practice* (Pacific Grove, CA: Brooks/Cole, 2002).

24. Karen K. Kirst-Ashman and Grafton H. Hull, Jr., *Understanding Generalist Practice,* 3d ed. (Pacific Grove, CA: Brooks/Cole, 2002), pp. 46–48.

25. Ibid., pp. 46–48.

26. Thomas Gordon, *Parent Effectiveness Training* (New York: Peter H. Weyden, 1970); Charles Zastrow, *The Practice of Social Work,* 6th ed. (Pacific Grove, CA: Brooks/Cole, 1999), pp. 386–91.

27. Charles Zastrow and Karen Kirst-Ashman, *Understanding Human Behavior and the Social Environment,* 6th ed. (Pacific Grove, CA: Brooks/Cole), pp. 310–12.

28. Ibid., p. 144.

29. Ibid., p. 156–57.

30. Zastrow, *Practice of Social Work,* pp. 387–89.

31. Ibid., p. 387.

32. Ibid., p. 388.

33. Thorman, *Helping Troubled Families,* p. 87. Herbert Goldenberg and Irene Goldenberg, *Counseling Today's Families,* 4th ed. (Pacific Grove, CA: Brooks/Cole, 2002).

34. Karpel, 1994; Kirst-Ashman and Hull, 2002.

35. Kirst-Ashman and Hull, 2002.
36. Michael P. Nichols and Richard C. Schwartz, *Family Therapy: Concepts and Methods* (Boston: Allyn & Bacon, 2004); Virginia Satir, *People Making* (Palo Alto, CA: Science & Behavior Books, 1972); Satir, *Family Therapy.*
37. Salvador Minuchin and H. C. Fishman, *Family Therapy Techniques* (Cambridge, MA: Harvard University Press, 1981); Minuchin, *Families;* Nichols and Schwartz, 2004.
38. Bradford W. Sheafor, Charles R. Horejsi, and Gloria A. Horejsi, *Techniques and Guidelines for Social Work*

Practice, 4th ed. (Boston: Allyn and Bacon, 1997), p. 361.
39. James Alexander and Bruce V. Parsons, *Functional Family Therapy* (Monterey, CA: Brooks/Cole, 1982); Irene Goldenberg and Herbert Goldenberg, *Family Therapy: An Overview,* 6th ed. (Pacific Grove, CA: Brooks/Cole, 2003), pp. 282–88.
40. Alexander and Parsons, *Functional Family Therapy,* pp. 16–19, Nichols and Schwartz, 2004.
41. Alexander and Parsons, p. 58.
42. Ibid., p. 67.

CHAPTER 10: ORGANIZATIONS, COMMUNITIES, AND GROUPS

1. A. Etzioni, *Modern Organizations* (Englewood Cliffs, NJ: Prentice-Hall, 1964), p. 1.
2. F. E. Netting, P. M. Kettner, and S. L. McMurtry, *Social Work Macro Practice,* 2d ed. (New York: Longman, 1998), pp. 193–94.
3. David W. Johnson and Frank P. Johnson, *Joining Together: Group Theory and Group Skills,* 8th ed. (Boston: Allyn and Bacon, 2003), p. 19.
4. K. Davis and J. W. Newstrom, *Human Behavior at Work,* 8th ed. (New York: McGraw-Hill, 1989), p. 31.
5. Ibid., p. 31.
6. Frederick Taylor, *Scientific Management* (New York: Harper & Row, 1947).
7. F. J. Roethlisberger and W. J. Dickson, *Management and the Worker* (Cambridge, MA: Harvard University Press, 1939).
8. Etzioni, *Modern Organizations,* pp. 34–35.
9. Netting, Kettner, and McMurtry, *Social Work Macro Practice,* pp. 202–03.
10. D. McGregor, *The Human Side of Enterprise* (New York: McGraw-Hill, 1960).
11. Davis and Newstrom, *Human Behavior at Work,* p. 34.
12. William Ouchi, *Theory Z: How American Business Can Meet the Japanese Challenge* (Reading, MA: Addison-Wesley, 1981).
13. Peter F. Drucker, *The Practice of Management* (New York: Harper, 1954).
14. Vincent K. Omachony and Joel E. Ross, *Principles of Total Quality* (Delray Beach, FL: St. Lucie Press, 1994), p. 1.
15. Ibid.
16. David Hower, "David Hower's Definition of Total Quality," *Reporter* (Whitewater, WI: University of Wisconsin–Whitewater, August 29, 1994): 10.
17. R. Knopf, *Surviving the BS (Bureaucratic System),* (Wilmington, NC: Mandala Press, 1979), pp. 21–22.
18. Ibid., p. 25.
19. Ibid.
20. This description highlights a number of negatives about bureaucratic systems, particularly their impersonalization. In fairness, an advantage of being part of a large bureaucracy is that the potential is there for changing a powerful system to the clients' advantage. In tiny or nonbureaucratic systems, the social worker may have lots of freedom but little opportunity or power to influence large systems or mobilize extensive resources on behalf of clients.
21. Knopf, p. 25.
22. Robert L. Barker, *The Social Work Dictionary,* 5th ed. (Washington, DC: NASW Press, 2003), p. 83.
23. Ibid., p. 219.
24. Johnson and Johnson, *Joining Together* p. 19.
25. Barker, *The Social Work Dictionary,* p. 83.
26. Jack Rothman and John E. Tropman, "Models of Community Organization and Macro Practice Perspectives: Their Mixing and Phasing," in *Strategies of Community Organization,* 4th ed., eds. Fred Cox, John Erlich, Jack Rothman, and John E. Tropman (Itasca, IL: F. E. Peacock, 1987), pp. 3–26.
27. Saul Alinsky, *Rules for Radicals* (New York: Random House, 1972), p. 27.
28. ———, *Reveille for Radicals* (New York: Basic Books, 1969), p. 42.
29. Dennis Saleeby, *The Strengths Perspective in Social Work Practice,* 2d ed. (New York: Longman, 1997).

CHAPTER 11: EDUCATIONAL GROUPS: STRESS MANAGEMENT AND TIME MANAGEMENT AS EXAMPLES

1. Herbert M. Greenberg, *Coping with Job Stress* (Englewood Cliffs, NJ: Prentice-Hall, 1980), pp. 39–49.
2. John A. Romas and Manoj Sharma, *Practical Stress Management* (Boston: Allyn and Bacon, 1995).
3. O. Carl Simonton and Stephanie Matthews-Simonton, *Getting Well Again* (Los Angeles: J. P. Tarcher, 1978).

4. Bernard Gauzer, "What We Can Learn from Those Who Survive AIDS," *Parade Magazine,* June 10, 1990, pp. 4–7.

5. Kenneth R. Pelletier, *Mind as Healer, Mind as Slayer* (New York: Dell, 1977), p. 310.

6. Donald A. Tubesing, *Kicking Your Stress Habits* (Duluth, MN: Whole Person Associates, 1981).

7. Hans Selye, *The Stress of Life* (New York: McGraw-Hill, 1956).

8. Ibid., pp. 25–46.

9. For an expanded description of the physiological reactions involved in stress, see Romas and Sharma, *Practical Stress Management,* pp. 35–64.

10. Tubesing, *Kicking Your Stress Habits,* pp. 9–52.

11. Hans Selye, *Stress without Distress* (New York: Signet, 1974), p. 83.

12. Ibid.

13. Jerry Edelwich, *Burn-Out* (New York: Human Sciences Press, 1980); Ayala Pines and Elliot Aronson, *Burn-Out* (New York: Free Press, 1981); Herbert Freudenberger, *Burn-Out* (Garden City, NY: Anchor, 1980); and Christina Maslach, *Burnout—The Cost of Caring* (Englewood Cliffs, NJ: Spectrum, 1982).

14. W. Ryan, *Blaming the Victim* (New York: Pantheon, 1971); and Christina Maslach and Ayala Pines, "The Burn-Out Syndrome in the Day Care Setting," *Child Care Quarterly* 6 (1977): 100–101.

15. Freudenberger, *Burn-Out,* pp. 90–91.

16. Edelwich, *Burn-Out,* pp. 44–142.

17. Christina Maslach, "Burned-Out," *Human Behavior* 5 (1976): 19.

18. Ibid., p. 20.

19. Christina Maslach, "The Client Role in Staff Burn-Out," *Journal of Social Issues* 34 (1978): 111–24.

20. Pines and Aronson, "Burn-Out Syndrome," pp. 45–81.

21. Alan Lakein, *How to Get Control of Your Time and Your Life* (New York: Signet, 1973).

22. These relaxation techniques are more fully described in Charles Zastrow, *You Are What You Think: A Guide to Self-Realization* (Chicago: Nelson-Hall, 1993).

23. Edmund Jacobson, *Progressive Relaxation,* 2d ed. (Chicago: University of Chicago Press, 1938).

24. D. L. Watson and R. G. Tharp, *Self-Directed Behavior* (Pacific Grove, CA: Brooks/Cole, 1973), pp. 182–83.

25. Herbert Benson, *The Relaxation Response* (New York: Avon, 1975).

26. Since any neutral word or phrase will work, Herbert Benson, in *The Relaxation Response* (New York: Avon, 1975), suggests repeating the word *one* silently to oneself.

27. Greenberg, *Coping with Job Stress,* pp. 142–45.

28. Anthony de Mello, *Sadhana: A Way to God* (Garden City, NY: Image Books, 1978), p. 140.

29. Albert Ellis and Robert Harper, *A New Guide to Rational Living* (North Hollywood, CA: Wilshire, 1977).

30. For case examples demonstrating how to change unwanted emotions, see Zastrow, *You Are What You Think.*

31. B. L. Seaward, *Managing Stress* (Boston: Jones & Bartlett, 1994).

32. Harold L. Taylor, *Making Time Work for You* (New York: Dell, 1981), p. 13.

33. Alan Lakein, *How to Get Control of Your Time and Your Life* (New York: Signet, 1973), p. 28.

34. Ibid., p. 47.

35. Ibid., p. 71.

36. Ibid.

37. Taylor, *Making Time Work for You,* p. 171.

■ CHAPTER 12: TREATMENT GROUPS

1. These therapy approaches are summarized in Chapters 7 and Appendix 1: Modules 1, 2 & 3.

2. These therapy approaches are described in Raymond J. Corsini and Danny Wedding, *Current Psychotherapies,* 5th ed. (Itasca, IL: F. E. Peacock, 1995); and Charles Zastrow, *The Practice of Social Work,* 7th ed. (Pacific Grove, CA: Brooks/Cole, 2003).

3. Frank Riessman, "The 'Helper Therapy' Principle," *Journal of Social Work* (April 1965): 27–34.

4. James A. Garland, Hubert Jones, and Ralph Kolodny, "A Model for Stages of Development in Social Work Groups," in *Explorations in Group Work,* ed. Saul Bernstein (Boston: Milford House, 1965), pp. 12–53;

James A. Garland and Louise A. Frey, "Applications of Stages of Group Development to Groups in Psychiatric Settings," in *Further Explorations in Group Work,* ed. Saul Bernstein (Boston: Milford House, 1973), p. 3.

5. Elizabeth Kübler-Ross, *On Death and Dying* (New York: Macmillan, 1969).

6. *Social Work Code of Ethics* (Ottawa: Canadian Association of Social Workers, 1994).

7. *Code of Ethics* (Washington, DC: National Association of Social Workers, 1996).

8. Irving D. Yalom, "The Therapeutic Factors: What It Is That Heals," *The Yalom Reader* (New York: Basic Books, 1998), pp. 5–41.

■ CHAPTER 13: TERMINATION AND EVALUATION OF A GROUP

1. Dean H. Hepworth and Jo Ann Larsen, *Direct Social Work Practice: Theory and Skills,* 2d ed. (Homewood, IL: Dorsey Press, 1986), p. 590.

2. Ibid.

3. See Martin Bloom and Joel Fischer, *Evaluating Practice: Guidelines for the Accountable Professional* (Englewood Cliffs, NJ: Prentice-Hall, 1982).

4. Bradford W. Sheafor, Charles R. Horejsi, and Gloria A. Horejsi, *Techniques and Guidelines for Social Work Practice* (Boston: Allyn and Bacon, 1988), p. 390.

5. Wallace J. Gingerich, "Evaluating Social Work Practice," in *The Practice of Social Work,* 7th ed., Charles Zastrow (Pacific Grove, CA: Brooks/Cole, 2003), pp. 253–74.

6. Sheafor, Horejsi, and Horejsi, *Techniques and Guidelines for Social Work Practice,* p. 391.

7. William Reid and Laura Epstein, *Task Centered Casework* (New York: Columbia University Press, 1972).

8. Sheafor, Horejsi, and Horejsi, *Techniques and Guidelines for Social Work Practice,* p. 403.

■ APPENDIX 1

1. Albert Ellis, "Rational-Emotive Therapy," in *Current Psychotherapies,* 4th ed., eds. Raymond Corsini and Danny Wedding (Itasca, IL: Peacock, 1989), pp. 197–239; Maxie C. Maultsby, Jr., *Help Yourself to Happiness* (Boston: Herman, 1975).

2. Charles Zastrow, *You Are What You Think: A Guide to Self-Realization* (Chicago: Nelson-Hall, 1993).

3. Maultsby, *Help Yourself to Happiness.*

4. Edward Thorndike, *The Psychology of Learning* (New York: Teachers College Press, 1913); E. R. Guthrie, *The Psychology of Learning* (New York: Harper & Row, 1935); C. L. Hull, *Principles of Behavior* (New York: Appleton-Century-Crofts, 1943); E. C. Tolman, *Purposive Behavior in Animals and Men* (New York: Appleton-Century-Crofts, 1932); and B. F. Skinner, *The Behavior of Organisms* (New York: Appleton-Century-Crofts, 1938).

5. R. E. Alberti and M. L. Emmons, *Your Perfect Right: A Guide to Assertive Behavior,* 7th ed. (San Luis Obispo, CA: Impact Publishers, 1995); A. Bandura, *Principles of Behavior Modification* (New York: Holt, Rinehart and Winston, 1969); B. F. Skinner, *Walden Two* (New York: Macmillan, 1948); J. B. Watson and R. Rayner, "Conditioned Emotional Reaction," *Journal of Experimental Psychology* 3, no. 1 (1920): 1–14; and Joseph Wolpe, *Psychotherapy by Reciprocal Inhibition* (Stanford, CA: Stanford University Press, 1958).

6. M. T. Orne and P. H. Wender, "Anticipatory Socialization for Psychotherapy: Method and Rationale," *American Journal of Psychiatry* 124 (1968): 1201–12.

7. Dianne L. Chambless and Alan J. Goldstein, "Behavior Psychotherapy," in *Current Psychotherapies,* 2d ed., ed. Raymond Corsini (Itasca, IL: Peacock, 1979), pp. 244–45.

8. Wolpe, *Psychotherapy by Reciprocal Inhibition.*

9. Alberti and Emmons, *Your Perfect Right;* and Herbert Fensterheim and Jean Baer, *Don't Say Yes When You Want to Say No* (New York: Dell, 1975).

10. Robert E. Alberti and Michael L. Emmons, *Stand Up, Speak Out, Talk Back!* (New York: Pocket Books, 1975), p. 24.

11. These training steps are a modification of assertiveness training programs developed in Alberti and Emmons, *Your Perfect Right,* and in Fensterheim and Baer, *Don't Say Yes When You Want to Say No.*

12. Alan Kazdin, *The Token Economy* (New York: Plenum, 1977).

13. James O. Prochaska, *Systems of Psychotherapy* (Homewood, IL.: Dorsey Press, 1979), pp. 324–25. Reprinted by permission of Wadsworth Publishing Co.

14. D. H. Hepworth and J. Larsen, *Direct Social Work Practice: Theory and Skills,* 2d ed. (Pacific Grove, CA: Brooks/Cole, 1993), p. 365.

15. Ibid., p. 381.

16. Albert Ellis, *Reason and Emotion in Psychotherapy* (New York: Lyle Stuart, 1962), and A. T. Beck, *Cognitive Theory and the Emotional Disorders* (New York: International Universities Press, 1976).

17. Note that the paradigm of cognitive behavior therapists [S (stimulus) → O (cognitions of organism) → R (response)] is similar to the following paradigm of rational therapists [Events → Self-Talk → Emotions and Actions].

18. D. Rimm and J. Masters, *Behavior Therapy* (New York: Academic Press, 1974).

19. M. J. Mahoney, "Clinical Issues in Self-Control Training," paper presented at the meeting of the American Psychological Association, Montreal, 1973.

20. A. T. Beck and M. E. Weishaar, "Cognitive Therapy," in *Current Psychotherapies,* 4th ed., eds. Raymond Corsini and Danny Wedding (Itasca, IL: Peacock, 1989), p. 309.

21. Ibid., pp. 309–10.

22. Ibid., p. 310.

23. Ibid.

24. William Glasser, *Reality Therapy* (New York: Harper & Row, 1965).

25. William Glasser, *Choice Theory: A New Psychology of Personal Freedom* (New York: Harper Perennial, 1998).

26. William Glasser, *Control Theory* (New York: Harper & Row, 1984), p. 32.

27. Ibid., p. 19.

28. Glasser, *Choice Theory.*

29. Ibid, pp. 137–38.

30. American Psychiatric Association, *Diagnostic and Statistical Manual of Mental Disorders,* 4th ed. Text Revision (Washington, DC: Author, 2000).

31. William Glasser, *Warning: Psychiatry Can Be Hazardous to Your Mental Health* (New York: HarperCollins, 2003), p. 114.

32. Losi Leyden-Rubenstein, *The Stress Management Handbook* (New Canaan, CT: Keats Publishing, 1998).

33. American Psychiatric Association, *Diagnostic and Statistical Manual.*

34. Glasser, *Warning.*

35. Robert Barker, *The Social Work Dictionary,* 5th ed. (Washington, DC: NASW Press, 2003), p. 349.

36. William Glasser, *Reality Therapy in Action* (New York: Harper Collins, 2000).

Index